MICROECONOMICS WITH CALCULUS

SECOND EDITION

Brian R. Binger
University of Illinois at Chicago

Elizabeth Hoffman
University of Illinois at Chicago

ADDISON-WESLEY

An imprint of Addison Wesley Longman, Inc.

Reading, Massachusetts • Menlo Park, California • New York • Harlow, England
Don Mills, Ontario • Sydney • Mexico City • Madrid • Amsterdam

Microeconomics with Calculus
Second edition
Brian R. Binger and Elizabeth Hoffman

Senior Editor: Denise Clinton
Editorial Assistant: Jennifer Vito
Senior Production Supervisor: Nancy H. Fenton
Marketing Manager: Quinn Perkson
Manufacturing Supervisor: Hugh Crawford
Cover Designer: Jeannet Leendertse
Project Coordination: Thompson Steele Production Services

Photo Credits:
Figure 5.16 from "Experimental Studies of Consumer Demand Behavior Using Laboratory Animals" by John H. Kagel, et al., *Economic Inquiry*, March 1975, vol. XIII, no. 1, published by the Western Economic Association. Reprinted by permission.

Applications 1 and 3 of Section 19.10 are excerpts from *Problems in Price Theory* by David de Meza and Michael Osborne, pp. 57 and 59. Reprinted by permission.

Section 20.4 adapted from "Moral Hazard and Observability" by Bengt Holmstrom from *The Bell Journal of Economics,* Spring 1979, vol. 10, no. 1. Reprinted by permission of the Rand Corporation.

Figure 21.1 from *Intermediate Microeconomics* 2nd ed. by James P. Quirk, Copyright © Science Research Associates, Inc. 1982, 1976. Reprinted by permission.

Library of Congress Cataloging-in-Publication Data

Binger, Brian R.
   Microeconomics with calculus/Brian R. Binger, Elizabeth Hoffman.
      —2nd ed.
         p.   cm.
   Includes bibliographical references and index.
   ISBN 0-321-01225-9
   1. Microeconomics. 2. Economics, Mathematical.
   I. Hoffman, Elizabeth.   II. Title.
   HB172.B52   1998   97-25855
   338.5'01'515—dc21   CIP

2 3 4 5 6 7 8 9 10-MA-01 00 99 98

MICROECONOMICS WITH CALCULUS

The Addison-Wesley Series in Economics

To James P. Quirk, cornetist, economist, teacher,

who introduced us to the beauty

of microeconomics with calculus

Contents

Chapter 3

CONSTRAINED OPTIMIZATION   56

Chapter 4

INTRODUCTION TO ECONOMIC THEORY AND THE MARKET ECONOMY   92

Chapter 5

CONSUMER PREFERENCE THEORY   107

Chapter 6

INTRODUCTION TO INDIVIDUAL CONSUMER AND MARKET DEMAND THEORY   136

Chapter 7

ELASTICITY OF INDIVIDUAL AND MARKET DEMAND FUNCTIONS   160

Chapter 8

COMPENSATED DEMAND FUNCTIONS AND INCOME AND SUBSTITUTION EFFECTS   174

Chapter 9

EFFICIENCY AND TRADE: AN APPLICATION OF CONSUMER DEMAND THEORY   215

Chapter 10

PRODUCTION THEORY   242

Chapter 11

COST FUNCTIONS   261

Chapter 17

TIME ALLOCATION, LABOR SUPPLY, AND LABOR MARKETS   455

Chapter 18

INTERTEMPORAL DECISIONS AND COMPETITIVE CAPITAL MARKETS   482

Preface

This book is designed to meet the needs of three different kinds of students: upper-level undergraduates who have had at least principles and an introduction to calculus; mathematically sophisticated undergraduates or beginning graduate students who have not had any economics courses before; and beginning graduate students who need a bridge between the graphical presentation of most intermediate courses and the highly abstract presentation of most graduate courses. This book demonstrates to students who have had economics presented only graphically how we use calculus to understand the fundamental principles behind familiar economic concepts and how we make use of actual economic information in policy analysis. It also allows mathematically sophisticated principles students to learn economics in a form they are likely to find comfortable.

In order to appeal both to mathematically advanced principles students and upper-level students who have already had some economics, this book consistently develops both graphical and mathematical analyses and ties them together at each stage. It also offers many numerical, mathematical, and graphical examples relating to actual economic decisions and policy issues. In keeping with the authors' backgrounds in experimental economics, many of the examples are drawn from the literature in experimental economics.

Our treatment of consumer theory, beginning with Chapter 5, illustrates the above approach. Chapter 5 first develops indifference curves and then presents revealed preference analysis and the lump-sum tax and subsidy principle with an application to per-unit gasoline taxes and lump-sum rebates. The chapter ends with a description of laboratory experiments on revealed preference. Chapter 6, on consumer demand, develops individual and market demand curves and shifts in individual and market demand, and then shows how demand functions can be derived mathematically by solving the consumer's constrained maximization problem. Chapter 7 presents elasticity of individual and market demand functions and the use of elasticity in policy analysis. Chapter 8 presents income and substitution effects, the consumer's dual problem, the Slutsky equation, and consumer's surplus analysis using compensated demand curves. Graphical and mathematical derivations complement one another at each step. The chapter ends with a graphical comparison of compensated and uncompensated consumer's surplus analysis and with discussion of the assumptions of "no income effects" in the estimation of consumer's surplus from market demand curves. Chapter 9 completes consumer theory. It presents Edgeworth boxes graphically and then shows students how to use calculus to solve for both the conditions characterizing Pareto optimality and the pure-trade competitive equilibrium, thus illustrating the fundamental theorems of welfare economics. Thus, Chapters 5 through 9 give students the traditional graphical presentation of consumer demand, an understanding of the use of calculus in consumer demand analysis, and an introduction to the sophisticated use of economic tools and reasoning in policy analysis.

The problems at the end of each chapter also combine the graphical and mathematical approaches. Problems are divided into three types: questions for discussion, problems, and logical and mathematical applications. The questions for discussion test a student's intuitive understanding of the material in the chapter. The problems are generally calculus problems with particular functional forms, which ask the students to use calculus tools to solve for such things as generalized demand functions and cost functions. Finally, the logical and mathematical applications ask students to use graphical, logical, and mathematical tools to make clearer the fundamental economic principles developed in the chapter. For example, the applications in Chapter 5 force students to think through and graph extensions of the lump-sum tax and subsidy principle, and the applications in Chapter 8 ask students to use the tools of income and substitution effects to analyze comparative statics effects in specific situations.

This book also highlights key concepts for students, making it easy for them to outline each chapter and review it later on. Each chapter begins with its own introduction to the student, outlining the basic theoretical and mathematical concepts to be developed in that chapter. It ends with a detailed list of key concepts, including definitions, important relationships, and economic principles; these concepts are generally given in bold in the text, alerting students to their importance.

The text is organized as follows. After a brief introduction, the first three chapters are a math review, beginning with very simple mathematical concepts and progressing to constrained maximization using the Lagrange technique. Students who are not accustomed to calculus probably will need all three chapters in order to be able to understand the use of calculus in economics. Students who have had a great deal of math and little economics, on the other had, may not need more than Chapter 3 and perhaps some of the multivariate calculus in Chapters 1 and 2. Instructors may simply assign these chapters as reading and develop the material in lecture as each mathematical concept is used later.

Chapter 4 is a nonmathematical overview of the entire book. It presents the basic economic problem, discusses the use of models in economic analysis, develops the basic assumptions underlying the competitive model, and previews problems of market failure. It uses no math and is entirely self-contained. Then, as discussed above, Chapters 5–9 develop consumer theory: indifference curves; demand theory; the consumer's dual problem; and trade among consumers. Chapters 10–12 develop producer theory: production functions, costs, and profit maximization by competitive firms. Next Chapters 13 and 14 consider competitive markets in some depth, including short-run and long-run partial equilibrium analyses, the general competitive equilibrium with production, partial and general equilibrium comparative statics, and competitive welfare principles. Instructors wishing to present producer theory first can assign Chapters 10–12 before Chapters 5–9, but some additional explanation will be necessary in lecture: In particular, cost functions in Chapter 11 are developed as a mathematical parallel to the consumer's dual problem from Chapter 8; and production functions in Chapter 10 are compared with utility functions from Chapter 5.

Chapters 15–21 are devoted both to extensions of the competitive model and examples of market failure. Chapter 15 is on monopoly, including price discrimination, peak-load pricing, and regulation. Chapter 16 describes industrial organization, including game theory. Chapter 17 is on time allocation and competitive and noncompetitive labor markets. Chapter 18 considers decisions over time, competitive capital markets, and extensions of the problems of resource allocation over time, with discussions of education and the exploitation of renewable and nonrenewable natural resources.

Chapters 19 and 20 are devoted to resource allocation under uncertainty. Chapter 19 develops the basics, including an introduction to markets with complete contingent claims, while Chapter 20 deals with moral hazard and adverse selection, including applications from insurance, the principal-agent problem, and the market for lemons.

The book concludes with Chapter 21 on externalities, public goods, and public decision making. After identifying the conditions for Pareto optimality and explaining how competitive markets fail to allocate externalities and public goods efficiently, we show how all proposed centralized and decentralized solutions to the resource allocation problem with externalities and public goods do not quite solve the problem successfully. The chapter ends with a brief introduction to public-choice problems regarding distributional issues: voting cycles, agenda manipulation, and the use of different voting rules to manipulate voting outcomes.

The second edition is substantially the same as the first edition, with the exception of Chapters 6–9, which have been reorganized to improve clarity. Chapter 6 now includes both individual and market demand functions, but does not include either elasticity or income and substitution effects. This puts individual and market demand curves in the same place. Chapter 7 now presents elasticity of both individual and market demand curves, following directly from the introduction of individual and market demand curves in Chapter 6. Edgeworth boxes, that used to be developed in Chapter 7, are now in Chapter 9. Chapter 8 now includes the complete development of income and substitution effects. Finally, the treatment of Edgeworth boxes, now in Chapter 9, has been reorganized. It now starts with Pareto optimality, and then develops the model of pure trade and the competitive equilibrium. This new organization has the advantage of introducing students to the goal of Pareto optimality before introducing trade as a means of reaching that goal.

Acknowledgments

We would like to thank the many people who have helped us at various stages in the writing of this book and in the preparation of the second edition. First, the following people read the first edition and gave us detailed, insightful comments. The book would not be the same without their help.

Dagobert L. Brito	*Rice University*
H. Lorne Carmichael	*Queen's University (Ontario)*
Kathleen M. Day	*University of Ottawa*
Joseph P. Hughes	*Rutgers University*
Steve Medema	*University of Colorado at Denver*
Len Nichols	*Wellesley College*
Michel Poitenin	*University of Montreal*
F. M. Scherer	*Harvard University*
Ravi Thomas	*Temple University*

In addition, the following friends and colleagues provided comments as we were writing the first edition: Kerry Back, Dennis G. Beckmann, Kenneth D. Boyer, David Brookshire, Elizabeth Clayton, David Conn, James Cox, Maxim Engers, Charles C. Griffin, Robert W. Hahn, Thomas Holmes, R. Mark Isaac, C. Michael Jones, Ken Kletzer, Richard McLean, Mark Machina, Stephen V. Marks, Charles Mason, James Moore, Catherine Morrison, Julianne Nelson, Owen Phillips, John Pomery, Stan Reynolds, Barbara Sands, Vernon Smith, and Paul Thomas. We would also like to thank the many students who used the first edition and gave us invaluable suggestions; the secretarial staffs at Purdue University, the University of Wyoming, and the University of Arizona; George Lobell who encouraged us from the beginning and supported us throughout the initial writing process; and John Greenman who encouraged us to undertake writing a second edition.

Brian R. Binger
Elizabeth Hoffman

Introduction

This book is designed to serve the needs of three different kinds of students. On the one hand, it is designed for both advanced undergraduates and beginning graduate students who have had economics before, but only from a graphical perspective. For those of you who fall into either of those categories, the book is designed to show you how calculus can be used to gain a fuller understanding of microeconomics than what can be gained from the graphical treatment alone. Further, since many of you may only have had a brief introduction to calculus, the book provides a substantial math review and lots of practice problems. On the other hand, this book is also designed for engineering, science, and math students who are comfortable with calculus, but may never have had economics before. For those of you who fall into that category, this book develops economic principles from the basic foundations and shows how calculus can be used to make those economic principles more understandable. Moreover, for all three groups of students, this book shows how graphical, logical, and mathematical tools of analysis can be used together to improve our understanding of fundamental economic principles.

Regarding the economic content, this book presents microeconomic theory with three related levels of analysis. First, each separate section of theory begins with a description of how individual economic actors might behave under certain specified circumstances. We refer to this description as a model of the actors' behavior. For example, we model consumers as choosing combinations of goods that give them the most satisfaction, given their incomes and the prices of the goods they purchase. Similarly, we model firms as hiring inputs and producing output in order to maximize the difference between the revenues they get from selling output and the costs of producing it; that is, we model firms as maximizing profits.

For the second level of analysis, we consider how the decisions of individual economic actors are aggregated into market outcomes. For example, in a competitive market, consumers and firms take market prices as given and make their choices as though those prices are fixed. Consumers' choices are reflected in demand curves, and firms' choices are reflected in supply curves. When we aggregate consumers' demand and firms' supply curves and then combine them into a model of how the competitive market for a particular good operates, we conclude that the intersection of the market demand and market supply curves determines an equilibrium price for the good and a quantity which is both produced and sold.

For the third level of analysis, we consider how markets are combined together into general economic systems and we develop criteria for judging the performance of economic systems. For example, in a competitive market system, individual competitive markets for individual goods are all interrelated. Given a set of resources that can be used to produce output, if consumers all suddenly want to buy more of one particular good, more of that good can be produced only if less of the other goods is produced, freeing up resources for the good in increased demand. Production and distribution in such an economy are said to be *efficient* or *Pareto optimal* if it is not possible to make one agent in the economy better off without making some other agent worse off.

The content of this book is organized as follows. Each chapter begins with an introductory section, "What You Should Learn from This Chapter," which highlights the key concepts to be developed in the chapter and provides some motivation for the mathematical analysis to follow. You should read this section at the beginning to preview what concepts will be particularly important and then reread it at the end as a summary of the chapter. Some of those concepts are italicized.

Throughout the chapter, key concepts are highlighted in bold. Each chapter concludes with a section reviewing the key concepts—including definitions, important relationships, and economic principles—and with three different sets of problems. Use the key concepts to outline and review the important material in the chapter. The problems then test different approaches to economics taken in the book. First, the *questions for discussion* test your intuitive understanding of the key concepts, asking you to describe in words how the concepts might be applied in real-world economic situations. Second, the *problems* test your ability to use calculus to find specific solutions to economic problems. Finally, the *logical and mathematical applications* test your ability to illustrate and extend fundamental economic principles using logic, graphs, and math.

The first three chapters provide a very complete review of all the math you will need to read the rest of the book. If your calculus is rusty or you feel anxious about using calculus, you should go through these chapters and do the problems even if your instructor has not assigned them. The presentation begins with the simplest mathematical statement—the function—and progresses all the way to solving constrained maximization problems. If you have had a substantial amount of math and are comfortable with multivariate calculus and constrained maximization, you can probably treat these chapters as a handy reference guide. Skim them somewhat carefully to familiarize yourself with the basic notation used in the book and give special attention to the Lagrange method in Chapter 3.

Chapter 4 presents a verbal introduction to the market economy and problems of market failure. Since it uses no math and is self-contained, your instructor may assign it before the math introduction. Chapters 5–8 develop the basic models of individual consumer choice and market demand (the second level of analysis). Chapter 9 develops a very simple model of trade among consumers (the second level of analysis) and considers whether that market is efficient (the third level of analysis). Chapters 10–12 return to individual decision making, focusing on firm (or producer) behavior.* Chapter 13 then aggregates producers into market supply curves and studies the interaction of consumers and producers in competitive markets (the second level of analysis, again). Chapter 14 finishes the study of competitive markets by considering the coordination and efficiency of a competitive market economy (the third level of analysis).

The remainder of the book focuses on applications, extensions, and criticisms of the competitive model. Chapters 15 and 16 develop models of noncompetitive markets; Chapters 17 and 18 consider competitive and noncompetitive markets for labor and capital; Chapters 19 and 20 consider resource allocation under uncertainty; and Chapter 21 considers the implications of producing and consuming goods that generate external harms or benefits (externalities and public goods).

---

*Your instructor may have assigned Chapters 10–12 before Chapters 5–9.

Chapter 1

Basic Mathematical Concepts

1.1   WHAT YOU SHOULD LEARN FROM THIS CHAPTER

This chapter is designed to introduce you to the mathematical concepts and notation that will be used throughout this book. If you are anxious about math or if your math is rusty, the few simple tools presented here will help you gain the confidence and skills to tackle the rest of the book. If your math background is strong, this chapter will be a quick review.

    The most important concepts covered in this chapter are concerned with slopes (or derivatives) of functions. One of the central concerns of economics is how economic actors make changes in their behavior in response to changes in their economic environments. To model how economic behavior changes in response to small changes in the economic environment, economists use the mathematical tools of differential calculus.

1.2   FUNCTIONS

Functions are among the basic building blocks of mathematics. We say that y is a **function** of x if there is a *relationship* between y and x that defines, for each value of x, a corresponding value of y.[1] Thus, functions specify in precise terms how different *variables* are related to one another. For example, in economics, a demand function tells how many units of a good will be purchased at each price.

    The general function, with no specific values, is written as

$$y = f(x).$$

In such a function, x is called the **independent variable** and y is called the **dependent variable** because y *depends* on x according to the relationship $y = f(x)$. When we graph a function, we generally put the independent variable (x) on the horizontal axis and the dependent variable (y) on the vertical axis.

    A simple example of a function is

$$y = 2x.$$

---

[1]Technically, to be a *function,* the relationship must define a *unique* value of y for each value of x. If there is more than one value, the relationship is referred to as a *correspondence*. Except where otherwise noted, all mathematical relationships used in this book are functions.

This function defines the relationship between y and x that says, for every x value, the corresponding y value is twice as large.

Often, when we use functions, we distinguish between *variables* (which may vary) and **parameters,** which are held constant at some particular values. For example,

$$y = \alpha x^{\beta}, \text{ for } \alpha = 3, \beta = 2,$$

is written as

$$y = 3x^2.$$

In this case, x is the independent variable (it is allowed to vary) and α and β are parameters fixed at 3 and 2, respectively. We write the function in general form as

$$y = f(x; \alpha, \beta),$$

where x before the semicolon is a variable and α and β after the semicolon are parameters. We say that y is a function of x, given α and β.

Linear and Nonlinear Functions When we use functions, we will make frequent distinctions between two types of functions: linear functions and nonlinear functions. In economics, linear functions describe, for example, budget and isocost lines. Nonlinear functions may describe, for example, short-run average and marginal cost functions.

We say that y is a **linear function** of x if the graph of the function is a straight line. The general linear function is written as

$$y = a + bx,$$

where a is the y value when $x = 0$ (the y intercept) and b is the slope of the function (see Section 1.3). The function $y = 2x$ is a linear function with a zero y intercept. Figure 1.1 shows examples of the linear functions $y = 2x$ and $y = 2 + 2x$.

Functions that are *not* linear are called **nonlinear functions.** A simple example of a nonlinear function is $y = 1/x$, whose graph is shown in Figure 1.2.

Inverse Functions Often in economics, we will want to redefine a new function to make x in the original function the dependent variable and y the independent variable. For example, when we graph demand curves, we always put price on the vertical axis and quantity on the horizontal axis. We do this because an important turn-of-the-century economist, Alfred Marshall, conceived of the demand function with market price as a function of the quantity available for sale. He observed English country markets with numerous sellers bringing their quantities to the marketplace. The demand function specified what price consumers, taken together, would pay for a given quantity.

Today we generally build up market demand curves from individual consumer demand curves. We assume that consumers take market prices as *given* and choose quantities that maximize their utility. However, Marshall's influence is still so strong that we continue to draw our graphs with price on the vertical axis. Marshall did this because, to him, the dependent variable was price and the independent variable was quantity. The modern theory generally conceives of the demand function with quantity as the dependent variable and price as the independent variable. Marshall's *demand*

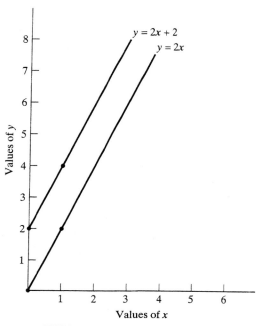

FIGURE 1.1   Linear Functions

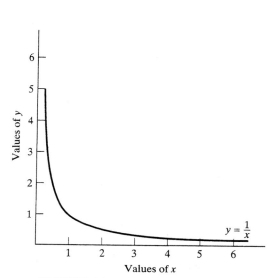

FIGURE 1.2   A Nonlinear Function

curve, therefore, is really the graph of a function other than the one we refer to as the *demand function*. We call this other function, with price as the dependent variable and quantity the independent variable, the *inverse demand function*.

More formally, we say that if $y = f(x)$ is a function of x, the **inverse function** defines an original x value for each y value.[2] The general form of the inverse function, with no specific values, is written as

$$x = f^{-1}(y) = h(y).$$

Some examples of functions and correspondences with their respective inverses are given below.

1. $y = 2x$ the function, $f(x)$ 2. $y = 1/x$ the function, $f(x)$

    $x = \dfrac{1}{2}y$ the inverse, $f^{-1}(y)$ $x = 1/y$ the inverse, $f^{-1}(y)$

3. $y = x^2$ the function, $f(x)$

    $x = \pm\sqrt{y}$ the inverse, which is not a function because there are two values of x for each nonzero y value

---

[2]You should note at this point, and be aware throughout the book, that the inverses of many functions are actually correspondences. That is because, in many cases, the inverse defines more than one value of x for each value of y.

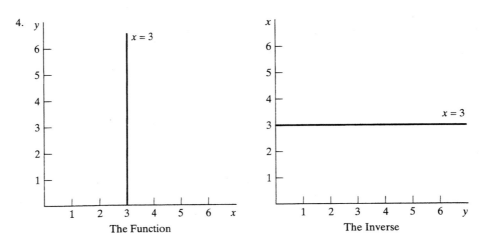

The Function   The Inverse

Continuity An important property of some functions and inverses is called continuity. Functions that exhibit this property are called continuous functions. To understand the concept of continuity, think of tracing the graph of a function with a pencil. If you can touch every point of the function without lifting the pencil from the paper, then the function is continuous. All the points of the graph are connected to one another.

To understand continuity more formally, we use the concept of the **limit of a function** as the independent variable approaches a particular value (say x_0): the value to which $f(x)$ approaches as x approaches x_0 is

$$\lim_{x \to x_0} f(x).$$

For example, suppose we wish to find the limit of the function $f(x) = x^2$ as x approaches 4. We can evaluate the function for values of x closer and closer to 4 to see what happens to $f(x)$ as x approaches 4.

$$f(3) = 3^2 = 9$$
$$f(3.5) = 12.25$$
$$f(3.9) = 15.21$$
$$f(3.99) = 15.9201$$
$$f(3.999) = 15.992001$$
$$f(3.9999) = 15.99920001$$

This suggests that the limit is $f(4) = 16$.

If a limit is actually equal to the value of a function at x_0, then the function is **continuous** at x_0:

$$\lim_{x \to x_0} f(x) = f(x_0)$$

implies that f is continuous at x_0. Thus, the function $y = x^2$ is continuous at $x = 4$ because

$$\lim_{x \to 4} x^2 = 4^2 = 16.$$

In fact, for every possible value of x, the limit of x^2 as x approaches all possible values is x^2.

On the other hand, the function $y = 1/x$ is undefined at 0. This means that there is a gap in the function at 0, and that the function is therefore not continuous everywhere.

$$\lim_{x \to 0} \frac{1}{x} = \pm\infty$$

Figure 1.3 illustrates another function that is not continuous everywhere. The function is constant at 1 for x values of 0 to 4, and then it jumps to 3 for x values greater than 4. Thus, the limit of the function is not well defined as x approaches 4.

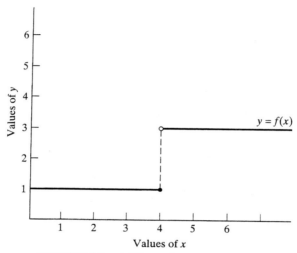

FIGURE 1.3   A Discontinuous Function

1.3   FUNCTIONS OF ONE INDEPENDENT VARIABLE: SLOPES AND DERIVATIVES

In economics, we are often concerned about the effect on the dependent variable of *changes* in the independent variable. For example, a retailer is interested in how much business he will lose if he raises the price of a product by $1. The ratio of the change in the dependent variable to the change in the independent variable is called the *slope*. Put in terms of x and y, the **slope** is equal to the change in y divided by the change in x. We use the notation Δy to denote the change in y and Δx to denote the change in x:

$$\frac{\Delta y}{\Delta x} = \frac{f(x_2) - f(x_1)}{x_2 - x_1}.$$

The distinction between linear and nonlinear functions becomes important when we begin to evaluate the slopes of functions. The **slope of a linear function** is simply b in the general form $y = a + bx$:

$$\frac{\Delta y}{\Delta x} = \frac{(a + bx_2) - (a + bx_1)}{x_2 - x_1}$$

$$= \frac{b(x_2 - x_1)}{x_2 - x_1}$$

$$= b.$$

Figure 1.4 shows the possible slopes of some straight lines.

Slopes of Nonlinear Functions In contrast to linear functions, which have constant slopes over all functional values, a nonlinear function does not have a constant slope and may, in fact, have a different slope at each point along the function. We could calculate $\Delta y/\Delta x$ over some range, but our choice of beginning and ending points would affect our calculation of the slope.

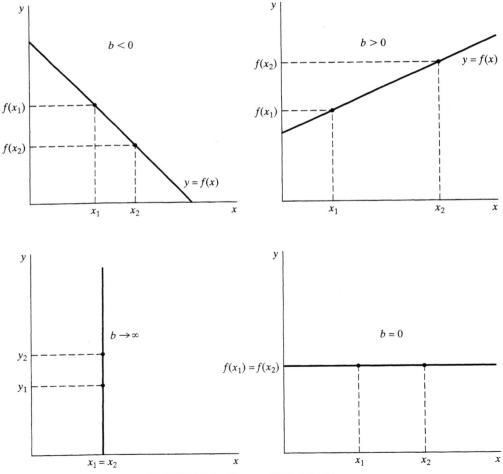

FIGURE 1.4   Slopes of Straight Lines

Suppose, for example, we wished to evaluate the slope of the function $y = f(x) = x^2$ at the point: $x = 2, y = 4$. Let's first evaluate the slope for $\Delta x = 2.5 - 2$ and $\Delta y = 6.25 - 4$, where $2.5 = x_2, 2 = x_1, 6.25 = f(x_2)$, and $4 = f(x_1)$:

$$\frac{\Delta y}{\Delta x} = \frac{6.25 - 4}{2.5 - 2} = \frac{2.25}{0.5} = 4.5.$$

Now, suppose that $\Delta x = 2.25 - 2$, then $\Delta y = 5.0625 - 4$, and

$$\frac{\Delta y}{\Delta x} = \frac{5.0625 - 4}{2.25 - 2} = \frac{1.0625}{0.25} = 4.25.$$

If we keep making Δx a little smaller, in this example $\Delta y / \Delta x$ would also keep getting smaller; as $\Delta x \to 0$, we would be evaluating better approximations of the slope at the point (2,4). For example, if $\Delta x = .125$, then $\Delta y = .5156$, and

$$\frac{\Delta y}{\Delta x} = \frac{.5156}{.125} = 4.125.$$

Similarly, if $\Delta x = .0625$, then $\Delta y = .2539$, and

$$\frac{\Delta y}{\Delta x} = \frac{.2539}{.0625} = 4.0625.$$

We can, however, find the slope at (2,4), without taking successive approximations, by noting that if two functions share a point in common, but do not cross, the two functions will have the same slope at that point.[3] With the exception of an inflection point, we say $f(x)$ is **tangent** to $g(x)$ at a particular point if the functions touch (without crossing) at that point. In particular, we can evaluate the slope of a nonlinear function at a point by finding the slope of a *linear* function that is just tangent at that point. The **slope of a nonlinear function** at a point is equal to the slope of a linear function that is tangent to the nonlinear function at that point. Figure 1.5 illustrates the line tangent to the function $y = x^2$ at the point (2,4). Thus, at (2,4), the slope of $y = x^2$ is 4, which is the slope of the linear function $y = -4 + 4x$.

The Slope Function Sometimes in economics, we want to find an entire function that specifies the slope of an original function corresponding to each value of the independent variable. In other words, we want to define a new function, $\Delta y / \Delta x = g(x)$. Graphically, we can sketch a *slope function* by finding the slopes of tangent linear functions at several points along the function. Figure 1.6 illustrates the graphical derivation of the slope function for the original function $y = x^2$. Connecting the points along the slope function reveals that the slope is the linear function $\Delta y / \Delta x = 2x$.

Derivatives Many mathematical arguments in economics require that we consider very small changes in the independent variable. To do this, we could evaluate the slope of the function at a point as we did above when we found the slope of the tangent to a nonlinear function. A more convenient way, however, is to find the derivative of the function. The **derivative of a function** at a given point is the limit of the slope of the

---

[3]This assumes the functions are smooth. The concept of smoothness is discussed at the end of this section.

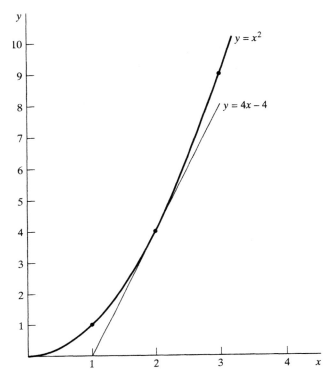

FIGURE 1.5   Derivation of the Slope of $y = x^2$ at $x = 2, y = 4$

function as the change in x approaches 0 (that is, as $\Delta x \to 0$). For linear functions, the derivative is everywhere b, the constant slope. For nonlinear functions, the derivative *at a point* is the slope of a tangent linear function at that point. We use the notations dy/dx (or $f'(x)$) to denote the derivative of the function $y = f(x)$:

$$\frac{dy}{dx} = f'(x) = \lim_{\Delta x \to 0} \frac{f(x + \Delta x) - f(x)}{\Delta x}.$$

In general, it is easier to derive the slope function by taking the derivative of the original function than by finding the slope at several points and then sketching a graph of the slope function. We will use graphical derivation for purposes of illustration, but will use derivatives to develop the formal theory. (Some simple rules for finding derivatives and other formulas are reviewed in the appendix to this chapter.) Returning to our example, the slope of the function $y = x^2$ is

$$\frac{dy}{dx} = \lim_{\Delta x \to 0} \frac{(x + \Delta x)^2 - x^2}{\Delta x}$$

$$= \lim_{\Delta x \to 0} \frac{x^2 + 2x\Delta x + (\Delta x)^2 - x^2}{\Delta x}$$

$$= \lim_{\Delta y \to 0} \frac{\Delta x \,(2x + \Delta x)}{\Delta y}$$

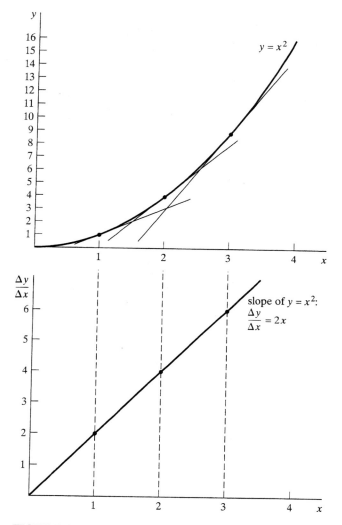

FIGURE 1.6   Derivation of the Slope Function for $y = x^2$

$$= \lim_{\Delta x \to 0} (2x + \Delta x)$$

$$= 2x,$$

as we derived graphically above.

The derivatives outlined above are often referred to as *first derivatives*. We can also define a function that is the derivative of the slope, or first derivative, function itself; it indicates the change in the slope of the function as the independent variable changes. This function is generally referred to as the **second derivative,** and we derive the notation for it in the following way. First, write it as the derivative of the derivative:

$$\frac{d}{dx}\left(\frac{dy}{dx}\right).$$

Now, remove the parentheses and note that dx times dx equals $(dx)^2$:

$$\frac{d}{dx}\left(\frac{dy}{dx}\right) = \frac{ddy}{dxdx} = \frac{d^2y}{(dx)^2}.$$

Finally, by convention, we drop the parentheses around dx in the denominator:

$$\frac{d}{dx}\left(\frac{dy}{dx}\right) = \frac{d^2y}{dx^2}.$$

For example, we have already seen that the first derivative of $y = x^2$ is $y = 2x$. The second derivative is

$$\frac{d^2y}{dx^2} = \frac{d(2x)}{dx} = 2.$$

Having defined first and second derivatives, higher-order derivatives follow analogously:

$$\frac{d^3y}{dx^3} = \frac{d}{dx}\left(\frac{d^2y}{dx^2}\right),$$

and, in general,

$$\frac{d^ny}{dx^n} = \frac{d}{dx}\left(\frac{d^{n-1}y}{dx^{n-1}}\right).$$

Smoothness The concept of continuity, introduced in Section 1.2, can also be applied to first and higher-order derivatives. A continuous function that has continuous, well-defined derivatives of every order is **smooth** in the sense that there are no gaps or kinks in the function. The concept of smoothness will have important applications later on.[4]

The upper graph of Figure 1.7 illustrates a function that is not smooth. The function is continuous, but the limit of the first derivative has two values at the peak, one as $\bar{x}$ is approached from above and one as it is approached from below. Along the straight lines, the function has constant derivatives equal to the slopes of the straight lines. However, at the point where the two lines meet, the derivative switches from one slope to the other. Thus, the derivative function (shown in the lower graph) consists of one constant positive function for x less than or equal to $\bar{x}$ and another constant negative function for x greater than or equal to $\bar{x}$.

---

[4]All we actually will need in most cases is for the function to have continuous second derivatives. In fact, nowhere in this book will we refer to third derivatives. As you progress in mathematical applications in economics, however, you may need to assume that functions have continuous higher-order derivatives as well.

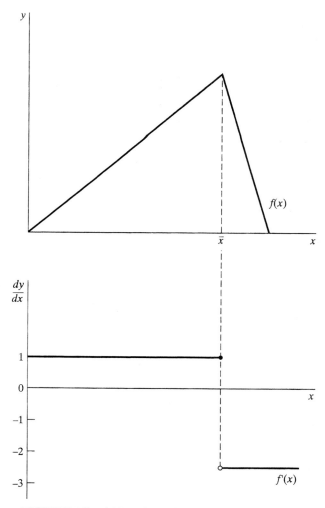

**FIGURE 1.7   A Function That Is Not Smooth and Its
First Derivative Function**

I.4   FUNCTIONS OF TWO OR MORE INDEPENDENT VARIABLES: PARTIAL AND TOTAL DERIVATIVES

While many interesting economic questions can be answered using functions of one independent variable, most of the economic problems requiring economic actors to make "trade-offs" can be analyzed effectively only with functions of two or more independent variables. For example, economists study how consumers maximize utility by purchasing different combinations of quantities of goods and services. Even if we restrict our attention to choices between two consumption goods, we still have a function in two independent variables and one dependent variable: the *first good*, the *second good*, and *utility*. Similarly, producers combine *capital* and *labor* to produce *output*.

Functions of Two Independent Variables Let's now consider a function of two independent variables in the general form

$$z = f(x, y).$$

This notation indicates z is a function of both x and y. An example of such a function is

$$z = 10x - x^2 + 20y - y^2. \tag{1.1}$$

Figure 1.8 illustrates a general, hill-shaped function in three dimensions.

Just as some questions in economics involve finding the slopes of functions of only one independent variable, other questions involve finding the slopes of functions of two or more independent variables. For example, how much does output change when labor or capital increases one unit? To illustrate the derivation of the slope of a function of more than one independent variable, let's focus on functions of two independent variables.

There are three ways of defining the slope of a function of two independent variables.

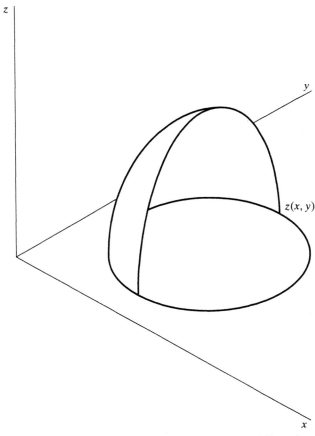

FIGURE 1.8   Graph of a General, Hill-shaped Function

1. We can hold x constant at the value $\bar{x}$ and find the slope of the function $z = f(y; \bar{x})$. This is called the **partial derivative of z with respect to y.** Letting $x = \bar{x}$, a constant, implies that $dx = 0$. Three notations for the partial derivative of z with respect to y are

$$\frac{\partial z}{\partial y} = \frac{dz}{dy}\bigg|_{dx=0} = f_y.$$

In our example (equation 1.1),

$$z = 10x - x^2 + 20y - y^2,$$

then

$$\frac{\partial z}{\partial y} = \frac{dz}{dy}\bigg|_{dx=0} = f_y = 20 - 2y. \tag{1.2}$$

Figure 1.9 illustrates dz/dy for a general, hill-shaped function.

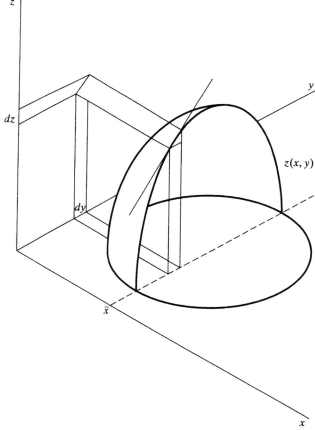

FIGURE 1.9   Illustration of the Partial Derivative of z with Respect to y

2. We can hold y constant at $\bar{y}$ and find the slope of the function $z = f(x; y)$. This is called the **partial derivative of z with respect to x.** Letting $y = \bar{y}$, a constant, three notations for the partial derivative of z with respect to x are

$$\frac{\partial z}{\partial x} = \frac{dz}{dx}\bigg|_{dy=0} = f_x.$$

In our example,

$$z = 10x - x^2 + 20y - y^2,$$

then

$$\frac{\partial z}{\partial x} = \frac{dz}{dx}\bigg|_{dy=0} = f_x = 10 - 2x. \tag{1.3}$$

Figure 1.10 illustrates $\partial z/\partial x$ for a general, hill-shaped function.

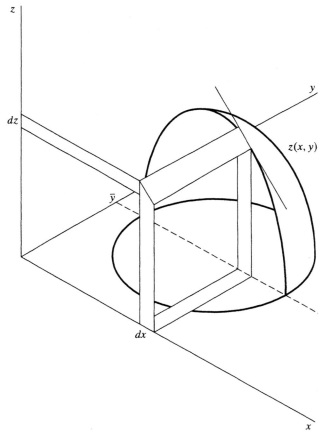

FIGURE 1.10 Illustration of the Partial Derivative of z with Respect to x

3. Finally, we can find the *total* change in z when both x and y change. This is called the *total differential* of the function z. We can think of the total differential as a weighted sum of the partial derivatives that adds up to the total change in z. To understand the intuition behind the concept of a total differential, think of the point-slope formula illustrated in Figure 1.11.

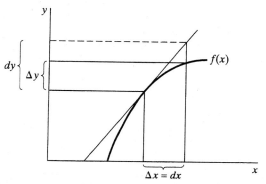

FIGURE 1.11   Illustration of the Point-Slope Formula

According to the point-slope formula, we can approximate Δy along a nonlinear function by multiplying the slope of a tangent linear function by Δx along the nonlinear function. Referring to the graph below,

$$dy = \frac{dy}{dx} \cdot dx$$

is an identity since $\Delta x = dx$; the approximation is

$$\Delta y \approx \frac{dy}{dx} \cdot dx.$$

Put in calculus notation, the point-slope formula becomes

$$\Delta y \approx f'dx.$$

When $\Delta x \to 0$, however, the slope of the function approaches the slope of the tangent function. We can write the point-slope formula as the identity

$$dy = f'dx.$$

Now, since a partial derivative is the same as a single-variable derivative when all but one independent variable is held constant, we can write dz, if x alone varies, by the following generalization of the single-variable point-slope formula:

$$dz|_{dy=0} = \frac{dz}{dx}\bigg|_{dy=0} dx = \frac{\partial z}{\partial x}\, dx = f'dx.$$

The **total differential** evaluates dz when all the independent variables are allowed to vary. It is expressed as the sum of the individual dz's when each independent variable is allowed to vary separately:

$$dz = \frac{dz}{dx}\bigg|_{dy=0} dx + \frac{dz}{dy}\bigg|_{dx=0} dy = \frac{\partial z}{\partial x} dx + \frac{\partial z}{\partial y} dy = f_x dx + f_y dy.$$

In our example,

$$z = 10x - x^2 + 20y - y^2,$$

then

$$dz = (10 - 2x)dx + (20 - 2y)dy. \tag{1.4}$$

Figure 1.12 illustrates a discrete approximation to dz for a general, hill-shaped function.

Functions of Several Independent Variables Having defined partial derivatives and the total differential for functions of two independent variables, the extension to functions of several (or n) independent variables follows.

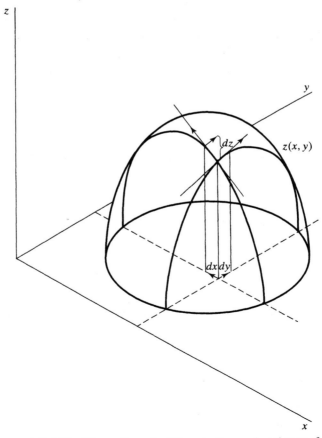

FIGURE 1.12   Illustration of a Discrete Approximation to dz

1. There are n partial derivatives of the dependent variable—one with respect to each of the independent variables.

$$z = f(x_1, \cdots, x_n)$$

$$\frac{\partial z}{\partial x_1} = \frac{dz}{dx_1}\bigg|_{dx_2 = \ldots = dx_n = 0}$$

$$\vdots$$

$$\frac{\partial z}{\partial x_i} = \frac{dz}{dx_i}\bigg|_{dx_1 = \ldots = dx_{i-1} = dx_{i-1} \ldots = dx_n = 0}$$

$$\vdots$$

$$\frac{\partial z}{\partial x_n} = \frac{dz}{dx_n}\bigg|_{dx_1 = \ldots = dx_{n-1} = 0}$$

2. The total differential is the generalization of the point-slope formula:

$$dz = \frac{\partial z}{\partial x_1} dx_1 + \cdots + \frac{\partial z}{\partial x_n} dx_n.$$

The Chain Rule and Continuity[5] When we work with functions of several variables in economics, we will often find that x and y are functions of another variable. For example, suppose x and y are both functions of α and z as a function of x and y. We can then write z as a function of α by substituting the functions $x(\alpha)$ and $y(\alpha)$ in the function $f(x, y)$:

$$z(\alpha) = f(x(\alpha), y(\alpha)).$$

To differentiate z with respect to α, we use the chain rule, taking account of how changes in α affect both x and y. The derivative of z with respect to α equals the derivative operating through a change in x *plus* the derivative operating through a change in y:

$$\frac{dz}{d\alpha} = \frac{\partial f}{\partial x}\frac{dx}{d\alpha} + \frac{\partial f}{\partial y}\frac{dy}{d\alpha} = f_x\frac{dx}{d\alpha} + f_y\frac{dy}{d\alpha}.$$

The concept of continuity may also be applied to functions of two or more independent variables and to their partial derivative functions. Just as with one independent variable, a function of several independent variables is continuous at a point if the limit of the function is equal to the value of the function as all the arguments approach that point. For example, in two dimensions,

$$\lim_{\substack{x \to x_0 \\ y \to y_0}} f(x, y) = f(x_0, y_0)$$

implies that f is continuous at (x_0, y_0).

Most of the functions developed in this book are functions of one or two independent variables. However, there are a few important functions of three or more independent variables. For example, after we derive what we call *ordinary demand curves* (quantity demanded is a function of price, holding income and other prices constant), we will derive a function called a *generalized demand function*. In this function,

---

[5]See Appendix 1.11 on the chain rule with functions of one variable.

quantity demanded is a function of all the variables assumed to affect it: own price, other prices, and income. Thus, we have a function of at least three independent variables.

1.5 SECOND PARTIAL DERIVATIVES AND SECOND TOTAL DIFFERENTIALS

Just as we defined second derivatives of functions of one independent variable, we can define second partial derivatives and second total differentials. For a function of two independent variables, for example, $z = f(x, y)$, there are four second derivatives and the second total differential.

1. The *second partial derivative* of z with respect to x is

$$\frac{\partial^2 z}{\partial x^2} = \frac{\partial}{\partial x}\left(\frac{\partial z}{\partial x}\right) = f_{xx}.$$

2. The *second cross partial derivative* of z with respect to x and y is

$$\frac{\partial^2 z}{\partial x \partial y} = \frac{\partial}{\partial x}\left(\frac{\partial z}{\partial y}\right) = f_{xy}.$$

3. The second partial derivative of z with respect to y is

$$\frac{\partial^2 z}{\partial y^2} = \frac{\partial}{\partial y}\left(\frac{\partial z}{\partial y}\right) = f_{yy}.$$

4. The second cross partial derivative of z with respect to y and x is equal to the second cross partial derivative of z with respect to x and y (that is, the order of differentiation does not matter) if both cross partial functions are continuous:[6]

$$\frac{\partial^2 z}{\partial y \partial x} = \frac{\partial}{\partial y}\left(\frac{\partial z}{\partial x}\right) = f_{yx} = \frac{\partial^2 z}{\partial x \partial y} = f_{xy}, \quad \text{if continuous.}$$

5. The *second total differential* is

$$d^2 z = d\left(\frac{\partial z}{\partial x} dx + \frac{\partial z}{\partial y} dy\right)$$

$$= \frac{\partial^2 z}{\partial x^2} dxdx + \frac{\partial^2 z}{\partial x \partial y} dydx + \frac{\partial^2 z}{\partial y \partial x} dxdy + \frac{\partial^2 z}{\partial y^2} dydy$$

$$= \frac{\partial^2 z}{\partial x^2}(dx)^2 + 2\frac{\partial^2 z}{\partial x \partial y} dydx + \frac{\partial^2 z}{\partial y^2}(dy)^2.$$

It can also be written as

$$d^2 z = f_{xx}(dx)^2 + 2f_{xy}dxdy + f_{yy}(dy)^2.$$

For example, consider the following function in two independent variables:

$$z = x^2 y^3 + 5xy^2 + 6y$$

---

[6]This is known as Young's theorem. For a discussion of Young's theorem, see, for example, Eugene Silberberg, *The Structure of Economics*, 2d ed. (New York: McGraw-Hill, 1990), pp. 73–74.

$$\frac{\partial z}{\partial x} = 2xy^3 + 5y^2$$

$$\frac{\partial^2 z}{\partial x^2} = 2y^3$$

$$\frac{\partial^2 z}{\partial x \partial y} = 6xy^2 + 10y$$

$$\frac{\partial z}{\partial y} = 3x^2y^2 + 10xy + 6$$

$$\frac{\partial^2 z}{\partial y^2} = 6x^2y + 10x$$

$$\frac{\partial^2 z}{\partial y \partial x} = 6xy^2 + 10y = \frac{\partial^2 z}{\partial x \partial y}$$

$$dz = (2xy^3 + 5y^2)dx + (3x^2y^2 + 10xy + 6)dy$$

$$d^2z = 2y^3 dx^2 + 2(6xy^2 + 10y)dydx + (6x^2y + 10x)dy^2.$$

We will also use the concept of smoothness of functions of several variables. Here, since we have only developed second partial derivatives, we will use smoothness to describe a function of several variables that has continuous second partial derivatives. The extension of the concept to higher-order partial derivatives would follow from a development of those derivatives.

1.6   MORE WORKED PROBLEMS INVOLVING PARTIAL AND TOTAL DERIVATIVES

In this section, we derive the first and second partial derivatives and the first and second total differentials for two more functions of two independent variables as further practice for students who are unfamiliar, or still uncomfortable, with partial derivatives.

1.

$$z = 4x^4y^3 - 5x^2y + xy^2$$

$$\frac{\partial z}{\partial x} = 16x^3y^3 - 10xy + y^2$$

$$\frac{\partial z}{\partial y} = 12x^4y^2 - 5x^2 + 2xy$$

$$dz = (16x^3y^3 - 10xy + y^2)dx + (12x^4y^2 - 5x^2 + 2xy)dy$$

$$\frac{\partial^2 z}{\partial x^2} = 48x^2y^3 - 10y$$

$$\frac{\partial^2 z}{\partial y^2} = 24x^4y + 2x$$

$$\frac{\partial^2 z}{\partial x \partial y} = \frac{\partial^2 z}{\partial y \partial x} = 48x^3y^2 - 10x + 2y$$

$$d^2z = (48x^2y^3 - 10y)dx^2 + 2(48x^3y^2 - 10x + 2y)dydx + (24x^4y + 2x)dy^2$$

2.

$$z = \frac{5x + 10y}{xy}, \quad xy \neq 0 \quad \text{see appendix for a review of the quotient rule}$$

$$\frac{\partial z}{\partial x} = \frac{5xy - y(5x + 10y)}{(xy)^2} = -\frac{10}{x^2}$$

$$\frac{\partial z}{\partial y} = \frac{10xy - x(5x + 10y)}{(xy)^2} = -\frac{5}{y^2}$$

$$dz = -\frac{10}{x^2}dx - \frac{5}{y^2}dy$$

$$\frac{\partial^2 z}{\partial x^2} = \frac{20}{x^3}$$

$$\frac{\partial^2 z}{\partial y^2} = \frac{10}{y^3}$$

$$\frac{\partial^2 z}{\partial x \partial y} = \frac{\partial^2 z}{\partial y \partial x} = 0$$

$$d^2z = \frac{20}{x^3}dx^2 + 2(0)dydx + \frac{10}{y^3}dy^2 = \frac{20}{x^3}dx^2 + \frac{10}{y^3}dy^2$$

1.7   SIMPLE INTEGRATION

Some of the mathematical applications in this book will require finding the area under a function. The technique used is *integration,* involving what is called an *antiderivative.* To develop integration, we begin with a function $F(x)$. Figure 1.13 illustrates such a function. We now define $f(x)$ to be the derivative of $F(x)$:

$$F'(x) = f(x).$$

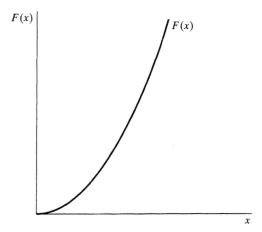

FIGURE 1.13   The Function $F(x)$

Figure 1.14 compares $F(x)$ and $f(x)$. Next, we divide the interval from a to b into n equal parts, each of which is designated Δx. Thus,

$$\Delta x = \frac{b - a}{n}.$$

Figure 1.15 illustrates this division for both $F(x)$ and $f(x)$.

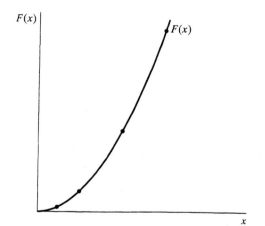

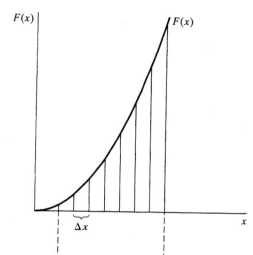

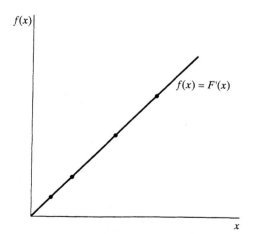

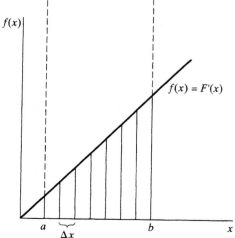

FIGURE 1.14   The Function $F(x)$ and Its Slope $f(x)$

FIGURE 1.15   Dividing the Interval from a to b into n Equal Segments

We now use the point-slope formula to approximate the changes in $F(x)$ associated with each interval Δx.

$$F(a + \Delta x) - F(a) \approx F'(a)\Delta x$$
$$F(a + 2\Delta x) - F(a + \Delta x) \approx F'(a + \Delta x)\Delta x$$
$$F(b) - F(a + (n - 1)\Delta x) \approx F'(a + (n - 1)\Delta x)\Delta x$$

Notice that if we add up all these equations, all the terms on the left-hand side cancel except $F(a)$ and $F(b)$. This happens because the other terms each enter the summation twice, once with a minus sign and once with a plus sign. For example, $F(a + \Delta x)$ is in the first equation with a plus sign and in the second equation with a minus sign. Thus, summing over all the $\Delta F(x)$ approximations yields

$$F(b) - F(a) \approx \sum_{i=0}^{n-1} F'(a + i\Delta x)\Delta x = \sum_{i=0}^{n-1} f(a + i\Delta x)\Delta x,$$

where the symbol Σ denotes that we are summing over values of F'.

Notice also that $f(a + i\Delta x)\Delta x$ is the area of the rectangle of width Δx and height $f(x)$ in the lower graph. Adding these up over the interval from a to b (as long as the functional values are nonnegative between a and b) gives an approximation to the area under the function $f(x)$ between a and b. This is illustrated in Figure 1.16. The shaded area represents the area measured by adding up the rectangles of width Δx.

As n goes to infinity (thus $\Delta x \to 0$), the area represented by the unmeasured triangles in Figure 1.16 goes to 0, and $F(b) - F(a)$ gives the actual area under f between a

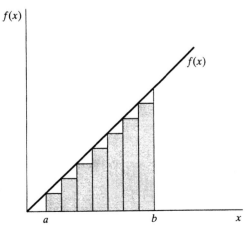

FIGURE 1.16 Approximating the Area Under the Function $f(x)$

and b. When we let Δx go to 0, we call the limit of the sum of the rectangles the **integral** of the function $f(x)$:

$$\int_a^b f(x)\, dx = \lim_{\Delta x \to 0} \sum_{i=0}^{n-1} f(a + i\Delta x)x = F(b) - F(a).$$

We call $F(x)$ the **antiderivative** of $f(x)$ because $F(x)$ is a function whose derivative is $f(x)$. Thus, to evaluate the integral of $f(x)$ between a and b, we try to find a function whose derivative is $f(x)$ and then evaluate that function at a and b. For example, if

$$f(x) = x^2,$$

then

$$F(x) = \frac{1}{3}x^3 + \text{ a constant } (C)$$

because

$$F'(x) = f(x) = x^2.$$

Therefore,

$$\int_1^3 x^2 dx = F(3) - F(1) = \frac{1}{3}3^3 - \frac{1}{3}1^3 = 9 - \frac{1}{3} = 8\frac{2}{3}.$$

Notice that the constant cancels in the subtraction. If

$$f(x) = 4x^2 + 3x + 2,$$

then

$$F(x) = \frac{4}{3}x^3 + \frac{3}{2}x^2 + 2x + C$$

$$F'(x) = f(x) = 4x^2 + 3x + 2$$

$$\int_a^b (4x^2 + 3x + 2)dx = F(b) - F(a)$$

$$= \left(\frac{4}{3}b^3 + \frac{3}{2}b^2 + 2b\right) - \left(\frac{4}{3}a^3 + \frac{3}{2}a^2 + 2a\right).$$

The general rule for a polynomial is that if

$$f(x) = a_0 + a_1x + a_2x^2 + \cdots + a_nx^n, n \neq -1,$$

then

$$F(x) = a_0x + \frac{a_1}{2}x^2 + \frac{a_2}{3}x^3 + \cdots + \frac{a_n}{n+1}x^{n+1} + C.$$

If n did equal -1 on the other hand, applying the above rule would give

$$F(x) = -1x^0 + C = -1 + C,$$

which is clearly not going to be true for all x. This case is taken care of with the **natural logarithm,** which (with the constant of integration) is *defined* to be the antiderivative of $1/x$:[7]

$$\ln(x) + C \equiv F\left(\frac{1}{x}\right) \quad \text{and} \quad \frac{d}{dx}\ln(x) = \frac{1}{x}.$$

1.8 REVIEW OF KEY CONCEPTS

This completes the set of fundamental mathematical tools you will need to read the rest of this book. Before beginning the next chapter on the mathematics of maximization, be sure you understand the following key concepts.

A *function* defines a precise mathematical relationship among variables.

A function is defined over values of *independent variables,* which are sometimes called right-hand side variables.

The value of the *dependent variable* depends on the values of the independent variables. Dependent variables are sometimes called left-hand side variables.

In defining a function, symbols designated as *variables* are allowed to vary, and symbols designated as *parameters* are held fixed at specific values.

The two-dimensional graph of a *linear function* is a straight line. Other kinds of functions are called *nonlinear functions*.

An *inverse function* defines values of the original independent variable as a function of values of the original dependent variable.

The *limit of a function* evaluated at a given value of the independent variable is the value the dependent variable approaches as the independent variable approaches the given value.

There are no gaps in the graph of a *continuous function*.

The *slope of a function* is the ratio of the change in the dependent variable to the change in the independent variable.

The *slope of a linear function* is constant.

A *function is tangent* to another function at a point if both functions touch at that point and do not cross.

The *slope of a nonlinear function* varies and equals the slope of a tangent linear function at each point.

The *derivative of a function* at a point is the same as the slope of the function at that point.

The *second derivative* is the derivative of the first derivative.

A function is *smooth* if it is continuous and has continuous first and higher-order derivatives.

The *partial derivative of z with respect to either x or y* is the same as the first derivative with respect to either x or y, holding all other independent variables constant.

The *total differential* evaluates a linear approximation to the change in the dependent variable when all the independent variables are allowed to vary simultaneously.

The *integral* of a function from point a to point b measures the area under the function from point a to point b.

The *antiderivative* of a function f is another function F, such that $f = F'$.

The integral from a to b is evaluated as the antiderivative evaluated at b minus the antiderivative evaluated at a.

The *natural logarithm* is the antiderivative of $1/x$.

---

[7]Tom M. Apostol, *Calculus,* 2d ed. (Lexington, MA: Xerox College, 1967), vol. 1, p. 229.

1.9 ___ QUESTIONS FOR DISCUSSION

1. Recall the material from your principles course and try to think of ten important economic relationships that could be expressed as functions. What are the dependent variables, the independent variables, and the parameters in each case? Write down a possible general formula for two of them.   .

2. Now, think of five important economic concepts that can be expressed as functions that are actually slopes of other functions.

3. Can you think of an economic concept that is properly expressed as an integral? Draw a graph to illustrate why it is an integral.

1.10 ___ PROBLEMS

(Consult the appendix for rules of differentiation.)

Problems 1–6 Graph the functions.

1. $y = -2x + 4$
2. $y = 3x + 1$
3. $y = 2/x$
4. $y = x^2 + 4$
5. $y = 16x - x^2$
6. $y = 4x - 1/x^2$

Problems 7–9 Find the inverses of the functions.

7. $y = -2x + 4$
8. $y = 3x + 1$
9. $y = 2/x$

10. Take each function in Problems 1–6 and indicate whether it is continuous or not. If it is not continuous, indicate at which points it is discontinuous and explain why.

11. Find the first and second derivative for each function in Problems 1–6.

12. Find the antiderivative $F(x)$ for each function in Problems 1–6.

Problems 13–16 Find the first and second derivatives for each function.

13. $y = 10 + 2x + 5x^2 - 4x^3$

14. $y = (5 - 3x)^4$
(Use the chain rule.)

15. $y = 12x^3(6x - 2)^5$
(Use the product rule and the chain rule.)

16. $y = \dfrac{x^2 + 5}{x^3}$
(Use the quotient rule.)

Problems 17–19 Find the partial derivatives and the total differential ($\partial z/\partial x$, $\partial z/\partial y$, and dz) for each function.

17. $z = 3x^3 + 15y^2 - x - 3y$

18. $z = x^3 y^4$

19. $z = \dfrac{x + y}{xy}$

20. Find the second partial derivatives (including cross partials) and the second total differential for each function in Problems 17–19.

1.11 ___ APPENDIX

REVIEW OF DIFFERENTIATION RULES AND SIMPLE FORMULAS

DERIVATIVES

1. Polynomials
   Let

$$y = f(x) = a_0 + a_1 x + a_2 x^2 + \cdots + a_n x^n,$$

   then

$$dy/dx = 0 + 1a_1 x^{1-1} + 2a_2 x^{2-1} + \cdots + na_n x^{n-1}$$

$$= a_1 + 2a_2x + \cdots + na_nx^{n-1}.$$

2. Chain rule
   Let

$$y = f(x) = g(h(x)),$$

then

$$dy/dx = g'(h(x))(dh/dx).$$

For example,

$$y = (a_0 + a_1x^n)^m, \quad m, n \neq -1$$
$$dy/dx = m(a_0 + a_1x^n)^{m-1}(na_1x^{n-1}).$$

3. Product rule
   Let

$$y = f(x) = g(x)h(x),$$

then

$$dy/dx = g'(x)h(x) + h'(x)g(x).$$

For example,

$$y = (q + rx)(s + tx), \quad q, r, s, t \text{ constant}$$
$$dy/dx = r(s + tx) + t(q + rx) = 2rtx + rs + qt.$$

4. Quotient rule
   Let

$$y = f(x) = g(x)/h(x),$$

then

$$\frac{dy}{dx} = \frac{g'(x)h(x) - h'(x)g(x)}{[h(x)]^2}.$$

For example,

$$y = \frac{q + rx}{s + tx}, \quad q, r, s, t \text{ constant}$$
$$\frac{dy}{dx} = \frac{r(s + tx) - t(q + rx)}{(s + tx)^2} = \frac{rs - qt}{(s + tx)^2}$$

5. Exponential functions
   If

$$f(x) = e^{ax},$$

then

$$f'(x) = ae^{ax}$$

and

$$F(x) = \frac{1}{a} e^{ax}.$$

OTHER USEFUL FORMULAS

1. Solution to a second-degree polynomial
   If

$$ax^2 + bx + c = 0,$$

then

$$x = \frac{-b \pm \sqrt{b^2 - 4ac}}{2a} .$$

2. Factoring

$$x^2 + 2xy + y^2 = (x + y)^2$$
$$x^2 - y^2 = (x + y)(x - y)$$

Chapter 2

UNCONSTRAINED MAXIMIZATION AND MINIMIZATION

2.1   WHAT YOU SHOULD LEARN FROM THIS CHAPTER

This chapter introduces the most important mathematical tools needed to read the rest of this book. In economics, we are always looking for the "best" way to do something. For example, we ask what combination of inputs and output will a firm choose in order to maximize profits? Alternatively, we might ask what output level allows the firm to produce that output at the lowest possible cost per unit? The first problem involves choosing a maximum (profit) and the second involves choosing a minimum (average cost). We use the calculus tools reviewed in Chapter 1 to make it relatively easy to choose a maximum or a minimum.

Sometimes we can choose the best alternative from all conceivable alternatives. We call this an *unconstrained* maximum or minimum. This chapter first reviews unconstrained maximization and minimization of functions of one variable. Then, the techniques of maximization and minimization allow us to relate such concepts as average cost and marginal cost and average product and marginal product. Next, we develop unconstrained maximization and minimization of functions of several independent variables.

The chapter ends with an introduction to two important mathematical tools used in economics. First, when we examine the effects of a change in a parameter (such as a consumer's income), we are doing what is called *comparative statics:* comparing one static equilibrium for one set of parameters with another equilibrium for another set of parameters. Second, when we evaluate functions at their optimal values, we can assume that all the conditions characterizing optimality are satisfied, which sometimes allows us to ignore certain kinds of indirect effects. This insight is made formal by the *envelope theorem.* Both comparative statics and the envelope theorem will be used throughout the book.

Most of you are probably somewhat familiar with unconstrained maximization and minimization of functions of one independent variable. Probably fewer of you are familiar with maximization and minimization of functions of more than one independent variable. Everyone should pay careful attention to comparative statics and the envelope theorem. As in the previous chapter, if your math is rusty or you still feel uncomfortable with math, study the entire chapter carefully. Begin with functions of one independent variable and do the one-variable problems at the end of the chapter. When you feel comfortable with those, go on to tackle functions of two or more independent variables. If your math background is strong, you can probably skim over the section on functions of one independent variable, making sure you can do the problems. However, be sure you have mastered the concepts in this chapter before going on to *constrained* maximization and minimization in Chapter 3.

2.2   FUNCTIONS OF ONE INDEPENDENT VARIABLE: UNCONSTRAINED MAXIMIZATION AND MINIMIZATION

Throughout this book, we will be concerned with maximizing and minimizing a number of functions of one independent variable. For example, in many cases, short-run average total cost is a U-shaped function of output, with some minimum average cost. On the other hand, a monopolist's profit as a function of output attains a maximum.

Optimization   A function attains a **local maximum** at a point that is *higher* than any other point nearby and a **local minimum** at a point that is *lower* than any other point nearby.[1] If the function is **smooth** at its maximum or minimum, the slope of the function will be 0 at that point. We call either a maximum or a minimum an **optimum** and the technique of finding an optimum, **optimization.** Thus, both *maximization* and *minimization* are referred to as optimization.

Maximization and minimization are both illustrated in Figure 2.1.[2] Notice that x^* determines the optimal value of the function being maximized or minimized, the **objective function** $y = f(x)$. It is a convention in economics to give "optimal" choices and outcomes the "*" notation. Thus, at the maximum or minimum, we write

$$y^* = f(x^*).$$

Critical Points   Looking at the problem from another perspective, we call a point where the slope of a function is 0 a **critical point** of the function. Such a point might be a maximum or a minimum, as above, but it might also be a temporary flat section in an otherwise increasing or decreasing function. In that case, the critical point is referred to as an **inflection point** of the function.[3] An inflection point of an increasing function, where the slope is 0, is illustrated in Figure 2.2. At x^*, the slope of the function is 0, as illustrated by the horizontal tangent function, but x^* is neither a maximum nor a minimum.

---

[1]We say that a function attains a **global maximum** if the maximum is the highest point over the entire function and a *global minimum* if the minimum is the lowest point over the entire function.

[2]The functions in Figure 2.1 are drawn only in the positive quadrant because economics typically concerns only positive values. But the maxima and minima of functions can occur at any values of the dependent or independent variables. In Chapter 3, we consider the consequences of restricting x and y to nonnegative values.

[3]Points of inflection do not necessarily occur at critical points of functions. An inflection point is defined to be a point at which the second derivative of a function changes sign.

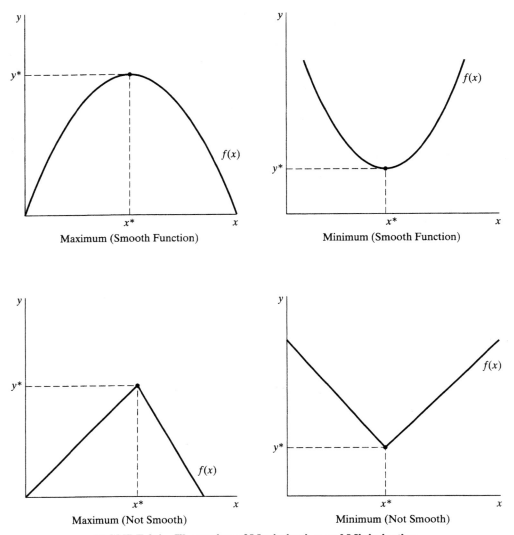

FIGURE 2.1 Illustration of Maximization and Minimization

Since the slope condition is the same for a maximum, a minimum, or a critical inflection point of a smooth function, we must have some other means of distinguishing among the three when we use calculus to find a critical point. We tell the differences among a maximum, a minimum, and an inflection point by looking at the behavior of the slope of the original function near x^*. If the slope is positive and falling for $x < x^*$, and negative and falling for $x > x^*$, the function is maximized at x^*. Conversely, if the slope is negative and rising for $x < x^*$, and positive and rising for $x > x^*$, the function is minimized at x^*. (These distinctions are illustrated in Figure 2.3.) Lastly, the slope of the slope function is 0 at an inflection point.

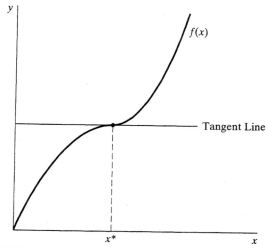

FIGURE 2.2   A Critical Point That Is an Inflection Point

These conditions can be translated into conditions on the second derivative of the original function. In the case of the maximum in Figure 2.3, the second derivative is negative because the slope function is downward sloping:

$$\frac{d^2y}{dx^2} < 0.$$

Similarly, in the case of the minimum, the second derivative is positive because the slope function is upward sloping:

$$\frac{d^2y}{dx^2} > 0.$$

In the case of an inflection point, the second derivative is 0.

First- and Second-order Conditions The condition that the derivative of the function is 0 is a **necessary condition** for a maximum or a minimum of a smooth function to occur. That means that if the function is smooth, it is *not* possible to attain a maximum or a minimum unless the derivative is 0. We call this condition the **first-order condition** for unconstrained maximization or minimization. Once the first-order condition is satisfied, the conditions on the second derivatives are **sufficient** for maximization or minimization to occur. That means that if the first derivative is 0 and the appropriate condition on the second derivative is satisfied, we know we have a maximum or a minimum. We call the conditions on the second derivative **second-order conditions** for unconstrained maximization and minimization. Thus, taken together, the first- and second-order conditions are necessary and sufficient for unconstrained maximization and minimization of smooth functions.

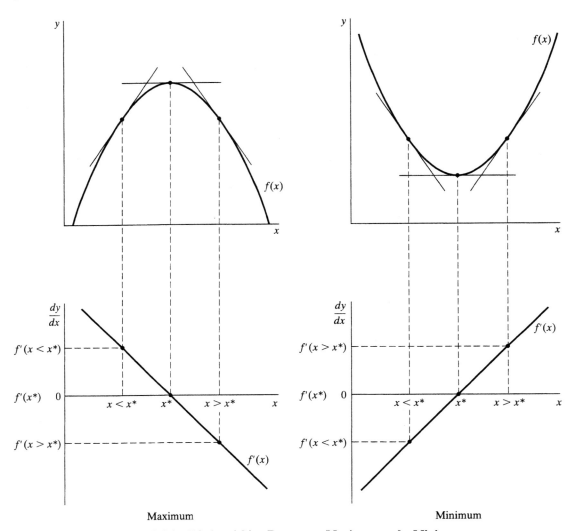

FIGURE 2.3 Distinguishing Between a Maximum and a Minimum

An inflection point cannot be identified by a zero second derivative alone, however, since a constant function and a few special cases of maxima and minima have zero second derivatives as well. In fact, an inflection point has the property that the second derivative actually changes sign at that point. This implies that the function increases in one direction away from the critical point and decreases in the other direction.

Examples In each of the following examples, we use the first-order condition to find a critical point, or critical points, of the function. Then we use the second-order condition to identify whether the critical point (or points) is a maximum or a minimum.

1. $y = 50x - 5x^2$

The first-order condition is

$$\frac{dy}{dx} = 50 - 10x^* = 0.$$

Therefore,

$$10x^* = 50 \Rightarrow x^* = 5$$
$$y^* = 50(5) - 5(5)^2 = 125.$$

The second-order condition is

$$\frac{d^2y}{dx^2} = -10 < 0.$$

Therefore, $x^* = 5$ is the value of x that maximizes the function $y = 50x - 5x^2$ at the point $y^* = f(5) = 125$. Moreover, 125 is the global maximum of the function: no other value of the function is higher.

2. $y = 25x + \dfrac{100}{x}$

The first-order condition is

$$\frac{dy}{dx} = 25 - \frac{100}{(x^*)^2} = 0.$$

Therefore,

$$\frac{100}{(x^*)^2} = 25 \Rightarrow (x^*)^2 = 4 \Rightarrow x^* = \pm 2$$

$$y^* = 25(+2) + \frac{100}{+2} = +100$$

or

$$y^* = 25(-2) + \frac{100}{-2} = -100.$$

The second-order condition is

$$\frac{d^2y}{dx^2} = \frac{200}{x^3}.$$

The second-order condition is positive for $+2$ and negative for -2. Therefore, $y^* = +100$ is a local minimum (positive second-order condition) and $y^* = -100$ is a local maximum (negative second-order condition). Figure 2.4 illustrates this function and its critical points.

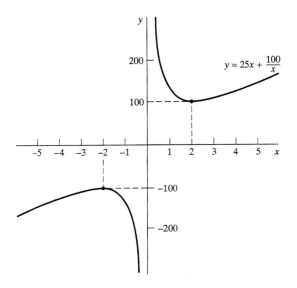

FIGURE 2.4   Graph of the Function $y = 25x + 100/x$

TOTAL, AVERAGE, AND MARGINAL FUNCTIONS OF ONE VARIABLE

Some of the most important concepts in economics are expressed as average or marginal functions derived from some original total function. For example, we speak of total cost, average cost, and marginal cost, and total product, average product, and marginal product of labor or capital. This section shows how total, average, and marginal functions are related to one another mathematically. The techniques of unconstrained optimization, developed above, make it easy to derive average and marginal functions and understand their mathematical interrelationships.

We begin with some **total function,** which is simply the original set of values of some particular function. For example,

$$\text{total} = 4x^2 + 3x + 2 = f(x) = y$$

might be a total cost function. The **average function,** derived from the original total function, is a function that describes the average value of the dependent variable for each value of the independent variable. It is derived by dividing the functional value corresponding to each value of the dependent variable by the value of the independent variable at each point:

$$\text{average} = \frac{f(x)}{x} = \frac{y}{x}.$$

For example, average cost is simply the total cost of producing each output level, or total cost, divided by output. In the above example,

$$\text{average} = \frac{\text{total}}{x} = \frac{4x^2 + 3x + 2}{x} = 4x + 3 + \frac{2}{x}.$$

The **marginal function** is the change in the total function for a given change in the independent variable. However, we have already seen that this is simply the slope function, or the first derivative of the original function:

$$\text{marginal} = \frac{d}{dx} f(x) = \frac{dy}{dx} = f'(x).$$

Thus, marginal cost is the slope or first derivative of the total cost function. In the above example,

$$\text{marginal} = \frac{d}{dx} (\text{total}) = \frac{d}{dx} (4x^2 + 3x + 2) = 8x + 3.$$

Marginal Functions There are some important ways that total, average, and marginal functions are related to one another. Figure 2.5 illustrates the relationship between a total and a marginal function, and the following facts help us to derive the marginal function.

1. When the total function $y = f(x)$ attains a maximum or a minimum, the slope, dy/dx, is 0. Thus, the marginal function is 0 when the total function attains either a maximum or a minimum. These points are identified as x_{max} and x_{min} in Figure 2.5.

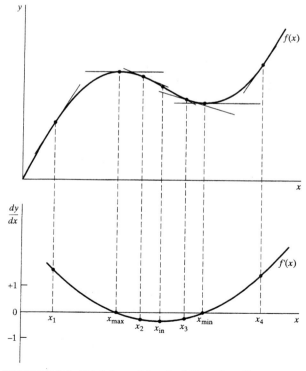

FIGURE 2.5   Deriving a Marginal Function Graphically

2. For points close to x_{max}, the slope should be positive and falling for $x < x_{max}$ and negative and falling for $x > x_{max}$. Points x_1 and x_2 illustrate positive and negative points on the decreasing part of the marginal function.

3. For points close to x_{min}, the slope should be negative and rising for $x < x_{min}$, and positive and rising for $x > x_{min}$. Points x_3 and x_4 illustrate negative and positive points on the increasing part of the marginal function.

4. The slope function must attain a maximum if the slope changes from rising to falling or a minimum if it changes from falling to rising. If the slope function itself is smooth, its slope should be 0 at that point. In Figure 2.5, x_{in} is the point of inflection, which identifies a minimum for this particular marginal function. Figure 2.6 illustrates the derivation of a marginal function that attains a maximum. In this case, x_{in} identifies a maximum along the marginal function.

Average Functions Figure 2.7 illustrates the relationship between the average and the total function, and the following facts help us to derive the average function.

1. The average function evaluated at a particular point is always equal to the slope of a line from the origin to the function at that point. To illustrate this

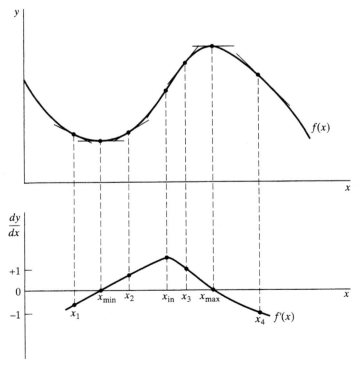

FIGURE 2.6 Derivation of a Marginal Function That Attains a Maximum

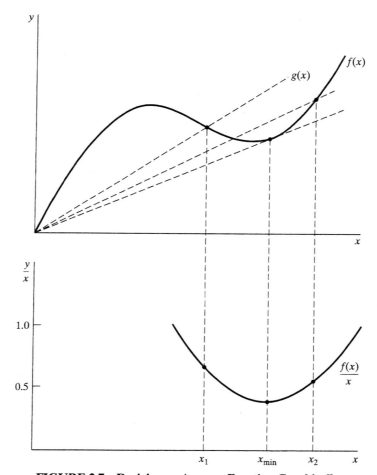

FIGURE 2.7   Deriving an Average Function Graphically

point, consider point x_1 in Figure 2.7. Let $g(x)$ represent a line from the origin to the function at x_1:

$$\frac{f(x_1)}{x_1} = \frac{f(x_1) - 0}{x_1 - 0} = \frac{d}{dx}g(x).$$

2. When the line from the origin to the function is just tangent to the function, the slope of the line from the origin becomes the slope of the total function at that point. Since the slope function is the same as the marginal function, and the average function is the same as the slope of a line from the origin, the average and marginal functions must be equal when the line from the origin is just tangent to the function. This would be true at point x_2 in Figure 2.6.

3. When the line from the origin is just tangent to the function, the average function attains either a maximum or a minimum. In Figure 2.7, the average function

attains a minimum at x_{min}. Up to the point of tangency the slope of the line from the origin falls. From the point of tangency on, it rises. Figure 2.8 illustrates the derivation of an average function that attains a maximum when the line from the origin is tangent to the function; the average function increases to the point x_{max} and then decreases thereafter.

Total, Marginal, and Average Functions Reviewed Figure 2.9 illustrates the relationships among all three functions: the total, the average, and the marginal. We have already seen that the average attains a maximum or a minimum when the line from the origin is just tangent to the function, or equivalently, when the average function is equal to the marginal function. This is shown as $x_{av=ma}$ in Figure 2.9. Notice also that the marginal function is everywhere less than the average function when the average is falling and everywhere greater than the average when the average is rising. Figure 2.10 illustrates these relationships when the average function attains a maximum. Once again, the marginal function is equal to the average function when the average is maximized, everywhere greater than the average when the average is rising, and everywhere less

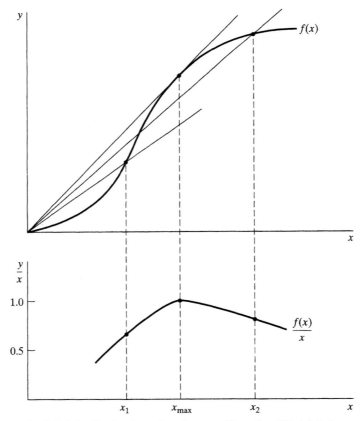

FIGURE 2.8 Derivation of an Average Function That Attains a Maximum

than the average when the average is falling. The following statements provide a summary of the relationships between average and marginal functions in general.

1. If x is greater than 0 ($x > 0$), the marginal function is less than the average function when the average is falling.

2. If x is greater than 0 ($x > 0$), the marginal function is greater than the average function when the average function is rising.

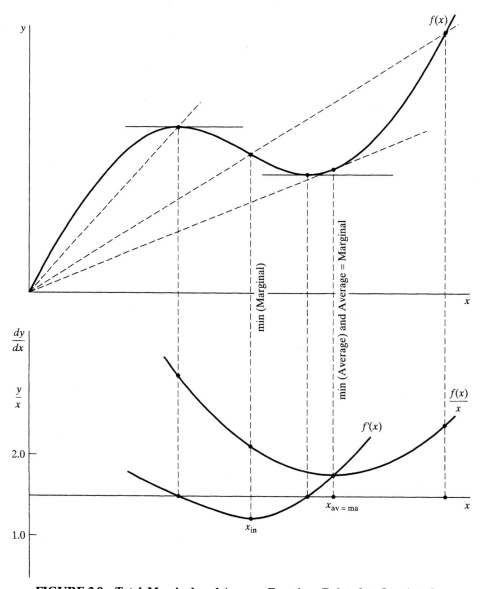

FIGURE 2.9   Total, Marginal, and Average Functions Related to One Another

3. The marginal function is always equal to the average function when the average attains either a maximum or a minimum.

The following simple mathematical proof shows that these statements are true for positive values of x. We wish to compare dy/dx and y/x. To do that we differentiate y/x (the average function) with respect to x:

$$\frac{d}{dx}\left(\frac{y}{x}\right) = \frac{(dy/dx)x - 1(y)}{x^2}.$$

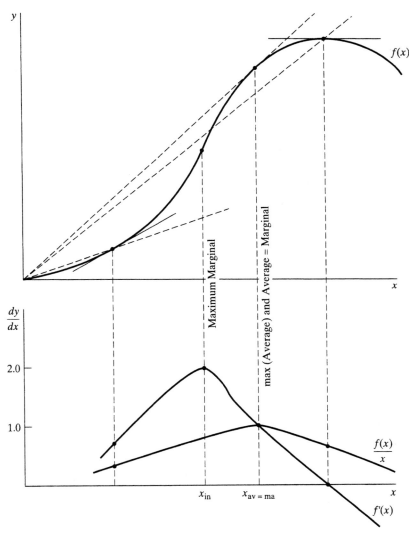

FIGURE 2.10   Total, Marginal, and Average Functions When the Average Attains a Maximum

Therefore,

$$\frac{d}{dx}\left(\frac{y}{x}\right) = \frac{(dy/dx)}{x} - \frac{y}{x^2}.$$

Multiply both sides by x:

$$x\,\frac{d}{dx}\left(\frac{y}{x}\right) = \frac{dy}{dx} - \frac{y}{x}.$$

Rearrange terms:

$$\frac{dy}{dx} = x\,\frac{d}{dx}\left(\frac{y}{x}\right) + \frac{y}{x}.$$

This relationship can now be expressed in words as

marginal $= x \cdot$ (slope of average) $+$ average.

Thus, statement 1 follows because the slope of the average is negative when the average is falling. Statement 2 follows because the slope of the average is positive when the average is rising. Statement 3 follows because the slope of the average is 0 when the average is maximized or minimized.

2.4   FUNCTIONS OF SEVERAL INDEPENDENT VARIABLES: UNCONSTRAINED MAXIMIZATION AND MINIMIZATION

This book will consider several unconstrained maximization problems in more than one independent variable. One in particular is the choice of production inputs for a profit-maximizing firm. In general, any economic agent that must make more than one unconstrained decision simultaneously potentially faces such an unconstrained maximization problem. For example, a firm may produce two different goods or engage in advertising in an attempt to affect its demand function. In the case of advertising, the firm must simultaneously choose both its output level and an appropriate amount of advertising.

Critical Points Finding a critical point of a function of several independent variables is analogous to finding a critical point of a one-variable function. To see the analogy, recall the first-order condition for single-variable optimization:

$$\frac{dy}{dx} = f'(x^*) = 0.$$

If we multiply each part of the expression by dx, we get the point-slope formula equated to 0:

$$dy = f'(x^*)\,dx = 0.$$

Now, recall that dz is the multivariate analog to dy in the point-slope formula. This suggests that to find a critical point of a smooth function of several variables, we look for a point on the function for which $dz = 0$. Figures 2.11 and 2.12 illustrate a maximum and a minimum of functions of two independent variables. In both cases, $dz = 0$ at the critical point.

The analog to a critical inflection point for a function of two or more independent variables is called a saddle point because the graph of such a critical point in three dimensions often resembles a saddle. Basically, a **saddle point** is defined as a critical point of a function of two or more independent variables where the function increases in some directions away from the critical point and decreases in other directions. Figure 2.13 illustrates a typical saddle point of a two-variable function.

First- and Second-order Conditions If we write out the total differential of the function $z = f(x, y)$,

$$dz = \frac{\partial z}{\partial x} dx + \frac{\partial z}{\partial y} dy,$$

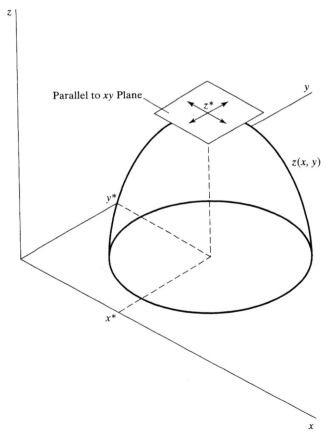

FIGURE 2.11   Maximization of a Function of Two Independent Variables

we see that $dz = 0$ requires that

$$\frac{\partial z(x^*, y^*)}{\partial x}dx + \frac{\partial z(x^*, y^*)}{\partial y}dy = 0$$

for all possible changes, dx or dy, away from (x^*, y^*). Otherwise, we could not be sure that $dz = 0$. To ensure that $dz = 0$ for every possible dx and dy, the following conditions must hold:

$$\frac{\partial z}{\partial x} = f_x = 0 \quad \text{and} \quad \frac{\partial z}{\partial y} = f_y = 0.$$

To see that these conditions are necessary, suppose $(\partial z/\partial x) \neq 0$ and $(\partial z/\partial y) \neq 0$, with $dz = 0$ for some combination of dx and dy. Then, for some *different* combination of dx and dy, dz will not be equal to zero. We call the conditions $(\partial z/\partial x) = 0$ and $(\partial z/\partial y) = 0$ the first-order, necessary conditions for unconstrained optimization of functions of two variables.

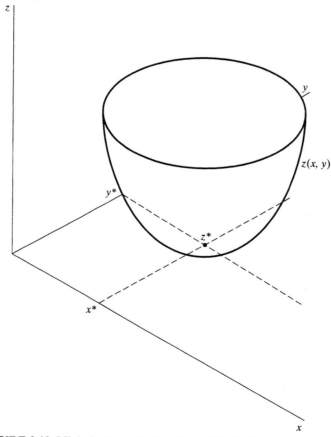

FIGURE 2.12 Minimization of a Function of Two Independent Variables

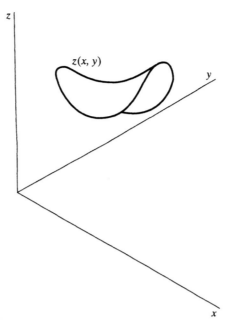

**FIGURE 2.13   Saddle Point of a
Function of Two Independent Variables**

Extending these first-order conditions to the case where there are several independent variables is straightforward. First-order, necessary conditions for unconstrained optimization of functions of several variables are satisfied when all the partial derivatives of the function are equal to 0:

$$f_1 = f_2 = \cdots = f_n = 0$$

for n independent variables. Like the first-order conditions for functions of one variable, they are *necessary but not sufficient* for unconstrained maximization or minimization.

Second-order, *sufficient* conditions, which allow us to distinguish between a maximum and a minimum, are also analogous to the single-variable case. In the two-variable case, for example, if all the partial derivatives are 0, the sufficient condition for a maximum is for the second total differential to be less than 0:

$$d^2z = f_{xx}(dx)^2 + 2f_{xy}\,dxdy + f_{yy}(dy)^2 < 0,$$

for any combination dx and dy when both are not equal to 0. Similarly, if the first-order conditions are satisfied, the sufficient condition for a minimum in the two-variable case is for the second total differential to be greater than 0:

$$d^2z > 0,$$

for any combination of dx and dy when both are not equal to 0. In addition, we show in the appendix to this chapter that the following conditions on the second partial and cross partial derivatives of a function of two independent variables imply that the total differential will be of the correct sign:[4]

1. $f_{xx} < 0$ and $f_{yy} < 0$ for a maximum,

2. $f_{xx} > 0$ and $f_{yy} > 0$ for a minimum,

3. $f_{xx}f_{yy} - (f_{xy})^2 > 0$ for either a maximum or a minimum.

The second-order conditions for a saddle point of a two-variable function are analogous to those for an inflection point of a one-variable function. Once again, if the first-order conditions are satisfied, a sufficient condition for a saddle point is for the function to both increase and decrease as x and y move in different directions away from (x^*, y^*).

Example The example set out in equation 1.1 illustrates how to find a critical point from the first-order conditions and how to use the second-order conditions to check for a maximum or a minimum. If

$$z = 10x - x^2 + 20y - y^2,$$

then the first-order conditions are the same as the partial derivatives set out in equations 1.2 and 1.3:

$$\frac{\partial z}{\partial x} = 10 - 2x^* = 0$$

$$\frac{\partial z}{\partial y} = 20 - 2y^* = 0.$$

Therefore,

$$2x^* = 10 \Rightarrow x^* = 5$$
$$2y^* = 20 \Rightarrow y^* = 10$$
$$z^* = 10(5) - 5^2 + 20(10) - 10^2 = 125.$$

The second-order conditions are

$$f_{xx} = -2 < 0$$
$$f_{yy} = -2 < 0$$

and, noting that $f_{xy} = 0$,

$$f_{xx}f_{yy} - (f_{xy})^2 = 4 > 0.$$

Thus, the second-order sufficient conditions for a maximum are satisfied. This implies that the maximum value for the function z occurs at the point $(x^* = 5, y^* = 10, z^* = 125)$.

---

[4]See A. C. Chiang, *Fundamentals of Mathematical Economics*, 3d ed. (New York: McGraw-Hill, 1984), pp. 332–337; or Silberberg, *Structure of Economics*, pp. 109–111, for the extension to three or more independent variables.

2.5   ONE-VARIABLE COMPARATIVE STATICS, IMPLICIT FUNCTIONS, AND THE UNCONSTRAINED ENVELOPE THEOREM

Comparative Statics It is often the case in economics that we wish to evaluate a change in an economic variable when one of the parameters changes. For example, what happens to the quantity demanded of a good when income, the price of the good, or the price of another good changes? The technique used, called **comparative statics,** is one of the most important mathematical tools used in economic analysis.

In microeconomics, we generally obtain comparative statics results by first assuming that a decision maker is maximizing an objective function by choosing values of the independent variables (which we refer to as **choice variables**). We then examine how the optimal values of both the choice variables and the objective function are affected by changes in the parameters.

To illustrate the technique of comparative statics when optimization is assumed, we will use the general function $y = f(x)$ with several parameters $(\alpha, \beta, \text{and } \gamma)$:

$$y = f(x; \alpha, \beta, \gamma).$$

Figure 2.14 illustrates a possible shape for this function with only one parameter (α) in two and three dimensions. In the left graph (three dimensions) we see that as α increases, the optimal values of both x and y also increase. This is made clearer in the right graph in two dimensions. Each curve represents the function y for a different value of α:

$$\alpha_3 > \alpha_2 > \alpha_1$$

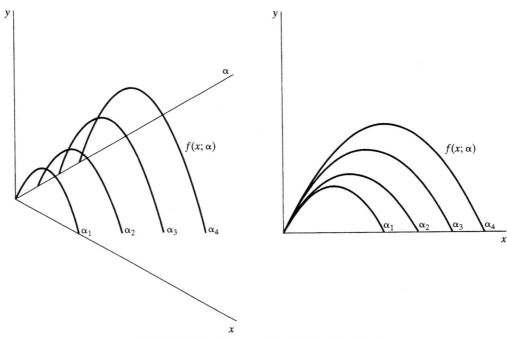

FIGURE 2.14   Comparative Statics Illustrated

As α increases, both x^* and y^* also increase:

$$x_3^* > x_2^* > x_1^*$$

and

$$y_3^* (x_3^*; \alpha_3) > y_2^*(x_2^*; \alpha_2) > y_1^*(x_1^*; \alpha_1).$$

Since α essentially shifts the relationship between y and x as it changes (that is, the nature of $y = f(x)$ changes), it is often referred to as a *shift parameter.*

We can illustrate comparative statics resulting from optimization in the case of one choice variable and one parameter with the following function:

$$y = \alpha x - x^2. \tag{2.1}$$

To find x^*, we start with the first-order condition:

$$\frac{dy}{dx} = \alpha - 2x^* = 0. \tag{2.2}$$

Thus,

$$x^* = \frac{\alpha}{2}, \tag{2.3}$$

and the comparative statics result for the choice variable is

$$\frac{\partial x^*}{\partial \alpha} = \frac{1}{2} > 0. \tag{2.4}$$

Equation 2.4 implies that as α increases the value of x^* increases.

Now, to find y^* as a function of α, we can substitute the function for x^* into the y function:

$$y^* = \alpha\left(\frac{\alpha}{2}\right) - \left(\frac{\alpha}{2}\right)^2.$$

Thus,

$$y^* = \frac{\alpha^2}{2} - \frac{\alpha^2}{4} = \frac{\alpha^2}{4}, \tag{2.5}$$

and the comparative statics result for the objective function is

$$\frac{\partial y^*}{\partial \alpha} = \frac{\alpha}{2}. \tag{2.6}$$

Implicit Functions Often in economics, however, we do not know what the specific functional form of the objective function is. What we do in that case is exploit what we know about the function when it is evaluated at its critical point. In the case of one choice variable, we know that the first-order condition is 0 and we assume that the second-order, sufficient condition is satisfied. Thus, if

$$y = f(x; \alpha),$$

then

$$\frac{\partial y}{\partial x} = f_x(x^*; \alpha) = 0;$$

and, given the first-order condition,

$$\frac{\partial^2 y}{\partial x^2} = f_{xx} < 0$$

is sufficient for x^* to be the maximizing choice.

Now, to find how x^* and y^* change when α changes, we use the fact that $f_x(x^*; \alpha) = 0$ implicitly defines a relationship between x^* and α that is called an **implicit function.**[5] In our example (equation 2.1), the first-order condition for $y = \alpha x - x^2$,

$$\alpha - 2x^* = 0$$

(equation 2.2), is the implicit function. While we can simply use this implicit function to find the explicit function $x^* = \alpha/2$ (equation 2.3) and the comparative statics results as we did in equations 2.4 and 2.6, we can also solve for the comparative statics results indirectly. This is done by totally differentiating the first-order condition and then solving for $\partial x^*/\partial \alpha$. Moreover, since we are always assuming the function is being optimized with respect to the choice variable (x), the first-order condition is always 0. Therefore, the total differential will also be 0. Thus, totally differentiating the first-order condition,

$$d\alpha - 2dx^* = 0.$$

Solving for $\dfrac{dx^*}{d\alpha}$,

$$\frac{dx^*}{d\alpha} = \frac{1}{2} = \frac{\partial x^*}{\partial \alpha},$$

which is the same comparative statics result we derived as equation 2.4 from the explicit function $x^*(\alpha)$ (equation 2.3).[6]

We can now extend this technique (of finding comparative statics results by totally differentiating the first-order condition) to the more general problem:

$$\text{maximize } y = f(x; \alpha, \beta, \gamma).$$

The first-order condition for this problem is

---

[5]What we are doing here is applying what is called the *implicit function theorem.* Basically, in this simple environment, the implicit function theorem states that if there is an implicit function $h(x^*, \alpha) = 0$ and h_x exists and is not equal to 0, then there exists an explicit function $x^*(\alpha)$. Further, the derivative $\partial x^*/\partial \alpha$ also exists and may be found by totally differentiating the implicit function, as described in the text. For a more formal discussion of the theorem, see Silberberg, *Structure of Economics,* pp. 144–148.

[6]At this point, $dx^*/d\alpha$ is usually written $\partial x^*/\partial \alpha$ because, in general, there may be other parameters that are being held constant.

$$f_x(x^*; \alpha, \beta, \gamma) = 0.$$

If we totally differentiate this first-order condition, we get

$$f_{xx}dx^* + f_{x\alpha}d\alpha + f_{x\beta}d\beta + f_{x\gamma}\, d\gamma = 0.$$

Thus, the comparative statics effect of a change in α on x^*, holding β and γ constant, is

$$\left.\frac{dx^*}{d\alpha}\right|_{\substack{d\beta=0 \\ d\gamma=0}} = -\frac{f_{x\alpha}}{f_{xx}} = \frac{\partial x^*}{\partial \alpha}.$$

Similarly, the comparative statics effects of changes in β and γ are

$$\left.\frac{dx^*}{d\beta}\right|_{\substack{d\alpha=0 \\ d\gamma=0}} = -\frac{f_{x\beta}}{f_{xx}} = \frac{\partial x^*}{\partial \beta} \quad \text{and} \quad \left.\frac{dx^*}{d\gamma}\right|_{\substack{d\alpha=0 \\ d\beta=0}} = -\frac{f_{x\gamma}}{f_{xx}} = \frac{\partial x^*}{\partial \gamma}.$$

To determine the signs of these comparative statics terms, we first note that f_{xx} is always less than 0 if we are assuming that the sufficient conditions for a maximum are satisfied.[7] Thus, with the negative sign in front, the sign of each term will be the same as the sign of its respective numerator.

$$\frac{\partial x^*}{\partial \alpha}$$ will have the same sign as $f_{x\alpha}$.

$$\frac{\partial x^*}{\partial \beta}$$ will have the same sign as $f_{x\beta}$.

$$\frac{\partial x^*}{\partial \gamma}$$ will have the same sign as $f_{x\gamma}$.

Finally, to find the comparative statics effect on the optimal value of the objective function, we assume the existence of the explicit function $x^*(\alpha)$, and we use the comparative statics result, $\partial x^*/\partial \alpha$, we just derived. First, we identify the function $y^*(\alpha)$ by substituting $x^*(\alpha)$ in the objective function. This new function is sometimes called the **indirect objective function.** It identifies the optimal values of the objective function: the values of y when the function (f) is evaluated at the optimal values of x, given the parameter α:

$$y^*(\alpha) = f(x^*(\alpha); \alpha).$$

Next, we differentiate y^* with respect to α, using the chain rule:

$$\frac{\partial y^*}{\partial \alpha} = \frac{\partial}{\partial \alpha} f(x^*(\alpha); \alpha) = f_x(x^*; \alpha)\frac{\partial x^*}{\partial \alpha} + f_\alpha(x^*; \alpha).$$

However, since

$$f_x(x^*; \alpha) = 0$$

---

[7]Notice that assuming that the second-order sufficient condition for a maximum is satisfied (so that $f_{xx} < 0$) is equivalent to assuming that the condition $h_x \neq 0$ is satisfied. That is because $h(x^*; \alpha) = f_x(x^*; \alpha)$, implying that $h_x = f_{xx}$. Moreover, we can see why the condition is important: in the equation above, $\partial x^*/\partial \alpha$ would not be defined if f_{xx} were 0.

is the first-order condition for an optimum, we get

$$\frac{\partial y^*}{\partial \alpha} = f_\alpha.$$

Thus, if we know the sign of f_α, we can determine the effect of a change in α on the optimal value of the objective function.

The Envelope Theorem   We have just derived the simplest version of one of the most important mathematical results used in economics: the *envelope theorem*. We will make use of it repeatedly throughout the book. Basically, the **envelope theorem** in the unconstrained case states that the comparative statics effect of a change in a parameter on the optimal value of the objective function is simply the partial derivative of the objective function with respect to the parameter (the direct effect), ignoring the effect of the change in the parameter on the choice variable (the indirect effect). The indirect effect can be ignored because the partial derivative of the optimal value of the choice variable with respect to the parameter is multiplied by the first-order condition, which is 0. Thus, in general,

$$\frac{\partial y^*}{\partial \alpha} = f_\alpha, \quad \frac{\partial y^*}{\partial \beta} = f_\beta, \quad \text{and} \quad \frac{\partial y^*}{\partial \gamma} = f_\gamma.$$

We should note, however, that the envelope theorem should be applied only when evaluating *derivatives* at the optimal value of the objective function. As soon as discrete changes are considered, the indirect effects can no longer be ignored.

2.6   MORE WORKED PROBLEMS INVOLVING OPTIMIZATION OF FUNCTIONS OF TWO INDEPENDENT VARIABLES

This section solves two more optimization problems with two independent variables and one more single-variable problem with a shift parameter.

1. $z = x^2 - xy + y^2$

   The first-order conditions are

   $$f_x = 2x - y = 0 \Rightarrow y = 2x$$
   $$f_y = -x + 2y = 0 \Rightarrow x = 2y.$$

   The only values for x and y that satisfy the first-order conditions are

   $$x^* = y^* = 0.$$

   Thus,

   $$z^* = 0.$$

   The second-order conditions are

   $$f_{xx} = 2 > 0$$
   $$f_{yy} = 2 > 0.$$

And, noting that $f_{xy} = -1$,

$$f_{xx} f_{yy} - (f_{xy})^2 = 4 - 1 = 3 > 0.$$

Thus, the second-order conditions for a *minimum* are satisfied at the point $(x^* = 0, y^* = 0, z^* = 0)$.

2. $z = 5x + 2y - x^2 - y^2 + xy$

The first-order conditions are

$$f_x = 5 - 2x + y = 0 \Rightarrow y = 2x - 5$$
$$f_y = 2 - 2y + x = 0 \Rightarrow x = 2y - 2.$$

Thus,

$$y = 2(2y - 2) - 5 = 4y - 9 \Rightarrow y^* = 3$$
$$x^* = 2(3) - 2 = 4$$
$$z^* = 5(4) + 2(3) - (4)^2 - (3)^2 + (4)(3) = 13.$$

The second-order conditions are

$$f_{xx} = -2 < 0$$
$$f_{yy} = -2 < 0$$

and, noting that $f_{xy} = 1$,

$$f_{xx} f_{yy} - (f_{xy})^2 = 4 - 1 = 3 > 0.$$

Thus, the second-order conditions for a *maximum* are satisfied at the point $(x^* = 4, y^* = 3, z^* = 13)$.

3. Find the comparative statics effects for the following problem.

$$\text{maximize } y = f(x; \alpha) = \alpha + 8\alpha x - 2x^2.$$

First, we solve this explicitly. The first-order condition is

$$f_x = 8\alpha - 4x = 0.$$

The second-order condition is

$$f_{xx} = -4 < 0. \quad \textbf{maximum}$$

Thus,

$$x^* = 2\alpha$$

$$\frac{\partial x^*}{\partial \alpha} = 2 > 0$$

$$y^* = \alpha + 8\alpha x^* - 2(x^*)^2 = \alpha + 8\alpha(2\alpha) - 2(2\alpha)^2$$
$$= \alpha + 16\alpha^2 - 8\alpha^2 = \alpha + 8\alpha^2$$

$$\frac{\partial y^*}{\partial \alpha} = 1 + 16\alpha > 0, \quad \text{if } \alpha > -\frac{1}{16}.$$

Second, we make use of the implicit function theorem. The first-order condition is

$$f_x = 8\alpha - 4x^* = 0. \quad \textbf{the implicit function}$$

Totally differentiating the first-order condition,

$$8d\alpha - 4dx^* = 0.$$

Therefore,

$$\frac{\partial x^*}{\partial \alpha} = 2 > 0$$

$$\frac{\partial y^*}{\partial \alpha} = f_\alpha \quad \textbf{by the envelope theorem}$$

$$= 1 + 8x^* > 0, \text{ for } x^* > -\frac{1}{8}.$$

Notice that if we substitute the explicit function

$$x^*(\alpha) = 2\alpha,$$

then

$$\frac{\partial y^*}{\partial \alpha} = 1 + 8(2\alpha) = 1 + 16\alpha,$$

the result we derived above.

2.7 _____ REVIEW OF KEY CONCEPTS

This completes our introduction to unconstrained optimization in economics. Before continuing to the next chapter on constrained optimization, be sure you understand and can use the following key concepts.

A function attains a _local maximum_ at a point that is _higher_ than any other point nearby, and a _local minimum_ at a point that is _lower_ than any other point nearby.

If a function is _smooth_, its slope will be 0 at a maximum or a minimum.

Optimization is the technique for finding either a maximum or a minimum.

A function being maximized or minimized is referred to as an _objective function_.

We denote the _optimum_ (maximum or minimum) by the notation "*".

At a _critical point_ of a function, the slope of the function is 0.

An _inflection point_ at which the slope of the function is 0 is a critical point that is neither a maximum nor a minimum.

At a _maximum_, the second derivative is negative; at a _minimum_, the second derivative is positive; and at a critical _inflection point_, the second derivative is 0.

A _necessary condition_ must hold for a particular result to follow.

The _first-order_, necessary condition for a maximum or a minimum is for the first derivative of a smooth function to be 0.

A _sufficient condition_ will guarantee a particular result will follow, but it might not be a necessary condition.

Once the first-order condition is satisfied, the _second-order condition_ for a maximum is for the second derivative to be negative. The second-order condition for a minimum is for the second derivative to be positive.

The first- and second-order conditions together are both necessary and sufficient for either a maximum or a minimum of a smooth function.

An *inflection point* is a point at which the second derivative of a function changes sign.

A *total function* is the original set of values of a particular function.

The *average function* is the total function divided by the value of the independent variable at each point.

The *marginal function* is the slope of the total function.

The marginal function attains a maximum or a minimum at the point of inflection of the total function.

The average function attains a maximum or a minimum at the point at which a line from the origin is tangent to the function. At that point, the marginal function is also equal to the average function.

At a critical point of a function of two or more independent variables, the total differential is 0. Such a critical point can be a maximum, a minimum, or a saddle point of the function.

The first-order conditions for maximization or minimization of a function of two or more independent variables are for all of the first partial derivatives of the function to be equal to 0.

The second-order condition for a maximum is for the second total differential to be negative.

The second-order condition for a minimum is for the second total differential to be positive. The function increases in some directions and decreases in others away from a saddle point.

Economists do what is called *comparative statics analysis* when they analyze the effects of a change in the value of a parameter on the optimal values of the choice variables and the objective function.

In economic analysis, independent variables are often called *choice variables*.

A *shift parameter* is a parameter that changes the relationship between the choice variables and the objective function as it takes on different parametric values.

The *implicit function theorem* states that if h is an implicit function of the optimal value of the choice variable x, given some parameter α, then there exists an explicit function $x^*(\alpha)$. Moreover, the derivative $dx^*/d\alpha$ can be found by totally differentiating the implicit function.

The *indirect objective function* describes the optimal values of the objective function, defined over values of the shift parameters.

By the *envelope theorem,* the comparative statics effect of a change in a parametric value on the optimal value of the objective function is equal to the partial derivative of the objective function with respect to the parameter, ignoring the effect of the parameter on the choice variables.

2.8 ____ PROBLEMS

Problems 1–5 For each function, find the average and marginal functions.

1. $y = 25 - 5x, x, y > 0$

2. $y = \dfrac{50}{x}, x, y > 0$

3. $y = 10x^2 + 5, x, y > 0$

4. $y = 25x - x^2, x, y > 0$

5. $y = 100x + \dfrac{1}{x}, x, y > 0$

Problems 6–9 Find the x value that identifies the maximum or minimum value of each function, and find the optimal value of the function itself.

In each case, use the second-order condition to show that the point is either a maximum or a minimum.

6. $y = 25x - x^2, x, y > 0$

7. $y = 100x + \dfrac{1}{x}, x, y > 0$

8. $y = 40x - 2x^2, x, y > 0$

9. $y = 40x + \dfrac{4}{x}, x, y > 0$

Problems 10 and 11 Find the point (x, y) that identifies a maximum or a minimum value of each function, and find the optimal value of the function itself. Use the second-order conditions to show that the critical point is either a maximum or a minimum.

10. $z = 3x^2 + 15y^2 - x - 3y$

11. $z = -5x^2 - 10y^2 + 5x + 4y$

2.9   APPENDIX

RELATIONSHIPS AMONG THE SECOND TOTAL DIFFERENTIAL AND THE SECOND PARTIAL AND CROSS PARTIAL DERIVATIVES FOR MAXIMA AND MINIMA FOR TWO-VARIABLE FUNCTIONS

1. For a maximum,

$$d^2z = f_{xx}(dx)^2 + 2f_{xy}\,dxdy + f_{yy}(dy)^2 < 0,$$

assuming dx and dy are not both 0.

$$dy = 0 \;\Rightarrow\; dx \neq 0 \text{ and } f_{xx} < 0$$
$$dx = 0 \;\Rightarrow\; dy \neq 0 \text{ and } f_{yy} < 0$$

To establish the third condition, factor f_{xx} in the expression for d^2z:

$$d^2z = f_{xx}\left[(dx)^2 + \frac{2f_{xy}\,dx\,dy}{f_{xx}} + \frac{f_{yy}(dy)^2}{f_{xx}}\right].$$

Now, add and subtract $(f_{xy}\,dy/f_{xx})^2$ inside the braces:

$$d^2z = f_{xx}\left\{(dx)^2 + \frac{2f_{xy}\,dxdy}{f_{xx}} + \left(\frac{f_{xy}\,dy}{f_{xx}}\right)^2 - \left(\frac{f_{xy}\,dy}{f_{xx}}\right)^2 + \frac{f_{yy}(dy)^2}{f_{xx}}\right\}$$

$$= f_{xx}\left\{\left[dx + \frac{f_{xy}\,dy}{f_{xx}}\right]^2 + \left(\frac{dy}{f_{xx}}\right)^2 [f_{yy}\,f_{xx} - (f_{xy})^2]\right\}.$$

Thus, since $f_{xx} < 0$, a sufficient condition for $d^2z < 0$ is

$$f_{xx}\,f_{yy} - (f_{xy})^2 > 0.$$

This would ensure that the term in braces is positive.

2. For a minimum,

$$d^2z > 0$$
$$dy = 0 \Rightarrow f_{xx} > 0$$
$$dx = 0 \Rightarrow f_{yy} > 0.$$

Thus,

$$f_{xx}\,f_{yy} - (f_{xy})^2 > 0$$

to ensure $dz^2 > 0$, by the same argument developed above.

   Those of you who have had some matrix algebra will recognize the third sufficient condition as a condition on the sign of the determinant of the matrix of partial derivatives:

$$\begin{vmatrix} f_{xx} & f_{xy} \\ f_{xy} & f_{yy} \end{vmatrix} > 0.$$

This matrix is derived by totally differentiating the first-order conditions (which are functions of the choice variables) and setting the resulting set of equations in matrix form. We start with

$$z = f(x, y).$$

The first-order conditions are

$$f_x(x^*, y^*) = 0$$
$$f_y(x^*, y^*) = 0.$$

Totally differentiating the first-order conditions,

$$f_{xx} \, dx^* + f_{xy} \, dy^* = 0$$
$$f_{xy} \, dx^* + f_{yy} \, dy^* = 0.$$

In matrix form:

$$\begin{bmatrix} f_{xx} & f_{xy} \\ f_{xy} & f_{yy} \end{bmatrix} \begin{bmatrix} dx^* \\ dy^* \end{bmatrix} = \begin{bmatrix} 0 \\ 0 \end{bmatrix}.$$

Chapter 3

CONSTRAINED OPTIMIZATION

WHAT YOU SHOULD LEARN FROM THIS CHAPTER

This chapter completes the introduction to optimization in economics begun in Chapter 2. Many important problems in economics deal with choices that are constrained in some way. The most obvious problem is the consumer's problem. Consumers try to purchase the combination of goods and services that give the greatest satisfaction, but they are constrained by their budgets. We say that consumers maximize utility subject to their budget constraints. In addition, many unconstrained problems may be easier to solve, or may provide useful additional insights, if they are expressed mathematically as constrained problems. For example, the firm's problem is to maximize profits, an unconstrained problem. However, as we will see, we may find it useful to solve the firm's problem in two stages, one of which is best expressed as a constrained problem. First, we find the least-cost combination of inputs to produce each possible output level. We express this as minimizing costs subject to an output constraint. Then, we choose the profit-maximizing output level, assuming costs have been minimized for every output level.

In contrast to the previous two chapters, the material in this chapter will probably be new to almost all of you. For that reason, and because the techniques developed in this chapter will be used in almost every subsequent chapter, this chapter should be studied carefully. Concentrate particularly on the Lagrange method, which is developed at the end.

Those students whose math was rusty at the beginning or who were uncomfortable with math should be gaining some facility by this time. If not, they should see their instructors for help or additional problems with which to practice.

3.2   ONE-VARIABLE CONSTRAINED OPTIMIZATION

Mathematically, the first thing we should note about constrained maximization or minimization is that the problem does not become interesting (there are no trade-offs) unless the function we are maximizing or minimizing has at least *two* independent variables. To see this, suppose we have a one-variable problem,

$$\text{maximize } y = f(x),$$

and we constrain x to equal some value, say $\bar{x}$. With only one independent variable, however, y is uniquely determined for the value $\bar{x}$:

$$y^* = f(\bar{x}).$$

For example,

$$\text{maximize } y = x^2$$
$$\text{subject to: } x = 2.$$

Therefore,

$$y^* = 4.$$

Figure 3.1 illustrates how one-variable constrained maximization is no different from simply evaluating the function at some specified point.

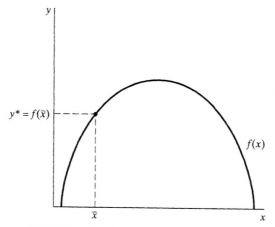

FIGURE 3.1   One-variable Constrained Maximization

3.3   ONE-VARIABLE CONSTRAINED OPTIMIZATION WITH A NONNEGATIVITY CONSTRAINT

One-variable constrained problems can provide a useful introduction to an important set of concepts in constrained optimization. Suppose, for example, that we wished to maximize a one-variable problem, with the constraint that x^* has to be greater than or equal to 0:

$$\max y = f(x)$$
$$\text{subject to: } x \geq 0.$$

We call the constraint that x has to be greater than or equal to 0 a **nonnegativity constraint.** Figure 3.2 illustrates this problem for a function that actually attains its unconstrained maximum at x less than 0. By imposing the constraint that x has to be greater than or equal to 0, we see that x^* has to be 0 and thus, $y^* = f(0)$.

Kuhn-Tucker Conditions Notice now that if the unconstrained maximum does not occur for values allowed by the constraint, the first-order condition will not be satisfied with equality. In fact, as we can see in Figure 3.2, the slope of the function is negative at x^*. This tells us that if we impose a nonnegativity constraint on a one-variable function, the first derivative will be less than or equal to 0 at the constrained maximum:

$$\frac{dy}{dx} \leq 0.$$

Another way of expressing this idea is:

$$f'(x^*) \leq 0.$$

If the first derivative is equal to 0 and the function attains a maximum, then the constrained maximum is equal to the unconstrained maximum.[1] If the first derivative is less than 0 under the constraint, then the constrained maximum occurs at $x^* = 0$ (as in Figure 3.2). The statement that the first derivative is less than or equal to 0, combined with the characterization of x^*, is called the **Kuhn-Tucker condition** for one-variable maximization with a nonnegativity constraint.[2]

The Kuhn-Tucker condition for one-variable *minimization* with a nonnegativity constraint can be defined analogously. Suppose we minimize $f(x)$ subject to a nonnegativity constraint:

$$\min f(x)$$

$$\text{s. t. } x \geq 0.$$

This problem is illustrated in Figure 3.3 for a function that attains its unconstrained minimum at $x < 0$. Notice in this problem that $x^* = 0$ (as in Figure 3.2), but the slope is positive at x^*. Thus, the condition for one-variable minimization with a nonnegativity constraint is

$$\frac{dy}{dx} \geq 0,$$

or

$$f'(x^*) \geq 0.$$

---

[1]Note that the constrained x^* would be 0 if the unconstrained maximum occured at $x^* = 0$. In that case, the first-order condition would be satisfied with equality at $x = 0$. Thus, at such a constrained maximum, either $x^* = 0$ or $f'(x^*) = 0$. This fact can be expressed as the condition $f'(x^*) x^* = 0$, since one or both of these terms must be zero.

[2]For a more detailed discussion of the Kuhn-Tucker condition, see Silberberg, *Structure of Economics*, pp. 470–476.

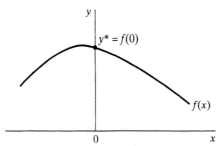

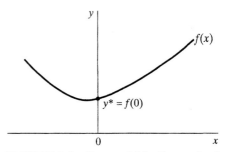

FIGURE 3.2   One-variable Constrained Maximization with a Nonnegativity Constraint

FIGURE 3.3   One-variable Constrained Minimization with a Nonnegativity Constraint

The Kuhn-Tucker condition is that the first-order condition is greater than or equal to 0; that $x^* \geq 0$ if the first-order condition is 0; and that $x^* = 0$ if the first-order condition is greater than 0:

$$f'(x^*)x^* = 0.$$

3.4   TWO-VARIABLE PROBLEMS WITH EQUALITY CONSTRAINTS

Suppose now that we wish to maximize a hill-shaped function, subject to the constraint that the sum of x and y is equal to some constant, say $\bar{k}$:

$$x + y = \bar{k}.$$

We call the line $x + y = \bar{k}$ an **equality constraint,** since we are requiring it to hold with equality. This implies that the solution to the constrained maximization problem must be on the constraint line.[3]

Figure 3.4 illustrates maximization subject to an equality constraint. If we consider all possible values of z that are consistent with the constraint $x + y = \bar{k}$, we can define a vertical plane that goes through that line. The highest value of the objective function located on that plane is z^*.

Level Surfaces of an Objective Function   To see this last point more clearly, think of a z function that is composed of circles which progressively decrease in diameter as z increases, forming a hill. The top of the hill is represented by a dot instead of a circle.

---

[3]In this section, we will develop the argument in terms of equality constraints first, and then return to inequality constraints and Kuhn-Tucker conditions later. We will also assume, for the time being, that there are no nonnegativity constraints; that is, optimal solutions could be positive, negative, or 0.

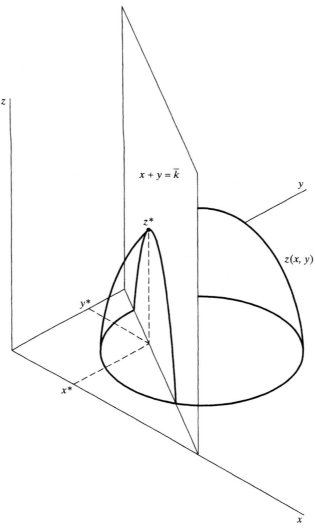

FIGURE 3.4 Maximization Subject to an Equality Constraint

Each circle represents all the (x, y) values that define one specific z value of the function, say $\bar{z}_i$:

$$f(x, y) = \bar{z}_i.$$

We can also write an equation for the circle at $\bar{z}_i$ with y as the dependent variable, x as the independent variable, and $\bar{z}_i$ as a parameter:

$$y = h(x; \bar{z}_1).$$

We call the circle at $\bar{z}_i$ **a level surface** of the z function.[4] That is, along each circle at $\bar{z}_i$, the value of z is constant.[5] In fact, we can graph the entire z function in the xy plane as a set of concentric circles or level surfaces. The unconstrained maximum is represented as a dot in the center of the graph. This is analogous to representing hills and valleys as contour lines and mountain tops as dots on a topographical map. Figure 3.5 illustrates

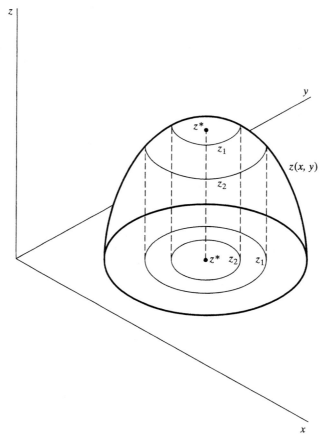

FIGURE 3.5   The Level Surfaces of a Hill-shaped Function Projected onto the xy Plane

[4]This relationship is, of course, not strictly speaking a function, since there are two values of y for every value of x around a circle. When we use the word "function" in this context, we are referring to the z function itself. In that case there is only one value of z for each combination of x and y.

[5]Since the circles are drawn in two dimensions, they are actually level curves, rather than level surfaces. In general, they are sometimes called level sets, encompassing both surfaces and curves. However, economists also often use the term level surface to describe combinations of the independent variables that combine to yield equal values of the dependent variable, even in two dimensions. Since this is a widely used convention, we adopt it in this book.

how the level surfaces of the z function are projected onto the xy plane, and Figure 3.6 shows the level surfaces of the z function in xy space.

Imposing the Constraint   The equality constraint $x + y = \bar{k}$ can now be imposed as a line in the xy plane by solving the equation $x + y = \bar{k}$ for y:

$$y = \bar{k} - x.$$

Figure 3.7 superimposes this constraint on the projections of the z function. Notice that the circle at z_c^*, which is just tangent to the equality constraint, is the highest value of the z function allowed by the constraint. The point of tangency, (x_c^*, y_c^*), is the (x, y) combination that yields z_c^*.

　　To see that (x_c^*, y_c^*) has to be the optimal choice, think of trying a level surface just a little lower than at z_c^* (say at z_1) and another one just a little higher than at z_c^* (say at z_2). At z_1, it is possible to make z higher (up to z_c^*) without violating the constraint. At z_2, we are outside the constraint. Thus, z_c^* is the best we can do, given the constraint. Since the constraint function and the level surface at z_c^* are tangent to one another at (x_c^*, y_c^*), we also know that the slope of the function $y = \bar{k} - x$ is equal to the slope of $y = h(x; \bar{z}_c^*)$ at that point. That fact forms the basis for one of the methods developed below, used to solve constrained optimization problems.

　　Figure 3.8 shows the constrained maximization problem in three dimensions once again. The vertical plane that goes through the line $x + y = \bar{k}$, which is tangent to the level surface at z_c^*, cuts through the side of the hill at exactly that value of the z function.

Constrained Minimization   Let's now consider a related problem that involves constrained minimization:

$$\min k = x + y$$
$$\text{s.t. } f(x, y) = \bar{z},$$

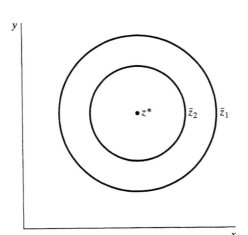

FIGURE 3.6   The Level Surfaces of a Hill-shaped Function on the xy Plane

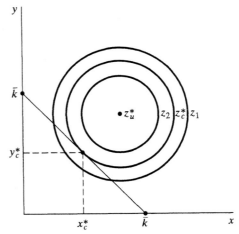

FIGURE 3.7   Constrained Maximization of z in xy Space

where $\bar{z} = z_c^*$ in the maximization problem outlined above. Figure 3.9 illustrates this problem in two dimensions. The level surfaces of the k function are just lines in xy space, and $\bar{z}$ is the same circle at z_c^* we found to be the constrained maximum in the previous problem. In this problem, however, the circle at $\bar{z}$ represents the equality constraint.

Duality   In the previous problem, z_c^* is the highest level surface allowed by the line defined by $x + y = \bar{k}$. In the minimization problem, however, the lowest level surface allowed by the constraint is the line at k_c^*, which is just tangent to the circle $f(x, y) = \bar{z}$. But we defined $\bar{z}$ to be equal to z_c^* in the previous constrained maximization problem.

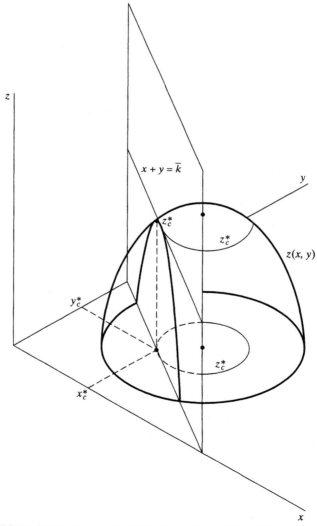

FIGURE 3.8   Constrained Maximization in Three Dimensions

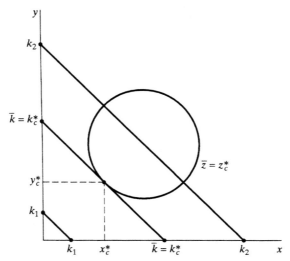

FIGURE 3.9   Constrained Minimization

Since z^*_c was tangent to x, $x + y = \bar{k}$ we know that $\bar{k}$ in the maximization problem must equal k^*_c in the minimization problem. The point (x^*_c, y^*_c) defines both constrained optimal values k^*_c and z^*_c. Thus,

$$\max z = f(x, y)$$
$$\text{s.t. } x + y = \bar{k}$$

is essentially equivalent to the problem

$$\min k = x + y$$
$$\text{s.t. } f(x, y) = \bar{z}$$

as long as $\bar{k}$ in the maximization problem equals k^*_c in the minimization problem or $\bar{z}$ in the minimization problem equals z^*_c in the maximization problem.

The examples developed above illustrate three important facts about maximization and minimization subject to constraint when both functions are smooth;[6] we will make use of these repeatedly throughout the book. In the examples below, we consider the maximization problem in two dimensions, with one of the choice variables on each axis and the objective function suppressed.

1. A function is maximized subject to the constraint that the choice variables must satisfy some other function with equality when the slope of a level surface of the objective function is equal to the slope of the constraint.

---

[6]For an introduction to optimization of nonsmooth functions, see W. J. Baumol, *Economic Theory and Operations Analysis* (Englewood Cliffs, N.J.: Prentice-Hall, 1977); A. Takayama, *Mathematical Economics* 2d ed. (New York: Cambridge University Press, 1985).

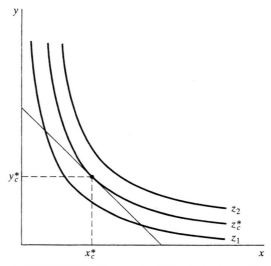

FIGURE 3.10   Constrained Maximization with Hyperbolic Level Surfaces

2. A function is minimized subject to the constraint that some other function of the choice variables must be equal to some constant when the slope of a level surface of the objective function is equal to the slope of the constraint.

3. For every maximization (or minimization) problem subject to constraint, there is a **dual problem,** which minimizes (or maximizes) the constraint function, subject to the original objective function being equal to its optimal value in the original problem. The original problem is called the **primal problem,** and the new problem is called the dual problem. The optimal values of the choice variables are the same in the two problems.

3.5   TECHNIQUES FOR SOLVING TWO-VARIABLE CONSTRAINED OPTIMIZATION PROBLEMS

This section outlines two methods for solving a two-variable constrained optimization problem with an equality constraint. Both methods will be illustrated by solving the following simple maximization problem:

$$\max \ z = x^{1/2}y^{1/2}$$
$$\text{s.t.} \ x + y = 4. \tag{3.1}$$

While this problem does not have an unconstrained maximum, it is possible to find a constrained maximum, illustrated in Figure 3.10. This graph shows that to maximize this function subject to the given constraint, find the point of tangency between the constraint and the highest constrained level surface of the objective function, just as with the circular level surfaces illustrated earlier.

We now turn to a consideration of two mathematical methods for solving such constrained optimization problems.

The Equal Slopes Method The equal slopes method involves finding the point of equal slopes.

Step 1 Since we know the solution will lie on the line $x + y = 4$, the equality constraint, we can rewrite the problem as two equations with y as the dependent variable:

$$z = x^{1/2}y^{1/2} \Rightarrow y|_{obj} = \frac{z^2}{x}, \qquad \text{objective function} \qquad (3.2)$$

$$x + y = 4 \Rightarrow y|_{con} = 4 - x. \qquad \text{constraint} \qquad (3.3)$$

Step 2 Find the derivative of each function with respect to x. Because we are looking for a point of tangency between the constraint function and *one* (as yet undetermined) level surface of the objective function, we can do this for any arbitrary level surface of the z function.

$$\frac{d}{dx}\left(\frac{z^2}{x}\right)\bigg|_{obj} = -\frac{z^2}{x^2} \qquad (3.4)$$

$$\frac{d}{dx}(4 - x)\bigg|_{con} = -1 \qquad (3.5)$$

Step 3 Substitute the function for z (equation 3.2) in the derivative of z^2/x with respect to x (equation 3.4):

$$-\frac{z^2}{x^2} = -\frac{(x^{1/2}y^{1/2})^2}{x^2} = -\frac{y}{x}. \qquad (3.6)$$

Step 4 Set the two slopes (equations 3.5 and 3.6) equal to one another:

$$-\frac{y}{x} = -1 \Rightarrow x = y. \qquad (3.7)$$

The equation $x = y$ defines a line that connects all the points of tangency between the level surfaces of the objective function, $x^{1/2}y^{1/2}$, and all possible straight lines of slope -1 and y intercept $\bar{k}_i$. In this particular problem, of course, $\bar{k}_i = 4$, but we have not yet imposed that constraint in solving the problem. Figure 3.11 illustrates how the function $y = x$ is constructed.

Step 5 Substitute $x = y$ in the constraint function:

$$y = 4 - x = 4 - y \Rightarrow 2y = 4$$

$$\Rightarrow y^* = 2 \qquad (3.8)$$

$$x^* = y^* = 2 \qquad (3.9)$$

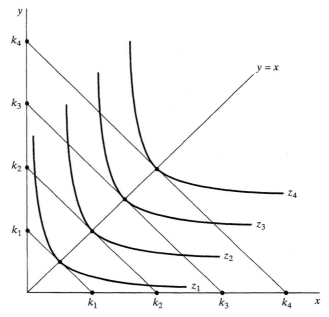

FIGURE 3.11 Construction of the Function $y = x$

$$z^* = (x^*)^{1/2}(y^*)^{1/2} = (2)^{1/2}(2)^{1/2} = 2. \tag{3.10}$$

In effect, this last step selects the point along the function $y = x$ that is consistent with the constraint $y = 4 - x$. Figure 3.12 illustrates this last step.

The Substitution Method The substitution method involves substituting the constraint function in the objective function. In any constrained maximization problem, it is always possible (in principle) to substitute the constraint in the objective function and then solve the problem as an unconstrained problem. The problem becomes unconstrained because the constraint is incorporated in the objective function being maximized or minimized.

Step 1 Express the constraint with either x or y as the dependent variable:

$$y = 4 - x,$$

as in equation 3.3.

Step 2 Substitute the constraint in the objective function:

$$z = x^{1/2}y^{1/2} = x^{1/2}(4 - x)^{1/2}. \tag{3.11}$$

This creates a plane in xy space on which lie all the values of z for combinations of x and y on the constraint line. The plane is, in effect, a vertical

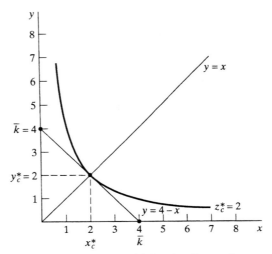

FIGURE 3.12 **Satisfying the Constraint**

slice out of the side of the graph of the function. Figure 3.13 illustrates the values of a general, hill-shaped function on a constraint line.

Step 3 Maximize the new z function (equation 3.11) with respect to the remaining independent variable (you will need to use both the product rule and the chain rule for this function):

$$\frac{dz}{dx} = \frac{1}{2} x^{-1/2}(4 - x)^{1/2} - \frac{1}{2} x^{1/2}(4 - x)^{-1/2} = 0.$$

Therefore,

$$\frac{(4 - x)^{1/2}}{x^{1/2}} = \frac{x^{1/2}}{(4 - x)^{1/2}} \Rightarrow 4 - x = x \Rightarrow x^* = 2$$

$$y^* = 4 - x^* = 2$$

$$z^* = 2^{1/2}(4 - 2)^{1/2} = (2)^{1/2}(2)^{1/2} = 2,$$

which are the same results as in equations 3.8–3.10.

Figure 3.14 illustrates the substitution method. As the upper graph shows, the intuition behind the substitution method is the idea that we are starting at some arbitrary point, say a or b, and then moving from one level surface of the z function to another (increasing z) along the constraint until we reach the highest level surface on the constraint line. Setting the derivative equal to 0 selects just that critical point. Moreover, this is exactly the same level surface that we identified as the optimum when we found the level surface that was tangent to the constraint in the equal slopes method. The lower graph shows the derivation of the constrained z function. Each value of z in the lower graph corresponds to a level surface in the upper graph. In principle, this method can be used to solve a problem with any number of independent

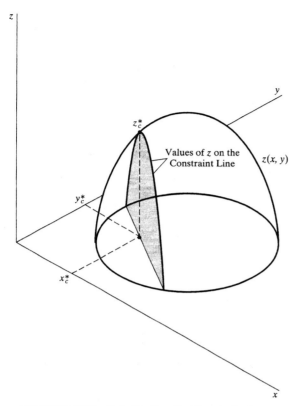

FIGURE 3.13   Substituting the Constraint in an Objective Function

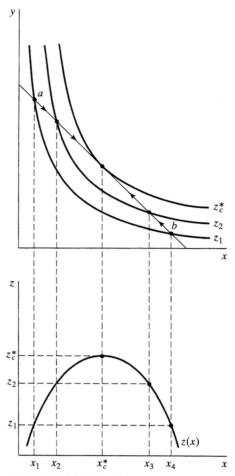

FIGURE 3.14 The Substitution Method for Solving a Constrained Maximization Problem

variables and constraints; however, it quickly becomes very complicated to apply. The next section outlines a simple, general method for solving constrained optimization problems.

3.6   THE LAGRANGE METHOD

The Lagrange method is the method most widely used by economists for solving constrained optimization problems with smooth functions. What it does, in essence, is create a new optimization problem that can be solved in a straightforward way, analogous to unconstrained optimization.

Maximizing the Difference Between Two Functions   Before we outline the Lagrange method, however, we should note a general property about problems that maximize the difference between two functions. We will use this property later on when we analyze profit maximization, where profits are expressed as the difference between revenues and costs. Suppose we wish to solve the following unconstrained maximization problem:

$$\max v = f(x, y) - g(x, y).$$

The first-order conditions are

$$\frac{\partial}{\partial x} v(x^*, y^*) = \frac{\partial}{\partial x} f(x^*, y^*) - \frac{\partial}{\partial x} g(x^*, y^*) = 0$$

$$\frac{\partial}{\partial y} v(x^*, y^*) = \frac{\partial}{\partial y} f(x^*, y^*) - \frac{\partial}{\partial y} g(x^*, y^*) = 0.$$

Thus,

$$\frac{\partial}{\partial x} f(x^*, y^*) = \frac{\partial}{\partial x} g(x^*, y^*) \quad \text{and} \quad \frac{\partial}{\partial y} f(x^*, y^*) = \frac{\partial}{\partial y} g(x^*, y^*).$$

Therefore, when the difference between two functions is maximized, the respective partial derivatives of the two functions are equal.

The Lagrangian   The Lagrange method creates a new optimization problem, of which some of the first-order conditions characterize the maximum difference (at the constraint) between the objective function and a plane that goes through the equality constraint line in the xy plane. Since the solution is the maximum difference at the constraint line, it is also the constrained maximum value of the objective function. This problem is developed by equating the respective partial derivatives of two functions: the objective function and an appropriate multiple of the constraint function. (How the constraint function is changed is explained shortly.) These equal partial derivatives then turn out to be some of the first-order conditions of another function, called the **Lagrange equation** or **Lagrangian,** which is the difference between the objective function and the function derived from the constraint. Thus, by finding a critical point of the Lagrangian, we will have characterized the highest value of the objective function consistent with the constraint.

To develop the Lagrangian, we first construct an entirely new plane in three dimensions. The constraint in our problem is one line in this new plane. We define the function for this new plane as

$$z = g(x, y).$$

The constraint line will describe all values of x and y for which $g(x, y)$ is 0. Thus,

$$g(x, y) = 0$$

along the constraint line. In our example (equation 3.1), the line $x + y = 4$ is the constraint. Rearranging terms, it is conventional to express the constraint in the following form:

$$4 - x - y = 0.$$

Thus, $g(x, y)$ has the form

$$g(x, y) = 4 - x - y$$

to ensure that $g(x, y) = 0$ along the constraint line. Figure 3.15 on the following page illustrates $g(x, y) = 4 - x - y$. Notice that outside the constraint (to the right of the line),

$$g(x, y) = 4 - x - y < 0.$$

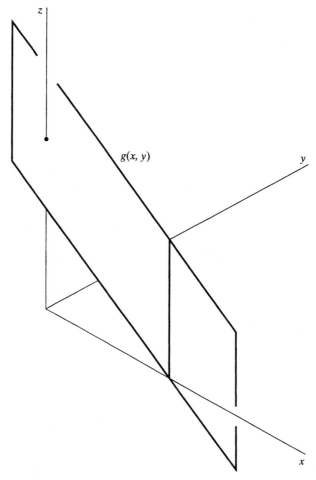

FIGURE 3.15   The Function $g(x, y) = 4 - x - y$

Similarly, inside the constraint (to the left of the line),

$$g(x, y) = 4 - x - y > 0.$$

Next, suppose we take the negative of $g(x, y)$, $[-g(x, y)]$ which gives us a plane that rises from left to right, and then pivot it about the line $g(x, y) = 0$. The new plane will still go through the line $g(x, y) = 0$. The object is to create another new plane with the property that this plane and the objective function have equal partial derivatives at the point (x_c^*, y_c^*). As we discussed above, equal partial derivatives would describe the greatest difference between the objective function and the xy plane along the constraint line. This greatest difference would also be the highest value of the objective function consistent with the constraint; that is, z_c^*. Thus, we want to "tilt" the $-g(x, y)$ function in such a way that the partial derivatives of the objective function are equal to the partial derivatives of the tilted $-g(x, y)$ function.

In Figure 3.16, the original function $-g(x, y)$ is outlined with a dashed line, and the tilted function is outlined with a solid line; $-g(x, y)$ is tilted until the new plane is

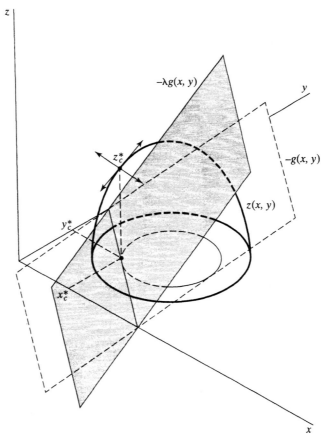

FIGURE 3.16   Equal Partial Derivatives Between $f(x,y)$ and a "Tilted" $-g(x,y)$

parallel to a plane that is tangent to the objective function at the constrained optimum (x^*, y^*). Since the planes are parallel, the partial derivatives of the objective function at the point of tangency are equal to the partial derivatives of the tilted $-g(x, y)$ function.

The Lagrange Multiplier   Suppose we simply multiply the $-g(x, y)$ function by a positive number (call it λ). This has the effect of tilting the constraint function, making the partial derivatives of $f(x, y)$ equal to the partial derivatives of $-\lambda g(x, y)$:

$$\frac{\partial f}{\partial x} = -\lambda \frac{\partial g}{\partial x} \quad \text{and} \quad \frac{\partial f}{\partial y} = -\lambda \frac{\partial g}{\partial y}.$$

We can rewrite these equations as

$$f_x = -\lambda g_x \quad \Rightarrow \quad f_x + \lambda g_x = 0$$
$$f_y = -\lambda g_y \quad \Rightarrow \quad f_y + \lambda g_y = 0.$$

Now, suppose we construct the new function

$$\mathcal{L}(x, y, \lambda) = f(x, y) + \lambda g(x, y). \tag{3.14}$$

If we were to find an unconstrained critical point of this function, the first-order conditions would be

$$\frac{\partial \mathcal{L}}{\partial x} = f_x(x^*, y^*) + \lambda^* g_x(x^*, y^*) = 0 \tag{3.15}$$

$$\frac{\partial \mathcal{L}}{\partial y} = f_y(x^*, y^*) + \lambda^* g_y(x^*, y^*) = 0 \tag{3.16}$$

$$\frac{\partial \mathcal{L}}{\partial \lambda} = g(x^*, y^*) = 0. \tag{3.17}$$

Thus, the first-order conditions of this new function characterize the maximum difference between the objective function and the tilted constraint plane. In other words, they characterize the constrained optimum. The solution $f(x^*, y^*)$ is the maximum difference, the constrained optimum, itself.

We call $\mathcal{L}(x, y, \lambda) = f(x, y) + \lambda g(x, y)$ the *Lagrangian,* and λ, the **Lagrange multiplier.** The number λ is simply the amount by which the partial derivatives of $-g(x, y)$ have to be multiplied to make the partial derivatives of the tilted constraint function equal to the partial derivatives of $f(x, y)$.

Economic Interpretations of $\mathcal{L}$ ***and*** λ The Lagrangian and the Lagrange multiplier also have important economic interpretations. To interpret $\mathcal{L}$, recall that $g(x, y) = 0$ along the constraint line. (That was how we defined it to begin with.) Thus,

$$\mathcal{L}(x^*, y^*, \lambda^*) = f(x^*, y^*) = f(x^*, y^*) + \lambda^* 0.$$

In other words, the critical value of the $\mathcal{L}(x, y, \lambda)$ function is simply the optimal value of the constrained $f(x, y)$ function itself.

To interpret λ^*, think of $g(x, y)$ as a function of x and y with some parameter, α, that determines the level of the constraint:

$$g(x, y; \alpha),$$

where $g(x^*, y^*; \alpha) = 0$. Each level of α will determine a different set of constrained optimal values of x, y, and z, which we write as $x^*(\alpha)$, $y^*(\alpha)$, and $z^*(\alpha)$. We can derive the comparative statics relationships, $\partial x^*/\partial\alpha$, $\partial y^*/\partial\alpha$, and $\partial z^*/\partial\alpha$, as we did in the unconstrained case in Chapter 2.[7] Recall that one step in finding comparative statics relationships is to totally differentiate the implicit function,

$$g(x^*, y^*; \alpha) = 0. \tag{3.18}$$

Thus,

$$g_x \, dx^* + g_y \, dy^* + g_\alpha \, d\alpha = 0. \tag{3.19}$$

Therefore,

$$-g_\alpha = g_x \frac{dx^*}{d\alpha} + g_y \frac{dy^*}{d\alpha}. \tag{3.20}$$

Now, to find the comparative statics relationship, $\partial z^*/\partial\alpha$, we first construct the indirect objective function from $x^*(\alpha)$ and $y^*(\alpha)$, remembering that we have constructed this problem so that α shifts only the constraint and not the objective function:

$$z^*(\alpha) = f(x^*(\alpha), y^*(\alpha)). \tag{3.21}$$

We then differentiate with respect to α, using the chain rule:

$$\frac{\partial z^*}{\partial\alpha} = f_x \frac{dx^*}{d\alpha} + f_y \frac{dy^*}{d\alpha}. \tag{3.22}$$

However, we know from the first two first-order conditions (equations 3.15 and 3.16) that

$$f_x = -\lambda g_x \quad \text{and} \quad f_y = -\lambda g_y.$$

Therefore, substituting for f_x and f_y in equation 3.22,

$$\frac{\partial z^*}{\partial\alpha} = -\lambda g_x \frac{dx^*}{d\alpha} - \lambda g_y \frac{dy^*}{d\alpha} = -\lambda\left(g_x \frac{dx^*}{d\alpha} + g_y \frac{dy^*}{d\alpha}\right).$$

Thus, substituting from equation 3.20,

$$\frac{\partial z^*}{\partial\alpha} = -\lambda(-g_\alpha) = \lambda g_\alpha. \tag{3.23}$$

---

[7]Since there are three first-order conditions instead of just one, we have to solve a system of three simultaneous equations to find the comparative statics relationships. This is usually done with matrices. For further information, interested students should consult Silberberg, *Structure of Economics*, pp. 180–187; or Chiang, *Fundamentals of Mathematical Economics*, pp. 404–409.

We now return to equation 3.13,

$$g(x, y; \alpha) = 4 - x - y,$$

where $4 = \alpha$. Thus,

$$g(x, y; \alpha) = \alpha - x - y, \tag{3.24}$$

Therefore,

$$g_\alpha = 1 \tag{3.25}$$

and, substituting for g_α in equation 3.23,

$$\frac{\partial z^*}{\partial \alpha} = \lambda(1) = \lambda. \tag{3.26}$$

Thus, we can interpret λ as the derivative of the optimal value of the objective function with respect to the constant in the constraint. In fact, whenever α enters $g(x, y)$ in this linear fashion, λ will have that interpretation. In later chapters, we will see that the economic interpretation of λ will be the marginal value (in terms of the objective function) of relaxing the constraint: applications include marginal utility of income and marginal cost.

The Envelope Theorem for Constrained Optimization   Notice that to derive the comparative statics relationship $\partial z^*/\partial \alpha$ (equation 3.26), we made use of the fact that the first two first-order conditions (equations 3.15 and 3.16) always hold with equality at the optimal values. This allowed us to substitute $-\lambda g_x$ for f_x and $-\lambda g_y$ for f_y. In doing so, we derived a version of the envelope theorem for the constrained case with two independent variables. Basically, in this context, the envelope theorem states that if $z = f(x, y; \alpha)$ is maximized or minimized subject to $g(x, y; \alpha) = 0$, then

$$\frac{\partial z^*}{\partial \alpha} = f_\alpha = \lambda g_\alpha, \tag{3.27}$$

where λ is the Lagrange multiplier of the constrained optimization problem. This is true because of the substitutions we can make for f_x and f_y based on the first-order conditions:

$$\frac{\partial z^*}{\partial \alpha} = f_x \frac{\partial x^*}{\partial \alpha} = f_y \frac{\partial y^*}{\partial \alpha} = f_\alpha = f_\alpha - \lambda \left(g_x \frac{\partial x^*}{\partial \alpha} = g_y \frac{\partial y^*}{\partial \alpha} \right)$$

$$= f_\alpha - \lambda(-g_\alpha) = f_\alpha + \lambda g_\alpha.$$

In our example, α did not enter the objective function (f); therefore, $f_\alpha = 0$. In addition, $g_\alpha = 1$. Thus, when $f(x, y)$ is maximized or minimized subject to $g(x, y; \alpha)$, and α enters in a linear fashion,

$$\frac{\partial z^*}{\partial \alpha} = \lambda.$$

We will make use of both the unconstrained and the constrained envelope theorems for deriving functions and proving propositions throughout this book.

Applying the Lagrange Method To complete our introduction to the Lagrange method, let's return to the example, equations 3.1:

$$\max z = x^{1/2}y^{1/2}$$

$$\text{s.t. } x + y = 4.$$

Step 1 Identify the objective function, $f(x, y)$, and the constraint, $g(x, y)$:

$$f(x, y) = x^{1/2}y^{1/2} \tag{3.28}$$

$$g(x, y) = 4 - x - y. \tag{3.29}$$

Step 2 Write down the Lagrangian:

$$\mathcal{L}(x, y, \lambda) = x^{1/2}y^{1/2} + \lambda(4 - x - y). \tag{3.30}$$

Step 3 Find the first-order conditions of the Lagrange equation:

$$\frac{\partial \mathcal{L}}{\partial x} = \frac{1}{2}x^{-1/2}y^{1/2} - \lambda = 0 \tag{3.31}$$

$$\frac{\partial \mathcal{L}}{\partial y} = \frac{1}{2}x^{1/2}y^{-1/2} - \lambda = 0 \tag{3.32}$$

$$\frac{\partial \mathcal{L}}{\partial \lambda} = 4 - x - y = 0. \tag{3.33}$$

Step 4 Find expressions for λ in terms of x and y and set them equal to one another:

$$\lambda = \frac{1}{2}x^{-1/2}y^{1/2} \tag{3.34}$$

$$\lambda = \frac{1}{2}x^{1/2}y^{-1/2} \tag{3.35}$$

$$\lambda = \lambda \quad \Rightarrow \quad \left(\frac{1}{2}\right)\frac{y^{1/2}}{x^{1/2}} = \left(\frac{1}{2}\right)\frac{x^{1/2}}{y^{1/2}} \quad \Rightarrow \quad y = x,$$

as in equation 3.7.

Step 5 Substitute the function $y = f(x)$, derived in step 4 ($y = x$ in this example), in the last first-order condition. Notice that the last first-order condition is simply the constraint function. Thus, step 5 is the same as satisfying the constraint in the previous two methods for solving these problems.

$$4 - x - y = 0 \Rightarrow \quad x + x = 4$$

$$\Rightarrow \quad x^* = 2 \qquad \text{same as equation 3.8}$$

$$y^* = x^* = 2 \qquad \text{same as equation 3.9}$$

$$z^* = (x^*)^{1/2}(y^*)^{1/2} \qquad \text{same as equation 3.10}$$

$$= (2)^{1/2}(2)^{1/2} = 2$$

$$\lambda^* = \frac{1}{2}(x^*)^{-1/2}(y^*)^{1/2}$$

$$= \frac{1}{2}(2)^{-1/2}(2)^{1/2} = \frac{1}{2}. \qquad (3.36)$$

First- and Second-order Conditions   The first-order conditions set out in step 3 (equations 3.31–3.33) are the *necessary* conditions for constrained optimization. In our example, we used two choice variables and one constraint. In the general case, we could have several choice variables and several constraints, each constraint with its own Lagrange multiplier. Thus, to take the first-order conditions in the general case, we take the partial derivative of the Lagrangian with respect to each of the choice variables and each of the multipliers and set each partial derivative equal to 0. In addition, regarding the general case, there must always be more choice variables than constraints. Otherwise the same problem arises as when we tried to do constrained optimization with a one-variable function. The constraints can uniquely determine the only possible value of the objective function if the number of constraints equals the number of choice variables. With more constraints than choice variables, some constraints may be inconsistent so that it is not possible to satisfy all the constraints simultaneously.

Second-order, *sufficient* conditions for constrained optimization with two choice variables and one constraint are presented in the appendix to this chapter. The intuition is that we want to guarantee that a critical point is either a maximum or a minimum. In the case of a maximum, as in the example developed above, sufficient conditions include having a linear constraint, level surfaces of the objective function that are convex to the origin at the point of tangency with the constraint, and the value of the function increasing in a northeastern direction from the origin. These conditions are illustrated in Figure 3.17; the convex level surface is tangent to a linear constraint, and the level surfaces increase in a northeastern direction.

The Dual Problem   Having learned the Lagrange method, it is now very easy to illustrate the dual problem and its relationship to the primal problem we just solved. Recall that the dual problem of a maximization problem, subject to a constraint, minimizes the constraint function, subject to the original function constrained at its optimal value.

The Primal Problem	The Dual Problem
$\max z = x^{1/2}y^{1/2}$	$\min c = x + y$
s.t. $x + y = 4$	s.t. $x^{1/2}y^{1/2} = 2$
$z^* = 2$	$c^* = 4$ (We will show this)
$\lambda^* = 1/2$	$\mu^* = 1/\lambda^* = 2$ (We will show this)
$x^* = 2$	$x^* = 2$ (We will show this)
$y^* = 2$	$y^* = 2$ (We will show this)

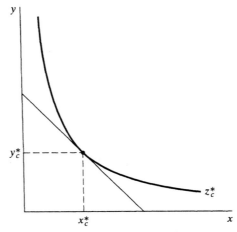

FIGURE 3.17 Sufficient Conditions for Constrained Maximization

The number μ will be the Lagrange multiplier for the dual problem. (We define a new Lagrange multiplier so that we will not confuse the Lagrange multipliers in the two problems.) To solve the dual problem we follow the same steps as above (equations 3.21–3.33).

Step 1   Write down the f and g functions:

$$f(x,y) = x + y \tag{3.37}$$

$$g(x,y) = 2 - x^{1/2}y^{1/2}. \tag{3.38}$$

Step 2   Write down the Lagrangian:

$$\mathcal{L}(x, y, \mu) = x + y + \mu(2 - x^{1/2}y^{1/2}). \tag{3.39}$$

Step 3   Find the first-order conditions:

$$\frac{\partial \mathcal{L}}{\partial x} = 1 - \mu\left(\frac{1}{2}x^{-1/2}y^{1/2}\right) = 0 \tag{3.40}$$

$$\frac{\partial \mathcal{L}}{\partial y} = 1 - \mu\left(\frac{1}{2}x^{1/2}y^{-1/2}\right) = 0 \tag{3.41}$$

$$\frac{\partial \mathcal{L}}{\partial \mu} = 2 - x^{1/2}y^{1/2} = 0. \tag{3.42}$$

Step 4   Find expressions for μ and set them equal to one another:

$$\mu = \frac{1}{1/2x^{-1/2}y^{1/2}} \tag{3.43}$$

$$\mu = \frac{1}{1/2x^{1/2}y^{-1/2}} \tag{3.44}$$

$$\mu = \mu \quad \Rightarrow \quad 2\frac{x^{1/2}}{y^{1/2}} = 2\frac{y^{1/2}}{x^{1/2}} = \quad \Rightarrow \quad y = x.$$

(Notice that we get the same function, $y = x$, as we got when we solved the primal problem. That is because the points of tangency are identical in the two problems.)

Step 5   Satisfy the constraint:

$$2 - x^{1/2}y^{1/2} = 0 \quad \Rightarrow \quad x^{1/2}x^{1/2} = 2 \quad \Rightarrow \quad x^* = 2$$

$$y^* = x^* = 2$$

$$c^* = 2 + 2 = 4$$

$$\mu^* = \frac{1}{1/2(x^*)^{-1/2}(y^*)^{1/2}} = 2\frac{(2)^{1/2}}{(2)^{1/2}} = 2.$$

Therefore, as promised, we get the same x^* and y^* as in the primal problem (equations 3.8 and 3.9) and c^* is the same as the value of the constraint constant in the primal problem (equations 3.1). Moreover, μ^* in the dual problem is the reciprocal of λ^* in the primal problem (equation 3.36), that is, $2 = 1/\frac{1}{2}$. This relationship between the λ^* and μ^* will also hold for all primal and dual problems. The reason they are reciprocals is because the roles of the objective function and the constraint have been reversed in the two problems. In the primal problem we write

$$\frac{\partial f}{\partial x} = \lambda^* \frac{\partial g}{\partial x}.$$

Therefore,

$$\lambda^* = \frac{\partial f/\partial x}{\partial g/\partial x}.$$

In the dual problem, however, g (in the primal problem) becomes the objective function, and f (in the primal problem) becomes the constraint. Therefore,

$$\frac{\partial g}{\partial x} = \mu^* \frac{\partial f}{\partial x}.$$

Thus,

$$\mu^* = \frac{\partial g/\partial x}{\partial f/\partial x} = \frac{1}{\lambda^*}.$$

3.7   NONNEGATIVITY AND INEQUALITY CONSTRAINTS: KUHN-TUCKER CONDITIONS FOR CONSTRAINED OPTIMIZATION WITH TWO CHOICE VARIABLES AND ONE CONSTRAINT

Up until now, we have assumed that the constraint always held with equality, and we did not impose nonnegativity constraints on the problem, even though we only drew our graphs in the first quadrant. However, in economics we generally (at least implicitly) impose nonnegativity constraints on the independent variables, as in the development of one-variable Kuhn-Tucker conditions in Section 3.3. We impose this assumption because, in many cases, it would not be economically meaningful to allow negative values of the independent variables. For example, inputs of capital and labor (the independent variables) cannot be negative, but profits (the dependent variable) might be. Similarly, a consumer cannot choose to consume negative quantities of goods or services. If all the independent variables are positive at the optimal solution, we call it an **interior solution.** If one or more of the independent variables is 0 at the optimal solution, we call it a **boundary** or **corner solution.**

Figure 3.18 illustrates two possible corner solutions. In the left graph, the level surface of the objective function is just tangent to the constraint at $x^* = 0$. In this case, we say that the nonnegativity constraint is not binding, since x^* would be 0 without imposing the extra constraint. In the right graph, on the other hand, the optimal solution would be negative without the nonnegativity constraint; thus, $x^* = 0$ because the nonnegativity constraint *is* imposed.

Developing the Kuhn-Tucker Conditions In Section 3.3, we developed Kuhn-Tucker conditions for a one-variable constrained maximization problem with a nonnegativity constraint. We can now develop analogous Kuhn-Tucker conditions for a two-variable constrained problem. To derive these new Kuhn-Tucker conditions, we will develop a new Lagrange problem with an additional constraint to represent nonnegativity, constructed so that it always holds with equality. To do that, we introduce a new variable, s^2. Since s^2 is always nonnegative, it is used to represent the value of x in the nonnegativity constraint and is sometimes referred to as a **slack variable.**[8] We can now

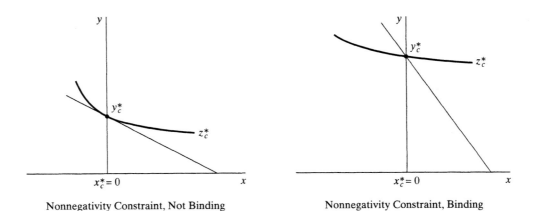

Nonnegativity Constraint, Not Binding   Nonnegativity Constraint, Binding

FIGURE 3.18 Boundary (Corner) Solutions

---

[8]We could also create another squared variable to represent a nonnegative, constrained value of y, but we will keep the problem simple by only imposing a nonnegativity constraint on x.

write this new problem with three choice variables (x, y, and s), two constraints, and two Lagrange multipliers (λ and μ):

$$\max f(x, y)$$
$$\text{s.t. } g(x, y) = 0$$
$$x - s^2 = 0.$$

The Lagrangian is

$$\mathcal{L}(x, y, s, \lambda, \mu) = f(x, y) + \lambda g(x, y) + \mu(x - s^2).$$

The relevant first-order conditions are

$$\frac{\partial \mathcal{L}}{\partial x} = f_x + \lambda g_x + \mu = 0$$

$$\frac{\partial \mathcal{L}}{\partial y} = f_y + \lambda g_y = 0$$

$$\frac{\partial \mathcal{L}}{\partial s} = -2\mu s = 0.$$

Now, let's consider the third first-order condition. Clearly, either $\mu = 0$ or $s = 0$ or they are both 0. Suppose $s = 0$, but $\mu \neq 0$. That is represented by point A in Figure 3.19. The nonnegativity constraint is binding (implying $\mu \neq 0$),[9] but the optimal value of x is $x^* = 0$. Thus, by the first first-order condition,

$$f_x + \lambda g_x + \mu = 0 \quad \Rightarrow \quad f_x + \lambda g_x < 0,$$

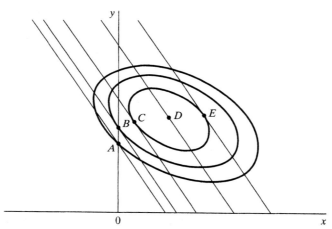

FIGURE 3.19 Two-variable Constrained Maximization with a Nonnegativity Constraint

---

[9]In fact, by the second-order conditions for constrained maximization, it can be shown that $\mu > 0$ if the constraint is binding. Interested students should consult Silberberg, *Structure of Economics*, pp. 470–476.

since $\mu > 0$ by the second-order conditions. Now suppose $s \neq 0$, implying $\mu = 0$. That is represented by the interior solution at point C. The nonnegativity constraint is not binding (implying $\mu = 0$), and $x^* > 0$. Thus,

$$f_x + \lambda g_x + 0 = 0 \quad \Rightarrow \quad f_x + \lambda g_x = 0.$$

If both s and μ are 0, we are at the "equal slopes" corner solution, represented by point B. The nonnegativity constraint is not binding, but $x^* = 0$ anyway. In this case, too,

$$f_x + \lambda g_x = 0.$$

The extension to y follows naturally:

$$f_y + \lambda g_y < 0 \quad \Rightarrow \quad y^* = 0$$
$$f_y + \lambda g_y = 0 \Rightarrow \quad y^* \geq 0.$$

Inequality Constraints Economic problems often do not require that the constraint be satisfied with equality. Consumers may not always spend all their incomes, and firms may not always exploit all possibilities for minimizing costs. We simply require that consumers spend no more than their incomes and that firms use technologically feasible input combinations. To describe a feasible set of choices in a constrained maximization problem, for example, the constraint $g(x, y) = 0$ might be written as $g(x, y) \geq 0$. In our specific example, $4 - x - y = 0$ becomes $4 - x - y \geq 0$, or $x + y \leq 4$. We refer to such a constraint as an **inequality constraint.** If the unconstrained optimum does not satisfy the constraint, then a problem with an inequality constraint is generally the same as a problem with an equality constraint. For example, in Figure 3.19, the unconstrained optimum is at point D, but at point C the (equality) constraint is binding. If the function is being maximized subject to an inequality constraint with the line at point C as the boundary, then the optimal solution is still point C, at a point of tangency with the constraint. But, if the constraint is lifted until the unconstrained optimum (point D) is inside the constraint, then the solution to a problem with an inequality constraint is simply the unconstrained optimum. The constraint is not binding. To develop Kuhn-Tucker conditions with an inequality constraint, we use another nonnegative slack variable (say t^2) to make the reformulated constraint hold with equality. Thus, we write the problem as

$$\max z = f(x, y)$$
$$\text{s.t. } t^2 - g(x, y) = 0.$$

The Lagrangian is

$$\mathcal{L}(x, y, \lambda, t) = f(x, y) + \lambda[t^2 - g(x, y)].$$

The relevant first-order conditions are

$$\frac{\partial \mathcal{L}}{\partial t} = 2\lambda t = 0$$

$$\frac{\partial \mathcal{L}}{\partial \lambda} = t^2 - g(x, y) = 0.$$

By the first condition given above, we know that $\lambda = 0$ or $t = 0$ or they are both 0. If $t = 0$, then the second condition implies that $g(x, y) = 0$, and the constraint holds with equality. If $t \neq 0, \lambda$ must be 0, and $g(x, y) > 0$; the constraint is not binding. If both λ and t are 0, then the unconstrained optimum is exactly equal to the constrained optimum; this is illustrated by the constraint line going through point D (the unconstrained optimum) in Figure 3.19. The constraint is not binding ($\lambda = 0$), but $g(x, y) = 0$ anyway since the solution is on the constraint line.

The General Problem   To summarize, we can write a two-variable constrained maximization problem with nonnegativity constraints *and* an inequality constraint as follows:

$$\max f(x, y)$$
$$\text{s.t. } g(x, y) \geq 0$$
$$x, y \geq 0.$$

The Lagrangian is

$$\mathcal{L}(x, y, r, s, t, \lambda, \mu, \tau) = f(x, y) + \lambda[t^2 - g(x, y)] + \mu(x - s^2) + \tau(y - r^2).$$

The first-order conditions are

$$\frac{\partial \mathcal{L}}{\partial x} = f_x + \lambda g_x + \mu = 0 \quad \Rightarrow \quad f_x + \lambda g_x \leq 0$$

$$\frac{\partial \mathcal{L}}{\partial y} = f_y + \lambda g_y + \tau = 0 \quad \Rightarrow \quad f_y + \lambda g_y \leq 0$$

$$\frac{\partial \mathcal{L}}{\partial \lambda} = t^2 - g(x, y) = 0 \quad \Rightarrow \quad g(x, y) \geq 0$$

$$\frac{\partial \mathcal{L}}{\partial t} = 2\lambda t = 0 \quad \Rightarrow \quad \lambda = 0, t = 0, \text{ or both}$$

$$\frac{\partial \mathcal{L}}{\partial s} = -2\mu s = 0 \quad \Rightarrow \quad \mu = 0, s = 0, \text{ or both}$$

$$\frac{\partial \mathcal{L}}{\partial r} = -2\tau r = 0 \quad \Rightarrow \quad \tau = 0, r = 0, \text{ or both}.$$

Kuhn-Tucker conditions for constrained minimization follow from the fact that μ can be shown to be negative in that case.[10] Thus, for constrained minimization,

$$f_x + \lambda g_x \geq 0$$

---

[10] An alternative way to state Kuhn-Tucker conditions is as follows:

$$x^*(f_x + \lambda g_x) = 0$$
$$y^*(f_y + \lambda g_y) = 0$$
$$\lambda^* g(x^*, y^*) = 0.$$

Since either the variable or the first-order condition is 0 in each of these equations, these Kuhn-Tucker conditions always hold with equality.

$$f_y + \lambda g_y \geq 0$$
$$g(x, y) \leq 0$$
$$f_x + \lambda g_x > 0 \quad \Rightarrow \quad x^* = 0$$
$$f_y + \lambda g_y > 0 \quad \Rightarrow \quad y^* = 0$$
$$g(x, y) < 0 \quad \Rightarrow \quad \lambda^* = 0.$$

We should note at this point that Kuhn-Tucker conditions are not generally used to solve constrained optimization problems. Rather, they characterize the constrained optimum with inequality and nonnegativity constraints. For practical purposes, it is easiest to solve a constrained optimization problem by assuming an interior solution and an equality constraint. If the calculated solution does not turn out to be a constrained interior solution, then proceed as suggested in the examples below.

Some Examples To illustrate these Kuhn-Tucker conditions, consider the following constrained maximization problem:

$$\max z = 10x - x^2 + 180y - y^2 \tag{3.45}$$
$$\text{s.t. } 80 - x - y \geq 0$$
$$x, y \geq 0.$$

First, let's solve for the unconstrained maximum. The first-order conditions for the unconstrained maximum are

$$\frac{\partial z}{\partial x} = 10 - 2x = 0 \quad \Rightarrow \quad x^* = 5 \tag{3.46}$$

$$\frac{\partial z}{\partial y} = 180 - 2y = 0 \quad \Rightarrow \quad y^* = 90. \tag{3.47}$$

Thus, at the unconstrained maximum, $x^* + y^* = 95$. This tells us that the constraint $80 - x - y \geq 0$ will be binding.

Returning to the constrained problem, begin by solving the problem without slack variables for the nonnegativity and inequality constraints. The Lagrangian with one constraint is

$$\mathcal{L} = 10x - x^2 + 180y - y^2 + \lambda(80 - x - y). \tag{3.48}$$

The first-order conditions for the constrained problem are

$$\frac{\partial \mathcal{L}}{\partial x} = 10 - 2x - \lambda \leq 0 \tag{3.49}$$

$$\frac{\partial \mathcal{L}}{\partial y} = 180 - 2y - \lambda \leq 0 \tag{3.50}$$

$$\frac{\partial \mathcal{L}}{\partial \lambda} = 80 - x - y \geq 0. \tag{3.51}$$

Now, assume the first two first-order conditions (equations 3.49 and 3.50) are satisfied with equality and solve for λ:

$$\lambda = 10 - 2x = 180 - 2y. \tag{3.52}$$

Thus,

$$2y = 170 + 2x \quad \Rightarrow \quad y = 85 + x. \tag{3.53}$$

Next, assume the third first-order condition (equation 3.51) is satisfied with equality and substitute for y:

$$80 - x - (85 + x) = 0 \quad \Rightarrow \quad x^* = -2.5, \tag{3.54}$$

without the nonnegativity constraint. Equation 3.54 tells us that to satisfy the nonnegativity constraint, we must set x^* equal to 0 and find the value of y that satisfies the constraint (equation 3.51).

$$80 - x - y = 0 \quad \Rightarrow \quad 80 - 0 - y = 0$$

Thus,

$$y^* = 80, \quad x^* = 0$$

with the nonnegativity constraint.

We can now characterize the solution using the Kuhn-Tucker conditions. Since $y^* > 0$, we know that the second first-order condition (equation 3.50) holds with equality:

$$180 - 2y - \lambda = 0.$$

Thus,

$$\lambda^* = 180 - 2(80) = 20.$$

Substituting for λ^* in equation 3.49,

$$10 - 2x - \lambda^* = 10 - 0 - 20 = -10 < 0,$$

which is what we expected since $x^* = 0$ and the nonnegativity constraint is binding.

To illustrate Kuhn-Tucker conditions further, suppose we raise the nonnegativity constraint to $85 - x - y \geq 0$. Thus, substituting in equations 3.49 and 3.50,

$$85 - x - (85 + x) = 0 \quad \Rightarrow \quad x^* = 0$$
$$y^* = 85$$
$$180 - 2y - \lambda = 0 \quad \Rightarrow \quad \lambda^* = 180 - 2(85) = 10$$
$$10 - 2x - \lambda = 10 - 0 - 10 = 0.$$

Both first-order conditions are satisfied with equality because the nonnegativity constraint is not binding, even though $x^* = 0$. For any value of the constraint between 85 and 95, both constraints will be binding, and x^*, y^*, and λ^* will all be positive.

Suppose now that the inequality constraint is $95 - x - y \geq 0$. Thus, substituting again in equations 3.49 and 3.50,

$$95 - x - (85 + x) = 0 \quad \Rightarrow \quad x^* = 5$$

$$y^* = 90 \qquad \qquad \text{the unconstrained maximum is } (5, 90)$$

$$\lambda^* = 180 - 2(90) = 0$$

because the constraint is not binding if the unconstrained maximum is attainable. For any value of the constraint greater than or equal to 95, if we were to solve the problem as if the constraint held with equality, the resulting value for λ^* would be less than 0. This would indicate that the point identified is beyond the constrained optimum, as is point E in Figure 3.19. In that case, the true solution is simply the unconstrained optimum itself, and $g(x, y) > 0$ and λ is 0, by the argument developed above.

For example, suppose the constraint were $110 - x - y \geq 0$. If we were to assume that the constraint held with equality, we would solve for the optimal solution as above:

$$110 - x - (85 + x) = 0 \quad \Rightarrow \quad x = 12.5$$

$$y = 85 + 12.5 = 92.5$$

$$\lambda = 180 - 2(92.5) = -5.$$

But since λ is negative, we know we have found a point of tangency that is past the unconstrained optimum. Thus, the correct solution is still $x^* = 5, y^* = 90$, implying $x^* + y^* = 95 < 110$ and $\lambda^* = 0$.

3.8 MORE WORKED PROBLEMS INVOLVING CONSTRAINED OPTIMIZATION

This section presents two more constrained optimization problems. One of the problems also reviews the dual problem, and the other reviews Kuhn-Tucker conditions.

1. $\max z = x + 2x^{1/2}y^{1/2} + y$ **the primal problem**

s.t. $x + y = 200$

The Lagrangian is

$$\mathcal{L} = x + 2x^{1/2}y^{1/2} + y + \lambda(200 - x - y).$$

The first-order conditions are

$$\frac{\partial \mathcal{L}}{\partial x} = 1 + \frac{y^{1/2}}{x^{1/2}} - \lambda = 0 \quad \Rightarrow \quad \lambda = \frac{x^{1/2} + y^{1/2}}{x^{1/2}}$$

$$\frac{\partial \mathcal{L}}{\partial y} = 1 + \frac{x^{1/2}}{y^{1/2}} - \lambda = 0 \quad \Rightarrow \quad \lambda = \frac{y^{1/2} + x^{1/2}}{y^{1/2}}$$

$$\frac{\partial \mathcal{L}}{\partial \lambda} = 200 - x - y = 0.$$

Finding expressions for λ and setting them equal to one another,

$$\frac{x^{1/2} + y^{1/2}}{x^{1/2}} = \frac{x^{1/2} + y^{1/2}}{y^{1/2}}.$$

Thus,

$$y^* = x^*.$$

Substituting this in the third first-order condition,

$$200 - x - y = 200 - x - x = 0 \quad \Rightarrow \quad x^* = 100$$

$$y^* = 100$$

$$z^* = 100 + 2(100)^{1/2}(100)^{1/2} + 100 = 400$$

$$\lambda^* = \frac{100^{1/2} + 100^{1/2}}{100^{1/2}} = \frac{10 + 10}{10} = 2.$$

Now, to set up the dual problem, we minimize the linear function $x + y = k$ (which played the role of the constraint in the primal problem), subject to $z = 400$:

$$\min k = x + y \qquad \textbf{the dual problem}$$

$$\text{s.t. } x + 2x^{1/2}y^{1/2} + y = 400.$$

The Lagrangian is

$$\mathcal{L} = x + y + \mu(400 - x - 2x^{1/2}y^{1/2} - y).$$

The first-order conditions are

$$\frac{\partial \mathcal{L}}{\partial x} = 1 - \mu\left(1 + \frac{y^{1/2}}{x^{1/2}}\right) = 0 \quad \Rightarrow \quad \mu = \frac{x^{1/2}}{x^{1/2} + y^{1/2}}$$

$$\frac{\partial \mathcal{L}}{\partial y} = 1 - \mu\left(\frac{x^{1/2}}{y^{1/2}} + 1\right) = 0 \quad \Rightarrow \quad \mu = \frac{y^{1/2}}{x^{1/2} + y^{1/2}}$$

$$\frac{\partial \mathcal{L}}{\partial \mu} = 400 - x - 2x^{1/2}y^{1/2} - y = 0.$$

Finding expressions for μ and setting them equal to one another,

$$\frac{x^{1/2}}{x^{1/2} + y^{1/2}} = \frac{y^{1/2}}{x^{1/2} + y^{1/2}} \quad \Rightarrow \quad y^* = x^*.$$

Substituting in the third first-order condition,

$$400 - x - 2x^{1/2}x^{1/2} - x = 0$$

$$\Rightarrow \quad x^* = 100 = x^* \text{ in the primal problem}$$

$$y^* = x^* = 100 = y^* \text{ in the primal problem}$$

$$k^* = 100 + 100 = 200 = \bar{k} \text{ in the primal problem}$$

$$u^* = \frac{100^{1/2}}{100^{1/2} + 100^{1/2}} = \frac{1}{2} = \frac{1}{\lambda^*}.$$

Thus, the optimal values of the choice variables are the same in the primal and the dual problems; the Lagrange multipliers are reciprocals; and the value of the constraint in each problem is the optimal value of the objective function in the other problem.

2. max $z = 100x - 5x^2 + 500y - 5y^2$

   s.t. $10x + 10y = 40$

   $x, y \geq 0$

Assuming an interior, constrained solution, the Lagrangian is

$$\mathcal{L} = 100x - 5x^2 + 500y - 5y^2 + \lambda(40 - 10x - 10y).$$

The first-order conditions are

$$\frac{\partial \mathcal{L}}{\partial x} = 100 - 10x - 10\lambda = 0 \quad \Rightarrow \quad \lambda = 10 - x$$

$$\frac{\partial \mathcal{L}}{\partial y} = 500 - 10y - 10\lambda = 0 \quad \Rightarrow \quad \lambda = 50 - y$$

$$\frac{\partial \mathcal{L}}{\partial \lambda} = 40 - 10x - 10y = 0.$$

Setting $\lambda = \lambda$,

$$10 - x = 50 - y \quad \Rightarrow \quad x = y - 40.$$

Substituting into the third first-order condition and assuming it holds with equality,

$$40 - 10(y - 40) - 10y = 0 \quad \Rightarrow \quad y^* = 22$$
$$x^* = 22 - 40 = -18.$$

Thus, to satisfy the nonnegativity constraint,

$$x^* = 0$$
$$0 + 10y = 40 \quad \Rightarrow \quad y^* = 4$$
$$\lambda^* = 50 - 4 = 46 > 0.$$

Substituting in the first first-order condition,

$$100 - 10(0) - 10(46) = -360 < 0$$
$$\Rightarrow \quad x^* = 0. \qquad \text{as above}$$

3.9   REVIEW OF KEY CONCEPTS

This completes our introduction to optimization in economics. From now on, we will use these methods (especially the Lagrange method and the envelope theorem) to develop economic concepts at every step. Before continuing to the theory chapters which follow, be sure you understand and can use the following key concepts.

Nonnegativity constraints require that the optimal values of the independent variables be greater than or equal to 0.

The Kuhn-Tucker condition for one-variable *maximization* with a nonnegativity constraint is that 1) the first-order condition is less than or equal to 0, and 2) that x^* is 0 if the first-order condition is negative, and greater than or equal to 0 if the first-order condition is 0.

The Kuhn-Tucker condition for one-variable *minimization* with a nonnegativity constraint is 1) that the first-order condition is greater than or equal to 0, and 2) that x^* is 0 if the first-order condition is positive and greater than or equal to 0 if the first-order condition is 0.

An *equality constraint* is a constraint that requires the constrained optimal values of the choice variables to satisfy the constraint equation.

A *level surface* of a function is the set of all combinations of values of the independent variables that define a given value of the dependent variable. Level surfaces are sometimes referred to as level curves (in two dimensions) or level sets (in general).

A function is maximized or minimized subject to constraint when the slope of the level surface of the objective function is equal to the slope of the constraint.

An original maximization or minimization problem subject to constraint is called a *primal problem*.

The *dual problem* to a maximization (minimization) problem minimizes (maximizes) the original constraint function, subject to the original objective function being equal to its optimal value in the primal problem. The optimal values of the choice variables are the same in both problems.

The *equal slopes method* for solving a two-variable, constrained optimization problem involves setting the slope of a level surface of the objective function equal to the slope of the constraint.

The *substitution method* for solving constrained optimization problems involves substituting the constraint in the objective function and then solving the resulting unconstrained optimization problem.

The *Lagrangian* is an equation that describes the maximum difference between the objective function and the constraint. Finding a critical point of the Lagrangian is equivalent to solving the constrained optimization problem of maximizing the objective function subject to the constraint.

The *Lagrange multiplier* is the derivative of the optimal value of the objective function with respect to the constraint when the shift parameter in the constraint function enters in a linear fashion.

The critical value of the Lagrangian equals the optimal value of the objective function.

The *envelope theorem in the constrained case* states that if $f(x, y; \alpha)$ is maximized subject to $g(x, y; \alpha) = 0$, then the derivative of the optimal value of the objective function with respect to α is equal to $f_\alpha + \lambda g_\alpha$.

Sufficient conditions for maximization subject to constraint include having a linear constraint, level surfaces of the objective function that are convex to the origin, and the value of the objective function increasing in a northeastern direction.

The Lagrange multiplier for the dual problem is the reciprocal of the Lagrange multiplier for the primal problem.

The solution to a constrained optimization problem is called an *interior solution* if the optimal values of all the choice variables are positive.

The solution is called a *boundary solution* or a *corner solution* if the optimal value of one or more of the choice variables is 0.

Slack variables are used to ensure that all constraints are equality constraints.

An *inequality constraint* is a constraint specifying that the optimal values of the choice variable must lie in a set that is either greater than or equal to or less than or equal to the set of values satisfying the constraint equation.

3.10 ___ PROBLEMS

Problems 1–5 Find the point (x, y, z) and the value of the Lagrange multiplier that solve each problem.

1. max $z = x^2 y^3$
   s.t. $4x + 5y = 40$
   $x, y \geq 0$

2. max $z = x^2 y^2$
   s.t. $x + y = 10$
   $x, y \geq 0$

3. max $z = \dfrac{xy}{x + y}$
   s.t. $x + 4y = 90$
   $x, y \geq 0$

4. max $z = 2x + 4x^{1/2} y^{1/2} + 2y$

s.t. $x + y = 400$
$x, y \geq 0$

5. max $z = 50x - 5x^2 + 100y - 10y^2$
   s.t. $10 - 2x - y \geq 0$
   $x, y \geq 0$

6. Find the solution to Problem 5 if the inequality constraint is $5 - 2x - y \geq 0$.

7. Find the solution to Problem 5 if the inequality constraint is $20 - 2x - y \geq 0$. Write down and solve the dual problem to each of Problems 1– 5. Show that you get the same optimal values of x and y and that the Lagrange multipliers are reciprocals of one another.

3.11 ___ APPENDIX

SECOND-ORDER CONDITIONS FOR TWO-VARIABLE CONSTRAINED OPTIMIZATION

Second-order conditions for constrained maximization and minimization are analogous to second-order conditions for unconstrained maximization and minimization, for values of dx and dy that satisfy the constraint. Given that the first-order conditions are satisfied, the second-order, sufficient condition for constrained maximization is for the second total differential of the objective function to be less than 0 for values of dx and dy consistent with the constraint. Similarly, the second-order, sufficient condition for constrained minimization is for the second total differential of the objective function to be greater than 0 for values of dx and dy consistent with the constraint.

Consider the general two-variable constrained maximization problem:

$$\max z = f(x, y)$$
$$\text{s.t. } g(x, y) = 0.$$

To find values of dx and dy consistent with the constraint, we totally differentiate the constraint function, $g(x,y)$:

$$dg = g_x dx + g_y dy = 0.$$

Thus,

$$dx = -\frac{g_y}{g_x} dy.$$

Now, as with unconstrained maximization,

$$dz^2 = f_{xx}(dx)^2 + 2f_{xy}\, dxdy + f_{yy}(dy)^2 < 0.$$

For a constrained maximum, substituting for dx,

$$d^2 z = f_{xx}\left(-\frac{g_y}{g_x} dy\right)^2 + 2f_{xy}\left(-\frac{g_y}{g_x} dy\right)dy + f_{yy}(dy)^2$$

$$= \left(\frac{dy}{g_x}\right)^2 [f_{xx}(g_y)^2 - 2f_{xy}g_xg_y + f_{yy}(g_x)^2] < 0.$$

Analogously, for a constrained minimum,

$$d^2z = \left(\frac{dy}{g_x}\right)^2 [f_{xx}(g_y)^2 - 2f_{xy}g_xg_y + f_{yy}(g_x)^2] > 0.$$

Those of you who have had some matrix algebra will recognize the terms in brackets as the determinant of the bordered Hessian matrix:

$$\begin{bmatrix} f_{xx} & f_{xy} & g_x \\ f_{yx} & f_{yy} & g_y \\ g_x & g_y & 0 \end{bmatrix} > 0,$$

for a constrained maximum. This is found by totally differentiating the first-order conditions of the Lagrangian with respect to x^*, y^*, and λ^*, and noting that g_{xx}, g_{xy}, and g_{yy} are all 0 if the constraint function is linear:

$$f_{xx}dx^* + f_{xy}dy^* + g_xd\lambda^* = 0$$
$$f_{yx}dx^* + f_{yy}dy^* + g_yd\lambda^* = 0$$
$$g_xdx^* + g_ydy^* = 0.$$

In matrix form, we have

$$\begin{bmatrix} f_{xx} & f_{xy} & g_x \\ f_{yx} & f_{yy} & g_y \\ g_x & g_y & 0 \end{bmatrix} \begin{bmatrix} dx^* \\ dy^* \\ d\lambda^* \end{bmatrix} = \begin{bmatrix} 0 \\ 0 \\ 0 \end{bmatrix}.$$

Chapter 4

INTRODUCTION TO ECONOMIC THEORY AND THE MARKET ECONOMY

4.1 WHAT YOU SHOULD LEARN FROM THIS CHAPTER

This chapter introduces you to the basic way economists think about economic problems. First, it discusses how we formulate and use theories to analyze complex economic issues. Then, it sets out the assumptions and basic structure underlying the model that is the focus of most of the theoretical portion of this book, *the competitive model.* At the same time, however, it points out the strengths and weaknesses of each assumption as a description of the way in which economic decisions are made. Finally, it discusses how we might create a more realistic model by relaxing some of those assumptions.

This chapter contains no math and thus may seem easier to read. It should, however, still be read with the same careful attention to detail with which you read the previous three chapters. The concepts are important and often subtle, and subsequent chapters will frequently refer back to the development of assumptions in this chapter.

4.2 THE ROLE OF MODELS IN ECONOMICS

This book stresses that economics does not have definitive answers for how the economy works or how individuals behave under all circumstances. Rather, what economists do is try to model economic processes, derive testable statements from the logical structures of their models, and then test whether the predictions of their models are consistent with observed outcomes. Economists begin by abstracting certain essential features about the economic environment and human motivation into a set of a priori statements called **assumptions.** Using those assumptions as a set of stylized "facts," economists develop logically consistent **economic models,** often expressed in mathematical terms, of the behavior of individuals and their interaction in economic circumstances. The models, then, can be used to follow through the logical consequences of some economic change, such as a new government policy, and to derive predictions about the economic effects of that change. These predictions are then compared statistically with outcomes occurring under conditions comparable to those specified in the model.

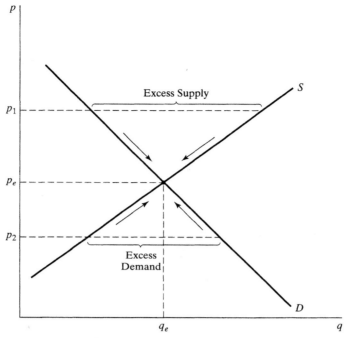

FIGURE 4.1   The Model of Supply and Demand

The Model of Supply and Demand   This process of model building utilizes what is called **deductive reasoning.** Logical conclusions are *deduced* from a set of initial assumptions. An example of a model based on deductive reasoning is the model of supply and demand developed in your principles classes. In its simplest form, the model of supply and demand might start by assuming that consumer purchases at different prices can be represented by a downward-sloping demand curve and that firm supplies at different prices can be represented by an upward-sloping supply curve. Having made those assumptions, supply and demand can be represented by the familiar supply and demand graph, reproduced in Figure 4.1.

As Figure 4.1 illustrates, if demand is downward sloping and supply is upward sloping, and if prices are adjusted on the basis of excess demand, then there exists a stable equilibrium price and quantity represented by the point (p_e, q_e). If price starts out above equilibrium, there will be excess supply, and firms will tend to reduce price. If price starts out below equilibrium, there will be excess demand, and consumers will tend to bid up price. Only at the equilibrium price will the quantity demanded by consumers exactly equal the quantity supplied by firms. The existence and stability of the equilibrium price and quantity are deduced as logical conclusions which follow from the initial assumptions of downward-sloping demand and upward-sloping supply. Having developed the concept of a stable equilibrium price and quantity, the next step in developing the model of supply and demand is generally to assume that one of the parameters determining either the demand curve or the supply curve changes and then

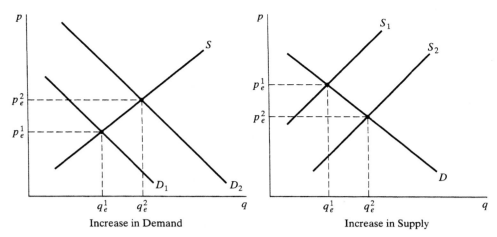

Increase in Demand   Increase in Supply

FIGURE 4.2   The Comparative Statics Effects of Changes in Demand and Supply

to deduce the comparative statics effect of the change in demand or supply. For example, Figure 4.2 illustrates an increase in demand on the left and an increase in supply on the right. As these graphs illustrate, the model logically predicts that if demand increases, both equilibrium price and equilibrium quantity also increase. On the other hand, if supply increases, equilibrium quantity increases, but equilibrium price falls. Deductive reasoning, illustrated above, can be contrasted with **inductive reasoning,** where general principles are *inferred* from observations of evidence. For example, we might collect data on prices, quantities, consumer incomes, input costs, and other variables that might affect either demand or supply and then estimate supply and demand curves from those data. If, in general, the estimated demand curves were downward sloping and the estimated supply curves were upward sloping, we might then infer a model of supply and demand similar to the one outlined above.

Both the deductive and the inductive approaches can lead to poorly developed theory. Beginning from a set of simplifying assumptions, the deductive method can fail to capture essential complexities of a problem being analyzed. In that case, the theory will be correct, given the assumptions, but not useful as a descriptive tool. The inductive method suffers from the opposite problem: there may be so much apparently conflicting evidence that one is tempted to develop a unique explanation for every event. Taken together, however, these "explanations" may be logically inconsistent with one another. In that case, there will be no "theory" and, therefore, no way of making sense of any new event. The best theory is developed as an interaction between these two techniques. First, we propose a set of assumptions and deduce theory as logical conclusions which follow from the assumptions. Next, we test whether observed phenomena conform to the predictions of the theory. If they do not, we alter the theory, derive a new set of conclusions, and test them again. In Chapter 13, we discuss one of the ways the model of supply and demand has been tested.

"As If" Assumptions   If the outcomes are consistent with the predictions of some particular model, then we say that economic actors, faced with the conditions being modeled, behave **as if** they satisfy the behavioral assumptions of that model. The reason we use the qualifying "as if" statement is because we cannot *know* what motivates individuals; we can only observe their behavior. We could ask them to explain why they behaved in some particular way, but there are two important reasons why economists argue that the responses will be unreliable. First, individuals may not understand their own motivation. Second, many individuals may wish to lie either because they think their motivation is socially unacceptable or because they do not think it is in their best interest to tell the truth. Thus, when we find their behavior is consistent with a model based on a set of assumptions about their motivation, we can still only speculate whether we have truly captured that motivation in those assumptions.

Recognizing this underlying ambiguity regarding behavioral assumptions, the "value" of a particular economic theory rests ultimately on two kinds of criteria: how well its assumptions capture the *essential* features of the environment being modeled and how accurately it predicts the economic consequences in some particular environment.

Seen in this light, the competitive model, summarized as the model of supply and demand, does not tell us how markets always *do* behave but rather how they *would* behave if certain rather restrictive assumptions were met. We study the competitive model because it is simple enough to understand at an introductory mathematical level and because it provides a benchmark against which to judge the performance of actual markets. Further, in many cases, the deviations from the competitive assumptions are not sufficient to negate crucial insights provided by a study of the competitive model.

4.3   THE ECONOMIC PROBLEM: RESOURCE ALLOCATION

Every economy faces the problem of **scarcity:** individuals in an economy always wish to consume more goods and services than the economy is capable of producing. Even primitive societies, which appear to have limited wants, and frontier societies, which appear to have unlimited resources, face scarcity. In both of these examples, time is still a scarce resource and it must be carefully allocated between production of goods and consumption of leisure. Everyone would prefer to have the same amount of goods and more leisure, but that is not possible because leisure time must be given up to get produced goods.

Because of scarcity, every economy must solve three **fundamental economic problems:**

1. what to produce;

2. how to produce it; and

3. how to distribute the production among competing demands.

Economists refer to this three-part economic problem as the problem of **resource allocation;** that is, the economy must allocate scarce inputs to the production of outputs and scarce outputs among competing uses. Given scarcity, one objective criterion for judging the performance of an economy might be whether it would be possible to produce more output by rearranging the allocation of inputs to production or by using some different production processes. We say that *production* is **efficient** if it is *not* possible to produce more of one good without taking resources away from the production of another good and, therefore, reducing its output. In general, however, as we shall see later, an economy will be able to produce many different combinations of goods and services that, according to this criterion, are efficient.

The Distributional Problem   Part of the resource allocation problem, therefore, is to decide which (possibly efficient) combination of goods and services to produce. This is the classic "guns and butter" problem many of you have been introduced to in principles courses. In the "guns and butter" problem, an efficient economy can gear up for war only by transferring peacetime resources to wartime uses and accepting a lower output of consumer goods. It cannot maintain its private consumption standard while it mobilizes for war.

The "guns and butter" problem illustrates how the distributional problem is an integral part of the overall resource allocation problem. In that problem, the mix of goods the economy will produce (relatively more guns or butter) is determined by the competing final use judged to be relatively more valuable at the time (war goods or peacetime consumer goods, respectively). In general, if the economy is at all responsive to the desires of final users, *what* gets produced will be strongly influenced by *who* gets to consume it, that is, by how the final output is distributed among users who may have different tastes.

Given scarcity, we might wish to use some objective criteria to judge the distributional performance of an economy as well. In particular, it seems reasonable to expect a distribution system to satisfy a criterion comparable to production efficiency: is it possible to redistribute resources in such a way that some final user or consumer can be made better off without making someone else worse off? We say that an allocation is efficient or **Pareto optimal** if it is *not* possible to make one person better off without making someone else worse off. In general, however, just as with production efficiency, there will be many possible distributions that are Pareto optimal.

To illustrate this last point, consider a simple two-person economy that has been given some quantity of one good to divide. Thus, this economy only has to solve the distribution problem. Now, consider all the possible ways this output might be divided: from person A getting everything and B getting nothing to B getting everything and A getting nothing, and every distribution in between. Suppose, in addition, that person A is given three-fourths to begin with. Thus, given that initial distribution, taking away from person A to create a more equal division would make most people in person A's position strictly worse off.[1] In other words, to make B better off if would be necessary to make A worse off. But, that implies that the original allocation of three-fourths to A and one-fourth to B was Pareto optimal. In fact, any a priori distribution on the continuum from all to A to all to B is Pareto optimal.

---

[1]Some people might be altruistic toward B and not be made worse off, but many other possible individuals in that position *would* be hurt. Thus, we consider this a reasonable hypothetical example.

Initial Endowments   This simple, one-good, purely distributional example provides an introduction to a fundamental difficulty with solutions to the resource allocation problem. In an economy that produces goods and must distribute final output, a number of efficient output combinations may be potentially Pareto optimal for a given distribution of consumer preferences. In fact, assuming an efficient point is actually chosen, *which* efficient point depends upon how claims to final output are distributed among consumers. For example, in an economy with two consumers and two goods, if the consumers have different tastes, the consumer who has more "purchasing power," a priori, will bias the distribution of final output toward his or her tastes. However, without having specified some a priori set of claims, it is generally not possible to predict which (possibly) efficient point will be the outcome of a resource allocation process. Thus, in order for an economy to solve the resource allocation problem, it is necessary to start from some a priori distribution of "purchasing power."

In the market economy, to which this book is devoted, each consumer is endowed with an a priori allocation of labor skills, capital, land, and goods, which determines his or her ability to trade for consumption goods in the marketplace. Together with consumer preferences, firm technologies, and the structure of the market, this a priori distribution determines both the production and the final distribution of goods and services. We call this distribution an **initial endowment** or **initial allocation.** The right to exchange one's initial endowment for other goods and services is one of the characteristics of a **property right.**

Once we have accepted that the initial allocation either evolves or is chosen independently, we can judge the performance of a particular economy by asking whether the production and distribution in that economy are efficient. That is, can we alter the allocation mechanism in any way that would make one person better off without making someone else worse off? If not, then we conclude that the economy could not do any better (although there might exist other mechanisms that could do just as well).

4.4   THE MARKET ECONOMY

This book will be concerned almost entirely with a model of an economy in which the government does not participate. It is assumed that the only roles for government are to protect property rights and enforce contracts and that the government uses up no resources in its operation. This may seem like an oversimplified assumption and, therefore, an oversimplified model. However, we justify it on two important grounds. First, in order to learn to construct and analyze economic models, we must begin somewhere; ideally we would use a model with a relatively simple mathematical structure. Otherwise, we get bogged down in the mathematics and miss the economic insights which the model offers.

Second, when certain competitive assumptions are met, the market economy turns out to be very good at solving the efficiency problem. We will show, for example, that when these assumptions are met, every competitive equilibrium is a Pareto optimum and vice versa. Thus, this economy can perform very well. Generally, however, actual economies do not perform quite that well. After developing the competitive model, we will discuss some specific reasons why it might fail to achieve Pareto opti- mally. Traditionally, these "market failures" have justified government intervention in the market economy. Unfortunately, however, in many cases nonmarket remedies do not necessarily achieve efficiency either.

Private Ownership   In a market economy, all factors of production are privately owned by consumers themselves. Thus, typical consumers will own their labor and skills (called *human capital*), some machines and buildings (called *physical capital*) which they rent to firms, some land, title to natural resources, shares in firms, and loan- able funds. Some consumers may own more or less or even none of any of these factors of production.

We begin with an initial assumption that in a **market economy,** there exists some initial distribution of inheritances of endowments of the factors of production among consumers. The market economy itself cannot alter that initial distribution, although individuals may increase or decrease their holdings by **investing** instead of spending for current consumption or by **disinvesting** (using up their investments). For example, the market cannot alter the fact that some people are born rich and others are born poor; however, the poor person can acquire the skills for a high-paying job, and the rich person can squander his or her fortune.

The combination of initial endowments and investment decisions determines a consumer's ability to produce income for the purchase of consumption goods and ser- vices. Labor and skills can be sold for wages; capital and land yield rents; funds yield interest; natural resources yield both prices and royalties; and shares of firms give title to firm profits.

Simultaneity of Individual Decisions and Market Outcomes   When we talk about microeconomic theory in the context of the market economy, we will be interested in two different topics. First, we will study the individual decisions made by consumers, firm managers, and owners of productive resources. Then, we will study the coordina- tion of all those economic decisions in the market allocation of scarce resources. Through markets, both individual and group decisions will be made *simultaneously.* On the one hand, market coordination among consumers, owners of factors of production, and firm managers will result both in observable market prices for all goods and ser- vices and in quantities transacted in each market. At the same time, those market prices will enter into the individual decision problems of consumers, owners of factors of production, and firm managers. Whenever markets are competitive, economic actors are assumed to take those market prices *as given.* That means those prices enter as parameters in the individuals' decision functions.

Figure 4.3 on the following page shows the coordination among consumers and firms in all the relevant output and input markets. This *circular flow* diagram shows, on the one hand, how firms pay consumers for the use of factors of production, and, on the other hand, how consumers use the income gained from selling and renting those fac- tors to purchase the goods and services provided by firms.

Self-interest   Microeconomic theory is based upon a fundamental assumption about how individual economic decisions are made. Economists generally assume that deci- sions are made in accordance with the self-interest of the decision maker. That does

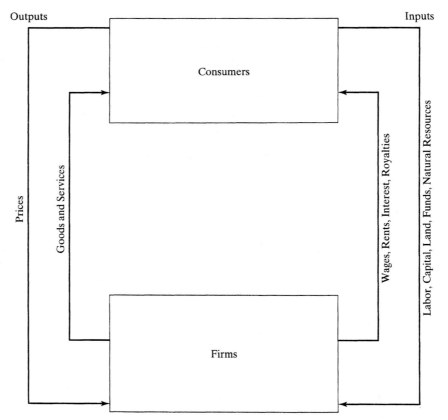

FIGURE 4.3   The Flow of Goods, Services, and Factors of Production in a Decentralized Economy

not imply, however, that economists assume that individuals are nasty, money grubbing, boring, calculating, or mechanical. **Self-interest** can encompass anything that makes the individual "feel good." Seen in that light, self-interest allows for altruism, laziness, indifference to monetary gain, interest in leisure-time activities, concern for others, and a host of other feelings and activities not usually associated with the caricature of the "economic man." What economists *do* mean is that they assume economic actors try to make the *best* decisions for themselves, given their preferences among different combinations of goods and services, their initial endowments, the available technology, and the prices they face in the marketplace. In other words, economic actors are assumed to behave as if they maximize subject to constraint.

Individual Versus Group Decision Making   In addition, simple microeconomic models generally are based on the admittedly restrictive assumption that all decisions are made by individuals and not by groups. That is to say, consumers are individuals, not families, and firm managers are individual entrepreneurs, not boards of directors. One reason why this assumption is made is illustrated by the following simple joint-decision

TABLE 4.1   **Voters' Preference Orderings**

	Voters		
Preference	A	B	C
1	X	Y	Z
2	Y	Z	X
3	Z	X	Y

problem. Suppose three people have to decide among three possible actions to take. Let the people be labeled A, B, and C and the alternative actions X, Y, and Z. Asked to rank the alternatives by first choice, second choice, and third choice, suppose each person would express a different **preference ordering** over them. Table 4.1 shows a possible set of preference orderings for the three individuals.

Now, notice that A and C prefer X to Y, A and B prefer Y to Z, and B and C prefer Z to X. If they vote in a pairwise election by majority rule, with the ordering of alternatives to be voted upon, the **agenda,** set as X against Y and the winner against Z, X would defeat Y and then Z would defeat X. That might suggest that the group decision would be Z. But, if the agenda were Z against Y and then the winner against X, the choice would be X. Moreover, if the agenda were Z against X and then the winner against Y, the choice would be Y. In other words, given the right agenda to order the votes, any of the three alternatives could be chosen by majority rule. This problem with group decision making is referred to as the **voting paradox** or the **Arrow paradox.**[2]

The voting paradox shows that a group may not be able to form a consistent preference ordering over alternatives, even though each individual member can. The group cannot maximize subject to constraint because it cannot choose a most preferred alternative from a set of possible alternatives. Thus, we cannot legitimately model its behavior as if it does maximize subject to constraint. More sophisticated models allow for some joint decision making, such as an agent working for another individual or a group of neighbors deciding to build a public park. The last few chapters will introduce you to a few simple models with joint decision making allowed.

The Small Economy   We will also restrict ourselves in this book to very simple economies with two consumers, two goods, and often only two factors of production, capital and labor. The reason is that *most* of the important insights of economic models can be obtained from studying such simple models. In particular, we will study how individuals make trade-offs among consumption goods and how firm managers make trade-offs among production inputs. A simple, constrained maximization problem that can be graphed in two dimensions as the level surfaces of the objective function and a constraint captures most of the insights that could be obtained from an n-good, m-input generalized model. In a few cases, such as the firm's short-run production decision, an extension to three choice variables adds to understanding; but the extension from three to any larger number almost never does.

---

[2]Kenneth Arrow, *Social Choice and Individual Values* (New York: Wiley, 1963).

We will assume in this book that markets exist for all the goods and services that our simple economy produces and for all the factors that it uses in production. This assumption will imply that each good, service, or factor of production has a market-determined price that can be entered as a parameter in all the relevant constraints. While this assumption is clearly restrictive, it is not unreasonable in the highly abstract, two-good, two-input model developed in this book.

4.5   THE MODEL OF PERFECT COMPETITION

Most of this book will be devoted to developing the formal structure of the model of perfect competition. While it is clearly oversimplified relative to actual economic environments, it provides the best possible introduction to formulating economic problems as mathematical models. It provides a logically consistent model of both individual behavior and market interaction, both of which can be deduced from a minimum of assumptions. Because the model of perfect competition is simple and logically consistent, it provides a basic model that can be understood fairly easily. Because it requires a minimum of simplifying assumptions, it provides a base on which to build more complicated models. We start with perfect competition and then relax each assumption to see how much, and in which directions, the predictions of the original model change. That way, our theories are always logically consistent, and we always know what assumptions (realistic or otherwise) underlie whatever predictions we make.

Price Taking   The crucial assumption of the competitive model is that individual economic actors have no effect on market prices and, therefore, must take market prices *as given* when making their individual decisions. This is often referred to as **price-taking behavior.** Thus, economists use the word *competition* to describe an anonymous acceptance of market forces and *not* aggressive "rivalry" among individuals. Since we will use simple, two-consumer, two-producer, two-good models in this book, we will assume that agents are price takers when developing the *competitive* model. As we will see in later chapters, however, agents cannot necessarily be expected to always be price takers when there are only small numbers on each side of the market.

Economists deal with this divergence between assumption and potential reality in two different ways. On the one hand, more complicated models generally assume that there are so many participants on each side of every market that no one buyer and no one seller has the power to unilaterally affect the price prevailing in that market. Consumers as a group or firms as a group can affect the price, but no *one* participant can. When we develop market supply and demand curves and the single-market competitive equilibrium, we will assume there are many buyers and sellers.

On the other hand, however, if economic agents in some markets were forced to behave as if there were many agents, even when it would seem as though there were few, then the model would be more widely applicable. Empirical work on markets suggests that in certain circumstances, even small numbers of economic agents behave as if they are price takers. For example, ordinarily we would model an industry with only one or two sellers as a monopoly or an oligopoly and not as a competitive industry. But if the product in question has many close substitutes, the one or two producers may be unable to affect its price. Instead, the price of the product will be determined in large part by the equilibrium price of its substitutes.

No External Effects   We also assume in building the competitive model that the consequences of individual actions do not fall on other individuals. For example, something I do personally does not help or hurt someone else personally. Similarly, the production by one firm does not produce by-products that either reduce or increase the potential production by other firms. This rules out, for example, both pollution and goods that jointly benefit consumers (such as public parks).

4.6   MONOPOLY, EXTERNALITIES, AND PUBLIC GOODS

After developing the competitive model, we consider the effects on the model's predictions of relaxing each of the competitive assumptions. First, we allow market participants to individually affect market price, arriving at models of **monopoly** and **monopsony.** A monopolist is the only seller in a market; a monopsonist is the only buyer. We find that relative to competitive markets, consumers tend to pay higher prices for consumer goods if firms can behave as monopolists and tend to receive lower wages if firms can behave as monopsonists. In addition, these markets generally fail to achieve efficiency.

Next, we allow the consequences of individual actions to fall on other individuals. For example, one person's consumption decisions may benefit other people. We call a good a public good if one person's enjoyment of it does not reduce others' ability to enjoy it simultaneously. A good example of a public good is a TV signal. Once a signal is broadcast, anyone with a TV can enjoy it without reducing anyone else's ability to enjoy it. Thus, if one person provides (broadcasts) a TV signal for his or her own consumption, everyone else can benefit.

Public goods also provide what are called *positive externalities* by allowing other consumers to benefit from one consumer's consumption decision. Positive externalities are also generated if, for example, a homeowner puts in a flower bed or paints his or her house, thereby raising the neighbors' property values and giving pleasure to people passing by. On the other hand, if a homeowner throws garbage in the yard, it has the opposite effect, and we refer to it as a *negative externality.* In general, an **externality** occurs when one agent's economic decision impinges on another economic agent directly; positive externalities benefit other agents and negative externalities harm other agents.

Efficiency with Externalities and Public Goods   A significant problem with public goods and positive and negative externalities is that competitive markets do not tend to allocate benefits and harms efficiently. In the case of a negative externality, for example, the efficient point is reached when the increased benefit to society (called the marginal social benefit) from further cleanup is exactly equal to the marginal cost of further cleanup. Thus, if nobody cares about garbage and it is relatively costly to remove it, the optimal reduction in garbage is slight. But if the neighbors do care about the garbage and it is not very costly to remove it, the optimal reduction could be quite large.

We call a good a **private good** if it can only be consumed privately and cannot be consumed jointly. In a private-goods competitive market, each person ends up paying a price that equates the marginal cost of production and the marginal private benefit from consumption. However, with a public good, each individual's marginal private benefit is less than the marginal social benefit to all. Thus, private cleanup will be less than the amount that would be socially optimal.

The TV signal provides a useful example of the problems that can ensue when marginal private benefits are less than marginal social benefits. For efficiency, TV signals should be provided until the marginal cost of further provision equals the *sum* of the marginal private benefits across all consumers with TV sets. In a competitive market, each person provides only until his or her *individual* marginal private benefit (very small relative to the marginal social benefit) equals the marginal cost. Suppose, for example, that a TV program costs $10,000 per minute to produce and broadcast. Hardly anyone would be willing to privately provide even one minute of programming, but everyone would be willing to contribute some small amount per minute if it were provided jointly. Thus, if TV is treated as a private good, very little gets provided even though most people would be willing to pay some small amount to get more. That outcome cannot be a Pareto optimum since everyone could be made better off by paying more and getting more TV in return.

The problem in allocating public goods and both positive and negative externalities is that only by joining together is it possible to provide a quantity of either an externality or a public good that equates marginal social cost and marginal social benefit. With a public good or a positive externality, for example, one way to equate marginal social cost and marginal social benefit is to find out the optimal quantity and collect from each person his or her marginal willingness to pay for that quantity jointly provided. Similarly, to clean up pollution, we might also collect the marginal willingness to pay from each person who would benefit from the cleanup. Unfortunately, however, competitive markets in goods, with both public goods and externalities, do not have mechanisms for determining the right set of prices and for collecting from those who benefit.

The Free-rider Problem   In addition, there is another problem, which further complicates any attempt to collect each person's marginal willingness to pay. In private-goods markets, you must pay the market price for a good or you are excluded from consuming it. With public goods, however, you can benefit from any amount provided by someone else. Similarly, if someone else pays to reduce negative externalities or increase positive ones, you benefit without having paid anything. If you believe that others will contribute, you have an incentive to "free ride" on their contributions, either by contributing nothing or by underrevealing your "true" willingness to pay. Economists call this phenomenon the **free-rider problem.** It leads to underprovision of public goods and positive externalities and to less cleanup of negative externalities than would be socially optimal.

There are many examples of the free-rider problem in action. Every year in every community in the United States, the United Fund exhorts everyone to contribute to worthy causes. While many do contribute, many others who verbally support the work of the fund do not. Similarly, public TV has a fund drive several times a year and rarely gets enough contributions to pay its operating costs. Many viewers of public TV do not contribute because they know they can watch the programs without paying.

Coercion and Exclusion If there were no free-rider problem, public goods could be optimally provided through subscription drives that collected a small amount from each beneficiary. However, because of the free-rider problem, some kind of coercion is generally necessary in order to get everyone who benefits to pay. In fact, this necessity for coercion is generally used to justify government provision of both public goods and pollution control. However, any signed, enforceable contract among the consumers of a public good will satisfy the coercion requirement, as long as those who benefit can exclude those who do not. Thus, for example, a TV signal that cannot be scrambled is called a *pure* public good because those who benefit cannot exclude those who do not, but cable TV is reserved for those who pay. Similarly, a pool or neighborhood park can be fenced with only members having keys. If the government provides a public good, the tax system is seen as *forcing* people to pay *approximately* what they would have been willing to pay. Membership fees for clubs or cable TV service provide similar incentives.

After showing that decentralized markets tend to be inefficient when the strict competitive assumptions are violated, we will suggest some centralized and decentralized remedies and discuss theoretical and practical problems with implementing those remedies. Traditionally, monopoly, externalities, and public goods have been viewed as justifying government intervention. Recently, however, economists have developed some decentralized remedies that may be more efficient than the traditional centralized ones.

4.7 REVIEW OF KEY CONCEPTS

We turn next to an analysis of the consumer's problem and the derivation of consumer demand functions. However, before continuing to Chapter 5, be sure you can recognize the following key concepts. Future chapters will develop all these concepts more fully, but this chapter provides the overview of what the book covers and tells why it is important. As you read the rest of the book, if you begin to lose the "big picture," return to this chapter and fit the details you have learned into the structure outlined above.

An *assumption* is an a priori statement about some feature of an economic environment that is being modeled.

An *economic model* is an abstract description of how an economic environment, such as a market, works.

When we use *deductive reasoning,* we begin with a set of prior assumptions and then deduce logical conclusions about the economic environment being modeled.

The existence of a stable equilibrium price and quantity follow logically from the assumptions of downward-sloping demand and upward-sloping supply.

When we use *inductive reasoning,* we infer general principles from evidence.

If the predictions of an economic model are found to be consistent with evidence, we say that economic agents behave *as if* the assumptions of the model are satisfied.

The problem of *scarcity* dictates that an economic system must satisfy the *fundamental problems* of deciding what to produce, how to produce it, and how to distribute production among competing demands.

Resource allocation refers to the allocation of inputs to the production of outputs and the allocation of outputs among competing uses.

Production is *efficient* if it is not possible to produce more of one good without taking resources away from the production of some other good.

An allocation is *Pareto optimal* if it is not possible to make one person better off without making another person worse off.

An *initial endowment* or *initial allocation* is an a priori distribution of goods, services, or inputs (that is, purchasing power).

Among other things, a *property right* gives an individual the right to exchange his or her initial endowments for goods and services he or she might wish to consume.

In a *market economy,* individuals begin with initial endowments and exchange those endowments with one another in markets.

Individuals may *invest,* by giving up consumption today in order to accumulate capital or skills, or *disinvest,* by using up portions of their endowments.

Markets simultaneously coordinate individual decisions and generate equilibrium prices which, in turn, are parameters in those individual decision functions.

Economic decisions are generally assumed to be made in accordance with the *self-interest* of the decision maker, encompassing anything that makes the individual "feel good."

The competitive model will be developed under the assumption that all decisions are made by individuals, not groups. By doing this, we avoid the problem illustrated by the *voting paradox.*

A *preference ordering* of alternatives is a ranking of those alternatives according to the order of preference (for example, X preferred to Y preferred to Z).

An *agenda* is an ordering of alternatives to be discussed and voted upon.

The *voting paradox* or *Arrow paradox* in group decision making is the possibility that a group may not be able to form a consistent preference ordering over alternatives, even though each individual member can.

In a *perfectly competitive* market, economic agents are assumed to take prices as given parameters in their decision functions. This is referred to as *price-taking behavior.*

A *monopoly* is an industry with one producer. A *monopsony* is a market with one buyer. Monopolists tend to produce less than competitive industries, and monopsonists tend to purchase less than competitive buyers.

A *public good* is a good that all consumers can consume jointly. No one person's consumption reduces another's ability to consume. Examples are national defense and TV signals.

An *externality* occurs when one agent's economic decision impinges on another economic agent directly. Positive externalities benefit other agents, and negative externalities, such as pollution, harm other agents.

A private good is consumed privately and cannot be consumed jointly. Food is a good example.

An optimal allocation of a public good equates the marginal cost of providing a unit of the public good and the sum of all the individual marginal benefits to consumers.

Competitive markets do not allocate externalities and public goods efficiently because competitive markets allocate all goods as though they were private goods.

Because of the *free-rider problem,* it is very difficult to provide public goods or pollution cleanup through subscription drives. Each person would benefit, but reasons that someone else is likely to pay.

If consumers who do not pay can be excluded from consuming a public good, then the free-rider problem may be overcome.

4.8 QUESTIONS FOR DISCUSSION

1. Suppose we lived in a society in which no individual had property rights. Would it be possible to have a market economy? Explain why or why not.

2. Suppose communities had property rights, but individuals did not. What special problems would have to be overcome in order for there to be a market economy? Compare those problems to the problems of joint decision making and the problems associated with allocating public goods and externalities.

3. A typical "solution" to the "problem" of public goods or externalities is for the government to provide the public goods or to clean up pollution. Discuss how the problem of joint decision making relates to the problem of deciding how much of a public good to provide or how much to spend on pollution control.

Chapter 5

CONSUMER PREFERENCE THEORY

WHAT YOU SHOULD LEARN FROM THIS CHAPTER

In this chapter, we introduce the assumptions underlying the economists' model of consumer behavior. From a few assumptions about consumer preference and indifference for different combinations of goods, subsequent chapters will develop consumer demand functions and the market demand functions upon which demand analysis is based. The theory of consumer choice is based on an assumption that consumers optimize subject to constraint.

In addition to the assumptions themselves, this chapter introduces new concepts and techniques that are important in economics. Economists model consumer behavior *as if* consumers maximize some *"utility" function* subject to constraint. This chapter argues that if consumer choices obey a set of reasonable assumptions, it is valid to represent consumer decision making as constrained optimization.

This chapter and Chapter 6 (Problems 1(a) and (b) and 4–9) also seek to dispel a myth that continues to be perpetuated in many principles courses. Many of you may have learned that demand curves are downward sloping because of diminishing marginal utility. While this explanation has some intuitive appeal, it turns out that the assumption of diminishing marginal utility is neither necessary nor sufficient for downward-sloping demand. Diminishing marginal utility simply has no place in consumer preference theory as it is now understood; the assumption is a holdover from turn-of-the-century theory. The text explains this important point, and reinforces it in the problems you will do at the ends of Chapters 5 and 6.

5.2 CARDINAL VERSUS ORDINAL UTILITY: AN HISTORICAL INTRODUCTION

In the approach to consumer utility to which many of you may have been exposed in a principles course, **utility** is viewed as some *measurable* level of satisfaction that a consumer gets from consuming a good. The idea goes back to Jeremy Bentham, an English economist-philosopher who wrote in the late eighteenth and early nineteenth centuries. Bentham argued that society should try to achieve the "greatest good for the greatest number" of people, and he assumed such a policy could be found by maximizing an aggregate social utility function. Since utility was viewed as measurable by some objective standard, it was both *comparable* and *additive* across individuals. In other words, Bentham believed that it was possible to say that person A got more "utils" from the consumption of some quantity of a particular good than person B. Furthermore, the "utils" enjoyed by person A could be added to the "utils" enjoyed by person B to help find society's total utility.

Cardinal Utility We say that an index, like utility, which assigns numerical values to items, is **cardinal** if the items making up the index can be objectively measured and compared. A cardinal utility index would allow utilities to be compared across consumers.

Since utility is not observable, however, there is an extremely difficult measurement problem in constructing a set of cardinal utility indices for individuals. Each person *might* be able to construct an index reflecting personal preferences. However, since person A cannot observe the utils person B enjoys and vice versa, there is no way to verify whether person A's utils have the same enjoyment value as person B's.

The problem can be illustrated with a simple example. Suppose you are traveling in Germany and you wish to buy some groceries. You would like to be able to compare the prices you are paying with the prices you are used to paying in the United States. However, the prices in the store are all in German marks; the prices you are familiar with are in U.S. dollars; and you don't know the correct exchange rate. Until you do know the exchange rate, any price comparison is not meaningful, but when you do know it, you can make a precise comparison. Moreover, the information you need can be readily obtained. Utility exchange information, however, does not exist because the items making up the individual indices cannot be observed and objectively compared. Two indices that are not constructed on comparable numerical scales cannot be added to form a meaningful, composite index. Adding A's utils and B's utils would be like adding dollars and marks without adjusting according to the exchange rate. Because utility indices are not objectively comparable, economists today say that we *cannot make interpersonal comparisons of utility.*

Marginalists By the turn of the twentieth century, most economists had come to realize this difficulty with Benthamite cardinal utility. Thus, the assumptions of comparability and additivity across consumers were dropped from the theory. However, an element of cardinality remained. While economists no longer assumed that utility could be added across individuals, they still assumed that each individual could construct a *personal* utility function, which retained some cardinal properties. Economists assumed that each consumer could assign numbers to goods consumed and that those numbers were comparable and additive within the personal utility function, even though one person's utility numbers could not legitimately be compared with another person's utility numbers. Thus, an individual could say that consuming one peanut butter sandwich gives 5 utils and consuming two gives 8.

In the example above, the first sandwich yielded 5 utils, but the **marginal utility** (the change in utility given the change in consumption) from the second sandwich was only 3 utils; that is, the second sandwich only added 3 utils to the individual's *total utility*. Since 3 is less than 5, we might say that the consumer got *diminishing marginal utility* from increasing consumption. This was the basic cardinality assumption maintained by the late nineteenth- and early twentieth-century economists, called *marginalists,* and they used this assumption to justify (incorrectly) downward-sloping demand curves.

Ordinal Utility   If you think about it, there is something strange about this theory. If utility is additive, each good can be treated in isolation from other goods. Thus, we could construct the utility of a peanut butter sandwich as the sum of the utility from the bread, the peanut butter, the jelly, and the butter. In particular, the utility of the peanut butter is not affected by how much bread or jelly there is in the sandwich, even though there would be no sandwich without the bread. At a minimum, we would like a theory that assigns utility numbers to combinations of consumption goods that cannot necessarily be separated into their components. For example, a peanut butter sandwich could be constructed with a variety of different proportions of bread, peanut butter, jelly, etc., and a consumer might have preferences among those combinations, but none of the goods stands alone. Economists call such a group of consumption goods a **consumption bundle.**

Today, economists go one step further, arguing that the concept of utility is only useful as a representation of a consumer's preferences over consumption bundles. All that is needed for a utility index is a rule that assigns higher numbers to more preferred consumption bundles and lower numbers to less preferred bundles. We say that an index is **ordinal** if it is only interpreted as representing a rank ordering among the items composing the index. Today's consumer theory is based on an assumption of ordinal utility. Such cardinal assumptions as diminishing marginal utility are no longer invoked in the development of demand theory. As we shall see, even downward-sloping demand does not depend on cardinal utility.

5.3 _____ THE MODERN THEORY OF CONSUMER PREFERENCE

In the modern theory, a utility index is simply a representation of a consumer's ordinal preferences. Economists model utility maximization mathematically because it is very convenient to do so, but what they have in mind is not choosing the highest number but, rather, choosing the *most-preferred consumption bundle* allowed by a consumer's budget.

To develop the modern theory of preference, let's assume, for the sake of simplicity, that there are only two consumption goods, good X and good Y. That way, we can represent a consumer's choices on a two-dimensional graph. Consumers are assumed to rank *consumption bundles* and choose among them. Each consumption bundle contains x units of X and y units of Y. Figure 5.1 on the following page shows two possible consumption bundles, described by points A and B. A consists of x_A and y_A. B consists of x_B and y_B.

Axioms of Consumer Preference: 1–4, on the Properties of Real Numbers   In order to represent consumer preferences among consumption bundles by an index expressed in real numbers, we must impose on those preferences consistency assumptions, which are similar to the consistency properties of real numbers. For example, from the fact

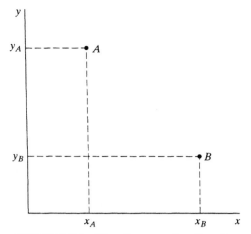

FIGURE 5.1 **Two Consumption Bundles**

that 3 is greater than 2 and 2 is greater than 1, we know that 3 is greater than 1. We begin with a set of assumptions, or *axioms,* that will allow a particular kind of mathematical representation of preferences.

AXIOM 1 *Preferences are complete.* For any two consumption bundles A and B, a consumer can make one of the following three comparisons:

1. A is *preferred* to B (denoted A^PB),
2. B is *preferred* to A (denoted B^PA), or
3. A is *indifferent* to B (denoted A^IB).

Preference means that the consumer would rather have the preferred bundle, and indifference means that the consumer doesn't care and would be willing to use a coin toss to decide. This axiom implies that a consumer can make such a comparison for *every possible* pair of consumption bundles. We refer to a ranking of consumption bundles for one consumer as that consumer's **preference ordering.**

AXIOM 2 *Preferences are reflexive.* If the consumer is presented with two *identical* consumption bundles, so that $A = B$ in all respects, A is *indifferent* to B. This simply means that if A and B are the same, the consumer has to rank them the same.

AXIOM 3 *Preferences are transitive.* If a consumer prefers A to B and B to C, then the consumer also prefers A to C: A^PB and $B^PC \Rightarrow A^PC$. Also, if a consumer is indifferent between A and B and between B and C, then the consumer is indifferent between A and C: A^IB and $B^IC \Rightarrow A^IC$.

This axiom simply says that consumer preferences are internally consistent. Thus, if A is assigned a number equal to or higher than the number assigned to B, and

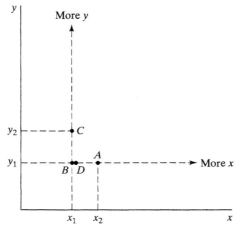

FIGURE 5.2 Lexicographic Preferences

B is assigned a number equal to or higher than C, then the numbers assigned to A and C (A equal to or higher than C) still describe the preference relationship between A and C.

> **AXIOM 4** *Preferences are continuous.* If bundle A is preferred to bundle B and bundle C is sufficiently close to bundle B (B is the limit of C), then A is also preferred to C: A^PB and $C \to B \Rightarrow A^PC$.

To see the importance of this assumption, suppose a consumer had the following preferences. First, look at the amount of X available; the bundle with more X is preferred to the bundle with less X, regardless of how much Y is available. But, if two bundles have the same amount of X, the bundle with more Y is preferred. Such preferences are called *lexicographic,* and they are illustrated in Figure 5.2. By the above criteria, A is preferred to B (because $x_2 > x_1$), and C is also preferred to B (because $y_2 > y_1$ and the x values are the same). Now consider point D, which is "close" to point B, but with slightly more X than at C. To satisfy continuity, C should also be preferred to D, but, by the statement of lexicographic preferences, even the smallest increase in X is preferred to any increase in Y for a given amount of X. The assumption of continuity rules out this and other such perverse discontinuities in preference.

Now, suppose consumption bundles are also continuous (or *infinitely divisible*). If these four axioms are satisfied, we can represent areas of consumer preference and indifference graphically. We call curves that connect all the consumption bundles that leave a consumer indifferent, **indifference curves.** Figure 5.3 illustrates possible indifference curves that satisfy the first four axioms.

The curves I_1 and I_2 describe consumption bundles over which the consumer is indifferent, that is,

$$A_1^IB_1^IC_1 \text{ and } A_2^IB_2^IC_2.$$

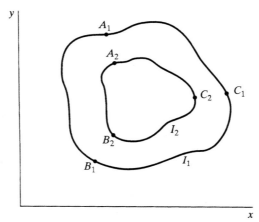

FIGURE 5.3 Indifference Curves for Complete, Reflexive, Transitive, and Continuous Preferences

In addition, if points on I_2 are preferred to points on I_1, then,

$$A_2^P A_1, A_2^P B_1, A_2^P C_1, B_2^P A_1, B_2^P B_1, B_2^P C_1, \ldots$$

Figure 5.4 illustrates indifference curves representing preferences that *do not* satisfy all the assumptions—in particular, they violate transitivity. Suppose all points on I_3 are preferred to all points on I_2, and all points on I_2 are preferred to all points on I_1. That would imply

$$A_3^P A_2 \text{ and } A_2^P A_1.$$

Thus, transitivity would imply

$$A_3^P A_1,$$

but if these curves satisfy reflexivity, it must be that

$$B_1^I B_2, C_2^I C_3, \text{ and } D_1^I D_3,$$

since $B_1 = B_2$, $C_2 = C_3$, and $D_1 = D_3$. Therefore, by transitivity,

$$A_3^I D_3^I D_1^I A_1,$$

and A_3 is *not* preferred to A_1, which is a contradiction.

Taken together, Axioms 1–4 are simply fundamental properties of real numbers, which we wish to use to construct the utility index. Axiom 1 says each point on the real number line is assigned some specific value. Axiom 2 says two identical points on the real line are assigned the same value. Axiom 3 says that if x is greater than y and y is greater than z, then x must be greater than z. The fourth axiom says that if $x > y$ on the real line, then there is another number, y' (between x and y), such that $x > y'$. If preferences did not obey the first three axioms, we *could not* represent them by real numbers, even ordinally. All four axioms, taken together, are necessary and sufficient for the existence of such a numerical representation. Such a functional relationship that

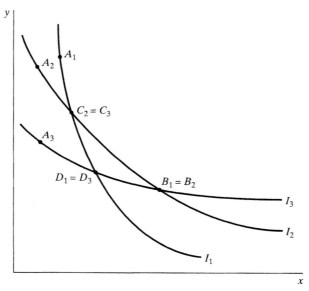

FIGURE 5.4   Intransitive Preferences Represented by Indifference Curves That Cross

assigns numbers to consumption bundles is called a **utility function.** For two goods it can be expressed as

$$U = U(x, y).$$

Nonsatiation and Diminishing Marginal Rates of Substitution   Economists also often make two additional assumptions that allow them to predict that consumers will choose unique consumption bundles, given their budgets, and not throw away any money. The assumptions are *not* necessary for representing consumer preferences in terms of utility functions over goods, but they allow economists to use the calculus of constrained maximization to analyze consumer choice.

> **AXIOM 5**   *Preferences exhibit nonsatiation.* Given two consumption bundles, *A* and *B*, with the property that the X in *A* is equal to the X in *B* and the Y in *A* is greater than the Y in *B*, the consumer will always prefer *A* to *B*. Similarly, if the Y in *A* is equal to that in *B* and the X in *A* is greater than that in *B*, the consumer will also prefer *A* to *B*.

In other words, if *A* is equal to *B* on one dimension and greater than *B* on the other dimension, then *A* is preferred to *B*. This assumption is generally referred to as "more is better."

Axiom 5 rules out "circular" indifference curves of the form shown in Figure 5.5. These indifference curves would describe the level surfaces of a hill-shaped function, such as we analyzed in Chapters 1–3 (Figures 1.8–1.10, 1.12, 2.11, 3.4–3.8, 3.13–3.16). The dot in the center, *U**, represents the highest utility level or **bliss point.** Point *A*, which contains more of both X and Y than at *U**, is on a lower indifference curve, and

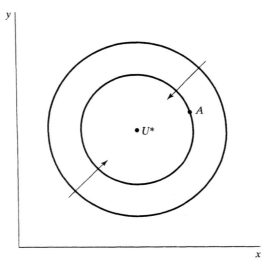

FIGURE 5.5 "Circular" Indifference Curves

therefore is not preferred to U^*. We say the consumer is *satiated* at U^*. Axiom 5 rules out such a bliss point.

The next axiom can be stated in a number of different ways. The basic idea is that indifference curves are smooth and convex to the origin. To introduce this axiom, we first define a concept called the *marginal rate of substitution* along an indifference curve. Consider that a single indifference curve can be described by a function

$$y = f(x; \overline{U}),$$

meaning that y is a function of x, holding utility constant at $\overline{U}$. The slope of an indifference curve is, therefore,

$$\frac{dy}{dx}\bigg|_{dU=0}.$$

We define the **marginal rate of substitution** of Y for X as the negative of the slope of the indifference curve:

$$\text{marginal rate of substitution } (MRS_{yx}) \equiv -\frac{dy}{dx}\bigg|_{dU=0}.$$

The idea of the marginal rate of substitution is to describe how much Y a person is willing to give up in order to get more X and remain indifferent between the two consumption bundles. One way to think of the marginal rate of substitution is as an individual's *internal rate of trade* between the two goods. Asked to trade Y for X, the marginal rate of substitution tells what rate of trade will keep the consumer just as well off as before the trade. We will see below that consumers make the best choices for themselves when the market rate at which they *must* trade just equals their respective internal rates of trade.

Now, recall that in Chapter 3 we said that a sufficient condition for constrained maximization with a linear constraint was for the level surfaces of the objective function to be convex to the origin.[1] For indifference curves to have that shape, they have to have negative slopes (first derivatives) and positive second derivatives:

$$\left.\frac{dy}{dx}\right|_{dU=0} < 0, \qquad \left.\frac{d^2y}{dx^2}\right|_{dU=0} > 0.$$

Translating that into marginal rates of substitution, if the slope is negative, the marginal rate of substitution is positive. If the second derivative is positive, the slope of the marginal rate of substitution must be negative:

$$MRS_{yx} = -\left.\frac{dy}{dx}\right|_{dU=0} > 0$$
$$(-)$$

$$\frac{d}{dx}(MRS) = \frac{d}{dx}\left(-\frac{dy}{dx}\right) = -\left.\frac{d^2y}{dx^2}\right|_{dU=0} < 0.$$
$$(+)$$

Thus, the *marginal rate of substitution is declining* or *diminishing.*[2]

AXIOM 6   *Indifference curves exhibit diminishing marginal rates of substitution.*

Figure 5.6 shows two representative examples of indifference curves that satisfy Axioms 1–5, but violate Axiom 6. The arrows denote the direction of increasing preference. In the left graph, the marginal rate of substitution is increasing, instead of decreasing, as x increases. In the right graph, the marginal rate of substitution is either constant (along the straight line segments) or undefined (at the corners).

Marginal Rates of Substitution and Marginal Utilities   We can also express the marginal rate of substitution as a ratio of marginal utilities. First, we consider a general utility function $U(x, y)$ and totally differentiate it:

$$dU = \frac{\partial U}{\partial x}dx + \frac{\partial U}{\partial y}dy,$$

---

[1]See Figure 3.15.

[2]Another way to express Axiom 6 is to develop the concept of a *strictly convex set.* To do that, consider two points on an indifference curve, for example, points A and B. Now, assuming nonsatiation, if we draw a straight line connecting A and B, all points on that straight line, except A and B, are on higher indifference curves. All such points can be represented as:

$$\alpha A + (1 - \alpha)B$$

for all values of α between 0 and 1. We say that indifference curves *bound strictly convex sets* if all points on such a linear combination of A and B not equal to A or B are preferred to A and B:

$$U[\alpha A + (1 - \alpha)B] > [U(A) = U(B)], 0 < \alpha < 1.$$

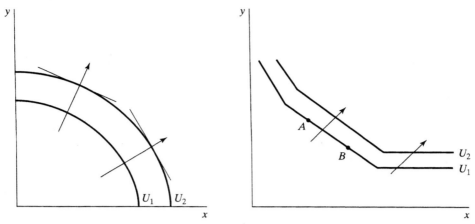

FIGURE 5.6   Indifference Curves That Do Not Exhibit Diminishing Marginal Rates of Substitution

where

$$\frac{\partial U}{\partial x} = \text{marginal utility of X } (MU_x)$$

$$\frac{\partial U}{\partial y} = \text{marginal utility of Y } (MU_y).$$

Now, notice that along an indifference curve, utility is constant, implying that $dU = 0$:

$$dU = 0 = \frac{\partial U}{\partial x} dx + \frac{\partial U}{\partial y} dy \quad \Rightarrow \quad MU_x dx + MU_y dy = 0. \tag{5.1}$$

Therefore,

$$\frac{MU_x}{MU_y} = -\frac{dy}{dx}\bigg|_{dU=0} = MRS_{yx}. \tag{5.2}$$

Equation 5.2 describes the only sense in which marginal utilities are meaningful. The *ratio* of marginal utilities must decline along an indifference curve in order for the marginal rate of substitution to decline. But that condition can be satisfied if both marginal utilities are increasing just as well as if both are diminishing. In fact, you will see in doing the problems at the end of Chapter 6 that whole families of utility functions, each with a different set of marginal utilities, may describe identical choices and yield the same demand functions. If two utility functions yield the same demand functions, we consider them to have identical ordinal properties.

Positive Monotonic Transformations   To begin to illustrate this point, consider two possible utility functions,

$$U = x^{1/2}y^{1/2} \quad \text{and} \quad U = x^2 y^2.$$

Their marginal utilities and the rates of change of those marginal utilities are described below. For

$$U = x^{1/2}y^{1/2}$$

$$MU_x = \frac{1}{2}x^{-1/2}y^{1/2} \implies \frac{d}{dx}MU_x = -\frac{1}{4}x^{-3/2}y^{1/2} < 0 \quad \text{diminishing}$$

$$MU_y = \frac{1}{2}x^{1/2}y^{-1/2} \implies \frac{d}{dy}MU_y = -\frac{1}{4}x^{1/2}y^{-3/2} < 0; \quad \text{diminishing}$$

and for

$$U = x^2y^2$$

$$MU_x = 2xy^2 \implies \frac{d}{dx}MU_x = 2y^2 > 0 \quad \text{increasing}$$

$$MU_y = 2x^2y \implies \frac{d}{dy}MU_y = 2x^2 > 0. \quad \text{increasing}$$

The marginal rates of substitution for these particular utility functions are

$$U = x^{1/2}y^{1/2}$$

$$MRS = \frac{MU_x}{MU_y} = \frac{\frac{1}{2}x^{-1/2}y^{1/2}}{\frac{1}{2}x^{1/2}y^{-1/2}} = \frac{y}{x}$$

and

$$U = x^2y^2$$

$$MRS = \frac{MU_x}{MU_y} = \frac{2xy^2}{2x^2y} = \frac{y}{x}.$$

Thus, the two functions have the same marginal rates of substitution, even though one has increasing marginal utilities and the other has decreasing marginal utilities. The only difference between the two functions is in the utility values assigned to the respective indifference curves. However, if utility is only ordinal, the differences in values assigned to indifference curves by different utility functions are not meaningful. The only important differences are those that change the order in which commodity bundles are ranked. Two functions that generate identically shaped indifference curves (that is, those for which the marginal rates of substitution are identical) and that number those indifference curves in the same order describe the same preferences.

Two functions with identical ordinal properties are called **positive monotonic transformations** of one another. In the above example, x^2y^2 is a positive monotonic transformation of $x^{1/2}y^{1/2}$ by the exponent 4:

$$x^2y^2 = (x^{1/2}y^{1/2})^4.$$

On the other hand, $-(x^{1/2}y^{1/2})$ is *not* a positive monotonic transformation of $x^{1/2}y^{1/2}$, even though they have the same marginal rates of substitution. The reason is that utility decreases as x and y increase if the utility function is $-(x^{1/2}y^{1/2})$. Thus, multiplying by a negative number is not a positive monotonic transformation because it does not preserve the order of preference.

While these do not exhaust the possibilities, if two functions differ only by a positive or negative additive constant, a positive multiplicative constant, or an exponential constant, they are positive monotonic transformations of one another. As other examples,

$$x^2y^2, 2x^2y^2, \text{ and } 2 + x^2y^2$$

are all positive monotonic transformations of one another. In the ordinal theory of consumer preferences, we say that utility functions are unique only up to positive monotonic transformations.

5.4   TWO UTILITY FUNCTIONS THAT SATISFY AXIOMS 1–6

In this section, we illustrate step by step how two particular utility functions satisfy all six axioms of consumer preference, using the functions

1. $U = xy$; $x, y > 0$
2. $U = x + 2x^{1/2}y^{1/2} + y$; $x, y \geq 0$.

Axioms 1–3, completeness, reflexivity, and transitivity: these are satisfied simply because preferences are represented by real-valued utility functions. Satisfying these axioms of real numbers is necessary for such a representation.

Axiom 4, continuity: this is satisfied because both functions are continuous.

Axiom 5, nonsatiation: proceed as follows.

1. $MU_x = \partial U/\partial x = y > 0$
   $MU_y = \partial U/\partial y = x > 0$

2. $MU_x = 1 + x^{-1/2}y^{1/2} > 0$
   $MU_y = x^{1/2}y^{-1/2} + 1 > 0$

Thus, for both functions, utility increases for any increase in x or y, guaranteeing that more is always preferred to less and, thereby, satisfying nonsatiation.

Axiom 6, diminishing marginal rate of substitution: proceed as follows.

1. $MRS = \dfrac{MU_x}{MU_y} = \dfrac{y}{x}$

   $\Rightarrow \dfrac{d}{dx}MRS = \dfrac{x(dy/dx) - y}{x^2}$ Take note that y cannot be treated as a constant along a level surface of the objective function.

   Since $MRS = -dy/dx, dy/dx = -MRS$, and

   $$\frac{d}{dx}MRS = \frac{x(-y/x) - y}{x^2} = -\frac{2y}{x^2} < 0.$$

2. $MRS = \dfrac{1 + x^{-1/2}y^{1/2}}{x^{1/2}y^{-1/2} + 1} = \dfrac{(x^{1/2} + y^{1/2})/x^{1/2}}{(x^{1/2} + y^{1/2})/y^{1/2}} = \dfrac{y^{1/2}}{x^{1/2}}$

$$\frac{d}{dx}MRS = \frac{\frac{1}{2}y^{-1/2}(dy/dx)(x^{1/2}) - \frac{1}{2}x^{-1/2}y^{1/2}}{(x^{1/2})^2}$$

$$= \frac{1/2(x^{1/2}y^{-1/2})(-x^{1/2}y^{1/2}) - 1/2(x^{-1/2}y^{1/2})}{x}$$

$$\frac{d}{dx}MRS = \frac{-1/2(1 + MRS)}{x} < 0.$$

Therefore, indifference curves exhibit diminishing marginal rates of substitution for both utility functions.

5.5   UTILITY MAXIMIZATION

We have just argued that if the six axioms are satisfied, we can represent consumer preferences by a utility function with level surfaces that are convex to the origin. Now, economists assume that the consumer will choose the *most-preferred* consumption bundle allowed within his or her budget. The same six axioms that allow us to represent preferences with convex indifference curves also allow us to represent consumer choice *as if* the consumer is maximizing the utility function used as a representation.

The Feasible Set   To develop the concept of utility maximization, we first need to develop the concept of what choices an individual consumer is *able* to make. Economists refer to the set of consumption bundles that are *not too expensive,* given a consumer's budget, as the consumer's **feasible set** of consumption bundles. The feasible set is determined by the consumer's income and the market prices of the goods consumed. For example, suppose a consumer spends all income on food and clothing. Food costs $3 per unit; clothing costs $2 per unit; and the consumer has $12 in income. If the consumer buys *only food,* the most food the consumer can purchase is 4 units. If the consumer buys *only clothing,* the most clothing the consumer can purchase is 6 units. Considering consumption bundles that combine food and clothing, a bundle consisting of 2 units of food and 3 units of clothing costs $12 and is, therefore, *not* too expensive and in the feasible set. However, a bundle consisting of 3 units of food and 3 units of clothing costs $15 and is, therefore, too expensive.

To derive the feasible set, let

$$p_x = \text{price of good X}$$
$$p_y = \text{price of good Y}$$
$$M = \text{consumer's income.}$$

To begin, we assume, for simplicity, that there is only one time period in this model. Each consumer has some income, M, but can't borrow any more because there is no future during which to pay it back. Thus, expenditure on consumption has to be less than or equal to the consumer's income:

$$p_x x + p_y y \leq M.$$

Figure 5.7 illustrates the feasible set.

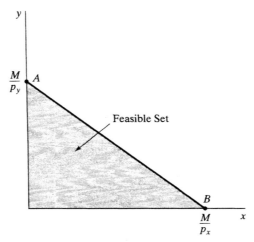

FIGURE 5.7 The Consumer's Feasible Set

The line AB is constructed by assuming the income equation holds with equality. This is the same as assuming that all income is spent on the two goods:

$$p_x x + p_y y = M.$$

Therefore,

$$y = \frac{M}{p_y} - \frac{p_x}{p_y} x$$

is the equation for the line AB, which we call the **budget line** or the **budget constraint.** Anything in the shaded area, including the line AB, is not too expensive and is, therefore, in the feasible set.

If the consumer spends all income on Y, the most that can be bought is

$$\frac{M}{p_y},$$

which is the y intercept $(x = 0)$ of the budget line. Similarly, if the consumer spends all income on X, the most that can be bought is

$$\frac{M}{p_x},$$

which is the x intercept $(y = 0)$ of the budget line. Finally, the slope of the budget line is

$$\frac{dy}{dx} = -\frac{p_x}{p_y}.$$

We now simply assume that a consumer always chooses the most-preferred consumption bundle from the feasible set.

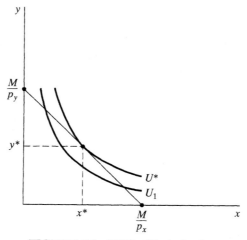

FIGURE 5.8   Utility Maximization

Utility Maximization over the Feasible Set   Figure 5.8 describes utility maximization over a consumer's feasible set when the consumer can choose between two goods X and Y, when the prices are p_x and p_y, and when the consumer's income is M. Just as with the general problem of constrained maximization developed in Chapter 3 (equations 3.1), the optimal choice (x^*, y^*) occurs at a point of tangency between the budget line and the indifference curve U^*. The slope of the budget line is

$$- \frac{p_x}{p_y},$$

and the slope of an indifference curve is the negative of the marginal rate of substitution:

$$\left. \frac{dy}{dx} \right|_{dU=0} = -MRS_{yx}.$$

Therefore, equating the slope of a budget line and the slope of an indifference curve,

$$\frac{p_x}{p_y} = MRS_{yx}, \tag{5.3}$$

at the consumer's most-preferred consumption bundle. In other words, the consumer equates the rate at which the market trades Y for X with the rate at which the consumer is *willing* to trade Y for X given his or her preferences.

The condition for **utility maximization,** in which the marginal rate of substitution is equal to the price ratio, is the first of many such "equal-slopes" equations you will learn in this book. In this example (equation 5.3), we can think of the consumer as equating the *internal rate of trade* (the consumer's marginal rate of substitution) with the market-determined or *external rate of trade* (the price ratio). Recall that we can think of the marginal rate of substitution as how much Y a consumer is *willing* to give up, or trade, in order to get more X and remain on the same indifference curve. The price ratio dictates the rate at which the consumer *must* give up Y in order to purchase more X in the market. Utility is maximized when the rate at which the consumer *must* give up Y is equal to the rate at which he or she is *willing* to give up Y in order to get more X. In fact, many of the equal-slopes equations will have a similar interpretation. In essence, equating internal and external rates of trade characterizes maximization subject to constraint in economics.

The Consumer's Constrained Maximization Problem   As a final illustration of the process of utility maximization, we set up the Lagrangian and go through an example. The next few chapters will carry through this example to the end. In general, the consumer's problem is

$$\text{maximize } U = U(x, y) \quad \text{the objective function} \tag{5.4}$$

$$\text{subject to: } M \geq p_x x + p_y y. \quad \text{the constraint}$$

Assuming the constraint holds with equality, the Lagrangian is

$$\mathcal{L} = U(x, y) + \lambda(M - p_x x - p_y y). \tag{5.5}$$

The first-order conditions are

$$\frac{\partial \mathcal{L}}{\partial x} = \frac{\partial U}{\partial x} - \lambda p_x = 0 \tag{5.6}$$

$$\frac{\partial \mathcal{L}}{\partial y} = \frac{\partial U}{\partial y} - \lambda p_y = 0 \tag{5.7}$$

$$\frac{\partial \mathcal{L}}{\partial \lambda} = M - p_x x - p_y y = 0. \tag{5.8}$$

Solving for λ from the first two first-order conditions (equations 5.6 and 5.7),

$$\lambda = \frac{\partial U / \partial x}{p_x} = \frac{\partial U / \partial y}{p_y}.$$

Therefore,

$$\frac{\partial U / \partial x}{\partial U / \partial y} = \frac{p_x}{p_y}.$$

However,

$$\frac{\partial U / \partial x}{\partial U / \partial y} = \frac{MU_x}{MU_y} = MRS_{yx}.$$

Thus, we get the same equal slopes result as in equation 5.3:

$$MRS_{yx} = \frac{p_x}{p_y}.$$

5.6 ___ THE REVEALED PREFERENCE APPROACH

An alternative way of developing preference theory is to observe consumer choices and see if any mathematical relationship can describe those choices. In this section, we argue that if observed choices are consistent in a particular way, we can represent those choices *as if* consumers have maximized utility functions that satisfy the six axioms, subject to the constraints imposed by their budgets. The approach of observing choices and then inferring properties of a consumer's preference from those choices is called revealed preference analysis.

Revealed Preference   To develop the concept of revealed preference, we return to a consideration of pairs of consumption bundles. If one bundle (x^*, y^*) is *chosen* when another bundle (x', y') is *available,* we say that (x^*, y^*) is **revealed preferred** to (x', y'). Figure 5.9 illustrates revealed preference. Both (x^*, y^*) and (x', y') are on the budget line and, therefore, available, but (x^*, y^*) is chosen.

On the other hand, if (x', y') is not available when (x^*, y^*) is chosen, we cannot say that (x^*, y^*) is revealed preferred to (x', y'). Figure 5.10 compares two points, neither of which is revealed preferred to the other. The choice is (x_1^*, y_1^*) at income M_1 and prices p_x^1 and p_y^1, but it is outside the budget line (too expensive) at income M_2 and prices p_x^2 and p_y^2. The shaded area within the first budget line describes the choices that are feasible for the first budget but too expensive for the second. Similarly, (x_2^*, y_2^*) is the choice at income M_2 and prices p_x^2 and p_y^2, and it is too expensive at income M_1 and prices p_x^1 and p_y^1. The shaded area within the second budget line describes choices that are feasible for the second budget but too expensive for the first.

Deriving Indifference Curves from Choices That Are Not Revealed Preferred to One Another   Suppose we now consider a series of choices on different budget lines where each choice is not revealed preferred to any other choice. In the limit, if we consider all

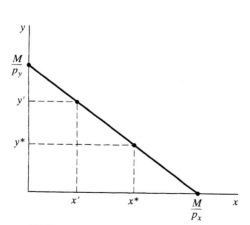

FIGURE 5.9   Revealed Preference

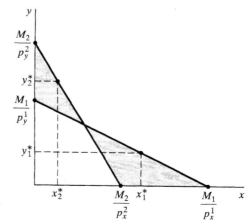

FIGURE 5.10   Choices That Are Not Revealed Preferred to One Another

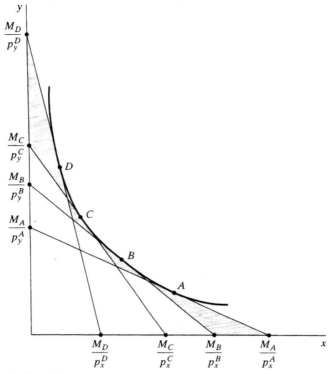

FIGURE 5.11 Choices That Are Not Revealed Preferred to One Another Forming an Indifference Curve Satisfying Diminishing Marginal Rates of Substitution

possible budget lines, choices that are not revealed preferred to one another can be represented as points along an indifference curve that satisfies diminishing marginal rates of substitution. In Figure 5.11, point A is the choice for income M_A and prices p_x^A and p_y^A; point B is the choice for income M_B and prices p_x^B and p_y^B; point C is the choice for income M_C and prices p_x^C and p_y^C; and point D is the choice for income M_D and prices p_x^D and p_y^D. Each is the choice along its own budget line, but is too expensive for every other budget. The shaded area below each budget line represents points feasible for that budget but too expensive for every other budget. In the limit, we could think of there being an infinite number of these points, each of which is not revealed preferred to any other point. If we connect these points with a smooth curve, we construct a function that could be thought of as an indifference curve satisfying diminishing marginal rates of substitution. The consumer has not stated indifference, so the title *indifference curve* is not quite appropriate, but the behavioral effect is the same: the consumer has not indicated a preference for one point over any of the others.[3]

---

[3]For a formal treatment of revealed preference, consult Hal R. Varian, *Microeconomic Analysis,* 3d edition (New York: Norton, 1992).

5.7   LUMP-SUM AND PER-UNIT TAXES AND SUBSIDIES: AN APPLICATION OF REVEALED PREFERENCE

We are now in a position to develop one of the most important propositions that follows from consumer theory. Suppose a consumer is given a choice of two possible ways of paying a tax to be collected by the government.

1. The government could institute an excise tax on some (but not all) goods a consumer purchases. If the tax is levied as a set amount (say $1) on each unit purchased, we call it a **per-unit tax.**

2. Alternatively, the government could simply collect the tax in a single sum, independent of the consumer's choices. We refer to this as a **lump-sum tax.**

It turns out that if the consumer can be guaranteed that both taxes will end up collecting exactly the same revenue, the consumer will prefer the lump-sum tax over the per-unit tax.[4] We show below, using a two-good example, that this statement is true, based simply on a revealed preference analysis.

The Revealed Preference Argument for Lump-sum Taxes   We begin the revealed preference argument for two goods by constructing three distinct budget lines: the original budget line before the tax, the budget line under the per-unit tax, and the budget line under the lump-sum tax. Assume that the consumer chooses (x_1^*, y_1^*) before the tax, (x_2^*, y_2^*) under the per-unit tax, and (x_3^*, y_3^*) under the lump-sum tax. Now, if we let t be the tax rate under the per-unit tax and T be the lump-sum tax, we can summarize the budget lines and choices as follows.

	Budget Line	Choice	
Original	$p_x x + p_y y = M$	(x_1^*, y_1^*)	(5.9)
Per-unit	$(p_x + t)x + p_y y = M$	(x_2^*, y_2^*)	(5.10)
Lump-sum	$p_x x + p_y y = M - T$	(x_3^*, y_3^*)	(5.11)

Next, we write the budget equation under the per-unit tax at the consumption bundle chosen along that budget line, (x_2^*, y_2^*):

$$(p_x + t)x_2^* + p_y y_2^* = M. \tag{5.12}$$

Expanding equation 5.12,

$$p_x x_2^* + t x_2^* + p_y y_2^* = M. \tag{5.13}$$

---

[4]In this simple, two-good economy, in which both goods are purchased in markets, the preference for a lump-sum tax can always be shown. Problems may arise in a more complicated world in which some goods (such as leisure) are not actually produced and sold in markets. When leisure is considered as a good, for example, there can never be a truly lump-sum tax since the government in a free society cannot forcibly take away part of someone's leisure. Moreover, as the Applications (Section 5.12) indicate, there may exist situations in which consumers are indifferent between the two taxes.

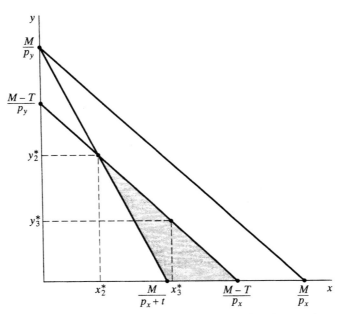

FIGURE 5.12 **Choices Along the Budget Lines Under the Lump-sum and Per-unit Taxes**

Notice that tx_2^* is the total tax paid. Now, rearranging equation 5.13,

$$p_x x_2^* + p_y y_2^* = M - tx_2^*. \tag{5.14}$$

Since tx_2^* is the total tax paid under the per-unit tax, the assumption that the taxes collect the same revenue requires that

$$T = tx_2^*. \tag{5.15}$$

Thus, by substituting equation 5.15 in equation 5.11, we can rewrite the budget line under the lump-sum tax as

$$p_x x + p_y y = M - tx_2^*. \tag{5.16}$$

But notice, by comparing equations 5.14 and 5.16, that the choice under the per-unit tax, (x_2^*, y_2^*), must satisfy equation 5.16. This means that the choice under the per-unit tax must *also* be a point on the budget line under the lump-sum tax. However, since the price ratios are different under the two taxes, the budget lines cannot be identical (equations 5.10 and 5.11 are different). This means that the choice under the per-unit tax must be at the intersection of the two budget lines, and it must be *available* when the choice under the lump-sum tax, (x_3^*, y_3^*), is chosen. Thus, (x_3^*, y_3^*) is revealed preferred to (x_2^*, y_2^*).

Figure 5.12 illustrates the choices under both the per-unit and the lump-sum taxes. By the above argument, the choice under the per-unit tax, (x_2^*, y_2^*), must be at the intersection of the two budget lines and must be available when (x_3^*, y_3^*) is chosen. In

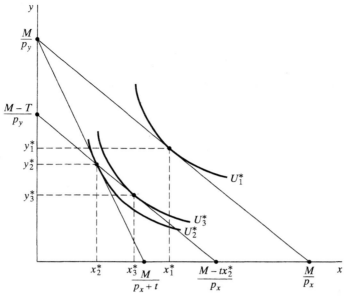

FIGURE 5.13   Consumer's Preference for a Lump-sum Tax over a Per-unit Tax

order to be consistent with the idea of revealed preference, the choice under the lump-sum tax, (x_3^*, y_3^*), must not be revealed preferred to the choice under the per-unit tax (x_2^*, y_2^*); it must be to the right, on a section of the budget line under the lump-sum tax that is too expensive at the income and prices under the per-unit tax.

A Graphical Illustration   Figure 5.13 illustrates this proposition graphically. The consumer starts at (x_1^*, y_1^*), at income M and prices p_x and p_y. The choice under the per-unit tax, (x_2^*, y_2^*), must be at the intersection of the two budget lines (since $T = tx_2^*$). The indifference curve under the per-unit tax, however, must be tangent to *its* budget line defined by $M, p_x + t$, and p_y; but, since the slope of the budget line under the lump-sum tax is different from the slope of the budget line under the per-unit tax, the indifference curve under the per-unit tax (U_2^*) must cut across the budget line under the lump-sum tax. Thus, the point of tangency with the budget line under the lump-sum tax must be on a higher indifference curve (U_3^*).

Lump-sum Subsidies   Two important corollaries follow from the above analysis. First, it can be shown that a consumer also prefers a lump-sum subsidy to a per-unit subsidy on some goods if the two subsidies are calculated to give the consumer the same amount. A shortened version of a revealed preference argument similar to the argument comparing lump-sum and per-unit taxes demonstrates this corollary. Assuming that there are only two goods, X and Y, and letting s be the per-unit subsidy rate and S be the lump-sum subsidy, we begin by constructing the three budget lines.

	Budget Line	Choice	
Original	$p_x x + p_y y + M$	(x_1^*, y_1^*)	
Per-unit	$(p_x - s)x + p_y y = M$	(x_2^*, y_2^*)	(5.17)
Lump-sum	$p_x x + p_y y = M + S$	(x_3^*, y_3^*)	(5.18)

Next, we rewrite the budget equation under the per-unit subsidy (equation 5.17), where (x_2^*, y_2^*) is the choice along that budget line:

$$(p_x = s)x_2^* + p_y y_2^* = M \implies p_x x_2^* - sx_2^* + p_y y_2^* = M$$

$$\implies p_x x_2^* + p_y y_2^* = M + sx_2^*. \tag{5.19}$$

Then, noting that if the two subsidies must be equal to one another,

$$sx_2^* = S. \tag{5.20}$$

Substituting equation 5.20 in the budget line under the lump-sum subsidy (equation 5.18),

$$p_x x + p_y y = M + sx_2^*.$$

Comparing equations 5.19 and 5.20, we see that the choice under the per-unit subsidy, (x_2^*, y_2^*), is a point on the budget line under the lump-sum subsidy and is available when the choice under the lump-sum subsidy, (x_3^*, y_3^*), is made. Thus, the choice under the lump-sum subsidy is revealed preferred to the choice under the per-unit subsidy.

Figure 5.14 illustrates this corollary. The consumer begins at (x_1^*, y_1^*) at income M and prices p_x and p_y. Since the two subsidies are identical, the indifference curve under the per-unit subsidy has to be tangent to its budget line at the intersection of the two budget lines. Since the slope of the budget line under the per-unit subsidy is different from that of the budget line under the lump-sum subsidy, the indifference curve under the per-unit subsidy (U_2^*) has to cut across the budget line under the lump-sum subsidy. Thus, the point of tangency with the budget line under the lump-sum subsidy is on a higher indifference curve (U_3^*), and the consumer prefers the lump-sum subsidy.

Rebating a Per-unit Tax For the second corollary, suppose the government wishes to discourage consumption of a good, say gasoline, but doesn't want to harm consumers in the process. What the government would like to do is raise the price of the good but simultaneously rebate the taxes to be collected in lump-sum payments. The consumer ends up choosing a consumption point on a new budget line that gives the same income as before (since the consumer's entire tax is rebated), but the price of one good is higher than it was before. The second corollary states that if a per-unit tax were instituted, the revenue collected from the tax would never be enough to restore the consumer to the original utility level if it were to be rebated in a lump sum.

This follows directly from the consumer preference for a lump-sum tax. In this case, we have two budget lines: the original budget line and a new one after the tax and

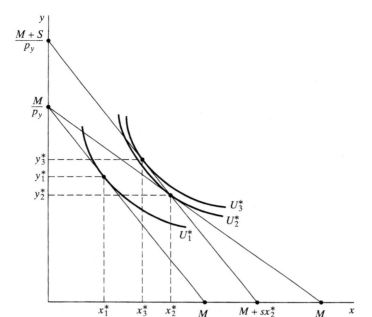

FIGURE 5.14   Consumer's Preference for a Lump-sum Subsidy over a Per-unit Subsidy

the rebate. If (x_2^*, y_2^*) is the choice after the tax and rebate, the tax and rebate must be equal to tx_2^*. Thus, the new budget line after the tax and rebate is

$$(p_x + t)x + p_y y = M + tx_2^*. \tag{5.21}$$

Writing equation 5.21 with the choice after the tax and rebate substituted for x and y,

$$(p_x + t)x_2^* + p_y y_2^* = M + tx_2^*.$$

Expanding and rearranging terms,

$$p_x x_2^* + p_y y_2^* = M.$$

Thus, the new choice, (x_2^*, y_2^*), is a point on the original budget line (equation 5.9) and is, therefore, available when the original choice, (x_1^*, y_1^*), is made. Since the prices are different, the budget lines must have different slopes, and the original choice, (x_1^*, y_1^*), is revealed preferred to the choice after the tax and rebate, (x_2^*, y_2^*).

Figure 5.15 illustrates this corollary. The consumer begins at (x_1^*, y_1^*) at income M and prices p_x and p_y. Since the full amount of the tax is to be rebated, the consumer's income at the choice under the tax has to be equal to the income at the original choice.

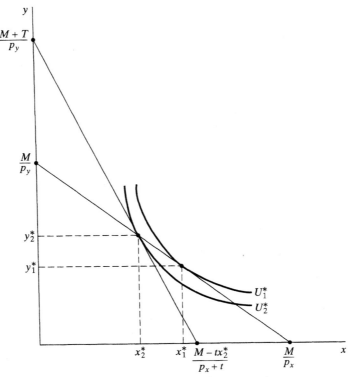

FIGURE 5.15   Illustration of Why a Per-unit Tax is Insufficient to Restore a Consumer to the Original Utility Level

This means that the new choice, (x_2^*, y_2^*), has to be a point on the original budget line. However, since the budget line under the tax has a different slope from that of the original budget line, the point of tangency under the tax has to be on a lower indifference curve.

5.8   USING REVEALED PREFERENCE TO DERIVE INDIFFERENCE CURVES: A CASE STUDY FROM EXPERIMENTS WITH RATS

While the revealed preference approach provides a simple, alternative way of understanding the axioms of consumer preference, the approach does depend on consumer choices being consistent with the axioms of consumer preference and the principles of revealed preference. From a scientific perspective, we would like to be able to verify that consumer choices are consistent before fully accepting the model of consumer preference for analyzing consumer choice.

One approach to studying choices came in the development of the field of economics known as experimental economics, pioneered by Vernon Smith.[5] The idea in experimental economics is to create a controlled economic environment that *parallels* some theoretical or naturally occurring environment. Typically, that is done by telling subjects they will be paid different cash amounts for different decisions they might make. We will be referring to a number of such experimental tests throughout this book.

Using Animals as Experimental Subjects   The first systematic experimental studies of preference theory did just that, using rats and pigeons instead of people as subjects![6] Rats, for example, were kept hungry and then had to pay for food and water by pressing two different levers. The concepts of income and relative prices were operationalized by the number of lever presses (income) each animal was allowed in an interval of time and the number of presses it took to get a pellet of food or a small cup of water (relative prices). At first, the animals were observed for a period of time under one set of parameters to get a baseline reading. The average consumption of food and water over several trials was then taken as the animal's choice at that income and price configuration.

Once an initial choice was established, the animals were presented with a new budget line, which was constructed so that the first choice was clearly too expensive along the new budget line. This is illustrated in Figure 5.16. The first budget line is labeled AA' and the choice is A^*. The new budget line (BB') is less steeply sloped, which means that the relative price of water has fallen, and income is adjusted to allow the rats some room to make choices which are consistent with the concept of revealed preference. A^* is in the shaded area of the first budget line and is not attainable along BB'. The question was, would the animals change their consumption of food and water in the predicted direction? That is, would they choose a combination, such as B^*, along the portion of budget line BB' that was itself too expensive at A^*? The answer was

[5]Smith's first experimental article will be discussed in some detail in Chapter 13: Vernon L. Smith, "An Experimental Study of Competitive Market Behavior," *Journal of Political Economy* 70(1962):111. For general discussions of the methodology of and literature in experimental economics, see Charles R. Plott, "Industrial Organization Theory and Experimental Economics," *Journal of Economic Literature* 20(1982):1485; Douglas Davis and Charles Holt, *Experimental Economics* (Princeton: Princeton University Press, 1993); John H. Kagel and Alvin Roth (eds.), *Handbook of Experimental Economics* (Princeton: Princeton University Press, 1995); Vernon L. Smith, "Experimental Economics: Induced Value Theory," *American Economic Review* 66(1976):274 and "Microeconomic Systems As An Experimental Science," *American Economic Review* 72(1982):923; and Elizabeth Hoffman and Matthew L. Spitzer, "Experimental Law and Economics: An Introduction," *Columbia Law Review* 85(1985):991.

[6]Raymond C. Battalio, John H. Kagel, Howard Rachlin, and Leonard Green, "Commodity-Choice Behavior with Pigeons as Subjects," *Journal of Political Economy* 89(1981):67; John H. Kagel and Raymond C. Battalio, "Token Economy and Animal Models for the Experimental Analysis of Economic Behavior," in Jan Kmenta and James B. Ramsey, (eds.), *Evaluation of Econometric Models* (New York: Academic Press, 1980); John H. Kagel, Raymond C. Battalio, Leonard Green, and Howard Rachlin, "Consumer Demand Theory Applied to Choice Behavior of Rats," in John E. R. Staddon, (ed.), *Limits to Action: The Allocation of Individual Behavior* (New York: Academic Press, 1980); John H. Kagel, Raymond C. Battalio, Howard Rachlin, Leonard Green, Robert L. Basemann, and W. R. Klemm, "Experimental Studies of Consumer Demand Behavior Using Laboratory Animals," *Economic Inquiry* 13(1975):22.

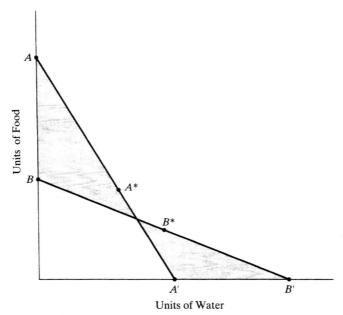

FIGURE 5.16   Choices of Food and Water by Rats Given Different "Income" and "Price" Parameters

clearly yes. The choices made by rats, and also pigeons in another study, were found to be consistent with revealed preference.

These experiments clearly do not *prove* that choices are consistent with revealed preference, since people are far more complex than rats or pigeons. However, they do suggest that making choices consistent with revealed preference does not require a lot of careful calculation. If animals can be shown to do it consistently, it almost seems as if the response is natural. If that is true, then representing consumer choices as if they result from maximizing a utility function that satisfies the axioms of consumer preferences does not imply we are imposing greatly restrictive assumptions on our analysis of consumer choice.

5.9 ____ REVIEW OF KEY CONCEPTS

We turn now to an analysis of consumer choice and a derivation of consumer demand functions, assuming preferences obey the axioms developed in this chapter. However, before continuing to Chapter 6, be sure you understand and can use the following key concepts.

Utility is an index of the satisfaction a consumer gets from consumption.

If utility were measurable, it would be both comparable and additive across consumers. We would call it *cardinal utility*.

Since utility cannot be compared across consumers we say that we *cannot make interpersonal comparisons of utility*.

Marginal utility is the change in utility for a given change in consumption.

A *consumption bundle* is a list of quantities of different consumption goods that a consumer might consume simultaneously.

Since utility cannot be compared across consumers, only a consumer's order of preference is meaningful. We say that utility is only an *ordinal* index of consumer satisfaction.

Consumers are modeled as choosing the most-preferred consumption bundles allowed by their budgets.

Preferences for consumption bundles are *complete* if a consumer can rank all pairs of consumption bundles as one preferred to the other or as one indifferent to the other (that is, ranked equally). (Axiom 1)

A *preference ordering* is a ranking of consumption bundles.

Preferences are *reflexive* if two identical consumption bundles are always ranked the same. (Axiom 2)

Preferences are *transitive* if A preferred to B and B preferred to C implies A preferred to C, for all triples of consumption bundles. Transitivity also applies to indifference. (Axiom 3)

Preferences are *continuous* if when A is preferred to B and B is the limit of C, then A is also preferred to C. (Axiom 4)

Preferences are *lexicographic* if, for one particular good, the consumer always prefers a bundle with more of that good, regardless of the quantities of other goods in the consumption bundles being compared. The quantities of other goods are only important if the quantities of the particular good are the same in the consumption bundles being compared.

An *indifference* curve connects all *infinitely divisible* consumption bundles that are indifferent to one another.

If preferences are transitive, indifference curves do not cross.

A *utility function* assigns numbers to consumption bundles by a functional relationship such that the numerical ranking generated by the utility function represents the ordinal ranking of consumption bundles.

Preferences exhibit *nonsatiation* if more goods are always preferred to less. (Axiom 5)

A *bliss point* of a utility function would be a consumption bundle giving a consumer the highest possible utility. The assumption of nonsatiation rules out bliss points.

The *marginal rate of substitution* is the negative of the slope of the indifference curve. It indicates the rate at which a consumer is willing to trade one good for another and remain at the same level of satisfaction.

The marginal rate of substitution can be thought of as an *internal rate of trade.*

If indifference curves are smooth and convex to the origin, we say that they exhibit *diminishing marginal rates of substitution.* (Axiom 6)

The marginal rate of substitution is also equal to the ratio of marginal utilities.

Utility functions with identical ordinal properties are called *positive monotonic transformations* of one another.

Utility functions are unique only up to positive monotonic transformations.

A consumer's *feasible set* is the set of all consumption bundles that are not too expensive, given a consumer's income and the market prices for consumption goods.

The *budget line* or *budget constraint* describes the set of all consumption bundles such that expenditures on the items in each consumption bundle exactly equal the consumer's income, given market prices.

At a *utility-maximizing* consumption bundle, the slope of the consumer's indifference curve is equal to the slope of the budget line. This implies that the consumer's marginal rate of substitution is equal to the market price ratio.

If one consumption bundle is chosen when another bundle is available, we say that the chosen bundle is *revealed preferred* to the other.

A *per-unit tax* is a tax that collects a fixed amount per unit of a good purchased. For example, the per-pack tax on cigarettes is a per-unit tax.

A *lump-sum tax* is a tax that is collected as one lump sum, independent of any purchases of any goods.

Lump-sum and per-unit subsidies are analogous to lump-sum and per-unit taxes.

Consumers generally prefer lump-sum taxes or subsidies to per-unit taxes or subsidies that collect or grant the same revenue.

5.10 _____ QUESTIONS FOR DISCUSSION

1. Suppose you choose to eat a different dinner each night, even though your income and the prices of different foods do not change from day to day. Does that violate the axioms of consumer preference? How would you have to modify the model to allow for such "normal" preferences?

2. How would you illustrate the indifference curves for goods that are perfect substitutes for one another?

3. How would you illustrate the indifference curves for goods that are consumed only in fixed proportions?

4. Does an addict have lexicographic preferences? Explain why or why not. Is an addiction to heroin or alcohol, for example, different from an addiction to mountain climbing or running when it comes to representing preferences? Explain.

5. Suppose someone's preferences really were intransitive. For example, each time he was presented with a new consumption bundle he preferred to the old, he would be willing to pay a little more to exchange his current bundle for the "preferred" bundle, as long as his budget were not exhausted. How could you take all that person's money away and leave him with nothing? (This is called the *money-pump* argument in favor of transitivity.)

6. What practical problems would be involved in using lump-sum taxes instead of per-unit and percentage taxes? Could we ever satisfy the requirements of the principle that lump-sum taxes are better?

7. Economists generally argue that we should do away with the food stamp program and just give poor people lump-sum grants. What principle is behind this argument, and is it always correct in this instance? (Application 3, Section 5.12, asks you to develop a formal argument.)

8. Could you extend the rat and pigeon experiments to humans in the laboratory? What experimental design problems would you have to overcome?

9. Suppose you worked for a market research firm that was testing the market for a new kind of candy. How could you use the tools of revealed preference analysis to help your client decide whether or not consumers like the new candy?

10. How would you expand the model of consumer preference to allow for altruism or envy?

5.11 _____ PROBLEMS

Problems 1–6   Take each utility function and show whether it satisfies the axioms of consumer preference.

1. $U = x^4 y^4, x, y > 0$
2. $U = x^{\frac{1}{2}} y^{\frac{1}{4}}, x, y > 0$
3. $U = xy^2, x, y > 0$
4. $U = 5x + 3y, x, y \geq 0$
5. $U = \dfrac{xy}{x + y}, x, y > 0$
6. $U =$ minimum of x and $y = \min(x, y), x, y > 0$

7. Find the function, if it exists, for the marginal rate of substitution for each utility function in Problems 1–6.

8. Are any of the above functions monotonic transformations of one another? Explain briefly.

9. Graph the indifference curve for $U = 100$ for each utility function in Problems 1–6.

10. Now, assume $p_x = \$2, p_y = \$4$, and $M = \$100$. Find the utility-maximizing consumption bundle for each utility function in Problems 1–6.

5.12   LOGICAL AND MATHEMATICAL APPLICATIONS

1. Show how you might formally represent a change in tastes in favor of good X.

2. Show how you might formally represent a set of preferences in which one person is altruistic toward, or envious of, another person.

3. Suppose that a per-unit subsidy is only allowed up to some maximum number of units purchased and that a consumer will always purchase more than that maximum number. Show that a lump-sum subsidy that would grant the same income to the consumer as the per-unit subsidy is identical to the per-unit subsidy from the consumer's point of view (that is, the consumer is indifferent between the two). (Note that, for most welfare recipients, food stamps cover less than the total food budget.)

4. Show that an equal percentage tax on all goods, collecting the same revenue from a consumer as a lump-sum tax, is identical to the lump-sum tax.

5. Show that if food stamps can be resold on a black market, giving food stamps is equivalent to giving a lump-sum grant.

Chapter 6

INTRODUCTION TO INDIVIDUAL CONSUMER AND MARKET DEMAND THEORY

6.1 WHAT YOU SHOULD LEARN FROM THIS CHAPTER

In this chapter, we introduce the development of demand functions. From the solution to the utility maximization problem, we derive a set of individual demand functions: quantity demanded as a function of price (the *ordinary demand curve*), quantity demanded as a function of income (the *Engel curve*), and quantity demanded as a function of the price of another good (the *cross-price demand function*). Additionally, we show that these one-variable demand functions can all be derived from a *generalized demand function,* which allows prices and income to vary. Finally, we show how a *market demand function* is constructed from individual ordinary demand functions.

6.2 CONSUMER DEMAND FUNCTIONS: GRAPHICAL DEVELOPMENT

To begin our analysis of consumer demand functions, recall from Chapter 3 that the equal-slopes equation (equation 3.7, for example) describes a function $y = f(x)$ that is derived as the locus of all points of equal slopes between level surfaces of the objective function and parallel constraint lines. This can be generated by holding prices constant and allowing the budget constraint to shift out in a parallel fashion.

In consumer theory, we have seen that the appropriate equal-slopes condition sets the marginal rate of substitution equal to the price ratio. From this equal-slopes condition, we can derive a function in xy space that describes the consumer's utility-maximizing consumption choice at each income level, holding prices constant. Economists call this function the **income-consumption curve** (or **income-consumption line** if the function is linear). Figure 6.1 illustrates how the income-consumption curve is derived. Note that p_x and p_y are held constant at $\bar{p}_x$ and $\bar{p}_y$ and income is allowed to vary (M_1, M_2, M_3). The consumer maximizes utility on each budget line, choosing quantities

$$(x_1^*, y_1^*) \text{ at } M_1, \quad (x_2^*, y_2^*) \text{ at } M_2, \quad (x_3^*, y_3^*) \text{ at } M_3.$$

The income-consumption curve is constructed by connecting the optimal consumption choices at each income level.

Quantity Demanded as a Function of Income The equation for the income-consumption curve expresses a function that graphs y^* against x^*, holding prices constant. The

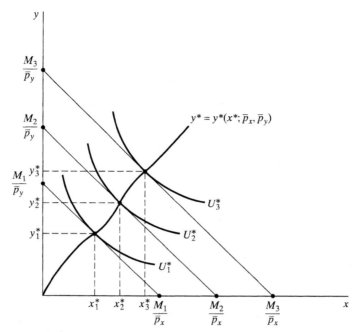

FIGURE 6.1   Deriving the Income-Consumption Curve

changes in both x^* and y^* are determined by the change in income, which is implicit in the following statement of the income-consumption curve:

$$y^* = y^*(x^*; p_x, p_y).$$

To find quantity demanded as a function of income, holding prices constant, we take the points on the income-consumption curve and summarize the relationship between income and either x^* or y^* on a graph with x^* or y^* as the dependent variable and income as the independent variable. For example, let's develop a graph of y as a function of income, assuming that x is always chosen optimally:

$$y^* = y^*(M; \bar{p}_x, \bar{p}_y).$$

Economists call this function an **Engel curve** for Y.[1]

Figure 6.2 illustrates how the Engel curve for Y is derived. The incomes M_1, M_2, and M_3, used to derive the income-consumption curve on the left graph, are the same as the points M_1, M_2, and M_3 on the horizontal axis of the right graph (the Engel curve). The utility-maximizing choices of y on the left graph, y_1^*, y_2^*, and y_3^*, are the same as the points y_1^*, y_2^*, and y_3^* on the vertical axis of the right graph. The Engel curve is con-

---

[1]This is named after Ernst Engel (1821–1896), a German statistician who studied the spending patterns of groups of people of different incomes. His conclusion is summarized in what is called *Engel's law,* the observation that people spend a smaller and smaller proportion of their incomes on food as those incomes increase. Ernst Engel should not be confused with Friedrich Engels, Karl Marx's friend.

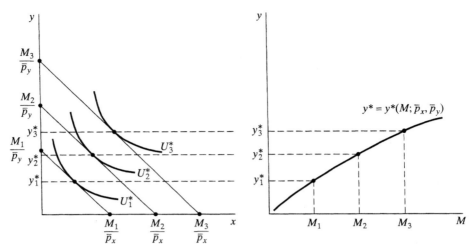

FIGURE 6.2   Deriving an Engel Curve for Y

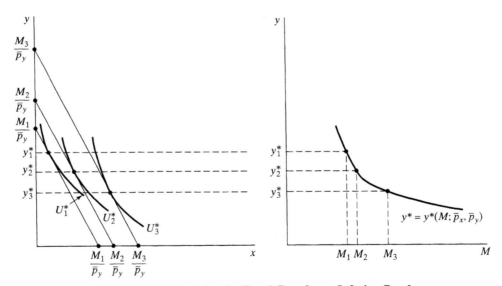

FIGURE 6.3   Deriving the Engel Cure for an Inferior Good

structed by connecting the points (M_1, y_1^*), (M_2, y_2^*), and (M_3, y_3^*). The Engel curve for X can be similarly constructed by placing the utility-maximizing choices of x on the vertical axis of a graph and the respective values of M on the horizontal axis.

Normal and Inferior Goods   Figure 6.2 illustrates the case of a **normal good:** quantity demanded increases as income increases. The theory also allows for the possibility that a good will be an **inferior good:** quantity demanded *decreases* as income *increases.* Figure 6.3 illustrates the case of an inferior good. Once again, the Engel curve for Y is

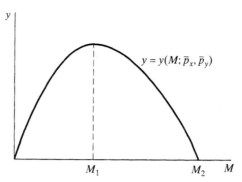

FIGURE 6.4   Engel Curve for a Locally Inferior Good

constructed by placing the income values on the left graph on the horizontal axis of the right graph and the utility-maximizing values of y on the vertical axis of the right graph and then by connecting the points (M_1, y_1^*), (M_2, y_2^*), and (M_3, y_3^*). In this case, however, y^* decreases as M increases. A good cannot be inferior over all possible ranges of income and still be classified as a "good," however. The argument is quite intuitive. At zero income a consumer can purchase nothing. As income increases a little, the consumer is able to purchase a little. In order for consumption of a good to be high enough to later decline as income continues to increase, consumption of that good must have increased over some range of income. Eventually, of course, if income gets high enough and a good is inferior, the consumer will simply cease to purchase it altogether. Consumption simply stays at 0 as income continues to increase. For these reasons, we say that goods can be **locally inferior** but not **globally inferior.**

Figure 6.4 illustrates a reasonable shape for the Engel curve of a good that is locally inferior. At low levels of income, quantity demanded of Y increases, but once income M_1 is attained, quantity demanded falls. At M_2 quantity demanded falls to 0 and remains at 0 thereafter.

The Price-Consumption Curve   To find quantity demanded as a function of a good's own price, we hold income and all other prices constant and observe how the utility-maximizing choices change as the price changes. We begin, as we did with the income-consumption curve, by connecting the utility-maximizing choices on the budget line and indifference curve graph. In this case, we will follow changes in the utility-maximizing choices as p_x changes, holding M and p_y constant. If income and the price of Y are constant, however, it means that $\overline{M}/\overline{p}_y$ is a constant. This implies that the y intercept remains fixed at that value as p_x changes. The x intercept and the slope, $\overline{M}/p_x$ and $-p_x/\overline{p}_y$, respectively, fall as p_x increases, generating a family of budget lines that are anchored on the constant y intercept but have falling x intercepts and steeper slopes. This is in contrast to the family of parallel budget lines that is generated when income

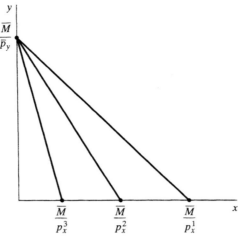

FIGURE 6.5   Budget Lines for Fixed Income and p_y

changes and prices remain fixed. A typical budget line with constant income and p_y, and variable p_x, has the following form:

$$y = \frac{\overline{M}}{\overline{p}_y} - \frac{p_x}{\overline{p}_y} x.$$

Figure 6.5 illustrates this family of budget lines. As p_x increases, $p_x^3 > p_x^2 > p_x^1$, the y intercept remains the same while the x intercept falls and the slope becomes steeper.

If we find the utility-maximizing choice for each budget line, we can construct another function with $y*$ graphed against $x*$ (with p_x varying implicitly), holding income and the price *of* Y constant:

$$y* = y*(x*; \overline{M}, \overline{p}_y).$$

Economists call this function the **price-consumption curve.** It is thus similar to the income-consumption curve, except that p_x is implicitly varying in this case.

Figure 6.6 illustrates the derivation of a price-consumption curve. As p_x rises (p_x^1, p_x^2, p_x^3), the price-consumption curve connects the utility-maximizing choices:

$$(x_1^*, y_1^*) \text{ at } p_x^1, \quad (x_2^*, y_2^*) \text{ at } p_x^2, \quad (x_3^*, y_3^*) \text{ at } p_x^3.$$

The Ordinary Demand Function   Having found the price-consumption curve, we can find quantity demanded of X as a function of its own price by taking the points along the price-consumption curve and converting them to a graph with x as the dependent variable and p_x as the independent variable, holding income and p_y constant:

$$x* = x*(p_x; \overline{M}, \overline{p}_y).$$

We call this function the **demand function** for X or the **ordinary demand function** for X. As we discussed in Section 1.2, however, economists by convention always graph

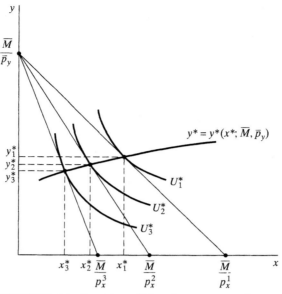

FIGURE 6.6   Deriving a Price-Consumption Curve

the demand function with price on the vertical axis and quantity demanded on the horizontal axis (which makes it, technically, the **inverse demand function**),

$$p_x = p_x(x^*; \overline{M}, \overline{p}_y),$$

even though quantity is usually the dependent variable in mathematical analysis.[2] Thus, to avoid confusion and preserve the traditional graphical treatment, we will develop the inverse demand function graphically. But, be careful to use the demand function with quantity as the dependent variable when that is appropriate in mathematical applications.

Figure 6.7 illustrates how the inverse of the ordinary demand function is derived. The values of p_x from the price-consumption curve in the upper graph $(p_x^1, p_x^2, \text{ and } p_x^3)$ are the same as the values of p_x along the vertical axis of the lower graph. The utility-maximizing values of x (x_1^*, x_2^*, x_3^*) derived in the upper graph are the same as the x values along the horizontal axis of the lower graph (x_1^*, x_2^*, x_3^*). The graph of the inverse ordinary demand function connects the points (x_1^*, p_x^1), (x_2^*, p_x^2), and (x_3^*, p_x^3).

Downward- and Upward-sloping Demand   Figure 6.7 illustrates downward-sloping demand: quantity demanded increases as the price falls. The axioms of consumer preference presented in Chapter 5 do not rule out the *possibility* that demand will be

---

[2]What is usually referred to as the *demand curve* is actually the inverse demand function. We will tend to use the terms demand curve and inverse demand function interchangeably. The meaning should be clear from the context.

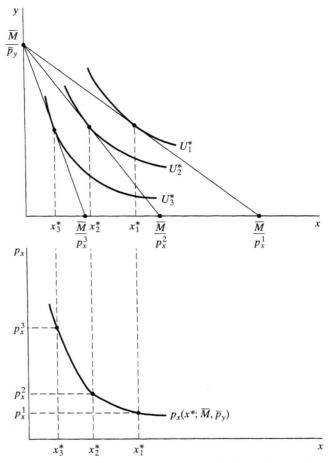

FIGURE 6.7   Deriving the Inverse Ordinary Demand Function for X

upward-sloping, however. Figure 6.8 illustrates the graphical derivation of an upward-sloping inverse demand function, where the indifference curves obey all the assumptions of consumer preference theory. Once again, the inverse demand function is constructed by locating the utility-maximizing choices of x from the price-consumption curve along the horizontal axis and the values of p_x associated with those respective choices along the vertical axis, and then connecting the points (x_1^*, p_x^1), (x_2^*, p_x^2), and $(x_3^*, p_{x,}^3)$. In this case, however, the utility-maximizing values of x increase as p_x increases.

The Cross-price Demand Function: Substitutes and Complements   Finally, we can use the price-consumption curve to develop quantity demanded as a function of the price of the other good, holding income and own price constant:

$$y^* = y^*(p_x; \overline{M}, \overline{p}_y).$$

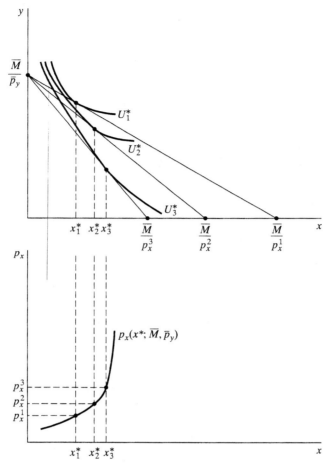

FIGURE 6.8   Deriving an Upward-sloping Inverse Demand Function

This can be referred to as a **cross-price demand function.**

Figure 6.9 illustrates quantity demanded of Y increasing as the price of X increases. The utility-maximizing choices of y (y_1^*, y_2^*, y_3^*) from the price-consumption curve are located along the vertical axis of the right graph, and the rising prices of X, (p_x^1, p_x^2, p_x^3), are located along the horizontal axis. The graph of quantity demanded of Y as a function of p_x, holding M and p_y constant, connects the points (p_x^1, y_1^*), (p_x^2, y_2^*), and (p_x^3, y_3^*). In this case, we say Y is a **gross substitute** for X since Y is substituted for X as the price of X increases.[3] For example, when the price of butter goes up, holding

---

[3]In your principles course, you were probably told that Y was simply a *substitute* for X in this case. In this book, however, we distinguish between gross substitutes and net substitutes, depending on whether income or utility is held constant. When income is held constant and utility varies, economists use the term *gross substitute.*

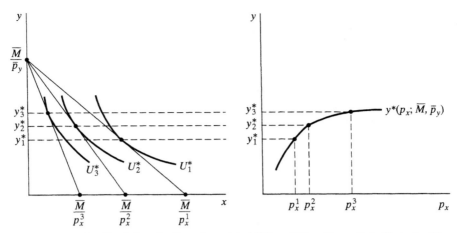

FIGURE 6.9 Deriving the Function $y^*(p_x)$ When Y Is a Gross Substitute for X

income and the price of margarine constant, some people substitute margarine for butter in some uses. Thus, they consume more margarine as the price of butter increases.

If the quantity demanded of Y *decreases* as p_x increases, holding income and the price of Y constant, we say that Y is a **gross complement** to X.[4] The idea is that, as the price of X increases, a consumer purchases less of both X and Y. For example, when the price of coffee increases, some consumers consume less cream and sugar as well as less coffee, since cream and sugar *complement* the consumption of coffee.

Figure 6.10 illustrates the derivation of y as a function of p_x when Y is a gross complement to X. Once again, the utility-maximizing choices of y from the price-

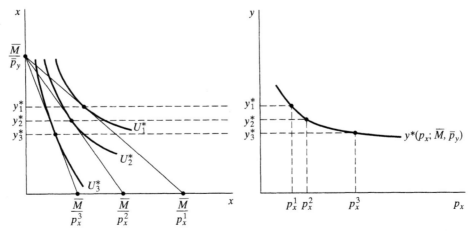

FIGURE 6.10 Deriving the Function $y^*(p_x)$ When Y Is a Gross Complement to X

---

[4]The same caveat about gross and net substitutes applies to gross and net complements. In this case, we use the term *gross complement* because income is held constant.

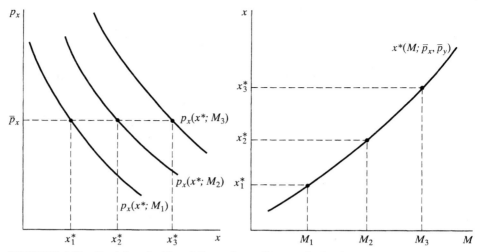

FIGURE 6.11   Deriving the Engel Curve from Changes in Ordinary Demand as Income Changes

consumption curve are paired with rising prices of X to form $y^*(p_x)$ by connecting (p_x^1, y_1^*), (p_x^2, y_2^*), and (p_x^3, y_3^*).

6.3   THE ORDINARY DEMAND FUNCTION: CHANGES IN DEMAND AND CHANGES IN QUANTITY DEMANDED

When you studied demand functions in principles, you probably focused on the ordinary demand curve. Changes in income and in other prices were probably analyzed as causing shifts in the demand curve. If a good's own price changes, we move along the ordinary demand function and say there has been a **change in quantity demanded.** For example, in Figure 6.7, when p_x increases from p_x^1 to p_x^2, quantity demanded decreases from x_1^* to x_2^*. In contrast, when one of the parameters affecting the ordinary demand function changes, moving the position of the function, we say there has been a **change in demand.** The Engel curve and cross-price demand functions can be derived from a set of ordinary demand functions for different incomes or other prices by keeping track of the quantity demanded for one particular value of the good's own price.

For example, suppose we consider a set of ordinary demand curves for a normal good, as illustrated in the left graph of Figure 6.11. Each demand curve represents the inverse of quantity demanded of good X as a function of p_x for a different parametric value of income, holding p_y constant throughout at $\bar{p}_y$. Since X is assumed to be a normal good, quantity demanded increases at each price as income increases. Thus, at a given price for X, such as $\bar{p}_x$, x^* increases as M increases: x_1^* at M_1, x_2^* at M, x_3^* at M_3, for $M_3 > M_2 > M_1$. In the right graph, the values of M from the demand functions in the left graph are plotted along the horizontal axis, and the values of x^* are plotted along the vertical axis. The Engel curve for p_x fixed at $\bar{p}_x$ and p_y fixed at $\bar{p}_y$ is con-

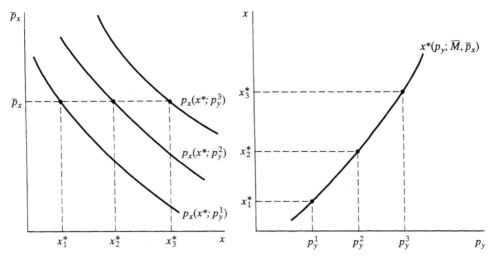

FIGURE 6.12 **Deriving the Cross-price Demand Function from Changes in Ordinary Demand as the Other Price Changes**

structed by simply connecting the combinations of income and x^* already identified. It is upward sloping, reflecting the fact that X is a normal good.

Similarly, the cross-price demand function can be constructed from a set of demand curves for different values of the other price. Figure 6.12 illustrates this point when X is a gross substitute for Y. As with income and the Engel curve in Figure 6.11, each demand function in the left graph represents quantity demanded of X as a function of p_x for a different parametric value of p_y, holding M constant at $\overline{M}$. Since X is a gross substitute for Y, x^* increases as p_y increases. The right graph then constructs the cross-price demand function for p_x fixed at $\overline{p}_x$. The values of p_y from the demand functions on the left are plotted on the horizontal axis of the right graph, and the corresponding values of x^* at $\overline{p}_x$ are plotted along the vertical axis. The cross-price demand function is constructed by connecting the points (p_y^1, x_1^*), (p_y^2, x_2^*), and (p_y^3, x_3^*). It is upward sloping, reflecting the fact that X is a gross substitute for Y.

6.4   GENERALIZED DEMAND FUNCTIONS

To derive mathematical expressions for the demand curves derived graphically above, we can start by maximizing utility subject to a budget constraint (which, at this point, is assumed to hold with equality),

$$M = p_x x + p_y y.$$

From this we can derive an expression for quantity demanded as a function of all prices and income; we call this the **generalized demand function.** Then, from the generalized demand function, we can derive the ordinary demand function, the Engel curve, and the cross-price demand functions by simply allowing each price or income to vary in turn.

Deriving a Generalized Demand Function   For example, suppose a consumer's utility function is

$$U = xy + x + y, \quad x, y \geq 0.$$

The consumer's maximization problem is

$$\max U = xy + x + y \tag{6.1}$$
$$\text{s.t.} \quad M - p_x x - p_y y = 0$$
$$x, y \geq 0.$$

We will assume that the budget constraint holds with equality, and following the illustration of the application of Kuhn-Tucker conditions in Section 3.7, we will solve this problem assuming the nonnegativity constraints are not binding. The Lagrangian is

$$\mathcal{L} = xy + x + y + \lambda(M - p_x x - p_y y). \tag{6.2}$$

The first-order conditions are

$$\frac{\partial \mathcal{L}}{\partial x} = y^* + 1 - \lambda^* p_x = 0 \quad \Rightarrow \quad \lambda^* = \frac{y^* + 1}{p_x} \tag{6.3}$$

$$\frac{\partial \mathcal{L}}{\partial y} = x^* + 1 - \lambda^* p_y = 0 \quad \Rightarrow \quad \lambda^* = \frac{x^* + 1}{p_y} \tag{6.4}$$

$$\frac{\partial \mathcal{L}}{\partial \lambda} = M - p_x x^* - p_y y^* = 0. \tag{6.5}$$

Equating the values of λ^* from the first two first-order conditions (equations 6.3 and 6.4),

$$\frac{y^* + 1}{p_x} = \frac{x^* + 1}{p_y} \quad \Rightarrow \quad y^* + 1 = \frac{p_x}{p_y}(x^* + 1).$$

Therefore, we can derive the income-consumption curve by solving for y:

$$y^* = \frac{p_x}{p_y}(x^* + 1) - 1. \qquad \text{the income-consumption curve}$$

Substituting for y in the third first-order condition (equation 6.5),

$$M - p_x x - p_y \left[\frac{p_x}{p_y}(x + 1) - 1 \right] = 0$$

$$\Rightarrow \quad M - p_x x - p_x x - p_x + p_y = 0$$

$$\Rightarrow \quad 2p_x x = M - p_x + p_y.$$

Thus, the generalized demand function for X is

$$x^* = \frac{M - p_x + p_y}{2p_x}. \tag{6.7}$$

To find the generalized demand function for Y, we substitute for x^* in equation 6.6:

$$y^* = \frac{p_x}{p_y}\left(\frac{M - p_x + p_y}{2p_x} + 1\right) - 1 = \frac{M - p_x + p_y}{2p_y} + \frac{2p_x}{2p_y} - \frac{2p_y}{2p_y}.$$

Thus, the generalized demand function for Y is

$$y^* = \frac{M - p_y + p_x}{2p_y}. \tag{6.8}$$

Deriving Single-variable Demand Functions Now, to find each of the single-variable demand functions illustrated above, we can start by assuming fixed, parametric values for each of the possible independent variables and then by allowing them to vary one at a time. For example, suppose M, p_x, and p_y are fixed at $\overline{M}, \overline{p}_x$, and $\overline{p}_y$. Then, by the generalized demand function,

$$x^* = \frac{\overline{M} - \overline{p}_x + \overline{p}_y}{2\overline{p}_x} \quad \text{and} \quad y^* = \frac{\overline{M} - \overline{p}_y + \overline{p}_x}{2\overline{p}_y}.$$

To find the Engel curves, the ordinary demand functions, and the cross-price demand functions, we simply let each parameter vary in turn: the Engel curves are

$$x^* = \frac{M - \overline{p}_x + \overline{p}_y}{2\overline{p}_x} \quad \text{and} \quad y^* = \frac{M - \overline{p}_y + \overline{p}_x}{2\overline{p}_y};$$

the ordinary demand functions are

$$x^* = \frac{\overline{M} - p_x + \overline{p}_y}{2p_x} \quad \text{and} \quad y^* = \frac{\overline{M} - p_y + \overline{p}_x}{2p_y};$$

and the cross-price demand functions are

$$x^* = \frac{\overline{M} - \overline{p}_x + p_y}{2\overline{p}_x} \quad \text{and} \quad y^* = \frac{\overline{M} - \overline{p}_y + p_x}{2\overline{p}_y}.$$

A Specific Example Now, suppose we use the following parametric values:

$$\overline{M} = \$100, \quad \overline{p}_x = \$5, \quad \overline{p}_y = \$10.$$

If all three of the possible parameters are fixed at these values simultaneously, then we can identify one specific utility-maximizing choice, (x^*, y^*), from equations 6.7 and 6.8.

$$x^* = \frac{\overline{M} - \overline{p}_x + \overline{p}_y}{2\overline{p}_x} = \frac{100 - 5 + 10}{2(5)} = 10.5$$

$$y^* = \frac{\overline{M} - \overline{p}_y + \overline{p}_x}{2\overline{p}_y} = \frac{100 - 10 + 5}{2(10)} = 4.75$$

The Engel curves for price parameters are, for X and Y, respectively,

$$x^* = \frac{M - \overline{p}_x + \overline{p}_y}{2\overline{p}_x} = \frac{M - 5 + 10}{2(5)} = \frac{M}{10} + \frac{1}{2} \tag{6.9}$$

$$y^* = \frac{M - \bar{p}_y + \bar{p}_x}{2\bar{p}_y} = \frac{M - 10 + 5}{2(10)} = \frac{M}{20} - \frac{1}{4}. \qquad (6.10)$$

To see whether X and Y are normal or inferior goods, we differentiate the Engel curves (equations 6.9 and 6.10) with respect to income:

$$\frac{\partial x^*}{\partial M} = \frac{1}{2\bar{p}_x} = \frac{1}{10} > 0 \quad \Rightarrow \quad \text{upward sloping} \quad \text{X is normal good}$$

$$\frac{\partial y^*}{\partial M} = \frac{1}{2\bar{p}_y} = \frac{1}{20} > 0 \quad \Rightarrow \quad \text{upward sloping.} \quad \text{Y is normal good}$$

The ordinary demand functions for income and other-price parameters are

$$x^* = \frac{\bar{M} - p_x + \bar{p}_y}{2p_x} = \frac{100 - p_x + 10}{2p_x} = \frac{110 - p_x}{2p_x} = \frac{55}{p_x} - \frac{1}{2} \qquad (6.11)$$

$$y^* = \frac{\bar{M} - p_y + \bar{p}_x}{2p_y} = \frac{100 - p_y + 5}{2p_y} = \frac{105 - p_y}{2p_y} = \frac{105}{2p_y} - \frac{1}{2}. \qquad (6.12)$$

To see whether the ordinary demand functions are downward sloping, we differentiate the ordinary demand functions (equations 6.11 and 6.12) with respect to their own prices:

$$\frac{\partial x^*}{\partial p_x} = -\frac{\bar{M} + \bar{p}_y}{2(p_x)^2} = -\frac{55}{(p_x)^2} < 0 \quad \Rightarrow \quad \text{demand is downward sloping}$$

$$\frac{\partial y^*}{\partial p_y} = -\frac{\bar{M} + \bar{p}_x}{2(p_y)^2} = -\frac{105}{2(p_y)^2} < 0 \quad \Rightarrow \quad \text{demand is downward sloping.}$$

Finally, the respective cross-price demand functions for income and own-price parameters are

$$x^* = \frac{\bar{M} - \bar{p}_x + p_y}{2\bar{p}_x} = \frac{100 - 5 + p_y}{2(5)} = 9.5 + \frac{p_y}{10} \qquad (6.13)$$

$$y^* = \frac{\bar{M} - \bar{p}_y + p_x}{2\bar{p}_y} = \frac{100 - 10 + p_x}{2(10)} = 4.5 + \frac{p_x}{20}. \qquad (6.14)$$

Thus,

$$\frac{\partial x^*}{\partial p_y} = \frac{1}{10} > 0 \quad \Rightarrow \quad \text{X is a gross substitute for Y}$$

$$\frac{\partial y^*}{\partial p_x} = \frac{1}{20} > 0 \quad \Rightarrow \quad \text{Y is a gross substitute for X.}$$

Homogeneity of Degree 0   Returning to the generalized demand function with all prices and income variable, suppose that we multiply all prices and income by the same positive constant, say α. This would be equivalent to a general inflation that leaves all *relative prices* the same:

$$\frac{\alpha p_x}{\alpha p_y} = \frac{p_x}{p_y}.$$

The budget constraint would go from

$$p_x x + p_y y = M \quad \text{to} \quad \alpha p_x x + \alpha p_y y = \alpha M.$$

Since α enters each term, it cancels, and the second budget line is the same as the first. If the budget constraint is unchanged, the choices must be unchanged because the utility function is only defined over quantities of goods and services, not over prices and income. In essence, the general inflation has not affected the feasible set. Therefore, the consumer chooses the same utility-maximizing consumption bundle as before.

In mathematical terms, we say that demand functions are *homogeneous of degree 0* in all prices and income. We say that a function is **homogeneous of degree k** if multiplying each of the arguments of the function by α multiplies the function by α^k, that is,

$$f(\alpha x, \alpha y) = \alpha^k f(x, y).$$

Thus, homogeneity of degree 0 means that

$$f(\alpha x, \alpha y) = \alpha^0 f(x, y) = f(x, y)$$

since $\alpha^0 = 1$. In the case of demand functions as functions of all prices and income, we have

$$x = f(p_x, p_y, M).$$

Homogeneity of degree 0 implies

$$x(\alpha) = f(\alpha p_x, \alpha p_y, \alpha M) = f(p_x, p_y, M) = x.$$

An Application of Homogeneity of Degree 0   An important applied use of the property that demand functions are homogeneous of degree 0 is in testing whether a particular, estimated, individual demand relationship *could* come from an underlying utility-maximization problem. If an estimated demand relationship is not homogeneous of degree 0, then it cannot be derived from utility maximization. For example, suppose we tried to estimate a demand relationship of the following form:

$$x = a_0 + a_1 M + a_2 p_x + a_3 p_y.$$

If we multiply all prices and income by α, we can see that it is not homogeneous of degree 0:

$$x(\alpha) = a_0 + \alpha a_1 M + \alpha a_2 p_x + \alpha a_3 p_y$$
$$= a_0 + \alpha(a_1 M + a_2 p_x + a_3 p_y)$$
$$\neq x.$$

Thus, in doing individual demand estimation, applied economists need to be careful to use only demand functions that are consistent with our underlying assumptions about consumer behavior. In contrast to the simple, linear, generalized demand function just proposed, the particular generalized demand functions we developed from utility maximization (equations 6.7 and 6.8) are homogeneous of degree 0 in all prices and income. Considering equation 6.7, for example,

$$x^* = \frac{M - p_x + p_y}{2p_x}$$

$$x(\alpha) = \frac{\alpha M - \alpha p_x + \alpha p_y}{2\alpha p_x} = x.$$

Therefore,

$$x(\alpha) = x,$$

implying that homogeneity of degree 0 is satisfied.

6.5   COBB-DOUGLAS UTILITY FUNCTIONS

As the discussion at the end of Section 6.4 makes clear, it is important for economists to use functional forms for demand equations that are homogeneous of degree 0 in all prices and income. One particular utility function, which yields very simple demand functions, has a long history in the applied economics literature:

$$U = x^\alpha y^\beta, x, y > 0. \tag{6.15}$$

It is called a generalized Cobb-Douglas utility function.[5]

Deriving Demand Functions   To find the generalized demand function for the generalized Cobb-Douglas utility function, we maximize utility subject to the budget constraint with all prices and income variable:

$$\max U = x^\alpha y^\beta \tag{6.16}$$
$$\text{s.t. } M - p_x x - p_y y \geq 0.$$

We do not need to apply the nonnegativity constraints in this case because the indifference curves are rectangular hyperbolas and asymptote to the axes. This rules out corner solutions. Thus, assuming the budget constraint holds with equality, the Lagrangian is

$$\mathcal{L} = x^\alpha y^\beta + \lambda(M - p_x x - p_y y). \tag{6.17}$$

The first-order conditions are

$$\frac{\partial \mathcal{L}}{\partial x} = \alpha(x^*)^{\alpha-1}(y^*)^\beta - \lambda^* p_x = 0 \quad \Rightarrow \quad \lambda^* = \frac{\alpha(x^*)^{\alpha-1}(y^*)^\beta}{p_x} \tag{6.18}$$

$$\frac{\partial \mathcal{L}}{\partial y} = \beta(x^*)^\alpha(y^*)^{\beta-1} - \lambda^* p_y = 0 \quad \Rightarrow \quad \lambda^* = \frac{\beta(x^*)^\alpha(y^*)^{\beta-1}}{p_y} \tag{6.19}$$

$$\frac{\partial \mathcal{L}}{\partial \lambda} = M - p_x x^* - p_y y^* = 0. \tag{6.20}$$

Solving for λ^* from equations 6.18 and 6.19,

$$\lambda^* = \frac{\alpha(x^*)^{\alpha-1}(y^*)^\beta}{p_x} = \frac{\beta(x^*)^\alpha(y^*)^{\beta-1}}{p_y} \quad \Rightarrow \quad \frac{\alpha(x^*)^{-1}}{p_x} = \frac{\beta(y^*)^{-1}}{p_y}.$$

---

[5]C. W. Cobb and P. H. Douglas, from P. H. Douglas, *The Theory of Wages* (New York: Macmillan, 1934).

Thus, the income-consumption curve (or line) is

$$y^* = \frac{\beta p_x}{\alpha p_y} x^*. \tag{6.21}$$

Substituting equation 6.21 in equation 6.20,

$$M - p_x x^* - p_y\left(\frac{\beta p_x}{\alpha p_y} x^*\right) = 0.$$

Thus,

$$\left(1 + \frac{\beta}{\alpha}\right)p_x x^* = M \quad \Rightarrow \quad x^* = \frac{M}{(1 + \beta/\alpha)p_x}.$$

Rearranging

$$\left(1 + \frac{\beta}{\alpha}\right)$$

to yield

$$\left(\frac{\alpha + \beta}{\alpha}\right),$$

and inverting this expression when moving it from the numerator to the denominator, the generalized demand function for X is

$$x^* = \frac{\alpha M}{(\alpha + \beta)p_x}. \tag{6.22}$$

Thus, substituting equation 6.22 in equation 6.21, the generalized demand function for Y is

$$y^* = \frac{\beta p_x}{\alpha p_y} x^* = \frac{\beta p_x}{\alpha p_y}\left[\frac{\alpha M}{(\alpha + \beta)p_x}\right] = \frac{\beta M}{(\alpha + \beta)p_y}. \tag{6.23}$$

Now, notice some interesting characteristics of these demand functions. First, note that each good's exponent, divided by the sum of the exponents, is the share of income spent on each good:

$$\frac{\alpha}{(\alpha + \beta)} = \textit{share of income spent on } x^*.$$

$$\frac{\beta}{(\alpha + \beta)} = \textit{share of income spent on } y^*.$$

Next, the demand functions can easily be transformed into a linear form by rewriting them and then taking logs:

$$x^* = \frac{\alpha}{\alpha + \beta} M(p_x)^{-1}$$

$$\Rightarrow \quad \ln(x^*) = \ln\left(\frac{\alpha}{\alpha + \beta}\right) + \ln(M) - \ln(p_x) \tag{6.24}$$

$$y^* = \frac{\beta}{\alpha + \beta} M(p_y)^{-1}$$

$$\Rightarrow \ln(y^*) = \ln\left(\frac{\beta}{\alpha + \beta}\right) + \ln(M) - \ln(p_y). \qquad (6.25)$$

Thus, the shares of income spent on the two goods can be estimated as the intercepts of two log-linear demand functions.

6.6   MARKET DEMAND FUNCTIONS

We turn now to the development of market demand functions. The **market demand function** is a schedule describing the total quantities demanded by all consumers at each price. It is found by adding up the *individual* demand functions developed in Section 6.4. Thus, if

$$x_i = x_i(p_x; \overline{M}_i, \overline{p}_y) \qquad (6.26)$$

is person i's ordinary demand function for X, then the market demand function is found by adding these functions over all *n* individuals:

$$X_d = \sum_{i=1}^{n} x_i = \sum_{i=1}^{n} x_i(p_x; \overline{M}_i, \overline{p}_y). \qquad (6.27)$$

This equation is illustrated for two consumers in Figure 6.13. At price p_x^1, consumer A demands x_A^1 and consumer B demands x_B^1. The market demand at price p_x^1 is, therefore, $x_A^1 + x_B^1$. Similarly, at price p_x^2, the market demand is $x_A^2 + x_B^2$.

Some Examples   As an example, assume all consumers have the Cobb-Douglas utility function, $U_i = x_i y_i$, where $\alpha = \beta = 1$. Recall that we derived the demand function for X for this utility function as equation 6.22:

$$x_i = \frac{\overline{M}_i}{2p_x}. \qquad (6.28)$$

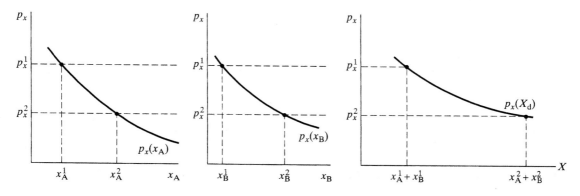

FIGURE 6.13   Constructing a Market Demand Curve from Two Individual Demand Curves

Summing (6.28) over i, the market demand function is,

$$X_d = \sum_{i=1}^{n} x_i = \sum_{i=1}^{n} \frac{\overline{M}_i}{2p_x} = \frac{1}{2p_x} \sum_{i=1}^{n} \overline{M}_i. \tag{6.29}$$

As another example, suppose there are three consumers, each of whom has a simple linear individual demand function:

$$x_1 = 10 - p_x \tag{6.30}$$

$$x_2 = 20 - 6p_x \tag{6.31}$$

$$x_3 = 50 - 4p_x. \tag{6.32}$$

The market demand function is the sum of equations 6.30–6.32 over nonnegative quantities:

$$X_d = \begin{cases} x_1 + x_2 + x_3 = 80 - 11p_x, & 0 \le p_x \le 3.33 \\ x_1 + x_3 = 60 - 5p_x, & 3.33 < p_x \le 10 \\ x_3 = 50 - 4p_x, & 10 < p_x \le 12.50. \end{cases} \tag{6.33}$$

Notice that when we add to find the market demand function, the x_i's are on the left-hand side and p_x is on the right-hand side of each equation. Quantity, the dependent variable, is a function of price. Adding up the functions $x_i(p_x)$ on the right-hand side is what we mean by adding up the quantities demanded at each price. Notice also that the market demand function is a piecewise linear function. This ensures that we only add over nonnegative quantities: $x_1 \ge 0$ if $p_x \le 10$; $x_2 \ge 0$ if $p_x \le 3.33$; $x_3 \ge 0$ if $p_x \le 12.50$.

6.7   CHANGES IN THE PARAMETERS OF MARKET DEMAND: THE CASE OF THE BABY BOOM

In Section 6.2 we discussed the parameters that affect individual demand: income, the prices of other goods, and (implicitly) an individual consumer's tastes. A change in tastes can be represented as a change in the parameters of the utility function. For example, we have seen (equation 6.28) that if the function is $U_i = x_i y_i$, then the generalized demand function for X is $x_i = M_i/2p_x$. But, if for some reason a consumer's utility function were to change to $U_i = (x_i)^2 y_i$, then the generalized demand function for X would increase to $x_i = 2M_i/3p_x$. (Substitute $\alpha = 2$, $\beta = 1$ in equation 6.22.) If all consumers were to experience a similar shift in preferences, then market demand for X would rise also.

This change in demand due to a change in the utility function is illustrated in Figure 6.14. The change in utility functions $U_i = x_i y_i$ to $U_i = (x_i)^2 y_i$ results in the increase in demand: $x_i = M_i/2p_x$ to $x_i = 2M_i/3p_x$.

Changes in Market Demand When we consider market demand functions, the process of adding up across consumers introduces three important additional parameters: the number of consumers, the distribution of tastes among consumers, and the distribution of income among consumers of different tastes. Holding all other parameters constant, if the population of consumers increases, all goods will experience an

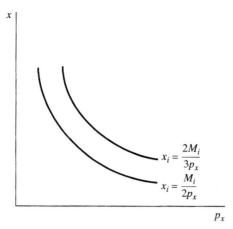

FIGURE 6.14   Shift in Demand from a Change in Tastes

increase in demand. Even if population remains constant, if the distribution of tastes among consumers changes, demand for some goods will increase, while for others it will decrease. Similarly, if the income distribution were to change in favor of a group with especially strong tastes for some particular good, there would be an increase in demand for that good relative to other goods. An example of changes in the composition of the population resulting in significant changes in demand is illustrated by the changes in demand as the baby boom generation ages.

The Baby Boom   In the 1950s, the United States experienced an unprecedented rise in average family size from just over two children per family to well over three children by 1960. Then, just as suddenly, average family size fell to under two children per family by the mid-1970s. The most rapid decline came in the 1960s. This change in the age distribution of the population has had profound effects on the structure of consumer demand. Moreover, as long as the baby boom generation continues to constitute a relatively large proportion of the population, it will continue to be important in shaping consumer demand.

In the 1950s, baby food, baby clothes, and baby toys experienced rapid increases in demand. Housing was also in great demand as families expanded. In the late 1950s and early 1960s, there was great pressure on our elementary school system, and school boards across the country responded by building new schools. But, almost as soon as the new capacity was completed, the "baby bust" of the 1960s was under way, and schools were faced with both excess capacity at the elementary school level and rising demand at the high school level, as the baby boom generation reached its teens.

In the late 1960s and early 1970s, the baby boom generation entered college and miniskirts were the hallmark of female fashion. Even older professional women found themselves wearing fashions designed essentially for the young. By the early 1980s, the baby boom generation was entering its 30s and goods appealing to young professionals experienced an unprecedented increase in demand at that time. In women's fashions, for example, "success dressing" was popular. At the end of the 1990s the baby boom generation is turning 50, creating a surge in demand for products purchased by the "mature" consumer. More than seven million baby boomers in the United States turned 50 in 1996 alone. Moreover, the target age for mass marketing has increased noticeably as the baby boom has aged. This is evidenced by a profound change in the character of television commercials. In the early 1970s, female models over 30 years old had to retire; in the early 1980s, models in their 30s (and even 40s) suddenly found themselves very much in demand; in the late 1990s models in their late 40s and early 50s are still working.

In the future, the voice of the baby boom generation will continue to be heard in the marketplace. Taking age 65 as an average retirement age, the baby boom generation will begin to retire in the year 2011 and continue retiring until 2026. The market will have to respond to a rapid increase in demand for goods purchased by elderly and retired people.

6.8 ANOTHER WORKED PROBLEM: FINDING THE GENERALIZED DEMAND FUNCTION

In this section, we work through one more utility-maximization problem, finding the generalized demand functions.

Suppose the consumer's utility function is

$$U = \frac{xy}{x + y}.$$

Maximizing utility subject to the budget constraint, the Lagrangian is

$$\mathcal{L} = \frac{xy}{x + y} + \lambda(M - p_x x - p_y y).$$

The first-order conditions are

$$\frac{\partial \mathcal{L}}{\partial x} = \frac{y^*(x^* + y^*) - x^* y^*}{(x^* + y^*)^2} - \lambda^* p_x = 0$$

$$\frac{\partial \mathcal{L}}{\partial y} = \frac{x^*(x^* + y^*) - x^* y^*}{(x^* + y^*)^2} - \lambda^* p_y = 0$$

$$\frac{\partial \mathcal{L}}{\partial \lambda} = M - p_x x^* - p_y y^* = 0.$$

Solving for λ^* from the first two first-order conditions,

$$\lambda^* = \frac{(y^*)^2/(x^* + y^*)^2}{p_x} = \frac{(x^*)^2/(x^* + y^*)^2}{p_y}.$$

Thus,

$$\frac{(y^*)^2}{(x^*)^2} = \frac{p_x}{p_y} \quad \Rightarrow \quad y^* = \left(\frac{p_x}{p_y}\right)^{1/2} x^*.$$

Substituting for y* in the third first-order condition,

$$M - p_x x^* - p_y\left[\left(\frac{p_x}{p_y}\right)^{1/2} x^*\right] = 0.$$

Thus,

$$M = x^*\left[p_x + (p_x p_y)^{1/2}\right]$$

$$\Rightarrow \quad x^* = \frac{M}{p_x + (p_x p_y)^{1/2}} \qquad \text{the generalized demand function for X}$$

$$y^* = \left(\frac{p_x}{p_y}\right)^{1/2}\left(\frac{M}{p_x + (p_x p_y)^{1/2}}\right)$$

$$\Rightarrow \quad y^* = \frac{M}{p_y + (p_x p_y)^{1/2}}. \qquad \text{the generalized demand function for Y}$$

6.9   REVIEW OF KEY CONCEPTS

This completes the introduction to ordinary demand functions and market demand functions. In Chapter 8, for reasons which will be made clear then, we will refer to these ordinary demand functions as *uncompensated demand functions*. The next chapter introduces elasticity of individual and market demand functions. Before continuing to Chapter 7, be sure you understand and can use the following key concepts.

The *income-consumption curve* describes a consumer's utility-maximizing choices at different income levels, holding prices constant. It is constructed by connecting all the points of tangency between the consumer's budget lines and corresponding indifference curves, holding prices constant.

The *Engel curve* for a particular good describes a consumer's utility-maximizing choices of that good at different income levels, holding prices constant. It is constructed by plotting quantities of that good from the income-consumption curve on a graph comparing income and the quantity of that good consumed.

A *normal good* is a good that a consumer buys more of as income increases.

An *inferior good* is a good that a consumer buys less of as income increases.

Goods cannot be inferior over all income ranges. We say that goods can only be *locally inferior*.

The *price-consumption curve* describes a consumer's utility-maximizing choices at different prices for one particular good, holding income and other prices constant.

The consumer's *demand function* or *ordinary demand function* for a particular good describes the quantities demanded of the good at different values of the good's own price, holding income and other prices constant.

Graphically, economists generally represent ordinary demand as the *inverse demand function* (price represented as a function of quantity).

Demand curves can be upward sloping and still satisfy the axioms of consumer preference.

A *cross-price demand function* describes the quantity demanded of one good for different prices of some other good.

Y is a *gross substitute* for X if the quantity demanded of Y increases when the price of X increases. For example, butter and margarine tend to be gross substitutes.

Y is a *gross complement* to X if the quantity demanded of Y decreases when the price of X increases. For example, coffee and cream tend to be gross complements.

If only a good's own price changes, then we move along the ordinary demand curve and say there has been a *change in quantity demanded*.

If income or the price of another good changes, the entire ordinary demand curve shifts. We say there has been a *change in demand*.

The *generalized demand function* for a particular good describes the quantities demanded of that good, allowing income and all prices to vary.

A function is *homogeneous of degree k* if multiplying all the arguments of a function by a positive constant (for example, α) multiplies the value of the function by α^k.

Generalized demand functions are homogeneous of degree 0 in all prices and income.

The *market demand function* for a good is a schedule describing the total quantities of that good demanded by all consumers at each price.

A change in tastes can be represented as a change in the parameters of the utility function.

The parameters affecting market demand include the number of consumers, the distribution of tastes among consumers, and the distribution of income among consumers of different tastes. These parameters are in addition to the parameters affecting individual demand: income and prices.

6.10 ___ QUESTIONS FOR DISCUSSION

1. Can all goods a consumer purchases be inferior at the same time? Explain why or why not.

2. For what kinds of goods might a consumer have upward-sloping demand curves?

3. Between 1890 and 1910, hundreds of thousands of immigrants from eastern and southern Europe poured into New York City through Ellis Island. While some continued on to other destinations, most stayed in New York for some period of time. Analyze the effect of this immigration of people from different cultures on the demand in New York

City for such products as pasta and rye bread. What other markets do you think would have been affected and how?

4. The immigrants discussed in Question 3 were also very poor. What effect would a sudden influx of very poor people have on the demand for such goods as rental housing? What other markets would you expect to be affected by the change in income distribution brought about by immigration? How would demand for government services be affected?

6.11 ___ PROBLEMS

Problems 1–3 Consider the following utility functions.

(a) $U = x^4y^4$, $x,y > 0$

(b) $U = x^{1/4}y^{1/4}$, $x,y > 0$

(c) $U = xy^2$, $x,y > 0$

(d) $U = 5x + 3y$, $x,y \geq 0$

(e) $U = $ minimum of x and $y = \min(x,y), x, y \geq 0$

1. Let $p_x = \$2$ and $p_y = \$3$. Derive the income-consumption line for each utility function. (Note that (d) and (e) cannot be solved with calculus; graph them. Hint: use your answers from Chapter 5.)

2. Let $p_x = \$2, p_y = \$3$, and $M = \$100$. Find the utility-maximizing consumption bundle for each utility function. (Hint: use your answers to Problem 1.)

3. Suppose $p_x = \$4, p_y = \$6$, and $M = \$200$. Would any of your answers to Problem 2 be different? Explain why or why not.

Problems 4–14 Now just consider functions (a) and (b).

4. Explain why your answers to Problems 1 (a) and (b) were identical.

5. Find a function for λ as a function of M for each utility function. (Hint: use the first-order conditions of the Lagrangian Problems 1 (a) and (b) and 2 (a) and (b)).

6. Find a function for the marginal utility of income for each utility function. Is marginal utility increasing or decreasing in M for each utility function? Compare your answers with your answers to Problem 5.

7. Derive generalized demand functions for X and Y as functions of $p_x, p_y,$ and M. Compare the generalized demand functions in terms of the modern theory of utility.

8. Are the own-price, ordinary demand functions downward sloping? Verify your answer.

9. Do your answers to Problems 1 (a) and (b) and 4–8 provide a contradiction to the proposition that diminishing marginal utility is a necessary condition for downward-sloping demand? Discuss in terms of the modern theory of utility.

10. Are the goods normal or inferior? Verify your answer.

11. What are the cross-price effects of p_y on X? Is X a substitute for or a complement to Y? Verify your answer.

Problems 12–13 Suppose there are 2000 consumers, each with an income of $500 and utility function

$$U_i = (x_i)^2 y_i.$$

The price of Y is $1.

12. Derive the own-price market demand function for X.

13. Now let M vary and let p_x = $4. Derive a market demand function as a function of the sum of consumer incomes.

6.12   LOGICAL AND MATHEMATICAL APPLICATIONS

1. A utility function is said to be homothetic if the marginal rates of substitution of the indifference curves are equal along any straight line from the origin. Show that a *homothetic* utility function always represents a normal good.

2. Interpret the meaning of λ as a marginal function from the utility maximization problem. Use the envelope theorem to illustrate your interpretation.

Chapter 7

ELASTICITY OF INDIVIDUAL AND MARKET DEMAND FUNCTIONS

7.1 WHAT YOU SHOULD LEARN FROM THIS CHAPTER

In this chapter, we introduce the concept of elasticity and show how it is used in economic policy analysis. In one sense, the material in this chapter is a review of principles material and should, therefore, be relatively easy to learn. That should not lead you to take this material less seriously, however: elasticity is one of the most useful concepts for simple economic analysis. Differences in price elasticity determine differences in changes in consumers' total expenditures and producers' total revenues as price changes. For example, if supply increases, reducing price, price elasticity of demand determines whether consumers will spend, in total, more or less on the good. Differences in income elasticity determine the differential effects of economic growth on the market demands for different goods. Differences in cross-price elasticities determine the differential effects of changes in relative prices on the markets for substitutes and complements.

7.2 ELASTICITY DEFINED

The slope of each of the respective demand functions developed in Chapter 6 indicates the *absolute* change in quantity relative to a change in own price, income, or other price. Often, however, we wish to evaluate the *relative* change in quantity with respect to one of the independent variables with a measure that is not affected by the units used. The measure economists use for such comparisons is called **elasticity,** measuring the percentage change in one variable divided by the percentage change in another. Elasticity is defined for both individual and market demand functions.

Own-price Demand Elasticity For example, **own-price elasticity** of demand measures the percentage change in quantity demanded for a given percentage change in price along the ordinary demand function or the own-price market demand function. If we let $\epsilon_{xo}^{d} = $ own-price elasticity of demand for good X, then

$$\epsilon_{xo}^{d} = \frac{\% \ \Delta \ \text{in} \ x}{\% \ \Delta \ \text{in} \ p_x}.$$

Percentage change can be represented as the change from one point to another divided by the average value over the range between the points, multiplied by 100. For example, the percentage change in x from x_1 to x_2 is

$$\% \, \Delta \text{ in } x = \frac{x_2 - x_1}{(x_1 + x_2)/2} \cdot 100.$$

Similarly, the percentage change in p_x from p_x^1 to p_x^2 is given by

$$\% \, \Delta \text{ in } p_x = \frac{p_x^2 - p_x^1}{(p_x^1 + p_x^2)/2} \cdot 100.$$

Putting these together, we have what is called the *arc elasticity,* elasticity measured for a discrete change in price along the demand function:

$$\epsilon_{xo}^d = \frac{\% \, \Delta \text{ in } x}{\% \, \Delta \text{ in } p_x} = \frac{\dfrac{x_2 - x_1}{(x_1 + x_2)/2} \cdot 100}{\dfrac{p_x^2 - p_x^1}{(p_x^1 + p_x^2)/2} \cdot 100.}$$

$$= \frac{\dfrac{x_2 - x_1}{(x_1 + x_2)}}{\dfrac{p_x^2 - p_x^1}{(p_x^1 + p_x^2)}}$$

If we are evaluating elasticities at single points, however, the changes will be infinitesimal, and the averages over the ranges can be replaced by the values at the points themselves. Thus, we can write the infinitesimal percentage changes as

$$\% \, \Delta \text{ in } x = \frac{\Delta x}{x} \cdot 100$$

$$\% \, \Delta \text{ in } p_x = \frac{\Delta p_x}{p_x} \cdot 100.$$

We can now define the own-price elasticity at a point as

$$\epsilon_{xo}^d = \frac{\% \, \Delta \text{ in } x}{\% \, \Delta \text{ in } p_x} = \frac{\dfrac{\Delta x}{x} \cdot 100}{\dfrac{\Delta p_x}{p_x} \cdot 100} = \frac{\Delta x}{\Delta p_x} \frac{p_x}{x}.$$

Thus, in calculus notation,

$$\epsilon_{xo}^d = \frac{dx}{dp_x} \frac{p_x}{x} = (\text{slope of ordinary demand function}) \cdot \frac{p_x}{x}.$$

If we assume demand is downward sloping, economists divide own-price elasticity into three categories. We say demand is **elastic** if the percentage change in quantity is greater than the percentage change in price. Since the slope of a downward-sloping demand function is negative, that would imply that the elasticity is less than -1:

$$\text{demand is elastic if } \epsilon_{xo}^d < -1.$$

We say demand is **unitary elastic** if the percentage change in quantity is equal to the percentage change in price, making price elasticity equal to -1:

$$\text{demand elasticity is unitary if } \epsilon_{xo}^d = -1.$$

Demand is **inelastic** if the percentage change in quantity is less than the percentage change in price, making elasticity between 0 and -1:

$$\text{demand is inelastic if } 0 > \epsilon_{xo}^d > -1.$$

Income Elasticity and Cross-price Elasticity   Having defined own-price elasticity, it is very simple to define income elasticity and cross-price elasticity. **Income elasticity** is simply the percentage change in quantity demanded for a given percentage change in income, and **cross-price elasticity** is the percentage change in quantity demanded for a given percentage change in the price of the other good. Thus, if we let

$$\epsilon_{xM}^d = \text{income elasticity of demand for X}$$

and

$$\epsilon_{xc}^d = \text{cross-price elasticity of demand for X},$$

then by analogy with own-price elasticity,

$$\epsilon_{xM}^d = \frac{\% \, \Delta \text{ in } x}{\% \, \Delta \text{ in } M} = \frac{dx}{dM} \frac{M}{x} = (\text{slope of Engel curve}) \cdot \frac{M}{x}$$

$$\epsilon_{xc}^d = \frac{\% \, \Delta \text{ in } x}{\% \, \Delta \text{ in } p_y} = \frac{dx}{dp_y} \frac{p_y}{x} = \left(\begin{array}{c}\text{slope of cross-price} \\ \text{demand function}\end{array}\right) \cdot \frac{p_y}{x}$$

While it is a valid concept for both normal and inferior goods, income elasticity is typically used only to describe normal goods. We say that a good is income elastic if the percentage change in quantity is greater than the percentage change in income, and we say a good is income inelastic if the income elasticity is less than 1. Income elasticity is unitary at 1.

$$\epsilon_{xM}^d > 1 \text{ if elastic}$$
$$\epsilon_{xM}^d = 1 \text{ if unitary}$$
$$\epsilon_{xM}^d < 1 \text{ if inelastic}$$

For cross-price elasticity, note that substitutes have negative cross-price elasticities and complements have positive cross-price elasticities.

7.3   ELASTICITY OF DEMAND ALONG LINEAR AND NONLINEAR DEMAND CURVES

To understand the concept and uses of elasticity more fully, we begin with an analysis of the elasticity of linear demand curves. Since the slope of a linear demand curve is constant, one might conclude that the elasticity should be constant as well. In actuality, however, the elasticity along a linear demand function varies all the way from 0 to $-\infty$. This happens because the slope is constant, but the ratio p_x/x varies from 0 when p_x is 0 (the x intercept) to $-\infty$ when x is 0 (the p_x intercept). These extremes of elasticity are illustrated with a linear inverse demand function in Figure 7.1.

The formula for the demand function whose inverse is illustrated in Figure 7.1 is

$$x = a - \frac{a}{b}p_x. \tag{7.1}$$

Thus, the elasticity of demand is

$$\epsilon_{\mathrm{d}} = \frac{dx}{dp_x}\frac{p_x}{x} = -\frac{a}{b}\frac{p_x}{x}. \tag{7.2}$$

Substituting for x and p_x in equation 7.2, at

$$
\begin{array}{lll}
x = a, & p_x = 0, & \text{and } \epsilon_{\mathrm{d}} = 0; \\
x = 0, & p_x = b, & \text{and } \epsilon_{\mathrm{d}} = -\infty; \\
x = \dfrac{1}{2}a, & p_x = \dfrac{1}{2}b, & \text{and } \epsilon_{\mathrm{d}} = -1.
\end{array} \tag{7.3}
$$

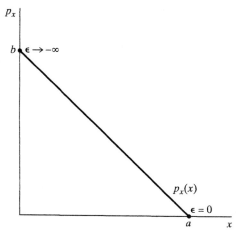

FIGURE 7.1   Extremes of Elasticity Along a Linear Demand Curve

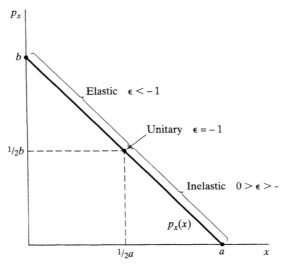

FIGURE 7.2 Ranges of Elasticity Along a Linear Demand Curve

The ranges of elasticity indicated in equations 7.3 are illustrated in Figure 7.2. The midpoint of the function $((\frac{1}{2})a, (\frac{1}{2})b)$ is the point of unitary elasticity. Demand is elastic when p_x is greater than $(\frac{1}{2})b$ and inelastic when x is greater than $(\frac{1}{2})a$.

Perfectly Inelastic and Perfectly Elastic Demand There are two specific linear demand curves that do not have a different elasticity at every point. These are the limiting cases of the vertical demand curve (quantity demanded is independent of price) and the horizontal demand curve (quantity demanded is not uniquely determined at a particular price). These demand curves are illustrated in Figure 7.3. With the vertical demand curve on the left, Δx is always 0. Thus, $\Delta x/\Delta p_x$ is also 0 and elasticity is everywhere equal to 0. We say the vertical demand curve is **perfectly inelastic.** With the horizontal demand curve on the right, on the other hand, Δp_x is always 0. In that case, $\Delta x/\Delta p_x$ is $-\infty$ and elasticity is everywhere $-\infty$. We say the horizontal demand curve is **perfectly elastic.**

Constant Elasticity Demand Functions Along a nonlinear demand function, elasticity may be either the same or different at every point. First, let's consider a *constant-elasticity demand function*. Along such a demand function, elasticity is always the same. This happens because the changing slope along the function is always equal to the changing ratio, p_x/x. The general form for a constant-elasticity demand function is

$$x = A(p_x)^{-k}, \tag{7.4}$$

where A and k are positive constants.

$$\frac{dx}{dp_x} = -kA(p_x)^{-k-1} \tag{7.5}$$

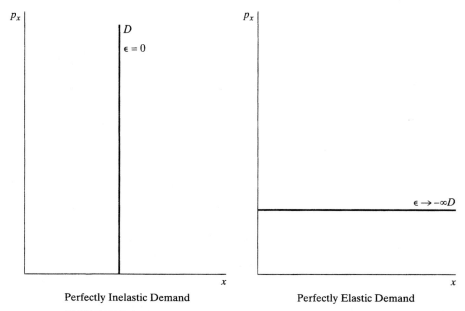

FIGURE 7.3   Perfectly Inelastic and Perfectly Elastic Demand

Therefore, multiplying (7.5) by p_x/x,

$$\epsilon_d = -kA(p_x)^{-k-1}\frac{p_x}{x} = -kA(p_x)^{-k-1}\frac{p_x}{A(p_x)^{-k}} \qquad (7.6)$$

$$= -k.$$

Equation 7.6 indicates that for

$$
\begin{aligned}
&k > 1, \quad \text{demand is elastic everywhere;} \\
&k = 1, \quad \text{demand is unitary everywhere;} \qquad (7.7)\\
&k < 1, \quad \text{demand is inelastic everywhere.}
\end{aligned}
$$

Other nonlinear demand functions have different elasticities at different points along the functions.

7.4   ELASTICITY AND TOTAL REVENUE

The own-price elasticity of demand has important implications for total consumer expenditures (which become total revenues to producers) as price changes along an own-price demand function. To illustrate the importance of elasticity, we need to introduce the concepts of total revenue, average revenue, and marginal revenue. **Total revenue** is the total amount consumers pay for a given number of units of a good, or the price paid times the quantity purchased. Since total revenue is usually expressed as a function of quantity, we express price as a function of quantity (the inverse demand function) to derive the total revenue function:

$$\text{total revenue} = TR(x) = p_x(x)x. \tag{7.8}$$

Average revenue is simply the revenue per unit, or the price:

$$\text{average revenue} = AR(x) = \frac{TR(x)}{x} = \frac{p_x(x)x}{x} = p_x(x). \tag{7.9}$$

Marginal revenue is the slope of the total revenue function:

$$\text{marginal revenue} = MR(x) = \frac{d}{dx} TR(x) = \frac{d}{dx} [p_x(x)x]. \tag{7.10}$$

Using the product rule to expand (7.10),

$$MR(x) = x \frac{d}{dx} p_x(x) + p_x(x). \tag{7.11}$$

Multiplying the right-hand side of (7.11) by p_x/p_x,

$$MR(x) = \frac{p_x}{p_x} x \frac{d}{dx} p_x(x) + \frac{p_x}{p_x} p_x(x) = p_x \left(\frac{x}{p_x} \frac{d}{dx} p_x(x) + 1 \right). \tag{7.12}$$

Thus, since

$$\frac{x}{p_x} \frac{d}{dx} p_x(x) = \frac{1}{\dfrac{p_x}{x} \dfrac{dx}{dp_x}} = \frac{1}{\epsilon_d},$$

(7.12) reduces to

$$MR(x) = p_x \left(\frac{1}{\epsilon_d} + 1 \right). \tag{7.13}$$

Equation 7.13 indicates that if demand is

$$\text{elastic,} \ \epsilon_d < -1, MR > 0, \text{ and } TR \text{ increases} \tag{7.14}$$

as price falls;

unitary, $\epsilon_d = -1$, $MR = 0$, and TR does not change

as price changes;

inelastic, $0 > \epsilon_d > -1$, $MR < 0$, and TR falls

as price falls.

Marginal Revenue and Linear Demand To find marginal revenue for a linear demand function, let

$$p_x(x) = b - \frac{b}{a} x, \tag{7.15}$$

as in the inverse of (7.1). Then

$$TR(x) = p_x(x)x = \left(b - \frac{b}{a}x\right)x = bx - \frac{b}{a}x^2 \tag{7.16}$$

$$MR(x) = \frac{d}{dx}TR(x) = b - 2\frac{b}{a}x. \tag{7.17}$$

Thus, the marginal revenue function for a linear demand function has the same price intercept and twice the slope as the inverse demand function. The quantity intercept is half that of its demand curve:

$$p_x = 0 \Rightarrow 0 = b - 2\frac{b}{a}x \Rightarrow x = \tfrac{1}{2}a. \tag{7.18}$$

Notice that the value of x in (7.18) coincides with the quantity at the point of unitary elasticity (equations 7.3).

Note also that, since marginal revenue is the slope of the total revenue function, total revenue is maximized when elasticity is unitary. That is because marginal revenue is 0 at that point. These relationships are illustrated in Figure 7.4. The demand

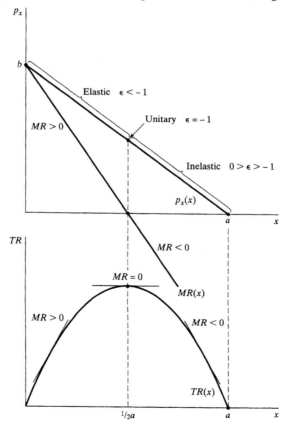

FIGURE 7.4   Comparing Elasticity, Total Revenue, and
Marginal Revenue

curve and the marginal revenue curve have the same price intercept, but the marginal revenue curve is twice as steeply sloped, crossing the quantity axis at the point of unitary elasticity along the demand curve. Total revenue is 0 when x is 0 and rises as a function of quantity when marginal revenue is positive and demand is elastic. It reaches a maximum at $(\frac{1}{2})a$, when marginal revenue is 0 and demand is unitary. Then, it falls when marginal revenue is negative and demand is inelastic, returning to zero when p_x is 0.

7.5 TOTAL, AVERAGE, AND MARGINAL REVENUE ALONG NONLINEAR DEMAND CURVES

Nonlinear demand curves may have either constant or changing elasticities. Along a constant-elasticity demand function, marginal revenue is everywhere either positive, 0, or negative. This implies that total revenue is everywhere either increasing, constant, or decreasing as x increases.

$$x = A(p_x)^{-k} \Rightarrow p_x = \left(\frac{x}{A} \right)^{-1/k} \tag{7.19}$$

$$TR = \left(\frac{x}{A} \right)^{-1/k} x = \left(\frac{1}{A} \right)^{-1/k} x^{1-1/k} \tag{7.20}$$

$$MR = \left(1 - \frac{1}{k} \right)\left(\frac{x}{A} \right)^{-1/k} = \left(1 - \frac{1}{k} \right)p_x \tag{7.21}$$

Equation 7.21 indicates that if $k > 1$ (elastic), marginal revenue is positive; if $k = 1$ (unitary), marginal revenue is 0; and if $k < 1$ (inelastic), marginal revenue is negative.

7.6 EXAMPLES OF LINEAR AND NONLINEAR DEMAND FUNCTIONS

To further illustrate these relationships among total revenue, marginal revenue, and elasticity, we consider two demand functions, one linear and one constant elasticity.

Linear demand function:

$$x(p_x) = 10 - p_x \Rightarrow p_x = 10 - x$$
$$TR(x) = (10 - x)x = 10x - x^2$$
$$MR(x) = 10 - 2x. \qquad \text{same intercept and twice the slope as } p_x(x)$$

To maximize total revenue,

$$MR = 0 = 10 - 2x$$

$$x^* = 5. \quad \text{half the } x \text{ intercept}$$

Constant-elasticity demand function:

$$x(p_x) = 20(p_x)^{-1} \Rightarrow p_x(x) = 20x^{-1}$$
$$TR(x) = (20x^{-1})x = 20, \quad \text{everywhere}$$
$$MR(x) = 0, \quad \text{everywhere.}$$

7.7   THE FARM PROBLEM IN HISTORICAL PERSPECTIVE: THE EFFECT OF PRICE AND INCOME INELASTICITY

Three hundred years ago, more than 75 percent of the world's population made its living from farming. Most of these people were subsistence farmers, but some (particularly in England and the Netherlands) produced for the growing urban market. Then, as today, being a farmer was a very risky business, and the degree of risk was strongly affected by the fact that demand for basic foodstuffs (such as grain) was inelastic. In any given year, a farmer would have to sink a fairly large fixed cost into planting, tending, and harvesting, but his revenues were highly dependent on the weather. If the weather was especially good everywhere, there would be a bumper crop. Quantity sold would be high, but price would be low, and, because demand was inelastic, revenues would also be low. On the other hand, when the weather was generally bad, overall supply would be low and prices high. If a particular farmer were fortunate in that bad year, that farmer's revenue would be much higher than during a good year because demand was inelastic. The worst situation, however, was to be unlucky in a bad crop year. The farmers whose crops failed in a famine year received no revenue, paid high fixed costs, and still had to buy their own food at famine prices. For such farm families, the choice was often to abandon farming or starve.

Today, many of the same problems remain. Farmers still pay high fixed costs for planting and harvesting, still depend on worldwide weather conditions to determine their revenues, and still dread a real bumper year. The reason is that demand for basic foodstuffs is still quite price inelastic.

In the last two hundred years, incomes have risen rapidly in Europe, North America, Australia, and in some areas of Asia and Latin America. This rapid rise in income has had a profound effect on farmers and farming as a way of life. In particular, as incomes have risen, demand for income-elastic goods has increased much faster than the demand for income-inelastic goods, such as basic foodstuffs. This process has forced a massive change in the structure of production and the employment of resources in those countries that have experienced this rise in income. Demand for industrial products and services has grown much more rapidly than the demand for agricultural products, and resources have shifted from farming to manufacturing and services. At the same time, improved agricultural technology has made it possible for each farmer to feed many other people who are not employed in farming. Today in the United States, less than 3 percent of the population is engaged in farming. Much of this change is due to improved agricultural technology, but some is due to the income inelasticity of demand for farm products.

The risks associated with farming and the rapid displacement of farmers due to technological change and rising demand for nonfarm products relative to farm products led farmers in the nineteenth century to lobby for farm regulation. The Grangers of the 1870s and 1880s pressed for state and federal assistance in forming cooperatives to restrict supply and thus raise prices. They also wanted their cooperatives to store grain in bumper crop years to smooth price fluctuations. The cooperative movement spread throughout the country and succeeded in passing a series of federal farm regulations in the 1920s that culminated in the New Deal agricultural regulations of the 1930s. These regulations, that lasted virtually intact until the mid-1990s, included acreage restrictions for primary food products, target prices with government purchase and storage of excess supply, and considerable federal government control over production decisions.

7.8   HOW ESTIMATES OF ELASTICITY ARE USED FOR POLICY ANALYSIS

Estimates of demand elasticities are very important in applied microeconomics and in microeconomic policy analysis. For example, suppose the government is considering changing the tax on gasoline. By estimating the short-term and long-term own-price elasticity of demand for gasoline, the government can predict the effect of the tax on consumption of gasoline, holding income and other prices constant. In addition, the income elasticity of demand for gasoline indicates the potential effect of possible income changes on gasoline consumption at a given price. The cross-price elasticity indicates the potential effects of changes in other prices on gasoline consumption at a given price. For example, an increase in the price of automobiles reduces the demand for gasoline. By estimating these elasticities, the government (and others), can predict the change in gasoline consumption for different assumptions about future incomes and changes in other prices.

Estimates of own-price elasticity are also important for developing policy when differences in total revenue are important. For example, most public transportation systems in this country typically lose money. So does the U.S. Postal Service. The costs of running a transportation system or the Postal Service do not vary much as the number of riders or pieces of mail change, but their respective revenues are highly dependent on those factors. This has led to debates over pricing of these services which can only be resolved if estimates of elasticity of demand are made. In the transportation case, the companies typically argue that they have to raise fares in order to raise revenue, while the riders argue that if they lower fares, enough more people will ride that revenues will increase. Similarly, the Postal Service argues it has to raise stamp prices, and consumers argue that enough more mail will be sent to raise revenue if the price of stamps is lowered. Clearly who is right depends on the own-price elasticity of demand. If demand for transportation or postal services is inelastic, the providers of these services are right; they will get more revenue if they raise their prices. On the other hand, if demand is elastic, the consumer groups are right; the providers will get more revenue if they lower their prices. Policy with regard to the pricing of these services cannot be made without estimates of own-price elasticity of demand.

Estimates of income elasticity are particularly important when firms are making major investment decisions. Suppose, for example, that a firm is contemplating building a new plant to produce gourmet frozen dinners. Current demand for the frozen dinners is significant, but not enough to keep the plant operating at full capacity. On the other hand, if the demand for gourmet frozen dinners is income elastic and incomes are expected to rise, the firm might decide to build for an expected growth in demand. Thus, the firm will very likely conduct a market study before building the plant and collect enough data to estimate the income elasticity of demand.

The government also makes investment decisions that require estimates of income elasticity. For example, if the government is going to build a dam that will create a recreational lake or make new investments in our national parks, it would like to know whether recreational travel is income elastic. If it is, the government can expect that use of lakes and parks will increase fairly rapidly over time as incomes increase.

Estimates of cross elasticity are useful for predicting the secondary effects of policy changes. For example, if a tax is imposed on gasoline, what effect will that policy have on the market for cars, trucks, planes, boats, and anything else that uses gasoline? Similarly, dairy price supports keep the market price of butter higher than it would be otherwise. The cross-price elasticity of demand for margarine when the price of butter changes indicates the secondary effect of that policy on the market for margarine.

7.9   REVIEW OF KEY CONCEPTS

This chapter continues the presentation of consumer theory. Before continuing to Chapter 8 on compensated demand, be sure you understand and can use the following key concepts.

Elasticity measures the percentage change in one variable divided by the percentage change in some other variable.

Own-price demand elasticity is the percentage change in quantity demanded divided by the percentage change in own price.

Demand is *elastic* if the percentage change in quantity is greater than the percentage change in price: elasticity is less than −1.

Demand is *inelastic* if the percentage change in quantity is less than the percentage change in price: elasticity is between 0 and −1.

Demand is *unitary elastic* if the percentage change in quantity is equal to the percentage change in price: elasticity is equal to −1.

Income elasticity is the percentage change in quantity demanded divided by the percentage change in income.

A good is said to be income elastic if the income elasticity is greater than 1, income inelastic if the income elasticity is less than 1, and unitary elastic if the income elasticity is equal to 1.

Cross-price elasticity is the percentage change in quantity divided by the percentage change in the price of another good.

Substitutes have negative cross-price elasticities. Complements have positive cross-price elasticities.

Elasticity of demand along a linear demand curve varies from − ∞ at the price intercept to 0 at the quantity intercept.

Along a linear demand curve, demand is elastic on the upper portion, unitary at the midpoint, and inelastic on the lower portion.

We say that demand is *perfectly inelastic* if quantity demanded is independent of price (vertical demand curve) and *perfectly elastic* if there is only one price and no unique quantity (horizontal demand curve).

Total revenue is the quantity of goods sold in a market times the price per unit.

Average revenue is total revenue per unit and it equals the market price.

Marginal revenue is the slope of the total revenue function. If demand is elastic, total revenue increases as quantity increases, and marginal revenue is positive. If demand is inelastic, total revenue decreases as quantity increases, and marginal revenue is negative. If demand is unitary, total revenue is constant and marginal revenue is 0.

Marginal revenue for a linear demand curve is also linear. It has the same price intercept, half the quantity intercept, and twice the slope of the corresponding demand curve.

Total revenue is maximized at the point of unitary demand elasticity.

7.10 QUESTIONS FOR DISCUSSION

1. Suppose you were on a diet and consumed only 1500 calories of food per day. Taking a sample of individual foods that you might combine to make up your 1500 calories a day, can we say anything about your own-price or income elasticity of demand for these individual foods?

2. Think of the goods that you either do consume or might consume. For which ones do you think your individual own-price demand is relatively inelastic or relatively elastic? What about your income elasticity? Are there pairs of goods with strong cross-price elasticities? Are they substitutes or complements?

3. What factors would contribute to a good's having a relatively elastic or inelastic demand? Explain your choices.

4. Suppose you are an economist working for your state government. There is a small state park that is currently accessible only by a dirt road that is impassable in winter. The state is currently considering upgrading the facilities at the park, paving the road, and charging admission to visit the park. You have been asked to study the question and make a recommendation as to whether the state should go ahead with its plan. If your answer is yes, the state wants to know how much admission to charge. Considering only the revenues the state can expect to receive over the next ten years, what would you have to know in order to make an informed recommendation and why?

5. Suppose you are an economist working for the public utilities commission in your state. A major electric company comes to the commission requesting a rate increase, claiming it needs more revenues to keep from losing money. Assuming that the company's costs will not be affected by a change in usage, what demand information will you need in order to make a recommendation to the commission regarding this case? Explain your answer. What would be your expectations about the characteristics of demand for electricity in the short term and the longer term? Explain.

6. Suppose you are an economist working for a major conglomerate that is considering acquiring a toy manufacturing company that makes expensive educational toys. What economic data would you have to collect in order to make an informed recommendation to your company about the expected long-term profitability of the toy manufacturer?

7.11 PROBLEMS

Problems 1–3 Calculate the own-price elasticities, the income elasticities, and the cross-price elasticities associated with the generalized demand function calculated as the answer to Problem 7 for utility function (a)–(e) in Chapter 6.

Problems 4–5 Derive functions for the own-price elasticity of demand and the income elasticity as a function of x along the market demand functions derived as the answers to Problems 12–13 in Chapter 6.

Problems 5–8 Now consider the following market demand functions.

(a) $x(p_x) = 50 - 10p_x$
(b) $x(p_x) = 100/p_x$
(c) $x(p_x) = 50 - 2(p_x)^{1/2}$

5. Derive the inverse demand function, $p_x(x)$, for each demand function.

6. Derive the total revenue and marginal revenue functions as functions of x.

7. Find the price and quantity combinations that maximize total revenue.

8. Show that the elasticity of demand is -1 at the point of maximum total revenue.

7.12   LOGICAL AND MATHEMATICAL APPLICATIONS

1. Show that an Engel curve that is a straight line from the origin has an income elasticity of 1.

2. Suppose the demand for wheat (measured in bushels) is given by

$$w(p_w) = 50{,}000 - 500p_w,$$

and the current market price for wheat is $2 per bushel. Show that demand for wheat is inelastic at the current price and that the total revenue going to farmers would decline if the quantity of wheat available on the market were to increase.

3. The demand function for local bus service (measured in rides per day) is given by

$$r(p_r) = 5000 - 1000p_r,$$

and the current price per ride is $1. The bus company is losing money and it has applied to the local public service commission for a rate increase. A citizens' committee testifies that the price should be lowered to attract more riders and thus increase revenues. Which side is correct?

Chapter 8

Compensated Demand Functions and Income and Substitution Effects

8.1   WHAT YOU SHOULD LEARN FROM THIS CHAPTER

In this chapter, we extend the analysis of demand functions developed in Chapter 6. We introduce the idea of a *compensated demand function* and show how it is related to important analytical and policy tools used by economists. We develop the compensated demand function by hypothetically compensating the consumer's income every time price increases until the consumer is exactly indifferent between the combination of the old, lower prices and income and the new, higher prices and income. We then identify the consumer's choice after compensation. The relationship between the hypothetical, compensated quantities demanded and the respective prices is called the *compensated* or *income-compensated demand function*. (Points along that function leave the consumer just exactly as well off as at the original price.)

Next, we introduce an important analytical tool that relies on the concept of compensated demand. We divide the ordinary demand function into the *substitution effect,* which measures the effect on quantity demanded of simply changing relative prices, and the *income effect,* which measures the effect on quantity demanded of changing only the "purchasing power" associated with the price change. We show that the substitution effect involves a movement along the compensated demand curve and the income effect involves a movement along the Engel curve defined for the new prices.

Finally, we show how compensated demand and income and substitution effects can be used to analyze the impacts on consumers of policy changes that affect income or relative prices. To do this we introduce the concept of *consumer's surplus* and show how it is related to compensated demand.

Throughout this chapter, we use the dual to utility maximization (that is, expenditure minimization) as the mathematical tool for developing and illustrating the theory. Deriving the compensated demand function involves minimizing the income necessary to keep a consumer on the same indifference curve every time price changes. Setting up the dual to utility maximization is a straightforward approach to that problem.

Since this is the first application of the dual problem since it was developed as a concept in Sections 3.4 and 3.6 and in equations 3.37–3.44, pay special attention to how it is used. By the end of this chapter, you will have been introduced to applications of almost all the important mathematical tools used in this book. From now on, we will

repeatedly derive demand, supply, and cost functions using the constrained maximization problem and its dual, the constrained expenditure minimization problem.

8.2   THE COMPENSATED DEMAND FUNCTION

In sections 6.2 and 6.4 and in equations 6.11 and 6.12, we derived quantity demanded
as a function of price, holding income and other prices constant, but allowing utility to
vary. The consumer ended up on a different indifference curve as a result of each price
change. Figure 8.1 reviews how utility changes when price changes. When the price of
X increases from p_x^1 to p_x^2, the consumer suffers a loss in utility from U_1^* to U_2^*.

Compensation for Price Changes   Now, suppose every time the price changes, the
consumer's income is adjusted in such a way as to keep him or her on the same indifference curve as before the price change. If price increases, income is increased, and if
price declines, income is reduced. Figure 8.2 illustrates the appropriate change in
income for one such price change. For example, if price were to increase from p_x^1 to p_x^2,
the consumer's income would be increased from M_1 to M_2 so that utility stays at U_1^*.
Since price is still p_x^2, the new budget line represents a parallel increase relative to the
budget line with p_x^2 and M_1. Economists refer to the change in income as **compensation**
for a price change.

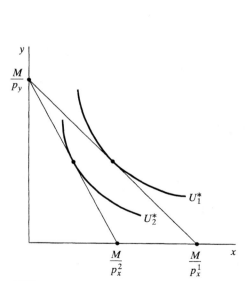

**FIGURE 8.1   A Change in Price Leading
to a Change in Utility**

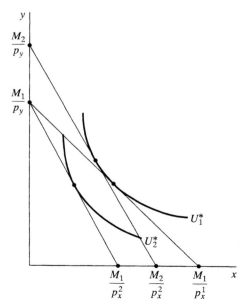

**FIGURE 8.2   A Compensated Price
Change**

Optimal Consumption Choices After Compensation If we keep track of the optimal choices of x after compensation (x_c) from the utility-maximization graph on a graph with x_c on the horizontal axis and p_x on the vertical axis, we can derive the inverse graph of the quantity demanded of X as a function of p_x, holding utility and p_y constant and (implicitly) allowing income to vary:

$$x_c^* = x_c^*(p_x; \overline{U}, \overline{p}_y).$$

Economists call this function the **income-compensated,** or simply, **compensated,** demand function for X. The income-compensated demand function for Y is represented analogously.

Figure 8.3 derives the inverse compensated demand function for X for one possible indifference curve. The optimal values of x_c from the upper graph are the same as

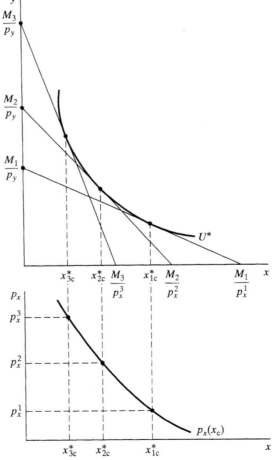

FIGURE 8.3 Deriving the Compensated Demand Curve for X

the values of x_c^* along the horizontal axis of the lower graph. The values of p_x associated with those optimal values in the upper graph are the same as the values of p_x along the vertical axis of the lower graph. The income-compensated demand curve is constructed by connecting the respective (x_c^*, p_x) points on the lower graph.

Compensated Demand Curves Are Always Downward Sloping   An important property of the compensated demand function is clear from Figure 8.3. Since the optimal values of x_c must lie along the indifference curve, which is convex to the origin, the quantity demanded of X after compensation must fall as p_x increases and must rise as p_x decreases. In other words, the compensated demand function is *always* downward sloping. That is illustrated by a comparison of x_{1c}^* and x_{2c}^* in Figure 8.3. As the price rises from p_x^1 to p_x^2, the budget line becomes steeper and quantity demanded falls from x_{1c}^* to x_{2c}^*. This always happens when price goes up and when the indifference curve satisfies diminishing marginal rate of substitution, because the indifference curve must be downward sloping and convex to the origin. Therefore, as the budget line becomes steeper (that is, as p_x increases), points of tangency involve increasing y and decreasing x. Thus, compensated demand curves are always downward sloping if the indifference curves satisfy the assumptions of the preference model developed in Section 5.3. This property stands in sharp contrast to the property that ordinary demand curves might be upward sloping even if indifference curves are convex to the origin.

8.3   INCOME AND SUBSTITUTION EFFECTS

The compensated demand curve, developed in Section 8.2, illustrates the effect of a change in relative prices on quantity demanded, holding utility constant. Sometimes in economic analysis it is useful to divide the movement along the ordinary demand curve into two separate effects: one due to the change in relative prices and the other due to the change in the feasible set associated with a change in the good's own price. This separation is important because two different things happen when the price of a good increases. First, the price ratio between X and Y changes, changing the slope of the budget line. Second, the feasible consumption set gets smaller, effectively reducing the consumer's "real" income. Figure 8.4 illustrates this point for an increase in the price of X. The budget rotates in, reducing the feasible set by the shaded area. In effect, the consumer has less "real" income to spend as a result of the increase in price.

Income and Substitution Effects   Economists refer to two distinct changes in a consumer's choices as

> 1. the **substitution effect:** the effect on consumer choice of changing the price ratio, leaving utility unchanged; and

> 2. the **income effect:** the effect on consumer choice of changing the feasible set, leaving the price ratio unchanged.

This distinction helps to make very clear some perhaps counterintuitive predictions of economic theory. In this chapter, we use income and substitution effects to show when our intuition that ordinary demand curves are downward sloping is correct

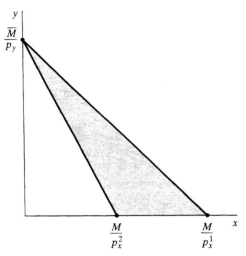

FIGURE 8.4 The Feasible Set Reduced as a Result of an Increase in p_x

and when that intuition may fail us. In addition, Sections 17.2, 17.3, 18.2, and 18.3 use income and substitution effects to show why individuals may choose to work less as their wages increase or why they may choose to save less as their incomes increase.

Figure 8.5 illustrates how income and substitution effects are developed for a particular price change: p_x increases from p_x^1 to p_x^2. At the original combination of prices and income, $p_x^1, \bar{p}_y$, and M_1, the consumer chooses (x_1^*, y_1^*) and is on indifference curve U_1^*. To identify the substitution effect, follow the derivation of the compensated demand curve along indifference curve U_1^* at the new price ratio. As the graph shows, if income is $M_2 > M_1$ and prices are p_x^2 and $\bar{p}_y$, the consumer maximizes utility along the original indifference curve, U_1^*, as in the derivation of the compensated demand curve. The new (implied) choice is (x_2^*, y_2^*). The change from (x_1^*, y_1^*) to (x_2^*, y_2^*) is referred to as the substitution effect.

To identify the income effect, we suppose that the (hypothetical) additional income, which allowed the consumer to remain on the original indifference curve, is no longer available, but p_x remains at p_x^2. This is equivalent to a movement along the Engel curve from M_2 back to M_1 at prices p_x^2 and $\bar{p}_y$. The consumer moves from point (x_2^*, y_2^*) to (x_3^*, y_3^*), and utility is allowed to decline from U_1^* to U_2^*. This change from (x_2^*, y_2^*) to (x_3^*, y_3^*) is referred to as the income effect. The entire change along the ordinary demand curve is the full change from (x_1^*, y_1^*) to (x_3^*, y_3^*).

Sometimes we want to focus on the effect of a change in the price of X on quantities demanded of good X alone. In that case, we would decompose the change along the ordinary demand curve for good X from x_1^* to x_3^* into the substitution effect (the change from x_1^* to x_2^*) and the income effect (the change from x_2^* to x_3^*). We use this decomposition in the next section.

The Negative Substitution Effect In general, what can we say about ordinary demand functions by looking at income and substitution effects? First, we have already

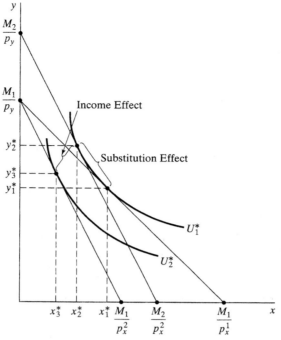

FIGURE 8.5   Income and Substitution Effects

seen that an increase in p_x reduces x by the substitution effect as we move along an indifference curve that bounds a strictly convex set. This was illustrated in Figure 8.5 with the change from x_1^* to x_2^*: as p_x rises, $x_2^* < x_1^*$. The same is true for y if p_y increases. In mathematical terms,

$$\left. \frac{dx^*}{dp_x} \right|_{\substack{dU=0 \\ dp_y=0}} < 0 \quad \text{and} \quad \left. \frac{dy^*}{dp_y} \right|_{\substack{dU=0 \\ dp_x=0}} < 0. \tag{8.1}$$

Since the partial derivatives are negative, we say that the substitution effect must always be *negative*. Figure 8.6 illustrates this important implication of diminishing marginal rate of substitution. The consumer begins with income M_1 and prices p_x^1 and $\bar{p}_y$ and chooses x_1^*. When the price of X increases to p_x^2, income is increased to M_2, and the consumer chooses x_2^*, which is less than x_1^*. Similarly, when p_x and M are again increased to p_x^3 and M_3, respectively, the consumer chooses x_3^*, which is less than x_2^*, and so on.

Normal Goods and Downward-sloping Demand   Although the substitution effect must be negative, the income effect can be either positive or negative, depending on whether the good is a normal or an inferior good. If the good is normal, when the feasible set is reduced as the result of a price increase, quantity demanded declines due to the income effect. That is because a decline in income implies a decline in quantity

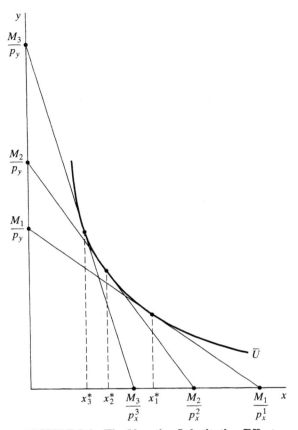

FIGURE 8.6 The Negative Substitution Effect Illustrated

demanded for a normal good. A price reduction has the opposite effect. We express this mathematically as follows:

$$\frac{dx^*}{dM}\bigg|_{\substack{dp_x=0\\dp_y=0}} > 0 \quad \text{for a normal good.} \tag{8.2}$$

Thus, in the case of a normal good, when price increases, quantity demanded declines due to the substitution effect and then further declines due to the income effect. Therefore, the combined effect on quantity demanded along the ordinary demand function must be that quantity demanded declines when the good's own price rises.

Figure 8.7 illustrates the income and substitution effects for a normal good. The consumer begins at x_1^* and utility level U_1^*, with income M_1 and prices p_x^1 and $\bar{p}_y$. When p_x and M rise to p_x^2 and M_2, respectively, keeping utility and p_y at U_1^* and $\bar{p}_y$, respectively, x^* falls to x_2^* by the substitution effect. Keeping p_x at p_x^2, if income falls back to M_1, x^* and utility fall to x_3^* and U_2^*, respectively, by the income effect. Thus, the overall

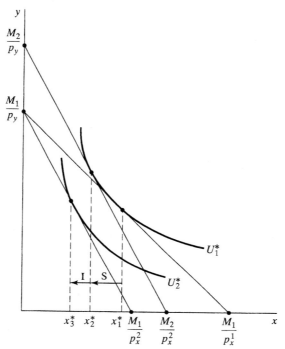

FIGURE 8.7   Income and Substitution Effects for a Normal Good

change in x as a result of the increase in price from p_x^1 to p_x^2 has been that x^* falls from x_1^* to x_3^*.

Inferior Goods   If, on the other hand, the good is an inferior good, quantity demanded increases if income declines. That implies that a reduction in the feasible set as a result of a price increase actually *increases* quantity demanded due to the income effect. An increase in the feasible set has the opposite effect. Mathematically, we express this as follows:

$$\frac{dx^*}{dM}\bigg|_{\substack{dp_x=0\\dp_y=0}} < 0 \quad \text{for an inferior good.} \tag{8.3}$$

If the price increases, for example, the substitution effect always reduces quantity demanded because of diminishing marginal rate of substitution. However, for an inferior good, the feasible set is reduced when the price increases, and the income effect increases quantity demanded for an inferior good. The overall, uncompensated effect, therefore, can be either to increase or decrease quantity demanded, depending on whether the substitution effect or the income effect is larger.

Figure 8.8 illustrates both possibilities. In both graphs, when p_x increases from p_x^1 to p_x^2, quantity demanded falls from x_1^* to x_2^* due to the substitution effect, and then quantity demanded rises to x_3^* due to the income effect. In the left graph, the increase

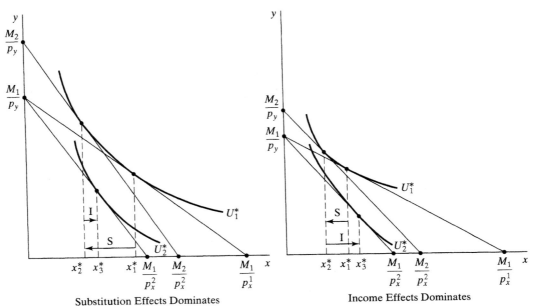

Substitution Effects Dominates · **Income Effects Dominates**

FIGURE 8.8 Income and Substitution Effects for Inferior Goods

from x_2^* to x_3^* is not sufficient to make x_3^* greater than x_1^*. Thus, the overall effect of the increase in p_x is to reduce quantity demanded from x_1^* to x_3^*. We say in this case that the *substitution effect outweighs the income effect.* However, as the right graph shows, if the good is an inferior good and if the *income effect outweighs the substitution effect,* the overall effect can be to increase x^* from x_1^* to x_3^*. Thus, if the income effect outweighs the substitution effect for an inferior good, the ordinary demand curve will be upward sloping, even if all the assumptions of the consumer preference model are satisfied. We refer to a good with an upward-sloping demand curve as a Giffen good. Figure 8.8 illustrates that for a good to be a **Giffen good,** it has to both be inferior and have a larger income effect than a substitution effect.

Summary of Income and Substitution Effects Figure 8.9 summarizes what we have just learned about income and substitution effects for normal and inferior goods. Beginning from x_1^*, if p_x rises, the substitution effect always moves x^* to the left (to x_2^*). If the good is a normal good, the income effect moves x^* further to the left. Thus x_3^* is always less than x_1^*, implying the ordinary demand curve is always downward sloping *if the good is normal.* On the other hand, if the good is inferior, the income effect moves x^* back to the right of x_2^*, and x_3^* is greater than x_2^*. If x_3^* falls in the region between x_2^* and x_1^*, then x_3^* is still less than x_1^*, and the ordinary demand curve is still downward sloping. In this case, the negative substitution effect outweighs the income effect. If, however, x_3^* falls to the right of x_1^*, then x_3^* is greater than x_1^*, and the ordinary demand curve is upward sloping. In this case, the income effect outweighs the substitution effect.

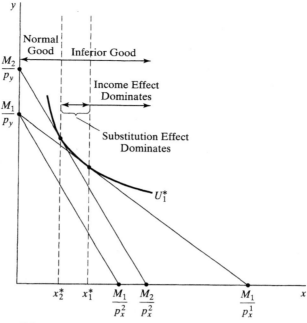

FIGURE 8.9   Summary of Income and Substitution Effects for Normal and Inferior Goods

8.4   THE EXPENDITURE MINIMIZATION PROBLEM

In Section 6.4, we solved the consumer's utility maximization problem to derive the generalized demand functions. The solution to the utility-maximization problem would be $U^* = U^*(x^*, y^*)$.[1] Moreover, since U^* changes every time prices and income change, we can think of U^* itself as being a function of prices and income. The way we construct a U^* function is to use the generalized demand functions, which are functions of prices and income, to represent the optimal choices for x and y. Then, we express U^* as a function of x^* and y^*, where x^* and y^* are the generalized demand functions for X and Y. The problem (with two consumption goods) is

$$\max U(x, y) \tag{8.4}$$
$$\text{s.t. } p_x x + p_y y = M.$$

The generalized demand functions are

$$x^* = x^*(p_x, p_y, M) \quad \text{and} \quad y^* = y^*(p_x, p_y, M). \tag{8.5}$$

The optimal solution can be expressed as

$$U^* = U^*(x^*(p_x, p_y, M), y^*(p_x, p_y, M)). \tag{8.6}$$

---

[1]Technically, this function should be expressed as $U^* = U(x^*, y^*)$, where U is the original utility function *evaluated* at the optimal values (x^*, y^*). To avoid confusion, however, we refer to U evaluated at the optimal values as $U^*(x^*, y^*)$.

This last function, U^*, can also be written simply as a function of all prices and income. In that form, it is called the **indirect utility function** (because the *choices* x^* and y^* have been suppressed):

$$U^* = U^*(p_x, p_y, M). \tag{8.7}$$

The Consumer's Dual Problem   The dual to utility maximization is expenditure minimization. Recall from Section 3.4 that to set up a dual problem, we minimize the constraint in the original (or primal) problem subject to the original objective function constrained at its optimal value. The primal problem is to maximize the *objective function* given by $U = U(x, y)$, subject to the *constraint* $M = p_x x + p_y y$. The solution to that problem is U^*. Applying the rules for setting up the dual problem, we make the objective of the problem to minimize the original constraint function. Thus, we minimize the *objective function* given by

$$M = p_x x + p_y y,$$

subject to the *constraint* (from the primal problem's objective function)

$$U = U(x, y).$$

The solution to that problem is M^*. Moreover, for each U^* with income constrained at $\overline{M}$ in the primal problem, there is a corresponding M^* with utility constrained at $\overline{U}$ in the dual problem. In each of such paired problems

$$U^* \text{ in primal} = \overline{U} \text{ in dual}$$

$$M^* \text{ in dual} = \overline{M} \text{ in primal.}$$

Just as in the primal (utility-maximization) problem, solving the dual (expenditure-minimization) problem involves finding a set of demand functions. Because utility is held constant and income is allowed to vary, these demand functions turn out to be the income-compensated demand functions we have already illustrated graphically. We have seen the two-dimensional versions corresponding to the ordinary demand functions from the utility-maximization problem. To derive M^* (the solution to the expenditure-minimization problem), however, we need **generalized compensated demand functions,** just as we needed generalized versions of the ordinary demand functions to derive the indirect utility function (the solution to the utility-maximization problem). The generalized versions of these compensated (dual) demand functions will be

$$x_c^* = x_c^*(p_x, p_y, U) \quad \text{and} \quad y_c^* = y_c^*(p_x, p_y, U). \tag{8.8}$$

Finally, just as in the primal problem, the optimal solution can be expressed as a function of the generalized demand functions:

$$M^* = p_x x_c^* + p_y y_c^* \tag{8.9}$$
$$= p_x x_c^*(p_x, p_y, U) + p_y y_c^*(p_x, p_y, U).$$

The function $M*$ is called the **expenditure function;** and again, by suppressing the choices x_c^* and y_c^*, it can be written as a function of prices and utility:

$$M* = M*(p_x, p_y, U). \tag{8.10}$$

Comparing the Primal and Dual Problems   Now, recall from Sections 3.4 and 3.6 that for given values of M and U, the optimal values of x and y will always be the same. This means that

$$x*(p_x, p_y, M*(p_x, p_y, \overline{U})) = x_c^*(p_x, p_y, U*(p_x, p_y, \overline{M})) \tag{8.11}$$

and

$$y*(p_x, p_y, M*(p_x, p_y, \overline{U})) = y_c^*(p_x, p_y, U*(p_x, p_y, \overline{M})), \tag{8.12}$$

where

$$M* = \overline{M} \quad \text{and} \quad U* = \overline{U}.$$

Figure 8.10 reviews this concept. The solution to the utility-maximization problem with $M*$ as the income constraint is the indifference curve $U*$. The solution to the expenditure-minimization problem with $U*$ as the utility constraint is the budget line with income $M*$. Needless to say, $(x*, y*)$, the optimal values in the primal problem, are the same as (x_c^*, x_c^*), the optimal values in the dual problem:

$$x* = x_c^* \quad \text{and} \quad y* = y_c^*.$$

In the future, we will often refer to the ordinary demand functions as *uncompensated demand functions* in order to distinguish them from the compensated demand

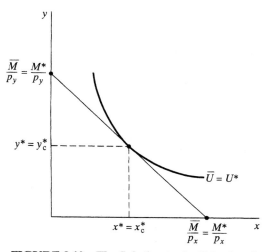

FIGURE 8.10   The Solution to the Primal and Dual Problems

functions. Points along the ordinary demand functions are, therefore, denoted *uncompensated* choices of x and y.

8.5   DERIVING COMPENSATED DEMAND FUNCTIONS AND THE EXPENDITURE FUNCTION: AN EXAMPLE

In this section, we derive the compensated demand functions and the expenditure function for the Cobb-Douglas utility function $U = xy$. Substituting $\alpha = \beta = 1$ in equations 6.16, the utility-maximization problem is

$$\max U = xy \tag{8.13}$$

$$\text{s.t. } p_x x + p_y y = M.$$

And, substituting $\alpha = \beta = 1$ in equations 6.22 and 6.23, the uncompensated generalized demand functions are

$$x^* = \frac{M}{2p_x} \quad \text{and} \quad y^* = \frac{M}{2p_y}. \tag{8.14}$$

Finally, if we substitute the generalized demand functions (equations 8.14) in the utility function, $U = xy$, we can derive the indirect utility function from the optimal values of x and y defined by the generalized demand functions:

$$U^* = x^* y^* = \frac{M}{2p_x} \frac{M}{2p_y} = \frac{M^2}{4p_x p_y}.$$

Thus, the indirect utility function is

$$U^* = \frac{M^2}{4p_x p_y}. \tag{8.15}$$

Solving the Dual Problem   The dual problem is

$$\min M = p_x x + p_y y \tag{8.16}$$

$$\text{s.t. } xy = U.$$

The Lagrangian is

$$\mathcal{L} = p_x x + p_y y + \mu(U - xy). \tag{8.17}$$

The first-order conditions are

$$\frac{\partial \mathcal{L}}{\partial x} = p_x - \mu y = 0 \quad \Rightarrow \quad \mu = \frac{p_x}{y} \tag{8.18}$$

$$\frac{\partial \mathcal{L}}{\partial y} = p_y - \mu x = 0 \quad \Rightarrow \quad \mu = \frac{p_y}{x} \tag{8.19}$$

$$\frac{\partial \mathcal{L}}{\partial \mu} = U - xy = 0. \tag{8.20}$$

Solving for μ,

$$\mu = \frac{p_x}{y} = \frac{p_y}{x} \quad \Rightarrow \quad y = \frac{p_x}{p_y}x. \tag{8.21}$$

Therefore,

$$U - x\left(\frac{p_x}{p_y}x\right) = 0 \quad \Rightarrow \quad x^2\frac{p_x}{p_y} = U$$

$$\Rightarrow \quad x_c^* = \left(\frac{p_y}{p_x}U\right)^{1/2}. \qquad \text{the generalized compensated demand function for X} \quad (8.22)$$

Substituting (8.22) in (8.21)

$$y_c^* = \frac{p_x}{p_y}\left(\frac{p_y}{p_x}U\right)^{1/2}$$

$$= \left(\frac{p_x}{p_y}U\right)^{1/2}. \qquad \text{the generalized compensated demand function for Y} \quad (8.23)$$

Now, to find the optimal solution to the dual problem, we substitute the optimal choices, defined by the compensated demand functions (equations 8.22 and 8.23), in the objective function $M = p_x x + p_y y$:

$$M^* = p_x x_c^* + p_y y_c^* \tag{8.24}$$

$$= p_x\left(\frac{p_y}{p_x}U\right)^{1/2} + p_y\left(\frac{p_x}{p_y}U\right)^{1/2}$$

$$= (p_x p_y U)^{1/2} + (p_x p_y U)^{1/2}$$

$$= 2(p_x p_y U)^{1/2}. \qquad \text{the expenditure function} \quad (8.25)$$

Anchoring   To derive the two-dimensional income-compensated demand functions, which we illustrated graphically in Section 8.2, we need to hold utility constant in order to find points of tangency along one indifference curve. One way to do this is to start at the utility-maximizing choice for a given income and prices (for example, $\overline{M}$, $\overline{p}_x$, and $\overline{p}_y$). We can then "anchor" the compensated demand functions around that point. Figure 8.11 illustrates this technique. The constant utility, $\overline{U}$, is the utility from choices x^* and y^* at prices and income p_x^1, p_y^1, and M_1. To maintain that utility level as p_x increases or decreases, holding p_y constant, the consumer needs M_2 at p_x^2, M_3 at p_x^3, and so on.

Deriving Anchored Compensated Demand Functions   Returning to the example derived in equations 8.13–8.25, we can evaluate utility for a given income and prices, $\overline{M}, \overline{p}_x$, and $\overline{p}_y$, by evaluating the indirect utility function (equation 8.15) for those parameters:

$$\overline{U} = \frac{\overline{M}^2}{4\overline{p}_x\overline{p}_y}. \tag{8.26}$$

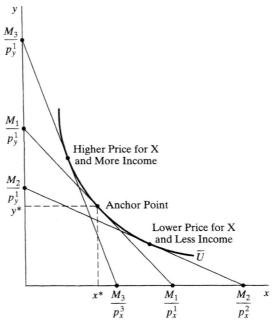

FIGURE 8.11   Deriving Compensated Demand Functions by "Anchoring" on One Point

We can now "anchor" the two-dimensional compensated demand functions on the value $\overline{M}^2/\overline{p}_x\,\overline{p}_y$, which defines the utility constraint, $\overline{U}$. By using the anchoring technique, we can derive compensated demand functions that do not explicitly depend on utility. This is important in demand estimation, since utility is unobservable.

To derive income-compensated demand functions around the anchor point, we first distinguish between the income and prices used to calculate the utility constraint $(\overline{M}, \overline{p}_x,$ and $\overline{p}_y)$ and the variable prices and income used to construct the compensated demand functions. In the example below we will keep p_y fixed at $\overline{p}_y$ and let p_x vary relative to $\overline{p}_x$. Each time p_x changes, we will find M^*, the minimum income necessary to keep utility constant at $\overline{U}$.

Keeping utility and p_y fixed at $\overline{U}$ and $\overline{p}_y$, respectively, we can derive the compensated demand for X as a function of p_x by substituting $\overline{U}$ and $\overline{p}_y$ in the generalized compensated demand function for X. When we do this, we must maintain the parameter $\overline{p}_x$, used to anchor the utility constraint, because that was the price of X used to calculate $\overline{U}$. The function is then derived relative to that point. The actual functional form will involve both $\overline{p}_x$ and the variable p_x.

Substituting $\overline{U}$ (equation 8.26) and $\overline{p}_y$ in the generalized compensated demand for X (equation 8.23) gives

$$x_c^* = \left(\frac{\overline{p}_y}{p_x}\,\overline{U}\right)^{1/2} = \left(\frac{\overline{p}_y}{p_x}\,\frac{\overline{M}^2}{4\overline{p}_x\,\overline{p}_y}\right)^{1/2}$$

$$= \frac{\overline{M}}{2}\left(\frac{1}{p_x \overline{p}_x}\right)^{1/2}. \tag{8.27}$$

And, substituting equation 8.22 in equation 8.20, the compensated demand for Y is

$$y_c^* = \left(\frac{p_x}{\overline{p}_y}\overline{U}\right)^{1/2} = \left(\frac{p_x}{\overline{p}_y}\frac{\overline{M}^2}{4\overline{p}_x\overline{p}_y}\right)^{1/2}$$

$$= \frac{\overline{M}}{2\overline{p}_y}\left(\frac{p_x}{\overline{p}_x}\right)^{1/2}. \tag{8.28}$$

We can now find M^*, the minimum income necessary to maintain utility at $\overline{U}$, by substituting equations 8.27 and 8.28 in the dual objective function, $M = p_x x + p_y y$. Holding p_y constant at $\overline{p}_y$,

$$M^* = p_x\frac{\overline{M}}{2}\left(\frac{1}{p_x \overline{p}_x}\right)^{1/2} + \overline{p}_y\frac{\overline{M}}{2\overline{p}_y}\left(\frac{p_x}{\overline{p}_x}\right)^{1/2}$$

$$= \overline{M}\left(\frac{p_x}{\overline{p}_x}\right)^{1/2}. \qquad \textbf{the minimum income} \tag{8.29}$$

To achieve the minimum income necessary to maintain a given level of utility, the consumer would have to be given a **subsidy** equal to the difference between that (hypothetical) minimum income and his or her actual income, $\overline{M}$. To find the minimum subsidy required to achieve that minimum income after compensation, we subtract the original income from the minimum income after compensation. Let S^* be the minimum subsidy required to maintain $\overline{U}$. Then,

$$S^* = M^* - \overline{M} = \overline{M}\left(\frac{p_x}{\overline{p}_x}\right)^{1/2} - \overline{M}$$

$$= \overline{M}\left[\left(\frac{p_x}{\overline{p}_x}\right)^{1/2} - 1\right]. \tag{8.30}$$

A Numerical Example   To clarify the example developed in equations 8.27–8.30, let's introduce some specific numerical parameters. We begin by evaluating $\overline{U}$ for a given initial income and set of prices. Thus, let

$$\overline{M} = \$100, \quad \overline{p}_y = \$5, \quad \text{and} \quad \overline{p}_x = \$4 \tag{8.31}$$

Therefore, substituting (8.31) in (8.14), the original choices of x and y are

$$x^* = \frac{\overline{M}}{2\overline{p}_x} = \frac{100}{2(4)} = \frac{25}{2} \tag{8.32}$$

$$y^* = \frac{\overline{M}}{2\overline{p}_y} = \frac{100}{2(5)} = 10. \tag{8.33}$$

These choices generate utility of

$$U^* = 10\left(\frac{25}{2}\right) = 125. \tag{8.34}$$

Now, if we hold utility fixed at 125 and p_y fixed at \$5, we can find compensated demand functions for X and Y as functions of p_x by substituting (8.31) in (8.27) and (8.28). To find x_c^*,

$$x_c^* = \frac{\overline{M}}{2}\left(\frac{1}{p_x \overline{p}_x}\right)^{1/2} = \frac{100}{2}\left(\frac{1}{4p_x}\right)^{1/2}$$

$$= \frac{25}{(p_x)^{1/2}}. \tag{8.35}$$

Alternatively, we could substitute (8.34) in (8.22):

$$x_c^* = \left(\frac{\overline{p}_y}{p_x}\overline{U}\right)^{1/2} = \left[\frac{(5)(125)}{p_x}\right]^{1/2} = \left(\frac{625}{p_x}\right)^{1/2} = \frac{25}{(p_x)^{1/2}}.$$

To find y_c^*,

$$y_c^* = \frac{\overline{M}}{2\overline{p}_y}\left(\frac{p_x}{\overline{p}_x}\right)^{1/2} = \frac{100}{2(5)}\left(\frac{p_x}{4}\right)^{1/2} \tag{8.36}$$

$$= 5(p_x)^{1/2}.$$

Alternatively, substituting (8.34) in (8.23),

$$y_c^* = \left(\frac{p_x}{\overline{p}_y}\overline{U}\right)^{1/2} = \left(\frac{125p_x}{5}\right)^{1/2} = (25p_x)^{1/2}$$

$$= 5(p_x)^{1/2}.$$

To find the minimum income, substitute (8.35) and (8.36) in the objective function:

$$M^* = p_x x_c^* + \overline{p}_y y_c^* \tag{8.37}$$

$$= p_x\left[\frac{25}{(p_x)^{1/2}}\right] + 5[5(p_x)^{1/2}] = 25(p_x)^{1/2} + 25(p_x)^{1/2}$$

$$= 50(p_x)^{1/2}.$$

Alternatively, substituting (8.34) in (8.25),

$$M^* = 2(p_x \overline{p}_y \overline{U})^{1/2} = 2[p_x(5)(125)]^{1/2}$$

$$= 50(p_x)^{1/2}.$$

To find the optimal subsidy, substitute (8.37) in (8.30):

$$S^* = M^* - \overline{M} \tag{8.38}$$

$$= 50(p_x)^{1/2} - 100.$$

Recall now that we anchored the compensated demand curve by fixing $\overline{p}_x$ at \$4. That means that if p_x were to increase above \$4, the optimal subsidy would be positive, and if p_x were to fall below \$4, the optimal subsidy would be negative. If p_x remains at \$4, the optimal subsidy would be 0. This is reflected in equation 8.38.

$$50(4)^{1/2} - 100 = 0 \qquad \textbf{same price}$$

$$50(9)^{1/2} - 100 = 50 \qquad \textbf{higher price}$$

$$50(1)^{1/2} - 100 = -50 \qquad \textbf{lower price}$$

8.6   MATHEMATICAL TREATMENT OF INCOME AND SUBSTITUTION EFFECTS

The example developed in Section 8.5 can be extended to calculate the income and substitution effects associated with a change in the price of good X. In that example, the initial parameters are $\overline{M} = \$100$, $\overline{p}_y = \$5$, and $\overline{p}_x = \$4$. Given those parameters, the initial choices of x and y are $x^* = 25/2 = 12.5$ and $y^* = 10$, from equations 8.32 and 8.33. Suppose p_x were to increase to \$5. We can now evaluate x_c^* and y_c^* (equations 8.35 and 8.36) at the new price for X:

$$x_c^* = \frac{25}{(p_x)^{1/2}} = \frac{25}{(5)^{1/2}} = 5(5)^{1/2} \approx 5(2.24) = 11.18 \tag{8.39}$$

$$y_c^* = 5(p_x)^{1/2} = 5(5)^{1/2} \approx 5(2.24) = 11.18. \tag{8.40}$$

Thus, the substitution effect is

$$(x^*, y^*) \rightarrow (x_c^*, y_c^*) = (12.5, 10) \rightarrow (11.18, 11.18).$$

Again, focusing on good X, alone, the substitution effect associated with an increase in p_x from \$4 to \$5 is the decline in quantity demanded along the compensated demand curve from 12.5 units to approximately 11.18 units.

In order to maintain the original level of utility, the consumer needs more income than before. This is found by substituting $p_x = \$5$ in equation 8.37:

$$M^* = 50(p_x)^{1/2} = 50(5)^{1/2} \approx 50(2.24) = \$112.$$

Thus, the subsidy that would be necessary to restore the consumer to $\overline{U}$ after the price increase is

$$S^* = M^* - \overline{M} = \$112 - \$100 = \$12.$$

At $p_x = 5$, if we were to take back the (hypothetical) \$12 subsidy, the new uncompensated choices would be

$$x_u^* = \frac{\overline{M}}{2p_x} = \frac{100}{2(5)} = 10 \text{ and } y_u^* = \frac{\overline{M}}{2\overline{p}_y} = \frac{100}{2(5)} = 10. \tag{8.41}$$

Thus, the income effect is:

$$(x_c^*, y_c^*) \rightarrow (x_u^*, y_u^*) = (11.18, 11.18) \rightarrow (10, 10).$$

Again, focusing on good X, the income effect associated with the increase in p_x from \$4 to \$5 is the further decline in quantity demanded along the Engel curve at $p_x = \$5$ from approximately 11.18 units to 10 units.

Notice that y^* and y_u^* are both 10. That is because, for the utility function, $U = xy$, there are no cross-price effects. In other words, the uncompensated choices of y are independent of changes in the price of X. Thus, if income remains at \$100 and p_y remains at \$5, $y*$ will always be 10, regardless of the value of p_x. The compensated choice of y, on the other hand, must change as p_x changes in order to satisfy the condition of diminishing marginal rate of substitution. Since the indifference curve must be downward sloping and convex to the origin, as p_x increases, x must decline and y must rise.

We can summarize the compensated and uncompensated changes derived in equations 8.39–8.41 as follows. We begin at

$$(x_1^*, y_1^*) = (12.5, 10),$$

with income of \$100 and prices of \$5 for Y and \$4 for X. Next, p_x is raised to \$5. If the consumer is simultaneously given a \$12 subsidy, that subsidy would be enough to keep the consumer on the original indifference curve at the higher price for X. With the higher price and the subsidy, the consumer would choose

$$(x_c^*, y_c^*) = (11.18, 11.18).$$

Since the price of X has risen, the new compensated choice must involve less X and more Y along a downward-sloping, convex indifference curve. This condition is clearly satisfied. x_c^* decreases from 12.5 to 11.18, and y_c^* increases from 10 to 11.18. Finally, if the (hypothetical) \$12 subsidy were taken back, the consumer would be forced to move back to the lower indifference curve along the income-consumption line for prices \$5 and \$5. At the old income of \$100 and the new higher price for X, the consumer chooses

$$(x_u^*, y_u^*) = (10, 10).$$

Summarizing these changes for good X, alone, the total change from 12.5 units to 10 units can be decomposed into the substitution effect (the change from 12.5 units to approximately 11.18 units) and the income effect (the change from approximately 11.18 units to 10 units): 12.5 → 11.18 → 10.

8.7   THE SLUTSKY EQUATION

As we saw in Section 8.3, income and substitution effects can be used to study the relationship between normal goods and downward-sloping demand. At that time, we showed graphically in Figures 8.6–8.8 that *one* of the following two conditions is sufficient to guarantee that an ordinary demand curve will be downward sloping:

1. the good in question is a normal good, or

2. for inferior goods, the substitution effect outweighs the income effect.

This proposition about the slope of the ordinary demand curve can be illustrated by an equation of the slopes of the respective demand functions, known as the **Slutsky equation.** We first state the equation below and discuss how it illustrates the above proposition. Then we will show how the equation can be derived from the solution to the expenditure minimization problem developed in Section 8.5 and equations 8.16–8.25. The Slutsky equation is

$$\frac{dx^*}{dp_x}\bigg|_{\substack{dM=0\\dp_y=0}} = \frac{dx^*_c}{dp_x}\bigg|_{\substack{dU=0\\dp_y=0}} - x^* \frac{dx^*}{dM}\bigg|_{\substack{dp_x=0\\dp_y=0}}. \tag{8.42}$$

Stated in words,

$$\begin{matrix} \text{slope of} \\ \text{ordinary} \\ \text{demand function} \end{matrix} = \begin{matrix} \text{slope of} \\ \text{compensated} \\ \text{demand function} \end{matrix} -x^* \text{ (slope of the Engel curve)}$$

or

$$\text{full effect} = \text{substitution effect} - \text{income effect.}$$

An Example   We can illustrate the Slutsky equation by substituting the slopes of the demand functions derived from the utility function $U = xy$ into equation 8.42. From equations 8.14, we know that the ordinary (uncompensated) demand function for X is $x^* = \overline{M}/2p_x$. Thus

$$\frac{dx^*}{dp_x}\bigg|_{\substack{dM=0\\dp_y=0}} = -\frac{\overline{M}}{2(p_x)^2}. \tag{8.43}$$

The anchored compensated demand function is $x^*_c = \overline{M}/2(p_x, \overline{p}_x)^{1/2}$ (equation 8.27). Thus,

$$\frac{dx^*_c}{dp_x}\bigg|_{\substack{dU=0\\dp_y=0}} = -\frac{\overline{M}}{4(\overline{p}_x)^{1/2}(p_x)^{3/2}}. \tag{8.44}$$

The Engel curve can also be derived from equations 8.14: $x^* = M/2\overline{p}_x$. Thus,

$$\frac{dx^*}{dM}\bigg|_{\substack{dp_x=0\\dp_y=0}} = \frac{1}{2\overline{p}_x}. \tag{8.45}$$

Thus, substituting (8.44–8.45) in (8.42), the Slutsky equation is

$$\frac{dx^*}{dp_x}\bigg|_{\substack{dM=0\\dp_y=0}} = -\frac{\overline{M}}{4(\overline{p}_x)^{1/2}(p_x)^{3/2}} - x^* \frac{1}{2\overline{p}_x}. \tag{8.46}$$

Substituting the ordinary demand function for x^* (equations 8.14) in equation 8.46 and letting $\overline{p}_x = p_x$, (since it is evaluated for an infinitesimal change in p_x),

$$\frac{dx^*}{dp_x}\bigg|_{\substack{dM=0\\dp_y=0}} = -\frac{\overline{M}}{4(p_x)^2} - \frac{\overline{M}}{2p_x}\frac{1}{2p_x} = -\frac{\overline{M}}{4(p_x)^2} - \frac{\overline{M}}{4(p_x)^2}$$

$$= -\frac{\overline{M}}{2(p_x)^2},$$

which is exactly what we found in equation 8.43 when we simply differentiated the ordinary demand function with respect to p_x.

Downward- and Upward-sloping Demand   The sign of the slope of the ordinary demand function can be derived by signing each of the components of the Slutsky equation and then comparing the income and substitution effects if the good is inferior. First, we sign each of the components.

1. The slope of the compensated demand function is negative by diminishing marginal rate of substitution.

2. x^* is positive, since X is a consumption good.

3. The slope of the Engel curve is positive if X is a normal good and negative if X is an inferior good.

We can then summarize the sign pattern of the slopes of the demand functions as follows.

Normal Good

uncompensated	= compensated	$-x^* \cdot$ (Engel curve)	
$(-)$	$=$ $(-)$	$-(+)\cdot$ $(+)$	**downward sloping**

Inferior Good

uncompensated	= compensated	$-x^* \cdot$ (Engel curve)	
$(-)$	$=$ $(-)$	$-(+)\cdot$ $(-)$	**downward sloping**

(substitution effect outweighs income effect)

$(+)$	$=$ $(-)$	$-(+)\cdot$ $(-)$	**upward sloping**

(income effect outweighs substitution effect)

Deriving the Slutsky Equation   To derive the Slutsky equation, we begin with the solution to the expenditure minimization or dual problem, equations 8.9 and 8.10:

$$M^*(p_x, p_y, U) = p_x x_c^* + p_y y_c^*.$$

We know from equations 8.11 and 8.12 that the optimal solutions to the primal and dual problems have to generate the same x^* and y^* values for the same indifference curve and budget line. Thus, for $\overline{M} = M^*$ and $\overline{U} = U^*$, the compensated and uncompensated demand functions have to give identical values for x and y. Maintaining these equalities, (8.11) can be written as

$$x_c^*(p_x, p_y, \overline{U}) = x^*(p_x, p_y, M^*(p_x, p_y, \overline{U})). \tag{8.47}$$

Differentiating both sides of equation 8.47 with respect to p_x,

$$\frac{\partial x_c^*}{\partial p_x} = \frac{\partial x^*}{\partial p_x} + \frac{\partial x^*}{\partial M}\frac{\partial M^*}{\partial p_x}, \tag{8.48}$$

which can be rewritten as

$$\left.\frac{dx_c^*}{dp_x}\right|_{\substack{dU=0\\dp_y=0}} = \left.\frac{dx^*}{dp_x}\right|_{\substack{dM=0\\dp_y=0}} - \left(\left.\frac{dM^*}{dp_x}\right|_{\substack{dU=0\\dp_y=0}}\right)\left(\left.\frac{dx^*}{dM}\right|_{\substack{dp_x=0\\dp_y=0}}\right). \tag{8.49}$$

Rearranging the terms in (8.49),

$$\left.\frac{dx^*}{dp_x}\right|_{\substack{dM=0\\dp_y=0}} = \left.\frac{dx_c^*}{dp_x}\right|_{\substack{dU=0\\dp_y=0}} - \left(\left.\frac{dM^*}{dp_x}\right|_{\substack{dU=0\\dp_y=0}}\right)\left(\left.\frac{dx^*}{dM}\right|_{\substack{dp_x=0\\dp_y=0}}\right). \tag{8.50}$$

Notice that equation 8.50 is identical to the Slutsky equation (8.42) except for the term,

$$\left.\frac{dM^*}{dp_x}\right|_{\substack{dU=0\\dp_y=0}}.$$

In the Slutsky equation, that term is simply x^*. Thus, if we can show that

$$\left.\frac{dM^*}{dp_x}\right|_{\substack{dU=0\\dp_y=0}} = x^*, \tag{8.51}$$

we will have shown that the Slutsky equation is correct. To do that, we simply recall the envelope theorem, developed in Section 3.6 and equations 3.18–3.26. We showed at that time that the derivative of the objective function with respect to one of the shift parameters is simply the partial derivative, ignoring any secondary effects of changes in the parameter. In other words, if

$$M^* = p_x x^* + p_y y^*,$$

then

$$\frac{\partial M^*}{\partial p_x} = x^*, \tag{8.52}$$

as in equation 8.51, and

$$\frac{\partial M^*}{\partial p_y} = y^*.$$

This conclusion, called **Hotelling's lemma,**[2] shows that the Slutsky equation is correct.

Interpretation of the Slutsky Equation   The interpretation of the Slutsky equation is basically that an infinitesimal change along the ordinary demand curve can be divided into two parts. The infinitesimal change along the compensated demand curve is the substitution effect. The infinitesimal change along the Engel curve, *weighted by the amount of the good actually purchased,* is the income effect. In the case of an inferior

---

[2]Harold Hotelling, "Edgeworth's Taxation Paradox and the Nature of Demand and Supply Functions," *Journal of Political Economy* 40(1932):577–616.

good, the income effect *might* outweigh the substitution effect, and the ordinary demand curve might be upward sloping, if the consumer were to consume a large quantity of a strongly inferior good.

8.8 SUBSTITUTION ELASTICITY AND THE SIZE OF THE SUBSTITUTION EFFECT

Consumers with differently shaped indifference curves will have different substitution effects for a given price change. When the price of X increases, for example, some would be quite willing to substitute Y for X after compensation. Others would not be willing to reduce their consumption of X by very much. Figure 8.12 illustrates these two possibilities. In the left graph, the indifference curve is relatively "*flat*" and the consumer reduces x and increases y by a relatively large amount when p_x increases and when income is compensated. In the right graph, however, the indifference curve bends sharply and the consumer reduces x and increases y by very little.

To compare substitution effects across consumers, we use a measure called the substitution elasticity or the elasticity of substitution along an indifference curve. **Substitution elasticity** measures the percentage change in the ratio of y to x purchases in response to a percentage change in the price ratio. In the left graph of Figure 8.12, the substitution elasticity is relatively high. Going from (x_1, y_1) to (x_2, y_2) entails a fairly large percentage increase in y/x.

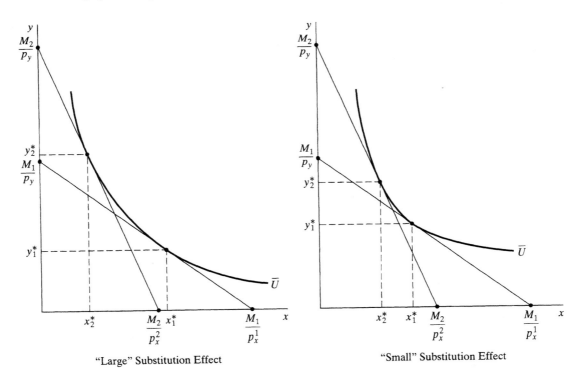

"Large" Substitution Effect   "Small" Substitution Effect

FIGURE 8.12 Differences in the Size of the Substitution Effect

On the other hand, the increase in y/x in the right graph is very small; thus, the substitution elasticity is small.

Deriving Substitution Elasticity   Mathematically, we let

$$\sigma_{yx} = \text{the substitution elasticity of Y for X}$$

$$\frac{y}{x} = \text{the purchase ratio of Y to X}$$

$$\frac{p_x}{p_y} = \text{the price ratio.}$$

For simplicity, we define new variables

$$\Psi \equiv \frac{y}{x} \text{ and } \mathcal{P} \equiv \frac{p_x}{p_y}. \tag{8.53}$$

Thus,

$$\sigma_{yx} = \frac{\text{percentage change in } y/x}{\text{percentage change in } p_x/p_y} = \frac{\Delta\Psi/\Psi}{\Delta\mathcal{P}/\mathcal{P}} = \frac{\Delta\Psi}{\Delta\mathcal{P}} \frac{\mathcal{P}}{\Psi}.$$

Expressed in terms of calculus,

$$\sigma_{yx} = \frac{d\Psi}{d\mathcal{P}} \frac{\mathcal{P}}{\Psi} = \frac{d(y/x)}{d(p_x/p_y)} \frac{p_x/p_y}{y/x}. \tag{8.54}$$

In our example derived from equation 6.15, we know that

$$\frac{y}{x} = \frac{p_x}{p_y}. \tag{8.55}$$

This is found by rearranging terms in equation 8.21, the income-consumption line for the utility function $U = xy$. (You should take careful note that this equation is not generally true. Only some utility functions have this income-consumption line.) Therefore, for this utility function,

$$\Psi = \mathcal{P} \quad \Rightarrow \quad \frac{d\Psi}{d\mathcal{P}} = 1 \tag{8.56}$$

$$\Rightarrow \quad \sigma_{yx} = 1\frac{\mathcal{P}}{\Psi} = \frac{\mathcal{P}}{\mathcal{P}} = 1. \tag{8.57}$$

The condition that $\sigma_{yx} = 1$ is characteristic of Cobb-Douglas utility functions (equation 6.15): $U = x^\alpha y^\beta$, for $\alpha, \beta > 0$. To show that, recall the income-consumption line that was derived as equation 6.21:

$$y = \frac{\beta p_x}{\alpha p_y} x.$$

Rearranging terms in equation 6.21,

$$\frac{y}{x} = \frac{\beta}{\alpha}\frac{p_x}{p_y},$$

(8.58)

or

$$\Psi = \frac{\beta}{\alpha}\mathcal{P} \implies \frac{d\Psi}{d\mathcal{P}}\frac{\mathcal{P}}{\Psi} = \frac{\beta}{\alpha}\frac{\mathcal{P}}{(\beta/\alpha)\mathcal{P}} = 1.$$

(8.59)

Other utility functions generally have different elasticities of substitution, however. For example, suppose

$$U = \frac{xy}{x + y}.$$

(8.60)

Then

$$MRS = \frac{MU_x}{MU_y} = \frac{\dfrac{y(x+y) - xy}{(x+y)^2}}{\dfrac{x(x+y) - xy}{(x+y)^2}} = \frac{y^2}{x^2} = \frac{p_x}{p_y}.$$

(8.61)

Taking the square root of both sides of equation 8.61,

$$\frac{y}{x} = \left(\frac{p_x}{p_y}\right)^{1/2} \implies \Psi = \mathcal{P}^{1/2}$$

$$\sigma_{yx} = \frac{d\Psi}{d\mathcal{P}}\frac{\mathcal{P}}{\Psi} = \tfrac{1}{2}\mathcal{P}^{-1/2}\frac{\mathcal{P}}{\mathcal{P}^{1/2}} = \frac{1}{2}.$$

(8.62)

Limiting Cases of Elasticity of Substitution   In fact, σ_{yx} can vary all the way from 0 to infinity. Figure 8.13 illustrates the two limiting cases. In the left graph, with "square"

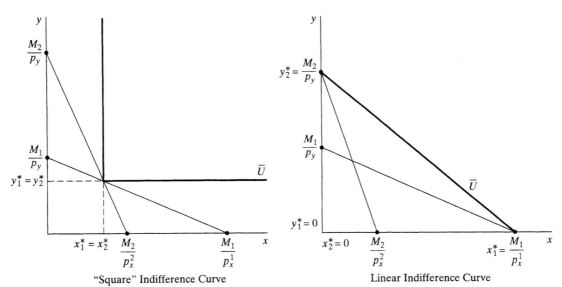

"Square" Indifference Curve   Linear Indifference Curve

FIGURE 8.13   Limiting Elasticities of Substitution

indifference curves, y/x never changes. Thus, σ_{yx} is 0. In the right graph, with linear indifference curves, y/x is either 0 (when the budget line is less steep than the indifference curve and y^* is 0), undefined (when the budget line is steeper than the indifference curve and x^* is 0), or indeterminate, not unique, (when the budget line lies on the indifference curve). Therefore,

$$\frac{d(y/x)}{d(p_x/p_y)} = \begin{cases} 0 \text{ as long as the budget line is less steep;} \\ \text{undefined as long as the budget line is steeper;} \\ \text{indeterminate on the indifference curve itself.} \end{cases}$$

To summarize, we speak of elasticity as moving from 0 to infinity as we go from square to linear indifference curves.

8.9   CONSUMER'S SURPLUS ANALYSIS

We turn now to an application of compensated demand theory. Consumer's surplus, an important topic in consumer theory, is a widely used concept in policy analysis, but the theoretical underpinnings of the version typically used in policy analysis are somewhat shaky.

The Optimal Subsidy and the Compensated Demand Curve The basic idea can be derived directly from things we already know about the compensated demand curve. Recall that when we were deriving the Slutsky equation in Section 8.6, we found Hotelling's lemma (equation 8.52) by applying the envelope theorem: $dM^*(p_x)/dp_x = x_c^*(p_x)$. Thus, by rearranging terms in equation 8.52,

$$dM^*(p_x) = x_c^*(p_x)\,dp_x, \tag{8.63}$$

where dM^* is the optimal subsidy for an infinitesimal change in price. Recall that

$$\frac{dM}{dp_x} = x_c,$$

by Hotelling's lemma. That allows us to rewrite equation 8.63 as

$$dM^*(p_x) = \frac{d}{dp_x}M^*(p_x)\,dp_x = x_c^*(p_x)\,dp_x. \tag{8.64}$$

Now, recall from Section 1.7 that we can "add up" a series of infinitesimal changes by taking the integral over those infinitesimal changes. Thus, if price increases from p_x^1 to p_x^2, the optimal subsidy required to maintain a given level of utility would be the integral over all the infinitesimal income changes as price changes (the integral of equation 8.64 from p_x^1 to p_x^2).

$$S^* = \int_{p_x^1}^{p_x^2} \frac{d}{dp_x}M^*(p_x)\,dp_x = \int_{p_x^1}^{p_x^2} x_c^*(p_x)\,dp_x \tag{8.65}$$

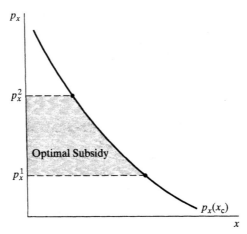

FIGURE 8.14   The Optimal Subsidy as an Integral Along the Vertical Axis of the Compensated Demand Curve

As Figure 8.14 illustrates, however, measured this way, the optimal subsidy is simply the integral between p_x^1 and p_x^2, measured along the vertical axis of the inverse compensated demand function.

A Numerical Example   To illustrate this equality, let's return to the utility function, $U = xy$. We showed in equation 8.30 that the optimal subsidy is $S^* = \overline{M}[\,(p_x/\overline{p}_x)^{1/2} - 1]$. Now, suppose we begin with the following parameters:

$$\overline{p}_x = \$1, \quad \overline{p}_y = \$1, \quad \overline{M} = \$8. \tag{8.66}$$

Then, substituting (8.66) in (8.30),

$$S^* = 8[(p_x)^{1/2} - 1]. \tag{8.67}$$

We also know that the compensated demand function is $x_c^* = \overline{M}/2(p_x\overline{p}_x)^{1/2}$. Evaluating the compensated demand function at the parameters given in equations 8.66,

$$x_c^* = \frac{8}{2(p_x)^{1/2}} = 4(p_x)^{-1/2}. \tag{8.68}$$

Now, suppose we let p_x increase to $4 in equation 8.67:

$$S^* = 8[(4)^{1/2} - 1] = 8(2 - 1) = \$8. \tag{8.69}$$

And if we integrate the compensated demand function (equation 8.68) over the price change,

$$\int_1^4 x_c^* dp_x = \int_1^4 4(p_x)^{-1/2} dp_x = 2(4)(p^{1/2})\big|_1^4$$
$$= 8[(4)^{1/2} - (1)^{1/2}] = 8(2 - 1) = \$8, \tag{8.70}$$

which is the same as the value of S^* derived in equation 8.69.

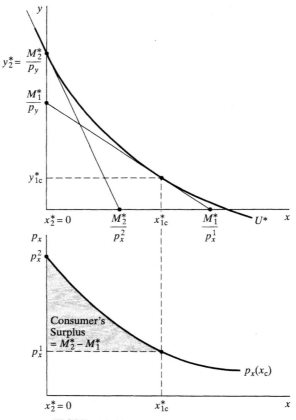

FIGURE 8.15   Consumer's Surplus

Compensation and Consumer's Surplus   Suppose now that we could find the income compensation such that the consumer would be just indifferent between the original consumption at the original price and zero units of X at the price at which the consumer demands zero units. In order for a consumer to choose zero units of a good, however, the consumer's compensated demand curve must cross the price axis. We have drawn the compensated demand curve approaching the axes asymptotically because we often draw indifference curves this way; however, the theory does not rule out the possibility that indifference curves could cross the axes, as we showed in developing Kuhn-Tucker conditions in Section 3.7 and Figures 3.17 and 3.18. Moreover, this situation actually is more plausible with many goods, since it allows for the possibility that a consumer would choose zero units of a good for some income and price combinations. If the indifference curves and the compensated demand curve do cross the vertical axis, it turns out that the compensating income change is the same as the area above the original price line and beneath the compensated demand curve. Figure 8.15 illustrates this point. The consumer begins at (x_{1c}^*, y_{1c}^*) with utility U^*, income M_1^*, and prices p_x^1 and p_y. If price were to go up to p_x^2, the consumer would choose zero units of X and y_{2c}^* units of Y, with compensation to an income of M_2^* in order to stay at utility level U^*. The optimal subsidy $S^* = M_2^* - M_1^*$ is equal to the shaded area in the bottom graph.

We call the shaded area **consumer's surplus.** The idea is that the consumer is indifferent between two situations: one in which the consumer has a low income M_1^*, pays a low price p_x^1, and consumes x_1^*; and the situation in which the consumer has a high income M_2^*, but the price is so high that zero units of X are consumed. The difference between the two incomes can be thought of as an implied benefit (or surplus) the consumer receives from making purchases at p_x^1.

Marginal Willingness-to-Pay and Marginal Benefit   Another way of looking at consumer's surplus is to suppose the consumer begins with M_2^* income and zero units of X. The consumer is then asked, on a take-it-or-leave-it basis, what the maximum is that he or she would be willing to pay for the right to purchase x_1^* units at a price of p_x^1. The consumer would be willing to pay up to $CS = S^* = M_2^* - M_1^*$ because at income M_1^* and price p_x^1, the consumer is just indifferent between x_1^* at that income and price and zero units of X with an income of M_2^*.

Alternatively, we could analyze a consumer's willingness-to-pay one unit at a time. At a sufficiently high price for good X, the consumer is not willing to purchase any units of X. The price falls by Δp_x and the consumer is now willing to purchase 1 unit at the lower price. The new lower price is the consumer's willingness to pay for the first unit. If the price falls again, the consumer is willing to purchase a second unit. The second lower price is the consumer's willingness to pay for the second unit and the total willingness to pay for the two units is the consumer's willingness to pay for the first unit plus the consumer's willingness to pay for the second unit. It turns out that each time the price drops, the compensated demand curve indicates how much the consumer is willing to pay to purchase an additional unit. The total willingness to pay is the sum of the individual willingnesses to pay for successive individual units.

For this reason, the compensated demand curve is often referred to as a **marginal willingness-to-pay** function or a **marginal benefit** function. It is called a marginal willingness-to-pay function because points along the compensated demand curve tell the maximum price a consumer is willing to pay for each additional unit of a good purchased. The reason the consumer is willing to pay that additional amount is because, having paid that amount and gotten an additional unit, the consumer is just as well off as before that last purchase was made. The compensated demand curve is called a marginal benefit function because each additional amount the consumer pays would represent additional consumer's surplus if the price were 0.

Continuing with the example illustrated in Figure 8.15, suppose the consumer starts with income M_2^*. This time the consumer is presented with each unit, one at a time, and forced to pay the maximum he or she would be willing to pay for that unit or not get it. For each unit, the consumer would pay the price along the vertical axis associated with that unit; and, ending up purchasing a total of x_1^* units, the consumer would pay in all $p_x^1 x_1^* + S^* = p_x^1 x_1^* + CS$, that is, the usual amount for $x_1^*(p_x^1 x_1^*)$ *plus* the consumer's surplus ($S^* = CS$). Figure 8.16 illustrates this point. The consumer is willing to pay p_x^1 for unit 1, p_x^2 for unit 2, p_x^3 for unit 3, and so on down to p_x^n for unit n. For discrete units, the consumer ends up paying the area under the step function connecting the

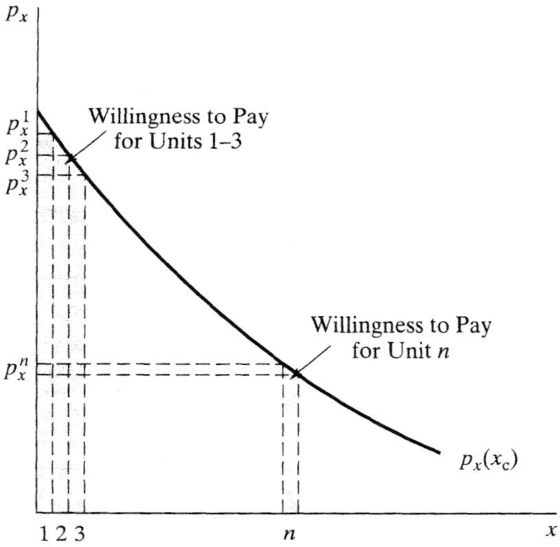

FIGURE 8.16   The Compensated Demand Curve as a Willingness-to-pay Function

combinations of unit price and quantity. However, if the units were infinitesimally small, each unit would be represented as a point on the demand curve and the consumer would end up paying the entire area under the demand curve.

A Change in Consumer's Surplus and the Optimal Subsidy   Since consumer's surplus represents the maximum additional amount a consumer would pay along the compensated demand curve, consumer's surplus is taken to be a measure of the net benefit a consumer gets from being able to make all purchases at market prices. Changes in consumer's surplus resulting from changes in price are taken to represent losses or gains in "welfare" associated with price changes. Figure 8.15 shows the optimal subsidy as the integral along the vertical axis of the demand curve between p_x^1 and p_x^2. Since a change in consumer's surplus between two prices will be the same as the optimal subsidy for the same price change, the change in consumer's surplus is also equal to the integral over that range:

$$\Delta CS = S^* = \int_{p_x^1}^{p_x^2} x_c^*(p_x)\,dp_x. \tag{8.71}$$

Figure 8.17 illustrates the change in consumer's surplus. The consumer begins at (x_{1c}^*, p_x^1) along the compensated demand curve. At that price, the consumer's surplus is the area under the demand curve above p_x^1. If price goes up to p_x^2, the new consumer's surplus is the area under the demand curve above p_x^2. The change in consumer's surplus is the shaded area.

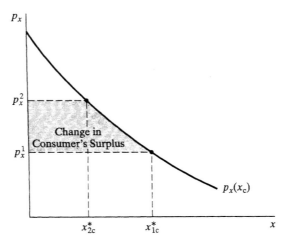

FIGURE 8.17 **Illustration of a Change in Consumer's Surplus**

PRACTICAL APPLICATIONS OF CONSUMER'S SURPLUS ANALYSIS

As derived in Section 8.9, the concept of consumer's surplus is a useful measure of consumer benefits or losses from policy changes. Specifically, a change in consumer's surplus tells exactly how much a consumer would have to be compensated in order to be just as well off after the price change as before. If price falls, it tells how much the consumer would be willing to pay to enjoy the lower price. If price rises, it tells how much compensation there would have to be. As a practical matter, compensated demand curves for individual consumers are not directly observable; however, they can be estimated by first estimating the ordinary demand function and the Engel curve for that consumer and then by finding the slope of the compensated demand function as the remainder from the Slutsky equation.

Estimating Compensated Demand Elasticity Typically, when this technique is used, the own-price and income elasticities are estimated empirically, and then a compensated own-price elasticity is estimated using the empirical estimates plus data on the share of income devoted to a particular good. The equation used to estimate the compensated own-price elasticity is derived from the Slutsky equation (equation 8.42). Rewriting (8.42) in partial derivatives,

$$\frac{\partial x}{\partial p_x} = \frac{\partial x_c}{\partial p_x} - x^* \frac{\partial x}{\partial M}. \tag{8.72}$$

To convert (8.72) to elasticities, we first multiply both sides by p_x/x:

$$\frac{\partial x}{\partial p_x} \frac{p_x}{x} = \frac{\partial x_c}{\partial p_x} \frac{p_x}{x} - x^* \frac{\partial x}{\partial M} \frac{p_x}{x}. \tag{8.73}$$

Now, let

$$\epsilon_u = \text{uncompensated own-price demand elasticity}$$

ϵ_c = compensated own-price demand elasticity

ϵ_M = income elasticity.

Then, (8.73) becomes

$$\epsilon_u = \epsilon_c - \frac{\partial x}{\partial M} p_x. \tag{8.74}$$

Now, multiply the income term in (8.74) by $(M/x) \cdot (x/M) = 1$:

$$\epsilon_u = \epsilon_c - \frac{\partial x}{\partial M} p_m \frac{M}{x} \frac{x}{M} \tag{8.75}$$

$$= \epsilon_c - \epsilon_M \frac{p_x x}{M}.$$

Therefore, after rearranging terms in (8.75),

$$\epsilon_c = \epsilon_u + \epsilon_M \frac{p_x x}{M}. \tag{8.76}$$

This means that the compensated own-price demand elasticity equals the uncompensated own-price demand elasticity plus the income elasticity times the percentage of income spent on good X. These elasticities might be estimated as the coefficients of a log-linear demand function. The resulting estimate for the compensated elasticity can then be used to construct a generalized, Cobb-Douglas, compensated demand function.

Uncompensated Consumer's Surplus   In practice, however, the technique summarized in equation 8.76 is rarely used, largely because it is too costly to collect enough data about individual consumers to make those estimates. Instead, policy analysts typically use market ordinary (uncompensated) demand curves to estimate consumer's surplus and then treat the estimate as though it were the true measure derived above. So, given that consumer's surplus is generally estimated from the market ordinary demand curve, we need to know how much difference it makes to use this imperfect indicator of welfare change.

Figure 8.18 illustrates the difference between compensated and uncompensated consumer's surplus loss for a single consumer if price increases for a normal good. The consumer begins at x_1^* along indifference curve U_1^* at income M_1 and prices p_x^1 and p_y. When price goes up to p_x^2, if income is simultaneously increased to M_2, the consumer chooses x_{2c}^* along U_1^*. But, if income is still M_1, the consumer chooses x_{2u}^* along U_2^* instead. Moreover, because the income effect is to reduce quantity demanded when price increases, x_{2u}^* must be less than x_{2c}^*. Similarly, if p_x were to increase once again, the uncompensated choice would be less than the compensated choice. Thus, the uncompensated demand curve must lie to the left of the compensated demand curve for prices greater than the price at the anchor point. This means that the loss of *uncompensated* consumer's surplus from a price increase for a normal good must always be *less* than the loss of *compensated* consumer's surplus.

This point is also illustrated by continuing the numerical example used to show that the optimal subsidy is the same as the compensated change in consumer's surplus.

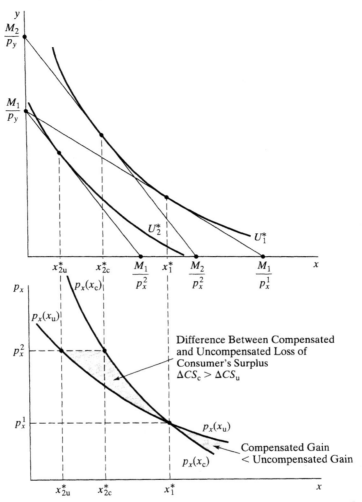

FIGURE 8.18 **Comparison of Compensated and Uncompensated Consumer's Surplus for a Normal Good**

We found in equation 8.69 that if the utility function is $U = xy$, income is $8, and if the price of X increases from $1 to $4, the optimal subsidy or compensated loss of consumer's surplus is $8. Now, to find the uncompensated loss of consumer's surplus, we integrate the ordinary demand curve for X from equations 8.5 from $1 to $4:

$$\Delta CS_u = \int_1^4 \frac{M}{2p_x} \, dp_x = \frac{8}{2} \ln p_x \big|_1^4 = 4(1.386 - 0). \tag{8.77}$$

Thus, comparing equations 8.70 and 8.77,

$$\Delta CS_u = 5.544 < 8 = \Delta CS_c.$$

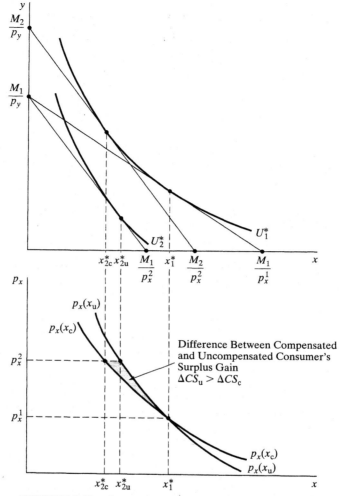

FIGURE 8.19   Comparison of Compensated and Uncompensated Consumer's Surplus for an Inferior Good

Notice also in Figure 8.18 that if price falls for a normal good, the uncompensated demand curve lies above the compensated demand curve. That means that the *uncompensated gain* from a price reduction will always be *greater* than the *compensated gain*. Thus, to the extent that government projects will tend to change the prices of goods that are normal for all consumers, the use of market uncompensated consumer's surplus consistently *understates losses* and *overstates gains*. This means that, overall, more projects would be recommended than would be justified by the "correct" measure.

Figure 8.19 illustrates that the opposite is true if the good is inferior. In this case, the uncompensated choice at each price above the anchor price must be *greater* than the compensated choice. That means that the uncompensated demand curve will lie above the compensated demand curve for price increases and uncompensated consumer's surplus will be *greater* than compensated consumer's surplus.

The use of market instead of individual demand curves further complicates our interpretation of consumer's surplus. The problem is that a market demand function is constructed by adding up the quantities demanded by each consumer at each price. When uncompensated consumer's surplus is used as the measure for one consumer, it biases the result by the income effect for that individual. Adding up across individuals adds all the different consumer income effects.

No Income Effects   The only time that uncompensated consumer's surplus calculated along a market demand curve correctly measures welfare gains and losses is when there are no income effects associated with a price change for any consumer. This is illustrated for one consumer in Figure 8.20. In the upper graph, we see that quantity

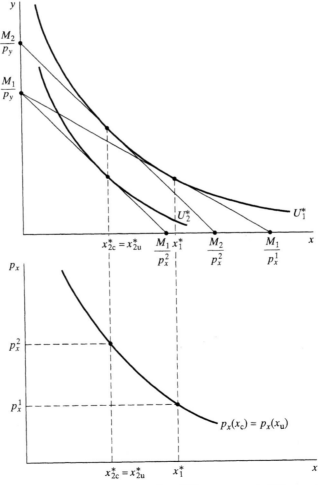

FIGURE 8.20   Compensated and Uncompensated Demand Curves Are Identical When There Are No Income Effects

demanded of X is independent of income. This implies, in the lower graph, that $x_c^* = x_u^*$ at every price and the two demand curves are identical. If this is true for every consumer, then there is no problem adding across consumers because each individual consumer's surplus change is expressed in monetary terms.

In effect, when uncompensated consumer's surplus analysis is used in policy analysis, there is an implied assumption that income effects are either very small or nonexistent.[3] Since it is unlikely that everyone would have no income effects, the question is whether there are reasonable circumstances under which income effects can appropriately be ignored. Basically, it comes down to how much the price will be affected by the policy change and how much the quantity will be affected by the price change. For example, if a policy is only going to change price by a small amount, and if the income and price elasticities are relatively small (or if the good in question represents a small proportion of the average consumer's budget), then there is not likely to be much difference between the compensated and the uncompensated demand curves in the relevant price range. In that case, uncompensated consumer surplus loss or gain is not likely to be a poor estimate of compensated loss or gain. On the other hand, if a policy is going to result in a large change in the price of a good on which people spend a high proportion of their incomes (for example, housing), then the uncompensated estimate may very well be seriously biased.

8.11   ANOTHER WORKED PROBLEM INVOLVING EXPENDITURE MINIMIZATION

In this section, we develop another example, using a different utility function. Suppose the consumer's utility function is

$$U = \frac{xy}{x + y}.$$

The Lagrangian for the expenditure minimization problem is

$$\mathcal{L} = p_x x + p_y y + \lambda \left(U - \frac{xy}{x + y} \right).$$

The first-order conditions are

$$\frac{\partial \mathcal{L}}{\partial x} = p_x - \lambda \left[\frac{y(x + y) - xy}{(x + y)^2} \right] = 0$$

$$\frac{\partial \mathcal{L}}{\partial y} = p_y - \lambda \left[\frac{x(x + y) - xy}{(x + y)^2} \right] = 0$$

$$\frac{\partial \mathcal{L}}{\partial \lambda} = U - \frac{xy}{(x + y)} = 0.$$

Solving for λ,

$$\lambda = \frac{p_x(x + y)^2}{y^2} = \frac{p_y(x + y)^2}{x^2}.$$

---

[3]For an example of this argument, see Robert Willig, "Consumer's Surplus Without Apology," *American Economic Review* 66(1976):589–97.

Thus,

$$\frac{y^2}{x^2} = \frac{p_x}{p_y} \quad \Rightarrow \quad y^* = \left(\frac{p_x}{p_y}\right)^{1/2} x^*$$

$$U - \frac{x[(p_x/p_y)^{1/2}x]}{x + (p_x/p_y)^{1/2}x} = 0.$$

And

$$U = \frac{x^2(p_x/p_y)^{1/2}}{\dfrac{x[(p_x)^{1/2} + (p_y)^{1/2}]}{(p_y)^{1/2}}} = x\frac{(p_x)^{1/2}}{(p_x)^{1/2} + (p_y)^{1/2}}$$

$$x^* = U\frac{(p_x)^{1/2} + (p_y)^{1/2}}{(p_x)^{1/2}} \qquad \text{the compensated demand function for X}$$

$$y^* = \left(\frac{p_x}{p_y}\right)^{1/2} x^* = U\frac{(p_x)^{1/2} + (p_y)^{1/2}}{(p_y)^{1/2}} \qquad \text{the compensated demand function for Y}$$

$$M^* = p_x\left[U\frac{(p_x)^{1/2} + (p_y)^{1/2}}{(p_x)^{1/2}} \right] + p_y\left[U\frac{(p_x)^{1/2} + (p_y)^{1/2}}{(p_y)^{1/2}} \right]$$

$$= U[(p_x)^{1/2} + (p_y)^{1/2}]^2. \qquad \text{the expenditure function}$$

8.12 ___ REVIEW OF KEY CONCEPTS

This completes the development of the basic theory of consumer demand. In the next chapter, we introduce the concepts of Edgeworth boxes and Pareto optimality. Before continuing to Chapter 9, however, be sure you understand and can use the following key concepts.

When price increases along the ordinary demand curve, the consumer suffers a loss in utility.

Compensation for a price increase is the amount of additional income a consumer would require in order to suffer no loss in utility from a price increase.

The *income-compensated demand function* describes the quantities of a good that a consumer would purchase at different prices if his or her income were changed just enough each time price changed to ensure that he or she remained on the original indifference curve.

The *compensated demand curve is always downward sloping* if preferences obey the axioms of consumer preference.

Diminishing marginal rate of substitution guarantees that quantity demanded decreases as the slope of the tangent price line becomes steeper (that is, as price increases).

The *substitution effect* associated with a price change describes how a consumer's utility-maximizing choice changes if only the price of a good changes, holding utility constant and allowing income to change to keep the consumer on the original indifference curve.

The *income effect* associated with a price change describes how a consumer's utility-maximizing choice changes as a result only of the change in the feasible set. An increase in price reduces the feasible set, while a reduction in price increases it.

The substitution effect is always negative. This means that if the price of a good increases, a consumer *always* demands less of the good according to the substitution effect: he or she always substitutes in favor of the cheaper good along an indifference curve.

The income effect is to reduce quantity demanded if the price of a normal good increases and to increase quantity demanded if the price of an inferior good increases. This happens because the feasible set is reduced if the price increases.

A normal good always has a downward-sloping demand curve because both the income and substitution effects act to reduce quantity demanded when price increases.

An inferior good can have an upward-sloping demand curve if the income effect of increasing quantity demanded when income falls outweighs the substitution effect of reducing quantity demanded when price increases. On the other hand, if the substitution effect outweighs the income effect, demand will be downward sloping even for an inferior good.

A good with an upward-sloping demand curve is referred to as a *Giffen good*. Giffen goods must always be inferior goods.

The substitution effect is a movement along the income compensated demand curve, and the income effect is a movement along the Engel curve.

The *indirect utility function* describes the maximum utility for every combination of income and prices. It is the solution to the utility maximization problem, expressed as a function of what were originally parameters, prices and income.

The dual to utility maximization is to minimize expenditures, subject to a utility constraint.

The solution to the consumer's dual problem (M^*) is the minimum income required to maintain utility at $\overline{U}$.

Generalized compensated demand functions are found as part of the solution to the consumer's dual problem. They are functions of prices and utility.

The consumer's *expenditure function* describes the minimum income (M^*) as a function of prices and utility.

If U^* in the primal problem equals $\overline{U}$ in the dual problem and if M^* in the dual problem equals $\overline{M}$ in the primal problem, then the generalized uncompensated quantities demanded must equal the generalized compensated quantities demanded since the primal and dual optimal choices must be the same.

One way to solve for compensated demand functions, holding utility and all but one price constant, is to "anchor" the compensated demand functions around the utility-maximizing choice for one particular combination of income and prices. This generates compensated demand curves that do not depend explicitly on utility.

Using the anchoring method requires that an original parametric price and a variable price be kept separate. Otherwise the anchoring feature is lost.

An optimal *subsidy* can be calculated as the difference between the minimum income required to maintain a constant level of utility and the original income used to anchor the compensated demand functions. This describes the amount of money that must be rebated (if prices rise) or taken away (if prices fall) in order to maintain a given level of utility.

The *Slutsky equation* summarizes the relationships among the slope of the ordinary demand curve, the slope of the income-compensated demand curve, and the slope of the Engel curve.

By *Hotelling's lemma*, the derivative of the expenditure function with respect to each of the prices is equal to each of the individual quantities demanded. This result follows from the envelope theorem.

The existence of a Giffen good requires both that the good be inferior and that it be consumed in relatively large quantities.

The *substitution elasticity* or *elasticity of substitution* along an indifference curve measures the percentage change in the ratio of y purchases to x purchases in response to a given percentage change in the price ratio, p_x/p_y.

The elasticity of substitution can vary from 0, with "square" indifference curves, to infinity, with indifference curves that are linear.

The optimal subsidy required to maintain a given level of utility as price increases from p_x^1 to p_x^2 is the same as the integral over the compensated demand function from p_x^1 to p_x^2.

Consumer's surplus is the amount of income a consumer would need as compensation in order to be just indifferent between consuming a positive quantity of a good at a lower price *and* zero units of the good at a sufficiently high price. It is calculated as the integral over the compensated demand function between the lower price and the price intercept.

Intuitively, consumer's surplus represents the (implied) benefit a consumer gets from consuming positive units of the good at a lower price.

The compensated demand curve is often referred to as a *marginal willingness-to-pay* function because it describes the maximum a consumer is willing to pay for each unit of a good (including the reduction in income compensation each time price falls).

The compensated demand curve is also often called a *marginal benefit* function because it represents the marginal consumer's surplus (if the good were provided at no cost).

A change in consumer's surplus associated with a price change is taken as representing the net gain or loss in "welfare" (expressed as the change in compensating income) associated with that price change.

A change in consumer's surplus tells exactly how much a consumer would have to be compensated to be just as well off after a price change as before. In other words, consumer's surplus is equal to the optimal subsidy.

The compensated demand curve can be estimated by combining own-price, uncompensated demand elasticity, income elasticity, and the share of income spent on the good. Compensated elasticity equals uncompensated elasticity plus income elasticity times the share of income.

Many policy applications substitute the ordinary demand curve for the compensated demand curve in consumer's surplus calculations.

Using uncompensated consumer's surplus underestimates welfare losses and overestimates welfare gains if a good is normal.

The use of uncompensated consumer's surplus is accurate only if there are no income effects.

Uncompensated consumer's surplus analysis may legitimately be used as an estimate of welfare changes in situations where income effects are judged to be "small."

8.13 QUESTIONS FOR DISCUSSION

1. Suppose you are hired by your state government to study the benefits of developing a new state park. The state has an estimate of how much it will cost to develop the park and will only undertake the project if the benefit to consumers (even if they pay no user fees) exceeds the cost. What information would you need to develop an accurate benefit estimate, and what technique would you use once the data are collected?

2. Suppose you are working as a consultant to Congress on the development of tax policy. You have been asked to estimate the cost to

consumers of an increase in the federal gasoline tax, but the only information available to you is market demand information. Can you use this information to make a reasonably accurate estimate of the cost? If so, how? If not, why not?

3. Is the substitution effect or the income effect more important in accounting for downward-sloping demand? Explain.

4. Can you think of decision problems that would be made more understandable if you analyzed them in terms of income and substitution effects? Illustrate one such choice.

8.14 _____ PROBLEMS

Problems 1–4 Let $U = xy^2$.

1. Derive the indirect utility function as a function of p_x, p_y, and M.
2. Derive the generalized compensated demand functions for X and Y as functions of p_x, p_y, and U.
3. Derive the expenditure function as a function of p_x, p_y, and U.
4. Derive the function for the subsidy necessary to keep a consumer on one indifference curve.

Problems 5–9 Using the utility function $U = xy^2$, let $p_x = \$2, p_y = \$3$, and $M = \$200$ to begin with.

5. Find the utility-maximizing consumption bundle at those prices and income.
6. Now, let p_x increase to \$4, leaving p_y at \$3. Find the income and substitution effects of that price change, the income necessary to maintain the original indifference curve at the higher price, and the subsidy necessary to restore the consumer to that indifference curve.
7. Find the substitution elasticity.
8. Find the compensated loss of consumer's surplus associated with the price increase.
9. Find the uncompensated loss of consumer's surplus associated with the price increase and compare it with your answer to Problem 8.

8.15 _____ LOGICAL AND MATHEMATICAL APPLICATIONS

1. Suppose that as a student you receive ten tickets to home basketball games for free. You may either use them to attend the games or sell them at the going "scalpers'" price. Assume that, in one year, you attend some of the games and sell some of your tickets. Assume also that your decision to attend individual games does not depend on such factors as standing or opponents. If the price at which you can sell your tickets increases, analyze the effect of this increase in price on the number of games you choose to attend.

2. Suppose you are a collector (cars, cameras, coins, etc.). Sometimes you buy items for your collection, and sometimes you sell items in your collection to other collectors. You are "in equilibrium" as a collector if you are currently neither a buyer nor a seller. Show that if you are in equilibrium, you cannot suffer a loss in utility from an increase in the price of items you generally collect.

3. Suppose two consumers have the same income and choose the same utility-maximizing consumption bundle. They have different substitution elasticities, however. Now, suppose that the price of X increases and that they also both choose the same utility-maximizing consumption bundle _after_ the price increase. Show graphically that the consumer with the smaller substitution elasticity requires the _larger_ income subsidy to restore him to his original indifference curve after the price increase.

4. Let $U = x^{1/2} + y$. Show that for good X, compensated and uncompensated consumer's surplus would be the same and explain why they are the same.

5. Suppose X is an inferior good. Show that if p_x falls, the uncompensated consumer's surplus gain is less than the compensated consumer's surplus gain.

6. Suppose the estimated ordinary demand function for local bus service (measured in rides per day) is given by

$$r(p_r) = 5000 - 1000p_r.$$

The current price per ride is \$1, the average rider spends about 0.5% of his or her income on bus service each year, and the income elasticity of demand for bus service is about 0.2. Find an estimate for the compensated elasticity of demand at the current price, and then construct a linear approximation for the compensated demand function based on that elasticity estimate. (Hint: Use the current price to convert elasticity into slope.) Then, calculate an estimate for the compensated loss of consumer's surplus if the price of a ride is increased to $1.50, and compare that to the uncompensated loss of consumer's surplus for the same price increase. Explain why the difference is so small.

Chapter 9

EFFICIENCY AND TRADE: AN APPLICATION OF CONSUMER DEMAND THEORY

9.1 WHAT YOU SHOULD LEARN FROM THIS CHAPTER

This chapter introduces you to one of the most important concepts and most important results to be learned from microeconomic theory: *Pareto optimality,* or *efficiency* in consumers' allocations, and its connection to competitive markets. First, we introduce the concept of Pareto optimality in a simple exchange economy involving only two individuals. At an *efficient* or *Pareto optimal* allocation of goods it is not possible to make one person better off without making another person worse off. Next, we show that trade can make consumers better off than if they do not trade. There is no production in this very simple economy; consumers simply begin trading with a set of initial endowments of goods. In most cases, consumers can achieve higher levels of utility if they exchange portions of those endowments with one another. Before trading begins, we say that there exist gains from trade. We show that, if the trading process exhausts all those gains, the resulting allocation is Pareto optimal. Given the allocation of initial endowments, the trading process does an efficient job of allocating goods among consumers: it is no longer possible to make one person better off without making another person worse off.

One difference between the material presented in previous chapters on consumer demand and the material presented in this chapter is that previous chapters used *partial equilibrium* analysis and this chapter introduces *general equilibrium* analysis. In a partial equilibrium analysis all variables except the price of one good or consumer income are held constant and we study the impact of a price or income change on the quantity demanded of one good, assuming all other variables are held constant. In a general equilibrium analysis, all relevant variables are allowed to change simultaneously until a *general competitive equilibrium,* in which supply and demand are equated in all markets, is reached.

By the end of this chapter, you should understand the concept of Pareto optimality, have an appreciation for some of the benefits of trade, and have some understanding of how prices get established in simple markets. The only new tool developed in this chapter is graphical: the Edgeworth box. Everything else simply uses the tools of demand theory developed in Chapters 6, 7, and 8. If that material is clear, this chapter should not be technically difficult. If that material is still not clear, you should review it before beginning this chapter.

9.2 ___ EFFICIENCY

Recall that in Section 4.3 we said that an allocation is **efficient,** or **Pareto optimal,** if it is not possible to make one person better off without making at least one other person worse off. To better understand the concept of Pareto optimality, we begin by developing the two-consumer, two-good case graphically. Next, we develop mathematically the properties of a Pareto optimum with two consumers and two goods. Finally, we expand to n consumers and m goods.

Constructing an Edgeworth Box   To illustrate a Pareto optimum we develop a new graphical tool. Consider a rectangle of dimensions $\bar{x}$ by $\bar{y}$ representing the total amounts of goods X and Y available for distribution to two consumers in a simple two-good economy. Economists call this rectangle an **Edgeworth box,** after a nineteenth-century economist who developed much of the graphical analysis of consumer demand theory that we use today.[1] This Edgeworth box, shown in Figure 9.1, describes all the feasible ways to allocate X and Y between A and B, given the total amounts available.

One way to understand how the Edgeworth box is constructed is to think of all the possible allocations for person A which range from $(0, 0)$ in the lower left-hand corner to $(\bar{x}, \bar{y})$ in the upper right-hand corner. There is a similar set of possible allocations for person B that has been turned 180° and then moved until the size of the Edgeworth box is $\bar{x}$ by $\bar{y}$; that is, all the X and Y available in this two-person, two-good example. Figure 9.2 illustrates how the Edgeworth box is constructed by turning the possible set of allocations for person B 180°. An allocation of $(0, 0)$ to person A and $(\bar{x}, \bar{y})$ to person B is represented by the lower left-hand corner, and an allocation of $(0, 0)$ to person B and $(\bar{x}, \bar{y})$ to person A is represented by the upper right-hand corner. A gets more of both goods as we move in a northeastern direction and B gets more of both goods as we move in a southwestern direction.

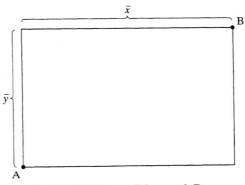

FIGURE 9.1   An Edgeworth Box

---

[1]Francis Ysidro Edgeworth, *Mathematical Psychics: An Essay on the Application of Mathematics to the Moral Sciences* (London, 1881).

Every point, either within the Edgeworth box or along any side, represents a possible division of goods X and Y between the two consumers that uses up all the X and Y available. For example, one possible division illustrated in the right panel of Figure 9.2 allocates (x_A, y_A), which represents 1/3 of the available X and 2/3 of the available Y, to person A, and (x_B, y_B), which represents 2/3 of the available X and 1/3 of the available Y, to person B. As we move right (east) from this point, A gets more X and B gets less. As we move left (west), B gets more X and A gets less. As we move up (north), A gets more Y and B gets less. As we move down (south), B gets more Y and A gets less.

Now, suppose both A and B have preferences that obey the assumptions of the model developed in Chapter 5. We can represent A's indifference curves as increasing in a northeastern direction from the lower left $(0,0)$ point toward the upper right corner $(\bar{x}, \bar{y})$. B's indifference curves are turned 180°, as in Figure 9.2, increasing in a southwestern direction from the upper right $(0, 0)$ point toward the lower left corner $(\bar{x}, \bar{y})$. This representation is appropriate because each consumer's allocation of both goods increases as we move in the respective direction of increasing preference. Figure 9.3 illustrates how we bring together A's and B's indifference curves to form two sets of indifference curves within the Edgeworth box. For person A, $U_{A5} > U_{A4} > U_{A3} > U_{A2} > U_{A1}$. Similarly, for person B, $U_{B5} > U_{B4} > U_{B3} > U_{B2} > U_{B1}$.

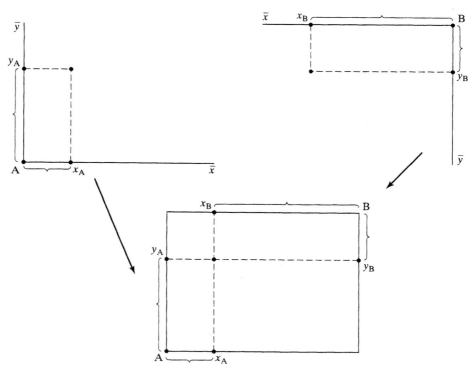

FIGURE 9.2   Constructing an Edgeworth Box by Turning Allocations for Person B 180° and Identifying a Point in the Box

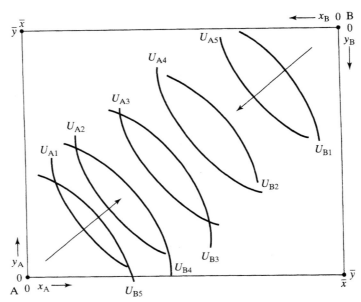

FIGURE 9.3 Indifference Curves in an Edgeworth Box

Finding a Pareto Optimum in an Edgeworth Box Now we develop an illustration of Pareto optimality in the Edgeworth box. We are looking for a point in the Edgeworth box that represents an allocation of X and Y between the two consumers that has the property that it is not possible to make one of the consumers better off without making the other consumer worse off. Let's start with the point (x_A, y_A), (x_B, y_B), illustrated in the bottom panel of Figure 9.2. One indifference curve for person A and one indifference curve for person B pass through that point. These indifference curves are shown in Figure 9.4 as U_A and U_B, passing through the point (x_A, y_A), (x_B, y_B). Notice the lens-shaped shaded area to the southeast of that point. Any point within the shaded area represents an alternative allocation that would place both consumers on higher indifference curves and thus make both consumers better off than on U_A and U_B. For now, we will refer to this area as representing potential gains from reallocating or redistributing goods X and Y. Later, we show why we also refer to this area as representing gains from exchange or **gains from trade.**

One way to find a point within the Edgeworth box with the property that it is not possible to make one person better off without making the other person worse off is to hold one person's utility constant and then maximize the other person's utility subject to the constraint that the first person's utility is held constant. For example, we could hold person B's utility in Figure 9.4 constant at $\overline{U}_B$ and then maximize person A's utility by moving to higher and higher indifference curves for person A along the surface of $\overline{U}_B$. This is shown in Figure 9.5. We start at the point (x_A, y_A), (x_B, y_B), identified in Figure 9.4, and number the indifference curve for person A passing through it as U_{A1}. We can increase person A's utility by moving to higher numbered indifference curves

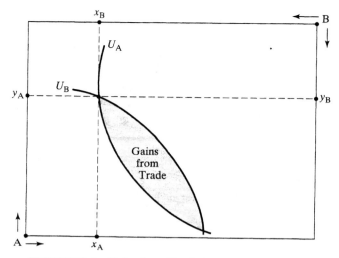

FIGURE 9.4   Gains from Trade in an Edgeworth Box

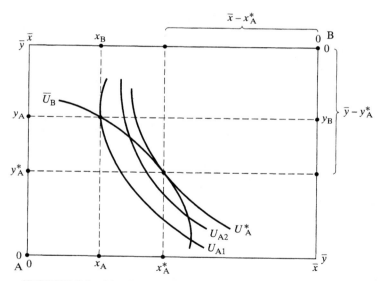

FIGURE 9.5   Identifying a Pareto Optimum by Maximizing A's Utility Subject to a Given Level of B's Utility

for person A along $\overline{U}_B$. The highest utility A can achieve without reducing B's utility below $\overline{U}_B$ is U_A^*, yielding allocation (x_A^*, y_A^*) for person A. This leaves $(\overline{x} - x_A^*, \overline{y} - y_A^*)$ for person B.

We have seen in previous discussions of constrained optimization that a constrained optimum is achieved when the level surface of the objective function is tangent

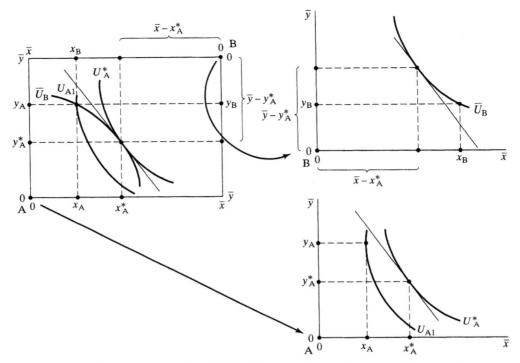

FIGURE 9.6 **Illustration that A's and B's Indifference Curves Have Equal Slopes at the Point of Tangency**

to the level surface of the constraint. In this example, a constrained optimum is achieved when the individuals' indifference curves are tangent to one another at the maximum of A's utility (U_A^*) subject to B's utility remaining at $\overline{U}_B$. In previous discussions we also have observed that the slopes of the two functions are equal at a point of tangency. In this case, however, the two functions are not illustrated on the same axes. Thus, to show that the slopes of the two indifference curves are indeed equal at the point of tangency illustrated in Figure 9.5, we must show that the slopes of the tangent functions are equal relative to the same axes. In the left panel of Figure 9.6 we show the tangency illustrated in Figure 9.5, with a tangent line sketched. In the right panel we rotate person B's indifference curves back 180° and show that the two tangent lines have the same slope. Moreover, since the slopes of the indifference curves are equal at the point of tangency, we know from Section 5.5 that the marginal rates of substitution are also equal at the point of tangency.

While the point $(x_A^*, y_A^*), (\overline{x} - x_A^*, \overline{y} - y_A^*)$ represents one possible Pareto optimum, in fact, every point of tangency between one of A's indifference curves and one of B's indifference curves also represents a Pareto optimum. Figure 9.7 illustrates this point. Each $\overline{U}_B$, from the point $(0, 0)$ for person B $(\overline{U}_{B0})$ in the upper right corner to the point $(\overline{x}, \overline{y})$ for person B $(\overline{U}_{B5})$ in the lower left corner, represents a level of B's utility against which to maximize A's utility. Maximization of A's utility against each possible given level of B's utility is illustrated by the series of U_A^*'s from U_{A0}^*, tangent

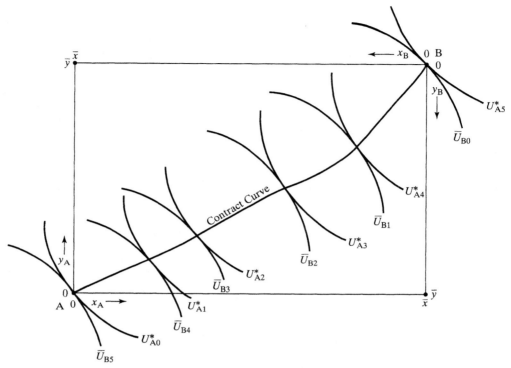

FIGURE 9.7   Pareto Optimal Points and the Contract Curve in an Edgeworth Box

to $\overline{U}_{B5}$, to U^*_{A5}, tangent to $\overline{U}_{B0}$. The curve running from the lower left corner to the upper right corner goes through all possible points of tangency. We refer to this curve as the **contract curve** for reasons that will be addressed below.

Mathematical Properties of a Pareto Optimum   We now consider the mathematical derivation of a Pareto optimum. We illustrated the derivation graphically by maximizing person A's utility subject to the constraint that person B's utility remained at a given level. In our two-person, two-good example, the mathematical problem is

$$\max U_A(x_A, y_A) \tag{9.1}$$
$$\text{s.t. } U_B(x_B, y_B) = \overline{U}_B$$
$$x_A + x_B \quad = \overline{x} \quad \Rightarrow \quad x_B = \overline{x} - x_A$$
$$y_A + y_B \quad = \overline{y} \quad \Rightarrow \quad y_B = \overline{y} - y_A.$$

The last two constraints, which must also be satisfied, guarantee that the total amounts of X and Y distributed to the two consumers equal the total amounts available.

Substituting for the last two conditions in person B's utility function, the Lagrangian is

$$\mathcal{L} = U_A(x_A, y_A) + \lambda[U_B(\overline{x} - x_A, \overline{y} - y_A) - \overline{U}_B]. \tag{9.2}$$

The first two first-order conditions are

$$\frac{\partial \mathscr{L}}{\partial x_A} = \frac{\partial U_A}{\partial x_A} + \lambda \frac{\partial U_B}{\partial x_B} \frac{\partial x_B}{\partial x_A} = 0 \qquad \text{by the chain rule} \qquad (9.3)$$

$$\frac{\partial \mathscr{L}}{\partial y_A} = \frac{\partial U_A}{\partial y_A} + \lambda \frac{\partial U_B}{\partial y_B} \frac{\partial y_B}{\partial y_A} = 0. \qquad \text{by the chain rule} \qquad (9.4)$$

But,

$$x_B = \bar{x} - x_A \implies \frac{\partial x_B}{\partial x_A} = -1 \qquad (9.5)$$

and

$$y_B = \bar{y} - y_A \implies \frac{\partial y_B}{\partial y_A} = -1. \qquad (9.6)$$

Therefore, substituting (9.5) in (9.3) and (9.6) in (9.4),

$$\frac{\partial \mathscr{L}}{\partial x_A} = \frac{\partial U_A}{\partial x_A} - \lambda \frac{\partial U_B}{\partial x_B} = 0 \qquad (9.7)$$

$$\frac{\partial \mathscr{L}}{\partial y_A} = \frac{\partial U_A}{\partial y_A} - \lambda \frac{\partial U_B}{\partial y_B} = 0. \qquad (9.8)$$

Solving for λ from equations 9.7 and 9.8,

$$\lambda = \frac{\partial U_A / \partial x_A}{\partial U_B / \partial x_B} = \frac{\partial U_A / \partial y_A}{\partial U_B / \partial y_B}.$$

Therefore,

$$\frac{MU_{Ax}}{MU_{Ay}} = \frac{MU_{Bx}}{MU_{By}} \implies MRS_A = MRS_B. \qquad (9.9)$$

Thus, the condition that the marginal rate of substitution for person A equals the marginal rate of substitution for person B is a characteristic of a Pareto optimal allocation of goods X and Y in this two-person economy.

The extension to n consumers and m goods is straightforward—maximize one person's utility subject to the constraint that everyone else's utility is kept at some given level for each individual:

$$\max U_1(x_{11}, \ldots, x_{1m})$$
$$\text{s.t } U_2(x_{21}, \ldots, x_{2m}) = \bar{U}_2$$
$$\vdots$$
$$U_n(x_{nl}, \ldots, x_{nm}) = \bar{U}_n$$
$$\left. \begin{array}{l} \vdots \\ \end{array} \right\} \left. \begin{array}{l} x_{nl} = \bar{x}_1 - x_{11} - \cdots - x_{n-1,1} \\ x_{nm} = \bar{x}_m - x_1 m - \cdots - x_{n-1, m} \end{array} \right\} \quad \text{equality constraints.}$$

The results from the first-order conditions for this problem are that the marginal rates of substitution are equal across consumers for all pairs of goods:

$$MRS_{1,\,ij} = \cdots = MRS_{n,\,ij} \qquad i, j = 1, \ldots, m, \quad i \neq j. \tag{9.10}$$

9.3   TRADE IN THE EDGEWORTH BOX

Let's turn now to a simple model of trade between two consumers with only two goods. Each consumer begins with an **initial endowment** of each of the two goods (see Section 4.3), and the two consumers then trade with one another. We can illustrate such an economy graphically and then explain how to extend the model to many consumers and many goods. We assume, for the purpose of developing the theory, that these two consumers behave competitively (that is, they are price takers, which means that they treat prices as parameters). While it is difficult to justify an assumption that two consumers would always behave competitively, this assumption becomes reasonable in the extension to many consumers.

Let

$$X, Y = \text{the goods in the economy,}$$
$$A, B = \text{the consumers in the economy,}$$
$$(\bar{x}_A, \bar{y}_A) = A\text{'s } \textit{initial endowment of } X \text{ and } Y,$$
$$(\bar{x}_B, \bar{y}_B) = B\text{'s } \textit{initial endowment of } X \text{ and } Y,$$
$$\bar{x}_A + \bar{x}_B = \bar{x} = \text{total } X \text{ available,}$$
$$\bar{y}_A + \bar{y}_B = \bar{y} = \text{total } Y \text{ available.}$$

Initial Endowments and Gains from Trade in an Edgeworth Box   Now, we return to Figures 9.2–9.4 and 9.7, in which we identified a point in the Edgeworth box; showed two indifference curves, one from each individual, intersecting at that point; identified a set of points between the two indifference curves representing gains from trade; and defined the contract curve representing all possible Pareto optima in the Edgeworth box. Now, suppose that a given point represents a set of initial endowments $(\bar{x}_A, \bar{y}_A)$ and $(\bar{x}_B, \bar{y}_B)$, in which both consumers have positive amounts of both goods.

Figure 9.8 locates this set of initial endowments as a point (IE) in an Edgeworth box, and shows that U_{A3} for person A and U_{B2} for person B both pass through that point. At this initial allocation, both A and B could be made better off simply by exchanging goods between themselves to reach any other allocation inside the shaded area. That is why we say that there are gains from trade inside the shaded area. Points along the contract curve inside the shaded area in Figure 9.8 exhaust the gains from trade, because at Pareto optimal points it is not possible to make one person better off without making the other person worse off.

Trade and Price Determination Facilitated by an Auctioneer   Suppose a third party were to announce prices for X and Y. (Economists often refer to this third party as the "*auctioneer,*" which could be either a person or a computer.) If A and B were to take

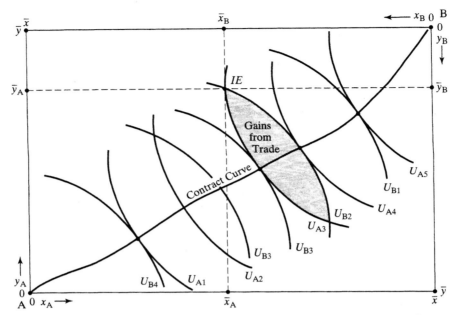

FIGURE 9.8 **The Initial Endowment, Gains from Trade, and the Contract Curve**

those prices as parameters, they could determine what their incomes would be by valuing their initial endowments at those prices. Then they could maximize their utilities subject to the budget constraints defined by those incomes and the announced prices. One way to think of this process (although not the only way) is to imagine that the consumers sell their endowments at the announced prices and then use the resulting incomes to buy their utility-maximizing consumption bundles back at those same prices.

However, since demand functions are homogeneous of degree 0 in income and prices, all sets of prices that preserve the announced price ratio are equivalent for predicting consumer behavior in this model. To see this point, suppose the auctioneer announced individual prices p_x and p_y. Consumer A would, therefore, have income

$$M_A = p_x \bar{x}_A + p_y \bar{y}_A.$$

However, as we showed in Chapter 6 in the discussion of functions that are homogeneous of degree 0, multiplying all prices and income by $1/p_y$ (or any other positive constant) leaves the budget line unchanged. Thus,

$$\frac{M_A}{p_y} = \frac{p_x}{p_y} \bar{x}_A + 1 \bar{y}_A$$

is the same budget equation as

$$M_A = p_x \bar{x}_A + p_y \bar{y}_A.$$

In other words, multiplying both prices by $1/p_y$, we also multiply income by $1/p_y$.

Consumer B's income would be determined in a similar fashion:

$$\frac{M_B}{p_y} = \frac{p_x}{p_y} \bar{x}_B + 1\, \bar{y}_B.$$

Since we can divide every term in the budget equation by p_y and leave the position of the budget line unchanged, only relative prices can be meaningful. Prices p_x and p_y, and the resulting income, M, are equivalent to prices p_x/p_y and 1, and the resulting income, M/p_y. Both sets of prices and income generate the same feasible set and, therefore, the same choices. For that reason, economists often set one of the prices (p_y, for example) equal to 1 and then quote income and other prices as ratios with p_y in the denominator. Of course, setting p_y equal to any other positive constant would have the same effect. This process of expressing income and prices as ratios with one of the prices equal to a positive constant is one example of what is called **normalization.** A common way to normalize prices is by setting one of the prices (for example, p_y) equal to 1.

Setting $p_y = 1$, the consumers' problems become

A: max $U_A(x_A, y_A)$ s.t. $p_x x_A + y_A = p_x \bar{x}_A + \bar{y}_A$

B: max $U_B(x_B, y_B)$ s.t. $p_x x_B + y_B = p_x \bar{x}_B + \bar{y}_B.$

The Consumer's Normalized Budget and Proposed Trades   After normalization, person A has the following budget equation:

$$M_A = p_x \bar{x}_A = \bar{y}_A = p_x x_A + y_A.$$

Person B's budget line is defined analogously:

$$M_B = p_x \bar{x}_B + \bar{y}_B = p_x x_B + y_B.$$

With prices and incomes represented in this way for each consumer, the initial endowment, $(\bar{x}_A, \bar{y}_A)$, and every other point that satisfies each consumer's budget constraint with equality, are points on their respective budget lines defined by those prices and incomes. Thus, we can think of each consumer trading in an Edgeworth box as having a budget line that goes through the initial endowment and has a slope equal to the announced price ratio. Figure 9.9 illustrates consumer A's budget line in just that way.

Consumer B's budget line is constructed the same way and then turned 180° in the Edgeworth box. It is important to note that in the Edgeworth box the two budget lines lie on top of one another, forming one line composed of two budget lines that coincide in the box. Figure 9.10 illustrates an Edgeworth box with an initial endowment and a line through the initial endowment representing both consumers' budget lines.

Each consumer then maximizes utility subject to his or her personal budget constraint and announces what affordable allocation he or she would like to purchase. Figure 9.11 illustrates the difference between the initial allocation and the utility-maximizing consumption bundle for person A. In this example, x_A^* is larger than $\bar{x}_A$, implying that A wants to buy $x_A^* - \bar{x}_A$, in addition to the initial endowment. Assuming positive prices, the budget line is downward sloping. Thus, if x_A^* is larger than $\bar{x}_A$, y_A^* must be less than $\bar{y}_A$, in order for consumer A to remain on this budget line. This implies that A wants to sell, on balance, $\bar{y}_A - y_A^*$. Thus, we say that A proposes to

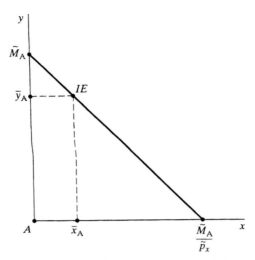

FIGURE 9.9　Consumer A's Budget Line, Given an Announced Price Ratio

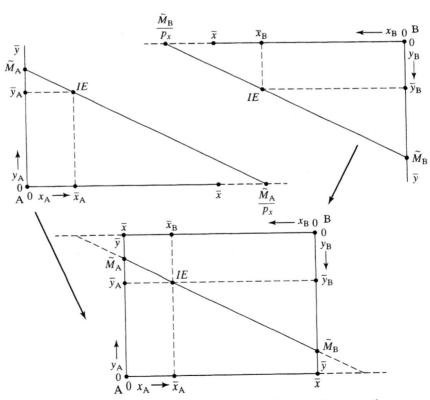

FIGURE 9.10　A Line Through the Initial Endowment Representing Both Consumers' Budget Lines

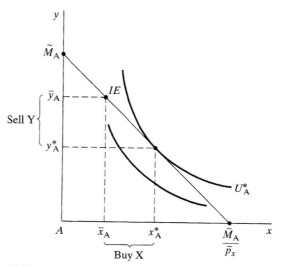

FIGURE 9.11   Choosing a Utility-Maximizing Consumption Bundle, Given an Initial Endowment and an Announced Price Ratio

exchange $(\bar{y}_A - y_A^*)$ for $(x_A^* - \bar{x}_A)$. Note that this notion of exchange (or trade) is equivalent to selling the entire initial endowment $(\bar{x}_A, \bar{y}_A)$ and then purchasing the utility-maximizing consumption bundle (x_A^*, y_A^*). From person A's perspective, we could think of this exchange as a **net purchase** of X and a **net sale** of Y.

Turning to B's choices, x_B^* might be less than $\bar{x}_B$ and y_B^* greater than $\bar{y}_B$, implying that B wants to sell $\bar{x}_B - x_B^*$ and buy $y_B^* - \bar{y}_B$. In other words, B might propose to exchange $(\bar{x}_B - x_B^*)$ for $(y_B^* - \bar{y}_B)$. This proposed exchange for person B is illustrated in Figure 9.12 The left graph illustrates the proposed trade from the normal graphical perspective. The right graph turns the left graph 180° in preparation for putting A and B together in the Edgeworth box.

Searching for an Equilibrium   We have seen in this example that, given the initially announced price ratio, A wants to buy X and sell Y, and B wants to buy Y and sell X. However, there is no reason to believe that the first price ratio announced would lead to a situation such that A would want to buy exactly as much X as B would want to sell and B would want to buy exactly as much Y as A would want to sell. In order for a set of trades to be in **equilibrium,** net supply and demand have to be equal in both markets. This implies that B must want to sell exactly as much X as A wants to buy and that A must want to sell exactly as much Y as B wants to buy. Such an equilibrium would imply the following equations:

$$\text{net } demand(x_A) = x_A^* - \bar{x}_A = \bar{x}_B - x_B^* = \text{net } supply(x_B)$$
$$\text{net } demand(y_B) = y_B^* - \bar{y}_B = \bar{y}_A - y_A^* = \text{net } supply(y_A).$$

If net supply does not equal net demand, the auctioneer must try another price ratio. Figure 9.13 illustrates a situation in which the announced price ratio results in a

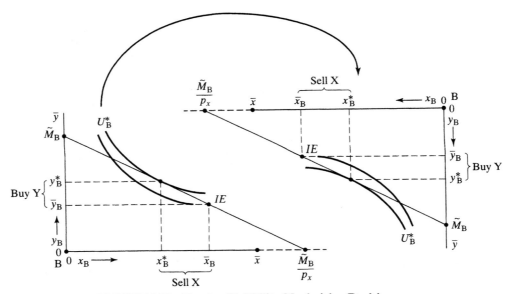

FIGURE 9.12 Turning B's Utility-Maximizing Decision

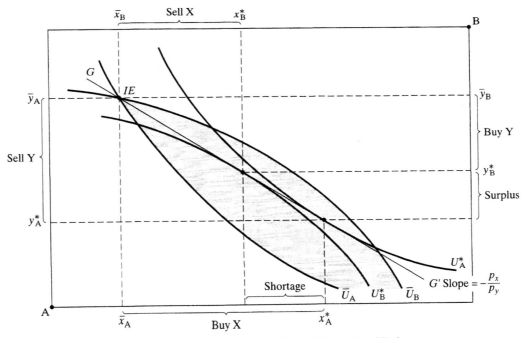

FIGURE 9.13 A Price Ratio That Is Not an Equilibrium

surplus of Y and a shortage of X. In other words, at those normalized prices, A is willing to supply more Y than B wishes to purchase, and B is not willing to supply as much X as A wishes to purchase. The line GG' represents a budget line of slope $(-p_x/p_y)$, which goes through the initial endowment point (IE). Along that budget line, Person A maximizes utility by choosing (x_A^*, y_A^*), and person B maximizes utility by choosing (x_B^*, y_B^*). That is not a feasible allocation, however, since more X is demanded than there is available and there is Y left over: there is a shortage of X and a surplus of Y at the current prices.

Returning to the idea that consumers sell their initial endowments and then express demands determined by their budgets, we can also check whether an allocation is in equilibrium by seeing whether total demand equals total supply in both markets. In this case, total demand in each market is the sum of the quantities demanded by the two traders, and total supply is the total quantity of each good available. Assuming that there is an underlying downward-sloping market demand curve for each good, which is the sum of the two consumers' individual demand curves, an equilibrium in each market would occur where the market demand curve crosses the fixed (vertical) supply. If demand exceeds supply at the given price, we say we have **excess demand** and the auctioneer should raise the price. If supply exceeds demand, we have **excess supply** and the auctioneer should lower the price. Figure 9.14 illustrates the situation portrayed in Figure 9.13 using demand and supply curves. The left graph shows that the price of X is too low, leading to excess demand and a shortage of X. In the right graph, the price of Y is too high, leading to excess supply and a surplus of Y. To bring prices into equilibrium, therefore, the auctioneer wants to raise the price of X relative to the price of Y, that is, increase p_x.

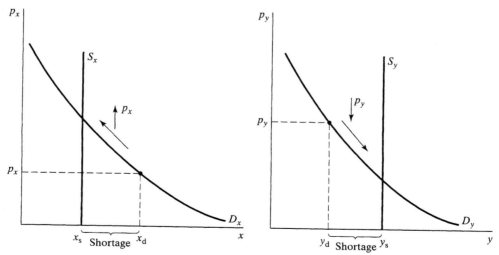

FIGURE 9.14 Using Excess Demand and Supply to Show a Price Ratio That Is Not an Equilibrium

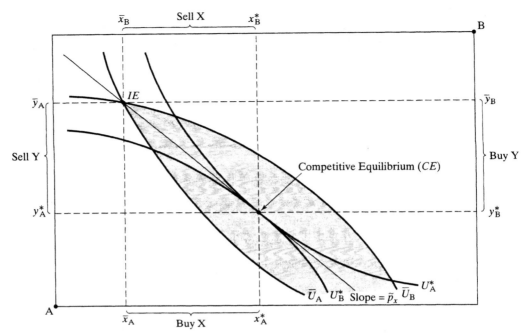

FIGURE 9.15 An Equilibrium Price Ratio in an Edgeworth Box

Now, suppose a higher normalized price of X is announced and demand *does* equal supply in the market for X. Figure 9.15 shows a very important result: when there are only two goods, equilibrium in the market for X automatically implies equilibrium in the market for Y. This happens because equilibrium in the market for X requires that the two consumers' indifference curves be tangent to one another. Once they are tangent, equilibrium in the market for Y follows.[2] The **equilibrium conditions** on supply and demand can be summarized as follows:

$$x_A^* + x_B^* = \bar{x} \quad \text{and} \quad y_A^* + y_B^* = \bar{y}.$$

---

[2]This result follows from what is known as Walras' law: Léon Walras (1834–1910), W. Jaffe, trans., *Elements of Pure Economics* (Homewood, IL: Richard D. Irwin, 1954) (originally published in French). Defining an excess demand function as the difference between quantity demanded and quantity supplied at each price, Walras' law states that the prices times the excess demands sum to 0 across all goods:

$$\sum_{j=1}^{m} p_j(q_j^d - q_j^s) = 0$$

This implies that if there are m different markets and m − 1 are in equilibrium, the mth market is automatically in equilibrium also. In this case there are only two markets, so if one is in equilibrium, the other must also be in equilibrium.

The Tâtonnement Process and the Competitive Equilibrium   The process of reaching an equilibrium we have just described is called a ***tâtonnement* process.**[3] The idea is that the auctioneer tries out prices and adjusts on the basis of excess demand and supply. If there is excess demand for a good, its relative price is raised; if there is excess supply of a good, it is lowered. The process stops when demand equals supply in all markets.

We call the allocation that emerges as an equilibrium of the *tâtonnement* process a **general competitive equilibrium.** More formally, a general competitive equilibrium is a set of price ratios and an allocation of goods among consumers that have the following properties:

1. demand equals supply in all markets, and

2. all consumers are maximizing utility subject to their budget constraints valued at those price ratios.

Property 2 implies that the marginal rates of substitution are equal across consumers as well as equal to the price ratio, since all consumers face the same price ratio:

$$MRS_A = MRS_B = \frac{p_x}{p_y}. \tag{9.11}$$

The First Fundamental Theorem of Welfare Economics   Equations 9.10 and 9.11 show that both a Pareto optimum and a competitive equilibrium have the property that the marginal rates of substitution are equal across consumers. In fact, it turns out that the competitive equilibrium is Pareto optimal.[4] This result holds whenever consumer preferences obey the assumptions of the model developed in Chapter 5 and whenever no consumers' preferences or consumption enter any other consumers' utility functions. In that case, we say there are no externalities in consumption: not altruism, envy, or physical externalities such as one person's smoking affecting another person. We refer to this result as the **first fundamental theorem of welfare economics** in the pure-trade case—if consumers have preferences that are complete, reflexive, transitive, and continuous and that exhibit nonsatiation and diminishing marginal rates of substitution, and if there are no externalities in consumption, then every pure-trade competitive equilibrium is Pareto optimal. Moreover, under these same conditions, this important result extends to many consumers and many goods. With the appropriate additional conditions, it also extends to the introduction of production into the model

---

[3]*Tâtonnement* is a French word meaning trial and error.

[4]The property that the marginal rates of substitution are equal across consumers at the competitive equilibrium follows from the fact that if each consumer is maximizing utility subject to the announced prices, the marginal rate of substitution is equal to the price ratio. Since all consumers face the same price ratio, their marginal rates of substitution are equal. The concept of Pareto optimality is defined independently of prices, however. It simply turns out that the operation of the competitive process drives consumers to choose an allocation that satisfies the conditions characterizing a Pareto optimum.

of trade developed in this chapter, to decisions over time, and to decisions under uncertainty.

9.4   SOLVING FOR A COMPETITIVE EQUILIBRIUM IN A TWO-PERSON, TWO-GOOD ECONOMY: AN EXAMPLE

In this section we give each consumer the simple utility function we used as an example in Chapter 6 and initial endowments of X and Y. From that information, we can solve for the competitive equilibrium price ratio and allocation of goods to consumers. Let the two consumers have the following utility functions:

$$U_A = x_A y_A \quad \text{and} \quad U_B = x_B y_B.$$

The initial endowments are

$$\bar{x}_A = 90, \quad \bar{y}_A = 35, \quad \bar{x}_B = 30, \quad \bar{y}_B = 25.$$

The total quantity available is

$$\bar{x}_A + \bar{x}_B = 120 = \text{supply of X}$$
$$\bar{y}_A + \bar{y}_B = 60 = \text{supply of Y}. \tag{9.12}$$

Thus, for an equilibrium, the quantities demanded must sum to the quantities available so that supply equals demand:

$$x_A^* + x_B^* = 120 = \bar{x}_A + \bar{x}_B \tag{9.13}$$
$$y_A^* + y_B^* = 60 = \bar{y}_A + \bar{y}_B. \tag{9.14}$$

We call these market-clearing requirements the equilibrium conditions. Normalizing so that $p_y = 1$, the budget constraints are

$$A: \quad p_x x_A + y_A = 90 p_x + 35$$
$$B: \quad p_x x_B + y_B = 30 p_x + 25.$$

Finding the Equilibrium Price Ratio   A's problem is

$$\max U_A = x_A y_A$$
$$\text{s.t.} \ p_x x_A + y_A = 90 p_x + 35.$$

A's Lagrangian is

$$\mathcal{L}_A = x_A y_A - \lambda_A (90 p_x + 35 - p_x x_A - y_A). \tag{9.15}$$

The first-order conditions are

$$\frac{\partial \mathcal{L}}{\partial x_A} = y_A - \lambda_A p_x = 0 \quad \Rightarrow \quad \lambda_A = y_A \frac{1}{p_x} \tag{9.16}$$

$$\frac{\partial \mathcal{L}}{\partial y_A} = x_A - \lambda_A = 0 \quad \Rightarrow \quad \lambda_A = x_A \tag{9.17}$$

$$\frac{\partial \mathcal{L}}{\partial \lambda_A} = 90 p_x + 35 - p_x x_A - y_A = 0. \tag{9.18}$$

Solving for λ_A from equations 9.16 and 9.17,

$$\lambda_A = x_A = y_A \frac{1}{p_x}. \tag{9.19}$$

Substituting equation 9.19 in equation 9.18,

$$90p_x + 35 - p_x\left(y_A \frac{1}{p_x}\right) - y_A = 0$$

$$\Rightarrow \quad y_A = 45p_x + 17.5 \qquad \textbf{A's demand function for Y} \tag{9.20}$$

Substituting (9.20) in (9.19),

$$x_A = \frac{1}{p_x}(45p_x + 17.5)$$

$$\Rightarrow \quad x_A = 45 + 17.5\frac{1}{p_x}. \qquad \textbf{A's demand function for X} \tag{9.21}$$

B's problem is

$$\max U_B = x_B y_B$$
$$\text{s.t. } p_x x_B + y_B = 30p_x + 25. \tag{9.22}$$

B's Lagrangian is

$$\mathcal{L}_B = x_B y_B + \lambda_B(30p_x + 25 - p_x x_B - y_B). \tag{9.23}$$

The first-order conditions are

$$\frac{\partial \mathcal{L}}{\partial x_B} = y_B - \lambda_B p_x = 0 \quad \Rightarrow \quad \lambda_B = y_B \frac{1}{p_x} \tag{9.24}$$

$$\frac{\partial \mathcal{L}}{\partial y_B} = x_B - \lambda_B = 0 \quad \Rightarrow \quad \lambda_B = x_B \tag{9.25}$$

$$\frac{\partial \mathcal{L}}{\partial \lambda_B} = 30p_x + 25 - p_x x_B - y_B = 0. \tag{9.26}$$

Solving for λ_B from equations 9.24 and 9.25,

$$\lambda_B = x_B = y_B \frac{1}{p_x}. \tag{9.27}$$

Substituting (9.27) in (9.26),

$$30p_x + 25 - p_x\left(y_B \frac{1}{p_x}\right) - y_B = 0$$

$$\Rightarrow \quad y_B = 15p_x + 12.5. \qquad \textbf{B's demand function for Y} \tag{9.28}$$

Substituting (9.28) in (9.27),

$$x_B = \frac{1}{p_x}(15p_x + 12.5)$$

$$\Rightarrow \quad x_B = 15 + 12.5\frac{1}{p_x}. \quad \text{B's demand function for X} \quad (9.29)$$

To find the actual equilibrium quantities and the normalized price of X, we can begin by adding up the two demand equations for Y (equations 9.20 and 9.28) and setting the sum equal to the total quantity of Y available (equation 9.12). The resulting equation describes an equilibrium in the market for Y: consumer demand equals available supply.[5]

$$y_A = 45p_x + 17.5$$
$$y_B = 15p_x + 12.5$$
$$y_A + y_B = 45p_x + 17.5 + 15p_x + 12.5 = 60 = \bar{y}_A + \bar{y}_B$$

Therefore,

$$60p_x + 30 = 60 \quad \Rightarrow \quad p_x = \frac{1}{2}. \quad (9.30)$$

Solving for the Competitive Equilibrium Allocation We now substitute the price found in equation 9.30 in the demand equations (equations 9.20, 9.21, 9.28, and 9.29) to find the actual quantities demanded:

$$y_A = 45(1/2) + 17.5 = 40$$
$$y_B = 15(1/2) + 12.5 = 20$$
$$x_A = 45 + 17.5(2) = 80$$
$$x_B = 15 + 12.5(2) = 40.$$

We can check these answers to see if they satisfy the equilibrium conditions given by equation 9.12:

$$x_A + x_B = 80 + 40 = 120$$
$$y_A + y_B = 40 + 20 = 60.$$

We can also check to make sure the price ratio equals the respective marginal rates of substitution. We know from Chapter 5 that if $U = xy$,

$$MRS = \frac{MU_x}{MU_y} = \frac{y}{x}$$

---

[5]Notice that we have six equations [the four demand functions (equations 9.20, 9.21, 9.28, and 9.29) plus the two equilibrium conditions (equation 9.12)], and six unknowns (the four allocations of X and Y plus the two prices). Thus, the number of equations equals the number of unknowns, and a solution can be found if it exists. We have already seen, however, that the solution is not unique; that is why we normalized the price of Y.

$$MRS_A = \frac{y_A}{x_A} = \frac{40}{80} = \frac{1}{2}$$

$$MRS_B = \frac{y_B}{x_B} = \frac{20}{40} = \frac{1}{2}.$$

Therefore,

$$MRS_A = MRS_B = \frac{p_x}{p_y} = \frac{1}{2}.$$

9.5   THE DISTRIBUTIONAL PROBLEM

While it is true that every competitive equilibrium is Pareto optimal, it is also the case that there are many Pareto optima, only some of which represent an improvement for both individuals as compared to their initial endowments. Return now to the two-person example we developed in Figures 9.1–9.8, and recall that Figure 9.7 illustrated all the possible points in a given Edgeworth box satisfying the condition that marginal rates of substitution are equal for the two consumers. We called the curve connecting all the Pareto optima the contract curve. The idea is that if the two individuals were to trade with one another, it would always be in their interest to exhaust the gains from trade, forming an agreement on the contract curve.

Pareto Optimality and Pareto Superiority   Now, consider an initial endowment and an area of gains from trade, as in Figure 9.16. All points on the contract curve between $\overline{U}_A$ and $\overline{U}_B$ represent Pareto optimal allocations that also have the property that both participants are better off than they were at the initial endowment. We refer to all points such that one or both individuals are better off and neither is worse off as the set of **Pareto superior** points (the complete shaded area, including the indifference curves, in Figure 9.16). Once an initial allocation is made, any point on the contract curve inside the shaded area (the competitive equilibrium, for example) is both Pareto optimal and Pareto superior. The allocations are efficient and no one is made worse off by exchange. Points on the contract curve outside the shaded area are Pareto optimal but not Pareto superior. At one of *those* Pareto optima, at least one participant would be strictly worse off than at the initial endowment. Figure 9.16 illustrates points that are Pareto superior, points that are Pareto optimal, and points that are both Pareto optimal and Pareto superior to an initial endowment (anything on the contract curve between C and D).

The Competitive Process and the Distribution of Initial Endowments   Consider two possible Pareto optima, C and D in Figure 9.17. Both points are on the contract curve; however, A would clearly prefer to be at D and B would clearly prefer to be at C. Even if we were to introduce a roughly equal allocation at E, A would still prefer D and B would still prefer C. The competitive equilibrium is one Pareto optimum that is both

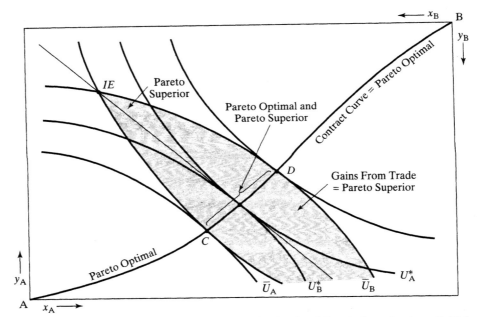

FIGURE 9.16 Points That Are Both Pareto Optimal and Pareto Superior to an Initial Endowment

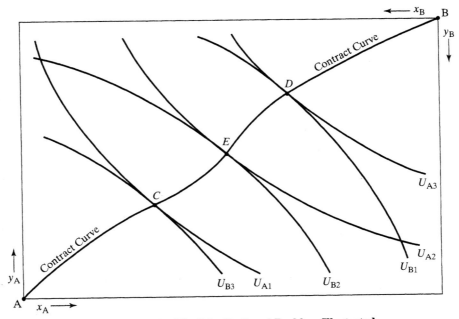

FIGURE 9.17 The Distributional Problem Illustrated

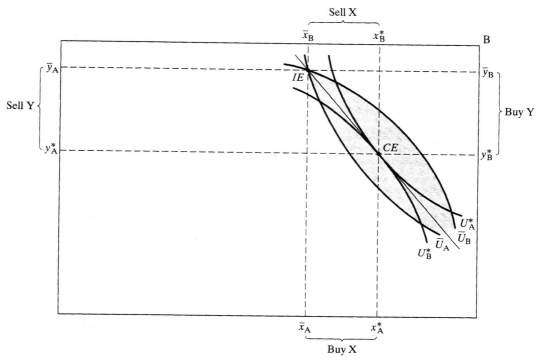

FIGURE 9.18   The Competitive Process Does Not Alter the Initial Distribution of Income

Pareto superior to the initial endowment and consistent with a budget line going through that initial endowment.[6] However, there are an infinite number of Pareto optima along the contract curve that are also Pareto superior to the initial endowment but are not competitive equilibria. Thus, there is nothing particular to recommend the competitive equilibrium as a final allocation, other than the fact it is relatively easily attained, as compared to other points that are both Pareto optimal and Pareto superior to the initial endowment.

The Pareto optimum the competitive process selects as an equilibrium depends on the initial endowment. If one person is relatively "rich" and the other is "poor" in initial endowments, for example, the competitive process will make both better off than at their initial endowments and will find a Pareto optimum; however, the inequality of purchasing power will not be affected by the competitive process. This point is illustrated in Figure 9.18. At the initial endowment, person A commands a relatively large share of both goods. At the competitive equilibrium both A and B are better off than at the initial endowment, but A still consumes a large proportion of both goods.

_____

[6]In some unusual circumstances there may be more than one competitive equilibrium for a particular initial endowment.

9.6 OTHER RESOURCE ALLOCATION PROCESSES AND PARETO OPTIMALITY

We have seen that the competitive process leads an economy to a Pareto optimum, but we have also seen that the Pareto optimum chosen could very well leave some people very poor and other very rich, depending on the distribution of initial endowments. While economists typically do not judge the "fairness" of any particular distribution of initial endowments, politicians and private citizens do. One of the goals of a planned or a welfare economy is to effect an efficient distribution of resources while ensuring a more equal distribution of claims to final consumption. In principle, if a planner knew the preferences of all members of a society and the total quantities of goods available, a Pareto optimum could be found that had the "desired" distribution of claims (possibly decided by some political process), and the goods could simply be distributed among the people. Then, even if people did decide to trade, there would not be any point in doing so; the original distribution would already have exhausted the gains from trade.

The Second Fundamental Theorem of Welfare Economics However, such a solution requires that the planner have far more information about consumer preferences than is ever likely to be obtained. An informationally simple solution to the redistribution problem is to change the initial endowments by taking some goods away from those deemed to have too much and giving them to those deemed to have too little. Once the transfer of initial endowments has been made, individuals trade among themselves to a new competitive equilibrium, which will also be Pareto optimal. In fact, under the same

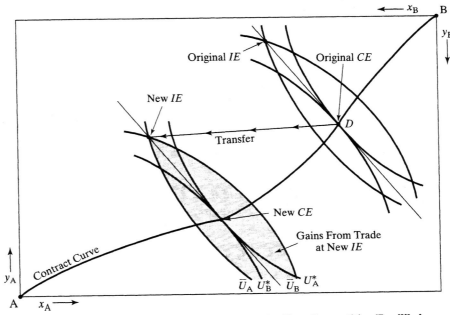

FIGURE 9.19 A Transfer of Endowments and a New Competitive Equilibrium

assumptions as those made for the first fundamental theorem of welfare economics, any point on the contract curve can be implemented as a competitive equilibrium by a suitable reassignment of initial endowments. This is called the **second fundamental theorem of welfare economics** in the pure-trade case.

Figure 9.19 illustrates the second fundamental theorem of welfare economics. Given the original initial endowments, the competitive equilibrium would be at point D, where A is relatively rich and B is relatively poor. The new competitive equilibrium (point F, New CE) can be achieved by simply taking some of each good away from A and giving it to B and then allowing A and B to trade.

9.7   REVIEW OF KEY CONCEPTS

Although some of the ideas introduced in this chapter may seem simple in comparison to those you have seen in the last few chapters, you should not lose sight of how important they are in economics. As was pointed out in Sections 4.3–4.5, efficiency, Pareto optimality, and the competitive equilibrium are the central concepts in this book. You have now seen them in a simple model without production. We will return to them again after we have developed the model of production. For now, you should understand the following key concepts in the context of a trading economy.

An allocation is *Pareto optimal* or *efficient* if it is not possible to make one person better off without making some other person worse off. (See Section 4.3.)

An *Edgeworth box* is a rectangle with length and width equal to the total quantities of two goods available in an economy of two goods and two consumers.

Gains from trade exist when some people can be made better off by trading without making anyone else worse off.

In an Edgeworth box, an allocation is *Pareto optimal* if the two consumers' indifference curves are tangent to one another

The *contract curve* in an Edgeworth box connects all the allocations that are Pareto optimal. The idea is that contracts are expected to exhaust the gains from trade.

An *initial endowment* is a list of the goods that a consumer has before any trading begins. (See Section 4.3.)

An *auctioneer* is a third party who facilitates trading by suggesting possible prices at which traders might exchange items with one another from their initial endowments.

The auctioneer may *normalize* by setting one price equal to 1 and then quoting only relative prices, because demand functions are homogeneous of degree 0.

In an Edgeworth box, each consumer's budget line goes through an initial endowment and has a slope equal to the announced price ratio.

After a price ratio is announced, each consumer proposes to sell some of one good and buy some of the other.

A *net purchase* is a purchase of a good in addition to the initial endowment.

A *net sale* is a sale of a portion of the initial endowment of a good.

At an *equilibrium* of a trading process supply equals demand in all markets.

There is *excess demand* if demand exceeds supply at a particular price and *excess supply* if supply exceeds demand.

Walras' law implies that, if all but one market is in equilibrium, the last market must also be in equilibrium.

When we solve for a competitive equilibrium, the *equilibrium conditions* are satisfied when the sum of the demands equals the sum of the initial endowments in all markets.

The *tâtonnement process* for finding an equilibrium set of price ratios involves having an auctioneer try out various prices, request information on demand and supply, and search for a set of prices such that demand equals supply in all markets.

A *general competitive equilibrium* is an allocation of goods to consumers and a set of price ratios, with the properties that demand equals supply in all markets at those prices and that consumers are maximizing utility subject to their budget constraints valued at those prices.

At a competitive equilibrium, the marginal rates of substitution are equal across consumers and are equal to the price ratio.

The pure-trade competitive equilibrium is Pareto optimal if there are no externalities in consumption. This is referred to as the *first fundamental theorem of welfare economics*.

Allocations that are *Pareto superior* to an initial endowment are allocations that make at least one person better off and make no individual worse off.

Allocations on the contract curve that are better than the initial endowment for both parties are both Pareto optimal and Pareto superior.

A *resource allocation process* is a process of allocating goods among consumers. The *tâtonnement* process is a resource allocation process.

A *competitive process* is a resource allocation process that leads an economy to a competitive equilibrium. Thus, the *tâtonnement* process is a competitive process as well.

A competitive process does not alter any inherent inequality in initial endowments. It simply finds a competitive equilibrium, given the initial endowments.

The *second fundamental theorem of welfare economics* in the pure-trade case states that if there are no externalities in consumption, every possible Pareto optimum can be implemented as a competitive equilibrium by a suitable reassignment of initial endowments.

9.8 QUESTIONS FOR DISCUSSION

1. Think of situations in which you and your friends or family benefited or might have benefited from trading with one another. For example, do you ever trade clothes with your roommate or your siblings? Do you use implicit prices? Explain.

2. Think of how the model of trade developed in this chapter might be applied to two countries that trade with one another. Label each end of the Edgeworth box as a country and illustrate how trade might take place if each country has certain endowments and if a set of indifference curves could represent preferences in a particular country.

3. Explain how the concepts of the competitive equilibrium and Pareto optimality are similar and different. Discuss in terms of the first and second fundamental theorems of welfare economics.

4. Explain how the concepts of Pareto optimality and Pareto superiority are similar and different. Why is the competitive equilibrium both Pareto optimal and Pareto superior to an initial endowment?

5. Were you ever asked to participate in a trade that would not have made you better off than if you had not traded at all? Were your belongings ever given to a sibling by family decision? Relate such an experience to the distributional problem discussed in Section 9.6. If you had the first experience, did you refuse to trade? If you had the second, did you trade again with your sibling? Discuss these reactions in light of the theoretical discussions presented in this chapter.

9.9 ___ PROBLEMS

1. In an exchange economy between A and B, the initial endowments are

$$\bar{x}_A = 50, \quad \bar{y}_A = 500,$$
$$\bar{x}_B = 200, \quad \bar{y}_B = 20.$$

Their utility functions are

$$U_A = (x_A)^2 y_A \quad \text{and}$$
$$U_B = x_B(y_B)^2.$$

Find the competitive equilibrium allocation and price ratio.

2. Show that $MRS_A = MRS_B = p_x/p_y$ at the competitive equilibrium in Problem 1.

3. Now, starting from the competitive equilibrium in Problem 1, suppose the government takes 100 units of Y away from A and gives it to B. Find the new competitive equilibrium and price ratio after the transfer of endowments.

4. Graph the changes you calculated in Problems 1–3. Sketch in the contract curve and some representative indifference curves for the two individuals. Show the initial endowment, the first competitive equilibrium, the transfer, and the second competitive equilibrium. Also indicate points that are Pareto optimal and Pareto superior to the initial endowment.

5. Now, suppose an advertising campaign in favor of good Y persuaded person A to change preferences to

$$U_A = (x_A)^2(y_A)^2.$$

Starting from the second competitive equilibrium, how would this change in A's utility function change the competitive equilibrium allocation and price ratio? (Find the new solutions.)

6. Can we use the Pareto superiority criterion to judge whether or not the advertising campaign made A or B better off? Why or why not?

Chapter 10

PRODUCTION THEORY

10.1   WHAT YOU SHOULD LEARN FROM THIS CHAPTER

In this chapter, we introduce you to the basic concepts and assumptions underlying the economist's model of production. We begin with a set of assumptions that allow us to represent equal output curves (*production isoquants*) as being convex to the origin. This analysis is similar to the development of indifference curves in Section 5.3. Next, we present an approach similar to revealed preference analysis in consumer theory. We show that if a firm manager always chooses a unique and different least-cost input combination to produce a given output level for all possible input price ratios, then the set of cost-minimizing input choices can be represented as an isoquant that is convex to the origin.

After developing the concept of a production function, we examine some important properties of production functions in the *long run* (when all inputs may vary) and in the *short run* (when some inputs are fixed). The mathematics of production theory are identical to what you have already learned in consumer theory, with one important exception. In consumer theory, the utility function is ordinal, but in production theory, the production function is cardinal. That is because in production we deal with measurable quantities of output.

Just as the material in Sections 5.3 and 5.5 laid the basic groundwork for consumer theory, the material in this chapter lays the basic groundwork for production theory. The end product of production theory will be the development of a set of cost functions and output choices for the firm.

10.2   THE PRODUCTION FUNCTION

In contrast to utility, which is purely ordinal, production is measurable. Firms combine observable inputs to produce measurable outputs, and the process can be described by precise engineering formulas; these formulas specify exactly how inputs are to be combined with one another at each stage in the production process. The end product, output, can then be expressed as a function of all the inputs used to produce it; the summary equation is derived from the production steps described by the engineering formulas. We call such a summary equation a **production function.** An example of a production function is

$$x = K^{1/2}L^{1/2}. \tag{10.1}$$

Put in words, this function (10.1) says that when capital and labor are combined to produce output, the quantity of output produced is always equal to the square root of the quantity of labor times the square root of the quantity of capital.

Input-Output Tables　Table 10.1 summarizes explicit calculations of outputs obtainable from different combinations of inputs, assuming the above production function accurately describes the engineering relationships. We refer to such a table as an **input-output table.** The columns represent quantities of capital employed, the rows represent quantities of labor employed, and the cell entries represent outputs obtainable from those combinations of inputs.

Notice in Table 10.1 that an output of 2 units can be produced using 4 units of capital and 1 unit of labor, 2 units of each, or 4 units of labor and 1 unit of capital. In fact, if units of labor and capital were infinitely divisible, any combination of labor and capital such that $K^{1/2}L^{1/2} = 2$ could be used to produce 2 units of output. These possible combinations of inputs to produce 2 units of output when the production function is $x = K^{1/2}L^{1/2}$ are graphed as a rectangular hyperbola in Figure 10.1.

TABLE 10.1　Input-Output Table for Production Function $x = K^{1/2}L^{1/2}$

L \ K	1	2	3	4	5
1	1	1.4	1.7	2	2.2
2	1.4	2	2.4	2.8	3.2
3	1.7	2.4	3	3.5	3.9
4	2	2.8	3.5	4	4.5
5	2.2	3.2	3.9	4.5	5

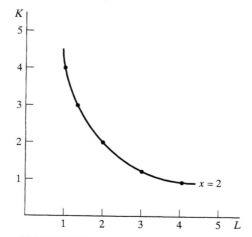

FIGURE 10.1　A Production Isoquant for Two Units of Output from Production Function $x = K^{1/2}L^{1/2}$

We call a curve describing all the input combinations that can be used to produce a given output a **production isoquant.** Another way of interpreting an isoquant is as an equal-output curve, from the Greek prefix *iso-*, which means equal or similar.

An Example Now, let's consider a more specific example. Suppose that an automobile manufacturing firm were contemplating building a new assembly plant and that its production technology could be summarized by the above equation. In this case, capital would represent the assembly line, buildings, and equipment, and labor would represent the labor hours employed in the plant per day. This equation would tell the manufacturer that many different kinds of plants could be built, each employing a different combination of capital and labor. On the one hand, the manufacturer could build a fully automated plant that could produce 100 cars per day, employing 1 labor hour per day and 10,000 units of capital:

$$100 = (10,000)^{1/2}(1)^{1/2} = (100)(1).$$

On the other hand, the manufacturer could build a plant in which most of the work is done by hand, producing 100 cars per day and employing 2500 labor hours per day and 4 units of capital:

$$100 = (2500)^{1/2}(4)^{1/2} = (50)(2).$$

Each of these two combinations of capital and labor would be a different point on the firm's 100-unit isoquant. Which plant the manufacturer would choose to build (among all the different possibilities summarized by the production function) is one of the subjects of the three chapters on production (10–12).

Technological Efficiency The basic assumption that economists make about production functions is that they are technologically efficient. When inputs (such as capital and labor) are combined to produce outputs (such as food and clothing), an input combination used to produce a particular output is **technologically efficient** if it is *not* possible to get the same output using *less* of one input and *no more* of any other input. Otherwise, some inputs would be wasted. Technological efficiency also implies that if one input is increased and all other inputs are held constant, output must increase. Once again, if output did not increase, then the increased input would simply be wasted.

$$\frac{\partial x}{\partial L} > 0 \quad \text{and} \quad \frac{\partial x}{\partial K} > 0. \tag{10.2}$$

Note that this is mathematically equivalent to the assumption of nonsatiation in consumer theory (Section 5.3):

$$\frac{\partial U}{\partial x} > 0 \quad \text{and} \quad \frac{\partial U}{\partial y} > 0.$$

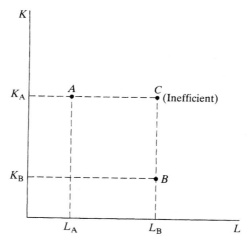

FIGURE 10.2   Technology Efficiency and Inefficiency

The basic production model assumes that firm managers would never choose technologically inefficient combinations of inputs, if we assume the managers have perfect information about those production possibilities.[1]

Figure 10.2 illustrates points that are technologically efficient and inefficient relative to one another. Points A, B, and C each represent a combination of capital and labor that might be used to produce 10 units of a good. Point A uses K_A capital and L_A labor, while B uses K_B capital and L_B labor. At point A, the firm uses more capital and less labor than at point B, but A and B are technologically efficient relative to one another. To move from A to B and back, the firm must use more of one input in order to use less of the other. Point C, on the other hand, uses K_A capital and L_B labor. The firm could use the same labor and less capital by moving to B or the same capital and less labor by moving to A. Thus, C is technologically *inefficient* relative to A and B.

Diminishing Marginal Rates of Technical Substitution   Another assumption generally made about production is that production isoquants are convex to the origin. The property that isoquants are convex to the origin is referred to as diminishing marginal

---

[1]The assumptions of perfect, costless information and no uncertainty about future events are used throughout the development of this simple model of production. Later on in the book, we will relax these assumptions to study the effects of imperfect information and random events on firm and consumer decisions. Thus, while in reality a manager may sometimes choose inefficient combinations out of ignorance, in a world of perfect, costless information, there is no reason to expect technological inefficiency.

Regarding the reality of the assumption of perfect information, there have been important recent advances in engineering modeling and in high-speed computing for running production simulations. These advances have made that kind of production information much easier for large manufacturing firms to obtain. Smaller firms and service industries still must rely more on rules of thumb and trial and error to approximate technological efficiency.

rates of technical substitution (*MRTS*). This is mathematically equivalent to the assumption of diminishing marginal rates of substitution in consumer theory (Section 5.3). We define the negative of the slope of the isoquant as the **marginal rate of technical substitution:**

$$MRTS = -\frac{dK}{dL} > 0, \tag{10.3}$$

since the isoquant is downward sloping. Thus,

$$\frac{d}{dL} MRTS = -\frac{d^2K}{dL^2} < 0, \tag{10.4}$$

since $d^2K/dL^2 > 0$ by convexity. For example, if

$$x = K^{1/2}L^{1/2} \Rightarrow K = \frac{x^2}{L} \tag{10.5}$$

$$MRTS = -\frac{dK}{dL} = -\left(-\frac{x^2}{L^2}\right) = \frac{x^2}{L^2} > 0 \tag{10.6}$$

$$\frac{d}{dL} MRTS = -2\frac{x^2}{L^3} < 0. \tag{10.7}$$

Comparison of Isoquants and Indifference Curves   The properties of a production function can be summarized in comparison to the axioms of consumer preference developed in Section 5.3. First, the production relationship is complete, reflexive, and transitive because it describes measurable quantities. Technological efficiency is mathematically equivalent to nonsatiation, and diminishing marginal rates of technical substitution in production are mathematically equivalent to diminishing marginal rates of substitution in consumer theory. Production functions are not necessarily continuous, but for the purposes of developing the model of production in this book, we will confine ourselves to continuous functions. In that case, therefore, we can treat production isoquants as being mathematically equivalent to indifference curves, except for the difference in cardinality.

10.3   RECOVERING ISOQUANTS BY OBSERVING PRODUCTION CHOICES

Economists estimate production isoquants by observing firm choices and assuming that, to produce a given output, firm managers always choose combinations of inputs that are both technologically efficient and cost minimizing. This is similar to the revealed preference approach to recovering indifference curves outlined in Section 5.6. The main difference is that isoquants can actually be estimated directly by this method, while indifference curves can only be inferred as points that are not revealed preferred to one another.

Economic Efficiency and Isocost Lines   The assumption that firm managers' input choices are cost minimizing for given outputs is referred to as an assumption of economic efficiency (in contrast to the assumption of technological efficiency outlined above). An input combination is said to be **economically efficient** if it is not possible to produce that combination at a lower cost, given the prevailing input prices. Given a set of input prices and a proposed quantity of output, the firm can use its engineering data to find the least-cost way of producing that quantity of output.

If a firm buys or rents inputs in competitive input markets, then input prices are parameters to the firm, and the cost of hiring those inputs is simply the sum of the expenditures on each input. Thus, if

$$TC = \text{total cost}$$
$$L = \text{labor}$$
$$K = \text{capital}$$
$$w = \text{market wage}$$
$$r = \text{market rental rate capital,}$$

then

$$TC = wL + rK. \tag{10.8}$$

Holding TC and the input prices fixed and varying K and L to satisfy equation 10.8 tells the firm all the combinations of capital and labor that can be hired for a certain total cost.

In a capital-labor graph, a firm's possible combinations of capital and labor that cost TC, given w and r, are represented by a line of slope $-w/r$ and capital intercept TC/r:

$$K = \frac{TC}{r} - \frac{w}{r}L. \tag{10.9}$$

The line described in (10.9) is called an **isocost line.** It is analogous to the budget line in consumer theory (introduced in Section 5.5) and is illustrated in Figure 10.3.

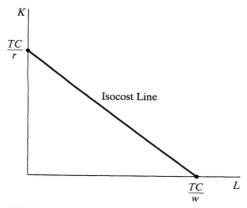

FIGURE 10.3   Possible Combinations of Capital and Labor, Given *TC*, *w*, and *r*

TABLE 10.2   Efficient Input Combinations to Produce 10 Units

Wage Rate	Rental Rate	Labor	Capital	Total Cost
w	r	L^*	K^*	$wL^* + rK^*$
$5	$10	24	3	$150
7	7	15	10	175
10	4	4	30	160

Estimating an Isoquant   To trace out a set of technologically efficient input combinations to produce a given level of output from engineering data, we begin by assuming that the firm, given a set of input prices, can identify the lowest cost combination of inputs, and the corresponding minimum cost, for producing that output. For example, Table 10.2 indicates hypothetical least-cost combinations of inputs to produce 10 units of output, and the associated total costs, for the set of input prices indicated.

Figure 10.4 plots the information summarized in Table 10.2 and illustrates how we estimate an isoquant. Point A (24 labor, 3 capital) describes the least-cost ($150) combination of capital and labor to produce $\bar{x}$ (10) units of output at input prices w_1

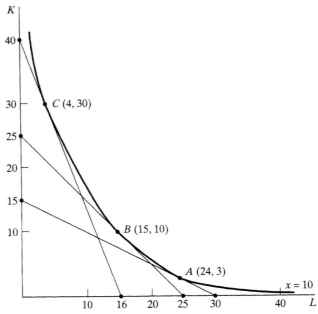

FIGURE 10.4   Least-cost Combinations of Capital and Labor, Given Different Sets of Input Costs

and r_1 ($5 and $10, respectively). The line through A is the isocost line for a total cost of $150 and input prices of $5 for labor and $10 for capital. Point B (15, 10) is the least-cost ($175) combination at ($7, $7), and point C (4, 30) is the least-cost ($160) combination at ($10, $4). Points A, B, and C are three points on the graph of the 10-unit isoquant.

Suppose the following three conditions are satisfied: inputs are infinitely divisible; there is only one cost-minimizing input combination for each input price ratio; and all possible input price ratios are tried. Then, an isoquant can be constructed by connecting all the cost-minimizing combinations that can produce the given output. The isoquant for $\bar{x} = 10$ units is sketched in Figure 10.4.

10.4   OUTPUT EXPANSION IN THE LONG RUN

Economists tend to separate production decisions into those made under two distinct planning horizons. In the **long run,** all inputs may vary. In the **short run,** some inputs are fixed, so the firm cannot optimize over the use of all inputs; this may happen because of long-term contracts for either labor or capital, or because it is not practical to adjust plant size or machinery on short notice.

While this distinction is sometimes oversimplified, it is also often useful. For example, the automobile manufacturer introduced in Section 10.2 will not easily be able to make adjustments in capital at the margin once the new plant is built. Over fairly wide ranges of output, the manufacturer will have to make production decisions assuming capital is fixed and will have to change output by changing the number of workers hired. In such a situation, we say that the manufacturer is operating in the short run. Only when the firm builds a new plant, adds to an existing one, or sells an old one can it be described as operating in the long run.

While the concepts of long run and short run are useful, you should keep in mind that they do not describe specific *time* horizons. They refer only to whether or not a firm can vary all its inputs simultaneously. For example, the automobile manufacturer above may operate in the short run for a long time, simply because it might take two or three years just to plan to build a new plant. A small retail firm, on the other hand, may rent its space, use part-time help, and buy all its inventory as needed. Such a firm can quickly vary all its inputs in response to market conditions and may essentially always operate in the long run.

Returns to Scale We begin by developing long-run production concepts and then turn to the short run. As output expands in the long run, production functions may exhibit the property of homogeneity defined in Section 6.4. Recall that a function is homogeneous of degree k if

$$f(\alpha x, \alpha y) = \alpha^k f(x, y) \quad \text{for all } \alpha \geq 0. \tag{10.10}$$

Homogeneous production functions are divided into three classes. First, if doubling all inputs exactly doubles output, we say the production function exhibits **constant returns to scale**—in other words, multiplying all inputs by the same positive constant multiplies output by that same constant. In that case, the production function exhibits *homogeneity of degree 1.*

$$f(\alpha K, \alpha L) = \alpha^1 f(K, L), \quad k = 1. \tag{10.11}$$

Second, if doubling all inputs *less* than doubles output, the function exhibits **decreasing returns to scale** and *homogeneity of degree less than 1.*

$$f(\alpha K, \alpha L) = \alpha^k f(K, L), \quad 0 < k < 1. \tag{10.12}$$

Finally, if doubling all inputs *more* than doubles output, the function exhibits **increasing returns to scale** and *homogeneity of degree more than 1.*

$$f(\alpha K, \alpha L) = \alpha^k f(K, L), \quad k > 1. \tag{10.13}$$

An Example   We can use the general Cobb-Douglas functional form for a production function (equation 6.15) to illustrate all three possibilities. If a general Cobb-Douglas form of the utility function is $U = x^\alpha y^\beta$, the analogous production function is

$$x = K^\alpha L^\beta. \tag{10.14}$$

We generally assume, in addition, that α and β are both greater than 0; otherwise, one of the inputs would simply be irrelevant ($K^0 = 1, L^0 = 1$). To check for homogeneity, we will multiply the inputs in (10.14) by θ:

$$x(\theta K, \theta L) = (\theta K)^\alpha (\theta L)^\beta = \theta^{\alpha + \beta} K^\alpha L^\beta. \tag{10.15}$$

Thus, (10.15) indicates that

$$\alpha + \beta = 1, \quad \text{the function is homogeneous of degree 1} \tag{10.16}$$
$$\text{(constant returns to scale)};$$
$$\alpha + \beta < 1, \quad \text{the function is homogeneous of degree} < 1$$
$$\text{(decreasing returns to scale)};$$
$$\alpha + \beta > 1, \quad \text{the function is homogeneous of degree} > 1$$
$$\text{(the increasing returns to scale)}.$$

10.5   OUTPUT EXPANSION IN THE SHORT RUN

In the short run, some factors of production are fixed as output expands. This situation is illustrated in Figure 10.5. Assume capital and labor are the only factors of production and capital is fixed in the short run at $\overline{K}$. If the firm wishes to expand, it must do so along the horizontal line at $\overline{K}$, since capital must equal $\overline{K}$. This line is called the firm's **short-run expansion path.** Thus, to produce x_1 units of output, the firm must use L_1 units of labor; to produce x_2, it must use L_2; and to produce x_3, it must use L_3. This graph might, for example, describe the amount of labor the automobile manufacturer would have to use to produce different numbers of cars per day once the plant is built.

Total, Average, and Marginal Physical Products   Taking the x values from the isoquants to the vertical axis of the lower graph in Figure 10.6, we can construct a function

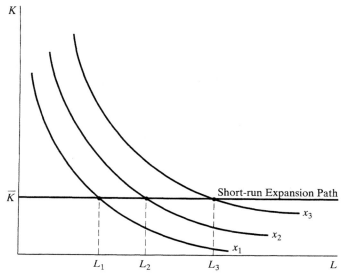

FIGURE 10.5   The Firm's Short-run Expansion Path

that describes how much output is obtained from given labor inputs, assuming capital is fixed at $\overline{K}$:

$$x = x(L; \overline{K}). \tag{10.17}$$

We refer to this function (10.17) as the **total physical product of labor** (abbreviated TP_L). If labor were fixed and capital were allowed to vary, we could also construct a **total physical product of capital** function in the same way:

$$x = x(K; \overline{L}) = TP_K. \tag{10.18}$$

Figure 10.6 on the following page illustrates the derivation of the total physical product of labor function from the short-run expansion path. Given that capital is fixed at $\overline{K}$, L_1 units of labor produce x_1 units of output, L_2 produces x_2, and L_3 produces x_3.

Having defined total physical products of labor and capital, we can also define average and marginal products of labor and capital in the same way we have defined average and marginal functions previously.

$$\text{average product of labor } (AP_L) = \frac{TP_L}{L} = \frac{x(L; \overline{K})}{L} \tag{10.19}$$

$$\text{average product of capital } (AP_K) = \frac{TP_K}{K} = \frac{x(K; \overline{L})}{K} \tag{10.20}$$

$$\text{marginal product of labor } (MP_L) = \frac{d}{dL} TP_L = \frac{\partial x}{\partial L} \tag{10.21}$$

$$\text{marginal product of capital } (MP_K) = \frac{d}{dK} TP_K = \frac{\partial x}{\partial K} \tag{10.22}$$

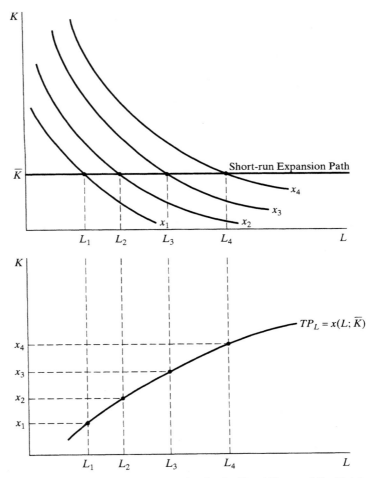

FIGURE 10.6 Output Expansion in the Short Run and the Total Physical Product of Labor

Mathematical and Graphical Examples For example, using the general Cobb-Douglas production function $x = K^\alpha L^\beta$, for $\alpha, \beta > 0$,

$$TP_L = \overline{K}^\alpha L^\beta$$

$$AP_L = \frac{\overline{K}^\alpha L^\beta}{L} = \overline{K}^\alpha L^{\beta-1}$$

$$MP_L = \frac{d}{dL}(\overline{K}^\alpha L^\beta) = \beta\overline{K}^\alpha L^{\beta-1}$$

$$TP_K = K^\alpha \overline{L}^\beta$$

$$AP_K = \frac{K^\alpha \overline{L}^\beta}{K} = K^{\alpha-1}\overline{L}^\beta$$

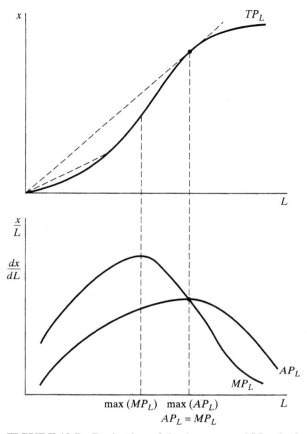

FIGURE 10.7   Derivation of the Average and Marginal Products of Labor

$$MP_K = \frac{d}{dK}\left(K^\alpha \overline{L}^\beta\right) = \alpha K^{\alpha-1}\overline{L}^\beta$$

Figure 10.7 illustrates the derivation of average and marginal products of labor from an idealized total product of labor function. Recall from Section 2.3 how to derive average and marginal functions from total functions. Deriving the average function first, the line from the origin to the total function rises until it is just tangent to the total function at the maximum of the average function, and it falls thereafter. The slope of the total function (which is the marginal function) rises to the inflection point, where the marginal function attains a maximum, and falls thereafter. The marginal and average functions are exactly equal at the point where the line from the origin to the total function is just tangent to that function. As we saw in Section 2.3, the marginal product is greater than the average product when the average product is rising and less than the average product when the average product is falling. Average and marginal products of capital can be derived analogously.

Marginal Physical Products and the Marginal Rate of Technical Substitution The marginal products of labor and capital are related to the marginal rate of technical substitution in the same way marginal utilities of X and Y are related to the marginal rate of substitution in consumer theory. Recall from Section 5.3 that we showed the relationship between marginal utilities and the marginal rate of substitution by totally differentiating the consumer's utility function, holding utility constant. To show the relationship between marginal products and the marginal rate of technical substitution, we totally differentiate the production function, assuming output is fixed. Let the production function be

$$x = x(K, L). \tag{10.23}$$

Totally differentiating (10.23),

$$dx = \frac{\partial x}{\partial L} dL + \frac{\partial x}{\partial K} dK = 0 \tag{10.24}$$

along an isoquant. Collecting terms in (10.24) and identifying the marginal rate of technical substitution,

$$MRTS = -\frac{dK}{dL} = \frac{\partial x/\partial L}{\partial x/\partial K} = \frac{MP_L}{MP_K}. \tag{10.25}$$

Thus, in consumer theory, the marginal rate of substitution is equal to the ratio of marginal utilities, and in production theory, the marginal rate of technical substitution is equal to the ratio of marginal products (equation 10.25). Diminishing marginal rate of technical substitution implies that as labor increases along an isoquant, the marginal product of labor must decline relative to the marginal product of capital. This is illustrated in Figure 10.8. At point B, more labor and less capital are used than at point

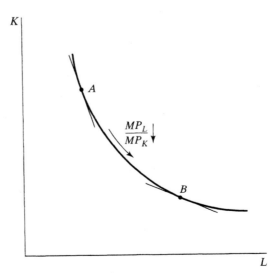

FIGURE 10.8   Diminishing Marginal Rates of Technical Substitution and Diminishing Ratio of Marginal Products

A. Thus, to satisfy diminishing marginal rates of technical substitution, the ratio of the marginal product of labor to the marginal product of capital must be lower at *B* than at *A*.

10.6   DIMINISHING RETURNS

An important property of most production functions is diminishing returns to variable inputs. If only one input is variable, **diminishing returns** is the same as diminishing marginal product. Returning to the general Cobb-Douglas production function $x = K^\alpha L^\beta$, for $\alpha, \beta > 0$ (equation 6.15),

$$MP_L = \beta \bar{K}^\alpha L^{\beta-1} \tag{10.26}$$

$$\frac{d}{dL} MP_L = (\beta - 1)\beta \bar{K}^\alpha L^{\beta-2}. \tag{10.27}$$

Equation 10.27 shows that this production function exhibits diminishing returns to labor if $\beta - 1 < 0$ $(\beta < 1)$. Similarly,

$$MP_k = \alpha K^{\alpha-1} \bar{L}^\beta \tag{10.28}$$

$$\frac{d}{dK} MP_K = (\alpha - 1)\alpha K^{\alpha-2} \bar{L}^\beta, \tag{10.29}$$

implying diminishing returns to capital if $\alpha < 1$. As we shall see in the next chapter, when there is only one variable input, diminishing returns to that variable input guarantee that short-run output supply is upward sloping and short-run input demand is downward sloping.

Diminishing Returns and Constant and Decreasing Returns to Scale   Moreover, if a production function exhibits constant or decreasing returns to scale, then the marginal products of labor and capital decline. This proposition is illustrated graphically in Figure 10.9 on the following page by showing that with constant returns to scale, the total product of labor is concave (slope declines as labor increases).[2] If a production function exhibits constant returns, then doubling inputs exactly doubles output. Along the 45° line in the upper graph, we can see that doubling all inputs exactly doubles output. Equal increases in output associated with equal increases in all inputs are recorded along the vertical axis of the lower graph. If capital is fixed at $\bar{K}$, however, diminishing marginal rates of technical substitution guarantee that the increase in labor needed to produce a specified increase in output must get larger. This increase in marginal labor input is recorded along the horizontal axes of the upper and lower graphs. As the lower graph shows, the marginal product of labor declines. The reason is illustrated by the following discrete version of the marginal product of labor: $MP_L = \Delta x/\Delta L$. Since the numerator is constant and the denominator is increasing, the ratio must fall. With decreasing returns, the effect is even stronger. The change in output (Δx) declines, and ΔL increases from one isoquant to the next if capital is fixed at $\bar{K}$. Thus, the numerator of the marginal product equation is decreasing while the denominator is increasing, and the ratio must fall. With increasing returns, Δx increases

---

[2]An outline of the proof for the constant-returns case is given in the appendix to this chapter.

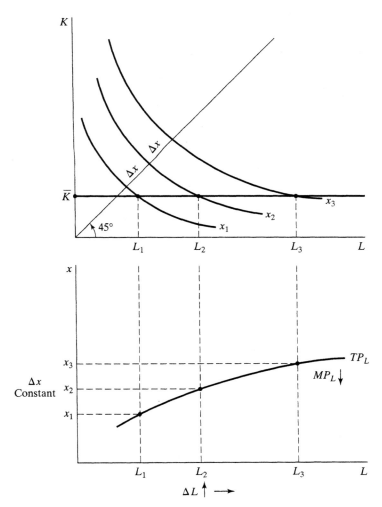

FIGURE 10.9   Diminishing Marginal Product of Labor and Constant Returns to Scale

from one isoquant to the next. Thus, both numerator and denominator of the marginal product equation increase, and marginal product can either increase or decrease.

An Example   The general Cobb-Douglas production function (equation 10.14) illustrates the different possibilities. We have already seen in equations 10.26–10.29 that if $x = K^\alpha L^\beta$, for α, $\beta > 0$,

   1. x exhibits constant returns if $\alpha + \beta = 1$, decreasing returns if $\alpha + \beta < 1$, and increasing returns if $\alpha + \beta > 1$;

   2. $dMP_L/dL = (\beta - 1)\beta K^\alpha L^{\beta-2}$;   **equation 10.27**

   3. $dMP_K/dK = (\alpha - 1)\alpha K^{\alpha-2}L^\beta$.   **equation 10.29**

Putting these together, we can see that if the production function exhibits constant or decreasing returns, then $\beta - 1 < 0$ and $\alpha - 1 < 0$, since $\alpha + \beta \leq 1$. This implies diminishing returns to both inputs. If, on the other hand, the production function exhibits increasing returns ($\alpha + \beta > 1$), it is possible to have increasing returns to one or both variable inputs in the short run.

10.6   REVIEW OF KEY CONCEPTS

We turn now to a development of a firm's cost function. Before continuing on, however, be sure you understand and can use the following key concepts.

A *production function* is a summary description of the outputs obtainable from different combinations of inputs used in production.

An *input-output table* is a tabular arrangement of the outputs obtainable from different combinations of inputs, as calculated from the production function.

A *production isoquant* describes combinations of inputs that can be used to produce a given (constant) amount of output.

An input combination used to produce a given output is *technologically efficient* if it is not possible to produce the same output using less of one input and no more of any other input.

In the basic model of production under certainty, we assume that managers use technologically efficient input combinations.

Isoquants, like indifference curves, are assumed to be downward sloping and convex to the origin. We say that isoquants exhibit *diminishing marginal rates of technical substitution*.

The *marginal rate of technical substitution* is the negative of the slope of the isoquant (just as the marginal rate of substitution for the consumer is the negative of the slope of the indifference curve).

If we assume continuity, isoquants are mathematically equivalent to indifference curves. The one exception to this statement is that output values are measurable (and thus cardinal), while utility values are only ordinal.

Input choices are *economically efficient* if they minimize the cost of producing a given output.

Given a set of input prices, an *isocost line* describes all the combinations of inputs that a firm can hire for a given total cost.

In the *long run,* all of a firm's inputs may vary.

In the *short run,* some of a firm's inputs are fixed. Typically, we think of fixed plant and equipment, but labor may be fixed as well if a firm has a long-term contract with its labor force.

A production function exhibits *constant returns to scale* if doubling all inputs exactly doubles output (homogeneity of degree 1).

A production function exhibits *decreasing returns to scale* if doubling all inputs less than doubles output (homogeneity of degree less than 1).

A production function exhibits *increasing returns to scale* if doubling all inputs more than doubles output (homogeneity of degree more than 1).

With capital and labor as the firm's inputs, the firm's *short-run expansion path* describes the quantities of labor it must use to produce different amounts of output if capital is fixed at $\overline{K}$.

The *total physical product of labor* describes the outputs obtainable from different labor inputs, holding all other inputs fixed. The *total physical product of capital* is defined analogously.

The *average physical product of labor* is the average output per unit of labor, assuming all other inputs are fixed; that is, average product is total product divided by labor.

The *marginal physical product of labor* is the additional amount of output produced by each additional unit of labor; that is, the marginal product is the slope of the total product function.

Most production functions exhibit the property of *diminishing returns* to, or *diminishing marginal products* of, variable inputs. If capital is fixed, for example, as more and more labor is added to that fixed capital, the marginal product of labor eventually declines.

10.7 ____ QUESTIONS FOR DISCUSSION

1. Consider two steel plants in two different countries. The plant in country A employs ten men for every ton of steel it produces, while the plant in country B employs only one man per ton of steel. Can we say that the plant in country B is more efficient than the plant in country A? Discuss in terms of both technological and economic efficiency.

2. It is generally observed that in relatively poor countries, firms use more labor and less capital to produce the same goods as are produced with a small amount of labor and much capital in richer countries. Are the firms in poor countries inefficient? Discuss in terms of both technological and economic efficiency.

3. Think of specific situations in which firms might be in short-run rather than long-run positions. Bear in mind in answering this question that labor could be a fixed factor of production.

4. What production processes do you think would be most likely to be subject to diminishing returns? Can you think of any that might actually have increasing returns to a variable input in the short run?

5. In the 1790s, Thomas Malthus predicted mass starvation because he believed population would always grow faster than our ability to increase agricultural production. Explain his theory in terms of diminishing returns in the short run.

6. Think of production processes that might not exhibit diminishing marginal rates of technical substitution. Explain your choices.

10.8 ____ PROBLEMS

Problems 1–6 Consider the following production functions.

(a) $x = 15K^{1/2}L^{1/2}$

(b) $x = 4K + 7L$

(c) $x = \dfrac{10KL}{K + L}$

(d) $x = K^2L$

(e) $x = \min(3K, 4L)$

1. Graph the isoquant for $x = 100$ for each production function.

2. Derive the function (if it exists) for the marginal rate of technical substitution for each production function.

3. Which functions exhibit diminishing marginal rates of technical substitution? Verify your answer.

4. Find functions (if they exist) for the total, average, and marginal physical products of labor for each production function.

5. Which functions exhibit diminishing marginal products of labor? Verify your answer.

6. What are the returns to scale of each production function? Verify your answer.

10.9 ____ LOGICAL AND MATHEMATICAL APPLICATIONS

1. Graph a production process requiring that capital and labor be used in exact (or fixed) proportions.

2. Graph a production process that allows capital and labor to be perfectly substituted for one another.

3. A homothetic production function has the property that the marginal rates of technical substitution are constant along every ray from the origin. Show that a homogeneous production function is also homothetic.

10.10 ___ APPENDIX

PROOF OF THE PROPOSITION THAT CONSTANT RETURNS IMPLY DIMINISHING MARGINAL PRODUCTS

To begin the proof, constant returns, or linear homogeneity, implies

$$f(\alpha K, \alpha L) = \alpha f(K, L). \tag{10.30}$$

Differentiating (10.30) with respect to α,

$$f_L L + f_K K = f. \tag{10.31}$$

Equation 10.31 is known as *Euler's equation.* Now we differentiate Euler's equation with respect to L:

$$f_{LL} L + f_L + f_{KL} K = f_L. \tag{10.32}$$

Collecting terms in (10.32),

$$f_{LL} + f_{KL} K = 0 \quad \Rightarrow \quad f_{LL} = -f_{KL} \frac{K}{L}. \tag{10.33}$$

Differentiating Euler's equation (10.31) with respect to K,

$$f_{LK} L + f_{KK} K + f_K = f_K \quad \Rightarrow \quad f_{LK} L + f_{KK} K = 0 \quad \Rightarrow \quad f_{KK} = -f_{KL} \frac{L}{K}. \tag{10.34}$$

Next, we totally differentiate the production function along an isoquant (output constant).

$$df = 0 = f_L dL + f_K dK \quad \Rightarrow \quad \frac{dK}{dL} = \frac{-f_L}{f_K} \tag{10.35}$$

$$\frac{d^2K}{dL^2} = \frac{-\left[\left(f_{LL} + f_{LK}\frac{\partial K}{\partial L}\right)f_K - \left(f_{KL} + f_{KK}\frac{\partial K}{\partial L}\right)f_L\right]}{f_K^2} \tag{10.36}$$

$$= \frac{-\left(f_{LK}\frac{-f_L}{f_K}f_K + f_{LL}f_K - f_{KK}\frac{-f_L}{f_K}f_L - f_{KL}f_L\right)}{f_K^2}$$

$$= \frac{-f_{LL}f_K^2 + 2f_{LK}f_L f_K - f_{KK}f_L^2}{f_K^3}$$

$$= \frac{f_{LK}\frac{K}{L}f_K^2 + f_{LK}f_K f_L \frac{L}{L} + f_{KL}f_L f_K \frac{K}{K} + f_{KL}\frac{L}{K}f_L^2}{f_K^3}$$

$$= \frac{\frac{f_K f_{LK}}{L}(f_K K + f_L L) + \frac{f_L f_{KL}}{K}(f_K K + f_L L)}{f_K^3}$$

$$= \frac{ff_{KL}\left(\dfrac{f_K K + f_L L}{LK}\right)}{f_K^3} = \frac{f^2 f_{KL}}{LK f_K^3}$$

$$\frac{d^2 K}{dL^2} = \frac{f^2 f_{KL}}{LK f_K^3}$$

Now, by diminishing marginal rates of technical substitution, $d^2 K / dL^2 > 0$. This means that $f_{KL} > 0$. Thus, if $f_{LL}L + f_{KL}K = 0$ (equation 10.33) and $f_{LK}L + f_{KK}K = 0$, then $f_{LL} < 0$ and $f_{KK} < 0$, which implies diminishing marginal products.

Chapter 11

COST FUNCTIONS

11.1   WHAT YOU SHOULD LEARN FROM THIS CHAPTER

In the next two chapters, we study the firm's decision problem in some detail. The basic assumption of production theory is that managers of firms maximize profits.[1] While we could just proceed directly to profit maximization, economists generally find it useful to treat the firm's problem as a two-stage decision problem. First, we study cost minimization and derive a set of *cost functions* describing the minimum cost of producing each output level. Then, assuming the firm always minimizes costs for whatever output level it is producing, we study how the firm chooses a profit-maximizing output level. This chapter deals with cost minimization, while Section 12.2 deals with a competitive firm's profit-maximizing output choice. The reason we can divide the firm's problem into cost minimization and profit maximization is because profit maximization implies that the firm has minimized costs for any output level it might choose.[2]

As we saw in Section 10.2, the feasible input combinations for every output level are determined by engineering knowledge that describes the available technology. The description of that technology is called a production function, the level surfaces of which are called isoquants. For a given level of production, the firm's cost-minimization problem is mathematically identical to the dual problem in consumer theory: find the lowest linear isocost line, subject to a production isoquant that is convex to the origin, or equivalently, find the least-cost input combination to produce a given output.

---

[1]This assumption has come under much criticism, but, like technological efficiency, it makes sense in a model based upon perfect, costless information and no uncertainty about future events. If a manager knows the firm's revenues and costs exactly for every output level and can costlessly compute profits, then the best the manager can do is maximize profits. Moreover, if information is costless, everyone else knows it as well. Thus, if the manager does not maximize profits, he or she will be fired by the owner of the firm. It is only under uncertainty that a manager might either purposefully or mistakenly do otherwise than maximize profits. Chapter 20, which deals with applications of uncertainty, considers what is called *moral hazard,* where a manager might use another objective function and then hide that fact from the owner of the firm. There are also cases in which a manager might wish to maximize profits, but have insufficient information. In those cases, other suggested objective functions, such as maximizing sales or maximizing the value of the firm, can be viewed as less than perfect rules of thumb a manager might use to approximate profit maximization.

[2]Profits (π) are simply equal to total revenues minus total economic costs. Thus, to maximize profits at a given output, the total cost of producing that output must be minimized.

We begin with the derivation of the firm's *long-run cost function.* This is mathematically equivalent to the generalized expenditure function developed in Sections 8.3 and 8.4. We then show how constant, increasing, and decreasing returns to scale are reflected in differently shaped long-run cost functions. Next, assuming that some inputs are fixed, we derive the firm's *short-run cost functions.* Finally, we develop some important properties of short-run cost functions and show how short-run and long-run cost functions are related to one another.

Mathematically, there is nothing new in this chapter. In fact, most of the math is exactly the same as the dual problem in consumer theory, except that the names of the variables have been changed. Thus, if you understood the math used in Sections 6.4, 6.6, 8.3, and 8.4, this material should be review. If you did not fully understand these sections, this material may help clarify the development of consumer theory.

II.2 _____ ECONOMIC COSTS

Before we go into the mathematics of cost minimization, we need to specify exactly what economists mean when they use the word *costs.* There are two equivalent ways of defining economic cost. One is to say that costs are the market value of all inputs used in production. Another is to say that economic cost is the market value of the best alternative employment of resources used in production. We define **opportunity cost** as the value of something in its next best alternative employment. Using the terminology of opportunity cost, economic cost is the sum total of the opportunity costs of all the inputs used in production. The idea is that all resources used in production have some market value or opportunity cost, whether the firm must pay cash for a particular resource or not. If the firm does not own a particular resource, it must buy or rent it and incur that market price. If the firm does own a resource, it may not pay a cash price, but it still uses the resource and, therefore, must forgo potential income that could be earned from selling or renting it to someone else. It is the *use* of the resource or the fact that someone else is not paying for its use that results in economic cost. Costs that must be paid directly are called **explicit costs;** economic costs not paid directly are called **implicit costs.** Implicit costs may be viewed as opportunity costs forgone.[3]

For example, an owner-manager may not draw a salary commensurate with what could be earned elsewhere but will get a periodic percentage of any revenues in excess of explicit costs. In addition, that owner-manager may have invested his or her own funds and be supplying his or her own land and capital equipment to the enterprise, without being paid market rates of interest or rent. While the firm's explicit cost might

---

[3]Sometimes in economics, the term *opportunity cost* is reserved to refer only to implicit costs. However, even explicit costs may be viewed as having opportunity costs. For example, the opportunity cost of hiring a particular worker is what that worker could earn in his next best alternative employment. In long-run equilibrium in a competitive market, explicit costs of inputs should equal their opportunity costs. But, if we are not in equilibrium, there might be a divergence. In that case, the economist values all resources at their opportunity costs, not their explicit costs.

be quite low (just materials and hired labor), the economic cost has to include the additional resource costs not being paid for directly: market salary to the owner-manager, market interest on the funds, market rent for the land and capital, and market prices for any other inputs the owner-manager supplies. These are the firm's implicit costs.

Whenever we speak of a firm's costs from now on, we always mean **total economic cost,** including both explicit and implicit costs:

$$\text{total economic cost} = \text{explicit cost} + \text{implicit cost}.$$

Thus, when economists refer to costs of production, they mean both direct costs and the opportunity cost of resources owned by the firm (implicit costs). Similarly, **economic profit** is the difference between total revenues and total economic cost:

$$\text{economic profit }(\pi) = \text{total revenue} - \text{total economic cost}$$
$$= \text{total revenue} - (\text{explicit cost} + \text{implicit cost}).$$

In other words, unless a firm's revenues exceed the total of explicit plus implicit costs, the firm is not making economic profits. The following example illustrates this point.

An Example of a Computer Software Company   Suppose a successful college professor, earning $40,000 per year, decides to quit academia to start a computer software business. The professor buys several different kinds of computers and converts the student apartment above the garage into a workshop. The apartment had been renting for $300 per month ($3600 per year), and the professor could rent all the computer equipment for $5000 per year. Five part-time student programmers are hired at $500 per month each ($30,000 total per year) and the utility bill runs $500 per month ($6000 per year). Table 11.1 summarizes the professor's costs. The explicit costs are hired labor plus utilities, for a total of $36,000 per year. However, to that we must add the implicit costs: income could have continued to be $40,000 per year in academia; the building could have been rented for $3600 per year; and the computer equipment could have been rented for $5000 per year. Thus, the implicit costs come to $48,600 per year. Until the professor's revenues exceed $84,600 per year, there is no economic profit.

TABLE 11.1   Explicit and Implicit Costs for a Software Business

Type of Cost	Resource	Amount
Explicit Costs	Hired Labor	$30,000
	Utilities	6,000
	Total Explicit Cost	36,000
Implicit Costs	Salary in Academia	40,000
	Rent on Buildings	3,600
	Rent on Computers	5,000
	Total Implicit Cost	48,600
Total Economic Cost		$84,600

11.3   COST MINIMIZATION

Having developed the concept of economic costs, we can now develop the concept of a **cost function** as the lowest possible economic cost to produce each possible output level. We begin by assuming the firm has a production function that can be described by isoquants which are convex to the origin. We also assume that wages and rents (both explicit and implicit) are parameters in the firm's decision problem. Under those assumptions, cost minimization for every output level is mathematically equivalent to expenditure minimization for every utility level in consumer theory. This is represented graphically in Figure 11.1. The isocost lines represent the level surfaces of the objective function for a given wage-rental ratio. The isoquant $\bar{x}$ represents the output constraint. The cost-minimizing input combination (K^*, L^*) is at the point of tangency between the isoquant and the isocost line at TC^*.

This tangency condition can be interpreted as follows:

$$\text{slope of isoquant} = \frac{dK}{dL} = -\frac{w}{r} = \text{slope of isocost line}$$

$$MRTS = -\frac{dK}{dL} = \frac{w}{r} = \frac{MP_L}{MP_K}. \tag{11.1}$$

As equation 11.1 shows, cost minimization implies that a firm adjusts its input mix until the technologically determined marginal rate of technical substitution equals the market-determined price ratio for those inputs. This is another example of a tangency condition which implies that the optimal solution is attained when the internal rate of trade (in this case the marginal rate of technical substitution) equals the external rate of trade (the input price ratio).

The cost-minimization condition summarized in (11.1) can also be viewed as a rule of thumb for optimal input choice. Without perfect information, a firm may not

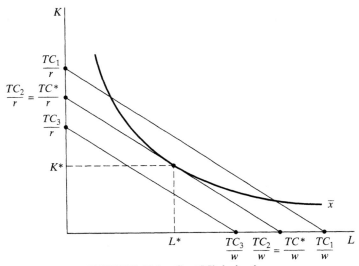

FIGURE 11.1   Cost Minimization

know enough about its production function to be able to construct an isoquant map and find a point of equal slopes. On the other hand, a firm may have local information about the marginal products of labor and capital. As the above equation shows, a firm can search for cost-minimizing input combinations by looking for combinations such that the ratios of marginal products are equal to factor price ratios.

A Mathematical Example To develop a mathematical example of cost-minimization, suppose we study one simple Cobb-Douglas production function,

$$x = K^{1/2}L^{1/2}. \tag{11.2}$$

We wish to minimize the cost of producing $\bar{x}$ units of output, given wages and rents of $\bar{w}$ and $\bar{r}$. The problem is

$$\min TC = \bar{w}L + \bar{r}K \tag{11.3}$$
$$\text{s.t. } \bar{x} = K^{1/2}L^{1/2}.$$

The Lagrangian is

$$\mathscr{L} = \bar{w}L + \bar{r}K + \lambda(\bar{x} - K^{1/2}L^{1/2}). \tag{11.4}$$

The first-order conditions are

$$\frac{\partial \mathscr{L}}{\partial L} = \bar{w} - \lambda * \left[\frac{1}{2} \frac{(K*)^{1/2}}{(L*)^{1/2}} \right] = 0 \implies \lambda* = \frac{2\bar{w}(L*)^{1/2}}{(K*)^{1/2}} \tag{11.5}$$

$$\frac{\partial \mathscr{L}}{\partial K} = \bar{r} - \lambda * \left[\frac{1}{2} \frac{(L*)^{1/2}}{(K*)^{1/2}} \right] = 0 \implies \lambda* = \frac{2\bar{r}(K*)^{1/2}}{(L*)^{1/2}} \tag{11.6}$$

$$\frac{\partial \mathscr{L}}{\partial \lambda} = \bar{x} - (K*)^{1/2}(L*)^{1/2} = 0. \tag{11.7}$$

Equating the values of $\lambda*$ from equations 11.5 and 11.6,

$$\frac{2\bar{w}(L*)^{1/2}}{(K*)^{1/2}} = \frac{2\bar{r}(K*)^{1/2}}{(L*)^{1/2}}. \tag{11.8}$$

Collecting terms in (11.8),

$$K* = \frac{\bar{w}}{\bar{r}} L*. \tag{11.9}$$

Substituting (11.9) in (11.7),

$$\bar{x} - \left(\frac{\bar{w}}{\bar{r}} L* \right)^{1/2} (L*)^{1/2} = 0. \tag{11.10}$$

Solving (11.10) for $L*$,

$$L* = \left(\frac{\bar{r}}{\bar{w}} \right)^{1/2} \bar{x}. \quad \text{the optimal choice of labor for producing } \bar{x} \tag{11.11}$$

Substituting (11.11) in (11.9),

$$K^* = \frac{\overline{w}}{\overline{r}}\left[\left(\frac{\overline{r}}{\overline{w}}\right)^{1/2}\overline{x}\right] \tag{11.12}$$

$$= \left(\frac{\overline{w}}{\overline{r}}\right)^{1/2}\overline{x}. \quad \text{the optimal choice of capital for producing } \overline{x}$$

Substituting (11.11) and (11.12) in the objective function in (11.3),

$$TC^* = \overline{w}L^* + \overline{r}K^* = \overline{w}\left(\frac{\overline{r}}{\overline{w}}\right)^{1/2}\overline{x} = \overline{r}\left(\frac{\overline{w}}{\overline{r}}\right)^{1/2}\overline{x} \tag{11.13}$$

$$= 2(\overline{w}\,\overline{r})^{1/2}\overline{x}. \quad \text{the minimum cost of producing } \overline{x}$$

11.4 ELASTICITY OF SUBSTITUTION

In the long run, the firm can optimally adjust its input combination in response to changes in the market wage-rental ratio. The extent to which the firm will adjust its input combination depends upon the engineering technology summarized by the isoquants. The measure of how responsive a firm's input choices are to changes in the wage-rental ratio is called the **elasticity of substitution** along an isoquant. This is mathematically equivalent to the elasticity of substitution along an indifference curve in consumer theory (Section 8.8), and it measures the responsiveness of the cost-minimizing capital-labor ratio to changes in the wage-rental ratio in the long run.

$$\sigma_{KL} = \frac{\%\Delta \text{ in the capital-labor ratio}}{\%\Delta \text{ in the wage-rental ratio}} = \frac{\%\Delta \text{ in } K/L}{\%\Delta \text{ in } w/r} \tag{11.14}$$

$$= \frac{\dfrac{\Delta(K/L)}{K/L}}{\dfrac{\Delta(w/r)}{w/r}} = \frac{\Delta(K/L)}{\Delta(w/r)}\frac{w/r}{K/L} = \frac{d(K/L)}{d(w/r)}\frac{w/r}{K/L}$$

Just as in Section 8.7, we can simplify this by forming new functions:

$$k = \frac{K}{L} \quad \text{and} \quad \omega = \frac{w}{r}, \tag{11.15}$$

where $k = f(\omega)$. Thus, substituting (11.15) in (11.14),

$$\sigma_{KL} = \frac{dk}{d\omega}\frac{\omega}{k}. \tag{11.16}$$

The function $k = f(\omega)$ is derived from the tangency condition, $MRTS = w/r$. For example, if $x = K^{1/2}L^{1/2}$, equation 11.9 can be written as

$$MRTS = \frac{K}{L} = \frac{w}{r} \Rightarrow k = \omega. \tag{11.17}$$

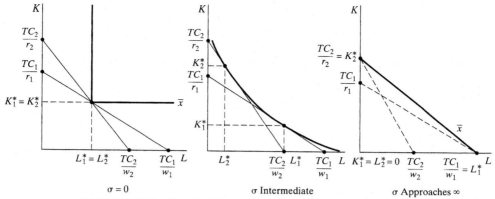

FIGURE 11.2   The Limiting Cases of Elasticity of Substitution

Substituting (11.17) in (11.16),

$$\sigma_{KL} = \frac{dk}{d\omega}\frac{\omega}{k} = 1\frac{\omega}{\omega} = 1. \qquad (11.18)$$

Thus, equation 11.18 shows that if the production function is $x = K^{1/2}L^{1/2}$, the elasticity of substitution equals 1.[4]

Limiting Cases of Elasticity of Substitution   Figure 11.2 shows that elasticity of substitution along an isoquant has the same limiting cases as elasticity of substitution along an indifference curve. In the left graph, the isoquants are "square," implying that the firm must use inputs in fixed proportions (referred to as **fixed proportions** or **Leontief technology**).[5] Thus, the firm uses (K^*, L^*), regardless of input prices, and the elasticity of substitution is 0. The middle graph shows an intermediate elasticity of substitution. When the wage-rental ratio changes from w_1/r_1 to w_2/r_2, the capital-labor ratio changes from K_1^*/L_1^* to K_2^*/L_2^*.

The right graph is the same as the one for linear indifference curves in consumer theory.[6] Recall from Figure 8.8 that if the slope of the isoquant is the same as the slope of the isocost line, the cost-minimizing input combination is indeterminate, and the

---

[4]Just as the marginal rate of substitution is not always y/x, the marginal rate of technical substitution is not always equal to K/L, and the elasticity of substitution is not always equal to 1. In fact, in general, production functions do not have constant elasticity of substitution along an isoquant. The functions are so simple only for the Cobb-Douglas-like functions we have been using as examples: $x = K^\alpha L^\beta$. These functions are a special case ($\sigma = 1$) of a class of functions called *constant elasticity of substitution* (CES) production functions. The general formula for a non-Cobb-Douglas constant-returns-to-scale CES production function is

$$x = A[\alpha K^{(\sigma-1)/\sigma} + (1 - \alpha)L^{(\sigma-1)/\sigma}]^{\sigma/(\sigma-1)}, \quad A > 0, \quad 0 < \alpha < 1.$$

(Note that if $\sigma = 1$, this formula cannot apply because of division by 0. Applying L'Hôpital's rule, the above formula reduces to $x = AK^\alpha L^{1-\alpha}$. See Chiang, *Fundamentals of Mathematical Economics*, pp. 429–430.)

[5]Wassily Leontief, *The Structure of the American Economy, 1919–1939*, 2d ed. (New York: Oxford, 1951).

[6]See Figure 8.8.

smallest change in the slope of the isocost line can move the optimal input choice from one axis to the other (that is, from $K = 0$ to $L = 0$). The elasticity of substitution approaches infinity.

LONG-RUN COST FUNCTIONS

In the example developed in Section 11.3 (equations 11.2–11.3), we found the optimal input combination (K^*, L^*) to produce a given output $\bar{x}$ and the minimum cost of producing that output, TC^*, given input prices $\bar{w}$ and $\bar{r}$. Now, if we allow x to vary, we can construct a function that describes the minimum cost of producing each output.

The Long-run Expansion Path First, we construct a function, from the points of tangency between the isocost lines and the isoquants, that describes the optimal combination of inputs at each output level as output expands:

$$K^* = K^*(L^*; \bar{w}, \bar{r}). \qquad (11.19)$$

We call this function the firm's **long-run expansion path,** and it is mathematically equivalent to the consumer's income-consumption curve developed in Sections 6.2 and 6.4.

Figure 11.3 illustrates graphically how the firm's long-run expansion path is constructed. The cost-minimizing input combination to produce x_1 is (K_1^*, L_1^*) at TC_1^*. To produce x_2, the optimal combination is (K_2^*, L_2^*) at TC_2^*; and to produce x_3, the optimal combination is (K_3^*, L_3^*) at TC_3^*. The expansion path is constructed by connecting

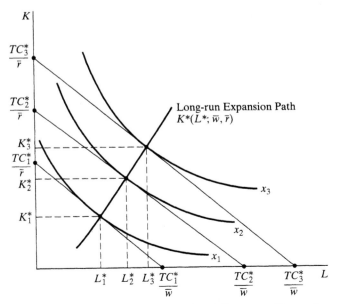

FIGURE 11.3 Derivation of the Firm's Long-run Expansion Path

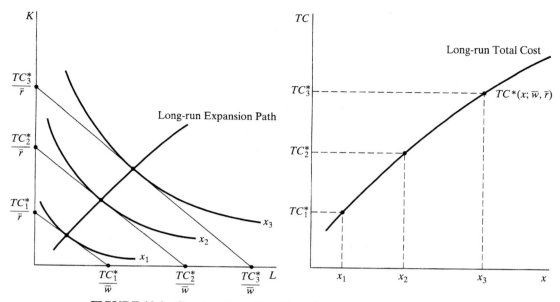

FIGURE 11.4   Construction of the Firm's Long-run Total Cost Function

the points of tangency, just as the income-consumption curve is constructed in consumer theory.

When we solved the problem stated in equations 11.3, we found that $K^* = (\overline{w}/\overline{r})L^*$ (equation 11.9) if $x = K^{1/2}L^{1/2}$. This function (11.9) is the firm's long-run expansion path, just as $y^* = (\overline{p}_x/\overline{p}_y) = x^*$ is the consumer's income-consumption curve for the utility function $U = x^{1/2}y^{1/2}$. (Substitute $\alpha = \beta = 1/2$ in equations 6.16 and 6.21.)

Long-run Total Cost   From the firm's long-run expansion path, we can also derive functions that describe the optimal inputs for each output level and the minimum cost of producing each output level:

$$K^* = K^*(x; \overline{w}, \overline{r}) \quad \text{and} \quad L^* = L^*(x; \overline{w}, \overline{r}). \qquad (11.20)$$

Thus, substituting (11.20) in (11.3),

$$TC^*(w; \overline{w}, \overline{r}) = \overline{w}L^*(x; \overline{w}, \overline{r}) + \overline{r}K^*(x; \overline{w}, \overline{r}). \quad \text{\small long-run total cost as a function of output}$$

Figure 11.4 illustrates graphically how the firm's **long-run total cost function** is constructed as the minimum cost of producing each output level when all inputs are variable. In the left graph, the minimum cost for x_1 is TC_1^*, for x_2 is TC_2^*, and for x_3 is TC_3^*. These total costs are plotted along the vertical axis of the right graph. The respective outputs are plotted along the horizontal axis of the right graph. The long-run total cost function connects each output and its respective minimum cost.

In the example set out in equation 11.2, $x = K^{1/2}L^{1/2}$, we already derived the optimal input combination for each given output level $\overline{x}$ and the total cost of producing $\overline{x}$.

Thus, if x is allowed to vary, we already have the functions for the optimal input combinations and the total cost at each output level:

$$L^* = \left(\frac{\bar{r}}{\bar{w}}\right)^{1/2}\bar{x} \quad \Rightarrow \quad L^*(x) = \left(\frac{\bar{r}}{\bar{w}}\right)^{1/2}x \qquad \text{equation 11.1 with } x \text{ variable} \qquad (11.21)$$

$$K^* = \left(\frac{\bar{w}}{\bar{r}}\right)^{1/2}\bar{x} \quad \Rightarrow \quad K^*(x) = \left(\frac{\bar{w}}{\bar{r}}\right)^{1/2}x \qquad \text{equation 11.12 with } x \text{ variable} \qquad (11.22)$$

$$TC^* = 2(\bar{w}\,\bar{r})^{1/2}\bar{x} \quad \Rightarrow \quad TC^*(x) = 2(\bar{w}\,\bar{r})^{1/2}x. \quad \text{equation 11.13 with } x \text{ variable} \qquad (11.23)$$

If we now let w and r vary, these expressions for L^* and K^* form generalized long-run demand functions for inputs, conditional on the level of output. Since these demand functions are conditional on the level of output, we refer to them as long-run **conditional input demand functions.**[7]

The generalized long-run total cost function is then constructed from the conditional input demand functions. The conditional input demand functions and the long-run total cost function are mathematically identical to the consumer's generalized compensated demand functions and the expenditure function, respectively (see Section 8.5).

Thus, allowing w and r to vary in equations 11.21–11.23,

$$L^* = \left(\frac{r}{w}\right)^{1/2}x \qquad \text{generalized conditional long-run demand for labor} \qquad (11.24)$$

$$K^* = \left(\frac{w}{r}\right)^{1/2}x \qquad \text{generalized conditional long-run demand for capital} \qquad (11.25)$$

$$TC^*(w, r, x) = 2(wr)^{1/2}x. \qquad \text{generalized long-run total cost} \qquad (11.26)$$

Notice that equations 11.24–11.26 are mathematically equivalent to

$$x^* = (p_y/p_x)^{1/2}U$$
$$y^* = (p_x/p_y)^{1/2}U$$
$$M^*(p_x, p_y, U) = 2(p_x p_y)^{1/2}U,$$

for the utility function $U = x^{1/2}y^{1/2}$.[8]

Comparison of Cost Minimization and Expenditure Minimization   To summarize the cost-minimization problem, recall once again that it is mathematically identical to the consumer's dual problem. To make this clear, consider the two problems side by side below.

---

[7]Just as the consumer's demand functions are homogeneous of degree 0 in prices and income, the conditional input demand functions are homogeneous of degree 0 in input prices. This is an important restriction imposed in the estimation of long-run cost. A discussion of long-run cost estimation can be found in Section 11.7.

[8]$U = x^{1/2}y^{1/2}$ is a positive monotonic transformation of $U = xy$ (equation 8.16). The generalized compensated demand functions and the expenditure function for both utility functions are derived as (8.22), (8.23), and (8.24), respectively, with $x^{1/2}y^{1/2} = (xy)^{1/2}$.

Consumer Dual Problem	Cost Minimization
$\min M = p_x x + p_y y$	$\min TC = wL + rK$
s.t. $U = U(x, y)$	s.t. $x = x(K, L)$

Compensated Demands	Conditional Demands
General demand functions $\begin{cases} x_c^* = x_c^*(p_x, p_y, U) \\ y_c^* = y_c^*(p_x, p_y, U) \end{cases}$	$K^* = K^*(w, r, x)$ $L^* = L^*(w, r, x)$
Solution $M^*(p_x, p_y, U) = P_x x_c^* + p_y y_c^*$	$TC^*(w, r, x) = wL^* = rK^*$

Long-run Average and Marginal Costs   Having derived the firm's generalized long-run total cost function, we can now derive a firm's long-run average cost and long-run marginal cost functions. Let

$$TC^* = LRTC, \quad \text{long-run total cost,} \tag{11.27}$$

then

$$\text{long-run average cost} \quad (LRAC) = \frac{LRTC}{x} \tag{11.28}$$

$$\text{long-run marginal cost} \quad (LRMC) = \frac{d}{dx} LRTC. \tag{11.29}$$

Thus, if $x = K^{1/2}L^{1/2}$ (equation 11.2), equation 11.26 can be restated as

$$LRTC = 2(wr)^{1/2}x, \tag{11.30}$$

and, from (11.30),

$$LRAC = LRMC = 2(wr)^{1/2}. \tag{11.31}$$

11.6   LONG-RUN COST FUNCTIONS AND RETURNS TO SCALE

Equations 11.30 and 11.31 illustrate an important property of long-run cost functions with constant-returns-to-scale (homogeneous of degree 1) production functions. Notice that if $x = K^{1/2}L^{1/2}$, long-run total cost is a linear function of output, and long-run average and marginal costs are equal and constant, independent of output. This happens whenever the production function exhibits constant returns to scale.[9] To see this point, note that long-run total cost as a function of capital and labor is always homogeneous of degree 1. In other words, long-run total cost and inputs always increase in the same proportion:

---

[9]See equations 10.14–10.16 for a reminder that $x = K^{1/2}L^{1/2}$ exhibits constant returns to scale. $x = K^{1/2}L^{1/2}$ is a Cobb-Douglas production function with $\alpha = \beta = 1/2$ and $\alpha + \beta = 1$.

$$w(\alpha L) + r(\alpha K) = \alpha(wL + rK). \tag{11.32}$$

Thus, from (11.32) and (10.15), when inputs are increased by any positive multiple, cost and output are increased by the same positive multiple. Changes in costs are proportional to changes in output:

$$\Delta LRTC = b(\Delta x), \tag{11.33}$$

where b is a constant factor of proportionality; or rearranging (11.33),

$$\frac{\Delta LRTC}{\Delta x} = b. \tag{11.34}$$

Converting (11.34) to calculus notation,

$$\frac{d}{dx} LRTC = LRMC = b. \tag{11.35}$$

Equation 11.35 implies that long-run total cost must be a linear function. Its slope, long-run marginal cost, is a constant, and, since the cost of producing zero output is 0 *in the long run,* long-run total cost must go through the origin:

$$LRTC = bx \tag{11.36}$$
$$LRMC = LRAC = b. \tag{11.37}$$

Figure 11.5 illustrates long-run cost functions for a constant-returns-to-scale production function. Long-run total cost is a linear function from the origin, and long-run average and marginal costs are constant.

Increasing Returns   The cost functions associated with increasing- and decreasing-returns-to-scale production functions can be understood by appealing to the same kind of argument. Beginning with increasing returns, we know from (10.13) that when the production function is homogeneous, multiplying all inputs by $\alpha > 1$ multiplies output by more than α:

$$x(\alpha K, \alpha L) = \alpha^k x(K, L) > \alpha x(K, L), \quad \text{for } \alpha, k > 1.$$

But, cost is always proportional to inputs (equation 11.32). Thus, if inputs are multiplied by a positive constant, costs are multiplied by the same constant, but output is multiplied by more than that constant. This means that output increases faster than costs and that

$$\frac{\Delta LRTC}{\Delta x} \approx \frac{d}{dx} LRTC$$

(which equals $LRMC$) must decline. Moreover, if the long-run marginal cost function is falling, the long-run total cost function must be concave. And, since zero inputs implies both zero output and zero cost, the long-run total cost function must be concave from the origin. This implies that the long-run average cost function must be falling and must be greater than the long-run marginal cost function at each output.

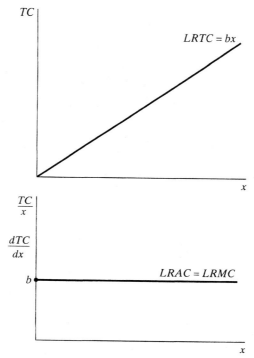

FIGURE 11.5   Long-run Cost Functions for a Constant-Returns-to-Scale Production Function

Figure 11.6 illustrates the cost functions for an increasing-returns-to-scale production function. The long-run marginal cost function is falling, implying a concave long-run total cost function. Concavity from the origin, in turn, implies that the long-run average cost function is falling and that the slope of the line from the origin (long-run average cost) is greater than the slope of the function (long-run marginal cost) at each output.

Decreasing Returns   If a homogeneous production function exhibits decreasing returns to scale, we know from (10.12) that

$$x(\alpha K, \alpha L) = \alpha^k x(K, L) < \alpha x(K, L), \quad k < 1, \quad \alpha > 1.$$

But, once again, cost is proportional to inputs (equation 11.32). Thus, if inputs are multiplied by a positive constant, costs are multiplied by the same constant, and output is multiplied by less than that constant. This means that output increases more slowly than costs and that

$$\frac{\Delta LRTC}{\Delta x} \approx \frac{d}{dx} LRTC$$

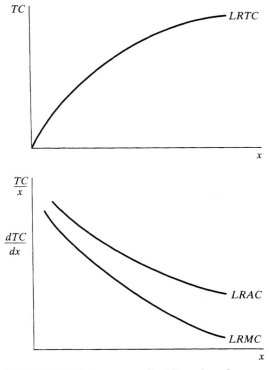

**FIGURE 11.6   Long-run Cost Functions for an
Increasing-Returns-to-Scale Production Function**

(which equals *LRMC*) must increase. If the long-run marginal cost function is rising from the origin, the long-run total cost function must be convex from the origin, and the long-run average cost function must be rising and less than the long-run marginal cost function at each output.

Figure 11.7 illustrates the cost functions for a decreasing-returns-to-scale production function. The long-run marginal cost function is rising, implying a convex long-run total cost function. Convexity from the origin, in turn, implies that the long-run average cost function is rising and that the slope of the line from the origin (average cost) is less than the slope of the function (marginal cost) at each output.

U-shaped Long-run Average Cost Functions and Scale Economies   When economists construct stylized long-run cost functions, they often conceive of the long-run average cost function as being U-shaped, first declining to some minimum long-run average cost and increasing thereafter. From the argument developed above, we know that this assumed shape also implies an assumption that production exhibits first increasing and then decreasing returns to scale.

The idea behind this stylized description of costs is as follows. In the production of certain goods, the production process that is cost-minimizing for a small number of units produced may have much higher unit (average) costs than a production process

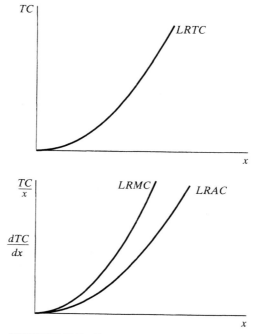

FIGURE 11.7   Long-run Cost Functions for a Decreasing-Returns-to-Scale Production Function

used for a large production run. For example, if an automobile company is only going to produce a few cars a year, it will not be cost-minimizing to use an assembly line, even though the assembly line can achieve a very low unit cost if a large number of cars are going to be produced each year. We say that an assembly line has large **economies of scale,** meaning that substantial unit cost savings can only be achieved at relatively high output levels.

In principle, once a firm has expanded until it is using its lowest unit-cost production process, it could continue to expand with constant returns to scale by simply replicating plants identical to the plant operating at minimum unit cost. This is what McDonald's does, for example. Every McDonald's is practically identical to every other McDonald's. On the other hand, many firms find that if they become too large, with many different plants or branches, it becomes difficult to coordinate the management of such a large firm. This coordination problem may cause unit costs to rise. In this case, the economist would say that there were **diseconomies** associated with managerial coordination of a large firm.

The scenarios described above imply two possible shapes for the long-run average cost curve. On the one hand, long-run average cost as a function of output might first decline as output expands, then be constant for some time as plants are replicated, and then eventually rise. On the other hand, the long-run average cost function might decline to a single minimum and then rise immediately. When we speak of a U-shaped

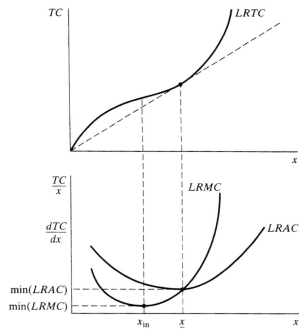

FIGURE 11.8 Long-run Cost Functions with a U-shaped Long-run Average Cost Function

long-run average cost function, we will be referring to the second possibility. Over some range of output, the first possibility can be analyzed "as if" there are constant returns to scale.

Figure 11.8 illustrates long-run cost functions where the long-run average cost function is U-shaped. The long-run total cost function is first concave and then convex, reflecting increasing returns followed by decreasing returns. Long-run average cost (the slope of the line from the origin) falls as output expands, reaching a minimum when the line from the origin is tangent to the function, and then rises. We will refer to the output corresponding to minimum long-run average cost as $\underline{x}$. Long-run marginal cost as a function of output falls to the inflection point (x_{in}) and then rises. Long-run marginal cost equals long-run average cost at $\underline{x}$, the output associated with minimum long-run average cost.

11.7   USING THE COBB-DOUGLAS PRODUCTION FUNCTION: ONE WAY ECONOMISTS ESTIMATE LONG-RUN COST FUNCTIONS

In Section 6.5, we saw how economists use the general Cobb-Douglas demand and utility functional forms to estimate demand functions and demand elasticities. Economists also use the Cobb-Douglas and the CES (see footnote 4, this chapter) production functions to estimate long-run costs when engineering data are not available or are insufficient. We have already derived the long-run cost function for the simple

Cobb-Douglas production function $x = K^{1/2}L^{1/2}$. The cost function for the general Cobb-Douglas production function $x = AK^{\alpha}L^{\beta}$ is somewhat more complicated to derive, but it is more useful in situations in which the exact relationship between capital and labor is not known but might be estimated empirically from the data. Moreover, as we saw in Section 10.4 and in equations 10.16, the estimates of α and β provide a direct estimate of the returns to scale of the underlying production process. Modelling with a simple functional form such that the exponents add to 1 *imposes* an assumption of constant returns to scale. Using a more flexible functional form allows us to *estimate* the actual returns to scale of the production function. For example, if estimated values for α and β *do* add to 1, then the assumption of constant returns to scale would be warranted. But if $\alpha + \beta > 1$, the production process exhibits increasing returns, and if $\alpha + \beta < 1$, the production process exhibits decreasing returns.

Mathematical Development   To find the conditional input demands and the long-run cost function for the general Cobb-Douglas production function, we set up and solve the firm's cost minimization problem subject to the general Cobb-Douglas production function as a constraint. The problem is

$$\min TC = wL + rK \tag{11.38}$$
$$\text{s.t. } x = AK^{\alpha}L^{\beta}.$$

The Lagrangian is

$$\mathscr{L} = wL + rK + \lambda(x - AK^{\alpha}L^{\beta}). \tag{11.39}$$

The first-order conditions are

$$\frac{\partial \mathscr{L}}{\partial L} = w - \lambda^*[\beta A(K^*)^{\alpha}(L^*)^{\beta-1}] = 0 \quad \Rightarrow \quad \lambda^* = \frac{w}{\beta A(K^*)^{\alpha}(L^*)^{\beta-1}} \tag{11.40}$$

$$\frac{\partial \mathscr{L}}{\partial K} = r - \lambda^*[\alpha A(K^*)^{\alpha-1}(L^*)^{\beta}] = 0 \quad \Rightarrow \quad \lambda^* = \frac{r}{\alpha(K^*)^{\alpha-1}(L^*)^{\beta}} \tag{11.41}$$

$$\frac{\partial \mathscr{L}}{\partial \lambda} = x - A(K^*)^{\alpha}(L^*)^{\beta} = 0. \tag{11.42}$$

Equating the values of λ^* from (11.40) and (11.41),

$$\lambda^* = \frac{w}{\beta A(K^*)^{\alpha}(L^*)^{\beta-1}} = \frac{r}{\alpha A(K^*)^{\alpha-1}(L^*)^{\beta}} \tag{11.43}$$

Solving (11.43) for K^*,

$$K^* = \frac{\alpha w}{\beta r} L^*. \tag{11.44}$$

Substituting (11.44) in (11.42),

$$x - A\left(\frac{\alpha w}{\beta r} L^*\right)^{\alpha}(L^*)^{\beta} = 0 \quad \Rightarrow \quad (L^*)^{\alpha+\beta} = \frac{x}{A}\left(\frac{\beta r}{\alpha w}\right)^{\alpha}. \tag{11.45}$$

Solving (11.45) for L^*,

$$L^* = \left(\frac{\beta r}{\alpha w}\right)^{\frac{\alpha}{\alpha+\beta}} \left(\frac{x}{A}\right)^{\frac{1}{\alpha+\beta}}. \qquad \text{the conditional input demand for } L \qquad (11.46)$$

Substituting (11.46) in (11.44),

$$K^* = \frac{\alpha w}{\beta r}\left(\frac{\beta r}{\alpha w}\right)^{\frac{\alpha}{\alpha+\beta}} \left(\frac{x}{A}\right)^{\frac{1}{\alpha+\beta}} \qquad (11.47)$$

$$= \left(\frac{\beta r}{\alpha w}\right)^{-1}\left(\frac{\beta r}{\alpha w}\right)^{\frac{\alpha}{\alpha+\beta}}\left(\frac{x}{A}\right)^{\frac{1}{\alpha+\beta}} = \left(\frac{\beta r}{\alpha w}\right)^{\frac{-\beta}{\alpha+\beta}}\left(\frac{x}{A}\right)^{\frac{1}{\alpha+\beta}}$$

$$= \left(\frac{\alpha w}{\beta r}\right)^{\frac{\beta}{\alpha+\beta}} \left(\frac{x}{A}\right)^{\frac{1}{\alpha+\beta}}. \qquad \text{the conditional input demand for } K$$

Substituting (11.46) and (11.47) in the objective function (11.38).

$$TC^* = wL^* + rK^* = w\left(\frac{\beta r}{\alpha w}\right)^{\frac{\alpha}{\alpha+\beta}}\left(\frac{x}{A}\right)^{\frac{1}{\alpha+\beta}} + r\left(\frac{\alpha w}{\beta r}\right)^{\frac{\beta}{\alpha+\beta}}\left(\frac{x}{A}\right)^{\frac{1}{\alpha+\beta}} \qquad (11.48)$$

$$= \left\{\frac{1}{A}\left[\left(\frac{\beta}{\alpha}\right)^{\alpha} + \left(\frac{\alpha}{\beta}\right)^{\beta}\right]\right\}^{\frac{1}{\alpha+\beta}}(r)^{\frac{\alpha}{\alpha+\beta}}(w)^{\frac{\beta}{\alpha+\beta}}(x)^{\frac{1}{\alpha+\beta}}.$$

Notice now that (11.48) can be expressed in logs:

$$\log TC = -\frac{1}{\alpha+\beta}\log A[(\alpha - \beta)(\log \beta - \log \alpha)] \qquad (11.49)$$

$$+ \frac{\beta}{\alpha+\beta}\log w + \frac{\alpha}{\alpha+\beta}\log r + \frac{1}{\alpha+\beta}\log x.$$

Equation 11.49 can now be estimated using cost, input price, and output data.[10]

Consistency Checks and Economic Interpretations   The coefficients estimated for equation 11.49 can now be checked for consistency, and they have important economic interpretations. To check for consistency, note the following relationships from (11.49):

$$\text{coefficient for } \log x = \frac{1}{\alpha+\beta} = \frac{\text{coefficient for } \log w}{\beta}. \qquad (11.50)$$

Solving (11.50) for β,

$$\beta = \frac{\text{coefficient for } \log w}{\text{coefficient for } \log x}, \qquad (11.51)$$

and by analogy,

$$\alpha = \frac{\text{coefficient for } \log r}{\text{coefficient for } \log x}. \qquad (11.52)$$

---

[10]Other, more general, functional forms for estimating cost functions are used, but the Cobb-Douglas functional form is a widely used form.

Therefore, we can empirically find α and β and then see if the estimates are consistent with the conditions implied by equations 11.50–11.52.

The important economic interpretations are as follows. First, $\alpha + \beta$ indicates the returns to scale of the production function, as discussed above and in Section 10.4. Moreover, by dividing the data into different ranges of output and estimating separate equations, it may turn out that a particular production process exhibits increasing returns over some ranges of output, constant returns over others, and decreasing returns over others still.

Planning and Policy Implications   Estimates of the degree of scale economies can have important policy and planning implications in situations in which the underlying engineering relationships are not sufficiently well understood to allow the estimation of a production function from process data. For example, a firm might wish to estimate whether its costs are likely to go up or down if it expands output further. It may have historical cost and output data, but not sufficient engineering information. With this formulation, it could estimate a projected cost function. Interestingly, many cost estimates have found that the firms studied had increasing returns at low levels of output followed by constant returns over wide ranges of output. With such information, the firm might estimate that if it expanded output, it would not face higher average costs.

From a policy perspective, a firm's returns to scale have important implications for market structure. Basically, if a production function exhibits increasing returns to scale over the relevant range of output, then there is a presumption among many economists that the firm is a monopolist and subject to antitrust laws. (See Section 13.5, Figures 13.8 and 13.9, and Section 15.6.) One of the jobs of economists employed by the Federal Trade Commission, for example, is to estimate economies of scale for firms under suspicion as monopolies.

Second, as we saw in equations 6.29–6.31, where the Cobb-Douglas coefficients turned out to be the demand elasticities, the coefficients for w and r provide estimates of the elasticity of total cost with respect to changes in the wage rate or the rental rate. If a firm faces an increase in input costs, it could use this formulation to estimate the impact of the increase in input costs on its overall costs.

II.8   SHORT-RUN COSTS WITH ONE VARIABLE INPUT

Turning now to short-run costs, we begin by assuming one input is fixed and the other is variable. We can then derive functions that describe short-run costs of production. We will derive these functions assuming capital is fixed and labor is variable, but the analysis is analogous if labor is fixed and capital is variable.

Short-run Total Cost   Short-run total costs can be derived from the firm's short-run expansion path. Figure 11.9 illustrates this derivation for a given wage and rental rate:

$$\text{short-run total cost } (SRTC) = SRTC(x(L; \overline{K}); \overline{w}, \overline{r}). \tag{11.53}$$

In the left graph, capital is fixed at $\overline{K}$, implying the firm must use L_1 to produce x_1, L_2 to produce x_2, and L_3 to produce x_3. Also on the left graph, we see that it costs

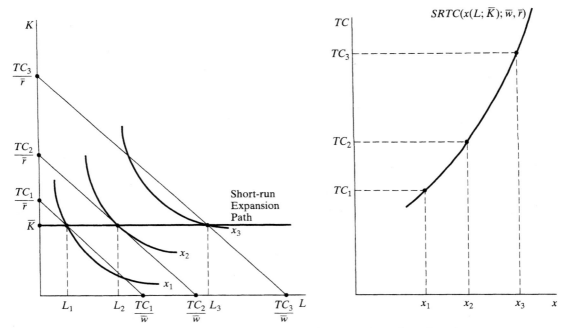

FIGURE 11.9 Derivation of the Firm's Short-run Total Cost Function

TC_1 to produce x_1 using $\overline{K}$ and L_1, TC_2 to produce x_2 using $\overline{K}$ and L_2, and TC_3 to produce x_3 using $\overline{K}$ and L_3. In the right graph, those total costs, TC_1, TC_2, and TC_3, are plotted along the vertical axis. The respective output levels, x_1, x_2, and x_3, are plotted along the horizontal axis. The short-run total cost function is constructed by connecting the points, (TC_1, x_1), (TC_2, x_2), and (TC_3, x_3).

Decomposing Short-run Total Cost Short-run total cost is often divided into fixed costs and variable costs:

short-run variable cost $\qquad (SRVC) = wL$ $\qquad\qquad$ (11.54)

fixed cost $\qquad\qquad (FC) = r\overline{K}$ $\qquad\qquad$ (11.55)

short-run total cost $\qquad\qquad = wL + r\overline{K} = SRVC + FC.$ $\qquad$ (11.56)

To derive the short-run variable cost, we begin with the firm's total product of labor function, $x = x(L; \overline{K})$. The inverse of the total product of labor is $x^{-1} = L = L(x; \overline{K})$. Figure 11.10 illustrates the formation of $L(x; \overline{K})$ from the total product of labor, $x(L; \overline{K})$. The values x_1, x_2, and x_3 from the vertical axis of the left graph are plotted along the horizontal axis of the right graph. L_1, L_2, and L_3 from the horizontal axis of the left graph are plotted along the vertical axis of the right graph. The function $L(x; \overline{K})$ is constructed by connecting the points (L_1, x_1), (L_2, x_2), and

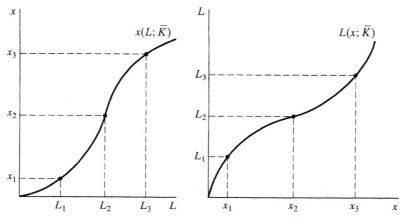

FIGURE 11.10   Derivation of the Firm's $L(x; \overline{K})$ Function

(L_3, x_3). Since the total product of labor function is first convex and then concave, its inverse $L(x; \overline{K})$ is first concave and then convex.

Short-run variable cost is then proportional to $L(x; \overline{K})$, since $SRVC = wL = wL(x; \overline{K})$. Figure 11.11 illustrates the relationship between $L(x; \overline{K})$ and $wL(x; \overline{K})$. Short-run variable cost is equal to 0 at $L = 0$ and is then w times $L(x; \overline{K})$ thereafter.

To reconstruct the short-run total cost function from the short-run variable cost function, we simply add the constant, fixed cost to the function derived in Figure 11.11.

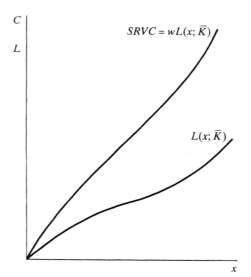

**FIGURE 11.11   Derivation of the Firm's
Short-run Variable Cost Function**

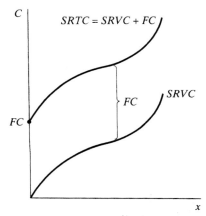

FIGURE 11.12   Derivation of the Firm's Short-run Total Cost Function from the Short-run Variable Cost Function and the Fixed Cost

(Notice that the cost intercept is simply fixed cost.) Thus, the short-run total cost function is always vertically parallel to the short-run variable cost function. This implies that the two functions have the same slope at every output level. Figure 11.12 illustrates this parallel relationship. At each output level, short-run total cost equals short-run variable cost plus fixed cost.

Short-run Average and Marginal Costs   Having defined the short-run total cost functions, we can, of course, define short-run average and marginal cost functions:

short-run average variable cost $$(SRAVC) = \frac{SRVC}{x} = \frac{wL(x)}{x} \qquad (11.57)$$

average fixed cost $$(AFC) = \frac{FC}{x} = \frac{r\overline{K}}{x} \qquad (11.58)$$

short-run average total cost $$(SRATC) = \frac{SRTC}{x} = \frac{wL(x)}{x} + \frac{r\overline{K}}{x} \qquad (11.59)$$

$$= SRAVC + AFC$$

short-run marginal variable cost $$= \frac{d}{dx} SRVC = w \frac{d}{dx} L(x) \qquad (11.60)$$

short-run marginal cost $$(SRMC) = \frac{d}{dx} SRTC = w \frac{d}{dx} L(x) + 0. \qquad (11.61)$$

Thus, from (11.60) and (11.61), $SRMC$ is short-run marginal (variable) cost, since variable cost and total cost are parallel functions. Because the two marginal functions are equal, we refer only to short-run marginal cost when referring to this function.

Graphical and Mathematical Derivations of Short-run Costs   The production function $x = K^{1/2}L^{1/2}$ may be used to illustrate the derivation of these short-run cost functions. Assuming capital is fixed at $\overline{K}$, the total product of labor is $x = \overline{K}^{1/2}L^{1/2}$. Therefore,

$$L = \frac{x^2}{\overline{K}} \tag{11.62}$$

$$SRVC = wL = \frac{wx^2}{\overline{K}} \tag{11.63}$$

$$SRTC = wL + r\overline{K} = \frac{wx^2}{\overline{K}} + r\overline{K} \tag{11.64}$$

$$SRAVC = \frac{wL}{x} = \frac{wx^2/\overline{K}}{x} = \frac{wx}{\overline{K}} \tag{11.65}$$

$$SRATC = \frac{wL}{x} + \frac{r\overline{K}}{x} = \frac{wx}{\overline{K}} + \frac{r\overline{K}}{x} \tag{11.66}$$

$$SRMC = \frac{d}{dx}SRTC = \frac{2wx}{\overline{K}}. \tag{11.67}$$

Figure 11.13 on the following page illustrates the derivation of the short-run average total, average variable, and marginal cost functions from the short-run total and variable cost functions illustrated in Figure 11.12. Each average function (the slope of the line from the origin) falls until the line from the origin is tangent to its respective total function. Each average function attains its respective minimum at that point and then rises thereafter. Since the two total functions are parallel to one another, there is one marginal function, which attains a minimum at the point of inflection and rises thereafter, intersecting with each average function at its respective minimum. Moreover, when the average functions are falling, the marginal function is lower; when the average functions are rising, the marginal function is higher.

We can use the production function $x = K^{1/2}L^{1/2}$ to show that marginal cost is equal to minimum short-run average total cost. To do that, we minimize short-run average total cost and show that at the output level that minimizes average cost, the two cost functions take on the same value.

$$(SRATC) = \frac{wx}{\overline{K}} + \frac{r\overline{K}}{x} \tag{11.68}$$

$$\frac{d}{dx}SRATC = \frac{w}{\overline{K}} - \frac{r\overline{K}}{x^2} = 0. \tag{11.69}$$

Solving (11.69) for x,

$$x^2 = \frac{r}{w}\overline{K}^2 \quad \Rightarrow \quad x = \left(\frac{r}{w}\right)^{1/2}\overline{K}. \tag{11.70}$$

Substituting (11.70) in (11.68),

$$\min(SRATC) = \frac{wx}{\overline{K}} + \frac{r\overline{K}}{x} = \frac{w\overline{K}(r/w)^{1/2}}{\overline{K}} + \frac{r\overline{K}}{\overline{K}(r/w)^{1/2}} \tag{11.71}$$

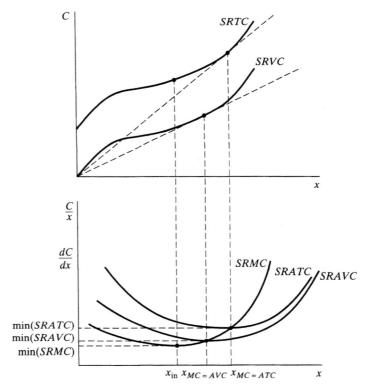

FIGURE 11.13   Derivation of a Firm's Short-run Average and Marginal Cost Functions

$$= w\left(\frac{r}{w}\right)^{1/2} + \frac{r}{(r/w)^{1/2}} = 2(wr)^{1/2}.$$

Substituting (11.70) in (11.67),

$$SRMC = \frac{2wx}{\overline{K}} = \frac{2w[\overline{K}(r/w)^{1/2}]}{\overline{K}} = 2(wr)^{1/2} = \min(SRATC). \text{ equation 11.71} \quad (11.72)$$

Notice that for $x = K^{1/2}L^{1/2}$, at minimum short-run average total cost (equations 11.71 and 11.72), these two short-run average and marginal costs are equal to long-run average and marginal cost, $2(wr)^{1/2}$ (equation 11.31). It turns out that this relationship holds for all constant-returns-to-scale production functions. We will return to this point when we discuss the relationships between short-run and long-run cost functions in Section 11.11.

Implications of Diminishing Returns   When there is only one variable input, three important properties of short-run cost functions follow from an assumption of diminishing returns to the variable input. Moreover, since constant and decreasing returns to scale also imply diminishing returns to a single variable input, these properties follow from constant and decreasing returns to scale as well.

1. The short-run marginal cost function is increasing with output.

To show that this property is true, recall from equation 11.61 that $SRMC = wdL(x)/dx$. Rearranging (11.61),

$$SRMC = \frac{w}{dx(L)/dL} = \frac{w}{MP_L}. \tag{11.73}$$

Equation 11.73 shows that if the marginal product of labor function is declining and w is a constant, the short-run marginal cost function must be rising.

2. The short-run average variable cost function will eventually rise.

Recall from Section 10.5 and Figure 10.7 that if the marginal product of labor function is falling, the average product of labor function eventually falls as well. This is because marginal product equals average product at maximum average product. The average product function must decline thereafter. To see how the average product function is related to the average variable cost function, recall from equation 11.57 that $SRAVC = wL(x)/x$. Rearranging (11.57),

$$SRAVC = \frac{w}{x(L)/L} = \frac{w}{AP_L}. \tag{11.74}$$

Equation 11.74 shows that if the average product of labor function is falling, the average variable cost function must be rising.

3. The short-run average total cost function is U shaped.

We have already shown in property 1 that the short-run marginal cost function eventually rises. If the short-run marginal cost function is rising, the short-run variable cost function is convex, and the short-run total cost function is higher than the variable cost function by the fixed cost. Figure 11.14 on the following page illustrates how this combination leads to a U-shaped short-run average total cost function. The short-run average variable cost function may be convex from the origin, with no minimum average variable cost. But, when fixed cost is added to the variable cost function, the short-run total cost function has an intercept equal to fixed cost. This implies that there will be a line from the origin that is tangent to the short-run total cost function and a minimum short-run average total cost. Thus, the short-run average total cost function is U shaped.

The Computer Software Company's Short-run Costs   The example of the computer software company outlined in Section 11.2 illustrates the development of short-run cost functions. In the short run, the computer software firm has fixed costs equal to the

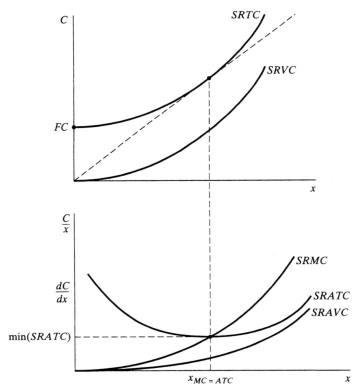

FIGURE 11.14   Derivation of a U-shaped Short-run Average Total Cost Function

implicit costs plus the utilities (Table 11.1).[11] These are summarized in Table 11.2. To the implicit costs of $48,600, we must add the utilities, for a total fixed cost of $54,600.

Now, suppose we measure the firm's output as the number of new software packages the firm can produce per year. Assume the firm sells the rights to another firm that handles distribution and sales. Also, assume the firm can produce 1 package if it hires 1 student programmer, 3 packages if it hires 2 students, and 7 if it hires 3, implying increasing returns over the first 3 programmers. This happens because they can compare notes and help one another solve problems. With the 4th student, marginal product begins to decline, however, as they begin to compete with one another for time on the different computers. Thus, output might be 10.5 packages with 4 students, 13.5 packages with 5 students, 16 packages with 6 students, and 18 packages with 7 students.

Table 11.3 summarizes this total product information in a table of costs, assuming each student hired earns $6,000 per year. Notice that the marginal cost is allocated to an output halfway between each output for which total and average costs are specified.

---

[11]Considering these as fixed costs is somewhat arbitrary, since the hypothetical software firm could avoid paying at least the utilities by simply ceasing operation. On the other hand, these costs do not vary over the range of output we are considering.

TABLE 11.2   Fixed Costs for the Computer Software Company

Type of Cost	Amount
Owner's Academic Salary	$40,000
Implicit Rent on Building	3,600
Implicit Rent on Computers	5,000
Utilities	6,000
Total Fixed Cost	$54,600

This is because, in this example, marginal cost refers to the change in costs measured over a discrete change in output.

Figure 11.15 graphs the information summarized in Table 11.3. Notice that, as we showed in Figure 11.13, the marginal cost function intersects minimum average variable cost and minimum average total cost. We will return to the computer software company in Section 12.8, when we consider its profit-maximization decision.

TABLE 11.3   The Computer Software Company's Short-run Costs

Output	Labor	SRVC	FC	SRTC	SRAVC	AFC	SRATC	SRMC
1	1	$ 6,000	$54,600	$ 60,600	$6,000	$54,600	$66,000	
2								$3,000
3	2	12,000	54,600	66,600	4,000	18,200	22,200	
5								1,500
7	3	18,000	54,600	72,600	2,571	7,800	10,371	
8.75								1,714
10.5	4	24,000	54,600	78,600	2,286	5,200	7,486	
12								2,000
13.5	5	30,000	54,600	84,600	2,222	4,044	6,266	
14.75								2,400
16	6	36,000	54,600	90,600	2,250	3,412	5,662	
17								3,000
18	7	42,000	54,600	96,600	2,333	3,033	5,367	
18.75								4,000
19.5	8	48,000	54,600	102,600	2,462	2,800	5,262	
20								6,000
20.5	9	54,000	54,600	108,600	2,634	2,663	5,297	
20.75								12,000
21	10	60,000	54,600	114,600	2,857	2,600	5,457	

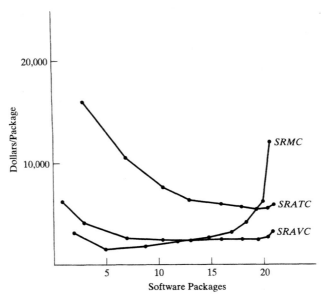

FIGURE 11.15   Graph of the Computer Software Company's Costs

11.9   SHORT-RUN COSTS WITH TWO OR MORE VARIABLE INPUTS

If the firm has more than one variable input in the short run, the analysis is somewhat more complicated and the results are not as clear-cut as in the case of one variable input. Suppose, for example, that physical capital (plant and machines) is fixed in the short run, but both labor and materials may vary. The firm's short-run problem now involves trade-offs similar to those analyzed for the long run above. If we let

$$\overline{K} = \text{the amount of fixed capital,}$$

$$m = \text{the quantity of variable materials hired, and}$$

$$p_m = \text{input price for variable materials,}$$

then

$$wL + p_m m = \text{short-run variable cost} \tag{11.75}$$

$$x = x(L, m; \overline{K}) = \text{production function with capital fixed.} \tag{11.76}$$

The cost-minimization problem is

$$\min (SRTC) = wL + p_m m + r\overline{K} \tag{11.77}$$
$$\text{s.t. } x = x(L, m; \overline{K}).$$

The Lagrangian is

$$\mathcal{L} = wL + p_m m + r\overline{K} + \lambda[x - x(L, m; \overline{K})]. \tag{11.78}$$

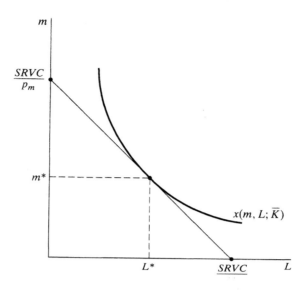

FIGURE 11.16   Optimal Variable Input Choice with Two Variable Inputs

The first two first-order conditions are

$$\frac{\partial \mathscr{L}}{\partial L} = w - \lambda \frac{\partial x}{\partial L} = 0 \quad \Rightarrow \quad \lambda = \frac{w}{MP_L} \tag{11.79}$$

$$\frac{\partial \mathscr{L}}{\partial m} = p_m - \lambda \frac{\partial x}{\partial m} = 0 \quad \Rightarrow \quad \lambda = \frac{p_m}{MP_m}. \tag{11.80}$$

Solving (11.79) and (11.80) for λ,

$$\lambda = \frac{w}{MP_L} = \frac{p_m}{MP_m} \quad \Rightarrow \quad \frac{MP_L}{MP_m} = \frac{w}{p_m}. \tag{11.81}$$

Equation 11.81 shows that this problem is equivalent to choosing the combination of labor and materials that minimizes short-run variable cost, subject to an output constraint. (Compare equations 11.1 and 11.81.) Figure 11.16 illustrates this choice, depicting the trade-off between labor and materials. The isocost lines represent the short-run variable cost, and the isoquant is now based on a fixed factor of production (physical capital). Given the constraint that one factor is fixed, the firm chooses the combination of labor and materials that minimizes short-run variable costs. Long-run total costs will not necessarily be minimized, however, because the firm cannot optimize over all three inputs simultaneously in the short run. But, as equation 11.81 shows, solving the problem stated in equations 11.77 implies that the firm will choose labor and materials so that the ratio of marginal products equals the ratio of variable input prices, just as in the long run.

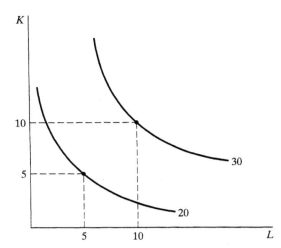

FIGURE 11.17   Short-run Diminishing Returns with Two Variable Inputs

Diminishing Returns to All Variable Inputs   If more than one input is variable, diminishing marginal products of individual inputs are no longer necessary and sufficient conditions for increasing short-run marginal cost functions and U-shaped short-run average total cost functions. Instead, production functions must exhibit diminishing returns to all variable inputs in combination when some inputs are fixed. This is illustrated in Figure 11.17. As labor and materials are doubled (from 5 units each to 10), holding capital fixed, output increases only 50% (from 20 units to 30). Thus, since variable costs double when variable inputs double, variable costs are increasing faster than output, and marginal costs are rising. Once marginal costs are rising, the short-run average total cost function is U shaped by the argument developed in the discussion of Figure 11.14.

11.10 _____ MULTIPRODUCT FIRMS

While some firms still only produce one product, most manufacturing firms produce many different products. Sometimes such diversification is justified solely from a marketing perspective, but other times the firm can achieve lower unit costs by diversifying than by producing only one product. These **economies of scope,** as they are called, may develop for a variety of reasons. The simplest type of economy of scope occurs when one good is produced virtually costlessly as a by-product of the production of another good. When beef is slaughtered for meat, hides are produced as well. Kerosene and heating oil are produced when oil is cracked for gasoline. Another kind of economy of scope may be achieved by a firm that produces its own intermediate inputs instead of purchasing everything used for production for final sale. For example, U.S. Steel used to mine coal and iron ore, combine those in blast furnaces, and then process a variety of finished steel products. We say that a firm is **vertically integrated** if it produces intermediate inputs as well as finished products. Vertical integration may save on the costs of transporting and distributing intermediate inputs and may thus lower the unit costs of finished products.

Other kinds of economies of scope may occur when a firm can use its fixed inputs to make a variety of different products to be sold in different markets. If there are scale economies, then the firm can achieve lower unit costs with larger production runs. Producing a variety of different products may allow the firm to produce a large enough output to take advantage of economies of scale. For example, a typical steel company will produce all different kinds of steel products in the same furnace and then pour the molten steel into different molds to make different specific products. An automobile company may produce several different car or truck models on the same assembly line.

Labor and management may also be able to achieve economies of scope by producing several different kinds of similar products. This may occur because many valuable skills are specific to the production of one kind of product. Thus, a group of engineers and workers who have been building cars will probably build better trucks than another group of engineers and workers who have been building office buildings, even if all the engineers had equal training before their work experience. This suggests that as new products are developed, existing firms that produce similar products may be able to achieve lower unit costs than new firms that might form solely to produce those new products.

The Multiproduct Firm's Decision Problem   The existence of economies of scope makes the construction of a cost function somewhat difficult because there is no longer a standard unit of measurement for output and because there will, in general, be an infinite number of output combinations that a multiproduct firm might produce. What the firm must do to develop a cost function is first to expand the decision space to include output combinations as well as input combinations and then to find the cost-minimizing way to produce feasible output combinations. The existence of economies of scope would then imply that there would exist specific output expansion paths involving specific combinations of outputs such that doubling all primary inputs less than doubles costs. By thinking in terms of primary inputs and costs, the firm reduces, to some extent, the measurement problem associated with trying to determine aggregate output when several different products are being produced.

In essence, the existence of economies of scope implies that there are *positive externalities* associated with producing several products simultaneously. Producing two or more goods simultaneously implies that the marginal products of some factors of production are higher with simultaneous production than if the goods were produced separately. In Section 21.2, we develop a formal model of firm decision making in the presence of externalities. At that time, we show that what the firm wants to do is choose a combination of outputs to maximize the difference between the sum of the revenues from selling different products and the overall cost of production, taking into account the externalities associated with producing two or more products simultaneously. Given that cost minimization for all output combinations may be a very difficult problem, it may be simpler to go directly to the profit-maximization problem and not try to develop a cost function first. Section 12.2 develops the basic one-product profit-maximization problem, and Section 21.2 provides an introduction to profit max-imization in the presence of externalities.

11.11   THE RELATIONSHIP BETWEEN SHORT-RUN AND LONG-RUN COSTS

Returning now to the case of a single-product firm using only one variable input, recall that, from equations 11.26, 11.71, and 11.72, we found that if $x = K^{1/2}L^{1/2}$, short-run marginal and average total costs were equal to long-run marginal and average costs at minimum short-run average total cost. These equations illustrate two important prop-erties of short-run and long-run cost functions.

    1. The long-run total cost functions are envelopes of the short-run total cost functions.

    The idea is as follows. For a given amount of capital (say $\overline{K}$), that fixed amount of capital is actually cost minimizing for some output level in the long run. In other words, $\overline{K}$ is equal to K^* for that output level. At every other output level, however, the firm cannot minimize long-run costs. We saw that in deriving the firm's short-run expansion path in Figure 11.3. Whenever the fixed capital is not equal to K^*, the firm is not at a point of tangency between an isoquant and an isocost line. Thus, when $\overline{K}$ is not equal to K^*, short-run total cost is higher than long-run total cost. When $\overline{K}$ is equal to K^*, the two costs are equal. The short-run total cost function is, therefore, just tangent to the long-run total cost function when $\overline{K}$ equals K^*, and the long-run cost function forms a lower "envelope" for the short-run function.

    This envelope concept is illustrated in Figure 11.18. The left graph shows the firm's short-run and long-run expansion paths. Along the long-run expansion path, the firm can produce x_1 at TC_1^*, x_2 at TC_2^*, and x_3 at TC_3^*. If capital is fixed at $\overline{K}$, on the other hand, the firm is able to minimize costs only for x_2 because at x_2, $\overline{K}$ is equal to K^*. To produce x_1 and x_3 using $\overline{K}$ units of capital, the firm uses L_1' and L_3' units of labor, and this costs the firm $SRTC_1$ and $SRTC_3$, respectively. $SRTC_1$ is higher than TC_1^*, and $SRTC_3$ is higher than TC_3^*. The right graph plots short-run and long-run total costs as functions of output. At x_2, short-run and long-run costs are equal, but at x_1 and x_3, short-run costs are higher. In the future, we will refer to the output level for which $\overline{K}$ is equal to K^* as $\hat{x}$.

    Since the long-run total cost function is an envelope of the short-run total cost functions, it must also be true that the long-run average total cost function is an enve-lope of the short-run average total cost functions. When long-run total cost is equal to short-run total cost (at $\hat{x}$), long-run average total cost must be equal to short-run aver-age total cost as well since we simply divide the two equal total costs by $\hat{x}$ to get the respective average costs. Everywhere else, while the output levels are equal, the short-run average total cost is higher because the short-run total cost is higher.

    In addition, since the short-run and long-run total cost functions are tangent at $\hat{x}$, short-run marginal cost also equals long-run marginal cost at that point. If x is less than $\hat{x}$, short-run marginal cost is lower than long-run marginal cost. If x is greater than $\hat{x}$,

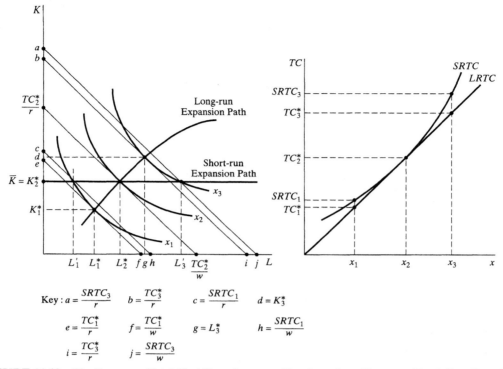

FIGURE 11.18   The Long-run Total Cost Function as an Envelope for a Short-run Total Cost Function

short-run marginal cost is higher. Before we illustrate this last point, we will state the second important property and then illustrate both together.

2. If the production function exhibits constant returns to scale, the point of tangency between the short-run and long-run cost functions is always at minimum short-run average total cost. At that point, all four average and marginal functions are equal to one another:

$$LRAC = LRMC = SRMC = \min(SRATC). \qquad (11.82)$$

The constant long-run average and marginal cost line forms a lower envelope, tangent to each short-run average total cost function at its minimum. This is the fact that was illustrated by comparing equations 11.26, 11.71, and 11.72.

Figure 11.19 on the following page illustrates property 2 and equation 11.82. The linear long-run total cost function forms the straight line from the origin that is just tangent to each short-run total cost function at $\hat{x}$ for that short-run function. We have seen several times that when a line from the origin is just tangent to a total function, the average function attains its maximum or minimum and the marginal function is equal to the average function at that point. Thus, when the linear long-run cost function is just tangent to the short-run total cost function, short-run average cost is at a

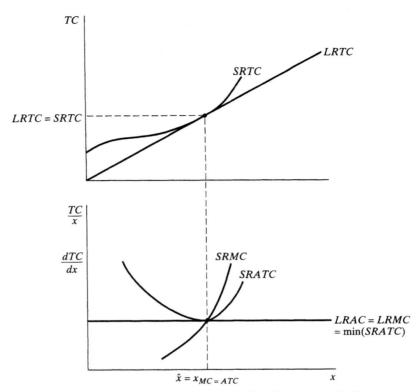

FIGURE 11.19   Short-run and Long-run Cost Functions with Constant Returns to Scale

minimum and short-run average cost equals short-run marginal cost. Moreover, since that is the point of tangency, short-run average cost equals long-run average cost, and short-run marginal cost equals long-run marginal cost.

Decreasing Returns   If the production function exhibits increasing or decreasing returns to scale, minimum short-run average total cost does not occur at $\hat{x}$ (the point of tangency between the short-run and the long-run cost functions). This idea is illustrated for decreasing returns to scale in Figure 11.20. Since the long-run total cost function is strictly convex from the origin, the slope of a line from the origin will always be different from the slope of the function. Since the short-run total cost function has a fixed-cost intercept, however, it does attain a minimum. But, it never does so at the point of tangency between the short-run and long-run total cost functions. At the point of tangency, $LRTC = SRTC$, $LRAC = SRATC$, and $LRMC = SRMC$. But, short-run marginal cost does not equal short-run average total cost, and long-run marginal cost does not equal long-run average total cost at that point. In addition, minimum short-run average total cost always occurs at x less than $\hat{x}$ for each set of short-run functions.

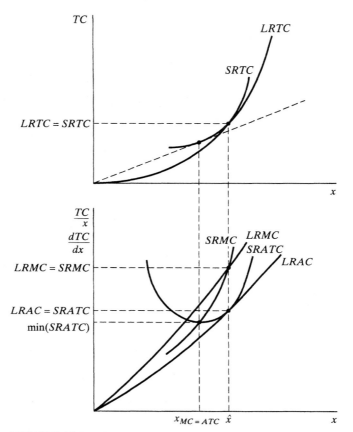

FIGURE 11.20   Short-run and Long-run Cost Functions with Decreasing Returns to Scale

Increasing Returns   The opposite happens with increasing returns to scale. Minimum short-run average total cost is always at x greater than $\hat{x}$ for each set of short-run functions. This is illustrated in Figure 11.21. Once again, the line from the origin defines the minimum short-run average total cost and the point where short-run marginal cost equals short-run average total cost. Moreover, $\hat{x}$, the point of tangency, is less than the x value determining minimum short-run average total cost. At the point of tangency, $SRTC = LRTC$, $SRATC = LRAC$, and $SRMC = LRMC$; but the four average and marginal functions are not all equal to one another.

U-shaped Long-run Average Cost Functions   In the stylized example, with U-shaped long-run average cost functions, all three types of short-run and long-run relationships can be seen. Figure 11.22 illustrates this point. In the region of increasing returns to scale (to the left of $\underline{x}$), minimum short-run average total cost occurs for x greater than $\hat{x}$.

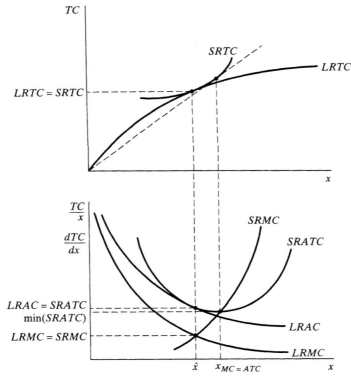

FIGURE 11.21   Short-run and Long-run Cost Functions with Increasing Returns to Scale

Thus, x_1 is greater than $\hat{x}_1$. At $\underline{x}$, there is a line from the origin that is tangent to both the short-run and the long-run total cost functions. Thus, all the conditions for constant returns to scale (equation 11.82) are satisfied at that point: $SRATC = SRMC = LRAC = LRMC$. Moreover, all these functions are also equal to minimum long-run average cost and minimum short-run average total cost at that point. Thus, $x_2 = \hat{x}_2 = \underline{x}$. Finally, in the region of decreasing returns (to the right of $\underline{x}$), minimum short-run average total cost occurs for x less than $\hat{x}$. Thus, x_3 is less than $\hat{x}_3$.

To understand these relationships, think of what it means for a firm to have constant, increasing, or decreasing returns to scale. With constant returns to scale, minimum average total cost is the same, regardless of firm size in both the short run and the long run. With increasing returns, on the other hand, at the output that minimizes short-run average total cost with a given amount of fixed inputs, long-run average cost is always lower than short-run average cost. For example, in Figure 11.22, when the firm is producing at minimum $SRATC_1$, the firm can always reduce average cost by expanding fixed inputs. With decreasing returns to scale, at the output that minimizes

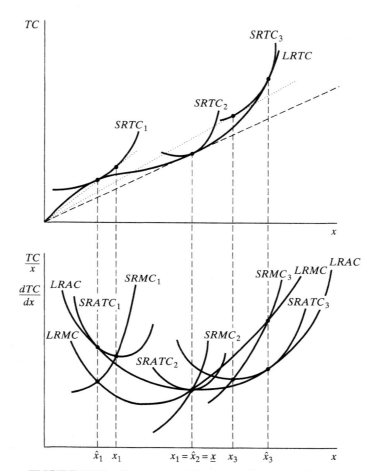

**FIGURE 11.22   Short-run and Long-run Costs with U-shaped
Long-run Average Cost**

short-run average total cost for a given amount of fixed inputs, long-run average cost is
also lower than short-run average cost. In this case, however, the firm reduces average
cost by *reducing* fixed inputs at that output. For example, in Figure 11.22, when the firm
is producing at minimum $SRATC_3$, the firm can reduce costs by reducing fixed inputs.
When long-run average cost is U-shaped, the firm reduces average costs by expanding
until it reaches minimum long-run average cost at $\underline{x}$. At that point, the firm is minimizing average costs in both the short run and the long run. Moreover, the firm has no incentive to expand further because adding fixed capital simply raises cost. In Section 13.5,
we will see that these relationships have important implications for the formation of a
long-run competitive equilibrium.

II.2 _____ REVIEW OF KEY CONCEPTS

This completes our development of cost functions. Before continuing on to supply functions and competitive equilibrium, be sure you understand and can use the following key concepts.

The _opportunity cost_ of a resource used in production is the value of that resource in its next best alternative employment.

Explicit costs are costs paid out directly.

Implicit costs are the opportunity costs of resources owned by the firm. While not paid out directly, they represent opportunity cost forgone.

Total economic cost is the sum of explicit costs and implicit costs, valuing all resources used by the firm at their respective opportunity costs.

Economic profit is the difference between total revenue and total economic cost including both explicit and implicit costs.

A firm's _cost function_ describes the lowest possible economic cost to produce each output level.

At a cost-minimizing input combination to produce a given output, the marginal rate of technical substitution will be equal to the input price ratio. This is another optimal condition which implies that the internal rate of trade (the marginal rate of substitution) is equal to the external rate of trade (the input price ratio).

The _elasticity of substitution_ along an isoquant measures the responsiveness of the capital-labor ratio to changes in the wage-rental ratio. It is mathematically equivalent to the consumer's elasticity of substitution along an indifference curve.

If inputs must be used in _fixed proportions_ to produce output, then the isoquants describing such a _fixed proportions technology_ are "square."

The firm's _long-run expansion path_ describes the cost-minimizing combinations of inputs, for a given set of input prices, as output expands.

The _long-run total cost function_ describes the minimum cost of producing each output when all inputs are variable.

Conditional input demand functions describe the least-cost quantities of inputs to hire, as functions of output and the input prices. They are called conditional input demand functions because they are conditional on output. They are mathematically equivalent to the consumer's generalized compensated demand functions.

The long-run total cost function is mathematically equivalent to the consumer's expenditure function, if input prices are allowed to vary.

Conditional input demand functions are homogeneous of degree 0 in input prices.

Long-run average cost is the cost per unit in the long run and equals long-run total cost divided by output.

Long-run marginal cost is the additional cost of producing each additional unit of output and equals the slope of the long-run total cost function.

If a firm's production function exhibits constant returns to scale, the long-run total cost function is linear, and the long-run average and marginal cost functions are constant, equal to one another, and equal to the constant slope of the total cost function.

If a firm's production function exhibits increasing returns to scale, the long-run total cost function is concave from the origin, the long-run average and marginal cost functions are both declining, and the long-run marginal cost function is less than the long-run average cost function at each output level.

If a firm's production function exhibits decreasing returns to scale, the long-run total cost function is convex from the origin, the long-run average and marginal cost functions are both increasing, and the long-run marginal cost function is greater than the long-run average cost function at each output level.

We say that a particular production process exhibits _economies of scale_ if the minimum unit cost associated with using that particular production process can only be achieved if a substantial number of units of a good are produced.

A large firm may eventually develop _managerial diseconomies_ that cause unit costs to rise.

Short-run variable cost is the cost of hiring variable factors (wL, if labor is the only variable factor).

A firm's _fixed cost_ is what it must pay for its fixed factors of production in the short run ($r\overline{K}$, if capital is fixed).

Short-run total cost is the sum of variable cost and fixed cost.

Short-run average variable cost is the variable cost per unit of output (variable cost divided by output).

Average fixed cost is the fixed cost per unit of output (fixed cost divided by output).

Short-run average total cost is the short-run total cost per unit of output (short-run total cost divided by output). It can also be calculated as average variable cost plus average fixed cost.

Short-run marginal cost is the additional cost associated with each additional unit of output in the short run (the slope of the short-run total cost function).

Since the short-run total cost and variable cost functions are parallel and have the same slope, and since fixed cost is independent of output, short-run marginal cost is also the slope of the short-run variable cost function.

Diminishing returns to a single variable input in the short run implies a rising short-run marginal cost function, a rising average variable cost function, and a U-shaped short-run average total cost function.

With two or more variable inputs, optimal input choice in the short run involves trade-offs similar to long-run input choices and thus involves minimizing costs for a given short-run production isoquant. At such a point of tangency, the ratio of marginal products will equal the input-price ratio.

With two or more variable inputs, a production function must exhibit diminishing returns to all variable inputs in combination in order for the marginal cost function to rise.

A multiproduct firm may be able to achieve lower unit costs through *economies of scope* by producing several different products.

Different kinds of economies of scope include producing by-products as well as original products; producing intermediate inputs as well as final products (*vertical integration*); producing different goods using the same capital to exploit economies of scale, and using the special skills of labor and management to produce a variety of similar products.

The existence of economies of scope makes the construction of a cost function difficult, since there is no longer a specific unit of measurement for output.

Identifying economies of scope involves identifying output expansion paths such that doubling all primary inputs less than doubles costs.

Economies of scope basically involve *positive externalities* in production: producing more than one good simultaneously implies higher marginal products of some factors of production (and no lower marginal products of others) than does producing each good individually.

Long-run total and average cost functions are lower envelopes of the short-run total and average cost functions. Long-run and short-run total cost functions are tangent to one another, as are long-run and short-run average cost functions at the output level such that short-run fixed capital is cost minimizing in the long run. At every other output level, short-run total and average costs are higher than long-run total and average costs, respectively.

If a firm's production function exhibits constant returns to scale, the constant long-run average and marginal cost line is tangent to each short-run average total cost function at minimum short-run average total cost. Moreover, at those points of tangency, all the average and marginal costs are equal:

$$LRMC = LRAC = SRMC = \min(SRATC).$$

If a firm's production function exhibits increasing or decreasing returns to scale, each short-run average total cost function is not tangent to the long-run average total cost function at minimum short-run average total cost. With increasing returns, tangency occurs at a lower output, and with decreasing returns, tangency occurs at a higher output than the output at which short-run average total cost is minimized.

If a firm has a U-shaped long-run average cost function, one particular minimum short-run average total cost function will be tangent at minimum long-run average cost. At that point the conditions characteristic of constant returns to scale will be satisfied:

$$LRMC = \min(LRAC) = SRMC = \min(SRATC).$$

II.13 QUESTIONS FOR DISCUSSION

1. If a firm wishes to estimate its cost function, does it have to know how much profit it would make at each output level? Explain why or why not.

2. Suppose that your current total revenue in farming is $120,000 per year and that your costs are $10,000 per year for seed and fertilizer, $12,000 for other supplies, and $15,000 interest on machinery loans. You have been offered another job that would pay $50,000 per year. If you took it, you could sell your farm and machinery and earn $70,000 per year interest on the money you had invested in land and machines. Should you take the other job? Explain your answer in terms of economic costs.

3. The current litigation crisis is raising insurance premiums for numerous activities subject to safety or malpractice lawsuits. Everyone from doctors to manufacturers of football helmets is paying higher rates. What effect is this increase having on the cost functions of firms facing higher insurance rates?

Under what circumstances is the rise in insurance premiums likely to affect fixed costs and not variable costs? Under what circumstances would variable costs also be affected? Explain your answer.

4. Suppose you are an economist working for a major manufacturing company. You have been asked to estimate the minimum cost of producing various possible output levels the firm is contemplating producing. You are working with a set of engineers who can tell you various combinations of capital and labor that can be used to produce those output levels. What other information would you need and how would you go about making your estimates?

5. In the situation depicted in Question 4, could you make an informed recommendation without having engineering data? If so, how would you make the necessary estimates?

6. Explain why long-run cost functions are envelopes of short-run cost functions.

II.14 PROBLEMS

Problems 1–3 Consider the following production functions.

(a) $x = 4K^{1/2}L^{1/2}$

(b) $x = 4K + 7L$

(c) $x = \dfrac{10KL}{K + L}$

(d) $x = K^2L$

(e) $x = \min(3k, 4L)$

1. Find the function for the firm's long-run expansion path for each production function.

2. Find the function for, or the value of, the elasticity of substitution for each production function.

3. With $w = \$1$ and $r = \$4$, find the cost-minimizing input combination to produce 10 units of output for each production function.

Problems 4–10 Concentrate on the following production function:

$$x = \frac{10KL}{K + L}.$$

4. Derive the conditional input demand functions.

5. Derive the generalized long-run total cost, marginal cost, and average cost as functions of w, r, and x.

6. Find λ as a function of w, r, and x from the Lagrange equation.

7. Interpret λ as a marginal function and show that your interpretation is correct.

8. With $w = \$1$ and $r = \$4$, find the long-run total, average, and marginal costs as functions of output.

Problems 9 and 10   Now let $w = \$1, r = \$4$, and $\overline{K} = 4$ units in the short run.

9. Derive the short-run variable cost, average variable cost, total cost, average total cost, and marginal cost as functions of output.

10. Show that the following four functions take on equal values at minimum short-run average total cost: short-run average total and marginal costs and long-run average and marginal costs.

11. Consider the following production function:

$$x = K^{1/4}L^{1/4}m^{1/4}.$$

Let $w = \$2, r = \$1, p_m = \$4$, and $\overline{K} = 8$ in the short run. Derive the short-run variable and average variable costs, short-run total cost, short-run average total cost, and short-run marginal cost as functions of output.

11.15   LOGICAL AND MATHEMATICAL APPLICATIONS

Applications 1 and 2   Suppose a firm that uses capital and labor to produce output under *constant returns to scale* is faced with an increase in the wage rate. Assume capital is fixed in the short run and the production function is such that as output expands, the firm always uses more of both capital and labor (we call these *normal inputs*, like normal goods).

1. Show that short- and long-run total, average, and marginal costs increase for every output level.

2. Show that the firm will use less labor and more capital at every output level *in the long run*.

3. Consider two firms that are producing along the same long-run expansion path. The only difference between the two firms is that firm A has a *smaller* elasticity of substitution than firm B. Show that if wages increase, firm A suffers a *larger* increase in long-run total cost than firm B.

4. Suppose you are given the following conditional input demands:

$$L^* = \left(\frac{(1 - \alpha)r}{\alpha w} \right)^{\alpha}(x)$$

$$K^* = \left(\frac{\alpha w}{(1 - \alpha)r} \right)^{1-\alpha}(x).$$

What is the underlying production function? (Hint: Work backward to find two different expressions for x, one in terms of L and one in terms of K, and then use these equations to find the long-run expansion path.)

5. Suppose a firm's fixed costs are \$50,000; 1 worker produces 20 units of output; and the marginal product of labor increases at a rate of 2 additional units of output per additional worker for the first 10 workers and then falls at a rate of 1 per additional worker. If the wage rate is \$20,000 per worker, calculate all the short-run costs for this firm over the first 20 workers hired.

Chapter 12

Profit Maximization by a Competitive Firm: Supply of Goods and Demand for Inputs

12.1 WHAT YOU SHOULD LEARN FROM THIS CHAPTER

In the previous chapter, we derived the cost-minimizing input combination for every possible output level. This chapter shows how a competitive firm chooses an output level to maximize profits (or minimize losses), given that it has minimized cost for every possible output choice. Moreover, choice of a profit-maximizing output level implies the choice of a profit-maximizing combination of inputs for the firm to hire. Choice of the output level for each output price derives the firm's output supply curve; choice of the input combination for each input price level derives the firm's input demand function.

The material developed in this chapter is the culmination of production theory for the individual competitive firm. The next chapter develops market supply and demand and the competitive equilibrium, the culmination of the central focus of this book. Pay particular attention to the derivation and properties of the firm's short-run supply function. Long-run supply and long-run equilibrium are developed in the next chapter.

12.2 COMPETITIVE PROFIT MAXIMIZATION AND SHORT-RUN SUPPLY

In the previous chapter, we developed functions that describe the minimum cost of production for every output level in both the short run and the long run. Now, we ask what output will a cost-minimizing firm produce in order to maximize profits? To answer that question, we construct the formula for profits (π) from the verbal development of the concept in Section 11.2:

$$\pi(x) = TR(x) - TC(x) = \text{total revenue} - \text{total economic cost.} \qquad (12.1)$$

To maximize profits, we differentiate the profit function (equation 12.1) and set the derivative equal to 0:

$$\frac{d}{dx}\pi(x) = \frac{d}{dx}TR(x^*) - \frac{d}{dx}TC(x^*) = MR(x^*) - MC(x^*) = 0. \qquad (12.2)$$

Therefore, at an interior profit maximum of (12.1), (12.2) implies

$$MR(x^*) = MC(x^*). \qquad (12.3)$$

Short-run Supply   Equation 12.3 shows that a profit-maximizing firm that produces a positive output chooses an output level such that the marginal cost associated with producing that output equals the marginal revenue associated with selling that output.[1] This fact turns out to be true regardless of whether the firm operates in a competitive market or not.

Differences in market structure are reflected in differences in the firm's marginal revenue function. Marginal revenue for a competitive firm is particularly simple. Since the firm's decisions are assumed to have no effect on its price, it must take price as a parameter in its decision function. We say the firm is a **price taker.** Thus, for a competitive firm,

$$TR(x) = \bar{p}_x x. \tag{12.4}$$

Differentiating (12.4) with respect to x,

$$MR(x) = \frac{d}{dx} TR(x) = \bar{p}_x. \tag{12.5}$$

If we now substitute (12.5) in (12.3), we see that the competitive firm maximizes profits by choosing an output level at which price is equal to the marginal cost associated with producing that particular output level:

$$p_x = MC(x^*). \tag{12.6}$$

Equation 12.6, in turn, implies that the firm treats its marginal cost curve as its supply curve, supplying output so that the marginal cost of producing each output level always equals price.

Figure 12.1 on the following page illustrates the competitive firm's output decision. Since price is a parameter, total revenue is a linear function. In the short run, the total cost function is eventually convex. Profits attain a minimum when marginal cost equals marginal revenue and when total cost is higher than total revenue; profits attain a maximum when marginal cost equals marginal revenue and when total revenue is higher than total cost. Profits are 0 when total cost equals total revenue; this is referred to as the **break-even point.** In the lower graph, marginal revenue is simply a constant equal to price, while the marginal cost function rises over the convex portion of the total cost function. The firm's optimal output (x^*) occurs at the point where price equals marginal cost on the rising portion of the marginal cost function.

Figure 12.1 can also be interpreted in terms of supply and demand. Since the firm treats price as a parameter in its decision function, it behaves as though it can sell any quantity of output at the market price. In other words, it behaves as though it faces a perfectly elastic demand curve at the market price.

An Example   We saw in equation 11.67 that if the production function is $x = K^{1/2}L^{1/2}$, the short-run marginal cost function is $SRMC = 2wx/\bar{K}$. Thus, equating price and marginal cost in (11.67),

$$p_x = \frac{2wx^*}{\bar{K}} \quad \text{the firm's short-run supply curve} \tag{12.7}$$

[1]As we will see below, if price is less than minimum average variable cost, a profit-maximizing firm shuts down and produces zero output. Thus, for price below minimum average variable cost, the firm no longer follows the rule of producing an output such that marginal cost equals marginal revenue: it simply produces nothing.

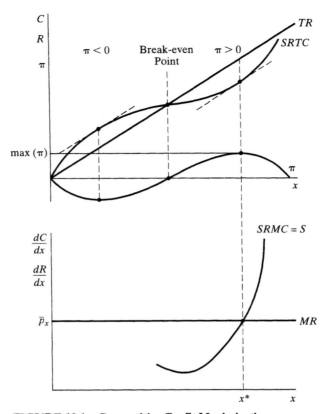

FIGURE 12.1 Competitive Profit Maximization

Figure 12.2 illustrates the firm's short-run supply curve.

Mathematical Development In general, we say that quantity supplied in the short run is a function of the good's own price, holding input prices, the prices of other goods the firm might produce, the amount of fixed inputs, and technology constant:

$$x^* = x^*(p_x; \overline{w}, \overline{r}, \overline{p}_y, \overline{K}), \tag{12.8}$$

where the technology is described by the shape of the production function from which the short-run supply function is derived. The graphed short-run supply curve is then simply the inverse short-run supply function (the inverse of equation 12.8):

$$MC(x) = p_x = p_x(x^*; \overline{w}, \overline{r}, \overline{p}_y, \overline{K}) = (x^*)^{-1}. \tag{12.9}$$

To see how the short-run supply function might be derived directly, we can think of a general profit function, where profit is a function of output, the parametric prices, and fixed inputs:

$$\pi = \pi(x; p_x, w, r, p_y, K). \tag{12.10}$$

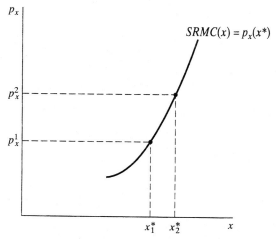

FIGURE 12.2   The Firm's Short-run Supply Curve

Profit maximization implies

$$\pi_x(x^*; p_x, w, r, p_y, K) = 0,$$ (12.11)

the first-order condition of equation 12.10. As we showed in Section 2.5, this first-order condition is an implicit function; and if we assume the firm is maximizing profits so that $\pi_{xx} < 0$, then there exists an explicit function $x^*(p_x)$, the firm's short-run supply function.

12.3 _____ CHANGES IN SHORT-RUN SUPPLY

If the parameters determining a firm's short-run supply function change, the function itself changes. For example, if there is only one variable input and its price increases, short-run marginal cost increases for every output level. To see this, recall from equation 11.73 that short-run marginal cost is simply the price of the input divided by the marginal product. Since the marginal product at a particular output does not change as a function of the price of the input, increasing the input price must increase short-run marginal cost at every output. For example, suppose labor is the only variable factor. In that case, the short-run marginal cost function is $SRMC = w[dL(x)/dx]$, from equation 11.61. Differentiating (11.61) with respect to w,

$$\frac{\partial}{\partial w} SRMC = \frac{d}{dx} L(x) > 0.$$ (12.12)

With two or more variable inputs, the effect of a change in input price on the short-run marginal cost function depends on whether or not the input is a normal input. A **normal input** (analogous to a normal good in consumer theory) is employed in increasing amounts as the firm expands output. In other words, labor is a normal input if $\partial L^*/\partial x > 0$. If the price of a normal input increases, short-run

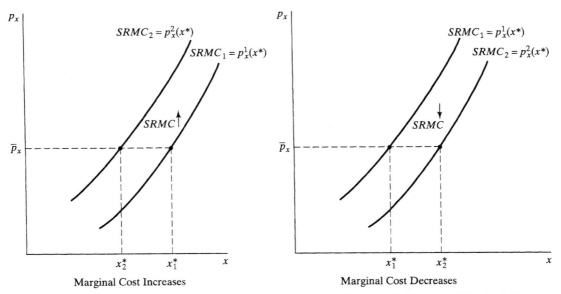

FIGURE 12.3   Shifts in Short-run Supply Curves as a Result of Changes in Short-run Marginal Cost

marginal cost increases for every output. If the price of an **inferior input** (use declines as output expands) increases, short-run marginal cost declines.[2]

Changes in Marginal Cost and Shifts in Supply   If short-run marginal cost increases for every output, the short-run supply curve shifts up (or to the left). If marginal cost declines for every output, the supply curve shifts down (or to the right). These cases are illustrated in Figure 12.3. In the left graph, short-run marginal cost is higher at every output level, implying a leftward shift in the short-run supply curve. From a quantity perspective, the firm is willing to supply less output at each price. In the right graph (marginal cost decreases), the firm is willing to supply more output at each price.

Changes in the Quantity of Fixed Inputs   The effect on short-run supply of an increase in the quantity of the firm's fixed input, with only one input variable, depends on the impact on the marginal product of the variable input of hiring more of the fixed input.[3] If increasing the fixed input raises the marginal product of the variable input at every input level, then increasing the fixed input decreases short-run marginal cost at every output level and increases the quantity the firm is willing to supply at each price. On the other hand, if increasing the fixed input reduces the marginal product of the variable input at every input level, increasing the fixed input increases short-run marginal cost at every output level and reduces the short-run supply curve.

---

[2]This point is not easily explained graphically, and the mathematics of showing it require multivariate comparative statics. Interested students can consult Silberberg, *Structure of Economics*, Figure 7.11 and pp. 197–198.

[3]The case of more than one variable input requires the use of multivariate comparative statics.

The relationship between the marginal product of the variable input and changes in the fixed input is described mathematically as, for example, the derivative of the marginal product of labor (if the variable input is labor) with respect to changes in the quantity of capital:

$$\frac{\partial}{\partial K} MP_L = \frac{\partial}{\partial K} \frac{\partial x}{\partial L} = \frac{\partial^2 x}{\partial L \partial K}, \tag{12.13}$$

which is the second cross partial of output with respect to labor and capital.

To see the relationship between changes in short-run marginal cost (as capital increases) and the second cross partial of output with respect to labor and capital, recall from equation 11.61 that $SRMC = w(\partial L/\partial x) = w[1/(\partial x/\partial L)]$. Differentiating (11.61) with respect to capital,

$$\frac{\partial}{\partial K} SRMC = -w \frac{\partial^2 x/\partial L \partial K}{(\partial x/\partial L)^2}. \tag{12.14}$$

Equation 12.14 indicates that if the second cross partial is positive, short-run marginal cost falls when capital increases, and vice versa. Therefore, Figure 12.3 could also illustrate the effect of an increase (right graph) or decrease (left graph) in a firm's hiring of a fixed input that decreases or increases, respectively, the marginal product of a single variable input.

Technological Changes   The other parameter of the firm's short-run supply function (engineering technology) is summarized in the form of the production function itself. A **technological change** is an improvement in engineering technology that allows the firm to produce more output from a given set of inputs.[4]

Economists distinguish between technological changes that leave the marginal rates of technical substitution unchanged for every input combination **(neutral technological changes)** and technological changes that change the marginal rates of technical substitution **(biased technological changes).** Neutral technological changes also increase output (and therefore reduce costs) for every possible combination of inputs. Biased technological changes *usually* reduce costs only for *some* combinations of inputs.

Neutral Technological Changes   To understand the effect of a neutral technological change, recall the discussion of positive monotonic transformations of utility functions in Section 5.3. Remember that a positive monotonic transformation changes the utility number assigned to each indifference curve, but leaves the marginal rates of substitution unchanged. A neutral technological change is simply a positive monotonic transformation of a production function, which increases the amount of production represented by each isoquant without changing the marginal rates of technical substitution.

---

[4]We only consider *improvements* because a profit-maximizing firm manager operating in a world of perfect information would never adopt a technology that *reduced* output per unit of each input.

For example, if the production function is $x = K^{1/2}L^{1/2}$ to begin with, a neutral technological change that doubles output for the same inputs would be represented as $x = 2K^{1/2}L^{1/2}$. Similarly, any other increase in the coefficient, or raising both capital and labor to the same exponential power, would represent a neutral technological change, since these are positive monotonic transformations.[5]

To take a more general example, suppose we start with a general Cobb-Douglas production function of the form $x = A(K^\alpha L^\beta)^\mu$, where A, α, β, and μ are all positive parameters. A neutral technological change could be represented by an increase in either A or μ. An increase in A leaves the returns to scale unchanged, while an increase in μ increases those returns.

For example, consider the constant-returns-to-scale Cobb-Douglas production function $x = AK^{1/2}L^{1/2}$. The short-run supply function is the inverse of (12.7) with the coefficient A added:

$$x^* = \frac{Ap_x \overline{K}}{2w}.\tag{12.15}$$

To see the effect of a parametric increase in the parameter A,[6] we differentiate (12.15) with respect to A, holding price, wage, and capital constant:

$$\frac{\partial x^*}{\partial A} = \frac{p_x \overline{K}}{2w} > 0.\tag{12.16}$$

Equation 12.16 indicates that as the parameter A increases, the firm is willing to supply more at each price.

The change described in (12.16) can also be analyzed as a parametric shift in the short-run marginal cost curve:

$$p_x = SRMC = \frac{2wx^*}{A\overline{K}}.\tag{12.17}$$

Differentiating (12.17) with respect to A,

$$\frac{\partial}{\partial A} SRMC = -\frac{2wx^*\overline{K}}{(A\overline{K})^2} < 0.\tag{12.18}$$

Thus, from (12.18), an increase in the parameter A also reduces short-run marginal cost at every output level, implying a rightward shift in the firm's short-run supply curve. This was the same kind of change as was illustrated in Figure 12.3.

Figure 12.4 illustrates a neutral technological change. The outer isoquant describes the input combinations that can produce output $\overline{x}$ under the old technology. The inner isoquant describes the input combinations that produce $\overline{x}$ units under the new technology. The inner isoquant represents a larger output under the new technology. Technological change is neutral because it can be represented by simply attaching

---

[5]While the addition of a positive constant would also be a positive monotonic transformation, it implies that positive output could be obtained from zero inputs, an unreasonable assumption in the case of production.

[6]The other kind of technological change (an increase in the parameter μ) would give this production function increasing returns to scale. To begin with, μ is implicitly 1.

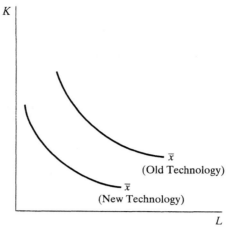

FIGURE 12.4   A Neutral Technological Change

new output numbers to the old isoquants, with no change in the marginal rates of technical substitution. Each isoquant now represents a higher output than it did before.

Biased Technological Changes   Biased technological changes can themselves be separated into those that raise the relative marginal product of labor (called **labor-using** or **capital-saving** technological changes) and those that raise the relative marginal product of capital (called **capital-using** or **labor-saving** technological changes). Whereas biased technological changes can be cost saving over all ranges of output, in many cases labor-using technological changes are cost saving only when labor is relatively inexpensive, and capital-using technological changes are cost saving only when capital is relatively inexpensive.

Figure 12.5 on the following page illustrates both kinds of biased technological changes when they are cost saving only over certain ranges of input prices. In the left graph (labor-using technological change), the isoquant becomes steeper, implying an increase in the relative marginal product of labor. Costs decline in the lower portion of the graph but rise in the upper portion. Thus, firms would never adopt in the shaded upper portion, but would adopt in the region where cost savings take place. In the right graph (capital-using technological change), the isoquant becomes less steep, implying an increase in the relative marginal product of capital. Costs fall in the upper portion of the graph but rise in the lower portion. In this case, firms adopt in the upper region but not in the shaded lower region. Notice also that labor is relatively inexpensive in the adoption region under labor-using technological change and that capital is relatively inexpensive in the adoption region under capital-using technological change.

A biased technological change will increase short-run supply under one of the following conditions. First, if it directly increases the marginal product of the variable input, it will reduce short-run marginal cost and increase short-run supply. Second, if adopting the new technology necessitates increasing the amount of the fixed input

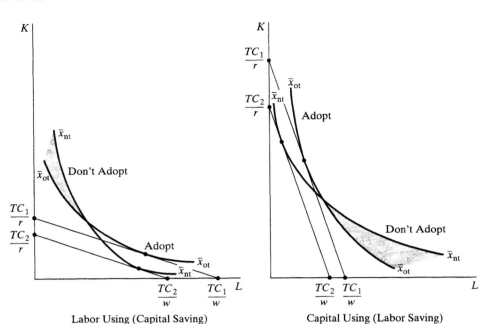

FIGURE 12.5 Biased Technological Changes

hired and if increasing the fixed input raises the marginal product of the variable input, short-run marginal cost will also decline.[7]

Summary   The following parametric changes result in an increase in short-run supply:

decrease in the price of an input when only one input is variable;

decrease in the price of a normal input (two or more inputs variable);

increase in the price of an inferior input (two or more inputs variable);

increase in a fixed input that raises the marginal product of a single variable input;

decrease in a fixed input that lowers the marginal product of a single variable input;

neutral technological change;

biased technological change that raises the marginal product of the variable input,

either directly or indirectly.

The following parametric changes result in a decrease in short-run supply:

increase in input price when only one input is variable;

increase in the price of a normal input (two or more inputs variable);

---

[7]Even though adopting new technology and changing capital are long-run decisions, once the new technology or capital is in place, the firm is in a short-run position with a short-run marginal cost function. What we are analyzing here are shifts in short-run supply resulting from long-run input changes.

decrease in the price of an inferior input (two or more inputs variable);

decrease in fixed inputs that raises the marginal product of a single variable input;

increase in fixed inputs that lowers the marginal product of a single variable input.

12.4   PROFITS AND SHORT-RUN SHUTDOWN

Returning to the profit-maximization decision, we now restate the firm's profit function:

$$\pi(x) = TR(x) - TC(x). \quad \text{equation 12.1}$$

If we multiply the right-hand side of (12.1) by x/x,

$$\pi(x) = x\left[\frac{TR(x)}{x} - \frac{TC(x)}{x}\right] = x\left[\frac{p_x x}{x} - ATC(x)\right]. \tag{12.19}$$

Thus, in the short run, (12.19) can be rewritten as

$$\text{short-run profits } [SR\pi(x)] = x(p_x - SRATC). \tag{12.20}$$

Stated in words, (12.20) says that short-run profit equals output times the difference between price and short-run average total cost.

Profits and Losses   Figure 12.6 illustrates short-run profits and losses.[8] In the left graph, with price equal to p_x^1, the firm produces x_1^* and makes maximum short-run profits equal to the shaded area:

$$SR\pi(x_1^*) = x_1^*[p_x^1 - SRATC(x_1^*)] > 0. \tag{12.21}$$

In the right graph, with price equal to p_x^2, the firm produces x_2^* and makes minimum losses equal to the shaded area:

$$SR\pi(x_2^*) = x_2^*[p_x^2 - SRATC(x_2^*)] < 0. \tag{12.22}$$

Notice that the rule "produce an output level in the short run so that price equals short-run marginal cost at that output level" applies whether the firm is making actual profits or losses. In the case of losses, following the rule minimizes the firm's losses (unless the firm decides to shut down).

The short-run profits for the production function $x = K^{1/2}L^{1/2}$ can be computed as follows. We know that $p_x = 2wx/\overline{K}$ (equation 12.7) and $SRACT(x) = wx/\overline{K} + r\overline{K}/x$ (equation 11.66). Substituting (11.66) and (12.7) in (12.20),

$$SR\pi(x) = x\left[\frac{2wx}{\overline{K}} - \left(\frac{wx}{\overline{K}} + \frac{r\overline{K}}{x}\right)\right] = x\left(\frac{wx}{\overline{K}} - \frac{r\overline{K}}{x}\right) \tag{12.23}$$

$$= \frac{wx^2}{\overline{K}} - r\overline{K}.$$

---

[8]Long-run profits will be considered in Section 13.5 in conjunction with the definition of long-run equilibrium under competition.

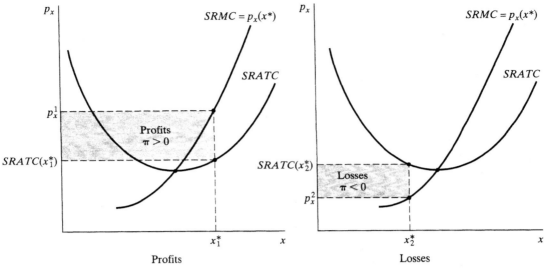

FIGURE 12.6 Profits and Losses

Short-run Shutdown The firm that makes losses may or may not continue to produce positive output in the short run. The objective function of a firm that is losing money is to minimize losses. To see how such a firm will decide whether to continue in operation, we break short-run average total cost into average variable cost plus average fixed cost: $SRATC = SRAVC + AFC$ (equation 11.59). Substituting (11.59) in (12.20),

$$SR\pi(x) = x\{p_x - [SRAVC(x) + AFC]\} \qquad (12.24)$$
$$= x[p_x - SRAVC(x) - AFC].$$

Equation 12.24 shows that if the firm were to shut down *in the short run,* implying no variable costs and no revenues, its losses would equal its fixed cost since fixed costs are incurred whether the firm produces any output or not. Thus, as long as price is greater than or equal to short-run average variable cost in the short run, the firm is doing at least as well as it could by shutting down.[9] Moreover, since price always equals marginal cost and since short-run marginal cost equals average variable cost at minimum average variable cost, the firm stays in business as long as price is greater than *minimum* average variable cost. Economists call the output level at which price equals minimum average variable cost the firm's **short-run shutdown point:**

$$p_x = \min(SRAVC) \qquad (12.25)$$

at the short-run shutdown point.

The Firm's Effective Supply Curve Since the firm is not producing if price is less than $\min(SRAVC)$, the firm's positive-output short-run supply curve is actually

---

[9]If price continues to be less than average total cost, the firm will go out of business in the long run. This possibility will be developed more fully in the next chapter.

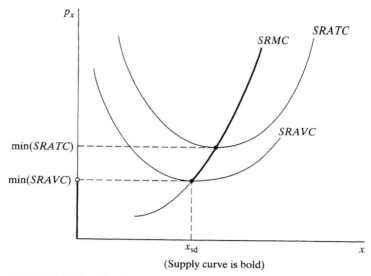

FIGURE 12.7   The Firm's Short-run Shutdown Point and Effective Short-run Supply Curve

restricted to the portion of the short-run marginal cost curve for outputs greater than or equal to minimum average variable cost. In fact, the short-run supply curve is discontinuous; it coincides with the vertical price axis (since output is 0) until price approaches minimum average variable cost, and then it coincides with the short-run marginal cost curve for prices greater than or equal to minimum average variable cost. Moreover, since short-run marginal cost rises through minimum average variable cost, the positive-output short-run supply curve is only defined over the rising portion of the short-run marginal cost curve. Thus, if short-run marginal cost eventually rises, short-run supply must be upward sloping, because only the upward-sloping portion of the firm's short-run marginal cost curve is ever observed as its positive-output short-run supply curve. These relationships are illustrated in Figure 12.7. Short-run marginal cost equals short-run average and average variable costs at their respective minima. Short-run shutdown occurs at minimum average variable cost, on the rising portion of the short-run marginal cost curve. The firm's short-run supply curve follows the vertical price axis at first, and then jumps to the short-run marginal cost curve for output levels greater than or equal to the shutdown point (x_{sd}).

A Numerical Illustration of the Shutdown Decision   The short-run shutdown decision can also be illustrated with a numerical example. Suppose a firm has fixed costs of $50,000, variable costs of $100,000, and revenues of $55,000. One might be tempted to suggest the firm would continue to produce in the short run, since it is covering fixed cost. But a comparison of the firm's losses if it produces or shuts down reveals that it minimizes losses by shutting down. Keep in mind that the firm incurs its fixed expenses of $50,000 whether it produces or not. Table 12.1 compares the

TABLE 12.1   Losses from Shutting Down and Continuing to Produce

	Firm Shut Down	Firm Still Producing
Total Revenue	$ 0	$ 55,000
Total Variable Cost	0	−100,000
Fixed Cost	−50,000	−50,000
Losses	−50,000	−95,000

firm's losses under the two scenarios. Notice that if it shuts down, it only loses $50,000, its fixed cost. If it continues to produce, however, it loses $95,000, or $45,000 more than if it shuts down. Thus, a profit-maximizing (loss-minimizing) firm facing these revenues and costs will shut down. Moreover, it will stay shut down unless price rises enough to generate revenues of at least $100,000 (its variable cost) for the same output level. At that point, losses are at least equal if the firm either produces or shuts down.

Implications of Diminishing Returns to Variable Inputs   We can now state another important property that follows from eventually diminishing marginal products of variable inputs. If there is only one variable input and the marginal product of that input eventually declines as more of the input is hired, the firm's short-run supply curve will be upward sloping. This follows directly from the argument developed above and the fact, shown in Section 11.8 at equations 11.73 and 11.74, that if the marginal product of labor function declines, the short-run average variable cost function must eventually rise. As long as the short-run average variable cost function eventually rises, short-run shutdown will be at minimum short-run average variable cost. Thus, as we mentioned in the discussion of Figure 12.7, the positive-output short-run supply curve will only be defined on the rising portion of the short-run marginal cost function for outputs greater than or equal to the shutdown point.

Note at this point that if the production function exhibits diminishing marginal product of *one* variable input *everywhere,* there will actually be no short-run shutdown point. That is because the short-run marginal cost and average variable cost functions both rise from 0, with marginal cost greater than average variable cost at every output. This is illustrated in Figure 12.8.

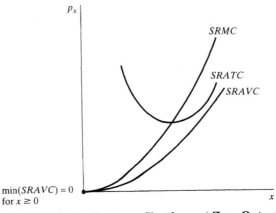

FIGURE 12.8   Short-run Shutdown at Zero Output

If the firm uses two or more variable inputs, the production function must exhibit diminishing returns to all variable inputs simultaneously in order to guarantee that short-run average variable cost and short-run marginal cost functions will be rising. That would happen if variable costs were rising faster than output as all variable inputs were increased.

12.5   SHORT-RUN DEMAND FOR ONE VARIABLE INPUT

With the development of the firm's short-run supply curve completed, the next three sections develop the concept of a firm's short-run demand for inputs. This section deals with short-run input demand with one variable input; the next focuses on input demand with two or more variable inputs; and Section 12.7 examines factors accounting for shifts in short-run input demand functions.

Derived Demand   Choosing a profit-maximizing output level implies a profit-maximizing choice of inputs needed to produce that output level. In fact, until an output is decided upon, there is no way of determining the correct set of inputs to be hired. In other words, input demand cannot be separated from output choice. Thus, the demand for inputs is *derived* from the demand for output. For that reason we refer to input demand as a **derived demand.**

To develop the properties of that input choice, we express the firm's profit function in terms of inputs:

$$\pi(L, K) = p_x x(L, K) - wL - rK. \tag{12.26}$$

To find the profit-maximizing choice of labor assuming capital is fixed, we take the partial derivative of (12.26) with respect to labor and set it equal to 0:

$$\frac{\partial \pi}{\partial L} = p_x \frac{\partial x}{\partial L} - w = 0. \tag{12.27}$$

Solving (12.27) for w,

$$w = p_x MP_L. \tag{12.28}$$

Similarly, to find the profit-maximizing choice of capital assuming labor is fixed, we take the partial derivative of (12.26) with respect to capital and set it equal to 0:[10]

$$\frac{\partial \pi}{\partial K} = p_x \frac{\partial x}{\partial K} - r = 0. \tag{12.29}$$

---

[10]While we develop short-run demand for capital in order to show the rule for profit-maximizing capital choice when labor is fixed, typically economists model capital as fixed in the short run and labor as the variable input.

Solving (12.29) for r,

$$r = p_x MP_K. \tag{12.30}$$

Marginal and Average Revenue Products   Equation 12.28 tells us that if labor is the only variable input, the short-run demand for labor under competition is proportional to its marginal product; and if capital is the only variable input, the short-run competitive demand for capital is proportional to its marginal product. Labor is hired until its marginal cost (w) is equal to its marginal contribution to the firm's total revenue, which is the price of output times the marginal product of labor. Capital is also hired until its marginal cost (r) is equal to its marginal contribution to the firm's total revenue, which is the price of output times the marginal product of capital. Economists refer to the marginal contributions to revenue as the **marginal revenue product of labor** (MRP_L) and the **marginal revenue product of capital** (MRP_K).

The production function $x = K^{1/2}L^{1/2}$ illustrates how the short-run demand for labor is derived. Differentiating the production function with respect to L,

$$MP_L = \frac{1}{2}\frac{K^{1/2}}{L^{1/2}}. \tag{12.31}$$

Substituting (12.31) in (12.28),

$$w = p_x\left(\frac{1}{2}\frac{K^{1/2}}{L^{1/2}}\right) = \frac{p_x K^{1/2}}{2L^{1/2}}. \tag{12.32}$$

We can now solve for labor from (12.32), generating the short-run labor demand function:

$$L^{1/2} = \frac{p_x K^{1/2}}{2w} \quad \Rightarrow \quad L^*(w; \overline{K}) = \frac{(p_x)^2 \overline{K}}{4w^2}, \tag{12.33}$$

which is the firm's short-run demand for labor with capital fixed at $\overline{K}$.

Just as we have defined average functions to accompany other marginal functions, we can also define an average revenue product as the total revenue per unit of the appropriate input:

$$\text{average revenue product of labor } (ARP_L) = \frac{TR}{L} = p_x \frac{x}{L} \tag{12.34}$$

$$\text{average revenue product of capital } (ARP_K) = \frac{TR}{K} = p_x \frac{x}{K}. \tag{12.35}$$

Figure 12.9 illustrates the relationships among the marginal product, average product, marginal revenue product, and average revenue product functions. Since p_x is a constant, the marginal revenue and average revenue product functions are simply proportional to the marginal and average product functions. This implies that maximum marginal revenue product occurs at the same input level as does maximum marginal product. Similarly, maximum average revenue product occurs at the same input

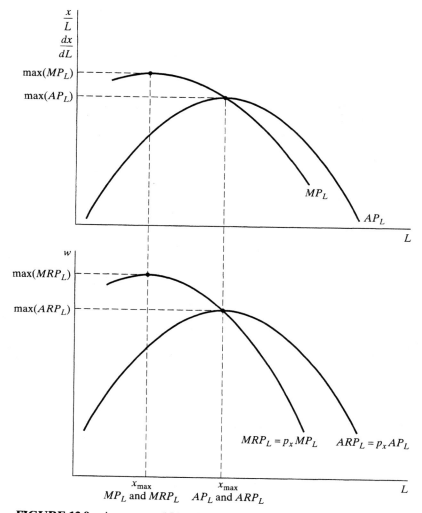

FIGURE 12.9   Average and Marginal Product and Average and Marginal Revenue Product of Labor

level as does maximum average product. When one function is simply changed (transformed) by a factor of proportionality, the value of the independent variable associated with the maximum point of the original function must be the same at the maximum of the transformed function.

Short-run Shutdown and the Effective Demand Curve for Labor   Now, recall from equation 12.25 that the firm's short-run shutdown point occurs when price equals minimum average variable cost. Holding price fixed and allowing the wage to vary, if labor

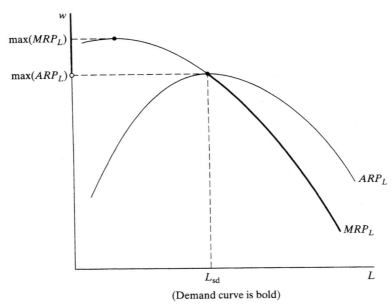

FIGURE 12.10 Labor Demand at the Short-run Shutdown Point and the Firm's Effective Short-run Demand Curve for Labor

is the only variable factor, $p_x = SRAVC = wL/x$ at the short-run shutdown point. Thus, at that point,

$$w = \frac{p_x x}{L} = ARP_L. \qquad (12.36)$$

However, since $w = MRP_L$ at every point on the short-run demand curve for labor, it must be that w equals maximum average revenue product at the short-run shutdown point. That is because marginal revenue product only equals average revenue product at maximum average revenue product. This means that the firm's short-run demand curve for labor follows the wage axis (since output is 0 and no labor is employed) for wages greater than maximum average revenue product and then jumps to follow the marginal revenue product curve for wages less than or equal to maximum average revenue product. In other words, the firm only hires positive quantities of labor if the wage is less than or equal to maximum average revenue product. Moreover, since marginal revenue product is falling when the wage is less than or equal to maximum average revenue product, short-run shutdown at that point also implies that the firm's short-run demand curve for labor will be downward sloping for positive production. Figure 12.10 illustrates these relationships. L_{sd} is the quantity of labor hired at the firm's short-run shutdown point. Thus, the firm's short-run demand curve for labor follows the wage axis (since labor input is 0) for wages greater than maximum average revenue product and then jumps to follow the marginal revenue product curve at maximum average revenue product. It is then defined for positive quantities of labor greater than or equal to L_{sd}. And, since marginal revenue product is falling for quantities of labor greater than or equal to L_{sd}, the firm's short-run demand for positive quantities of labor is downward sloping.

Short-run Shutdown in Terms of Labor Demand and Product Supply   Short-run shutdown for a competitive firm can be expressed either as minimum short-run average variable cost or as maximum average revenue product for the following reason. If prices are parameters and not decision variables, short-run shutdown can be viewed as a physical property of the production function itself, independent of either wage or price. That is to say, there is one quantity of labor input, or, equivalently, one total output at short-run shutdown. Changes in the parametric wage shift the shutdown price up or down without affecting the output at minimum average variable cost. Similarly, shifts in parametric output price shift the shutdown wage up or down without affecting the labor hired at maximum average revenue product. To see this point, consider the formulas for average variable cost and average revenue product: $SRAVC = wL/x(L; \overline{K})$ and $ARP_L = p_x x(L; \overline{K})/L$. To find the properties of each at their respective maxima and minima, differentiate each with respect to labor, treating input and output prices as parameters, and set the derivatives equal to 0:

$$\frac{\partial}{\partial L}(SRAVC) = w\left(\frac{x - (\partial x/\partial L)L}{x^2}\right) = 0 \quad \Rightarrow \quad x = \frac{\partial x}{\partial L}L \qquad (12.37)$$

$$\frac{\partial}{\partial L}ARP_L = p_x\left(\frac{(\partial x/\partial L)L - x}{L^2}\right) = 0 \quad \Rightarrow \quad x = \frac{\partial x}{\partial L}L. \qquad (12.38)$$

Equations 12.37 and 12.38 show that for a competitive firm, short-run shutdown implies a quantity of labor such that output is equal to labor input times the marginal product of labor, independent of either price or wage.

Further Implications of Diminishing Returns   Notice also that multiplying both sides of either (12.37) or (12.38) by p_x reinforces a previous observation:

$$x = \frac{\partial x}{\partial L}L \quad \Rightarrow \quad p_x x = p_x MP_L L. \qquad (12.39)$$

Thus, substituting $w = p_x MP_L$ in (12.39),

$$p_x x = wL. \qquad (12.40)$$

In other words, at the short-run shutdown point, revenues exactly equal variable costs.

The above discussion also illustrates the final important property that follows from eventually diminishing marginal products. If there is only one variable input and the production function exhibits eventually diminishing marginal product of that input, then the firm's short-run demand for positive quantities of that input will be downward sloping. Diminishing marginal product implies diminishing marginal revenue product, which implies downward-sloping short-run demand for positive quantities of an input, by the argument outlined above.

12.6 _____ SHORT-RUN INPUT DEMAND WITH TWO OR MORE VARIABLE INPUTS

With two or more variable inputs, the basic rule for profit maximization is the same as with one variable input: hire the input until its input price equals its marginal revenue product. For example, with three inputs (capital fixed, labor and materials variable) the profit function is

$$\pi(L, m; \overline{K}) = p_x x(L, m; \overline{K}) - wL - p_m m - r\overline{K}. \tag{12.41}$$

To find the profit-maximizing choice of labor and materials, we take the partial derivatives of (12.41) with respect to labor and materials and set them equal to 0:

$$\frac{\partial \pi}{\partial L} = p_x \frac{\partial x}{\partial L} - w = 0 \quad \Rightarrow \quad w = p_x MP_L \tag{12.42}$$

$$\frac{\partial \pi}{\partial m} = p_x \frac{\partial x}{\partial m} - p_m \quad \Rightarrow \quad p_m = p_x MP_m. \tag{12.43}$$

If the price of one of the variable inputs changes, there are "income" and "substitution" effects associated with the price change. Along an isoquant, a firm always substitutes the now cheaper input for the one whose price has gone up. But, as output changes, the firm may use more or less of a particular input. If the input is normal, the short-run input demand curve will be downward sloping. The reason is that short-run marginal cost increases at every output when the price of a normal input increases. This reduces the firm's profit-maximizing output for a given output price. If the input is normal, the reduction in the firm's profit-maximizing output implies a reduction in the optimal quantity of that input hired.

The reduction in the firm's profit-maximizing output as a result of an increase in short-run marginal cost at every output is illustrated in Figure 12.11. Since the firm

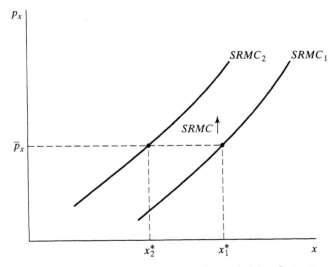

FIGURE 12.11   A Reduction in Profit-maximizing Output Resulting from an Increase in the Short-run Marginal Cost Curve

treats its short-run marginal cost curve as its short-run supply curve, the increase in marginal cost at every output implies a leftward shift in short-run supply and a decline in profit-maximizing output from x_1^* to x_2^*.

12.7   SHIFTS IN SHORT-RUN INPUT DEMAND FUNCTIONS

The parameters of short-run input demand functions are the price of output, the quantity of fixed inputs, and technology. As with supply and demand curves, short-run input demand curves shift when any of these parameters changes.

Changes in the Marginal Product of Labor   The effects of changes in fixed factors are indeterminate. However, if increasing the quantity of a fixed factor increases the marginal product of a single variable factor at all input levels, then increasing the quantity of a fixed factor will shift the short-run demand curve for the variable factor to the right. The effects of technological change depend on whether the technological change increases the marginal product of the variable factor. If it does, short-run input demand will increase, since an increase in marginal product must increase marginal revenue product for a given output price. These cases are illustrated in Figure 12.12. The increase in the marginal product of labor implies a rightward shift in the short-run demand curve for labor.

Changes in Output Price   With one variable input, if the price of output increases, short-run input demand must also increase at every input level. This is illustrated by recalling the expression for the short-run demand curve for labor from equation 12.28: $w = p_x MP_L$. If p_x increases, the firm is willing to pay a higher wage for each quantity of labor hired. But, since a competitive firm takes the market wage as given, the effect is

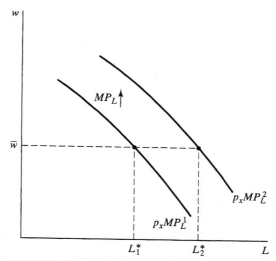

FIGURE 12.12   An Increase in Short-run Labor Demand from an Increase in the Marginal Product of Labor

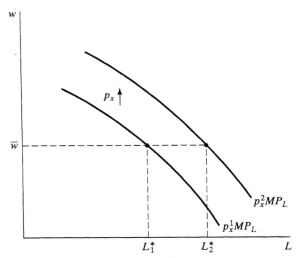

FIGURE 12.13 An Increase in Short-run Demand for Labor from an Increase in the Price of Output

to increase the quantity of labor the firm is willing to hire at each wage. This is illustrated in Figure 12.13. As the price of output increases, the short-run demand curve for labor shifts to the right.

   In general, if the short-run supply curve is upward sloping, and more of a variable input is employed as output increases, then an increase in output price will shift the short-run demand curve for the variable input to the right. This happens because output increases in response to an increase in price if short-run supply is upward sloping. To produce more output, the firm hires more of the input at each price.

12.8   THE COMPUTER SOFTWARE COMPANY'S SHORT-RUN SUPPLY CURVE AND SHORT-RUN LABOR DEMAND CURVE

Table 11.3 outlines the hypothetical computer software company's short-run costs. Using the profit-maximization rule developed in this chapter, the firm's short-run supply curve will follow the price axis at first and then jump to equal the firm's short-run marginal cost curve for prices greater than or equal to minimum average variable cost (approximately \$2,222 at 13.5 software packages per year). Table 12.2 summarizes the firm's short-run supply curve for output, and Figure 12.14 graphs it. Moreover, since minimum short-run average total cost is approximately \$5,262 at 19.5 software packages per year, the firm makes profits at any price above \$5,262.[11]

Short-run Labor Demand   The firm's short-run demand curve for labor is derived from the marginal product of labor, which can be constructed from the total product of

---

[11]Recall that this price is for the distribution rights to one software package. A distribution company would then make many copies that it would presumably sell for much less per package.

TABLE 12.2   The Computer Software Company's Short-run Supply Curve

Marginal Cost = Price	Output
$3,000	0
1,500	0
1,714	0
2,000	0
2,400	14.75
3,000	17
4,000	18.75
6,000	20
12,000	20.75

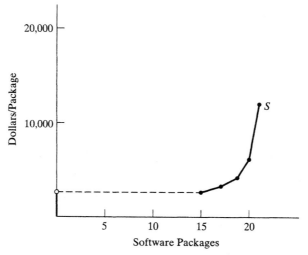

FIGURE 12.14   Graph of the Computer Software Company's Short-run Supply Curve

labor that is sketched out verbally in Section 11.8. Table 12.3 develops the marginal product of labor and the short-run labor demand function, assuming market price is $6,000.

Figure 12.15 illustrates the firm's short-run demand curve for labor. Notice that the average product of labor attains a maximum between 5 and 6 programmers. Since short-run shutdown occurs at maximum average product of labor, the firm's short-run demand curve for labor follows the wage axis for less than 6 student programmers and then follows the marginal revenue product curve for 6 or more.

TABLE 12.3   The Computer Software Company's Marginal Revenue Product

Labor	TP_L	AP_L	MP_L	Price	MRP_L
1	1	1			
1.5			2	$6000	$12,000
2	3	1.5			
2.5			4	6,000	24,000
3	7	2.3			
3.5			3.5	6,000	21,000
4	10.5	2.6			
4.5			3	6,000	18,000
5	13.5	2.7			
5.5			2.5	6,000	15,000
6	16	2.7			
6.5			2	6,000	12,000
7	18	2.6			
7.5			1.5	6,000	9,000
8	19.5	2.4			
8.5			1	6,000	6,000
9	20.5	2.2			
9.5			0.5	6,000	3,000
10	21	2.1			

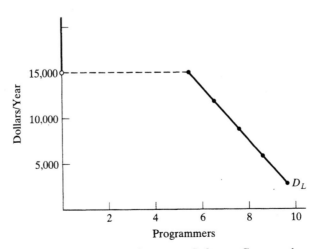

FIGURE 12.15   The Computer Software Company's Short-run Demand Curve for Labor

12.9 _____ "SUNK" COSTS AND ECONOMIC DECISION MAKING

Notice that in the above analysis we did not say that an increase in the price of a fixed factor of production would affect the short-run supply curve or short-run input demand curve. That is because fixed costs must be paid in the short run, regardless of how much output the firm produces or how many variable inputs the firm hires. When the price of a fixed factor increases, the firm simply absorbs the cost in the short run. Profits will be lower, but if the firm were to alter its output decision in response to the increase in cost, it would not be maximizing profits any more. Short-run marginal cost is unaffected by changes in fixed cost (marginal cost is the derivative of variable cost with respect to output) and the firm simply continues to equate its unchanged marginal cost and market price.

This implies a general principle of optimal economic decision making. Profit maximization always implies that a firm treats fixed costs as unrecoverable "sunk" costs in the short run and does not allow those sunk costs to affect decision making. The only important short-run variables are output price and the prices of variable inputs. Economists sometimes summarize this principle by saying that "sunk costs are sunk."

This principle applies more widely than simply to show that the short-run supply curve does not shift if fixed cost changes. It is also used to show that profit maximization implies that decisions made in the past do not directly affect what decisions are made in the future.[12] In other words, profit-maximizing decision makers do not respond differently to current incentives just because they have sunk investments into particular projects in the past. A profit-maximizing manager does not continue a course of action that is no longer profitable, despite decisions made in the past.

For example, suppose a store owner has an inventory of goods, some of which were purchased before a recent market price increase. The investment in that inventory is, therefore, a sunk cost, regardless of how much the owner paid for it. Profit maximization by a competitive firm in the present implies that the firm always sells at the prevailing market price, regardless of costs. A competitive firm cannot sell higher than the market price, and if it sells lower, it simply makes lower profits. Thus, the store owner should not distinguish between items purchased before the price increase and those purchased after if the owner is maximizing profits. All inventory should simply be sold at the new price. If the owner were to sell the old inventory at the old price, there would be lower profits on those particular items. Looking at it from the other side, if market price falls in a competitive market, a firm that still has inventory bought at the higher price must sell at the lower price or lose all its business. In grocery stores, the use of automatic scanners has made it much easier to maintain uniform prices on all inventory.

To take another example, suppose that a firm has to pay some entry fee to participate in a particular market.[13] Once a firm has paid that fee, it is a sunk cost and has no effect on a profit-maximizing firm's output decision in that market. Changes in the

---

[12]Past decisions may indirectly affect current decisions because past decisions determine how much capital a firm has in the present and perhaps even in the near future.

[13]Assume this market is still sufficiently competitive so that participating firms have no individual effect on market price.

entry fee might determine whether or not a profit-maximizing firm enters the market to begin with, but the fee change does not directly affect output decisions if the firm does participate.

12.10   REVIEW OF KEY CONCEPTS

This completes the introduction to the individual competitive firm's profit-maximizing output and input choices. Before continuing on to market supply and competitive equilibrium, be sure you understand and can use the following key concepts.

A profit-maximizing firm that produces a positive output always chooses that output so that the marginal cost of producing it is equal to the marginal revenue obtained from selling it.

A competitive firm cannot affect its price and thus must take price as a parameter in its profit-maximization decision. We say that a competitive firm is a *price taker.*

Price taking by a competitive firm implies that marginal revenue equals price. This, in turn, implies that a competitive firm chooses an output level such that the marginal cost of producing that output is equal to price.

Since a competitive firm chooses x^* so that $MC(x^*) = p_x$, the firm's short-run marginal cost curve acts as its short-run supply curve: points along the short-run supply curve indicate the profit-maximizing quantity at each price.

Profits are 0 at a firm's *break-even point.*

Typically in graphical exposition, we draw the firm's inverse supply function $[p_x(x^*)]$; but we model the firm as a price taker, choosing x^* as a function of a parametric price. Thus, the firm's supply function should be $x^*(p_x)$.

With only one variable input, an increase in an input price increases the firm's short-run marginal cost at every output level.

A *normal input* is used in increasing amounts as a firm expands, while an *inferior input* is used in decreasing amounts.

If a firm uses two or more variable inputs, an increase in the price of a normal input raises short-run marginal cost at every output level, while an increase in the price of an inferior input lowers short-run marginal cost.

An increase in short-run marginal cost at every output shifts the firm's short-run supply curve to the left, and a decrease in marginal cost shifts it to the right.

If a firm hires only one variable input (say labor), then hiring more fixed capital reduces short-run marginal cost if an increase in capital raises the marginal product of labor. Hiring more fixed capital increases marginal cost if an increase in capital reduces the marginal product of labor.

A *technological change* is an improvement in engineering technology that allows the firm to produce more output from a given set of inputs.

A *neutral* technological change leaves the marginal rates of technical substitution along an isoquant unchanged. Thus, the ratio of marginal products of labor and capital remains the same.

A *biased* technological change raises the marginal product of one factor of production by more than it does another and thus changes the marginal rates of technical substitution.

Neutral technological changes reduce unit costs for every possible input combination, while biased technological changes *generally* only reduce unit costs for *some* input combinations.

A neutral technological change can be represented by a positive monotonic transformation of the original production function.

With the adoption of a neutral technological change, marginal cost declines for every output and short-run supply shifts to the right; the firm is willing to supply more at each price.

Among biased technological changes, *labor-using* (or *capital-saving*) technological changes raise the marginal product of labor more than the marginal product of capital. *Capital-using* (or *labor-saving*) technological changes raise the marginal product of capital more than the marginal product of labor. Labor-using technological changes are generally cost saving when labor is relatively inexpensive, and capital-using technological changes are generally cost saving when capital is relatively inexpensive.

A biased technological change reduces short-run marginal cost if it directly raises the marginal products of variable inputs or if adoption of the new technology requires hiring more fixed inputs, perhaps indirectly raising the marginal products of variable inputs.

Adoption of new technology and expansion of capital are long-run changes that imply shifts in short-run supply.

Profits can be expressed as output times the difference between price and average total cost. Thus, profits are positive, 0, or negative as price is greater than, equal to, or less than average total cost, respectively.

A firm will continue to produce in the short run as long as price is greater than or equal to average variable cost. This decision is independent of fixed cost, since fixed costs are incurred whether or not the firm produces positive output.

Since price is always equal to marginal cost for a competitive firm, the lowest price at which a firm will continue producing is minimum average variable cost, where short-run marginal cost equals average variable cost. The output associated with minimum average variable cost is referred to as the firm's *short-run shutdown point.*

If there is only one variable input and the marginal product of that variable input declines, the firm's short-run supply curve is upward sloping.

If there is only one variable input, there will be no short-run shutdown point if the production function exhibits diminishing returns to that variable input over all ranges of output.

With two or more variable inputs, the short-run marginal cost curve (and thus short-run supply) will be upward sloping if there are diminishing returns to all inputs simultaneously.

Input demand is *derived* from the demand for output; it is referred to as a *derived demand.*

A profit-maximizing competitive firm hires labor so that output price times the marginal prod-uct of hiring that amount of labor is equal to the wage rate.

A profit-maximizing competitive firm hires capital so that output price times the marginal product associated with that amount of capital is equal to the rental rate on capital.

Price times the marginal product of labor (or capital) is called the *marginal revenue product* of labor (or capital) for a competitive firm.

Price times the average product of labor (or capital) is called the *average revenue product* of labor (or capital) for a competitive firm.

Average and marginal revenue products are proportional to average and marginal products for a given output price.

Short-run shutdown occurs at the labor input associated with maximum average revenue product. This amount of labor, in turn, produces the output associated with minimum average variable cost.

The firm's short-run demand curve for labor follows the vertical wage axis for wages greater than maximum average revenue product (since output is 0 and no labor is employed) and then jumps to follow the marginal revenue product curve for wages less than or equal to maximum average revenue product.

For a competitive firm, the short-run shutdown point can be viewed as a characteristic of the production function, independent of input and output prices. For a competitive firm using labor as its only variable factor, shutdown occurs when output equals the marginal product of labor times the quantity of labor hired. Labor at the shutdown point along the short-run labor demand curve then produces exactly the amount of output at the shutdown point along the short-run supply curve.

If a firm's production function exhibits diminishing returns to one variable input, then the short-run demand curve for positive quantities of that input will be downward sloping.

With two or more variable inputs, the short-run input demand curve for a *normal* input is downward sloping.

With one variable input, an increase in either the marginal product or output price will shift the short-run demand curve for that input to the right.

In general, with upward-sloping short-run supply and normal inputs, an increase in output price will result in an increase in the short-run demand curve for a variable input.

Changes in fixed costs do not affect the firm's short-run output decisions. That is because fixed costs must be paid, regardless of how much output is produced. Short-run marginal cost is independent of fixed cost.

The principle that *sunk costs are sunk* is a general rule that past decisions do not directly affect current decisions if a firm is maximizing profits. Current decisions are directly determined by current and projected future incentives.

12.11   QUESTIONS FOR DISCUSSION

1. Suppose you are the manager of a small firm that manufactures circuit boards for automated appliances. After two years in operation, you find that the market price for circuit boards is lower than your average variable cost, but still high enough to cover your rent and other fixed payments. You decide to continue producing because at least you are covering your fixed costs. Did you make the right decision? Explain why or why not. If you made the wrong decision, explain what you should have done.

2. You are the manager of a local grocery store. When the selling price of ketchup goes up, your stock manager argues that you should leave the old stock at the old price since you bought it at that price. Assuming that you have a scanning system (so that it does not cost you to change the prices on existing stock), analyze the stock manager's suggestion in terms of profit maximization.

3. You are the production manager of an assembly line. You lease your equipment on a long-term lease with a rental rate that changes as a function of the prime rate of interest. During the last quarter, the rental rate went up, and you therefore decided to reduce the production rate along the line. Did you make the right decision? Explain why or why not.

4. Suppose you are a Kansas wheat farmer and you have just harvested this year's crop. You are hoping to get $2 a bushel for your wheat. You figure your average cost per bushel is about $1.75. You go to the local co-op to sell, and the manager tells you that today's price is $1.75. Is there anything you can do to try to get $2 and make a profit? Explain.

5. Construct an example of a firm's output and input decisions to illustrate why we say that input demand is a *derived demand*.

6. In the nineteenth century, technological change in agriculture in the United States proceeded very differently than did technological change in Europe. In the U.S., farmers adopted labor-saving machines, such as tractors and combines, as soon as they were invented. Even though these machines were available in Europe, many European farmers were still not using them as late as the 1950s. Instead, European farmers were more likely to adopt diversified farming practices, which used more labor to raise yields. The number of farm laborers per acre of land was much higher in Europe than in the U.S. Given the difference in the laborer-land ratio and taking each kind of technological change separately, explain the differences in the direction of technological change. Could this process be viewed as a neutral technological change, with each area of the world producing on a different section of a new isoquant? Explain.

12.12   PROBLEMS

1. Consider the following production function,

$$x = \frac{10KL}{K + L},$$

and let $w = \$1$, $r = \$4$, and $\overline{K} = 10$ units in the short run. Derive the firm's short-run supply function.

Problems 2 and 3   Suppose there is a technological change that increases output to

$$x' = \frac{20KL}{K + L}.$$

2. Find the new short-run supply function.

3. Is the technological change neutral or biased? Explain briefly.

4. Now, return to the production function in Problem 1. What is the short-run shutdown point? Explain your answer briefly.

5. Using the production function in Problem 1, let the wage vary and let price equal $5 per unit. Derive the marginal revenue product and average revenue product function and the short-run demand function for labor.

6. Consider the following production function:

$$x = K^{1/4}L^{1/4}m^{1/4},$$

and let $w = \$1$, $r = \$4$, $p_m = \$2$, and $\overline{K} = 4$ units in the short run. Derive the short-run supply function for the firm.

12.13   LOGICAL AND MATHEMATICAL APPLICATIONS

1. Suppose a firm employs both skilled and unskilled labor as variable factors of production. Unskilled labor is a normal input. Show graphically the short-run effect of an increase in the wage for unskilled labor on the relative quantities of both kinds of labor hired to produce each output.

2. What happens to the total quantity of unskilled labor hired for a given output price as the wage rate for unskilled workers increases under the conditions in Application 1? Explain.

3. What does the analysis in Applications 1 and 2 tell us about the potential effect of an increase in the minimum wage on teenage unemployment?

4. Typically, skilled workers argue most strongly for increases in the minimum wage. Are they just being altruistic, or do they stand to gain? Explain.

5. Consider the following outputs obtainable at different labor inputs.

Labor	Output
1	10
2	15
3	25
4	35
5	40
6	44
7	47
8	49
9	50

If fixed costs are $100, the wage rate is $10, and the price of output is $5 per unit, how much output will the firm produce, how much labor will it hire, and how much profit will it make in the short run?

Chapter 13

COMPETITIVE MARKET SUPPLY, MARKET EQUILIBRIUM, AND COMPARATIVE STATICS

13.1 WHAT YOU SHOULD LEARN FROM THIS CHAPTER

This chapter brings you back to the supply and demand curves you learned to work with in your principles classes. First, we develop short-run *market-supply functions* by adding up the individual firm short-run supply functions developed in Section 12.2. Having developed short-run market supply functions, we next combine them with the market demand functions from Section 9.2 to develop the concept of a short-run competitive *market equilibrium*. Changes in the parameters determining demand or supply, which result in shifts in demand or supply curves, also imply changes in the competitive equilibrium. We refer to the comparison of equilibria as *comparative statics*.

The math used in this chapter is simple algebra and should present no problem. Concentrate, therefore, on the concepts, which are very important. The material in this chapter represents the culmination of all previous material. Everything you have learned about supply and demand curves underlies both the curves used in this chapter and the concept of competitive equilibrium.

13.2 SHORT-RUN MARKET SUPPLY FUNCTIONS

The **market supply function** is the schedule describing the total quantity that all firms are willing to supply at each price. The market supply function is derived by adding up across all firms the individual quantity each firm is willing to supply at each price:

$$X_s(p_x) = \sum_{j=1}^{m} x_j(p_x) \tag{13.1}$$

where there are *m* firms under consideration.

Recall from Section 6.6 that the market demand curve was found by adding up the functions with price on the right-hand side and quantity on the left-hand side because quantity demanded was a function of price. The situation is analogous to that of the market *supply* function. Since quantity supplied is a function of price, quantity must be on the left-hand side (the dependent variable) and price must be on the right-hand side (the independent variable).

Some Examples For example, suppose the jth firm has the production function $x_j = K_j^{1/2} L_j^{1/2}$ and that a different amount of capital is hired by each firm. We know from equation 12.7 that each firm's short-run supply curve is

$$p_x = \frac{2wx_j}{\overline{K}_j}. \tag{13.2}$$

Solving (13.2) for x_j to find x_j as a function of p_x,

$$x_j(p_x) = \frac{p_x \overline{K}_j}{2w}. \quad \text{firm } j\text{'s short-run supply function} \tag{13.3}$$

To find the short-run market supply function, we add (13.3) across all m firms:

$$X_s(p_x) = \sum_{j=1}^{m} x_j(p_x) = \sum_{j=1}^{m} \frac{p_x \overline{K}_j}{2w}. \tag{13.4}$$

Thus, rewriting (13.4), the short-run market supply function is

$$X_s(p_x) = \frac{p_x}{2w} \sum_{j=1}^{m} \overline{K}_j. \tag{13.5}$$

In another example, suppose there are three producers with linear short-run supply functions given by

$$x_1 = -2 + p_x, p_x \geq 2 \tag{13.6}$$

$$x_2 = -5 + 6p_x, \ p_x \geq 5/6 \tag{13.7}$$

$$x_3 = \quad 4p_x, \ p_x \geq 0. \tag{13.8}$$

The short-run market supply function is the sum of equations 13.6–13.8 over non-negative quantities:

$$\begin{aligned} X_s = x_1 + x_2 + x_3 &= -7 + 11p_x, & p_x \geq 2 \\ = x_2 + x_3 &= -5 + 10p_x, & 5/6 \leq p_x < 2 \\ = x_3 &= \quad 4p_x, & 0 \leq p_x < 5/6. \end{aligned} \tag{13.9}$$

Equation 13.9 is defined in segments to ensure that quantity supplied is always greater than or equal to 0.

Figure 13.1 illustrates the derivation of a short-run market supply curve when there are two firms in an industry. At price p_x^1, firm A supplies x_A^1 and firm B supplies x_B^1. The market quantity supplied at that price is $X_s^1 = x_A^1 + x_B^1$. Similarly, at p_x^2, firm A supplies x_A^2 and firm B supplies x_B^2. The market quantity supplied at p_x^2 is, therefore, $X_s^2 = x_A^2 + x_B^2$. The short-run market supply curve is, thus, the horizontal sum of the individual short-run supply curves. The graph is constructed by connecting the total quantities supplied at each price.

Elasticity of Supply Having defined market supply, we can also define the **elasticity of supply** as the percentage change in quantity supplied relative to a given percentage change in price. It is analogous to demand elasticity:

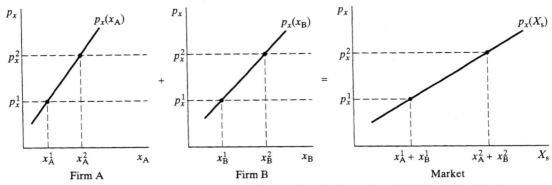

FIGURE 13.1   Constructing a Short-run Market Supply Curve from Individual Firm Short-run Supply Curves

$$\epsilon_s = \frac{p_x}{x} \frac{d}{dp_x} X_s(p_x). \tag{13.10}$$

Changes in Market Supply   Just as with individual firm supply functions, the market quantity supplied is a function of the own price of the good, holding several parameters fixed. In Section 12.3, we discussed the parameters affecting short-run individual supply: input prices, the amount of fixed inputs hired, and the technology. When we consider short-run market supply functions, the number of firms in an industry and the distribution of technologies among firms become parameters of short-run market supply. If firms enter the industry thereby increasing the number of firms, short-run market supply increases since the market sum is over more firms. Conversely, if firms exit from an industry thereby decreasing the number of firms, short-run market supply decreases. Regarding technology, at any point in time, not all firms may be using the same technology. Some may use a new, lower cost, technology, while others may still be using an older technology. Since adoption of a new technology increases short-run supply, the diffusion of a new technology to more and more firms also increases short-run market supply.[1]

13.3   SHORT-RUN COMPETITIVE EQUILIBRIUM

A short-run competitive **market equilibrium** is characterized by a market price and a quantity sold in that market such that market quantity demanded equals short-run market quantity supplied at that price, given the number of firms in the industry and the amount of capital employed by each firm. Figure 13.2 reviews the graph you should be familiar with from your principles courses. Assuming the good is not a Giffen good (to ensure that demand is downward sloping) and that there are diminishing returns to all variable inputs (so that short-run supply is upward sloping), $p_x(X_d)$ is the inverse

---

[1]We consider the effect of a technological change on long-run supply below.

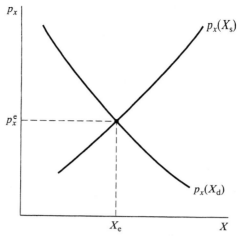

FIGURE 13.2   Short-run Competitive Equilibrium

demand function and $p_x(X_s)$ is the inverse short-run supply function. The equilibrium price (p_x^e) equates quantity demanded and short-run quantity supplied at p_x^e. Moreover, if none of the parameters underlying demand (income, prices of other goods, tastes, number of consumers, distribution of income or tastes) or short-run supply (input prices, quantity of fixed inputs, technology, number of firms, distribution of technology) changes, the same equilibrium price and quantity will be observed in the market every trading period.

An Example   For example, suppose all consumers have the utility function $U_i = x_i y_i$ and incomes of $\overline{M}_i$. All firms have production function $x_j = K_j^{1/2} L_j^{1/2}$ and fixed capital of $\overline{K}_j$ in the short run. The wage rate is $\overline{w}$. We have already seen in equation 6.29 that market demand is

$$X_d = \frac{1}{2p_x} \sum_{i=1}^{n} \overline{M}_i,$$

and we have seen in equation 13.5 that short-run market supply is

$$X_s = \frac{p_x}{2\overline{w}} \sum_{j=1}^{m} \overline{K}_j.$$

The equilibrium condition is

$$X_e = X_d = X_s. \tag{13.11}$$

Now, if we let SM represent the sum of the incomes and SK represent the sum of the capitals, we can restate (6.29) and (13.5) and substitute them in (13.11):

$$\frac{SM}{2p_x} = \frac{p_x SK}{2\overline{w}} \quad \Rightarrow \quad (p_x)^2 = \frac{\overline{w} SM}{SK}. \tag{13.12}$$

Solving (13.12) for p_x, the short-run equilibrium price is

$$p_x^e = \left(\frac{\overline{w}SM}{SK} \right)^{1/2}. \tag{13.13}$$

To find the short-run equilibrium quantity, we substitute (13.13) in either the market demand function (9.4) or the short-run market supply function (13.5). Substituting (13.13) in (9.4),

$$X_d = \frac{SM}{2(\overline{w}SM/SK)^{1/2}} = \frac{1}{2} \left(\frac{(SM)(SK)}{\overline{w}} \right)^{1/2}. \tag{13.14}$$

Alternatively, we can substitute (13.5) in (13.13):

$$X_s = \frac{(\overline{w}SM/SK)^{1/2}}{2\overline{w}} SK = \frac{1}{2} \left[\frac{(SM)(SK)}{\overline{w}} \right]^{1/2} = X_d. \tag{13.15}$$

Comparing (13.14) and (13.15), the short-run equilibrium quantity is

$$X_e = \frac{1}{2} \left[\frac{(SM)(SK)}{\overline{w}} \right]^{1/2}. \tag{13.16}$$

Thus, the short-run equilibrium is the price-quantity pair (p_x^e, X_e) derived as (13.13) and (13.16).

Individual Decisions and Market Equilibria Now, recall from Section 4.4 that under competition, individual consumers and firms simultaneously take this market equilibrium price as a parameter in their respective decision functions (utility maximization and profit maximization). Utility maximization subject to the market price generates individual quantities demanded, and the sum is market quantity demanded. Profit maximization subject to the market price generates individual quantities supplied, and the sum is market quantity supplied. In other words, the intersection of market demand and market supply generates the market price the individuals are simultaneously using as parameters.

Figure 13.3 illustrates the simultaneity of individual and market decisions. The consumer is represented in the left graph, the firm in the short run is in the right graph, and the market, which represents many consumers and many firms, is in the center. All the consumer demand curves combine to form the market demand, and the firm short-run marginal cost curves combine to form the market short-run supply. The short-run equilibrium price (p_x^e) is used by the consumer to choose x_i^* and by the firm to choose x_j^*. The market equilibrium quantity (X_e) is the sum of the x_i^*'s or the x_j^*'s, both of which must be equivalent in equilibrium.

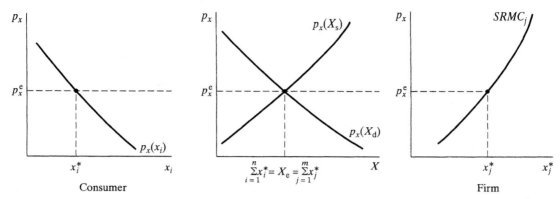

FIGURE 13.3   Individual and Market Decisions

13.4   EXPERIMENTAL MARKETS: AN ILLUSTRATION OF COMPETITIVE EQUILIBRIUM

The competitive model developed above has been criticized for not incorporating important features of naturally occurring markets. In particular, simultaneous individual and market decisions do not allow for the sequence of decisions that actually takes place in real time. What actually happens is that prices get formed in the market; individuals use those prices to make decisions; and their decisions combine to create a new set of market prices. Those new market prices may or may not be different from the old market prices. In addition, there is no institution specified in the model for bringing buyers and sellers together.

If all agents knew the demand and supply functions, they would all be able to determine the equilibrium price. Knowing that price, no buyer would be willing to pay more and no seller would accept less. Thus, no transactions would take place at any other price, and there would be no need for a trading institution to coordinate the activities of buyers and sellers. In the naturally occurring world, however, individuals do not have complete knowledge of supply and demand. Thus, there generally is need for institutions to bring buyers and sellers together. In Section 9.3, we used the *tâtonnement* process to generate an equilibrium between two traders. Recall that in that institution, an auctioneer tries out prices until an equilibrium is found and does not allow trades to take place out of equilibrium.

Most naturally occurring markets do not work that way, however.[2] Buyers and sellers find each other in a variety of ways, and no one checks to make sure that all trades are taking place at an equilibrium price. In stock and commodity markets, buyers and sellers call out prices. When a buyer and a seller agree on a price, they have a contract at that price. In the grocery store, the manager *posts* prices and buyers make purchases at their own discretion. However, it is not a usual practice for buyers to

---

[2]One notable exception is the international gold market. The morning and afternoon gold "fixings" are determined by a *tâtonnement* process in which buyers and sellers from all over the world call a central auctioneer who tries out prices in terms of U.S. currency until the quantity demanded of gold equals the quantity supplied.

make alternative price offers to grocery store managers. In open air markets, on the other hand, buyers and sellers may haggle over prices on a one-to-one basis. Each of these is a different trading institution, and these different institutions may have different implications for the applicability of the competitive model.

Testing the Competitive Model Testing the applicability of the competitive model using data from naturally occurring markets is difficult because we cannot observe individual demand and supply functions. All we can observe are market prices, which may or may not be competitive equilibrium prices.

In the late 1950s, Vernon Smith decided to try to test the competitive model in a laboratory experiment with human subjects.[3] In the simple supply and demand market, for example, Smith divided subjects into agents called buyers and agents called sellers and gave each agent a private payoff sheet. Each buyer was told that for each unit he or she bought in a trading period, he or she would be paid (by the experimenter) a redemption value for that unit listed on the payoff sheet. Profit on that unit (in cash) would be the difference between the redemption value and the price paid for the unit. Each seller was told that for each unit he or she sold, the experimenter would have to be paid the cost of that unit listed on the payoff sheet. The profit (in cash) was the difference between the price and the cost.

Figure 13.4 illustrates this simple experimental design. In this experiment there are 7 buyers (numbered 1 through 7) and 7 sellers (numbered 8 through 14). The numbers above the steps on the demand and supply functions represent the redemption values of the buyers and unit costs of the sellers. For example, buyer 1 has three units. The first pays $5, the second pays $3.70, and the third pays $3. Seller 8 also has three units. The first costs $3.20, the second costs $4.50, and the third costs $5.20. If we array these redemption values and costs along the step function as shown, we create *induced* demand and supply functions. And, assuming subjects will try to make as much money as they can, the competitive model predicts they will trade 9 or 10 units at the competitive equilibrium price of $4.10 and earn total profits equal to the shaded area.

The Double Oral Auction Smith used an auction mechanism similar to that used in commodity and stock markets to organize this first experimental market. Buyers were asked to submit oral bids and sellers were asked to submit oral offers to buy and sell single units at specified prices. An auctioneer kept track of all bids and offers on a blackboard so that all agents knew past and present bids and offers. If a buyer wished to accept a seller's offer or vice versa, the buyer or seller would signal the auctioneer, who would note on the blackboard that a contract had been made for one unit at the specified price. Since then, the institution has come to be known as the *double oral auction*.

Despite the difference between this institution and a market in which all agents have complete knowledge of supply and demand information, the experimental

---

[3]Vernon L. Smith, "An Experimental Study of Competitive Market Behavior," *Journal of Political Economy* 70(1962):111–137. Much of this discussion is adapted from Elizabeth Hoffman, James R. Marsden, and Andrew Whinston, "Laboratory Experiments and Computer Simulation: An Introduction to the Use of Experimental and Process Model Data in Economic Analysis," in Kagel and Green, eds., *Advances in Behavioral Economics* (Greenwich, CT: JAI Press, 1987); and Elizabeth Hoffman and Matthew L. Spitzer, "Experimental Law and Economics: An Introduction," *Columbia Law Review* 85(1985):991–1036.

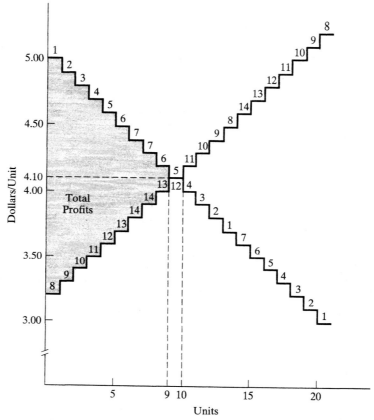

FIGURE 13.4   Induced Demand and Supply Functions

results conform closely to the theory. Smith found that after three or four trading periods, during which subjects learned about the institution, all trades occurred within a few cents of the equilibrium. Moreover, this experiment has been replicated many times, and the results are essentially the same each time. If subjects are paid a $0.05 commission per trade, the price will typically equal the equilibrium by the fourth or fifth trading period. Thus, we can conclude that in at least one kind of real-time market, predictions made by the simple supply and demand model accurately describe actual market transactions. Moreover, the double oral auction is an important market to study since its operation conforms closely to the operation of actual commodity and stock markets.

13.5   FROM SHORT-RUN TO LONG-RUN EQUILIBRIUM

Returning to the short-run equilibrium outlined in Section 13.3, firm j in Figure 13.3 is making profits $\pi_j(x_j^*) = x_j^*[p_x^e - SRATC_j(x_j^*)] > 0$. If we now assume there are no barriers to the entry of new firms in response to the short-run profits being made in

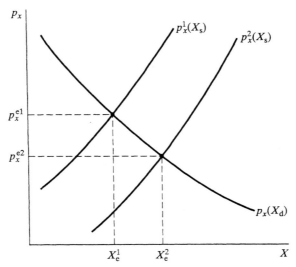

FIGURE 13.5 **The Effect of an Increase in Short-run Supply on Short-run Market Equilibrium**

this industry, competition implies that firms will enter the industry and some existing firms will expand[4] in order to gain some of these economic profits.

Recall from Section 11.2 that economic profits are in excess of both implicit and explicit costs. The firm illustrated in Figure 13.3 is making the market rate of return on all inputs, plus some additional return allowed by the short-run market condition. If firms in a competitive industry can make economic profits, even if only for a short time, other firms will try to capture some of those profits.[5]

As firms enter the industry, the number of firms increases, and consequently the short-run market supply shifts to the right. Assuming demand is downward sloping, as short-run supply increases, short-run market equilibrium price falls and market equilibrium quantity increases. This is illustrated in Figure 13.5. The inverse short-run supply function shifts rightward from $p_x^1(X_s)$ to $p_x^2(X_s)$ as a result of the increase in the number of firms. Market equilibrium price declines from p_x^{e1} to p_x^{e2} and equilibrium quantity increases from X_e^1 to X_e^2.

---

[4]See Section 12.3 for a discussion of the conditions under which capital expansion reduces short-run marginal cost.

[5]Think once again of a firm manager operating in a world of perfect information. Suppose the manager is producing good X and making only normal profits (that is, just covering opportunity costs). If producers of good Y suddenly start making economic profits, the owners of firm X will want the manager to switch from the production of X to the production of Y in order to make higher profits. This is simply an extension of the assumption of profit maximization developed in Section 12.2. The manager not only maximizes profits in the production of a particular good but also produces the mix of output that generates the highest profit, given market conditions.

Long-run Equilibrium Defined   The process of entry in response to economic profits continues until all opportunities to make further economic profits have been completely exhausted. At that point, there are no further incentives for firms to enter the industry or for existing firms to expand. We refer to a market condition in which short-run profits are 0 and all opportunities to make further economic profits have been completely exhausted as a **long-run competitive equilibrium.**

If firms were making short-run losses at a particular short-run equilibrium price, the reverse would occur. Firms would exit from the industry, reducing short-run supply and shifting the short-run supply curve to the left. With downward-sloping demand, a leftward shift in short-run supply raises price and reduces equilibrium quantity. Exit would continue until price equaled average total cost and normal profits were restored. This would also be a long-run competitive equilibrium.

Long-run Equilibrium with Constant Returns to Scale   A long-run equilibrium is illustrated in Figure 13.6 for a constant-returns-to-scale production function. The long-run equilibrium price (LRp_x^e) is equal to short-run marginal cost and minimum short-run average total cost, implying zero short-run profits at LRx_j^*:[6]

$$SR\pi_j(LRx_j^*) = LRx_j^*[LRp_x^e - SRATC_j(LRx_j^*)] = 0. \qquad (13.17)$$

Moreover, since minimum short-run average total cost is also equal to long-run average total cost with constant returns to scale, there are no opportunities to make further economic profits by expanding in the long run. Thus profits are also 0 in the long run:

$$LR\pi_j(LRx_j^*) = LRx_j^*[LRp_x^e - LRAC_j(LRx_j^*)] = 0. \qquad (13.18)$$

U-shaped Long-run Average Costs   Figure 13.7 illustrates long-run equilibrium with a U-shaped long-run average cost production function. In this case, there is only one possible long-run equilibrium quantity for the firm $(\underline{x}_j = LRx_j^*)$, since that is the only point at which short-run marginal cost equals both minimum short-run average total cost and minimum long-run average cost. Thus, it is the only point at which short-run and long-run profits can simultaneously be 0.

Nonexistence of Long-run Equilibrium with Increasing Returns   The concept of long-run competitive equilibrium, however, is well defined *only* for constant returns to scale and U-shaped long-run average total cost production functions. To see this point, suppose the production function exhibited either increasing or decreasing returns to scale over all ranges of output. Figures 13.8 and 13.9 illustrate the case of increasing returns everywhere.

---

[6]Note, however, that any output along the long-run average and marginal cost curve can be a long-run profit-maximizing output for an individual firm, even if there is only one long-run market equilibrium (LRX_e). That is because with constant returns to scale, long-run average cost is constant and thus every short-run average total cost function has the same minimum cost.

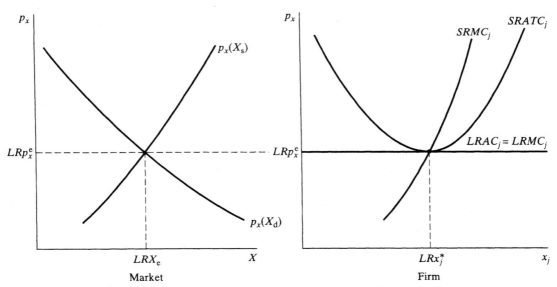

FIGURE 13.6   Long-run Equilibrium with Constant Returns to Scale

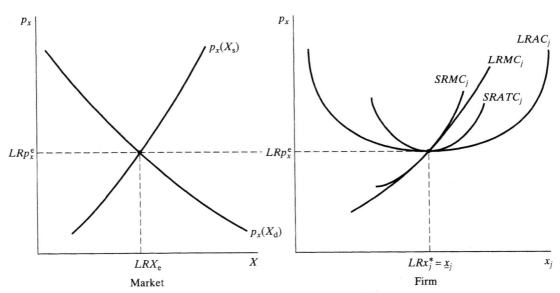

FIGURE 13.7   Long-run Equilibrium with U-shaped Long-run Average Cost

Suppose price starts out at p_x^1 (Figure 13.8), with the firm making short-run profits equal to

$$SR\pi_j^1(x_{j1}^*) = x_{j1}^*[p_x^1 - SRAC_j^1(x_{j1}^*)] > 0.$$

These short-run profits provide an incentive for the entry of other firms and for the expansion of firms already in the market. The combination of entry and expansion shifts the short-run inverse industry supply from $p_x^1(X_s)$ to $p_x^2(X_s)$, reducing market

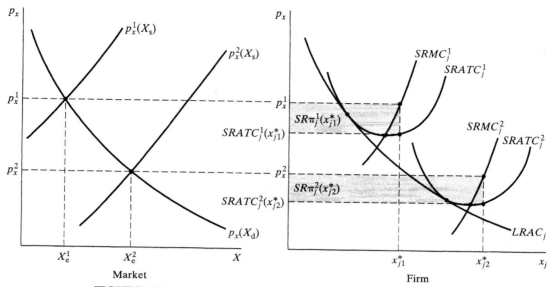

FIGURE 13.8   Long-run Expansion with Increasing Returns to Scale

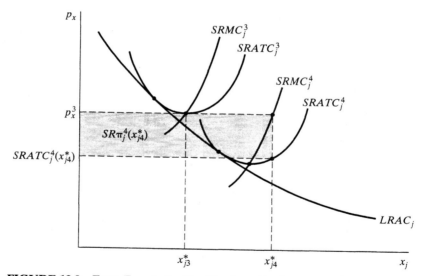

FIGURE 13.9   From Zero to Positive Short-run Profits with Increasing Returns to Scale

equilibrium price from p_x^1 to p_x^2. But, expansion by firm j has also reduced its short-run average total cost curve to $SRATC_j^2$. Thus, short-run profits are still positive:

$$SR\pi_j^2(x_{j2}^*) = x_{j2}^*[p_x^2 - SRATC_j^2(x_{j2}^*)] > 0.$$

In fact, since minimum short-run average cost is never equal to long-run average cost and since there is no minimum long-run average cost, there is no point at which all opportunities to make economic profits are exhausted. Even if price were p_x^3 (Figure 13.9)

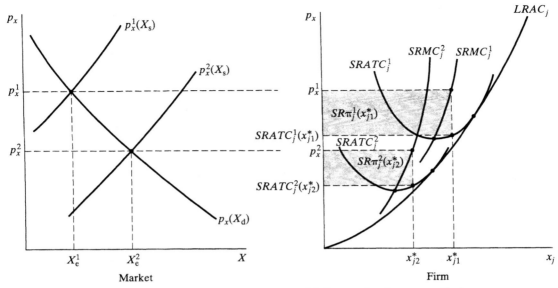

FIGURE 13.10   Long-run Expansion with Decreasing Returns to Scale

and were equal to minimum short-run average total cost momentarily, the firm could once again make profits at that market price by expanding output and reducing costs to $SRATC_j^4$.[7]

Nonexistence of Long-run Equilibrium with Decreasing Returns   If there really were decreasing returns to scale over all ranges of output, the only possible long-run equilibrium would be economically uninteresting, since each firm would produce zero output. Figures 13.10 and 13.11 illustrate this point.

Suppose price starts out at p_x^1 (Figure 13.10), with the firm making short-run profits equal to

$$SR\pi_j^1(x_{j1}^*) = x_{j1}^*[p_x^1 - SRATC_j^1(x_{j1}^*)] > 0.$$

The firm is not encouraged to expand (because that would lower profits), but other firms will enter the industry, shifting the short-run inverse market supply to the right from $p_x^1(X_s)$ to $p_x^2(X_s)$. Even though market equilibrium price falls from p_x^1 to p_x^2, the firm can still continue to make positive short-run economic profits by becoming smaller and reducing short-run average total costs from $SRATC_j^1$ to $SRATC_j^2$:

$$SR\pi_j^2(x_{j2}^*) = x_{j2}^*[p_x^2 - SRATC_j^2(x_{j2}^*)] > 0.$$

---

[7]In fact, in the long run with increasing returns to scale, one firm can eventually achieve lower costs by itself than any other number of firms can achieve under competition. Thus, since market equilibrium output is limited by the demand curve, eventually one firm will dominate with increasing returns and the industry will become a monopoly (one seller). We refer to an industry with increasing returns to scale over all ranges of output as a natural monopoly, and we will develop the concept in more detail in Section 15.6.

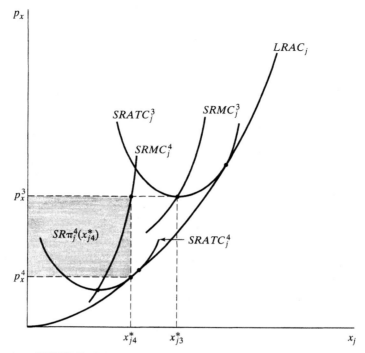

FIGURE 13.11   From Zero to Positive Short-run Profits with Decreasing Returns to Scale

In fact, the only equilibrium of this process is an infinite number of firms, each producing zero output. This is, of course, an equilibrium that would never be observed.[8] As with increasing returns, even if the price were to momentarily equal short-run average total cost (p_x^3 in Figure 13.11), the firm could always make positive short-run profits at that price by becoming smaller and reducing short-run average total cost (from $SRATC_j^3$ to $SRATC_j^4$).

13.6   LONG-RUN MARKET SUPPLY UNDER COMPETITION

The above discussion indicates some important properties of a competitive market. First, it is clear that if there are increasing returns to scale everywhere, competition cannot be sustained in the long run. Second, if production really exhibits decreasing returns to scale over all ranges of output, an industry cannot exist in the long run with free entry. Thus, competitive markets that persist in the long run must have either constant returns or U-shaped long-run average cost. Moreover, with U-shaped costs, in order for there to be many firms in the industry (to preserve competitive conditions),

---

[8]In fact, an industry with decreasing returns to scale everywhere can only exist in the long run if entry is limited and firms are allowed to make positive economic profits.

the output each firm produces $(\underline{x}_j)$ must be "very small" relative to the long-run market equilibrium output.[9] With constant returns, there must also be enough firms to preserve competitive conditions, even though a firm of any size is equally cost saving in the long run.

Long-run Equilibrium Price and Quantity   Given that, under competition, technology will be characterized by either constant returns or U-shaped long-run average cost, long-run equilibrium price is fully determined by technology and input prices. With constant returns to scale,

$$LRp_x^e = LRMC = LRAC = \min(SRATC). \tag{13.19}$$

With U-shaped long-run average cost,

$$LRp_x^e = \min(LRAC). \tag{13.20}$$

In either case, industry supply will simply be the sum of all individual firm quantities supplied *at that price*. With U-shaped costs, industry supply will be the sum of the quantities all firms will supply at minimum long-run average cost:

$$LRX_s = \sum_{j=1}^{m} \underline{x}_j. \tag{13.21}$$

Perfectly Elastic Long-run Supply   The industry expands or contracts in the long run by simply adding or subtracting firms (entry and exit, respectively), each producing exactly $\underline{x}_j$ at the long-run equilibrium price. Thus, we can think of long-run industry supply as being perfectly elastic at the long-run equilibrium price. As long as technology or input prices do not change, long-run equilibrium output increases or decreases at the same price.[10] Figure 13.12 illustrates this point. The firm represented in the right graph is "very small" relative to the market, represented in the left graph. The horizontal long-run supply curve (LRS) is constructed by adding up the $\underline{x}_j$'s along that line.

With constant returns to scale, every firm has a perfectly elastic long-run supply curve since every possible firm size is equally cost saving in the long run. Thus, the market long-run supply is just the same as the long-run supply for each firm. Market long-run supply is simply an extension of each firm's perfectly elastic long-run marginal and long-run average cost. This is illustrated in Figure 13.13. Both firm and industry can expand or contract along the firm's horizontal long-run marginal cost curve. Market

[9]Formally, each firm must be infinitesimally small so that no firm can have any individual effect on market equilibrium price. Actually, it is something of an open question how many firms are required to maintain competition. In the experimental markets discussed in Section 13.4, four buyers and four sellers are generally enough to ensure convergence to the competitive equilibrium.

[10]This analysis assumes that input prices do not change as an industry expands or contracts. If input prices do change, we can analyze the effects of those changes as changes in the parameters underlying long-run supply. (The comparative statics of changes in parameters are developed in Section 13.7.) We can, from a general equilibrium perspective, also analyze changes in input prices and in long-run supply as an industry expands. This perspective is presented in Section 14.6.

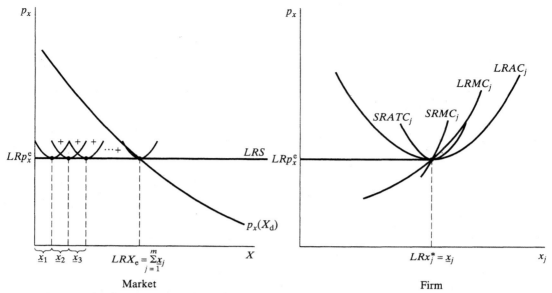

FIGURE 13.12   Long-run Supply with U-shaped Long-run Average Costs

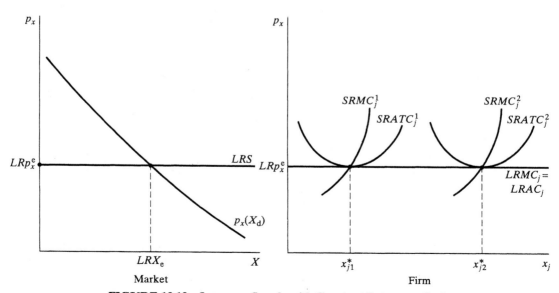

FIGURE 13.13   Long-run Supply with Constant Returns to Scale

long-run quantity is the sum of the firms' short-run optimal choices at the long-run equilibrium price. But, as Figure 13.13 illustrates, one firm could choose any output along the long-run supply: either x_{j1}^* or x_{j2}^*, for example. This implies an important indeterminacy that does not occur with U-shaped cost curves: we can never predict how many firms there will be in a constant-returns-to-scale industry in the long run.

13.7 SHORT-RUN AND LONG-RUN ADJUSTMENTS TO CHANGES IN DEMAND AND SUPPLY PARAMETERS: COMPARATIVE STATICS IN COMPETITIVE MARKETS

The equilibrium price-quantity pairs we have been considering represent **static equilibria;** that is, if the parameters determining supply and demand do not change, the market will generate the same equilibrium every trading period. When we compare different static equilibria as demand or supply parameters *do* change, we do what is called *comparative statics* (introduced in Section 2.5). We have already looked at the comparative statics of an increase or decrease in short-run supply, holding downward-sloping demand parameters constant, in Figure 13.5. We saw that if short-run supply increases (decreases), short-run equilibrium price decreases (increases) and equilibrium quantity increases (decreases).

A Change in Demand If the demand curve shifts to the right along a given upward-sloping short-run supply curve, short-run market equilibrium price and market equilibrium quantity will both increase. This is illustrated in Figure 13.14. Demand increases from $p_x^1(X_d)$ to $p_x^2(X_d)$, equilibrium price increases from p_x^1 to p_x^2, and equilibrium quantity increases from X_e^1 to X_e^2. A reduction in demand would have the opposite effect: equilibrium price and quantity would both fall.

An Increase in Consumer Income The long-run effect of an increase in demand is illustrated with the following more specific example and Figure 13.15. Suppose a constant-returns-to-scale industry producing a normal good is in long-run competitive equilibrium to begin with and suppose consumer incomes increase. This means that consumer demand for normal goods also increases. This is illustrated in the upper and lower left panels of Figure 13.15. As income increases from M_i^1 to M_i^2, the individual consumer's demand curve increases from $p_x^1(x_i)$ to $p_x^2(x_i)$. The combined increase in all consumer incomes shifts the market demand curve to the right from $p_x^1(X_d)$ to $p_x^2(X_d)$. Short-run equilibrium price increases from LRp_x^e to SRp_x^e, and market equilibrium quantity increases from X_e^1 to X_e^2 (lower middle graph). At the higher short-run equilibrium price, the firm, represented in the right graph, increases output from LRx_{j1}^* to SRx_j^* along its short-run marginal cost curve and starts to make economic profits

$$SR\pi_j(SRx_j^*) = SRx_j^*[SRp_x^e - SRATC_j^1(SRx_j^*)] > 0.$$

These profits provide the incentive for entry of new firms and expansion of existing firms. This possible expansion is illustrated by the shift from $SRMC_j^1$ and $SRATC_j^1$ to $SRMC_j^2$ and $SRATC_j^2$. The combination of entry and expansion shift the short-run market supply curve from $p_x^1(X_s)$ to $p_x^2(X_s)$, lowering the price. The process of entry and expansion continues until price is once again equal to the long-run equilibrium

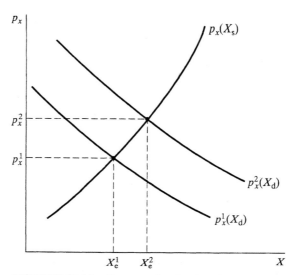

FIGURE 13.14   Comparative Statics of an Increase in Demand

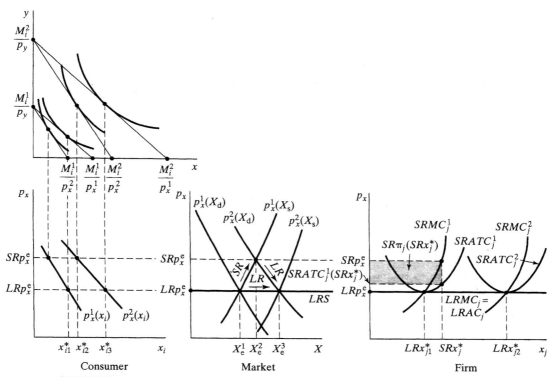

FIGURE 13.15   Long-run Comparative Statics of an Increase in Consumer Income

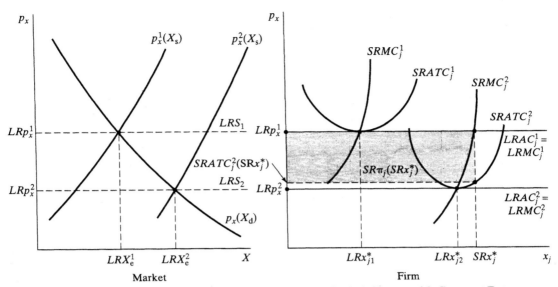

FIGURE 13.16   Comparative Statics of a Neutral Technological Change with Constant Returns to Scale

price and economic profits are once again 0. This happens at X_e^3, at the intersection of $p_x^2(X_d)$ and $p_x^2(X_s)$. Alternatively, one could suppress the short-run changes and simply view the long-run adjustment as a change from X_e^1 to X_e^3 along the long-run supply curve with price unchanged.

Technological Change   A neutral technological change with constant returns to scale provides an example of a long-run shift in supply. With constant returns to scale, we know from equations 11.36 and 11.37 that the long-run total cost is a linear function through the origin, $LRTC(x_1) = bx_1$, for $b > 0$, and that the long-run marginal cost is $LRMC_1 = b$. The original long-run supply is perfectly elastic at $LRMC_1$. If output were to increase by an arbitrary multiple $\alpha > 1$ for every combination of inputs, the new production function would be

$$x_2(K, L) = \alpha x_1(K, L) \quad \Rightarrow \quad x_1(K, L) = \frac{x_2(K, L)}{\alpha}. \tag{13.22}$$

Substituting for x_1 in equations 11.36 and 11.37,

$$LRTC(x_2) = b\frac{x_2}{\alpha} = \frac{b}{\alpha}x_2 \quad \text{and} \quad LRMC_2 = \frac{b}{\alpha} < b. \tag{13.23}$$

Equation 13.23 shows that the new long-run marginal cost is also perfectly elastic and lower than the old marginal cost. If $\alpha = 2$, the new marginal cost is $1/2$ the old; if $\alpha = 3$, the new marginal cost is $1/3$, and so on.

Figure 13.16 illustrates the effect of a neutral technological change on the firm and the industry, assuming the industry is in long-run equilibrium to begin with. Looking first at the individual firm (on the right), if firm j is the first to adopt a new technology, its short-run and long-run marginal and average cost curves shift down. But, since no one firm can affect the market equilibrium price individually, market price remains the same until other firms begin to adopt the new technology. Firm j simply maximizes profits by equating price and its new short-run marginal cost, making profits

$$SR\pi_j(SRx_j^*) = SRx_j^*[SRp_x^1 - SRATC_j^2(SRx_j^*)] > 0.$$

Profits, however, provide the incentive for the entry of new firms using the new technology and for existing firms to switch to the new technology. As firms enter and switch technologies, the short-run market supply increases, reducing price. Entry and switching continue until there are zero profits with all firms using the new technology. In the left graph, short-run market supply shifts out from $p_x^1(X_s)$ to $p_x^2(X_s)$, market price falls from LRP_x^1 to LRP_x^2, and market equilibrium increases from LRX_e^1 to LRX_e^2. No firms can be left using the old technology in the long run because they would make losses at the new (lower) long-run equilibrium price.

13.8   THE COMPARATIVE STATICS AND INCIDENCE OF A PER-UNIT TAX

Recall from Section 5.7 that a per-unit tax is a tax of a particular amount (say $\$t$) on each unit of a good purchased. Figure 13.17 illustrates the effect of such a tax levied on producers. Each time a producer sells a unit, he or she pays the government $\$t$. The effect is to raise the marginal cost of producing and selling each unit by t (from $SRMC_j$ to $SRMC_j + t$). This means short-run firm supply shifts up by t. If all firms are taxed equally, the entire short-run market supply also shifts up by t [from $p_x(X_s)$ to $p_x(X_s) + t$]. If demand is downward sloping, however, short-run market equilibrium price increases by less than the amount of the tax. Consumers now pay the price p_x^d, which is higher than the original equilibrium price; but, producers receive (net of the tax) only p_x^s, which is less than the original equilibrium price. The difference between the buyers' price and the sellers' price is the amount of the tax: $p_x^d - p_x^s = t$. The quantity under the tax (X_t) is found as the quantity such that demand price evaluated at X_t minus supply price evaluated at X_t equals t:

$$p_x^d(X_t) - p_x^s(X_t) = t. \tag{13.24}$$

A Consumer Tax   Now, suppose the tax were levied on consumers instead. In this case, every time a consumer buys a unit, he or she must pay the government $\$t$ per unit purchased. This has the effect of reducing the consumer's demand price (from the firm's point of view) by the amount of the tax. This is because the price paid to the firm plus the tax must equal the original demand price in order to satisfy the original demand relationship.

A consumer tax is illustrated in Figure 13.18. Each consumer's demand price decreases by t [from $p_x(x_i)$ to $p_x(x_i) - t$]. Since all consumers' individual demand curves are shifted down by t, the market demand also shifts down by t [from $p_x(X_d)$ to $p_x(X_d) - t$]. With upward-sloping supply, however, price does not go down by the full

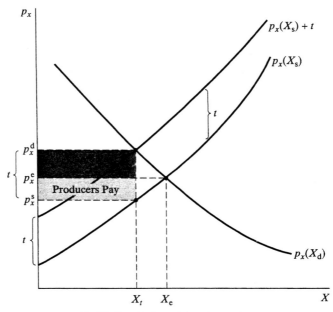

FIGURE 13.17   A Producer Tax

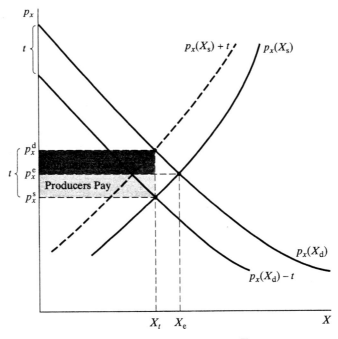

FIGURE 13.18   A Consumer Tax

amount of the tax. Producers receive p_x^s, which is less than the original equilibrium price; but, consumers must pay p_x^d, which is more than the original equilibrium price. Once again, the difference between the demand price evaluated at the quantity under the tax (X_t) and the supply price evaluated at X_t is equal to t, as in (13.24): $p_x^d(X_t) - p_x^s(X_t) = t$.

Equivalence of Producer and Consumer Taxes   Equation 13.24 implies, moreover, that the prices paid by consumers and received by producers must be the same under the producer and consumer taxes, since the equation for finding the equilibrium quantity is the same: the price is such that quantity demanded at p_x^d equals quantity supplied at p_x^s. This point is also illustrated in Figure 13.18. The dashed line above the supply curve represents the supply curve with the tax that would prevail under the producer tax. Notice that the equilibrium quantity and the net consumer and producer prices are all unaffected by whether the tax is imposed on producers or consumers.

A Numerical Example   The following numerical example also illustrates that consumer and producer taxes are equivalent. Suppose the demand and supply functions are given by

$$X_d = 10 - 2p_x \quad \text{and} \quad X_s = -2 + 2p_x. \tag{13.25}$$

Without a tax, the equilibrium price is found by equating X_d and X_s from (13.25):

$$X_d = X_s \Rightarrow 10 - 2p_x = -2 + 2p_x. \tag{13.26}$$

Solving (13.26) for the equilibrium price and quantity,

$$p_x^e = \$3 \quad \text{and} \quad X_e = 10 - 6 = 4. \tag{13.27}$$

If a \$1 per-unit tax were imposed on producers, it would raise the supply curve in (13.25) by \$1. To show the effect of the tax on the equilibrium, we first find the inverse supply function:

$$X_s = -2 + 2p_x \Rightarrow p_x^s = 1 + \frac{1}{2}X. \tag{13.28}$$

Adding \$1 to (13.28),

$$p_x^s + t = 1 + \frac{1}{2}X + 1 = 2 + \frac{1}{2}X. \tag{13.29}$$

To find the equilibrium under the tax, we first find the inverse demand function from (13.25):

$$p_x^d = 5 - \frac{1}{2}X. \qquad \text{\textbf{the inverse demand function}} \tag{13.30}$$

Now, to satisfy equation 13.24, we equate (13.29) and (13.30):

$$5 - \tfrac{1}{2}X = 2 + \tfrac{1}{2}X \quad \Rightarrow \quad X_t = 3 \qquad X_e = 4 > X_t \qquad (13.31)$$

$$p_x^d = 5 - \tfrac{1}{2}(3) = \$3.50 \qquad p_x^e = \$3 < p_x^d \qquad (13.32)$$

$$p_x^s = 1 + \tfrac{1}{2}(3) = \$2.50 \qquad p_x^e = \$3 > p_x^s \qquad (13.33)$$

$$p_x^d - p_x^s = \$3.50 - \$2.50 = \$1 = t.$$

If the tax were imposed on consumers, it would lower the demand curve in (13.25) by t:

$$p_x^d - t = 5 - \frac{1}{2}X - 1 = 4 - \frac{1}{2}X. \qquad (13.34)$$

To find the equilibrium under the consumer tax, equate (13.28) and (13.34):

$$4 - \frac{1}{2}X = 1 + \frac{1}{2}X \quad \Rightarrow \quad X_t = 3, \qquad (13.35)$$

which is the same as (13.31); and, as in (13.32) and (13.33), $p_x^d = \$3.50$ and $p_x^s = \$2.50$.

Elasticity and the Incidence of a Per-unit Tax   Notice that in the example above, consumers and producers each pay half of the tax (consumers' price increases by \$0.50 and producers' price decreases by \$0.50). In general, with linear demand and supply curves,[11] we could express the relative payments by the two sides of the market as the tax paid by consumers divided by the tax paid by producers:

$$\frac{t_d}{t_s} = \frac{p_x^d - p_x^e}{p_x^e - p_x^s} = -\frac{1/(p_x^e - p_x^s)}{1/(p_x^e - p_x^d)}.$$

Multiplying the right side of (13.36) by $\dfrac{X_e - X_t}{X_e - X_t} \dfrac{p_x^e/X_e}{p_x^e/X_e}$,

$$\frac{t_d}{t_s} = -\left(\frac{\dfrac{X_e - X_t}{p_x^e - p_x^s} \dfrac{p_x^e}{X_e}}{\dfrac{X_e - X_t}{p_x^e - p_x^d} \dfrac{p_x^e}{X_e}} \right) = -\left(\frac{\dfrac{\Delta X}{\Delta p_x^s} \dfrac{p_x^e}{X_e}}{\dfrac{\Delta X}{\Delta p_x^d} \dfrac{p_x^e}{X_e}} \right) \qquad (13.37)$$

$$= \frac{-\epsilon_s}{\epsilon_d} > 0, \qquad \text{since } \epsilon_d < 0.$$

Equation 13.37 implies that if

$$|\epsilon_d| > \epsilon_s, \qquad \qquad \text{demand more elastic than supply}$$

then $t_d < t_s$ (producers pay more of the tax): and if

$$|\epsilon_d| < \epsilon_s, \qquad \qquad \text{supply more elastic than demand}$$

---

[11]The following argument also applies to an infinitesimal change along nonlinear demand and supply curves.

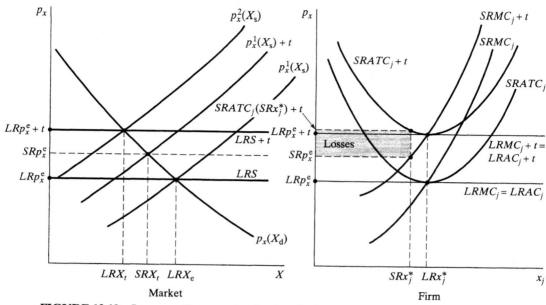

FIGURE 13.19   Long-run Comparative Statics of a Per-unit Tax in a Competitive Market

then $t_d > t_s$ (consumers pay more of the tax). Extending the argument to infinitesimal changes along nonlinear demand and supply curves, a general proposition follows: the *less* elastic side of the market pays a *higher* proportion of the tax.

The Long-run Effect of a Per-unit Tax   This proposition leads us to an understanding of the incidence of a per-unit tax in the long run in a competitive market, illustrated in Figure 13.19. Suppose we start out in long-run competitive equilibrium before the tax is imposed. The short-run effect of the tax is illustrated in Figures 13.17 and 13.18. Supply price declines and demand price increases, both by less than the amount of the tax. If the industry is in long-run equilibrium to begin with and supply price declines, firms will be making losses as a result of the tax. Firms will exit from the industry, shifting the short-run supply curve even further to the left. Exit continues until firms once again make zero economic profits. But, since firms were previously just covering average cost at minimum average cost, price must rise by the full amount of the tax to restore zero profits. In the left graph, the short-run effect (viewed as a tax imposed on producers) is the supply shift from $p_x^1(X_s)$ to $p_x^1(X_s) + t$. The long-run effect (after exit) is the shift from $p_x^1(X_s)$ to $p_x^2(X_s)$. Consumers' price increases in the short run from LRp_x^e to p_x^d and in the long run to $LRp_x^e + t$. Thus, consumers must pay the full amount of a per-unit tax in the long run in a competitive market.

The long-run effect is so one-sided under competition because long-run supply is perfectly elastic. If one side of the market is perfectly elastic, it pays nothing, and if one side is perfectly inelastic, it pays the entire tax. These two extremes are illustrated in Figure 13.20. In the left graph (perfectly elastic supply), consumers' price increases by

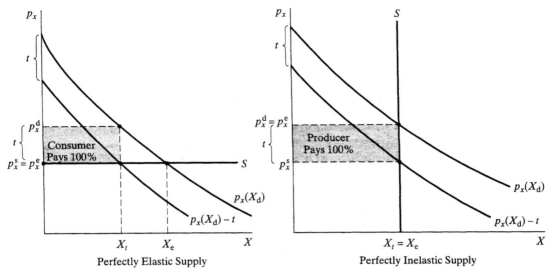

FIGURE 13.20 Incidence of a Per-unit Tax with Perfectly Elastic or Perfectly Inelastic Supply

the full amount of the tax. In the right graph (perfectly inelastic supply), producers' price falls by the full amount of the tax.

13.9 DEADWEIGHT LOSS FROM A PER-UNIT TAX

Recall from Section 5.7 that consumers generally prefer lump-sum taxes to per-unit taxes. Another way to analyze the welfare effect of a per-unit tax is to consider the effect of the tax on output, consumer's surplus, and firm profits. Before we begin that analysis, however, let us think of measuring firm profits as the sum of the profits earned on each unit. The cost of each additional unit is marginal cost. If a firm were to sell all its units at one price, the profit earned on each additional unit would be the difference between that price and the marginal cost of producing that unit. Total profits would be the integral over output between the marginal cost at zero units and the market price:

$$\pi = \int_{MC(0)}^{MC=p_x} x(MC)dMC, \qquad (13.38)$$

where $MC(0)$ is the marginal cost at zero units. In a competitive market, measured along the market supply curve, the profit characterized in (13.38) is often referred to as **producer's surplus** and is analogous to consumer's surplus. Rewriting (13.38),

$$PS = \int_{p_x(0)}^{p_x^c} x_s(p_x)dp_x,$$

where p_x^c is the competitive equilibrium price. Producer's surplus is illustrated by the shaded area in Figure 13.21.

When a per-unit tax is imposed, there is a loss of both consumer's and producer's surplus. Some of that lost surplus gets transferred to the government as the tax revenue.

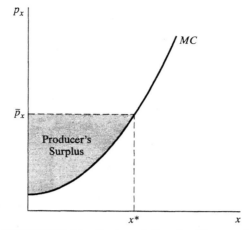

FIGURE 13.21   Producer's Surplus Illustrated

But, to the extent that a per-unit tax results in a reduction in output, some of that lost surplus is not recovered to any other economic agent. It simply represents a net loss, referred to as a **deadweight loss** from a per-unit tax. This deadweight loss is illustrated as the shaded area in Figure 13.22.

$$DWL = \Delta CS + \Delta PS - tX_t = \int_{p_x^e}^{p_x^d} x_d dp_x + \int_{p_x^s}^{p_x^e} x_s dp_x - tX_t \qquad (13.40)$$

Moreover, if income effects are small (so that uncompensated consumer's surplus loss represents an estimate of consumer welfare loss), the deadweight loss from a per-unit tax can be viewed as the social welfare loss from the imposition of a per-unit tax.

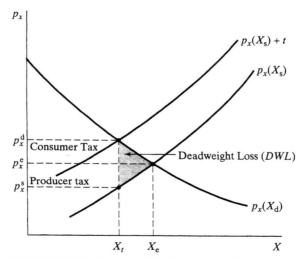

FIGURE 13.22   Deadweight Loss from a Per-unit Tax

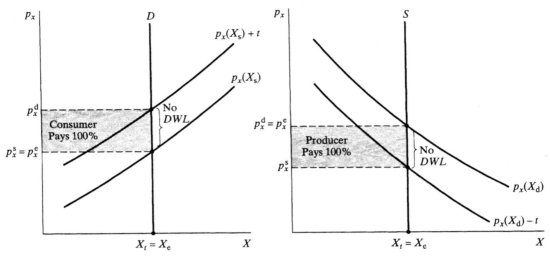

FIGURE 13.23   Illustration That There Is No Deadweight Loss with Perfectly Inelastic Demand or Supply

There will be no deadweight loss (and thus no net welfare loss) from a per-unit tax only if the tax results in no loss of output. This can only happen if either demand or supply is perfectly inelastic, as illustrated in Figure 13.23. In the left graph, with perfectly inelastic demand, price rises by the full amount of the tax and quantity stays the same. In the right graph, with perfectly inelastic supply, price falls by the full amount of the tax and quantity stays the same.[12] There is no deadweight loss in either case.

13.10   REVIEW OF KEY CONCEPTS

This completes our discussion of competitive equilibrium and comparative statics. Before continuing to the next chapter on the efficiency of competitive markets, be sure you understand and can use the following key concepts.

The *market supply function* is the schedule describing the total quantity that all firms are willing to supply at each price. It is the sum of the individual firm quantities supplied at each price.

The *elasticity of supply* is the percentage change in quantity supplied divided by the percentage change in price.

In addition to the parameters of individual short-run supply functions (input prices, fixed

inputs, and technology), the parameters of short-run market supply functions include the number of firms in an industry and the distribution of technologies among firms.

Entry of new firms into an industry increases short-run market supply; exit of firms from an industry decreases short-run market supply. Diffusion of a new technology also tends to increase short-run market supply.

A short-run competitive *market equilibrium* is characterized by a market price and a quantity sold in that market such that market quantity demanded equals short-run market quantity supplied at that price, given the

---

[12]Of course in the long run, in a competitive market, supply is perfectly elastic. Thus, the only way there can be no deadweight loss in the long run is for demand to be perfectly inelastic.

number of firms in the industry and the amount of capital employed by each firm.

Market equilibrium price is generated by the intersection of market demand and market supply; *simultaneously,* consumers and firms use this equilibrium price as a parameter in determining individual demands and supplies.

Economic profits (in excess of opportunity costs) encourage the entry of new firms into an industry.

Entry of new firms shifts short-run supply to the right and lowers equilibrium price.

At a *long-run competitive equilibrium,* economic profits are 0 and there is no longer any incentive for firms to enter an industry or expand.

If firms are making losses, some firms will *exit* from the industry. This will reduce short-run supply and increase price. Exit will continue until there are zero economic profits (long-run competitive equilibrium).

At a long-run competitive equilibrium, price equals minimum short-run and long-run average total cost as well as short-run and long-run marginal cost.

With constant returns to scale, any output along the perfectly elastic long-run average and marginal cost curve can be a long-run competitive equilibrium output for a firm. Industry long-run competitive output is determined as the market quantity demanded at a price equal to long-run average and marginal cost.

With U-shaped long-run average cost, the long-run equilibrium quantity for the firm occurs at minimum long-run average cost. Industry long-run competitive output is determined as the market quantity demanded at a price equal to minimum long-run average cost.

There is no long-run competitive equilibrium if there are increasing or decreasing returns to scale over all ranges of output.

Competitive markets that persist in the long run must have constant returns to scale or U-shaped long-run average cost curves. With U-shaped costs, each firm must be "small" relative to the long-run market equilibrium output.

If input prices do not change as an industry expands or contracts, long-run supply in a competitive market is always perfectly elastic at a price equal to minimum long-run average total cost.

With constant returns to scale, long-run supply under competition is perfectly elastic at a price equal to long-run marginal and average cost.

If the parameters affecting market demand and supply do not change, the same *static equilibrium* price and quantity will be observed every trading period.

The study of the effects of changes in demand or supply parameters on demand, supply, or market equilibrium is called *comparative statics.*

It does not matter whether a per-unit tax is levied on producers or consumers. Under either tax, consumers will pay the same price per unit, producers will receive the same revenue per unit, and the same quantity will be bought and sold.

The *less* elastic (more inelastic) side of the market always pays a *higher* percentage of a per-unit tax.

In a competitive market, the full amount of a per-unit tax will be passed on to consumers in the long run. This happens because long-run supply in a competitive market is perfectly elastic and because firms in a competitive market make zero economic profits in long-run equilibrium.

Total firm profits can be measured as the integral along the vertical axis of the firm's marginal cost curve from the marginal cost at zero output to the market price.

The integral of the market supply curve from the price associated with zero units to the market price is sometimes referred to as *producer's surplus.* It represents the total profits earned by all firms in that market.

The *deadweight loss* from a per-unit tax is the loss of consumer's and producer's surplus that is not transferred to the government as tax revenue.

There is no deadweight loss only if demand or supply is perfectly inelastic. In the long run, there is no deadweight loss only if demand is perfectly inelastic.

13.11   QUESTIONS FOR DISCUSSION

1. In the last 10 years, the number of personal computers sold per year has been increasing steadily and dramatically. At the same time, the price of a standard PC-type computer has fallen to less than one-third its original price. Can this result be due to an increase in demand for personal computers as incomes increase and more and more people discover the "joys" of personal computing? If so, show how. If not, explain what other changes must have been occurring and analyze the short-run and long-run changes in this market. Assume the market for PCs can be analyzed using the competitive model.

2. Suppose the government wishes to impose per-unit taxes on selected goods, but it does not wish to penalize consumers very much. Rather, it would like firms to pay most of the taxes. What kinds of goods should the government tax? Is this a feasible policy in the long run in a competitive market? Answer this question by analyzing the market for a representative good after the tax is imposed in both the short run and the long run.

3. There is a debate in economic history over the underlying causes of the Industrial Revolution of the eighteenth century. Some argue that rising demand encouraged firms to expand and produce more, while others argue that only rapid technological change increasing supply could account for the historical facts. The basic "fact" to be explained is that between 1790 and 1820 output increased dramatically and the prices of most manufactured goods fell equally dramatically. Use an analysis of short-run and long-run adjustments in a representative market to resolve which side of the debate is more likely to be correct.

4. One of the arguments used in favor of patents for inventors is that potential inventors will not make the investment if they then have to sell the new invention in a competitive market. Is this a reasonable argument? Explain.

5. It is often argued that during periods of rapid demand expansion, when prices are rising, poor people should be protected from rising prices by imposing price controls on "necessities." Analyze the short-run and long-run effect of imposing a maximum price below the equilibrium in a competitive market that is experiencing rising demand. Do price controls really protect poor people better than the operation of competitive markets does in the long run? Explain.

6. Suppose the city of Chicago were to impose a business-profits tax on firms operating inside city limits. How will firms operating in nationwide competitive markets respond in the short run and long run? On the basis of your answer, evaluate the use of business taxes as a way for cities to increase their revenues.

7. Would a competitive firm ever engage in advertising? Explain.

8. Suppose the government wishes to impose a per-unit tax, but also wishes to minimize the long-run deadweight loss from the tax. What kinds of goods should the government tax? Explain.

13.12   PROBLEMS

Problems 1–7   Begin with the following assumptions.

(a) There are 200,000 identical consumers, each with utility function

$$U_i = x_i^2 y_i;$$

$M_i = \$400$ for each consumer, $p_y = \$1$.

(b) There are 20,000 identical perfectly competitive firms producing good X. Each firm has the production function

$$x_j = 3K^{1/2}L^{1/2};$$

$w = \$4$, $r = \$9$, and $\overline{K}_j = 9$ in the short run for each firm.

1. Derive the short-run and long-run supply functions for each firm.

2. Derive the short-run and long-run market supply functions.

3. Find the competitive market equilibrium price and quantity for good X in the short run and long run.

4. How much profit will each firm make in the short run?

5. How much output will each firm produce and how many firms will be in the industry in the long run? Explain briefly.

6. How much profit will each firm make in the long run? Explain briefly.

7. Suppose the same 20,000 firms were still the firms in the industry in the long run. How much capital would each firm employ in the long run? What is each firm's short-run supply function at the long-run equilibrium?

Problems 8–13   Assuming (as in Problems 1–7) that the same 20,000 firms remain in the industry in the long run, suppose that a firm (k) adopts a new technology. The new production function is

$$x_k = 4K_k^{1/2}L_k^{1/2}.$$

At first, all other firms still use

$$x_j = 3K_j^{1/2}L_j^{1/2}, \quad j \neq k.$$

8. What is firm k's new short-run supply function, assuming it uses the same amount of capital as in Problem 7?

9. What is the industry short-run supply function, assuming all firms use the same amount of capital as in Problem 7?

10. What is the market equilibrium price and quantity? How does it compare to your answer to Problems 1–3? Explain briefly.

11. How much profit does firm k make? How much profit do the other firms $(j \neq k)$ make? Explain briefly.

12. Explain briefly how the industry adjusts to the change in technology in the long run.

13. What will be the new long-run equilibrium price and quantity?

Problems 14–19   Consider the following demand and supply functions:

$$X_d = 1000 - 10p_x$$
$$X_s = 10 + 200p_x.$$

14. Find the original competitive equilibrium price and quantity.

15. Impose a $1 per-unit tax and find the quantity transacted under the tax, the demand price, and the supply price, all in the short run.

16. Show that the tax can be viewed as either a producer tax or a consumer tax.

17. What proportion of the tax is paid by producer and consumer in the short run? Explain briefly.

18. What will be the long-run effect of the tax on price and quantity and on who pays the tax? Explain briefly.

19. Find the deadweight loss from the tax in the short run and long run.

13.13   LOGICAL AND MATHEMATICAL APPLICATIONS

1. Recently, the market for beef has been experiencing a major change. In general, there has been a decline in demand for beef as consumers have turned more to fish and chicken or have simply been eating less meat overall. On the other hand, there has been a dramatic increase in demand for "organic" or naturally raised beef. In fact, organic beef sells for a substantial premium over regular beef. Use comparative statics analysis to analyze the short-run and long-run effects of these shifts in demand. How much of a price differential would you expect to see when these markets achieve long-run equilibrium again?

2. After the Arab oil embargo of 1973, the world market price for oil more than doubled. Analyze the short-run and long-run effect of this price change on the market for a representative good that uses oil in its production process.

3. Show that in a competitive industry, the full amount of cost savings from a technological change will be passed on to consumers in the form of lower prices.

Chapter 14

PRODUCTION EFFICIENCY AND GENERAL EQUILIBRIUM OF COMPETITIVE MARKETS

14.1 WHAT YOU SHOULD LEARN FROM THIS CHAPTER

In Chapter 7, we explored the efficiency of competitive markets in which consumers simply traded goods with one another. In this chapter, we apply a similar kind of analysis to competitive markets with production. First, we assume that there are fixed amounts of labor and capital to be allocated to the production of two goods. Using a *production Edgeworth box,* we show that efficiency in production has similar properties to efficiency in distribution, discussed in Section 9.2. Then, from the optimal choices inside the Edgeworth box, we derive a **production possibilities frontier** that describes all the efficient combinations of X and Y that a two-good economy can produce. Next, using the production possibilities frontier and the solution to the distribution problem developed in Section 9.2, we develop the concept of a *general competitive equilibrium* as the simultaneous solution to both the production efficiency and the distributional efficiency problems.

Comparative statics in a general equilibrium framework points up some important long-run changes that cannot be adequately identified in a partial equilibrium analysis. In particular, if two goods use inputs in different proportions in their production functions, relative input prices may change as inputs are transferred from the production of one good to the production of the other. This change in relative input prices may change relative output prices in the long run as well. This means that in a general equilibrium framework, relative output prices may change, even though long-run supply would be perfectly elastic if input prices remained constant.

In developing general equilibrium with production and in developing comparative statics in a general equilibrium framework, we will sometimes need to use somewhat lengthy mathematical examples. Do not lose sight of the major thrust of this chapter in working through the examples: the competitive market solves the simultaneous production and distribution problem efficiently, without individual agents needing to "know" more than their own private preferences and technologies, as well as relevant market prices.

14.2 EFFICIENCY IN PRODUCTION

In Section 9.2, we analyzed solutions to the distributional problem using a two-person Edgeworth box. At that time, we defined a Pareto optimal allocation as an allocation of goods to consumers such that it was not possible to make one person better off without making some other person worse off. We also defined an allocation that was Pareto superior to an initial endowment as one at which some consumers were better off and no consumers were worse off than at their respective initial endowments. We argued that if the initial allocation was not Pareto optimal and if consumers traded with one another, they would end up choosing an allocation that was both Pareto optimal and Pareto superior. One such Pareto optimal and Pareto superior allocation was the pure-trade competitive equilibrium.

These pure-trade concepts have analogies when production is introduced. To begin, an **efficient allocation of inputs** refers to an allocation of inputs to the production of outputs such that it is not possible to produce more of one good without producing less of another. At an efficient allocation of inputs, we say that we have satisfied the basic criterion for *efficiency in production.*

The Production Edgeworth Box   To analyze efficiency in production, we use a **production Edgeworth box.** Recall from Section 9.3 that in a consumption Edgeworth box, the dimensions of the box are the total quantities of X and Y available. In using this technique in production, we assume there are given quantities of labor and capital to be allocated to the production of X and Y. The production functions of x and y are given by

$$x = x(K_x, L_x) \quad \text{and} \quad y = y(K_y, L_y), \tag{14.1}$$

where

$$K_x + K_y = \overline{K} = \text{maximum capital available} \tag{14.2}$$

$$L_x + L_y = \overline{L} = \text{maximum labor available.} \tag{14.3}$$

The dimensions of the Edgeworth box are the total amounts of capital and labor available. Figure 14.1 illustrates such an Edgeworth box.

In the consumption Edgeworth box, the lower left corner is one consumer's zero consumption point and the upper right corner is the other consumer's zero consumption point. In the production Edgeworth box, the lower left corner represents zero output of one good, while the upper right corner represents zero output of the other good.

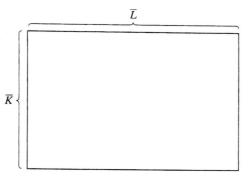

FIGURE 14.1   A Production Edgeworth Box

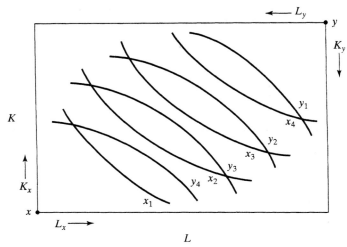

FIGURE 14.2   Production Isoquants in a Production Edgeworth Box

A movement from lower left to upper right represents an increase in output of the first good and a reduction in output of the second. This is illustrated in Figure 14.2. Isoquants x_1, x_2, x_3, and x_4 represent increasing output of good X, and y_1, y_2, y_3, and y_4 represent increasing output of good Y. As x increases, more capital and labor are allocated to the production of X, leaving less for the production of Y. As y increases, on the other hand, more capital and labor are allocated to Y, leaving less for the production of X.

The Efficient Production Set   In the consumption Edgeworth box, we started at an initial endowment to consumers and then analyzed how the market achieved a competitive equilibrium through the *tâtonnement* process. We could do the same thing with production, but the concept of an initial endowment to firms has little meaning since what gets produced depends upon consumer demand (that is, the allocation of inputs to firms is *derived* from underlying consumer demand). What does carry over from the consumption Edgeworth box are the properties of the set of efficient points inside the box. In consumption, it is not possible to make one person better off without making another person worse off when the indifference curves are tangent inside the Edgeworth box. In production, it is not possible to produce more of one good without reducing the production of another good when the isoquants are tangent to one another inside the Edgeworth box. This is illustrated in Figure 14.3. At point (x_1, y_4), for example, in order to increase x, it would be necessary to reduce the production of Y and vice versa. We will refer to the set of all points of tangency as the **efficient production set.** These points represent all the efficient allocations of inputs to the production of X and Y.

If the isoquants are tangent to one another, the marginal rates of technical substitution are equal. This is equivalent to saying that the ratios of marginal products are equal between goods:

$$MRTS_x = MRTS_y \quad \Rightarrow \quad \frac{MP_{Lx}}{MP_{Kx}} = \frac{MP_{Ly}}{MP_{Ky}}. \tag{14.4}$$

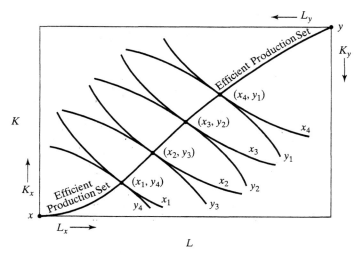

FIGURE 14.3   The Efficient Production Set

Further, since, by equation 11.1, the marginal rates of technical substitution are equal to the ratio of input prices, every point of tangency implies an input price ratio that would sustain that allocation of inputs to firms as a competitive equilibrium in the factor markets. This is mathematically equivalent to the finding in Section 9.6 that every point on the contract curve could be sustained as a competitive equilibrium for some set of initial endowments and a particular price ratio. This idea is illustrated in Figure 14.4. At point A on the efficient production set, the implicit input price ratio is w_1/r_1, while at point B, the implicit input price ratio is w_2/r_2.

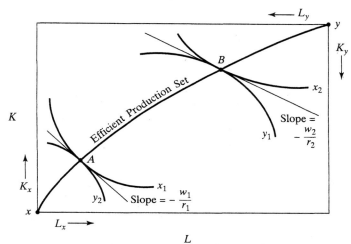

FIGURE 14.4   Implicit Input Price Ratios Along the Efficient Production Set

An Example To show mathematically that the marginal rates of technical substitution are equal for the two goods, we maximize the production of one good (say X) subject both to the constraint that y is no less than some given amount and to the input constraints. (This is comparable to maximizing one consumer's utility subject both to the constraint that the other's utility is made no lower than some level and to the quantities of X and Y available for distribution.)

$$\max x(K_x, L_x) \tag{14.5}$$
$$\text{s.t. } y = (K_y, L_y)$$
$$K_x + K_y = \overline{K}$$
$$L_x + L_y = \overline{L}$$

We can combine the three constraints by substituting the input constraints in the y production function:

$$y = y(\overline{K} - K_x, \overline{L} - L_x). \tag{14.6}$$

Thus, substituting (14.6) in the first constraint, the Lagrangian is

$$\mathcal{L} = x(K_x, L_x) + \lambda[y - y(\overline{K} - K_x, \overline{L} - L_x)]. \tag{14.7}$$

The relevant first-order conditions are

$$\frac{\partial \mathcal{L}}{\partial L_x} = \frac{\partial x}{\partial L_x} - \lambda \frac{\partial y}{\partial L_y} \frac{\partial L_y}{\partial L_x} = 0$$
$$\Rightarrow \quad \lambda = -\frac{MP_{Lx}}{MP_{Ly}}, \text{ since } \frac{\partial L_y}{\partial L_x} = -1 \tag{14.8}$$

$$\frac{\partial \mathcal{L}}{\partial K_x} = \frac{\partial x}{\partial K_x} - \lambda \frac{\partial y}{\partial K_y} \frac{\partial K_y}{\partial K_x} = 0$$
$$\Rightarrow \quad \lambda = -\frac{MP_{Kx}}{MP_{Ky}}, \text{ since } \frac{\partial K_y}{\partial K_x} = -1. \tag{14.9}$$

Solving for λ from (14.8) and (14.9),

$$\lambda = -\frac{MP_{Lx}}{MP_{Ly}} = -\frac{MP_{Kx}}{MP_{Ky}}. \tag{14.10}$$

Rearranging terms in (14.10),

$$\frac{MP_{Lx}}{MP_{Kx}} = \frac{MP_{Ly}}{MP_{Ky}} = MRTS_x = MRTS_y. \tag{14.11}$$

This equation indicates that we can solve for an efficient production set for two goods by setting the marginal rates of technical substitution for the two production functions equal to one another. Suppose, for example, that x and y have the following production functions:

$$x = (K_x)^{1/2}(L_x)^{1/2} \quad \text{and} \quad y = (K_y)^{1/4}(L_y)^{3/4}. \tag{14.12}$$

The marginal rates of technical substitution are

$$MRTS_x = \frac{K_x}{L_x} \quad \text{equation 11.17} \tag{14.13}$$

$$MRTS_y = \left[\frac{\frac{3}{4}(K_y)^{1/4}}{(L_y)^{1/4}} \middle/ \frac{\frac{1}{4}(L_y)^{3/4}}{(K_y)^{3/4}} \right] = \frac{3K_y}{L_y}. \tag{14.14}$$

Setting the marginal rates of technical substitution equal to one another, and substituting for K_y,

$$\frac{K_x}{L_x} = \frac{3K_y}{L_y} = \frac{3(\overline{K} - K_x)}{\overline{L} - L_x}. \tag{14.15}$$

Solving (14.15) for K_x,

$$K_x\overline{L} - K_x L_x = 3\overline{K}L_x - 3K_x L_x \quad \Rightarrow \quad K_x\overline{L} + 2K_x L_x = 3\overline{K}L_x$$

$$K_x = \frac{3\overline{K}L_x}{\overline{L} + 2L_x}. \quad \text{the efficient production set} \tag{14.16}$$

Linear and Nonlinear Efficient Production Sets   Notice that the efficient production set derived as equation 14.16 is nonlinear. In general, the efficient production set will be linear if the firms have constant and equal capital-labor ratios and nonlinear if their capital-labor ratios are different. In equations 14.13 and 14.14, firm X's capital-labor ratio is equal to its marginal rate of technical substitution, while firm Y's is equal to one third its marginal rate of substitution: $MRTS_x = K_x/L_x$, but $MRTS_y = 3K_y/L_y$, which implies that $K_y/L_y = (1/3)MRTS_y$. Thus, along the efficient production set, firm Y's capital-labor ratio is always less than firm X's. This is because the marginal rates of technical substitution are equal and firm Y's capital-ratio is one-third the marginal rate of technical substitution while firm X's is equal to the marginal rate of substitution.

If firm X had the production function $K_x^{1/2}L_x^{1/2}$ and firm Y had the production function $2K_y^{1/2}L_x^{1/2}$, on the other hand, they would have the same capital-labor ratio along the efficient production set (K/L constant) and a linear efficient production set.[1] To find the efficient production set, we equate the two marginal rates of technical substitution:

$$\frac{K_x}{L_x} = \frac{K_y}{L_y} = \frac{\overline{K} - K_x}{\overline{L} - L_x}. \tag{14.17}$$

Solving (14.17) for K_x,

$$K_x\overline{L} - K_x L_x = \overline{K}L_x - K_x L_x - \quad \Rightarrow \quad K_x = \frac{\overline{K}}{\overline{L}}L_x, \tag{14.18}$$

which is a linear function.

---

[1] We know they have the same marginal rates of technical substitution since they are just positive monotonic transformations of one another.

The Production Possibilities Frontier   If we now take points along the efficient production set and place them on a graph with x on the horizontal axis and y on the vertical axis, we can construct a function that describes all the efficient combinations of X
and Y that the economy can produce, given its resources and technology. We call such a
function the economy's **production possibilities frontier** (PPF). Figure 14.5 illustrates
the construction of a production possibilities frontier from an efficient production set.
The values of x (x_1, x_2, x_3, x_4) from the isoquants inside the Edgeworth box are plotted
along the horizontal axis of the lower graph, and the values of y (y_1, y_2, y_3, y_4) are plotted along the vertical axis. The points along the production possibilities frontier
$[(x_1, y_4), (x_2, y_3), (x_3, y_2), (x_4, y_1)]$, therefore, correspond exactly to the points of tangency
along the efficient production set.

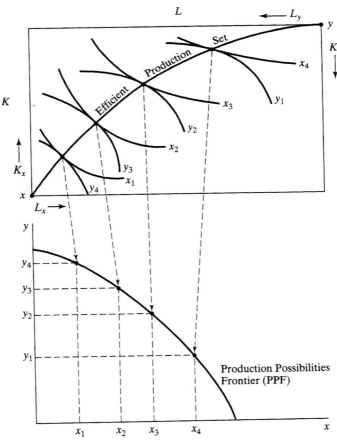

**FIGURE 14.5   Constructing the Production Possibilities Frontier
from the Efficient Production Set**

Linear and Nonlinear PPF's and the Marginal Rate of Transformation   The production possibilities frontier can be bowed out (as in Figure 14.5), bowed in, or linear. It will be bowed out under any one of the following three conditions: both production functions have decreasing returns to scale; one production function has decreasing returns and the other has constant returns; both production functions have constant returns but different capital-labor ratios along a (nonlinear) efficient production set. The production possibilities frontier might be bowed in if one of the production functions has increasing returns to scale, although with increasing returns to scale, any of the three shapes is possible. The production possibilities frontier will be a straight line if both production functions have constant returns to scale and equal capital-labor ratios along a (linear) efficient production set.

We refer to the negative of the slope of the production possibilities frontier as the **marginal rate of transformation** (MRT)[2] along the production possibilities frontier,

$$MRT_{yx} = -\frac{\Delta y}{\Delta x} = -\frac{dy}{dx}. \tag{14.19}$$

The idea is that the marginal rate of transformation is the rate at which the economy can efficiently transform Y into X by transferring resources from the production of Y to the production of X. Thus, if the production possibilities frontier is linear, the marginal rate of transformation is a constant: the economy can efficiently transform Y into X at a constant rate. On the other hand, if the production possibilities frontier bows out, the marginal rate of transformation increases as more and more X and less and less Y are produced.

When the marginal rate of transformation increases and the efficient production set bows out, it happens that one good is relatively more labor intensive and the other good is relatively more capital intensive. When both goods are being produced in significant quantities, the capital-intensive good uses a relatively high proportion of the capital and the labor-intensive good uses a relatively high proportion of the labor available in the economy. As more and more of the relatively capital-intensive good is produced, however, it is necessary to keep reducing the capital-labor ratio until it exactly equals the ratio of total capital $(\bar{K})$ to total labor $(\bar{L})$, at the corner, when only one good is being produced. Similarly, as more and more of the relatively labor-intensive good is produced, it is necessary to keep increasing the capital-labor ratio until it exactly equals the ratio of $\bar{K}$ to $\bar{L}$ at the other corner. However, as the capital-labor ratio changes along the isoquants, diminishing marginal rates of technical substitution imply that it is necessary to give up more and more of the good produced in relatively small amounts in order to get the same increment of the good being produced in relatively large amounts. Thus, as more and more X is produced, the marginal rate of transformation increases, implying the economy must give up more and more Y in order to get the same increment in x.

Figure 14.6 illustrates why the marginal rate of transformation increases. Suppose we consider two equal changes in x. On the graph, for example,

---

[2]Some economists refer to this concept as the **marginal rate of product transformation** $(MRPT)$ to emphasize that it refers to output production.

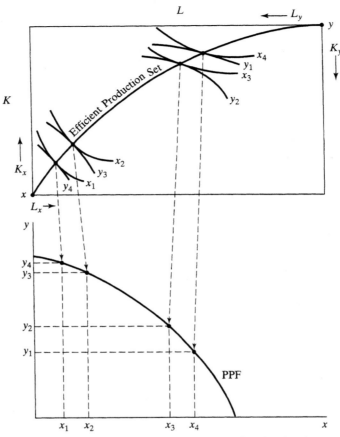

**FIGURE 14.6   Derivation of a Bowed Out Production
Possibilities Frontier**

$x_2 - x_1 = x_4 - x_3$. Notice, however, that because of diminishing marginal rates of technical substitution, $y_2 - y_1 > y_4 - y_3$. This translates into increasing marginal rates of transformation and a bowed out production possibilities frontier.[3]

    If the efficient production set is linear, on the other hand, the capital-labor ratio used in the production of each good is the same, regardless of how much of each good is being produced. This means that production of each good can simply change along a straight line from its respective origin, as though it were on a long-run expansion path. In this case, if both production functions also have constant returns to scale, the decrease in y necessary to get a given increment in x is constant. Hence, the marginal rate of transformation is constant, and the production possibilities frontier is linear. Figure 14.7 illustrates this point. Once again, $x_2 - x_1 = x_4 - x_3$. In this case, however,

---

[3]This is similar to what happens along the short-run expansion path. As output increases along the short-run expansion path, diminishing marginal rates of technical substitution make it necessary to use a larger and larger increment in labor to get the same increment in output.

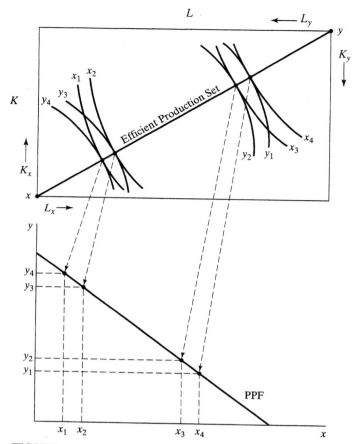

FIGURE 14.7   Derivation of a Linear Production Possibilities Frontier

the change in y is also the same: $y_4 - y_3 = y_2 - y_1$. This translates to a constant marginal rate of transformation and a linear production possibilities frontier.

Some Examples   The examples developed in equations 14.5–14.18 illustrate the implications of linear and nonlinear efficient production sets. First, consider the linear efficient production set $K_x = (\overline{K}/\overline{L})L_x$, derived as equation 14.18 from the production functions

$$x = (K_x)^{1/2}(L_x)^{1/2} \quad \text{and} \quad y = 2(K_y)^{1/2}(L_y)^{1/2}. \tag{14.20}$$

To find the production possibilities frontier, we first solve for L_x in terms of x from equations 14.20, 14.18, and an expression for L_y. First, we go through calculations similar to equations 14.17 and 14.18 to find that

$$K_y = \frac{\overline{K}}{\overline{L}}L_y. \tag{14.21}$$

Now, we substitute (14.18) and (14.21) in equations 14.20 to find expressions for x and y:

$$x = \left(\frac{\overline{K}}{\overline{L}}L_x\right)^{1/2}(L_x)^{1/2} = \left(\frac{\overline{K}}{\overline{L}}\right)^{1/2}L_x \tag{14.22}$$

$$y = 2\left(\frac{\overline{K}}{\overline{L}}L_y\right)^{1/2}(L_y)^{1/2} = 2\left(\frac{\overline{K}}{\overline{L}}\right)^{1/2}L_y. \tag{14.23}$$

Solving (14.22) for L_x,

$$L_x = \left(\frac{\overline{L}}{\overline{K}}\right)^{1/2}x. \tag{14.24}$$

Substituting (14.24) in (14.23), where $L_y = \overline{L} - L_x$ from equation 14.3,

$$y = 2\left(\frac{\overline{K}}{\overline{L}}\right)^{1/2}(\overline{L} - L_x) = 2\left(\frac{\overline{K}}{\overline{L}}\right)^{1/2}\left[\overline{L} - \left(\frac{\overline{L}}{\overline{K}}\right)^{1/2}x\right]. \tag{14.25}$$

$$= 2(\overline{K}\,\overline{L})^{1/2} - 2x,$$

which is a linear production possibilities frontier.

Notice in equation 14.25 that $2(\overline{K}\,\overline{L})^{1/2}$ is the y intercept, or the maximum attainable output of Y if all the capital and labor are employed in the production of Y, and that the marginal rate of transformation is equal to 2:

$$\frac{dy}{dx} = -2 \quad \Rightarrow \quad MRT_{yx} = 2. \tag{14.26}$$

Equation 14.26 implies that the technology is such that every time the output of Y is reduced by two units, the resources freed up can be used to produce one additional unit of X.

Turning now to the nonlinear case developed in equations 14.5-14.11, the efficient production set is $K_x = 3\overline{K}L_x/(\overline{L} + 2L_x)$ (equation 14.16) with production functions $x = (K_x)^{1/2}(L_x)^{1/2}$ and $y = (K_y)^{1/4}(L_y)^{3/4}$ (equations 14.12). Solving for the actual production possibilities frontier is computationally difficult and will not be included. Notice, however, that the production possibilities frontier will have to be nonlinear. When (14.16) is substituted in x in equations 14.12, the resulting equation will be exponential in both x and L_x.

14.3 UTILITY MAXIMIZATION OVER THE PRODUCTION POSSIBILITIES FRONTIER

As we pointed out in Section 4.3, producing output efficiently solves only part of the economic problem. As can be seen from the production possibilities frontier, there are countless possible efficient output combinations: every point on the frontier is an efficient output combination. The choice of an actual output combination involves the sticky distributional problem once again. We saw in Section 9.5 that without production, distribution is determined by consumer preferences and initial endowments of the goods themselves. The result is similar with production, except that the initial endowments are generally in terms of inputs rather than outputs. In this case, we will be looking for an allocation that is efficient in production, Pareto optimal (no consumer can be made better off without making some other consumer worse off), and Pareto superior to each consumer's initial endowments.

Robinson Crusoe and Pareto Optimality   To illustrate how to find an allocation with these three properties, we begin with the simplest possible complete economy: one consumer-producer who produces two goods with his or her own inputs for his or her own consumption. We might refer to this individual as Robinson Crusoe and, in keeping with the island theme, assume Robinson produces food for himself by collecting coconuts and fish. We also assume for simplicity that Robinson has some maximum number of tools and has allocated some number of hours per day to food collection.[4]

Given his labor and tools and the technology of collecting coconuts and fish, we can construct a production possibilities frontier that describes all the efficient combinations of coconuts and fish that Robinson can produce. This is illustrated as the production possibilities frontier in Figure 14.8. We assume now that Robinson has preferences over the consumption of coconuts and fish that can be represented by a set of indifference curves which obey the axioms of consumer preference. These are illustrated by the set of indifference curves U_1 through U_4. If Robinson is maximizing utility, he chooses the combination of coconuts and fish that puts him on the highest indifference curve, $(U_3 = U^*)$ at the point (C^*, F^*) where the slope of his indifference curve equals the slope of the production possibilities frontier. Moreover, this allocation

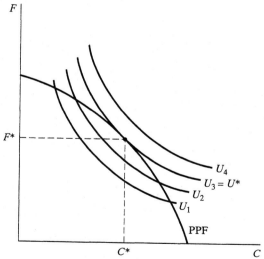

FIGURE 14.8   Utility Maximization over the Production Possibilities Frontier

---

[4]Sections 17.2 and 18.2 will consider labor and capital supply as part of the total consumer decision problem. Realistically, Robinson's labor and capital supply decisions are part of his overall utility-maximization decision. For now, however, we will consider only the choice of an output combination, assuming fixed labor and capital.

satisfies production efficiency (it is on the PPF) and Pareto optimality (there is only one consumer), and it is Pareto superior to any other feasible allocation, given resources and technology.

Since the negative of the slope of the indifference curve is the marginal rate of substitution, utility maximization implies that the efficient output combination that is actually chosen is the one that equates the marginal rate of substitution and the marginal rate of transformation:

$$MRT_{FC} = MRS_{FC}. \tag{14.27}$$

Equation 14.27 is another instance where equating the internal and external rates of trade determines the optimum. The marginal rate of transformation is the external rate of trade, determined by resources and technology. It represents the rate at which the economy can efficiently transform one good into the other by reallocating resources. The marginal rate of substitution is the consumer's internal rate of trade. Utility maximization occurs when the two rates of trade are made equal to one another.

Implicit Prices We know from consumer theory that when prices are taken as parameters, utility maximization also implies that the marginal rate of substitution is equal to the price ratio between the two goods:

$$MRS_{FC} = \frac{p_C}{p_F}. \tag{14.28}$$

Equation 14.28 tells us that when Robinson maximizes utility over his production possibilities frontier, the tangency between his maximum indifference curve and the production possibilities frontier creates an implicit price ratio between coconuts and fish, such that the marginal rate of transformation is also equal to the price ratio:

$$MRS_{FC} = MRT_{FC} = \frac{p_C}{p_F}. \tag{14.29}$$

Equation 14.29 is illustrated in Figure 14.9. The slope of the tangent line at the optimal output combination is the implicit output price ratio.

While Robinson Crusoe clearly would not need markets to facilitate his production and consumption decisions, all the necessary market prices can be inferred from the solutions to his decision problem. If he produces coconuts and fish efficiently, the tangency between the isoquants for coconuts and fish inside the production Edgeworth box determines an implicit price ratio for his inputs. If he maximizes utility, the tangency between his indifference curve and the production possibilities frontier determines an implicit output price ratio, and the rate at which inputs are changed into outputs determines an implicit ratio between input and output prices. Robinson could normalize by setting one of the four prices (labor, tools, coconuts, and fish) equal to 1 and by then paying himself for the value of both his inputs and his outputs. "Robinson the consumer" would pay "Robinson the producer" for coconuts and fish, while "Robinson the producer" would pay "Robinson the supplier of inputs" for his labor and tools. What he earned for his labor and tools would be his income for purchasing

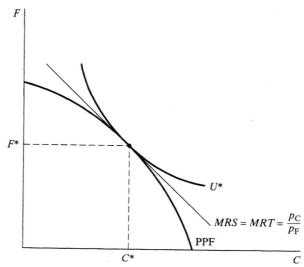

FIGURE 14.9 The Implicit Output Price Ratio at the Optimal Output Point

his food. It would be as though there were a competitive equilibrium between "Robinson the producer" and "Robinson the consumer."[5]

Solving Robinson's Decision Problem The following simple example illustrates both how to solve for an allocation that maximizes Robinson's utility over his production possibilities frontier and how to solve for a set of implicit prices that would support that allocation as a competitive equilibrium. Suppose coconuts and fish are produced using the constant-returns-to-scale production functions given as (14.20) in terms of x and y. Transforming (14.20) into functions for coconuts and fish, $C = (K_C)^{1/2}(L_C)^{1/2}$ and $F = 2(K_F)^{1/2}(L_F)^{1/2}$. Now let

$$\overline{K} = 100 \quad \text{and} \quad \overline{L} = 400. \tag{14.30}$$

Substituting (14.30) in (14.25), the production possibilities frontier is

$$F = 2(\overline{K}\,\overline{L})^{1/2} - 2C = 2(40{,}000)^{1/2} - 2C = 400 - 2C. \tag{14.31}$$

Now, if Robinson's utility function is $U = CF$, his maximization problem is

$$\max U = CF \tag{14.32}$$

$$\text{s.t. } F = 400 - 2C.$$

---

[5]Factor payments only exactly equal output expenditures with constant returns to scale (or at the minimum of a U-shaped long-run average cost curve). But, since we must have either constant returns or U-shaped cost curves to maintain competition in the long run, the assumption is not unwarranted in studying competitive markets. The single consumer-producer is only an example to prepare you to study the more complicated competitive world. In a more realistic model, for example, there might be short-run firm profits. In that case, shares of firms (and, hence, a distribution of profits) would be part of a consumer's initial endowments.

The Lagrangian is

$$\mathcal{L} = CF + \lambda(F - 400 + 2C). \tag{14.33}$$

The first-order conditions are

$$\frac{\partial \mathcal{L}}{\partial C} = F + \lambda 2 = 0 \quad \Rightarrow \quad \lambda = -\frac{F}{2} \tag{14.34}$$

$$\frac{\partial \mathcal{L}}{\partial F} = C + \lambda = 0 \quad \Rightarrow \quad \lambda = -C \tag{14.35}$$

$$\frac{\partial \mathcal{L}}{\partial \lambda} = F - 400 + 2C = 0. \tag{14.36}$$

Solving for λ from (14.34) and (14.35),

$$-\frac{F}{2} = -C \quad \Rightarrow \quad F = 2C. \tag{14.37}$$

Substituting (14.37) in (14.36),

$$2C - 400 + 2C = 0. \tag{14.38}$$

Solving (14.38) for C^* and substituting the result in (14.37),

$$C^* = 100 \quad \text{and} \quad F^* = 2(100) = 200. \tag{14.39}$$

To find the relative prices, we find the MRT_{FC} and the MRS_{FC},

$$MRT_{FC} = -\frac{d[2(\overline{K}\,\overline{L})^{1/2} - 2C]}{dC} = 2 \tag{14.40}$$

$$MRS_{FC} = \frac{F}{C} = \frac{200}{100} = 2. \tag{14.41}$$

Thus, from (14.29), (14.40), and (14.41),

$$\frac{p_C}{p_F} = 2. \tag{14.42}$$

To find the relative input prices, we first find the allocation of inputs to outputs by substituting (14.30) and (14.39) in (14.24) and analogous expressions for $K_C, L_F,$ and $L_C,$

$$K_C = \left(\frac{\overline{K}}{\overline{L}}\right)^{1/2} C^* = \left(\frac{100}{400}\right)^{1/2}(100) = 50 \tag{14.43}$$

$$L_C = \left(\frac{\overline{L}}{\overline{K}}\right)^{1/2} C^* = \left(\frac{400}{100}\right)^{1/2}(100) = 200 \tag{14.44}$$

$$K_F = \tfrac{1}{2}\left(\frac{\overline{K}}{\overline{L}}\right)^{1/2} F^* = \tfrac{1}{2}\left(\frac{100}{400}\right)^{1/2}(200) = 50 \tag{14.45}$$

$$L_F = \frac{1}{2}\left(\frac{\overline{L}}{\overline{K}}\right)^{1/2} \quad F^* = \frac{1}{2}\left(\frac{400}{100}\right)^{1/2}(200) = 200. \tag{14.46}$$

Next, we find the marginal rates of technical substitution by substituting equations 14.43–14.46 in (14.13):

$$MRTS_C = \frac{K_C}{L_C} = \frac{50}{200} = \frac{1}{4} \tag{14.47}$$

$$MRTS_F = \frac{K_F}{L_F} = \frac{50}{200} = \frac{1}{4}. \tag{14.48}$$

Thus, by equations 14.48 and 11.1,

$$\frac{w}{r} = \frac{1}{4}. \tag{14.49}$$

Now, suppose we let $\tilde{r} = 1$ be the normalization. That means

$$\tilde{w} = \frac{1}{4}. \tag{14.50}$$

Further, since we know from equation 12.28 that $w = p_C MP_{LC}$,

$$\frac{1}{4} = \tilde{p}_C\left[\frac{1}{2}\left(\frac{50}{200}\right)^{1/2}\right] = \frac{1}{4}\tilde{p}_C. \tag{14.51}$$

Solving (14.51) for $\tilde{p}_C$ and then deriving $\tilde{p}_F$ from (14.42),

$$\tilde{p}_C = 1 \quad \text{and} \quad \frac{\tilde{p}_C}{\tilde{p}_F} = 2 \;\Rightarrow\; \tilde{p}_F = \frac{1}{2}. \tag{14.52}$$

Finally, since the production functions both have constant returns to scale, factor payments should equal output expenditures, implying

$$\tilde{w}(L_C + L_F) + 1(K_C + K_F) = \tilde{p}_C C^* + \tilde{p}_F F^*$$

$$\tfrac{1}{4}(200 + 200) + (50 + 50) = 1(100) + \tfrac{1}{2}(200)$$

$$100 + 100 = 100 + 100.$$

To summarize, we have assumed that $\tilde{r} = 1$ and solved for the following equilibrium in equations 14.39, 14.42–14.46, 14.50, and 14.52:

$$\tilde{r} = 1, \quad \tilde{w} = \frac{1}{4}, \quad \tilde{p}_C = 1, \qquad \tilde{p}_F = \frac{1}{2},$$

$$C^* = 100 \quad F^* = 200, \quad L_C = L_F = 200, \quad K_C = K_F = 50.$$

This equilibrium is efficient in production in that it is not possible to produce more of one good without producing less of the other, and it maximizes the utility of the one consumer in the economy. In the next two sections, we consider efficiency and equilibrium with more than one consumer.

14.4 ___ PARETO OPTIMALITY WITH MORE THAN ONE CONSUMER

In the previous section, with only one consumer, we saw that utility maximization over the production possibilities frontier implied that the consumer's marginal rate of substitution was equal to the marginal rate of transformation along the production possibilities frontier. Moreover, in Section 9.2, we saw that with two consumers, Pareto optimality implies that the marginal rates of substitution are equal across consumers. In this section, we show that the two conditions together are necessary for both production efficiency and Pareto optimality when there are two consumers.[6]

To show this, we begin by fixing consumer A's utility at some level $\overline{U}_A$ and then maximizing consumer B's utility over the production possibility set. This is similar to what we did in Section 9.2 to find a Pareto optimum without production: we fixed one consumer's utility and then maximized the other consumer's utility given the total quantities of X and Y available for distribution.

Finding a Pareto Optimum Graphically   Figure 14.10 illustrates this process of finding a Pareto optimum with production. In each of the three panels, $\overline{U}_A$ represents a given utility for consumer A. In each panel, the small graph with its origin on consumer A's indifference curve represents consumer B's indifference map and the production possibilities frontier available to consumer B after ensuring that consumer A has enough of both X and Y to maintain utility level $\overline{U}_A$. In the top panel, if A consumes (x_1^A, y_1^A), then B could reach indifference curve U_B^1 and the economy could produce (x_1, y_1). In the center panel, A consumes (x_2^A, y_2^A), B achieves indifference curve U_B^3, and the economy could produce (x_2, y_2). In the bottom graph, A consumes (x_3^A, y_3^A), B achieves U_B^2, and the economy could produce (x_3, y_3). In principle, this exercise could be performed for every point along $\overline{U}_A$ until the highest possible indifference curve for consumer B was located. The result of this process is illustrated in Figure 14.10, where the center panel shows consumer B's maximum utility, given that consumer A's utility is fixed at $\overline{U}_A$. At (x_2, y_2), consumer B's utility is U_B^3, higher than at either (x_1, y_1) or (x_3, y_3).

Implicit Prices with Two Consumers   Notice in Figure 14.10 that the tangency between consumer B's indifference curve and the production possibilities frontier determines an implicit price ratio between X and Y, which is equal to both the marginal rate of transformation and consumer B's marginal rate of substitution, as in Figure 14.9 and equation 14.29:

$$\frac{p_x}{p_y} = MRS_{yx}^B = MRT_{yx}. \tag{14.53}$$

Figure 14.11 shows that this implicit price ratio is also equal to consumer A's marginal rate of substitution. This implies that the marginal rates of substitution are also equal across consumers and equal to an implicit price ratio. Thus, the conditions for Pareto optimality with production encompass the conditions for Pareto optimality in distribution developed in Section 9.2: at an allocation that is both efficient in production and

---

[6]These results extend to many consumers, goods, and inputs, but the analysis is beyond the scope of this book.

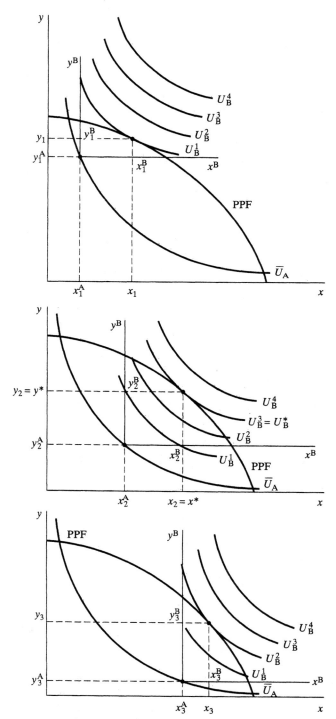

FIGURE 14.10   Utility Maximization over the Production Possibilities Frontier with Two Consumers

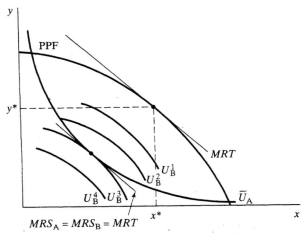

**FIGURE 14.11   Efficiency in Both Production and
Distribution with Two Consumers and Two Goods**

Pareto optimal, the marginal rates of substitution are equal across consumers and
equal to the marginal rate of transformation.

In Figure 14.11, consumer B's indifference map is turned 180° so that its origin is
at the optimal output choice (x^*, y^*), creating a pure trade Edgeworth box such as we
developed in Section 9.3, with dimensions x^* by y^*. Since turning consumer B's indifference map 180° does not change the slope of the tangency identified in Figure 14.10,
we can compare the slopes of the two indifference curves with the marginal rate of
transformation (the slope of the tangent line).[7]

Deriving the Pareto Optimality Conditions Mathematically   To show mathematically what is illustrated in Figures 14.10 and 14.11, we maximize consumer B's utility
subject to A's utility constraint and the production constraints:

$$\max U_B(x_B, y_B) \tag{14.54}$$
$$\text{s.t. } U_A(x_A, y_A) = \overline{U}_A$$
$$x_A + x_B = x$$
$$y_A + y_B = y$$
$$y = y(x). \qquad \textbf{the PPF}$$

---

[7]To convince yourself that Figures 14.10 and 14.11 work as we say they do, you can perform the following test
yourself. Take a piece of transparent plastic or other stiff, transparent material and a marker and trace B's
indifference map (including the axes) *and the tangent line* from the center panel of Figure 14.10. Put the origin of B's indifference map on A's indifference curve and move B's origin along A's indifference curve. The
point identified as the optimum should be on the highest indifference curve B can achieve. Then, turn your
tracing 180°, put the origin at point (x^*, y^*) in Figure 14.11, and square the sides of the Edgeworth box. A's
indifference curve should be tangent to U_B^3, with slopes equal to the tangent line from Figure 14.10.

To solve the problem stated in (14.54), we set up a Lagrange problem with four constraints instead of one. This creates a problem that may look long and complicated but that is actually very simple to work with.[8]

$$\mathcal{L} = U_B(x_B, y_B) + \lambda_1[\overline{U}_A - U_A(x_A, y_A)] - \lambda_2(x - x_A - x_B)$$
$$+ \lambda_3(y - y_A - y_B) + \lambda_4[y - y(x)]. \tag{14.55}$$

The relevant first-order conditions are

$$\frac{\partial \mathcal{L}}{\partial x_B} = \frac{\partial U_B}{\partial x_B} - \lambda_2 = 0 \quad \Rightarrow \quad MU_{Bx} = \lambda_2 \tag{14.56}$$

$$\frac{\partial \mathcal{L}}{\partial y_B} = \frac{\partial U_B}{\partial y_B} - \lambda_3 = 0 \quad \Rightarrow \quad MU_{By} = \lambda_3 \tag{14.57}$$

$$\frac{\partial \mathcal{L}}{\partial x_A} = -\lambda_1 \frac{\partial U_A}{\partial x_A} - \lambda_2 = 0 \Rightarrow -\lambda_1 MU_{Ax} = \lambda_2 \tag{14.58}$$

$$\frac{\partial \mathcal{L}}{\partial y_A} = -\lambda_1 \frac{\partial U_A}{\partial y_A} - \lambda_3 = 0 \quad \Rightarrow \quad -\lambda_1 MU_{Ay} = \lambda_3 \tag{14.59}$$

$$\frac{\partial \mathcal{L}}{\partial y} = \lambda_3 + \lambda_4 = 0 \quad \Rightarrow \quad \lambda_3 = -\lambda_4 \tag{14.60}$$

$$\frac{\partial \mathcal{L}}{\partial x} = \lambda_2 - \lambda_4 \frac{dy}{dx} = 0 \quad \Rightarrow \quad \lambda_2 = \lambda_4 \frac{dy}{dx}. \tag{14.61}$$

Therefore, from (14.60) and (14.61), and recalling from (14.19) that $MRT = dy/dx$,

$$\lambda_2 = \lambda_3 MRT. \tag{14.62}$$

Thus, from equations 14.56–14.59 and 14.62,

$$\frac{\lambda_2}{\lambda_3} = MRT = \frac{MU_{Bx}}{MU_{By}} = \frac{-\lambda_1 MU_{Ax}}{-\lambda_1 MU_{Ay}} = \frac{MU_{Ax}}{MU_{Ay}}. \tag{14.63}$$

Simplifying (14.63),

$$MRT_{yx} = MRS_{yx}^A = MRS_{yx}^B. \tag{14.64}$$

Equation 14.64 shows that the consumers' marginal rates of substitution are equal to one another and to the marginal rate of transformation.

14.5   GENERAL EQUILIBRIUM IN A COMPETITIVE ECONOMY

The actual level of utility each consumer can achieve and the actual output chosen along the production possibilities frontier will depend upon the initial endowments of inputs to consumers. Assuming consumers take all prices as parameters, they sell their inputs at market input prices, generating income to purchase goods at market output

---

[8]We could substitute the transformation function and the output constraints into consumer A's utility function, but that would create a much more complicated problem than is necessary.

prices. For example, given wage and rental rates w and r, consumer A can achieve income level

$$M_A = wL_A + rK_A.$$

Then, if prices are p_x and p_y, consumer A's budget line is

$$p_x x_A + p_y y_A = M_A = wL_A + rK_A.$$

Similarly, consumer B's budget line is

$$p_x x_B + p_y y_B = M_B = wL_B + rK_B.$$

Firm X produces $x_A + x_B$ using K_x and L_x and firm Y produces $y_A + y_B$ using K_y and L_y, where

$$K_A + K_B = K_x + K_y \quad \text{and} \quad L_A + L_B = L_x + L_y.$$

General Equilibrium and Partial Equilibrium   An equilibrium in this economy is a set of prices for both inputs and outputs, an allocation of inputs to firms, and an allocation of outputs to consumers such that demand equals supply in all input and output markets simultaneously, such that consumers are maximizing utility subject to their budget constraints defined by their initial endowments valued at the equilibrium prices, and such that firms are maximizing profits taking the equilibrium prices as given. We refer to such an equilibrium as a **general competitive equilibrium.** It differs from the equilibrium we developed in Sections 13.3 and 13.5, in that that is an equilibrium in the market for only one good, assuming no change in the markets for other goods. We call an equilibrium in a single market, ignoring any effects of changes in that market on other markets, a **partial competitive equilibrium.** When we study only one market by itself, we are doing a **partial equilibrium analysis,** and when we study all markets simultaneously, we are doing a **general equilibrium analysis.**

An important difficulty with a partial equilibrium analysis is that a change in the price of one good can have repercussions in other markets that are not included in the partial equilibrium analysis. For example, an increase in the price of X will increase the demand curve for Y if Y is a substitute for X. This increase in demand for Y will increase Y's price in the short run as well. A general equilibrium analysis allows for such market interactions and studies the simultaneous formation of equilibria in all markets. A partial equilibrium analysis ignores those interactions.[9]

Graphical Illustration of a General Competitive Equilibrium   To see graphically how a general competitive equilibrium is formed, assume as we did in Section 9.3 that there is an auctioneer who will call out prices, which consumers and firms will take as given,[10] and who will keep adjusting them in a *tâtonnement* process until all markets

---

[9]Sometimes general equilibrium effects are "small" and can be legitimately ignored. Then a partial equilibrium analysis is quite appropriate. Other times, the general equilibrium effects are quite large and must be considered. Section 14.6 considers some examples of each.

[10]Naturally, if there were really only two consumers and two goods, it would not be possible to justify the competitive assumption of price taking. We use this simple example merely for illustration and make the *assumption,* as we did in Section 7.2, that all market participants *behave competitively* (treat prices as parameters).

clear. Moreover, just as in the pure-trade economy analyzed in Section 9.3 and in the Robinson Crusoe economy outlined in Section 14.3, prices cannot be uniquely determined. This is because demand functions are homogeneous of degree 0 in all prices and income and because conditional input demands are homogeneous of degree 0 in input prices. Thus, to analyze a general equilibrium *tâtonnement* process, we normalize one of the output or input prices and express all other prices as price ratios relative to the normalized price.

Suppose, for example, we choose the price of capital (r) to be 1 and normalize all other prices on that. Thus, $\tilde{r} = 1$, $\tilde{w} = w/r$, $\tilde{p}_x = p_x/r$, $\tilde{p}_y = p_y/r$. Whether or not these price ratios are in equilibrium depends on consumer demand, given the price ratios. To find consumer demand, we first evaluate each consumer's income at the wage-rental ratio and then find the consumers' budget lines under the proposed output price ratios.

$$\tilde{M}_A = \tilde{w}L_A + K_A = \tilde{p}_x x_A + \tilde{p}_y y_A \tag{14.65}$$

$$\tilde{M}_B = \tilde{w}L_B + K_B + K_B = \tilde{p}_x x_B + \tilde{p}_y y_B \tag{14.66}$$

The consumers then maximize utility over the budget lines set out in equations 14.65 and 14.66. If, along the production possibilities frontier, $(x_A^* + x_B^*, y_A^* + y_B^*) = (x, y)$, then the economy is in equilibrium at those prices.

Figure 14.12 illustrates such an equilibrium. Consumer A's budget line has intercepts $\tilde{M}_A/\tilde{p}_x$ and $\tilde{M}_A/\tilde{p}_y$, and consumer A maximizes utility at (x_A^*, y_A^*). Consumer B's budget line can now be added to consumer A's, using up the potential output in the economy. The sum of the two budget lines is tangent to the production possibilities frontier at (X^*, Y^*), which is also where consumer B's indifference curve

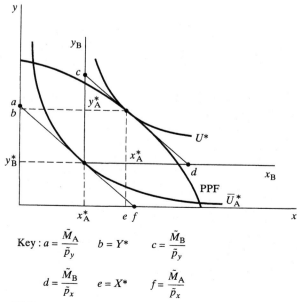

Key: $a = \dfrac{\tilde{M}_A}{\tilde{p}_y}$ $b = Y^*$ $c = \dfrac{\tilde{M}_B}{\tilde{p}_y}$

$d = \dfrac{\tilde{M}_B}{\tilde{p}_x}$ $e = X^*$ $f = \dfrac{\tilde{M}_A}{\tilde{p}_x}$

FIGURE 14.12   An Equilibrium Set of Price Ratios

is tangent. This means that at (x_A^*, y_A^*) and (x_B^*, y_B^*), the sums of A's and B's utility-maximizing quantities demanded at those prices are equal to the economy's efficient output of those goods: $x_A^* + x_B^* = X^*$ and $y_A^* + y_B^* = Y^*$, and the economy is in equilibrium.

Output and Input Prices   The choice of point (X^*, Y^*) implies both an allocation of inputs to the production of outputs along the efficient production set and an equilibrium price for labor. Figure 14.13 reiterates this idea. Point (X^*, Y^*) along the production possibilities frontier is mapped onto the point of tangency between X^* and Y^*

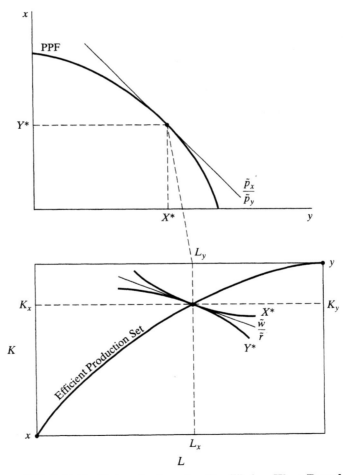

FIGURE 14.13   Determination of an Equilibrium Wage-Rental Ratio from an Equilibrium Output Choice

inside the production Edgeworth box. The equality of the marginal rates of technical substitution then determines the normalized wage rate, $\tilde{w}$. The ratio between output and input prices is determined by equating the normalized wage and the normalized marginal revenue product of labor: $\tilde{w} = \tilde{p}_x MP_{Lx}$. In order for all markets to be in equilibrium simultaneously, the normalized prices have to ensure that the above relationships hold.

The Fundamental Theorems of Welfare Economics   Notice in Figure 14.12 that the equilibrium satisfies the conditions for Pareto optimality developed in Sections 14.3 and 14.4: the marginal rate of transformation is equal to both consumers' marginal rates of substitution. This is accomplished through relative market prices $\tilde{w}$, $\tilde{p}_x$, and $\tilde{p}_y$. Thus, just as in the pure-trade case in Sections 9.2 and 9.3, we have the important result that the competitive market solves both the production and the distribution problems, given consumers' initial endowments and assuming that consumer preferences and technology satisfy the assumptions of the models developed in Sections 5.3 and 10.2, respectively.

In Section 9.2, we referred to this result as the first fundamental theorem of welfare economics in the pure-trade case. With production and distribution, the first fundamental theorem of welfare economics is extended as follows. If preferences are complete, reflexive, transitive, and exhibit nonsatiation and diminishing marginal rates of substitution; if there are no externalities in consumption; if production exhibits diminishing marginal rates of technical substitution and constant or decreasing returns to scale;[11] and if there are no externalities in production (such as pollution); then *every* general competitive equilibrium is both efficient in production and Pareto optimal.[12]

The second fundamental theorem of welfare economics also extends to the case with both production and distribution. Basically, every allocation along the production possibilities frontier implies implicit price ratios for outputs and inputs. This is illustrated for two different points in Figure 14.14. At point A along the production possibilities frontier, the implicit price ratio is p_x^1/p_y^1 and (x_1, y_1) is the competitive allocation. Taking that allocation inside the production Edgeworth box, we see that the implicit input price ratio is w_1/r_1. Similarly, at point B, the implicit price ratios are p_x^2/p_y^2 and w_2/r_2, and the allocation is (x_2, y_2). The second fundamental theorem of welfare economics in the general case states that under the same assumptions as for the first fundamental theorem,

---

[11]U-shaped costs are also possible if each firm is very small. If firms are not small, there may be a problem in that the total quantity demanded at minimum long-run average cost may not be exactly divisible by the number of firms. In that case, there may not be an exact, zero-profit long-run equilibrium. If there are decreasing returns, on the other hand, we assume a fixed number of firms so that entry does not drive firm size to 0. In this case, firms will make profits, but the profits are assumed to be distributed back to consumers in a private-ownership economy.

[12]Recall from Section 7.5, however, that Pareto optimality is consistent with every possible distribution of output from A gets all and B gets nothing to B gets all and A gets nothing. Which distribution is the actual outcome of the competitive process depends on the distribution of initial endowments. The concept of Pareto optimality describes a situation in which no individual can be made better off without hurting someone else.

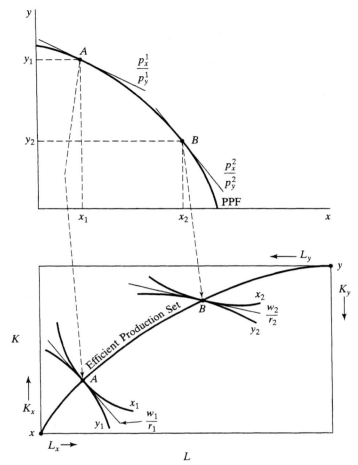

FIGURE 14.14   Different Allocations and Different Implicit Price Ratios Along the Production Possibilities Frontier

every allocation that is efficient in production and which could potentially be a Pareto optimal allocation can be supported as a general competitive equilibrium by a suitable assignment of initial endowments to consumers.

14.6   COMPARATIVE STATICS IN A GENERAL EQUILIBRIUM FRAMEWORK

In Section 13.6, we saw that, in a partial equilibrium framework, long-run supply is perfectly elastic if input prices do not change. On the other hand, it is clear that if the production possibilities frontier bows out, relative prices will change as the output of one good is increased and the other good is decreased. A change in tastes in favor of X, for example, would result in a movement along the production possibilities frontier that would increase x and reduce y. Output of Y must decrease in order to increase x if production were efficient to begin with. The only way to increase x is to transfer productive inputs from Y to X. Thus, increasing x also increases the marginal rate of transformation and, therefore, must increase the equilibrium price of X relative to the equilibrium price of Y as well. This is illustrated in Figure 14.14. At output combination (x_1, y_1), the relative output price is p_x^1/p_y^1. But at (x_2, y_2), with more X and less Y, the relative output price is p_x^2/p_y^2, which is greater than p_x^1/p_y^1.

If the efficient production set is nonlinear, the change in the output mix along the production possibilities frontier implies a change in relative input prices as well. This is also illustrated in Figure 14.14. As output of X increases from x_1 to x_2 and as Y decreases from y_1 to y_2, the wage-rent rate falls from w_1/r_1 to w_2/r_2. This happens because X is more capital intensive than Y (bowed up efficient production set), so increasing x increases the demand for capital relative to the demand for labor. With given quantities of capital and labor available in the economy, the increase in the relative demand for capital raises its relative price, and the wage-rental ratio falls.

We can reconcile the partial and the general equilibrium results by recalling our assumptions regarding input prices in the partial equilibrium analysis. In Section 13.6, we expressly assumed that input prices were fixed. But in a general equilibrium framework, we know that a different point on a bowed out production possibilities frontier also implies a different point on a curved efficient production set and a different wage-rental ratio.[13] Thus, long-run supply could be perfectly elastic for constant input prices, and there could still be a change in relative prices as relative input prices change.

Technological Changes A change that may or may not change relative prices, but that will increase attainable output, is technological change. For example, a neutral technological change that affects the output of all goods in the same proportion might have no effect on relative prices. First, looking at the production Edgeworth box, a neutral technological change that affects all goods proportionately would not change the marginal rates of technical substitution of any good. Moreover, if it affects all goods proportionately, it would simply shift the production possibilities frontier in a radial fashion without changing the marginal rates of transformation. This is illustrated in Figure 14.15. If, in addition, consumer preferences are such that all the marginal rates of substitution remain the same along any expansion path (identical homothetic preferences), then output of both goods will increase, and all relative prices will stay the same.

It is more likely, however, that a technological change will result in a general equilibrium change in relative prices as well as an increase in output of one or more goods. For example, suppose there is a neutral technological change that increases the maximum attainable output of one good and not the other, resulting in a change in the shape of the production possibilities frontier. Then, even with identical homothetic prefer-

---

[13]Prices stay the same only if the production possibilities frontier and efficient production set are linear.

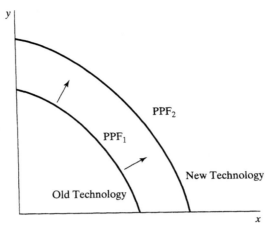

FIGURE 14.15   A Technological Change That Shifts the Production Possibilities Frontier Without Changing the *MRT*

ences, relative prices would change. If the technological change is biased or if preferences are not homothetic, the potential changes in relative prices are even greater.

Figure 14.16 illustrates the case of a technological change that increases the potential output of X but not the potential output of Y. Quantities $\bar{x}_1$ and $\bar{y}$ represent the maximum attainable outputs before the technological change, and $\bar{x}_2$ and $\bar{y}$ represent the maximum attainable outputs after. The shift in the production possibilities frontier has the effect of reducing the relative price of X when output increases from (x_1, y_1) to (x_2, y_2) along the straight line from the origin. Moreover, this result confirms

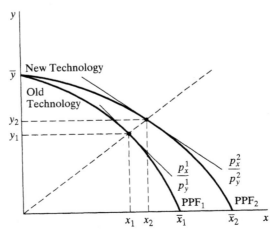

FIGURE 14.16   A Technological Change That Shifts the Production Possibilities Frontier and Does Change the *MRT*

our intuition that a technological change that reduces the cost of producing one particular good should reduce the general equilibrium relative output price of that good.

Partial and General Equilibrium Analysis   In analyzing economic policy, it is a matter of judgment and experience when to use a general equilibrium and when to use a partial equilibrium analysis to do comparative statics. In general, however, the best rule of thumb is to ask how substantial are the changes being analyzed in comparison to output and employment in the economy. If one industry is very small relative to labor, capital, and other output markets, for example, it is probably quite acceptable to ignore the effects of any changes in that industry on any other markets.

A change in tastes in favor of some particular food or item of clothing is not likely to have a measurable effect on relative output or input prices, although there are exceptions. For example, the recent craze for Cajun food has severely depleted populations of redfish (used to make blackened redfish) and has consequently raised its price. Similarly, demand for exotic furs is threatening the extinction of many large cat species, and demand for beaver hats in the eighteenth and early nineteenth centuries nearly brought about the extinction of the beaver in North America.

A technological change in steelmaking or an oil shortage can have profound general equilibrium effects. Steelmaking employs a large labor force and uses large quantities of capital. Moreover, steel is widely used in producing many other goods. Similarly, oil is used in making plastics and other synthetics in addition to being burned in automobiles and power plants. As we have already suggested in Section 6.5 and in Application 2, Section 13.3, an increase in the relative price of oil could increase the relative prices of numerous other goods. The shift toward the production of goods that do not use oil could, in turn, affect relative input prices. In the case of steel and oil, therefore, ignoring general equilibrium effects can lead to inaccurate and misleading predictions and, perhaps, inappropriate policy recommendations.

14.7   REVIEW OF KEY CONCEPTS

This completes our analysis of competitive output markets under certainty and with no specific time dimension incorporated in the model. The remainder of this book considers models of both output and input markets where one or more of these assumptions are violated: monopoly and imperfect competition, competitive and noncompetitive labor markets, decisions over time, decisions under uncertainty, and markets with externalities or public goods. Before continuing to these more advanced topics, however, be sure you understand and can use the following key concepts.

An allocation of inputs to the production of outputs is *efficient* if it is not possible to produce more of one good without being forced to produce less of another.

A *production Edgeworth box* is a rectangle of length and width equal to the total quantities of two inputs available for use in production in an economy. An increase in the output of one good is represented by increasing inputs in a northeastern direction, while an increase in the output of the other good is represented by increasing inputs in a southwestern direction.

The *efficient production set* in the Edgeworth box is the set of all input allocations such that it is not possible to produce more of one good without producing less of the other. At a point on the efficient production set, the production isoquants for the two goods are tangent to one another.

Since the isoquants are tangent along the efficient production set, the marginal rates of technical substitution for the two goods are equal to one another. This also implies that the ratios of marginal physical products of labor and capital are equal for the two goods.

Since the marginal rates of technical substitution are equal to the ratio of input prices, every point of tangency implies an input price ratio that would sustain that allocation of inputs to firms as a competitive equilibrium in the factor markets.

The efficient production set will be linear if both firms have constant and equal capital-labor ratios and nonlinear if their capital-labor ratios are different.

The *production possibilities frontier* describes all the efficient combinations of goods that an economy can produce. In a two-good economy, it is constructed by taking points along the efficient production set and placing them on a graph that compares the attainable quantities of the two goods.

The production possibilities frontier will be bowed out if both production functions have decreasing returns to scale, if one has decreasing and one has constant returns to scale, or if both have constant returns and different capital-labor ratios.

The production possibilities frontier will be a straight line if both production functions have constant returns to scale and equal capital-labor ratios along a (linear) efficient production set.

The *marginal rate of transformation* is the negative of the slope of the production possibilities frontier. It represents the rate at which an economy can transform Y into X by reallocating resources from the production of Y to the production of X.

If the production possibilities frontier bows out, the marginal rate of transformation increases as more X and less Y are produced.

At an output combination that is simultaneously efficient in production, Pareto optimal, and Pareto superior to an initial endowment, consumer marginal rates of substitution are equal to the marginal rate of transformation.

The tangency between the production possibilities frontier and consumer indifference curves creates an implicit price ratio that describes the rate at which Y can be traded for X at that allocation.

At the output combination that is efficient, Pareto optimal, and Pareto superior to an initial endowment, all output and input price ratios can be inferred. The input price ratio is equal to the marginal rate of technical substitution at the point on the efficient production set associated with the chosen point along the production possibilities frontier.

The allocation along the production possibilities frontier that is chosen as the result of a competitive process depends upon the allocation of inputs to consumers. Consumers owning inputs with higher equilibrium prices end up with more purchasing power, and the resulting output combination reflects their preferences.

A *general competitive equilibrium* is a set of prices for both inputs and outputs, an allocation of inputs to firms, and an allocation of outputs to consumers, such that demand equals supply in all input and output markets simultaneously, such that consumers are maximizing utility subject to their budget constraints defined by their initial endowments valued at the equilibrium prices, and such that firms are maximizing profits taking the equilibrium input and output prices as given.

An equilibrium in a single market, ignoring any effects of changes in that market on other markets, is called a *partial competitive equilibrium.*

Partial equilibrium analysis is the study of one market by itself. *General equilibrium analysis* is the study of all markets simultaneously.

The first and second fundamental theorems of welfare economics, developed in Sections 7.4 and 7.6, respectively, extend to the case of a general competitive equilibrium. Every general competitive equilibrium is both efficient in production and Pareto optimal. Every point on the production possibilities frontier, which could be a Pareto optimum, can be supported as a general competitive equilibrium by a suitable assignment of initial endowments to consumers.

If the efficient production set is curved, relative input and output prices must change as more of one good and less of another are produced.

A neutral technological change that affects the output of all goods in the same proportion shifts out the production possibilities frontier in a radial fashion.

In general, a technological change is likely to result in a change in relative prices.

If one market is "small" relative to its input markets and to other output markets, it may be correct to use a partial equilibrium analysis for policy analysis. Otherwise, a general equilibrium analysis should be considered.

14.8   QUESTIONS FOR DISCUSSION

1. Suppose population grows, increasing the total quantity of labor available in an economy that produces two goods, one that is produced using relatively labor-intensive technology and the other that is produced using relatively capital-intensive technology. Analyze the general equilibrium comparative statics effects of this population growth on input and output price ratios, assuming consumer preferences are identical and homothetic.

2. Suppose a one-consumer economy is producing inside its production possibilities frontier. Given the assumption of nonsatiation, graphically identify points that are both efficient in production and Pareto superior to the initial output point. Explain your answer.

3. Suppose there is a change in tastes in favor of a good that is relatively more capital intensive than the other good produced in a two-

good economy. There is no change in technology. Analyze the general equilibrium comparative statics effect of this change on output and input price ratios and comment on the change in the wage-rental ratio you identify.

4. Suppose we identify an allocation that satisfies the definition of Pareto optimality. Is it possible for that allocation to *not* be efficient in production as well? In other words, is production efficiency a necessary condition for Pareto optimality when there is both production and distribution? Is efficiency a sufficient condition? Explain.

5. Explain why, in the context of a general equilibrium model, it is not possible for input prices to change without some underlying change in preferences, technology, or the quantities of inputs available.

14.9   PROBLEMS

Problems 1–4 Suppose Robinson Crusoe uses only labor to produce coconuts and fish. His production function for fish is

$$F = 6L.$$

His production function for coconuts is

$$C - 5(L)^{1/2}.$$

His utility function is

$$U = F^2C.$$

He collects food for six hours per day.

1. Find the production possibilities frontier and graph it.
2. Find the utility-maximizing combination of coconuts and fish collected per day.

3. Show that the marginal rate of substitution is equal to the marginal rate of transformation at the utility-maximizing choice.
4. What is the implicit price ratio between coconuts and fish?

Problems 5 and 6 Consider a two-consumer, two-good, two-input economy. The production functions are

$$x = (K_x)^{1/2}(L_x)^{1/2} \quad \text{and}$$
$$y = 4(K_y)^{1/2}(L_y)^{1/2}.$$

The utility functions are

$$U_A = x_A(y_A)^2 \quad \text{and}$$
$$U_B = (x_B)^2 y_B.$$

The initial endowments are

$$\overline{K}_A = 800, \quad \overline{L}_A = 100,$$
$$\overline{K}_B = 400, \quad \overline{L}_B = 200.$$

5. Find the general competitive equilibrium input and output prices, allocation of outputs to consumers, and allocation of inputs to firms.

6. Show that each consumer's marginal rate of substitution is equal to the output price ratio and that each firm's marginal rate of technical substitution is equal to the input price ratio.

14.10   LOGICAL AND MATHEMATICAL APPLICATIONS

1. Use a production possibilities frontier to show why imposing a per-unit tax on only one good forces the economy to a non-Pareto optimal position.

2. An important theorem in international trade is called the Stolper-Samuelson theorem. One prediction of this theorem states that if countries sell their output at world market prices and if the market price of a relatively labor-intensive good increases, the equilibrium wage-rental ratio within each country must also increase. Use a graphical comparative statics analysis to show why this theorem is correct.[14]

---

[14]Paul A. Samuelson, "Prices of Factors and Goods in General Equilibrium," *Review of Economic Studies* 21(1953–1954):1–20.

Chapter 15

MONOPOLY

15.1   WHAT YOU SHOULD LEARN FROM THIS CHAPTER

This is the first chapter on noncompetitive markets. We begin with the simplest departure from the competitive model: we assume there is only one seller in a market (instead of many), but that there are still many consumers and competitive markets for inputs. If there is only one seller in a market, we call that firm a **monopolist.**

A monopolist still faces the cost functions we developed in Sections 11.5 and 11.8 and uses the same profit-maximization rule we developed in Section 12.2: the monopolist chooses an output level such that the marginal cost associated with that output level equals the marginal revenue associated with that output level. The difference between the monopolist and the competitive firm is that the monopolist faces a downward-sloping demand curve, while the competitive firm, which is a price taker, behaves as if its individual demand curve is horizontal.

From a general equilibrium perspective, the effect of monopoly is to raise the relative price of monopolized goods as compared to goods produced under perfect competition. Resources are transferred from the production of monopolized goods to the production of competitively priced goods. If the economy stays on its production possibilities frontier, the effect is to move in the direction of producing a larger quantity of competitively priced goods and a smaller quantity of monopolized goods than would be produced at a general competitive equilibrium. Since we know that at a general competitive equilibrium the marginal rates of substitution of consumers are equal to the economy's marginal rate of transformation, the effect of having some goods produced monopolistically is to create a situation in which the marginal rates of substitution are *not* equal to the marginal rate of transformation. Thus, even if the economy is on its production possibilities frontier, consumers could be made better off if the output mix moved in the direction of what would have been the general competitive equilibrium.

Only with increasing returns (decreasing marginal cost) is there any chance that a profit-maximizing monopolist will produce more and charge a lower price than a competitive industry would. We refer to a monopolist with increasing returns to scale over the relevant range of output as having a *natural monopoly.* The chapter ends with a discussion of some possible policies for regulating natural monopolies.

15.2   PROFIT-MAXIMIZING OUTPUT AND INPUT DECISIONS UNDER MONOPOLY

When we developed the firm's cost functions in Sections 11.5 and 11.8, we did not make any assumptions about the kind of market environment in which the firm operated. *Every* profit-maximizing firm minimizes cost. Similarly, when we first developed the firm's profit-maximizing decision in Section 12.2, we did not make any assumptions about the market. *Every* profit-maximizing firm produces an output such that the marginal cost associated with that output equals the marginal revenue associated with that output. The major difference between a monopoly and a competitive industry is that the single monopolist treats the entire industry demand curve as its demand curve. This means that the monopolist faces a downward-sloping demand curve instead of being a price taker. As we saw in Section 7.4, if demand is downward sloping, marginal revenue is everywhere lower than the demand curve itself. Thus, if a monopolist is maximizing profits, marginal revenue and marginal cost are always less than price. This is illustrated by the following mathematical argument, by Figures 15.1 and 15.2, and by the numerical example that accompanies these figures. As we showed in equation 7.8, the expression for a downward-sloping inverse demand function is $p_x(x)$, with $(dp_x/dx) < 0$, implying that total revenue is generally a nonlinear function of x: $TR(x) = p_x(x)x$. Marginal revenue is, therefore, generally not a constant:

$$MR(x) = \frac{d}{dx} TR(x) = x \frac{dp_x}{dx} + p_x. \quad \text{equation 9.19}$$

Equating marginal cost and marginal revenue,

$$MC(x) = MR(x) = x \frac{dp_x}{dx} + p_x. \quad (15.1)$$

Rearranging terms in (15.1),

$$p_x = MX(x) - x \frac{dp_x}{dx} > MC(x), \quad (15.2)$$

since $dp_x/dx < 0$. Thus, price is greater than both marginal cost and marginal revenue.

In Figure 15.1 and in the numerical example, we assume for simplicity that the monopolist faces a linear, downward-sloping demand curve and constant long-run marginal cost. While an industry with constant returns to scale could be competitive, we assume that a single firm is able to prevent the entry of other potential competitors. One way to prevent entry might be to secure a **patent** on a particular product. In the United States, for example, a patent gives a single firm the legal right to produce a product without competition for a period of 17 years.

A Numerical Example   We know from Section 7.4 that a downward-sloping linear demand curve has a downward-sloping linear marginal revenue curve with the same price intercept and half the quantity intercept as the demand curve. The profit-maximizing monopolist chooses the output x^* that equates marginal cost and marginal revenue and then charges the price at which that output will be

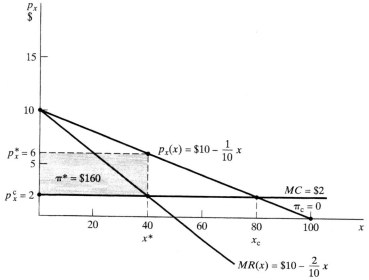

FIGURE 15.1   Profit-maximizing Output Choice Under Monopoly

demanded $[p_x^* = p_x(x^*)]$.[1] This is illustrated in Figure 15.1 and in the following numerical example. Suppose the market demand function is given by

$$x_d(p_x) = 100 - 10p_x, \tag{15.3}$$

and long-run marginal cost is constant at \$2. To find the profit-maximizing output and price, we first construct the firm's profit function as a function of output by substituting (9.16) in (12.1) and letting $TC(x) = 2x$:

$$\pi(x) = TR(x) - TC(x) = p_x(x)x - 2x. \tag{15.4}$$

To find $p_x(x)$, we find the inverse demand function from (15.3):

$$X_d(p_x) = 100 - 10p_x \Rightarrow p_x(x) = 10 - \tfrac{1}{10}x. \tag{15.5}$$

Substituting (15.5) in (15.4),

$$\pi(x) = (10 - \tfrac{1}{10}x)x - 2x = 10x - \tfrac{1}{10}x^2 - 2x \tag{15.6}$$
$$= 8x - \tfrac{1}{10}x^2.$$

To maximize long-run profits, we differentiate (15.6) with respect to x, set the derivative equal to 0, and solve the first-order condition

$$\frac{d\pi}{dx} = 8 - \tfrac{2}{10}x^* = 0. \tag{15.7}$$

---

[1]Alternatively, we could view the firm as choosing a profit-maximizing price p_x^* and then selling the output consumers will buy at that price. To avoid confusion, however, throughout this chapter we will maintain the convention that the firm chooses a profit-maximizing quantity.

Solving (15.7) for x^*,

$$x^* = 40 \quad \Rightarrow \quad p_x^* = 10 - \tfrac{1}{10}(40) = \$6. \tag{15.8}$$

The values of 40 for x^* and $6 for p_x^* are identified in Figure 15.1.

Monopoly and Competitive Outputs and Prices   Figure 15.1 also contrasts price and quantity in the long run under monopoly and competition. The long-run competitive price is always equal to long-run marginal cost, which is less than p_x^*, and the competitive output (x_c) is greater than x^*. Thus, the monopolist produces less and charges a higher price than a competitive industry would. To find the long-run equilibrium price and quantity under competition, we first note that the long-run equilibrium price would equal long-run marginal cost:

$$p_x^c = \$2 < \$6. \tag{15.9}$$

To find the long-run equilibrium price, we substitute long-run marginal cost into the market demand function (equation 15.5):

$$X_d = 100 - 10(2) = 80.$$

Thus,

$$x_c = 80 > 40. \tag{15.10}$$

The values of 80 for x_c and $2 for p_x^c are also identified in Figure 15.1.

The monopolist in Figure 15.1 makes profits in the long run:

$$LR\pi(x^*) = x^*(p_x^* - LRMC) = 40(6 - 2) = \$160 > 0. \tag{15.11}$$

This is in contrast to the competitive industry, where each firm earns zero economic profits in the long run (see Section 13.5). For firm i,

$$LR\pi(x_i) = x_i[p_x^c - LRMC(x_i)] = 0, \tag{15.12}$$

since $p_x^c = LRMC$ in long-run equilibrium under competition.

Monopoly and the Elasticity of Demand   As long as marginal cost is positive, equating positive marginal cost and positive marginal revenue implies that the monopolist will always produce on the *elastic* portion of its demand curve. This point is illustrated by recalling equation 7.13, which relates marginal cost and elasticity, and by recalling from equation 7.14 that demand is *elastic* when marginal revenue is positive. Thus, equating marginal cost and marginal revenue as defined in (7.4),

$$MC = MR = p_x\!\left(1 + \frac{1}{\epsilon_d}\right) > 0, \quad \epsilon_d < -1. \quad \textbf{\small elastic demand} \tag{15.13}$$

Recall now from Figure 7.4 that we can divide a linear demand curve into two sections according to whether demand is elastic or inelastic (marginal revenue is positive or negative). In Figure 15.2, as well, demand is elastic on the upper portion where marginal revenue is positive, unitary where marginal revenue is 0, and inelastic on the lower portion where marginal revenue is negative. With positive marginal cost, the profit-maximizing output is always to the left of the revenue-maximizing output (the output

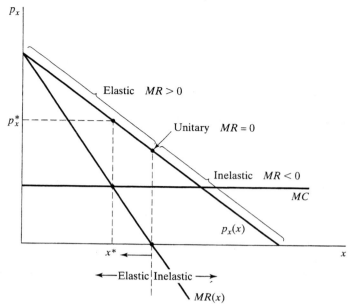

**FIGURE 15.2   A Monopolist Always Produces on the Elastic
Portion of the Demand Curve**

corresponding to zero marginal revenue) and thus is on the elastic portion of the
demand curve.

Notice also that a monopolist does not have a supply curve in the sense that the
competitive firm does. The competitive firm is a price taker, implying that it equates
price and marginal cost. Thus, in the competitive case, the marginal cost curve indicates
the quantity the firm will supply at each price (the supply curve). The monopolist, on
the other hand, chooses a profit-maximizing price and quantity given a demand curve
and a marginal cost curve. There is no function that describes the relationship between
price and quantity; price and quantity are simultaneously determined by the profit-
maximization decision.

Short-run and Long-run Shutdown   While a monopolist is free to choose the price-
quantity combination that generates the maximum profit, simply having a monopoly
does not guarantee that a firm can make profits producing and selling a particular
product. For example, in most communities, a particular company will have a monopoly on public transportation. Many such companies are unable to make a positive
profit at any price. In other instances, there are many products invented and patented
but never produced for want of positive profits.

Faced with a monopoly that cannot make positive profits, the manager of such a
firm makes shutdown decisions in a manner similar to the manager of a competitive
firm. In the short run, the monopolist that has already begun production continues to
produce as long as the loss-minimizing price is greater than or equal to short-run average variable cost. In the long run, the monopolist continues to produce as long as the

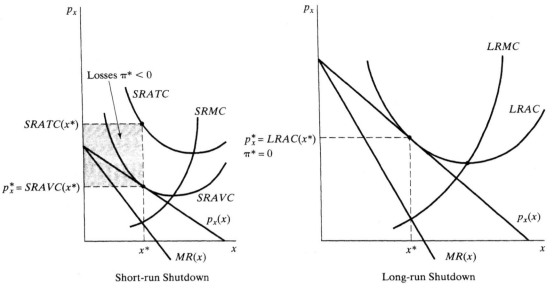

FIGURE 15.3 Short-run and Long-run Shutdown Under Monopoly

"profit-maximizing" price is at least equal to long-run average cost, guaranteeing at least zero profits in the long run.[2]

Figure 15.3 illustrates these short-run and long-run monopoly shutdown decisions. The left graph illustrates the case where demand is just tangent to short-run average variable cost. The monopolist is indifferent between producing and shutting down in the short run, but demand is insufficient to cover average total cost in the long run. The right graph illustrates the case of a zero-profit monopoly in the long run. Demand is just sufficient to cover long-run average cost at the tangency between the demand curve and the long-run average cost curve, generating zero profits.

Input Demand The monopolist's short-run input decision can also be compared to the competitive firm's short-run input decision. If we assume that labor and capital markets are competitive,[3] the monopolist must take the wage and rental rates as parameters in the monopoly profit-maximization decision. However, since price of output is *not* a parameter, the monopolist's marginal revenue products of labor and capital will be different from the competitor's. To find the profit-maximizing choice of labor, we express the profit function in terms of labor, holding capital fixed:

$$\pi(L; \overline{K}) = p_x(x(L; \overline{K}))x(L; \overline{K}) - wL - r\overline{K}. \tag{15.14}$$

The first-order condition is

$$\frac{\partial \pi}{\partial L} = \frac{dp_x}{dx}\frac{\partial x}{\partial L}x + p_x\frac{\partial x}{\partial L} - w = 0. \tag{15.15}$$

---

[2]This situation is not to be confused with a long-run competitive equilibrium, however, since price is still greater than marginal cost.

[3]This assumption will be discussed in Sections 17.6, 17.7, and 18.5.

Solving (15.15) for w,

$$w = \frac{\partial x}{\partial L}\left(\frac{dp_x}{dx}x + p_x\right) = MP_L(MR) = MRP_L. \tag{15.16}$$

Similarly, the short-run demand for capital can be derived from the following first-order condition:

$$\frac{\partial \pi}{\partial K} = \frac{dp_x}{dx}\frac{\partial x}{\partial K}x + p_x\frac{\partial x}{\partial K} - r = 0. \tag{15.17}$$

Solving (15.17) for r,

$$r = \frac{\partial x}{\partial K}\left(\frac{dp_x}{dx}x + p_x\right) = MP_K(MR) = MRP_K. \tag{15.18}$$

Comparing Monopoly and Competitive Input Demand   While the basic form of the monopoly and competitive input decisions appear similar (marginal revenue product equals marginal revenue times marginal product), the results are different. (Compare equations 12.28 and 12.30 with equations 15.16 and 15.18, respectively.) Under competition, marginal revenue is equal to output price, so the profit-maximizing input choice equates the input price and *price* times the marginal physical product. Since marginal revenue is always less than price along any downward-sloping market demand curve, the monopolist's marginal revenue product curve lies below the competitor's. This implies that for the same amount of fixed capital and for any given market input price, the monopolist hires less labor than a competitive firm would. This is illustrated in Figure 15.4. For a given industry-wide marginal product of labor (determined by the technology and the quantity of capital employed in the industry), the monopolist's

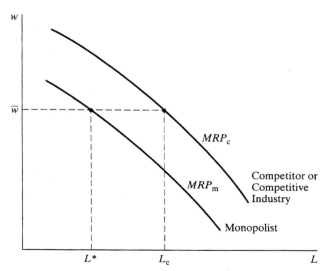

FIGURE 15.4   A Comparison of a Monopolist's and a Competitive Industry's Short-run Labor Demand

marginal revenue product is less than the competitor's at each quantity of labor hired. This implies that if the wage is given by the equilibrium wage in a competitive labor market, the competitive industry hires more labor (L_c) than a monopolist would (L^*).

15.3 WELFARE LOSS FROM MONOPOLY

When an industry is organized as a monopoly instead of as many competitive firms, some of the competitive consumer's and producer's surplus is lost at the monopoly output choice.[4] Some of that surplus gets transferred to the monopolist in the form of additional profits, but some is lost altogether. Figure 15.5 illustrates this loss for the monopolist with constant marginal cost, depicted in Figure 15.1 and in the numerical example. The loss of uncompensated consumer's surplus at the monopoly output as compared to the competitive output is

$$\Delta CS = \int_{p_x^c}^{p_x^*} X_d(p_x)dp_x = \int_2^6 (100 - 10p_x)dp_x \qquad (15.19)$$

$$= [100p_x - 5(p_x)^2]\big|_2^6 = 100(4) - 5(36 - 4) = 240.$$

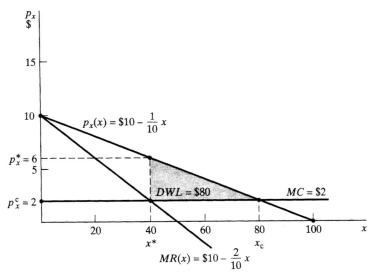

FIGURE 15.5 Deadweight Loss from Monopoly with Constant Cost

---

[4]The following analysis assumes there are no income effects, thus uncompensated and compensated consumer's surplus measures are the same. If there are income effects, the correct measure of welfare loss is in terms of the *compensated* consumer's surplus loss for each consumer, added across consumers, as we showed in Chapter 8.

However, some of that lost consumer's surplus is simply transferred to the monopolist in the form of monopoly profits. Restating (15.11) by substituting p_x^c for $LRMC$,

$$\pi^* = x^*(p_x^* - p_x^c) = 160. \tag{15.20}$$

The rest is lost because output is smaller. This lost surplus is referred to alternately as the **welfare loss from monopoly,** the **excess burden of monopoly,** or the **deadweight loss from monopoly.** With constant marginal cost, the deadweight loss (which is shaded in Figure 15.5) would be

$$\text{deadweight loss from monopoly } (DWL) = \Delta CS - \pi^* \tag{15.21}$$
$$= 240 - 160 = 80.$$

Increasing Marginal Cost   With increasing marginal cost, the concept of deadweight loss is somewhat problematical if the monopolist's costs are such that only one firm can make a positive profit. In that case, we compare the output that would prevail if price equaled marginal cost with the output produced by the monopolist. The output at which price equals marginal cost is still often referred to as the competitive output, even though it is recognized that a competitive industry could not be sustained.

Figure 15.6 illustrates deadweight loss with increasing marginal cost. In this case, some of the shaded welfare loss comes from an implied loss of producer's surplus; the deadweight loss is the loss of consumer's surplus plus the (implied) loss of producer's surplus minus the rectangle $x^*[p_x^* - MC(x^*)]$:

$$DWL = \Delta CS + \Delta PS - x^*[p_x^* - MC(x^*)]. \tag{15.22}$$

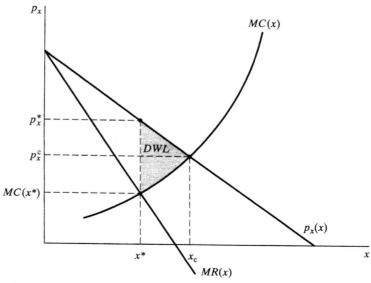

FIGURE 15.6   Deadweight Loss from Monopoly with Increasing Marginal Cost

Estimates of Deadweight Loss for the U.S. Economy The actual size of the dead-weight loss from monopoly in the U.S. economy is a matter of considerable controversy among professional economists. In a 1954 article, Harberger[5] estimated the welfare loss to be very small, only 0.1% of national income. He assumed, however, that all monopolies produce with constant marginal cost and that the elasticity of demand is unity. With constant marginal cost, there is no implied loss of producer's surplus. Moreover, assuming unitary elasticity of demand violates the observation we have already made that a profit-maximizing monopolist always produces on the elastic portion of its demand curve. Since the publication of Harberger's article, others have reestimated the loss using different assumptions about demand and cost and have come up with estimates ranging from 0.5% to over 5% of national income.[6]

Despite the intuitive appeal of this welfare measure, however, it should be clear from our discussion of uncompensated consumer's surplus in Section 8.10 that there are problems with using uncompensated consumer's surplus as an indicator of consumer welfare loss when there are income effects. To be correct, the consumer's surplus loss should be calculated for each consumer using his or her *compensated* demand curve, and then the totals should be added across consumers. In situations where there are no income effects, this measure coincides with the (uncompensated) deadweight loss developed above.

Monopoly in a General Equilibrium Analysis The existence of a welfare loss from monopoly implies that the monopoly output is inefficient. While this inefficiency may be analyzed from a partial equilibrium perspective (deadweight loss is a partial equilibrium concept, for example), it is perhaps best understood from a general equilibrium perspective.

With general equilibrium analysis, we notice some other effects that were not captured in the previous analysis. For one thing, the owners of a monopoly earn economic profits in the long run. This changes the distribution of purchasing power in the economy relative to a general competitive equilibrium. The partial equilibrium analysis outlined above assumes that the demand curve for the monopolized good is not affected by the presence or absence of monopoly power. This would not be true, however, if the owners of the monopoly demand more or less of the monopolized good relative to the demand at a general competitive equilibrium. The demand for other goods is affected by both the changes in relative prices and the change in the distribution of income.

To begin a general equilibrium analysis, we should note that the effect of monopoly is to induce consumers to consume less of the monopolized good than they would have consumed at a general competitive equilibrium and to pay a higher relative price for it. If all other markets are competitive, the resources not employed by the monopolist will be employed in producing other goods, and the economy will be moved to a

---

[5]A. C. Harberger, "Monopoly and Resource Allocation," *American Economic Review,* Papers and Proceedings 54(1954):77–87.

[6]See, for example, D. R. Kamerschen, "An Estimation of the 'Welfare Losses' from Monopoly in the American Economy," *Western Economic Journal* 4(1966):221–236; and D. A. Worcester, Jr., "New Estimates of the Welfare Loss to Monopoly, United States: 1956–1969," *Southern Economic Journal* 40(1973):234–245.

different point on the production possibilities frontier where less of the monopolized good and more of other goods are produced. Thus, from a general equilibrium perspective, *production* will be efficient, even if there is some monopoly, as long as other goods are produced competitively and inputs are competitively priced.

Even though production will be efficient, however, the resulting distribution of output will not be Pareto optimal. That happens because the monopolist changes the price ratio relative to a general competitive equilibrium price ratio. Assuming that consumer tastes have not changed and that consumers continue to purchase combinations of goods such that their marginal rates of substitution are equal to the market price ratio, those marginal rates of substitution will no longer be equal to the marginal rate of transformation at the general competitive equilibrium. In fact, if the output mix is forced away from the general competitive equilibrium, marginal rates of substitution will not be equal to the marginal rate of transformation at all. This will be true even if the output mix with monopoly is on the production possibilities frontier. This point is illustrated in Figure 15.7, assuming a single consumer in the economy for simplicity. The general competitive equilibrium is at (X^*, Y^*), where the consumer's indifference curve is tangent to the production possibilities frontier. If good X is produced by a monopoly and good Y is produced competitively, the monopolist restricts output and raises the price of good X. Resources are made available for the production of good Y, which is now relatively less expensive. With the decline in the relative price of Y, the

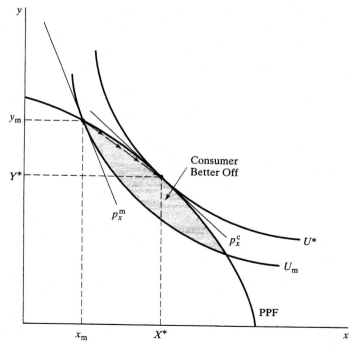

FIGURE 15.7   General Equilibrium Inefficiency with Monopoly

consumer purchases the increased production of Y and the economy remains on its production possibilities frontier.

Despite the continued efficiency in production, however, the consumer is no longer able to attain the maximum indifference curve U^*. The consumer still maximizes utility over the budget constraint, implying that his or her marginal rate of substitution is equal to the monopoly price ratio, but the tangency between the indifference curve and the budget line is no longer also a tangency between the indifference curve and the production possibilities frontier. At the monopoly output mix (x_m, y_m), the consumer would always be better off if the output mix would move back in the direction of (X^*, Y^*). The inefficiency associated with the monopoly output is represented by the possibility of moving the consumer to a higher indifference curve.

15.4   PRICE DISCRIMINATION

Up until now, we have assumed that a monopolist will charge the same price to every customer. But if demand elasticities in separate markets differ, a monopolist can sometimes raise monopoly profits by charging different prices in those different markets. This practice is called **price discrimination** when it is unrelated to differences in the cost of selling in the different markets, and it is effective only if the monopolist can *prevent resale of the lower priced units to the people who would have purchased the higher priced units.*

Actual Examples of Price Discrimination   Before health insurance became almost universal, doctors who knew their patients' incomes used price discrimination.[7] Since only a doctor can legally dispense medical advice and prescribe drugs, and since operations and tests can only be performed on one person at a time by hospitals and laboratories, one group of patients cannot "resell" most medical services to another. Doctors typically charged different fees to different income groups: indigent patients received small amounts of virtually free care, and wealthy patients paid the most. In fact, any kind of service that only a trained person can dispense can be priced that way.

Other examples of price discrimination include markets that are separated by some distance and markets where distinctions among customers can be made. Movie theaters, buses, trains, airplanes, amusement parks, and even some restaurants charge children, students, and elderly people less than they do working-age adults. In each case, the favored group must present proof of age or student status and the service provided cannot easily be transferred to another consumer. Clearance sales distinguish between customers who are willing to wait until next season and those who must have the latest fashion. Season ticket and quantity discounts distinguish between customers who are willing to buy large quantities and those who only buy a few units at a time. In

---

[7]R. A. Kessel, "Price Discrimination in Medicine," *Journal of Law and Economics* 1(1958):20–53.

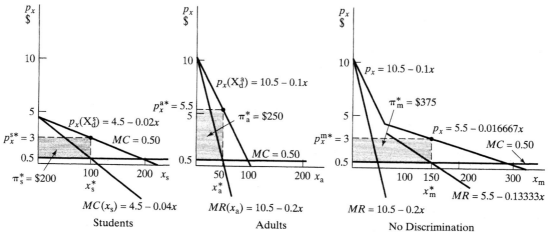

FIGURE 15.8   Price Discrimination with Two Distinct Demand Curves

each of these examples, different prices are charged even though there may be little or no difference in the cost of providing the service to the different groups of people.[8]

A Numerical Example   Figure 15.8 and a numerical example illustrate a simple case of price discrimination when there are two groups of consumers with distinct demand curves for a particular good (say tickets at the local movie theater). The left graph represents a group of consumers whose maximum price is relatively low and whose elasticity of demand is relatively high (for example, students).

$$X_d^s = 225 - 50p_x, \quad 0 \le p_x \le 4.50 \tag{15.23}$$

Solving for p_x from (15.23), the inverse demand function for students is

$$p_x(X_d^s) = 4.5 - 0.02x. \tag{15.24}$$

The middle graph represents a group of consumers whose maximum price is relatively high and whose elasticity of demand is relatively low (for example, adults).

$$X_d^a = 105 - 10p_x, \quad 0 \le p_x \le 10.50 \tag{15.25}$$

Solving for p_x from (15.25), the inverse demand function for adults is

$$p_x(X_d^a) = 10.5 - 0.1x. \tag{15.26}$$

---

[8]Typically, the firms producing the services used in these examples are not monopolies in the sense of only one seller in the market. On the other hand, since each either produces a unique product or has little competition, they are not price takers either. Rather, each of these kinds of firms has some individual downward-sloping demand curve that is not the entire industry demand curve. We will discuss such "imperfectly competitive" markets in Section 16.7. For now, we need only note that we can view such firms as having some *monopoly power* by virtue of having downward-sloping demand curves. And if they can accurately determine their individual demand curves, they can make pricing and output decisions that resemble monopoly decisions over those individual demand curves. In particular, they can practice price discrimination.

The right graph adds (15.23) and (15.25) to form one market demand curve (that is, for movie tickets).

$$X_d^m = X_d^a + X_d^s = 330 - 60p_x, \quad 0 \leq p_x < 4.50 \qquad (15.27)$$

Solving (15.27) for p_x, the inverse demand function for tickets at a single price less than \$4.50 is

$$p_x = 5.5 - 0.0166667x \qquad (15.28)$$

$$X_d^m = X_d^a = 105 - 10p_x, \quad 4.50 \leq p_x < 10.50 \Rightarrow p_x = 10.5 - 0.1x. \qquad (15.29)$$

The marginal cost is the same in both markets (\$0.50 per theater-goer for cleanup).

If the theater owner could practice price discrimination, the students would be charged p_x^{s*} and the adults p_x^{a*}; $x_s^* + x_a^*$ tickets would sell for a profit of $\pi_s^* + \pi_a^*$. To find p_x^{s*}, we set up the profit function for selling to students:

$$\pi_s = (4.5 - 0.02x)x - 0.5x = 4x - 0.02x^2. \qquad (15.30)$$

The first-order condition is

$$\frac{d\pi_s}{dx} = 4 - 0.04x = 0 \quad \Rightarrow \quad x_s^* = 100. \qquad (15.31)$$

Substituting (15.31) in (15.24),

$$p_x^{s*} = 4.5 - 0.02(100) = \$2.50. \qquad (15.32)$$

Substituting (15.31) in (15.30),

$$\pi_s^* = 4(100) - 0.02(100)^2 = \$200. \qquad (15.33)$$

The profit function for selling to adults is

$$\pi_a = (10.5 - 0.1x)x - 0.5x = 10x - 0.1x^2. \qquad (15.34)$$

The first-order condition is

$$\frac{d\pi_a}{dx} = 10 - 0.2x \quad \Rightarrow \quad x_a^* = 50. \qquad (15.35)$$

Substituting (15.35) in (15.26),

$$p_x^{a*} = 10.5 - 0.1(50) = \$5.50. \qquad (15.36)$$

Substituting (15.35) in (15.34),

$$\pi_a^* = 10(50) - 0.1(50)^2 = \$250 \qquad (15.37)$$

$$x_s^* + x_a^* = 100 + 50 = 150 \qquad (15.38)$$

$$\pi_s^* + \pi_a^* = \$200 + \$250 = \$450. \qquad (15.39)$$

Equations 15.31, 15.35, 15.38, and 15.39 show that with price discrimination, the theater owner charges students \$2.50 and adults \$5.50, sells 150 tickets a night, and makes a profit of $450. These prices, numbers of tickets, and profits are indicated in Figure 15.8.

On the other hand, if the theater owner could not prevent resale between students and adults, all movie goers would have to be charged the same price (p_x^{m*} in the right graph). That would imply selling x_m^* tickets and making a profit of π_m^*, which would be less than the sum of the individual market profits. To find that price, we first find a profit-maximizing price-output combination along the joint demand curve for prices less than $4.50 and then compare the profit earned at that price to the profit earned if all tickets were $5.50 and only adults went to the movies. If the theater owner can earn more profits by selling to both students and adults at less than $4.50, the owner will do so. Otherwise, the owner will charge $5.50, earn $250 in profits, and sell only to adults. From equation (15.28), $p_x(X_d^m) = 5.5 - 0.0166667x$, for $0 \le p_x < 4.50$. This implies a profit at one price less than $4.50 of

$$\pi_m = (5.5 - 0.0166667x)x - .5x = 5x - 0.0166667x^2. \tag{15.40}$$

The first-order condition is

$$\frac{d\pi}{dx} = 5 - 0.033333x = 0 \Rightarrow x_m^* = 150. \tag{15.41}$$

Substituting (15.41) in (15.28),

$$p_x^{m*} = 5.5 - 0.0166667(150) = \$3. \tag{15.42}$$

Substituting (15.41) in (15.40),

$$\pi_m^* = 5(150) - 0.0166667(150)^2 = \$375 > \$250. \tag{15.43}$$

Equations 15.42 and 15.43 show that if one price must be charged, the theater owner makes higher profits by charging $3 and selling to both students and adults than by charging $5.50 and selling only to adults. However, comparing (15.39) and (15.43), if one price must be charged, the owner makes lower profits than if students were charged $2.50 and adults $5.50 ($450 with price discrimination, as compared to $375 without).[9]

Multipart Tariffs   If a monopolist charges a lower price to consumers who are willing to buy larger quantities of a good, we refer to the pricing policy as a **multipart tariff** or a **declining block tariff.** In other words, the price declines as larger and larger quantities are purchased. Figure 15.9 illustrates the effect of using a declining block tariff as compared to charging one price, assuming there are no income effects. If the monopolist charges one price, it chooses p_x^*, produces x^*, and makes profits equal to the lightly shaded area. With a four-part declining tariff, profits are higher on the first blocks of

---

[9]Notice that the theater owner sells 150 tickets whether or not price discrimination is practiced. It turns out that if a monopolist with a linear demand curve and constant marginal cost sells in both markets, both with and without price discrimination, it is always the case that price discrimination with two different groups of consumers does not increase output. Application 8, at the end of the chapter, asks you to show that this is true.

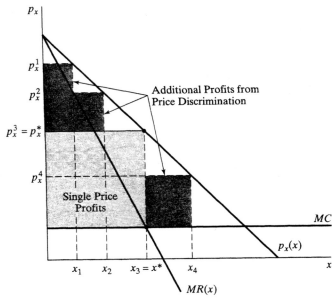

FIGURE 15.9   Price Discrimination with a Four-part Tariff

units, which are priced at p_x^1 and p_x^2, and more units are sold. In this example with no income effects, the monopolist makes higher profits (darkly shaded area) by price discrimination.[10]

Perfect Price Discrimination   Figures 15.8 and 15.9 illustrate price discrimination with discrete groups of consumers. Now, suppose that a monopolist could segment the market perfectly and charge a different price for each consumer for each unit purchased (**perfect price discrimination**). While this is a purely hypothetical example, since a monopolist would neither have enough information to determine the appropriate prices nor be able to perfectly prevent resale, it provides useful insight into the costs and benefits of price discrimination.

Assuming no income effects once again, the monopolist practicing perfect price discrimination charges each consumer the highest possible price for the first unit, the next highest price for the next unit, and so on. The monopolist will continue to produce until the marginal revenue obtained from selling the last unit is just equal to the marginal cost of producing it. Moreover, since the marginal revenue from each successive unit is equal to the price received for that unit, the monopolist will continue to expand output until the price of the last unit is just equal to marginal cost. Total monopoly profits will then be equal to consumer's plus producer's surplus at the out-

---

[10]If there are income effects, paying a higher price for the first few units reduces consumer income and causes the demand curve on subsequent units to shift. The monopolist will use such a pricing scheme if the additional profits it can get on the first blocks and on the additional units produced exceed the loss in profits attributed to the income effect of charging more for the first blocks.

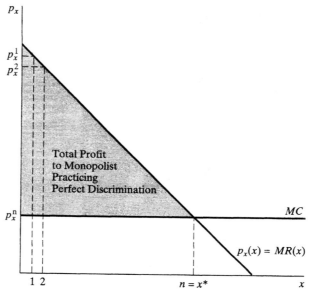

FIGURE 15.10 **Perfect Price Discrimination with Constant Marginal Cost**

put that equates marginal cost and price along the demand curve (the implied competitive output).[11]

Figure 15.10 illustrates perfect price discrimination for an individual consumer, assuming constant marginal cost for the firm and no income effects. The consumer pays p_x^1 for the first unit, p_x^2 for the second unit, and so on. The monopolist continues selling to the consumer until the lowest price (p_x^n) exactly equals marginal cost. For each of these units, the price the monopolist receives is at least as much as it costs to produce one more unit of the good, so the monopolist increases its profits by producing that extra unit.

In other words, to the monopolist practicing perfect price discrimination, price is equal to marginal revenue, just as in the case of perfect competition. However, with perfect price discrimination, that price is different for each unit, whereas with perfect competition, that price is always equal to the market equilibrium price. As long as marginal revenue is greater than marginal cost, the monopolist using perfect discrimination continues to expand. After the nth unit, however, the marginal revenue the monopolist can get becomes less than the marginal cost of producing it. Thus, the monopolist produces exactly n units, since it would lose money at the margin by adding

---

[11]As in the example of the four-part tariff illustrated in Figure 15.9, if there are income effects, the monopolist will not be able to sell all the units along the uncompensated demand curve. That is because the consumer's income falls as he or she pays higher than competitive prices for each successive unit purchased. This causes the demand curve with price discrimination to be different from the demand curve without price discrimination.

that extra unit. Moreover, at *n* units, each charged a different price, the monopolist gets the entire consumer's surplus as profits.[12]

Welfare Effects of Perfect Price Discrimination   The effect of perfect price discrimination on consumer welfare is negative. If the monopolist were to charge one price, there would still be some consumer's surplus. Perfect price discrimination transfers all the consumer's and producer's surplus to the monopolist, making consumers actually *worse off* than they would be at the monopoly price. But, by appropriating all the consumer's and producer's surplus in the form of monopoly profits, the monopolist using perfect discrimination expands output until the deadweight loss from monopoly has been eliminated and the competitive output is produced. Since the competitive output is Pareto optimal, the trade-off is Pareto optimality at the expense of consumer welfare.

Moreover, since all the consumer's surplus has been transferred to the monopolist, the entire *structure* of demand in the economy changes at the same time. In particular, more of the goods preferred by the owners of the monopoly practicing perfect discrimination will be produced than at a general competitive equilibrium. The resulting allocation will be Pareto optimal in the sense that no individual could be made better off without hurting someone else, but it will not be the same allocation as would be observed if all markets were perfectly competitive.

15.5   PEAK-LOAD PRICING

In the above discussions of the different kinds of price discrimination, the unifying theme was that the monopolist would segment the market into different groups of consumers with different demand characteristics or into geographically separated markets. Sometimes, however, a monopolist's markets may be different across time rather than across space or different groups of consumers. During some time periods (called *peak-demand periods*), demand is relatively high, while in others (*off-peak-demand periods*), it is relatively low. This situation implies a special kind of pricing decision, called **peak-load pricing,** since the monopolist must hire fixed inputs sufficient to accommodate both peak and off-peak demand. In this case, the problem is to decide how much fixed input to hire and what price to charge during each time period.

An Example   To illustrate how the monopolist solves the peak-load pricing problem, consider the following very simple example. Suppose you are setting up a restaurant, and you know that different groups of people will eat at your restaurant at lunch and dinner. The lunch group will consist only of people who work nearby; the dinner group will consist only of people who live nearby; and there is no overlap between the two groups. In addition, having more space available at the off-peak time will have no effect on the productivity of your staff during the off-peak time.

Your demand curves for lunch (off-peak) and dinner (peak) are given in Figure 15.11, and your costs are as follows. The marginal cost of adding enough space

---

[12]Keep in mind, that with discrete units, the monopolist cannot capture the series of little triangles above each revenue rectangle along the demand curve. In theory, perfect discrimination means that the set of different prices is continuous.

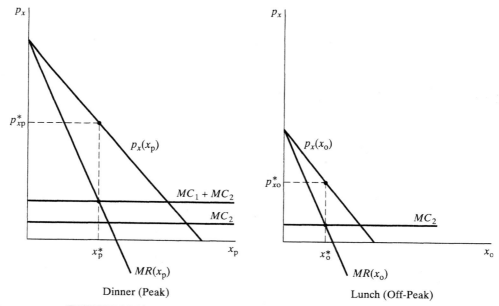

FIGURE 15.11   The Restaurant's Simple Peak-load Pricing Decision

to accommodate another customer is MC_1, and the marginal cost of cooking the food and serving that additional customer is MC_2. During the peak period, the pricing and output decision should be clear: equate marginal revenue and long-run marginal cost ($MC_1 + MC_2$). This implies serving x_p^* customers and charging p_{xp}^* per meal. This is also an implicit decision to hire sufficient fixed inputs to serve x_p^* customers.

During the off-peak hours on the other hand, extra space has no value to you. You can't sell more meals; you already have unused space; and having that space does not improve the marginal product of your variable inputs. You can essentially expand output at zero fixed cost if you want to simply by using more of the space that is already there. Thus, the marginal cost of space is 0 and should not be included in the off-peak pricing decision. The monopolist equates off-peak marginal revenue and the marginal cost of cooking and serving (MC_2) to find the profit-maximizing output and price during the off-peak period (x_o^* and p_{xo}^*). Moreover, there is no implicit decision about how much fixed input to hire since at x_o^* there is still unused space.

Peak-load Pricing with Cross-price Effects   The peak-load pricing decision becomes considerably more complicated if we cannot make the simplifying assumptions we made above. For example, suppose peak and off-peak demands are substitutes for one another, so that raising the peak price increases off-peak demand and lowering the off-peak price reduces peak demand. In that case, finding the right combination of prices involves taking account of the cross elasticities of demand between time periods. Airlines and movie theaters face that problem and so do restaurants that serve some of the same people at lunch and dinner. In addition, suppose having more of the fixed input actually raises the marginal product of the variable inputs during the off-peak period, even though the amount of the fixed input is not optimal for the off-peak period. In that case the marginal value of the fixed input is not 0, although it is likely to be less than the marginal cost of increasing the fixed input. In this more general case, the pricing and capacity decisions involve equating the sum of the marginal revenues affecting each market and the sum of the marginal costs actually incurred in each market.

15.6   NATURAL MONOPOLY AND REGULATION

In the discussions above, we assumed that the monopolist has constant or increasing marginal cost. In many cases, however, a monopoly develops because of increasing returns to scale over the relevant range of output. In that case, one producer can always produce more cheaply than two or more competing with one another. Such a firm is said to have a **natural monopoly.** Historically, the government has tried to regulate the prices charged by natural monopolies. On the other hand, the government has tried to break up monopolies with constant or increasing marginal costs when these monopolies produce nonpatented goods with few substitutes. The argument has been that, if a good has many substitutes, even a monopolist has little power to raise price because demand will be very elastic. If a good has few substitutes, however, demand will be *relatively* inelastic[13] and a monopolist will have considerable power to raise price.

The Problem with Marginal-cost Regulation   Figure 15.12 illustrates the case of a natural monopoly and also illustrates one of the problems encountered in regulation. The firm with increasing returns to scale would produce x^* and charge p_x^* if it were allowed to operate as a profit-maximizing monopoly. The decision usually associated with a competitive market—to equate price and marginal cost—might be considered to be in the public interest. Unfortunately, however, as Figure 15.12 shows, at (p_x^c, x_c) the firm loses money because marginal cost is always less than average cost with increasing returns to scale. Thus, if the monopolist is forced to price at marginal cost, it goes out of business in the long run.

Regulation with Multipart Tariffs   One way to compensate the monopolist and still preserve marginal-cost pricing is to allow the monopolist to practice price discrimination by charging some kind of multipart tariff. For example, each consumer might pay either an entry fee just to purchase any units or a fee in the form of higher prices on the first units. The entry fee or higher prices on the first units would be designed to make up the regulated monopolist's losses so that long-run economic profits would be approximately 0. All purchases at the margin would be at marginal cost.

Multipart tariffs are actually used in the regulation of a number of public services around the country. For example, water usage in southern California is typically priced using a declining block tariff. The first few cubic feet are fairly expensive, but the price per cubic foot declines as usage increases. Electricity prices in Baltimore and other cities

---

[13] A monopolist still produces on the *elastic* portion of the *relatively inelastic* demand curve.

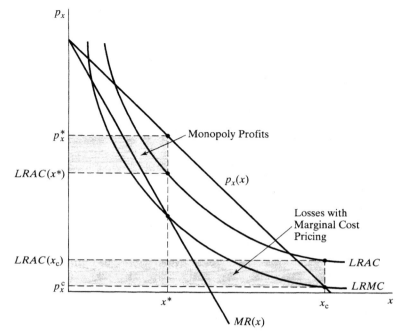

FIGURE 15.12 Regulating a Natural Monopoly

are also regulated so that price per kilowatt hour declines with usage. Both water and electricity rates may also vary by time of day in a regulated form of peak-load pricing.

Sometimes, however, multipart tariffs are used in regulation in a clearly nonoptimal way. For example, before the recent breakup of AT&T, a two-part tariff was allowed in regulated telephone service, but the rates were the reverse of what would be expected from the above analysis. Consumers paid a relatively low flat rate for local service and then more than the marginal cost by the minute for calls out of the immediate area. In other words, local service was priced below the fixed cost of providing it and long distance service was priced above marginal cost. One argument was that low-priced local service protected poor consumers. However, this pricing scheme also opened the way for competing long distance companies like MCI and Sprint to offer lower-priced long distance service at marginal cost. With more competition in telephone service accompanying the breakup of AT&T, two-part tariffs continue. But, local service rates are higher and long distance rates are lower, reflecting the high fixed and low marginal cost of providing telephone service.

Franchise Monopoly Regulation From a partial equilibrium perspective, a scheme that is equivalent to a multipart tariff is to sell the right to be a monopolist in a competitive market, rebate the proceeds of the sale to consumers, and then allow the monopolist to practice perfect price discrimination. Ignoring possible income effects, the *franchise* scheme allows the monopolist to extract all the consumer's surplus and to price the marginal unit at marginal cost. But, in a competitive auction, competition would drive up the price of the franchise right until there were zero economic profits, that is, until the price of the franchise equaled the total monopoly profits with perfect price discrimination. In reality, monopoly cable TV rights are sold to the highest bidder, although communities do not rebate the proceeds (except implicitly through lower taxes) and typically do not allow price discrimination by the winner of the franchise.[14]

A similar scheme is to provide a subsidy to a monopolist equal to the consumer's surplus for whatever single price the monopolist chooses and then to sell the right to be the monopolist in a competitive auction.[15] Since the largest subsidy the monopolist could get is equal to consumer's plus producer's surplus at the implied competitive price and quantity, the monopolist would choose that (optimal) price-quantity combination. And, as in the case of the monopoly franchise practicing perfect discrimination, the competitive auction would simply return the subsidy to the government. Consumers would pay the marginal cost of the last unit for all units, and there would be none of the income effects associated with perfect price discrimination.

While this may seem like a somewhat unconventional scheme, it finds some support in the experimental laboratory. Harrison and McKee[16] gave subjects induced cost schedules, like the sellers' cost schedules in the experimental market described in Section 13.4, and used a computer to simulate buyers with induced demand schedules, like the buyers' redemption schedules in that market. Each monopolist was allowed to choose any price it wanted and the experimenter paid the monopolist a subsidy equal to the consumer's surplus available at that price, given the number of units purchased along the simulated demand curve at that price. There were several subjects in each experiment and several trading periods. Before each trading period, the right to be the monopolist was sold at a sealed-bid auction, in which the highest bidder won the auction but paid only the second highest bid price.[17] Then for that trading period, the winner of the auction was the only subject allowed to participate in the market. The researchers found that after a few periods of learning, the franchise right sold for a

---

[14]Moreover, once a particular cable company is established in a particular community, it tends to perpetuate itself and to renegotiate its contract without having to compete with other bidders. For a discussion of the problems of cable TV and franchise monopoly in general, see Oliver E. Williamson, "Franchise Bidding for Natural Monopolies—in General and With Respect to CATV," *The Bell Journal of Economics* 7(1976):73–104.

[15]This scheme was first proposed by Demsetz, "Why Regulate Utilities," *Journal of Law and Economics* 11(1968):55–65, and formalized by M. Loeb and W. A. Magat, "A Decentralized Method for Utility Regulation," *Journal of Law and Economics* 22(1979):399–404.

[16]G. W. Harrison and M. McKee, "Monopoly Behavior, Decentralized Regulation, and Contestable Markets: An Experimental Evaluation," *The Rand Journal of Economics* 16(1985):51–69.

[17]This kind of auction was first suggested by W. Vickrey, "Counterspeculation, Auctions, and Competitive Sealed Tenders," *Journal of Finance* 16(1961):8–37. It is called a *second-price auction,* and the mechanism has the effect of encouraging all bidders to bid the most they are willing to pay. Since you don't have to pay what you bid, there is nothing to gain by bidding less than your maximum. There is no reason to bid more than your maximum, on the other hand, because you might win and have to pay more than you were really willing to. We say this auction has a *dominant strategy* to tell the truth; that is, you bid the amount you are actually willing to pay. We will discuss this kind of auction and its implication for the design of allocation mechanisms in some detail in Section 21.11.

price almost identical to the optimal subsidy and that subjects set prices at marginal cost and offered the implicit competitive output for sale when they won the franchise right. Thus, while this is a very simple experiment in which the regulator knew the correct consumer's surplus to provide as a subsidy, it does illustrate the power of this mechanism to encourage monopolies to behave in the public interest. The net result was that the monopolists priced at marginal cost and earned zero economic profits.[18]

Rate-of-Return Regulation   Despite the optimality properties of multipart tariffs, with marginal cost pricing of marginal units and with franchise monopolies when firm costs are known, the most common form of regulation involves a form of average cost pricing, even when different prices are allowed for different consumers. Basically, the idea is to determine a pricing scheme that allows the firm to earn enough profits to cover the opportunity cost of having the amount of fixed inputs it has. The regulation scheme is generally referred to as **rate-of-return regulation,** and the approach is to allow the firm to earn profits just large enough to provide an implicit return on capital a little larger than the market rate of return on invested funds. The object is to approximate normal profits, that is, zero *economic* profits.

If one price were charged for all units, the price the regulators would aim for is illustrated in Figure 15.13. If that single price is equal to long-run average cost at the point where the long-run average cost curve crosses the demand curve ($LRAC_s$), the firm makes zero profits and produces as much output (x_s) as it can without making losses.

This average cost regulated price is determined by a review process in which the firm submits cost and demand estimates to a panel of reviewers who also take testimony from consumer advocates. The consumer advocates typically dispute the firm's cost and demand estimates, claiming the regulated firm will actually make larger profits at the firm's proposed price. Since the regulators do not actually know the cost and demand figures, they must try to determine from the adversarial testimony of the firm and the consumer advocates how much to allow the firm to charge. Once a regulated price or price structure (peak-load pricing and multipart tariffs are often included) is agreed upon, it usually stands for several years because the review process is quite expensive. But, if the firm thinks its costs have gone up too much or consumer groups feel they have gone down, either side can request another review before the agreed-upon time has elapsed.

The A-J Effect   In an influential article, Averch and Johnson[19] argued that the effect of regulation that provides a certain implicit return on capital as a rate of return is to encourage the firm to hire more capital than would be cost minimizing in an attempt to

---

[18]The basic problem with the Loeb and Magat scheme is that it presumes the regulator has information that is private to the firm: the firm's cost. The regulator needs that information in order to calculate the appropriate subsidy at each output level. In a world of perfect information, that would present no problem. But, as we show in Section 21.11, if information is not perfect, it may be in the firm's interest to lie about its costs. In that case, a regulatory scheme that provides incentives for firms to reveal their true costs would be more appropriate. That topic is discussed, at least briefly, in Section 21.11.

[19]H. Averch and L. Johnson, "Behavior of the Firm Under Regulatory Constraint," *American Economic Review* 52(1962):1025–69.

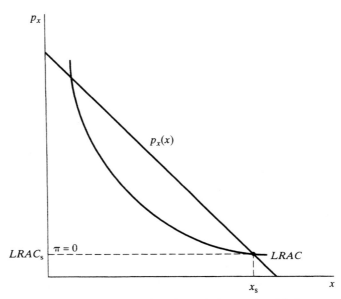

FIGURE 15.13 **Regulating a Natural Monopoly with Average Cost Pricing**

increase its allowed profits. This effect has come to be known as the **A-J effect** in the economics literature.

While Averch and Johnson did not quite get the argument correct, a number of subsequent papers have refined and corrected the argument.[20] The basic (corrected) argument is illustrated in Figure 15.14. The upper graph represents the firm's concave profit function as a function of both capital and labor. If the firm can maximize profits without regulation, it hires K^* units of capital and L^* units of labor and makes π^* in profits.

The regulatory constraint is represented by the plane sK in the upper graph. In effect, the firm is not allowed to earn profits above that plane; but, since the plane has positive slope, the effect of the regulatory constraint is to allow the firm to earn higher profits by hiring more capital. However, the firm cannot simply make higher profits by hiring more capital indefinitely; the profit function itself places a limit on how much capital the firm can profitably hire. The maximum regulated profit (π_s) is obtained at the maximum amount of capital (K_s) consistent with an intersection between the regulatory constraint and the profit surface.

In the lower graph, the circles superimposed on the firm's isoquant map represent level surfaces of the firm's unconstrained profit function for different combinations of capital and labor. The vertical lines represent level surfaces of the firm's allowed (constrained) profits as a function of the amount of capital it hires. Lines further to the right represent higher profits (up to the point that higher profits would be allowed by the firm's unconstrained profit function). Given the wage-rent ratio (w/r),

---

[20]See, for example, W. J. Baumol and A. K. Klevorick, "Input Choices and Rate of Return Regulation: An Overview of the Discussion," *The Bell Journal of Economics* 1(1970):162–190; and A. Takayama, "Behavior of the Firm Under Regulatory Constraint," *American Economic Review* 59(1969):255–260.

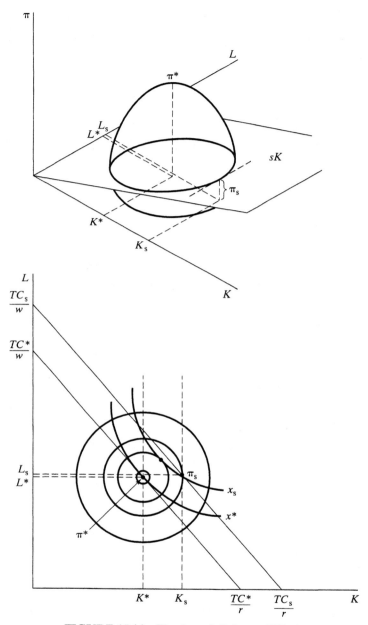

FIGURE 15.14   The Averch-Johnson Effect

the unconstrained firm expands output along its expansion path, maximizing profits by hiring (K^*, L^*) and producing x^* for a profit of π^*, as shown in the top graph. The constrained firm, on the other hand, earns π_s in profits by producing x_s units of output using K_s units of capital. This occurs at the tangency between the π_s level surface of the constrained profit function and the π_s level surface of the unconstrained profit function.

In contrast to the profit-maximizing choice of capital, however, the firm is not minimizing costs at the regulated choice. Instead, the firm is using more capital and less labor than would be cost minimizing for that output level. Alternatively, we could say that the regulation encourages the firm to choose an inefficient, high cost, high capital-labor ratio in order to get more profits under the regulatory constraint. This is illustrated by the fact that the x_s isoquant is not tangent to its respective isocost line at K_s. Instead, the point of tangency occurs at a lower capital-labor ratio.

The A-J effect has sparked considerable controversy among professional economists. For the purposes of understanding the problems associated with rate-of-return regulation, it is important to remember that this regulation gives firms an incentive to distort their capital-labor decisions in favor of combinations that do not minimize costs. For that reason, economists have long argued that some alternative scheme be tried instead.

15.7   REVIEW OF KEY CONCEPTS

Before going on to Chapter 16 on imperfect competition, be sure you understand and can use the following key concepts.

A *monopolist* is a firm that is the single seller of a particular good in a particular market.

The market demand curve is the monopolist's demand curve. This means that a monopolist is *not* a price taker.

A *patent* guarantees a firm the legal right to be the sole producer of a particular product for a period of 17 years.

A monopolist always charges a higher price and produces a lower quantity than a competitive industry would.

A monopolist, which can prevent entry in response to profits, can make profits in the long run.

A monopolist with positive marginal cost always produces on the *elastic* portion of the demand curve. This is because marginal cost equals marginal revenue, and marginal revenue is positive when demand is elastic.

A monopolist does not have a supply curve. It simply chooses the profit-maximizing price-quantity combination for each demand curve and marginal cost curve.

A monopolist making losses will continue to produce in the short run as long as it can cover its short-run variable costs. It will continue to produce in the long run only if it can make at least zero economic profits.

A monopolist hires labor until the wage rate is equal to the marginal revenue product of labor.

But, since marginal revenue is always less than price for a monopolist, the monopolist ends up hiring less labor than would be hired by a competitive industry producing the same product.

When a monopolist restricts output and raises price relative to that of a competitive industry, there is a loss of consumer's and producer's surplus. Some of that loss gets transferred to the monopolist as higher profits, but some gets lost altogether. That lost surplus is called the *deadweight loss from monopoly*.

With constant marginal cost, deadweight loss is equal to the loss of consumer's surplus minus the monopoly profits.

With increasing marginal cost, the deadweight loss is equal to the sum of the loss of consumer's surplus plus the (implied) loss of producer's surplus minus the monopoly output times the quantity, monopoly price minus the marginal cost of producing the monopoly output.

From a general equilibrium perspective, the presence of monopoly transfers resources from the production of monopolistically produced goods to those produced competitively, raises the relative output prices of monopolistically produced goods, and increases the relative incomes of owners of monopolies.

If inputs are priced competitively, an economy remains on its production possibilities frontier despite the presence of monopoly. The effect of the monopoly is to create an inefficiency in the distribution of output. Consumer marginal rates of substitution are not equal to the marginal rate of transformation, and consumers would prefer the output mix at the general competitive equilibrium.

If demand elasticities in separate markets differ, a monopolist may charge different prices in those different markets. This practice is called *price discrimination* when it is unrelated to differences in the cost of selling in the different markets.

Price discrimination can only be profitable if the monopolist can prevent resale by those who purchase at low prices to those who purchase at high prices.

One form of price discrimination involves dividing consumers into different groups who cannot resell to one another and charging a different price to each group. For example, students, children, and the elderly pay lower prices for many services than do working-age adults.

Another form of price discrimination involves charging different prices for different quantities of a good purchased. Such a pricing scheme is called a *multipart tariff* or a *declining block tariff.*

Multipart tariffs can also be used to separate consumers into groups. For example, some consumers will only buy small quantities, while others will buy large quantities at a time.

A monopolist that can charge a different price for every unit sold to every different consumer practices *perfect price discrimination.*

A monopolist may face different demand curves at different times of the day, on different days of the week, or at different times of the year. In that case, it may be profit maximizing to practice *peak-load pricing:* charging different prices at different times.

Part of the peak-load pricing decision involves deciding how much fixed capacity to build for the peak period.

During the off-peak period, the marginal cost of adding capacity is 0 because there is already excess capacity for that demand period. That implies that the off-peak price is generally based only on the marginal operating cost.

If the technology of producing a particular good is characterized by increasing returns to scale over the relevant range of output, we say that one firm producing that product has a *natural monopoly.*

The government historically has tried to regulate the prices charged by natural monopolies.

One problem posed by the regulation of a natural monopoly is that requiring the firm to price at marginal cost results in the firm's losing money.

One solution to the problem of pricing at marginal cost is to allow the natural monopolist to charge an entry fee or higher prices for the first units purchased in order to make up its losses. Marginal units are then priced at marginal cost.

Another possible solution to the problem of pricing at marginal cost is to sell the right to be a subsidized monopolist in a franchise auction.

Most regulation, called *rate-of-return regulation,* involves allowing a regulated firm to earn a return on its invested capital approximately equal to the market rate of return on invested funds.

Rate-of-return regulation encourages firms to use more capital to produce their chosen output levels than would be cost minimizing. This is referred to as the Averch-Johnson effect or the *A-J effect.*

15.8 QUESTIONS FOR DISCUSSION

1. The maintenance of a monopoly requires that a firm prevent the entry of potential competitors. In addition to acquiring a patent on a product, what strategies might a firm use to prevent entry?

2. One theory of regulation hypothesizes that regulation actually creates monopolies instead of controlling them. The idea is that one way for a group of competitors to act as a monopolist is to become regulated and then to use the regulatory process to earn higher than competitive profits. How would a group of firms go about doing that? Why would regulation be seen as better than competition from the firms' point of view?

3. A similar theory of regulation sees firms as willing to pay some positive amount to acquire monopoly status through regulation.

This is referred to as a form of **rent seeking.** How much would a rent-seeking firm be willing to pay for that privilege? Explain.

4. When the airlines were regulated, they could not compete on price, but they could compete on nonprice differences such as meals, on-time service, leg room, and so on. After deregulation, prices fell dramatically, but so did the quality of certain kinds of services. Explain this change as a consequence of deregulation.

5. Suppose you are the manager of a movie theater and you are trying to decide on a pricing scheme by day of the week, by time of day, and by different groups of consumers. How would you go about setting up your pricing decision problem, and what factors would you have to take into account if you decided to use some form of price discrimination? Would your pricing problem be different if you were the only theater in town compared to the problem if you were in competition with other theaters? How would competition from theaters in nearby towns affect your decisions?

6. It is commonly observed that prices are higher in small towns than in large cities for the same products. It is also generally observed that when a large shopping mall opens up in a large city, the business districts in neighboring small towns lose a substantial amount of business. Explain this scenario in terms of the theory of monopoly developed in this chapter.

15.9   PROBLEMS

Problems 1–12 A monopoly faces the demand curve

$$x = 250 - p_x.$$

It has the production function

$$x = K^{1/2}L^{1/2},$$

and $w = \$1, r = \$4$.

1. If $\overline{K}$, is fixed at 25 units, what is the firm's short-run profit-maximizing price-quantity combination?

2. What is its short-run demand function for labor?

3. How much profit does the firm make in the short run?

4. What is its long-run profit-maximizing price-quantity combination?

5. How much profit does the monopolist make in the long run?

6. How much labor and capital does it hire in the long run?

7. How much output would a competitive industry with that production function produce and what would be the long-run competitive price?

8. How much profit does the competitive industry make in the long run?

9. How much labor and capital would a competitive industry hire in the long run?

10. What is the deadweight loss from having a monopoly in this problem?

11. How much profit would a monopolist practicing perfect price discrimination make if we ignore the possible income effects?

12. How much output would the monopolist practicing perfect price discrimination produce and what would be its lowest price?

Problems 13–16 Suppose a monopolist sold good X in two markets. The demand curve in one market is

$$x_1 = 32 - \tfrac{1}{2}p_x^1.$$

The demand curve in the other market is

$$x_2 = 42 - p_x^2.$$

The marginal cost is $4.

13. What is the profit-maximizing price-quantity combination in each market if the monopolist is able to use price discrimination?

14. How much profit can it make from price discrimination?

15. How much output will it produce and what price will it charge if it cannot use price discrimination?

16. How much profit can it earn without price discrimination?

15.10   LOGICAL AND MATHEMATICAL APPLICATIONS

1. You are advising a group of investors who intend to build a new indoor tennis center. During the prime playing hours (evenings), the demand curve for courts per hour is estimated to be

$$q_e = 30 - p_e.$$

During the daytime hours (when most potential players are at work), demand per hour drops to

$$q_d = 16 - p_d.$$

Assuming that the investment per court works out to $6 per hour, that the center is expected to be full, and that lighting, heating, and maintenance costs work out to $4 per hour at all times, how many courts would you advise the investors to build and what price should be charged for an hour of each type of court time?

2. Suppose a natural monopoly had the cost curves and faced the demand curve as shown in the graph below.

   (a) Indicate what would be an optimal two-part tariff, ignoring possible income effects.

   (b) How much output would be produced if the optimal two-part tariff were used, ignoring income effects?

   (c) What price and output would be produced if average cost price regulation were used?

3. You have been hired to advise a monopolist on its pricing and output policy. An independent market research firm has estimated its elasticity of demand to be -0.5. Would you recommend that the monopolist change its output? If so, in what direction? Explain your answer and illustrate it with appropriate graphs.

4. An author and a publisher are deciding how many copies of the author's book to print and what price to charge per book. The author receives royalties, calculated as a percentage of the *revenues* received from selling books. The publisher wants to maximize profits and must incur positive marginal cost to print books. If the author is trying to maximize his or her royalties, will the author and the publisher agree on the number of copies to print and the price to charge? Explain your answer and illustrate it with appropriate graphs.

5. Suppose a per-unit tax is imposed on a monopolist. Show that if the monopolist has constant or increasing marginal cost, the profit-maximizing quantity decreases and the profit-maximizing price increases by *less* than the amount of the tax.

6. Suppose an industry is characterized by increasing returns to scale. Show that a profit-maximizing monopolist might charge a lower price than would prevail if the industry were forced to be competitive, with each firm earning zero short-run profits.

7. Suppose that a monopolist can sell in both a low-price and a high-price market. The low-price demand curve is

$$X_d^1 = 1000 - 100p_x,$$

and the high-price demand curve is

$$X_d^h = 100 - p_x.$$

Show that the monopolist will sell in the low-price market only if price discrimination can be practiced.

8. Show that a monopolist who faces two different linear demand curves in two different markets, with the same constant marginal cost in each market, sells the same output with and without price discrimination as long as he or she continues to sell in both markets.

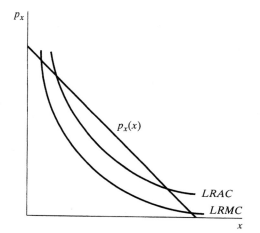

Chapter 16

OLIGOPOLY AND IMPERFECT COMPETITION

16.1 WHAT YOU SHOULD LEARN FROM THIS CHAPTER

Most markets are neither monopolies nor purely competitive but fall somewhere in between. Even a monopolist in the sale of one particular product will often have some competition from producers of substitute products. Thus, a typical market will have more than one seller of the same or very similar products, but not enough to justify the assumption that sellers simply take prices as given. Thus, each firm will have an individual, downward-sloping demand curve and is, therefore, said to have some **monopoly power.**

Oligopoly (few sellers) and **imperfect competition** (more sellers, but not perfect competition) are distinguished from perfect competition and monopoly in that the oligopolistic or imperfectly competitive firm must take account of its rivals' actions in making its own pricing decisions. A perfectly competitive firm does not have to worry about other firms because no one firm can have any effect on market prices, and a monopoly has no rivals to worry about.

Traditionally, oligopoly and imperfect competition have been studied by constructing a series of very specific models for specific types of industries, as extensions of the monopoly and perfect competition models. The more modern approach is to model such firms as choosing "strategies" or playing "games" with one another. This approach is called (appropriately) *game theory.* This chapter will first develop some basic concepts in game theory and then show how some of the standard textbook models of oligopoly and imperfect competition fit into a game-theoretic framework.

We assume in this chapter that each firm has perfect knowledge of all firm costs and demand. Sections 20.6 and 20.7 introduce some new models that allow for uncertainty and differences in information among firms.

Oligopoly and imperfect competition theory is developing rapidly and is constantly changing. This means that what you might learn today could very well not be widely accepted tomorrow. To get the most out of this chapter, you should view it as an introduction to what economists really do with the tools you are learning from this book. They try to use the basic optimization methods to understand what happens in naturally occurring markets. Knowledge about these markets is constantly growing and developing.

16.2   INTERDEPENDENT FIRMS AND NONZERO SUM GAMES

To be successful in a world of interdependent firms, a firm manager has to plan a production strategy that takes account of what other firms producing the same or similar products are doing. In addition, he or she must not only anticipate what the firm's rivals have already planned to do but must also anticipate how they will react to any change in the firm's own production plan. In more abstract terms, a manager needs to plan a strategy that involves both a planned sequence of moves and a set of reactions to moves that the rivals might make. Thus, we can view the manager as *playing a game* with the firm's rivals. This similarity between a manager's strategies and the strategies that might be used in a complicated game such as chess has led economists to study rivalry among interdependent firms by using a branch of mathematics known as **game theory.**[1]

The Payoff Matrix of a Game   Basically, a **game** in economics consists of a set of players (firms or consumers), a set of alternative strategies available to each player, and a set of payoffs (profits or utilities) obtainable as a function of the strategies simultaneously played by all the players. For example, suppose there are two firms (X and Y) and two possible strategies (play A or play B). The **payoff matrix** shown in Figure 16.1 indicates the possible profits going to each firm. In this payoff matrix, if firm X plays A, it receives 10 if Y also plays A and 0 if Y plays B. If firm X plays B, it receives 12 if Y plays A and 1 if Y also plays B. The payoffs to firm Y are exactly symmetric.

X's Possible Strategies

		A	B
	A	X earns 10 Y earns 10	X earns 12 Y earns 0
	B	X earns 0 Y earns 12	X earns 1 Y earns 1

Y's Possible Strategies

FIGURE 16.1   Payoffs in a Two-person Game

---

[1]The classic works in game theory are John von Neumann and Oscar Morgenstern, *Theory of Games and Economic Behavior* (Princeton, N.J.: Princeton University Press, 1944); and R. Duncan Luce and Howard Raiffa, *Games and Decisions* (New York: Wiley, 1957). Guillermo Owen, *Game Theory* (Philadelphia: W. B. Saunders, 1968), provides an easy introduction to the subject. Martin Shubik, *Game Theory in the Social Sciences: Concepts and Solutions* (Cambridge, MA: The MIT Press, 1983), provides a more advanced contemporary treatment.

Game theory is not limited to analyzing firm behavior, either. In many situations, consumers can also be modeled as if they are playing games both with one another and with firms.

Notice that if both firms play A, they can earn 20 between them, as opposed to 12 if one plays A and the other plays B and only 2 if both play B. Thus, if the firms can agree (*cooperate*) and both choose A, they can make more joint profits than with any other individual strategies. We call a game that has higher joint profits if firms cooperate a **nonzero sum game.** Games that have the property that one player's gain is always another player's loss are called **zero sum games.** The oligopoly models discussed in this chapter are by nature nonzero sum games.

Cooperative Games and Cartels   There are two basic theoretical approaches to the study of nonzero sum games. On the one hand, we can model firms as playing a **cooperative game,** where the object is to maximize the joint profits of the group and then distribute them in such a way that no player is made worse off than if he or she did not cooperate with the others. On the other hand, a nonzero sum game can be viewed as a **noncooperative game,** in which the players try to do the best for themselves without cooperation.

Whenever there exists a potential profit-maximizing price-quantity combination for a monopoly, there exists the potential for a cooperative game. By definition, the monopoly choice maximizes the joint profits which all firms could get by cooperating. However, in order to gain those maximum profits as a group, the firms have to agree to produce no more than the monopoly output in total and to charge exactly the monopoly price. When a group of firms tries to cooperate (or **collude**) with one another, we refer to the group as a **cartel.**

In order for a cartel agreement to benefit all members, each member has to make in profits at least as much as it could make if the firms did not cooperate. For example, suppose a perfectly competitive industry were to form a cartel and act as a monopoly. In the long run under competition, each firm makes zero economic profits. Thus, the cartel arrangement would have to guarantee each firm *at least* zero economic profits in the long run. We say that the solution to a cooperative game is in the *core* of the game if the solution maximizes the joint profits and guarantees each firm at least as much as it could get by itself or by cooperating with *any* smaller group among the other firms. (A group of players within a game is called a **coalition.**)

The difference between the total profits all firms can get without cooperating (zero in the case of a competitive industry) and the monopoly profit is the **surplus from cooperation.** Once a group of firms has determined what the joint maximizing output is and the amount of surplus available, they have to decide how to divide that surplus among themselves. Deciding on a division of the surplus is often the most difficult problem a cartel faces, since, of course, each firm would like to have all of it.[2]

One way a cartel might work is for one of the firms to manage the entire operation as a monopolist and then to distribute profit shares to the other participants. This would involve estimating a demand curve for the entire industry and having each firm

---

[2]One proposed "fair division" is called the **Nash bargaining solution,** John F. Nash, "The Bargaining Problem," *Econometrica* 18(1950):155–162. If money can be transferred (as in the case of profits) and participants have identical attitudes towards risk (an idea we develop in Section 19.3), then the Nash bargaining solution is to simply divide the surplus equally.

produce output in such a way that industry-wide marginal revenue equals marginal cost for each firm. This can be seen by setting up the joint-profit problem. Joint profits are

$$\left[p_x\left(\sum_{j=1}^{m} x_j \right) \right]\left(\sum_{j=1}^{m} x_j \right) - \sum_{j=1}^{m} TC_j(x_j). \tag{16.1}$$

The first-order conditions are

$$\frac{\partial \pi}{\partial x_j} = \frac{\partial p_x}{\partial X} X = p_x - MC_j = 0, \quad \text{for all } j, \tag{16.2}$$

where X is the sum of the x_j's. Thus,

$$MR = MC_j, \text{ for all } j. \tag{16.3}$$

Equation 16.3 indicates that, at a joint-profit maximum, each firm will produce an output such that the industry-wide marginal revenue associated with total output is equal to the firm's marginal cost associated with its output. This is in contrast to the individual firm's profit-maximization rule to produce an output such that the individual firm's marginal revenue at the profit-maximizing output is equal to the marginal cost of producing it. The potential difference between these decision rules is spelled out in the next few pages.

From a practical standpoint, most cartels form because a group of competitive firms decides to try to act as a monopolist. This is, for example, how OPEC was formed. This means that each firm starts by producing the competitive output and all firms are selling at the competitive price. As we saw in Section 15.2, the monopoly output is less than the competitive output and the monopoly price is higher. Thus, for a competitive industry to cartelize, each firm must agree to reduce its output enough so that the sum of all firm outputs is just equal to the monopoly output. As all firms reduce their output, market price increases. In order for all firms to agree to produce a reduced quantity, however, each firm will have to be making more profits at the higher price and lower output than it would be making without the cartel. If the firms have different cost structures, ensuring a core allocation of reduced outputs may require that some firms actually transfer profits to other firms.

If firms can observe one another's outputs and if they can enforce their quantity restrictions in the courts, then the cooperative cartel solution can be quite stable. In Germany and Japan, for instance, cartels are legal and many industries are organized as cartels. In the U.S., on the other hand, it is a felony to form a cartel under the Sherman Antitrust Act. Thus, firms that do (illegally) form cartels cannot enforce their agreements in the courts. While OPEC is not illegal, it suffers from the same basic problem: lack of enforcement of quantity agreements.

Cheating   Without contract enforcement, once a cooperative agreement has been made and each firm is assigned a quantity of output, there is a powerful incentive to cheat on the agreement. This is because each firm can gain by expanding output. If a cartel cannot observe each firm's output changes and enforce the agreed upon set of outputs, then all firms have an incentive to cheat. If all firms cheat, however, all firms lose profits. This point is illustrated in Figure 16.2. At (x^*, p_x^*) the entire industry is maximizing joint profits

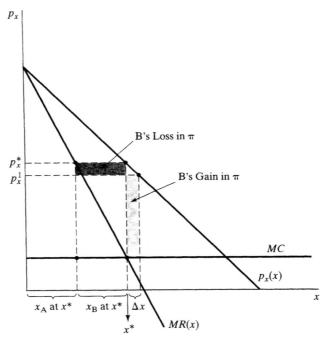

FIGURE 16.2 Profit Gain from Cheating by One Firm

(π^*). Each firm reasons, however, that if it increased output a little (Δx on the graph), its profits would increase even though market price would fall slightly to p_x^1. For example, with two firms producing equal output at the joint maximum, firm B loses the darkly shaded area of profits when it increases output and drives down price, but gains the lightly shaded area of profits. For small increases in output, the gain in B's profits will exceed its loss. Moreover, in general, there will exist an optimal output expansion for B (one that maximizes the increase in profits), assuming A stays at the cartel output.

Figure 16.3 illustrates what happens when both firms increase output by Δx. Total quantity increases by $2\Delta x$ and price falls to p_x^2. Because price has fallen by more than if only B cheats, firm B now loses a larger darkly shaded area and gains a smaller lightly shaded area than in Figure 16.2. In this case, the losses for B are substantially more than the gains.

The points—that both firms have an incentive to cheat on any cooperative agreement and that cheating leads to lower profits for both—can also be illustrated with the following simple numerical example. Suppose the market demand curve is given by

$$p_x = 20 - x. \tag{16.4}$$

Assume that marginal cost is 0 and the firms agree to each produce half the monopoly output and receive half the monopoly profits. To find the monopoly output, we set up the profit function by multiplying (16.4) by x and take the first-order condition.

$$\pi_{\mathrm{m}} = 20x - x^2 \tag{16.5}$$

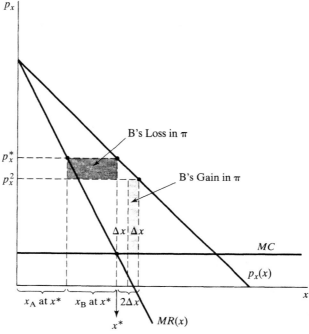

FIGURE 16.3   Profit Loss When Both Firms Cheat

$$\frac{d\pi_m}{dx} = 20 - 2x = 0 \tag{16.6}$$

Thus, solving (16.6), (16.4), and (16.5) for x^*, p_x^*, and π_m^*, respectively, yields

$$x^* = 10, \quad p_x^* = \$10, \quad \text{and} \quad \pi_m^* = \$100. \tag{16.7}$$

Equation 16.7 indicates that if the firms agree to an equal division, each produces 5 units and makes $50 profit at a price of $10.

Now, suppose firm 1 decides to cheat by producing 6 units instead of 5. If firm 2 continues to produce 5, market output will be 11, and the price will fall to $9. At $9 and no cost, firm 1 makes $54 (6 × 9), which is more than $50, and firm 2 makes $45 (5 × 9), which is less than $50. Thus, firm 1 has an incentive to increase output to 6 and firm 2 has exactly the same incentive. However, if they both increase output to 6 units, they both lose: total output increases to 12, market price falls to $8, and each firm makes only $48.

The Prisoner's Dilemma   The cheating problem just outlined is an example of a general problem that occurs whenever firms try to play cooperatively but cannot enforce contracts. The problem is called the **prisoner's dilemma** and the usual scenario goes like this. Suppose two friends are arrested on a minor charge, but the police suspect they are both guilty of a much more serious offense. If they both keep quiet, they will be convicted on the minor charge and serve a short sentence. If they are both convicted on the major charge, they will serve long sentences. The only proof the police have is what they can get out of the prisoners. The police promise each separately that if *he* confesses and his buddy does not, he will get off altogether and his buddy will get the maximum sentence. Put in terms of years, if both keep quiet they get 1 year; if both confess they get 10 years; but if one confesses and the other doesn't, the one who confesses gets 0 and the other gets 15. We can summarize the prisoner's dilemma game with the payoff matrix shown in Figure 16.4. The elements of the matrix represent the prison terms each will receive as a function of the joint strategies played.

To see what each prisoner will do, we find his best response against each of his buddy's possible responses. Take prisoner A, for example. If his buddy doesn't confess, he should confess, because he gets 0 instead of 1. If his buddy confesses, he should still confess, because he gets 10 instead of 15. It is thus a **dominant strategy** for A to confess; it is best against both possible responses by B. B's decision is exactly analogous. The end result is for both to confess and serve 10 years, even though both would have been better off serving only 1 year if neither confessed. We say that the result (confess, confess) is a **strong Nash equilibrium** of the game.[3] It is an equilibrium because neither prisoner can unilaterally improve his position, even though both could improve their profits jointly. It is called a strong equilibrium because the equilibrium strategies are dominant strategies.

The Cartel Problem as a Prisoner's Dilemma   The structure of the cartel game discussed above is analogous. If both firms abide by the cartel agreement, they share the joint maximum profits. If both cheat, they get somewhat lower profits. However, if one firm cheats and the other does not, the cheating firm gets more than its share of the joint profits and the other firm gets less. Indeed, just as in the prisoner's dilemma, it is a dominant strategy to cheat on the cartel agreement. This is illustrated by putting the profits outlined above into the payoff matrix shown in Figure 16.5. Looking first at firm A's decision, if firm B doesn't cheat, firm A gets higher profits by cheating ($54

B's Strategies

		Don't Confess	Confess
Don't Confess		A serves 1 year	A serves 15 years
		B serves 1 year	B gets off (0 yrs)
Confess		A gets off (0 yrs)	A serves 10 years
		B serves 15 years	B serves 10 years

A's Strategies

FIGURE 16.4   The Prisoner's Dilemma

[3]John F. Nash, "Equilibrium Points in *n*-Person Games," *Proceedings of the National Academy of Science U.S.A.* 36(1950):48–49; and "Two-Person Cooperative Games," *Econometrica* 21(1953):128–140.

		Firm B's Strategies	
		Don't Cheat	Cheat
Firm A's Strategies	Don't Cheat	A gets \$50 B gets \$50	A gets \$45 B gets \$54
	Cheat	A gets \$54 B gets \$45	A gets \$48 B gets \$48

FIGURE 16.5 The Cartel as a Prisoner's Dilemma

instead of \$50). Similarly, if firm B does cheat, firm A still gets higher profits by cheating (\$48 instead of \$45). Firm B's decision is identical. Thus, each firm does better by cheating against each possible choice by the other firm. It is a dominant strategy to cheat, and both firms end up with lower profits than if they did not cheat.

16.3 THE COURNOT DUOPOLY MODEL AND EXTENSIONS

Since cartels are illegal in the United States, most U.S. firms can be modeled as playing noncooperative games with one another. There have been numerous attempts at outright collusion, but few have been very successful for very long.[4] Given this bias toward noncooperative play, we devote our attention in the remainder of this chapter to consideration of several important and influential noncooperative models of oligopoly and imperfect competition. We cannot, however, present all the important models in the space available.[5]

You should approach these models as an introduction to the process of building economic models to describe particular markets or circumstances. Each model is based on a particular set of simplifying assumptions, which may or may not be appropriate in any particular market. Where the assumptions are generally met, the models may be accurate predictors of behavior and market outcomes. Where they are not, some other model should be applied. In many cases, an economist needs to construct a new model with its own special set of assumptions to describe the market he or she is studying. When you have finished this chapter, you should have at least an introductory notion of how to set up a model and derive its important characteristics.

The Cournot Model with Linear Demand and Zero Marginal Cost We begin with the simplest nonmonopoly model, the **Cournot duopoly model.** This was first described

---

[4]We discuss *tacit collusion* in the context of repeated games in Section 16.9.

[5]Students interested in more thorough treatments of this subject should consult F. M. Scherer, *Industrial Market Structure and Economic Performance,* 2d ed. (Chicago: Rand McNally, 1980); and Martin Shubik and R. E. Levitan, *Market Structure and Behavior* (Cambridge, MA: Harvard University Press, 1980).

by the French economist-mathematician Augustin Cournot.[6] In this model, we assume there are two firms that produce a homogeneous product. Each firm makes its output decision assuming the other firm's behavior is fixed. And to further simplify this first model, we begin with the assumption of a linear demand curve for the homogeneous good and zero marginal cost. The extension to positive marginal cost follows the initial discussions.

One way of deriving the Cournot model is to start with a monopolist and then allow additional firms to enter. If the demand curve is linear with quantity intercept of a and price intercept of b, the demand function is

$$x = a - \frac{a}{b}p_x. \tag{16.8}$$

With zero marginal cost, a monopolist would maximize profits where marginal revenue is also 0 (or where revenue is maximized, since there are no costs). This is at $(x^*, p_x^*) = ((1/2)a, (1/2)b)$, as illustrated in Figure 16.6.

Now, suppose a second firm assumes the monopolist will produce $(1/2)a$. The entering firm treats the remaining $(1/2)a$ of the demand curve as its demand curve

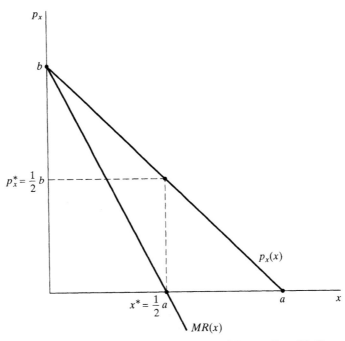

FIGURE 16.6 Profit Maximization by a Monopolist with Zero Marginal Cost

[6]Augustin Cournot (1801–1877), *Researches Into the Mathematical Principles of the Theory of Wealth* (in French, 1838), trans. N. T. Bacon (Homewood, IL: Irwin, 1963).

and behaves as a monopolist on that segment. This is illustrated in Figure 16.7. The original monopolist produces $(1/2)a$, leaving the lower right-hand portion of its demand curve unsatisfied. The entrant treats that lower portion as its residual demand curve. The profit-maximizing output choice along that lower portion is

$$\tfrac{1}{2}\left(a - \tfrac{1}{2}a\right) = \tfrac{1}{4}a.$$

But, if firm 2 is producing $(1/4)a$, firm 1 is no longer a monopolist. Thus, the original $(1/2)a$ output decision is no longer profit maximizing. Following the assumption of the model, firm 1 now treats firm 2's $(1/4)a$ as fixed and assumes the remainder of the demand curve. Given that, firm 1's profit-maximizing choice is

$$\tfrac{1}{2}\left(a - \tfrac{1}{4}a\right) = \tfrac{3}{8}a.$$

This reaction process continues until neither firm has an incentive to change its output decision. Suppose each firm offers $(1/3)a$. If firm 1 offers $(1/3)a$, firm 2 offers

$$\tfrac{1}{2}\left(a - \tfrac{1}{3}a\right) = \tfrac{1}{3}a.$$

Firm 1, in turn, offers

$$\tfrac{1}{2}\left(a - \tfrac{1}{3}a\right) = \tfrac{1}{3}a.$$

Thus, neither firm has an incentive to change. The equilibrium total output is

$$x = \tfrac{1}{3}a + \tfrac{1}{3}a = \tfrac{2}{3}a,$$

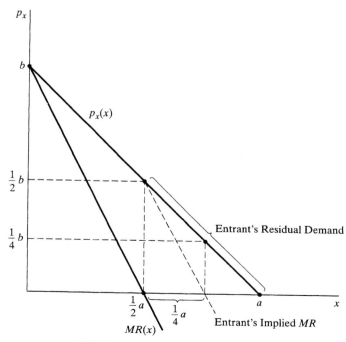

FIGURE 16.7   Entry by a Second Firm

and the equilibrium price is

$$p_x = b - \frac{b}{a}\left(\tfrac{2}{3}a\right) = \tfrac{1}{3}b.$$

This is illustrated in Figure 16.8. The monopolist produces $(1/2)a$ at a price of $(1/2)b$, while the duopoly equilibrium is at an output of $(2/3)a$ and a price of $(1/3)b$.

Reaction Functions and Equilibrium   We can also find the Cournot duopoly equilibrium with a linear demand curve and zero marginal cost by formally deriving how each firm reacts to changes in the output produced by the other firm. To begin this analysis, take the inverse of equation 16.8 and let p_x be a function of x_1 and x_2:

$$p_x = b - \frac{b}{a}(x_1 + x_2). \tag{16.9}$$

Multiplying (16.9) by x_1, firm 1's profits are

$$\pi_1 = \left[b - \frac{b}{a}(x_1 + x_2)\right]x_1. \tag{16.10}$$

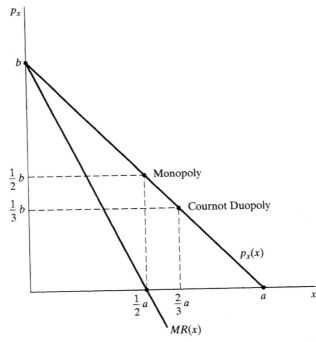

FIGURE 16.8   Comparison of the Monopoly and Duopoly Outputs and Prices

Differentiating (16.10) with respect to x_1 and setting the derivative equal to zero characterizes firm 1's profit-maximizing decision.

$$\frac{d\pi_1}{dx_1} = b - 2\frac{b}{a}x_1 - \frac{b}{a}x_2 = 0 \tag{16.11}$$

Solving (16.11) for x_1,

$$x_1 = \tfrac{1}{2}(a - x_2). \tag{16.12}$$

We refer to (16.12) as firm 1's **reaction function,** which describes how much firm 1 will produce (x_1) as a function of each given output by firm 2 (x_2). By analogy with (16.10), firm 2's profit function is

$$\pi_2 = \left[b - \frac{b}{a}(x_1 + x_2) \right] x_2. \tag{16.13}$$

The first-order condition is

$$\frac{d\pi_2}{dx_2} = b - 2\frac{b}{a}x_2 - \frac{b}{a}x_1 = 0. \tag{16.14}$$

Solving (16.14) for x_2, firm 2's reaction function is

$$x_2 = \tfrac{1}{2}(a - x_1). \tag{16.15}$$

At an equilibrium of this reaction process, neither firm would wish to change its behavior, given the equilibrium output of the other firm. This is referred to as a **weak Nash equilibrium** of the noncooperative game,[7] and the assumption that firms take their rivals' outputs as given is called the **Cournot-Nash** behavioral assumption.

To solve for an equilibrium of this process, we substitute the equation for x_1 (16.12) in the equation for x_2 (16.15):

$$x_2 = \tfrac{1}{2}[a - \tfrac{1}{2}(a - x_2)] = \tfrac{1}{2}a - \tfrac{1}{4}a + \tfrac{1}{4}x_2. \tag{16.16}$$

Solving (16.16) for x_2,

$$x_2 = \tfrac{1}{3}a. \tag{16.17}$$

Substituting (16.17) in (16.12),

$$x_1 = \tfrac{1}{2}\left(a - \tfrac{1}{3}a\right) = \tfrac{1}{3}a. \tag{16.18}$$

This equilibrium is illustrated in Figure 16.9, with x_1 on the horizontal axis and x_2 on the vertical axis. The reaction functions are shown as $x_2(x_1)$ and $x_1^{-1}(x_2)$. The Nash equilibrium $(x_1^e, x_2^e) = ((1/3)a, (1/3)a)$ is at the intersection of the two reaction functions.

---

[7]John F. Nash, "Noncooperative Games," *Annals of Mathematical Economics* 45(1951):286–295. The equilibrium is weak because the strategies are not dominant strategies. They are only appropriate under the assumption that rivals' outputs do not change.

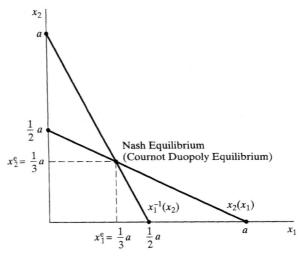

FIGURE 16.9   Reaction Functions and the Nash Equilibrium for a Duopoly

Extension to n Firms   Suppose now that there are three firms and the first two offer $(1/4)a$. The third firm maximizes profits over the rest of the demand curve, offering

$$x_3 = \tfrac{1}{2}\left(a - \tfrac{1}{4}a - \tfrac{1}{4}a\right) = \tfrac{1}{4}a$$

and firms 1 and 2 respond with the same:

$$x_1 = x_2 = \tfrac{1}{2}\left(a - \tfrac{1}{4}a - \tfrac{1}{4}a\right) = \tfrac{1}{4}a.$$

In fact, with n firms, each firm offers

$$x_j = \frac{1}{n+1}\,a. \tag{16.19}$$

Each other firm then offers

$$x_k = \tfrac{1}{2}\left(a - \sum_{j \neq k}\frac{1}{n+1}\,a\right) = \tfrac{1}{2}\,a - \frac{n-1}{2(n+1)}\,a$$

$$= \frac{n+1-n+1}{2(n+1)}\,a = \frac{1}{n+1}\,a,$$

and the respective outputs are in equilibrium. Summing equation 16.19 over j yields a market quantity of

$$X = \sum_{j=1}^{n}\frac{1}{n+1}\,a = \frac{n}{n+1}\,a. \tag{16.20}$$

Substituting (16.20) in (16.9) then yields a price of

$$p_x = b - \frac{b}{a}\left(\frac{n}{n+1}\,a\right) = \frac{1}{n+1}\,b. \tag{16.21}$$

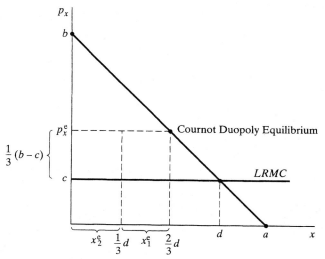

FIGURE 16.10　Cournot Duopoly Equilibrium with Positive Marginal Cost

Now, suppose we allow entry of new firms, as in a perfectly competitive market. To find the limiting quantity and price as entry proceeds, we let the number of firms go to infinity in the expressions for quantity and price:

$$\lim_{n \to \infty} \frac{n}{n + 1} a = a, \quad \lim_{n \to \infty} \frac{1}{n + 1} b = 0. \tag{16.22}$$

Thus, as n goes to infinity, output goes to a and price goes to 0, which is equal to marginal cost (the competitive price). Therefore, the Cournot model with entry becomes the competitive model when the number of entrants goes to infinity.

Extension to the Case of Positive Marginal Cost　The Cournot duopoly model extends directly to the case of positive and constant marginal cost. Figure 16.10 illustrates the more general solution for two firms. If long-run marginal cost is c, then the competitive quantity would be d. We can derive the Cournot equilibrium by treating the horizontal marginal cost as if it were the quantity axis in the zero-marginal-cost model. In that case, d would play the role of the quantity intercept and a duopoly equilibrium would have each firm producing $(1/3)d$ at a price of $c + (1/3)(b - c)$. Generalizing equations 16.19 and 16.21 to the case of positive marginal cost, the Cournot equilibrium would be

$$x_j = \frac{1}{n + 1} d, \quad p_x = c + \frac{1}{n + 1} (b - c). \tag{16.23}$$

The Bertrand Model　The Cournot equilibrium is intuitively appealing for at least two reasons. First, it provides predicted solutions that are between the monopoly and the competitive solutions. And second, it reduces to the competitive model when entry is allowed and the number of firms goes to infinity (equation 16.22), and it reduces to the monopoly model when there is only one firm. Moreover, the equilibrium quantity becomes larger and larger as the number of firms increases. However, its assumptions are quite restrictive. In 1883, Joseph Bertrand[8] wrote a review of Cournot's book in which he criticized the model's basic assumption of what firms do. The Cournot model assumes that firms commit themselves to quantities and then let the market determine the market-clearing price. Bertrand argued that in many cases at least, firms commit themselves to prices and then adjust their rates of production to fit consumer demand at those prices.

This simple change leads to a complete turnaround in the market prediction. If firms produce a homogeneous product, consumers care only about the price in choosing between one firm and another. Given any price above marginal cost charged by one firm in a duopoly, for example, the other firm can increase its profits by lowering its price and taking all the business away from the other firm. Assuming neither firm is capacity constrained, this process continues as long as price is greater than marginal cost. The Nash equilibrium, therefore, is for price to equal marginal cost. At that point, neither firm has an incentive to lower its price because it will make negative profits on the marginal units if it does. Thus, Bertrand argued that the competitive solution is the appropriate equilibrium, even with only two firms.

The correct approach depends on the particular characteristics of each market being studied. Firms that sell from catalogues and then produce flows of output in response to orders from the catalogues are probably better described by the Bertrand model. Since catalogues are expensive to print, prices are probably set for some time. On the other hand, there certainly exist industries in which firms commit themselves to production runs and then sell the output for whatever they can get for it. Seasonal clothing and automobiles are good examples. These industries are probably better described by the Cournot model.

16.4   CONJECTURAL VARIATION

Another problem with the simple Cournot model developed above is that the assumption that firms in a small industry take their rivals' actions as given is unrealistic. In fact, when we derived the Cournot model, we saw that the assumption was incorrect everywhere except at equilibrium. When firm 2 enters, taking firm 1's $(1/2)a$ output as given, firm 1 changes its output in response. Change and response continue until equilibrium is reached. In an actual market, a firm would expect its rivals' behavior to change in response to the firm's output decisions. Thus, as in the game of chess, firm managers can be expected to plan sequences of moves in response to *conjectures* about how their rivals will respond. We refer to a set of such conjectures for all firms as *conjectural variations*.

Reaction Functions with Conjectural Variations   To see how introducing conjectural variation changes the Cournot equilibrium, consider the situation in which firms

---

[8]This review can be found in French in *Journal des Savants,* Sep. 1883.

look one move into the future. Firm 1 makes a conjecture about what firm 2 will do in response to any move firm 1 makes, and firm 2 makes a set of conjectures about firm 1's responses. We can express firm 1's conjectures by the function

$$x_2 = x_2(x_1) \tag{16.24}$$

and firm 2's conjectures by the analogous function

$$x_1 = x_1(x_2). \tag{16.25}$$

With a linear demand curve and constant marginal cost, firm 1's profit function (equation 16.10) can now be rewritten as

$$\pi_1 = \left\{ b - \frac{b}{a} [x_1 + x_2(x_1)] \right\} x_1 - cx_1. \tag{16.26}$$

The first-order condition is

$$\frac{d\pi_1}{dx_1} = b - 2\frac{b}{a}x_1 - \frac{b}{a}x_2 - \frac{b}{a}x_1\frac{dx_2}{dx_1} - c = 0. \tag{16.27}$$

Collecting terms in equation 16.27, firm 1's reaction function with conjectural variation is

$$x_1(x_2) = \frac{ab - bx_2 - ac}{2b + b(dx_2/dx_1)}. \tag{16.28}$$

Firm 2's reaction function with conjectural variation will be symmetric:

$$x_2(x_1) = \frac{ab - bx_1 - ac}{2b + b(dx_1/dx_2)}. \tag{16.29}$$

Cooperative Conjectural Variations   Now, consider three possible assumptions about the firms' conjectural variations. At one end, we might assume that firms will match one another's quantity restrictions and achieve the monopoly solution. This implies a conjectural variation of $+1$ for each firm. Substituting $+1$ for the derivatives in equations 16.28 and 16.29 yields the following reaction functions:

$$x_1(x_2) = \frac{ab - bx_2 - ac}{3b} \tag{16.30}$$

$$x_2(x_1) = \frac{ab - bx_1 - ac}{3b}. \tag{16.31}$$

To show that these reaction functions lead to the monopoly output, we first find the monopoly output by maximizing the monopoly's profit function, assuming $x_1 + x_2 = x_m$:

$$\pi_m = p_x(x_m)x_m - cx_m = \left(b - \frac{b}{a}x_m \right)x_m - cx_m \tag{16.32}$$

$$= (b - c)x_m - \frac{b}{a}(x_m)^2$$

$$\frac{d\pi}{dx_m} = b - c - 2\frac{b}{a}x_m = 0. \tag{16.33}$$

Solving (16.33) for x_m^*,

$$x_m^* = \frac{ab - ac}{2b}. \tag{16.34}$$

Now, we add together the firm reaction functions (equations 16.30 and 16.31) and solve for the equilibrium output:

$$x_1 + x_2 = \frac{ab - bx_2 - ac}{3b} + \frac{ab - bx_1 - ac}{3b} \tag{16.35}$$

$$= \frac{2ab - b(x_1 + x_2) - 2ac}{3b}.$$

Solving (16.35) for the sum of the firm outputs,

$$x_1 + x_2 = \frac{ab - ac}{2b}, \tag{16.36}$$

which is the monopoly output (equation 16.34).

Competitive Conjectural Variations At the other extreme, suppose each firm assumes that if it reduces output by one unit, the other firm will simply increase output by one unit to make up the difference. This is an assumption that each of the derivatives is equal to -1 (a decrease of one unit by one firm implies an increase of one unit by the other firm):

$$\frac{dx_2}{dx_1} = \frac{dx_1}{dx_2} = -1. \tag{16.37}$$

Substituting (16.37) in (16.28) and (16.29) makes the reaction functions

$$x_1(x_2) = \frac{ab - bx_2 - ac}{b} \tag{16.38}$$

$$x_2(x_1) = \frac{ab - bx_1 - ac}{b}. \tag{16.39}$$

We can show now that if the firms have the reaction functions given by equations 16.38 and 16.39, the total output produced by the two firms is equal to the competitive output. To find the competitive output, we let price equal marginal cost (as it would in a competitive industry) and solve equation 16.9 for the total market output:

$$p_x = c = b - \frac{b}{a}(x_1 + x_2). \tag{16.40}$$

Solving (16.40) for $x_1 + x_2$ and collecting terms,

$$x_1 + x_2 = \frac{ab - ac}{b}. \qquad \text{the competitive output} \tag{16.41}$$

Now, to find the total output produced by the firms with conjectural variations of -1, we add (16.38) and (16.39):

$$x_1 + x_2 = \frac{ab - bx_2 - ac}{b} + \frac{ab - bx_1 - ac}{b} \tag{16.42}$$

$$= \frac{2ab - b(x_1 + x_2) - 2ac}{b}.$$

Solving (16.42) for total output,

$$x_1 + x_2 = \frac{ab - ac}{b}, \tag{16.43}$$

which is the competitive output (equation 16.41).

Notice in equations 16.41 and 16.43 that the individual firm outputs are not specified, even though the total output is. This is exactly analogous to long-run equilibrium under competition with constant returns to scale. Every output costs the same per unit in the long run, and, since there are zero profits, the firms do not care how the output is distributed.

Cournot Conjectural Variations   An intermediate assumption about conjectural variations is the Cournot assumption that each firm takes the other's output as given. That is an implicit assumption of zero conjectural variation:

$$\frac{dx_2}{dx_1} = \frac{dx_1}{dx_2} = 0. \tag{16.44}$$

Substituting (16.44) in (16.28) and (16.29) makes the reaction functions

$$x_1(x_2) = \frac{ab - bx_2 - ac}{2b} \tag{16.45}$$

$$x_2(x_1) = \frac{ab - bx_1 - ac}{2b}. \tag{16.46}$$

Adding (16.45) and (16.46) and solving for the equilibrium output,

$$x_1 + x_2 = \frac{ab - bx_2 - ac}{2b} + \frac{ab - bx_1 - ac}{2b} \tag{16.47}$$

$$= \frac{2ab - b(x_1 + x_2) - 2ac}{2b}.$$

Solving (16.47) for $(x_1 + x_2)$,

$$x_1 + x_2 = \frac{2(ab - ac)}{3b}. \tag{16.48}$$

Notice that the output implied by equation 16.48 is 2/3 the competitive output (equation 16.41), as the Cournot model predicts. Thus, this analysis has shown that with conjectural variations from +1 to −1, it is possible to generate perfect collusion, Cournot duopoly, or perfect competition.

16.5   CONSISTENT CONJECTURAL VARIATIONS

The conjectural variations of +1 (perfect collusion), 0 (Cournot duopoly), and −1 (perfect competition) set reasonable bounds on the range of plausible conjectural variations. Perfect collusion generates the highest price and the lowest output, while perfect competition generates the lowest price and the highest output. If firms' conjectural variations lie between +1 and −1, price and total market quantity will fall somewhere in between. Choosing among models based on conjectural variations seems to come down to a judgment of what each firm will reasonably believe of its rivals. That imprecision concerns some economists who are more comfortable looking for the equilibria of complex processes.

An Equilibrium Set of Conjectural Variations   Suppose, instead of guessing about conjectural variations, we look for an equilibrium set of conjectural variations. Such an equilibrium would have the property that if each firm acted on a particular set of conjectural variations, no one firm would have an incentive to change either its behavior or its conjectural variations. This would be like a Nash equilibrium in conjectural variations. We call such an equilibrium a set of *consistent conjectural variations*.

To derive a set of consistent conjectural variations, let

$$k_1 = \frac{dx_2}{dx_1} \text{ and } k_2 = \frac{dx_1}{dx_2}. \qquad (16.49)$$

Substituting for k_1 from (16.49) in (16.28), firm 1's reaction function can now be written as

$$x_1 = \frac{ab - bx_2 - ac}{2b + bk_1}, \qquad (16.50)$$

and k_2 can be found by differentiating (16.50) with respect to x_2:

$$k_2 = \frac{dx_1}{dx_2} = \frac{-b}{2b + bk_1} = -\frac{1}{2 + k_1}. \qquad (16.51)$$

Analogously, we can derive k_1 by differentiating x_2 with respect to x_1:

$$k_1 = -\frac{1}{2 + k_2}. \qquad (16.52)$$

To find the equilibrium, we substitute k_1 (16.52) in the equation for k_2 (16.51):

$$k_2 = -\frac{1}{2 - \dfrac{1}{2 + k_2}} = -\frac{2 + k_2}{3 + 2k_2}. \qquad (16.53)$$

Collecting terms, (16.53) can be rewritten as

$$(k_2)^2 + 2k_2 + 1 = 0. \tag{16.54}$$

Equation (16.54) is a perfect square that can be factored:

$$(k_2 + 1)^2 = 0. \tag{16.55}$$

Thus,

$$k_2 = -1. \tag{16.56}$$

Substituting (16.56) in (16.52),

$$k_1 = -\frac{1}{2 - 1} = -1 = k_2. \quad \text{equation 16.56} \tag{16.57}$$

Equations 16.56 and 16.57 show that the equilibrium (or consistent) conjectural variations are for both firms to assume -1, which leads firms to the competitive solution. This argument suggests the possibility that the behavior of firms that produce a homogeneous product may fit the competitive model even when there are very few firms in the market. Experimental data, which we discuss in Section 16.10, provide some support for that contention. If that were the case, we would say that firms behaved as if the assumptions of the competitive model were satisfied.

16.6   THE STACKELBERG MODEL

Another kind of conjectural variations model is called the **dominant firm model** or the **Stackelberg equilibrium model**.[9] One version of this model can be developed in two different ways. On the one hand, in a duopoly, one firm can act as a leader while the other firm acts as a follower. The follower takes the price set by the leader as given and behaves competitively. The leader sets price by choosing a profit-maximizing quantity over the difference between market demand and the quantity offered by the other firm.[10]

On the other hand, there might be an industry with one large firm that possesses some monopoly power and several small firms that are forced to behave as price takers because they are too small to individually affect the market. Since they must take prices as given, they will behave competitively and will produce where marginal cost is equal to the market price. The dominant firm then sets the price by choosing a profit-maximizing quantity, as outlined in the duopoly dominant firm model, and maximizes profits over the difference between market demand and the sum of the outputs offered

---

[9]H. F. von Stackelberg, *The Theory of the Market Economy* (London: W. Hodge, 1952) (originally published in German in 1934).

[10]An alternative version of the Stackelberg model is analogous to the Bertrand model: the leader firm chooses price instead of quantity. Note that the equilibria in the two possible Stackelberg models are not necessarily the same, any more than the Cournot equilibrium is the same as the Bertrand equilibrium.

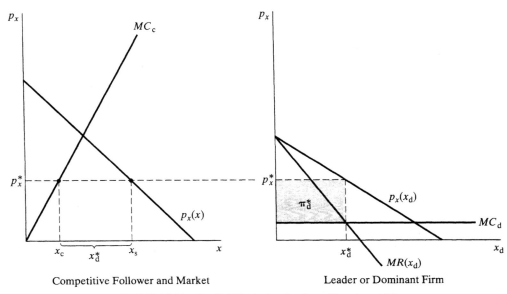

Competitive Follower and Market   **Leader or Dominant Firm**

FIGURE 16.11   Profit Maximization by a Dominant Firm

by the **competitive fringe,** the group of small firms. The resulting equilibrium in both the duopoly and the multifirm case is often called a **Stackelberg equilibrium.**

Figure 16.11 illustrates the dominant firm's decision in a duopoly dominant firm model. The left graph shows industry demand and the follower firm's marginal cost curve. The right graph shows the dominant firm's residual demand curve and profit-maximizing decision. The dominant firm's demand curve is constructed by subtracting the quantity supplied by the follower firm from the total market demand at each price. The dominant firm then maximizes profits by producing the output that equates its marginal cost and residual marginal revenue (at x_d^*) and by charging the profit-maximizing price along its residual demand curve (p_x^*). Returning to the left graph, if the price is p_x^* and the dominant firm produces x_d^*, the competitive follower takes p_x^* as given and produces x_c. Therefore, total industry output at the Stackelberg equilibrium is

$$x_s = x_d^* + x_c$$

and the price is p_x^*. The Stackelberg equilibrium price tends to be higher than the competitive price, even though competitive behavior by one firm makes it lower than either the monopoly or the Cournot-Nash equilibrium price. This happens because the leader firm is able to restrict output somewhat, relative to the competitive output.

16.7   THE MODEL OF MONOPOLISTIC COMPETITION

The models developed above all assume that firms in an industry produce a homogeneous product. That is a reasonable assumption for many products, such as graded lumber and other building materials and graded primary agricultural products. But most firms produce products that are distinguished (or differentiated) in some way from the products produced by other firms. Products may be differentiated by their manufacture: a General Motors car is different from a Ford car, and each car manufacturer produces many different models that compete with one another. Identical products may also become differentiated by the service package offered by the seller: two gas stations may sell the same gas, but you must pump your own at one, while at the other you get your gas pumped for you and your windshield washed at the same time. Most consumer products we purchase on a regular basis also come in many different brands that are only slightly differentiated from one another. A few examples include breakfast cereals, toothpaste, laundry soap, beer, and computer software.

Advertising and U-shaped Long-run Average Cost   The existence of differentiated products and imperfect information of product characteristics among consumers means there is a positive value to both the consumer and the firm for advertising each product's characteristics.[11] The consumer learns about a product's characteristics and is thus better able to choose the set of products that maximizes utility. The firm may sell more units to consumers who might not have known all of a product's characteristics without advertising.[12]

Firms that advertise are likely to have decreasing average costs over some ranges of output in the long run. This is because the same expenditure on advertising can be used to sell a few units of output or many thousands of units. Thus, for a given expenditure on advertising, the average cost of advertising a few units is very high, while the average cost of advertising a large number of units may be quite low.[13]

Whether because of advertising or because of inherent economies of scale in the production function itself, we assume in the model of **monopolistic competition**[14] that a large number of firms produce differentiated products with either increasing returns to scale or U-shaped long-run average costs. Each firm is a monopolist in its own particular product, but demand for each firm's product is relatively elastic, since there are so many potential substitutes among the slightly differentiated products produced by the other firms. Thus, each firm's decision problem can be modeled in a manner similar to the monopolist's problem. Assuming the firm knows or can estimate the demand curve for its particular product, it maximizes profits by choosing the price-quantity combination that equates marginal cost and marginal revenue. This decision is illustrated in Figure 16.12. The firm produces x_j^* and sells it for a price of p_x^*.

---

[11]Notice that at this point, we stray a bit from the assumption of perfect information. If there really were perfect information, consumers would already be informed and there would be no value to advertising. Despite the assumption that information is imperfect, we consider this model in this chapter instead of in Chapter 20 because it is one of the classic models of imperfect competition.

[12]We assume for the purpose of constructing this model that advertising is truthful and informative. False advertising and advertising that tries to associate a product with something unrelated would be modeled differently.

[13]Notice also that this model blurs the distinction between short run and long run. In Chapter 10, we assumed there were no fixed inputs in the long run. With advertising, there is an inherent fixed cost even in the long run, although the firm can avoid those fixed costs by shutting down.

[14]Edward Chamberlin, *The Theory of Monopolistic Competition: A Re-orientation of the Theory of Value* (Cambridge, MA: Harvard University Press, 1933).

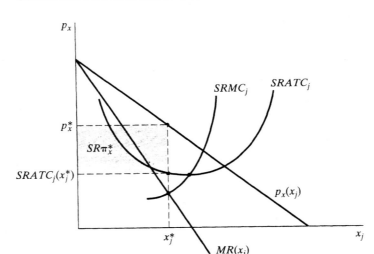

FIGURE 16.12   The Monopolistically Competitive Firm's Short-run Decision Problem

Long-run Equilibrium with Monopolistic Competition   The firm illustrated in Figure 16.12 is making profits. In the monopoly model, we allowed the firm to continue making profits in the long run, assuming the firm has some way of restricting the entry of new firms (for example, patents, geographical isolation, increasing returns to scale). In contrast, in the model of monopolistic competition, we recognize that profits encourage other firms to try to produce competing products. These products need not be identical to those already available to have an effect on existing firms' profits. What we assume is that consumers have preferences over consumption characteristics, which might be more or less satisfied by a variety of differentiated products.[15]

When a new product is introduced, consumers find that it may have some consumption characteristics satisfied by existing firms and (perhaps) some new ones. In any event, to the extent that it is a new-product substitute for other products, introducing it has the effect of changing the demand curves of existing products in two possible ways. Existing demand curves may simply shift back parallel, implying that consumers are willing to buy less of the existing products at each price. In addition, existing demand curves may become more elastic in the relevant range of output, reflecting the increased range of substitutes available. The combination would mean that existing demand curves would shift back and become flatter at the same time. This is illustrated

---

[15]Gary S. Becker, *The Economic Approach to Human Behavior* (Chicago: University of Chicago Press, 1976); and Kelvin Lancaster, *Consumer Demand: A New Approach* (New York: Columbia University Press, 1971). Both authors develop theories of consumer behavior that assume preferences over characteristics rather than over specific goods. They both use indifference maps and utility maximization, just as we did in Section 6.2. They simply derive results about choices, over combinations of consumption characteristics, that maximize utility subject to budget constraints appropriately defined. Becker's model is discussed in some detail in Section 17.5, because it deals with the allocation of time among market work, home work, and consumption (or leisure).

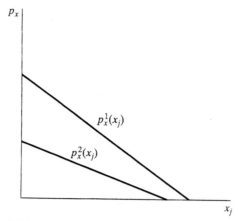

FIGURE 16.13   The Effect of Entry on a Existing Firm Under Monopolistic Competition

in Figure 16.13. Entry of firms producing slightly differentiated products causes the market demand curve for good j to change from $p_x^1(x_j)$ to $p_x^2(x_j)$.

Assuming free entry, firms will continue to enter as long as there are positive economic profits to be earned. As in perfect competition, entry will cease when long-run profits are 0. At that point, there are no longer any potential profits to be earned by producing another similar product. We call this situation a long-run equilibrium in a monopolistically competitive market.

An important difference between perfect competition and monopolistic competition, however, is that under monopolistic competition, price is still higher than marginal cost and higher than minimum long-run average cost, even in long-run equilibrium. This happens because each firm still has a downward-sloping demand curve and thus some monopoly power, even though profits have been eliminated.

The long-run equilibrium under monopolistic competition is illustrated in Figure 16.14. Long-run average cost is tangent to the demand curve (just as at the long-run shutdown point for a monopolist), implying zero economic profits. However, the price (p_x^*) is higher than marginal cost at that output, and the output $(\underline{x}_j^*)$ is less than $\underline{x}_j$, the output that minimizes long-run average cost.

Long-run Equilibrium and Competition   What happens as the number of firms goes to infinity? In the Cournot model, we were able to show quite conclusively that the solution would converge to the competitive solution. In the model of monopolistic competition, the same limiting argument can be made if long-run costs are U-shaped and if individual firm demand curves become more and more elastic as new firms enter. The intuition is that as demand curves become more and more elastic, eventually no individual firm will have any market power: all firms will be forced to be price takers as in a perfectly competitive market. This long-run equilibrium is reviewed in Figure 16.15. Firm j is now a price taker, implying its individual demand curve is now perfectly elastic at one price, the market equilibrium price. Thus, as we saw in Figure 13.7, tangency

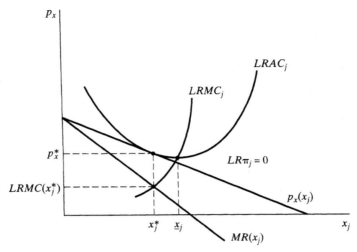

FIGURE 16.14 **Long-run Equilibrium for the Firm Under Monopolistic Competition**

between the demand curve and long-run average cost occurs at $\underline{x}_j$, where price equals marginal cost.[16]

The model of monopolistic competition provides some useful insights into the behavior of markets. On the one hand, we might argue that when long-run equilibrium occurs at a price higher than the long-run competitive price, the difference between price and marginal cost may reflect an implicit long-run price that we pay for

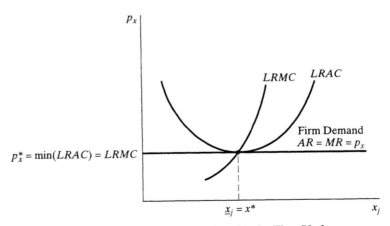

FIGURE 16.15 **Long-run Equilibrium for the Firm Under Monopolistic Competition As Demand Elasticity Goes to Infinity**

---

[16]Notice that this conclusion requires that the firm *not* have increasing returns over the entire relevant range of output. With increasing returns (instead of U-shaped costs), there would be no minimum long-run average cost.

product variety. The argument is that consumers are willing to pay a little extra in the long run to sustain diversity. On the other hand, the results on convergence in the limit illustrate the power of entry and "competition" to eliminate inefficiency, even when each firm is a little monopoly in its own particular product. The imperfectly competitive equilibrium is inefficient in the sense that price does not equal marginal cost and is higher than minimum long-run average cost. However, if products become so similar that they are "almost homogeneous," then market forces drive out even that slight inefficiency.

16.8   THE THEORY OF CONTESTABLE MARKETS

Recently, a new theory of monopoly has carried this efficiency argument one step further. The theory of **contestable markets**[17] argues that the "threat" of entry is often as good as entry itself in forcing firms to behave competitively.

Suppose, for example, that a firm produces a good under decreasing cost so that we might describe it as a natural monopoly, but it does not have large sunk costs which could not be recovered if it shut down. This would mean that another firm could inform customers of its intent to undersell the monopolist, enter quickly (perhaps before the monopolist could respond), charge a lower price, make a quick profit, and then exit, without having to forgo a large sunk cost. In such a situation, the first firm could not afford to charge a price that allowed it to earn positive economic profits. If it did, another firm would enter and take over the market by charging a slightly lower price.

A similar argument can be applied to a market with a few firms already in it, as long as new firms would not have to incur high sunk costs. Existing firms would have to produce so as to earn zero economic profits or an entrant could take over the entire market. This is a natural extension of the Bertrand model to a situation in which entry is only threatened and need not be carried out.

The theory of contestable markets is controversial because it implies that government regulation is unnecessary, even when there is a natural monopoly. This provides a powerful argument for deregulation, which may or may not be justified. In fact, it has already been invoked to justify deregulation in telecommunications, airlines, and trucking.

The problem in evaluating all these models is that crucial assumptions may be violated in actual markets. In the case of the theory of contestable markets, for example, the assumption of negligible sunk costs may be unwarranted in the presence of increasing returns to scale. The question is, do any major industries have such a cost structure? The answer is probably yes, but we must be careful in applying the theory too widely. For example, if scale economies arise from the use of capital that is not specific to the production of any particular good (computers, large office buildings), then a firm could purchase or rent the capital, use it for a short time to enter the contestable market, and then resell it or release it to another firm producing another product. In such a situation, there are virtually no sunk costs, since capital is quickly bought and sold.

---

[17]William J. Baumol, John D. Panzar, and Robert D. Willig, *Contestable Markets and the Theory of Industry Structure* (San Diego: Harcourt, Brace, Jovanovich, 1980).

On the other hand, if scale economies arise from very specific capital (such as an electric generating plant, a large dam constructed by a water company, or a gas pipeline), there may be high sunk costs because there is little or no resale market for the capital if the potential entrant wanted to exit. Some activities, like oil drilling, involve sunk costs that can never be recovered in any markets. In such a situation, the market would not be contestable, because existing firms would know that potential entrants would have a difficult time making profits in a short period of time.

Thus, the value of the model as a policy tool depends on finding industries that conform to the basic contestability assumption. Critics of this theory as a policy tool can point to the public utility examples cited above (electricity, water, and natural gas). These are all examples of natural monopolies that are or have been regulated and that probably should not be deregulated on the basis of contestable-markets arguments alone.

16.9   REPEATED GAMES AND TACIT COLLUSION

At this point we might begin to wonder whether there is any meaning to the term "imperfect competition." Unless cartels are legal, the above theoretical development appears to lead to the conclusion that market forces may drive even a small number of firms to the competitive equilibrium. Recent theoretical research on games that are played repeatedly, however, suggests that the cooperative approach may not be unreasonable, even if firms cannot communicate with one another.[18]

Infinitely Repeated Games The basic repeated-game argument is as follows. Suppose two firms produce a homogeneous product and they expect to continue to produce over an infinite time horizon into the future. We now analyze the infinitely many future plays of the game as one **supergame** and look at a sequence of moves each firm will make contingent on what the other firm does. This is similar to conjectural variations, but it makes more explicit the long-term relationship inherent in the concept of a supergame.

Now, suppose one firm adopts the following long-term strategy for playing the supergame: produce half the joint-profit maximum output each period as long as the other firm does the same thing; if the other firm *once* cheats, produce the competitive output every period for the rest of time. The best the other firm can do in the long run against that strategy is to adopt exactly the same strategy. As long as the other firm produces half the joint profit-maximizing output, it will get half the joint maximum profits every play of the game. But if it cheats once, it gets zero profits for the rest of time. Because of the punishment aspect of this strategy, it is referred to as a **punishment strategy.** Since the game is played infinitely many times, the potential profits from one-time cheating can never outweigh the loss of half the monopoly profits from all future plays of the game. Thus, it is a Nash equilibrium of the supergame for the

---

[18]Mordecai Kurz, "Reconsideration of Duopoly Theory: A Cooperative Perspective," in G. R. Feiwel, ed., *Issues in Contemporary Microeconomics and Welfare* (Albany: State University of New York Press, 1985), pp. 245–281, provides a technical introduction to the subject. Robert Axelrod, *The Evolution of Cooperation* (New York: Basic Books, 1984), provides a very readable, nontechnical introduction.

firms to maximize joint profits on each play of the game, even though they cannot explicitly collude with one another. We say that they engage in **tacit collusion** instead.

There are at least two fundamental problems with the simple repeated-game approach summarized above. First, there are many other Nash equilibria in the supergame, many of which do not predict that firms will tacitly collude. For example, the single-play prisoner's dilemma outcome is also a Nash equilibrium. If one player cheats each play, the best the other player can do is cheat also. With many plausible Nash equilibria with diametrically opposed predictions, can we make any useful predictions on the basis of the theory of repeated games?

Finitely Repeated Games   The second problem with the repeated-game approach is that if the game is only to be played a finite number of times, the cooperative outcome "unravels" from the last play backward. Suppose we take a reverse approach to deciding how to play the supergame: we start at the last play. Since there are no future plays in which to be punished, it is a dominant strategy to defect, as we showed in the development of the single-play prisoner's dilemma. Thus, everyone knows everyone will defect on the last play. But, if everyone defects on the last play, then it is a dominant strategy to defect on the next-to-last play, since there are no future joint profits to protect. Similarly, it is a dominant strategy to defect on the play before that, and so on all the way back to the first play. By *backward induction,* therefore, we conclude that on any play, all future plays will involve everyone else cheating. So, the only thing to do is cheat.

Axelrod[19] took a novel approach to studying finitely repeated prisoner's dilemma games. He solicited computer programs for supergame strategies from a number of famous game theorists and social scientists around the world. He then "played" a computerized round-robin prisoner's dilemma tournament, pitting each program against each other program. The winning program, the one that accumulated the most total points, was a much less draconian punishment strategy than the one described above. The strategy, since nicknamed **tit-for-tat,** involved simply repeating your opponent's current move on your next move. You cooperate on the first move and then if your opponent cooperates, you cooperate. If your opponent defects, you defect.

This result was so astonishing that Axelrod conducted another tournament, only this time he challenged scholars to beat tit-for-tat. It won again and its success prompted Axelrod to develop a nontechnical theory of how cooperation develops because people learn that tit-for-tat maximizes their long-run profits.[20]

16.10   MONOPOLY AND OLIGOPOLY EXPERIMENTS

Even without allowing for uncertainty, the theories we have developed thus far suggest a number of possible market outcomes when there are a small number of firms. This makes the task for both the analyst and the policy maker particularly difficult. If cooperative

---

[19]Axelrod, *The Evolution of Cooperation.*

[20]Formal theories that allow the cooperative tit-for-tat solution as an equilibrium of the *finitely* repeated game depend upon either discounting the future or uncertainty about whether one is playing against a utility-maximizing opponent.

game theory or repeated game theory is correct, then the monopoly solution will often be observed, even when explicit collusion is illegal. In that case, if maintenance of the competitive price is an important political goal, then some government intervention or regulation might be deemed necessary. On the other hand, if the theory of consistent conjectural variations or the Bertrand model predicts behavior correctly, markets will appear to be competitive, even with only a few sellers. If the small-numbers Cournot model is correct, the solution will be in between.

Experimental research sheds some light on this controversy and also raises some further questions. The pioneering experimental work in this area is by Fouraker and Siegel.[21] In their experiments, duopolists were given profit tables showing what profits they would make as a function of own price and competitor's price. The good was "homogeneous" in the sense that if your price was above your competitor's, you lost a great deal. They were then asked to set prices (as in the Bertrand model). The results of this set of experiments were mixed. If subjects did not know one another's profits, the results converged to the competitive solution over time. If they did know one another's profits, some of the groups were able to find and sustain the cooperative solution in the repeated game, but the majority were still at or near the competitive solution. Thus, under certainty (which is the assumption of this chapter), some subjects reached the competitive outcome while others reached the joint maximum. Without information on the other firms' profits, however, all the markets converged to the competitive equilibrium or to a price closer to the competitive equilibrium than to the joint maximum.

Monopoly and Oligopoly in the Double Oral Auction   More recent research on monopoly and oligopoly has explored the role of the trading institution in markets with a small number of sellers. Fouraker and Siegel's experiments had not actually involved a market between buyers and sellers. The demand curve was assumed to be known with certainty and was incorporated into the profit functions. In contrast, Smith[22] placed a monopolist in the double-oral-auction trading institution described in Section 13.4. In this auction, the monopolist would make verbal offers to sell and buyers would make verbal bids. When the monopolist and any individual buyer agreed on a price, there would be a contract for one unit.

In these double-oral-auction markets, some of the monopolists made offers at the monopoly price, but buyers bid low and simply refused to buy at that price. Eventually, the monopolist was forced to reduce its offer price or sell no (or very few) units. In some of these markets, the price actually converged down to the competitive equilibrium price.

---

[21]Laurence E. Fouraker and Sidney Siegel, *Bargaining Behavior* (New York: McGraw-Hill, 1963); and Sidney Siegel and Laurence Fouraker, *Bargaining and Group Decision Making: Experiments in Bilateral Monopoly* (New York: Macmillan, 1960).

[22]Vernon L. Smith, "An Empirical Study of Decentralized Institutions of Monopoly Restraint," in G. Horwich and J. P. Quirk, eds., *Essays in Contemporary Fields of Microeconomics* (W. Lafayette, IN: Purdue University Press, 1981), pp. 83–106.

Isaac and Plott[23] conducted a similar experiment in which they allowed a number of sellers to actively "conspire" about price before each trading period. Trading actually took place under the double oral auction, however. They found that sellers would agree on a joint-maximizing price, but would then be unable to sustain it in the competitive environment of the double oral auction.

Posted Prices   A slight change in the trading institution had rather dramatic results. When selling prices were posted at the beginning of each trading period and sellers could not change those prices during the trading period, it suddenly became easier for both monopolists and larger groups of sellers to maintain higher than competitive prices, even without overt collusion. Several studies[24] found that simply changing from the double oral auction to the posted-price institution allowed sellers to maintain prices somewhat above the competitive equilibrium. The joint maximum was not observed, however. Isaac, Ramey, and Williams[25] used the posted-offer institution in a replication of the monopoly and conspiracy experiments discussed above. While not all their subjects in the monopoly experiments set the monopoly price, those who did were able to maintain it over a number of trading periods. With several subjects conspiring, prices tended to be between the monopoly and the competitive prices. On the other hand, even with posted prices, the threat of entry (as in a contestable market) helped to keep a monopolist's prices well below the theoretical monopoly prediction.[26]

The experimental results summarized above have prompted some economists to suggest some rather different hypotheses about the effects of market structure on market outcomes. Until recently, despite the Bertrand model and consistent conjectural variations, economists had acted on the assumption that if a market were dominated by a few large firms, prices would be higher than the competitive price. They might not be at the monopoly price, because of the prisoner's dilemma, but they might be at the Cournot or Stackelberg equilibrium.

The experimental results suggest that the trading institution may be at least as important as the number of firms in determining whether market prices are closer to the monopoly or the competitive price. The double oral auction seems to promote con-

[23]R. Mark Isaac and Charles R. Plott, "The Opportunity for Conspiracy in Restraint of Trade: An Experimental Study," *Journal of Economic Behavior and Organization* 2(1981):448–459.

[24]Elizabeth Hoffman and Charles R. Plott, "The Effect of Intertemporal Speculation on the Outcomes in Seller Posted Offer Auction Markets," *Quarterly Journal of Economics* 92(1981):223–241; James T. Hong and Charles R. Plott, "Rate Filing Policies for Inland Water Transportation," *Bell Journal of Economics* 13(1982):1–19; Charles R. Plott and Vernon L. Smith, "An Experimental Study of Two Exchange Institutions," *Review of Economic Studies* 45(1978):133–153.

[25]R. Mark Isaac, Valerie Ramey, and Arlington W. Williams, "The Effects of Market Organization on Conspiracies in Restraint of Trade," *Journal of Economic Behavior and Organization* 5(1984):191.

[26]Don L. Coursey, R. Mark Isaac, and Vernon L. Smith, "Natural Monopoly and Contestable Markets," *Journal of Law and Economics* 27(1984):91; and Glenn W. Harrison and Michael McKee, "Monopoly Behavior, Decentralized Regulation, and Contestable Markets: An Experimental Evaluation," *Rand Journal of Economics* 16(1985):51–69.

vergence to the competitive price, even with only one seller.[27] The seller posted-offer institution seems to allow prices to remain above the competitive price, even with a large number of sellers and no opportunity for explicit collusion. Convergence does eventually occur with several sellers and no conspiracy, but it is very slow in comparison to the double oral auction.

The Federal Trade Commission, which investigates markets suspected of being noncompetitive, has become very interested in these experimental results and invited experimentalists to attend a symposium devoted to a variety of recent approaches to antitrust.[28] Currently, the commissioners consider these results in making their recommendations and they have some experimental economists working on the economics research staff. They are continuing to test these conclusions about the effects of trading institutions.

16.11   REVIEW OF KEY CONCEPTS

This completes our introduction to models of oligopoly and imperfect markets when firms know one another's costs and profits and to experimental results on markets with a small number of sellers. Before continuing on to Chapter 17 on labor markets, be sure you understand and can use the following key concepts.

An *oligopoly* is an industry with few sellers (generally more than two).

We say that an industry is characterized by *imperfect competition* if there are many sellers, but the market price and quantity outcomes are not the same as those that would prevail under perfect competition.

We say that a firm has *monopoly power* if it faces a somewhat downward-sloping individual demand curve.

Game theory in economics is the study of strategies by economic rivals and the outcomes of their rivalry, framed in the context of a complicated game of mental skill, such as chess.

A *game* in economics consists of a set of players (firms or consumers), a set of alternative strategies available to each player, and a set of payoffs (profits or utilities) obtainable as a function of the strategies simultaneously played by all the players.

The *payoff matrix* for a game indicates the profits or utilities that each player can earn for each combination of possible plays by each of the other players. In a two-person game with two possible plays, there are four possible payoffs for each player.

We say that economic agents *cooperate* if they all play strategies that lead to outcomes with the highest possible joint payoffs.

Games with payoff structures such that there exist higher joint profits associated with cooperation are called *nonzero sum games*.

Games with payoff structures such that one player can only make higher payoffs at the expense of other players are called *zero sum games*.

In a *cooperative game* model of a nonzero sum game, players are modeled as trying to maximize joint payoffs.

---

[27]Unpublished work by Charles Holt, Anne Villamil, and Loren Weeks, "Market Power in Double Auctions: Convergence to Competitive Equilibrium," University of Virginia, Charlottesville, Virginia, 1984, provides a counterexample to this statement, however. They set up a market supply curve that has the property that, if one particular seller sells one less than his or her competitive output, the market equilibrium price would increase enough to more than compensate him or her (on the units he or she sold at the higher price) for the profit lost on the unit not sold. With this design, they are able to generate market prices above the competitive equilibrium.

[28]Steven C. Salop, ed., *Strategy, Predation, and Antitrust Analysis* (Washington, DC: Federal Trade Commission, Bureau of Economics, Bureau of Competition, 1981).

In a *noncooperative game* model of a nonzero sum game, players are modeled as trying to make the highest individual payoffs without forming contracts with the other players.

Cooperation among firms to restrict output and raise prices is often referred to as *collusion*.

A group of firms that tries to act as a monopolist is called a *cartel*.

The solution to a cooperative game is in the *core* of the game if the solution maximizes the joint profits and guarantees each firm at least as much as it could get by itself or by cooperating with *any* smaller group among the other firms.

A *coalition* is any group of players within a game.

The *surplus from cooperation* is the difference between the total profits all firms can get without cooperating and the monopoly (or joint maximum) profit.

The *Nash bargaining solution* to a cooperative game divides a monetary surplus from cooperation equally among symmetric cooperating players.

Contract enforcement is an important ingredient in any cooperative agreement because individual firms can generally make higher profits than at the joint maximum by cheating on the agreement if all other firms continue to cooperate.

The *prisoner's dilemma* describes a two-person nonzero sum game in which there is a joint-profit maximum, but each player has an individual incentive to *cheat* and play a noncooperative strategy. When both players cheat, they end up with the lowest joint payoff in the game. In the prisoner's dilemma, each player makes more profits by cheating than by cooperating for every possible strategy played by the other player.

A *dominant strategy* is a strategy that is always best, regardless of what the other players play. Cheating is a dominant strategy in the prisoner's dilemma game.

A *Nash equilibrium* of a cooperative game is a set of strategies for each player with the property that no player can unilaterally make a higher payoff by playing another strategy. Some games have more than one Nash equilibrium.

A *strong Nash equilibrium* is a Nash equilibrium in which each player plays a dominant strat-egy. There can only be one strong Nash equilibrium in a particular game.

Cartels often fail because of the prisoner's dilemma: all firms benefit from cooperation, but each has an individual incentive to cheat by expanding output.

A *duopoly* is an industry with exactly two sellers.

In the *Cournot duopoly model,* there are two firms that produce a homogeneous product. Each firm makes its output decision assuming the other firm's behavior is fixed.

A firm's *reaction function* describes how much it will produce as a function of the outputs that its rivals might produce.

At a *weak Nash equilibrium* of a game, players play strategies that are only appropriate if their rivals' strategies do not change.

We say that firms play *Cournot-Nash* strategies if they make output decisions as though their rivals were not going to change their output decisions in response. In other words, they take their rivals' output *as given*.

In a Cournot model with n firms, a linear demand curve, and constant marginal cost, at a Nash equilibrium, each firm produces $1/n$ times the competitive quantity, and the price is equal to marginal cost plus $1/n$ times the difference between the price intercept and marginal cost. With two firms, this means the equilibrium output is $2/3$ the competitive output.

In the limit, as the number of firms goes to infinity, the Cournot equilibrium becomes the competitive equilibrium.

In the duopoly model proposed by Bertrand, firms commit themselves to prices and then adjust rates of production to meet consumer demand at those prices, as with goods sold from a catalogue.

In the *Bertrand model* with homogeneous goods, equilibrium price and quantity are equal to the competitive price and quantity for any number of firms greater than 1.

If firm managers plan a sequence of moves in response to projected responses by their rivals (instead of taking their rivals' outputs as given), we model their rivalry as a model of *conjectural variations*.

If both firms in a duopoly have conjectural variations of +1, implying each firm matches its rival's quantity restrictions, the market output will be the monopoly output. If both have conjectural variations of 0, implying each takes its rival's output as given, the outcome will be the Cournot duopoly. And if each assumes -1, implying its rival will increase output exactly in response to all output restrictions, the equilibrium market quantity will be the competitive quantity.

At a Nash equilibrium in conjectural variations, each firm assumes -1 and the market price and quantity are equal to the competitive price and quantity, regardless of the number of firms.

In the *Stackelberg model,* one firm acts as a *leader* (or *dominant firm*) and one or more firms behave competitively. In a duopoly, the other firm is called the *follower firm.* If there is more than one follower, we refer to the group of (small) follower firms as the *competitive fringe.*

At a *Stackelberg equilibrium* as described in Section 16.6, market price is higher and market quantity is lower than at a competitive equilibrium.

In the model of *monopolistic competition,* firms are assumed to produce differentiated products with increasing returns to scale or U-shaped long-run average costs.

At a long-run equilibrium under monopolistic competition, each firm makes zero profits and produces a quantity such that the demand price for that quantity equals the long-run average cost of producing it.

In general, long-run equilibrium price under monopolistic competition will be higher than marginal cost, and quantity will be less than the long-run competitive equilibrium quantity.

In the limit, if the number of firms goes to infinity, if individual firm demand curves become infinitely elastic, and if each firm has a U-shaped long-run average cost curve, then, the monopolistically competitive equilibrium goes to the competitive equilibrium. This assumes that differences among firm products become sufficiently small as to be unobservable or unimportant to consumers.

The difference between long-run equilibrium price under monopolistic competition and long-run marginal cost can be viewed as the equilibrium value consumers place on having a variety of similar products to choose from.

In the theory of *contestable markets,* monopolies and oligopolies are viewed as being unable to earn positive profits because of the threat of entry from potential rivals. This means that with constant or increasing marginal cost, price and quantity will be the same as the competitive price and quantity. With decreasing marginal cost, price would equal long-run average cost.

The predictions of the theory of contestable markets depend on the assumption that there are not substantial sunk costs to entering an industry. If there are sunk costs, rapid entry and exit in response to short-run profits is costly.

If a game among rivals is repeated over time, all future plays of the game can be analyzed as one *supergame.*

Punishment strategies in supergames often involve cooperating as long as one's rival cooperates and then behaving competitively for the rest of time if one's rival cheats once.

In an infinitely repeated game, if all players commit themselves to punishment strategies, one Nash equilibrium is for all players to cooperate for all infinitely repeated plays.

When firms play cooperative strategies without communicating with one another, we say they engage in *tacit collusion.*

In a finitely repeated prisoner's dilemma game, the only Nash equilibrium is for all players to cheat. This is because the game unravels from the last play backward: once you know everyone will cheat on the last play, there is no benefit to cooperation on the next-to-last play, and so on.

The *tit-for-tat* strategy for playing a two-person repeated game involves always matching your opponent's move on the last play. This strategy generated the highest profits in a round-robin tournament among programmed players of the prisoner's dilemma game.

Experimental results suggest that market institutions are also important in promoting either competition or cooperation. The double oral auction tends to lead to competitive outcomes, while posting of prices by sellers tends to foster more cooperation.

16.12 QUESTIONS FOR DISCUSSION

1. Suppose you are the manager of a supermarket in a medium-sized city. There are already six supermarkets in town and another national chain is opening a store, which will make the total seven. Analyze the effect of this change on your demand, pricing strategy, and profits. Would it be more appropriate to use the Cournot model, the Bertrand model, or the model of monopolistic competition to model this situation? Explain.

2. Make lists of products that might appropriately be modeled by the Cournot model, the Bertrand model, or the model of monopolistic competition and justify your choices. Might any of these industries also be modeled with tacit collusion? Explain.

3. Why do people tip waitresses after they have been served? Should the analysis be different for restaurants you visit often in contrast to those you only visit once?

4. Overexploitation of a resource that is "common property" for a number of firms is a serious problem in such industries as fishing and oil. Analyze the overexploitation problem as a prisoner's dilemma and think of other examples of joint decisions that might be modeled as prisoner's dilemmas.

5. The theory of contestable markets was developed as part of the accumulation of testimony during the AT&T antitrust case and was used to argue against forcing AT&T to be broken up into competing telephone companies. Explain how the theory could be used for that purpose and also why it might not be a compelling argument in this case.

6. Critics of government regulation argue that even if the strict competitive assumptions are not satisfied, it is still appropriate to model most industries as if the competitive assumptions were satisfied. Under what circumstances is this a reasonable approach to analyzing imperfectly competitive markets?

7. Explain the similarity between the Cournot model and the model of monopolistic competition when there is entry and there are many firms in the industry.

16.13 PROBLEMS

Problems 1–6 An industry faces the demand curve

$$x = 250 - p_x,$$

and each firm has a constant marginal cost of $4.

1. Find the Cournot reaction functions for the two firms.

2. What are the Cournot duopoly equilibrium price and quantity?

3. What are the Bertrand duopoly equilibrium price and quantity?

4. What will be the Cournot equilibrium if the number of firms goes to infinity?

5. What is the consistent conjectural variations equilibrium?

6. What is the competitive equilibrium?

16.14 LOGICAL AND MATHEMATICAL APPLICATIONS

1. Consider the following game, which is often referred to as the "battle of the sexes." A couple is deciding what to do on a Saturday night. The husband wants to go to the fights, but the wife wants to go to the opera. Neither particularly likes the other's choice, but prefers going with his or her spouse to going to the preferred choice alone. Set up a payoff matrix that describes this game and analyze the Nash equilibrium. Is it unique? Is it a nonzero sum game? What other joint decisions are analogous to this game?

2. You are the owner of a firm that produces ball bearings and there is one other firm that makes identical ball bearings. You would like to make profits in excess of your opportunity costs, but you find that, no matter how much you produce, your economic profits are

always 0. What should you conclude about the strategy your rival is playing against you? Explain. How might you get the other firm to begin to collude with you without bringing on an antitrust suit?

3. The steel industry consists of U.S. Steel and a number of smaller firms. For many years, every time U.S. Steel changed its price, all the other firms followed within a few days. Some argued this was clear evidence that the steel companies were conspiring to fix prices. Is this necessarily the correct interpretation? What model might account for this observed behavior? Explain and illustrate your answer graphically.

Chapter 17

TIME ALLOCATION, LABOR SUPPLY, AND LABOR MARKETS

17.1 ___ WHAT YOU SHOULD LEARN FROM THIS CHAPTER

This chapter is devoted to an analysis of models of time allocation and labor markets. We begin by extending the consumer model developed in Sections 6.2 and 6.4 to a choice between consumption and leisure. In this simplest time allocation model, consumers have preferences over consumption and leisure and they maximize utility by choosing a combination of purchased goods and leisure, subject to a budget constraint defined by the wage rate, market prices, nonlabor income, and time. Time not consumed as leisure is spent in the labor market, allowing us to derive an individual's supply curve of labor as the result of a utility-maximizing decision. The comparative statics of this simple model provide insight into some interesting features of labor markets.

Once we have constructed a labor supply curve, we can analyze labor markets using the labor demand curves developed in Sections 12.5 and 12.6. A market labor demand curve is derived as the total quantity of labor demanded by all firms at each wage, and a market labor supply curve is derived as the total quantity of labor supplied by all consumers at each wage. In a competitive labor market, a market equilibrium wage rate is determined at the intersection of the market demand and the market supply curves. This market wage is simultaneously the wage parameter in firms' and consumers' competitive decision problems.

There are at least three reasons why a labor market might not be competitive, however. First, one firm might be the only employer of a particular kind of a labor in a particular location. We call a firm that is a single buyer a *monopsonist* and a market with only one buyer a *monopsony*. Second, workers might join together in unions to act as monopoly sellers of their labor. Third, some workers have unique factor endowments which allow them to behave as monopolists in their respective labor markets. Prime examples are performing artists and athletes.

17.2 ___ THE SIMPLE MODEL OF TIME ALLOCATION AND LABOR SUPPLY

In the simplest model of time allocation, we treat leisure time as a consumption good that is "purchased" by spending time not working. A worker, for example, *forgoes* wages in order to consume leisure, and the cost of leisure is the amount of **forgone wages.** Given the ultimate time constraint of 24 hours per day, market wages, and a consumer's nonlabor income, we can construct a budget constraint that defines the consumer's attainable combinations of purchased consumption goods and leisure.

The Time Allocation Budget Line To maintain a two-dimensional example that we can graph, we lump all purchased consumption goods together and give them a price index (p). We now define the following variables and parameters.

$$C = \text{purchased consumption goods}$$
$$p = \text{price index for consumption goods}$$
$$\ell = \text{leisure}$$
$$w = \text{market wage rate}$$
$$I = \text{nonlabor income}$$
$$L = 24 - \ell = \text{labor}$$

The budget constraint stipulates that expenditures on consumption goods cannot exceed labor plus nonlabor income:

$$pC \leq I + w(24 - \ell). \tag{17.1}$$

Figure 17.1 illustrates the budget line. The horizontal axis depicts time, and the vertical axis depicts quantity of consumption goods. The vertical line at 24 from the time axis represents the ultimate time constraint, and the horizontal line at I/p represents the consumption level that the consumer can attain without working; that is, if leisure is 24 hours and the budget equation is satisfied with equality, then $C = I/p$. The intercept along the vertical axis represents the maximum attainable consumption level if zero hours of leisure are consumed; in other words, if leisure is 0 and the budget line

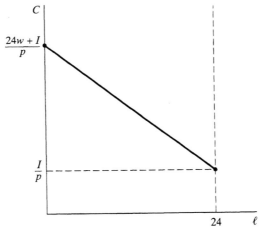

FIGURE 17.1 Time Allocation Budget Line

is satisfied with equality, then $C = (24w + I)/p$. The straight line connecting the vertical axis intercept and the point $(24, I/p)$ depicts all the attainable combinations of consumption goods, which can be purchased by earning income in the labor market, and leisure, which can be "purchased" by not working.

As Figure 17.2 shows, I/p need not be positive. For example, an individual might have more outstanding loans than savings. The interest on the loans would constitute a fixed cost before any consumption goods could be bought. Alimony and child support are other examples. In that case, if the budget equation is satisfied with equality when consumption is 0, leisure can only be $\ell = (24w + I)/w$. The budget line will go from the consumption intercept to the leisure intercept described above. Further leisure is unobtainable because of the prior financial commitments. This budget line is bold in Figure 17.2.

The Utility-maximizing Choice of Consumption and Leisure   Now, if we assume a consumer has preferences over combinations of consumption goods and leisure that satisfy the assumptions of the preference model developed in Section 5.3, we can represent the consumer's choice of a combination of consumption goods and leisure by our standard utility-maximization model. This is illustrated in Figure 17.3, assuming positive nonlabor income. The consumer chooses (C^*, ℓ^*) on the highest indifference curve (U^*), where the slope of the budget line is equal to the slope of the indifference curve. The optimal number of hours worked (L^*) is the difference between the maximum time (24) and ℓ^*: $L^* = 24 - \ell^*$. The equation for the budget line is

$$C = \frac{24w + I}{p} - \frac{w}{p}\ell. \tag{17.2}$$

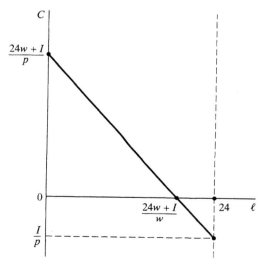

FIGURE 17.2 Time Allocation Budget Line with Negative Nonlabor Income

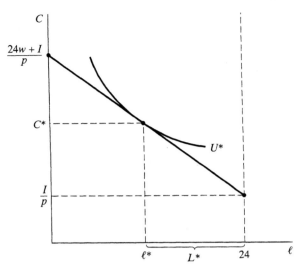

FIGURE 17.3 A Utility-maximizing Choice of Consumption and Leisure

Differentiating (17.2) with respect to ℓ, the slope of the budget line is

$$\frac{dC}{d\ell} = -\frac{w}{p}. \tag{17.3}$$

We refer to the right-hand side of (17.3) as the **relative wage** or the **real wage.** The idea is that this is the "purchasing power" of an hour's work. The tangency condition, therefore, stipulates that the marginal rate of substitution between consumption and leisure will equal the real wage:

$$MRS_{C\ell} = \frac{w}{p}. \tag{17.4}$$

Mathematical Treatment To derive equation 17.4 mathematically, we maximize utility, defined over consumption and leisure, subject to the budget constraint:

$$\max U(C, \ell) \tag{17.5}$$
$$\text{s.t. } pC = w(24 - \ell) + I.$$

The Lagrangian is

$$\mathcal{L} = U(C, \ell) + \lambda[w(24 - \ell) + I - pC]. \tag{17.6}$$

The first-order conditions are

$$\frac{\partial \mathcal{L}}{\partial C} = \frac{\partial U}{\partial C} - \lambda p = 0 \quad \Rightarrow \quad \lambda = \frac{MU_C}{p} \tag{17.7}$$

$$\frac{\partial \mathcal{L}}{\partial \ell} = \frac{\partial U}{\partial \ell} - \lambda w = 0 \quad \Rightarrow \quad \lambda = \frac{MU_\ell}{w} \tag{17.8}$$

$$\frac{\partial \mathcal{L}}{\partial \lambda} = w(24 - \ell) + I - pC. \tag{17.9}$$

Solving for l from equations 17.7 and 17.8,

$$\lambda = \frac{MU_C}{p} = \frac{MC_\ell}{w} \quad \Rightarrow \quad \frac{MU_\ell}{MU_C} = \frac{w}{p}. \tag{17.10}$$

Thus, rewriting (17.10),

$$MRS_{C\ell} = \frac{w}{p}. \qquad \textbf{equation 17.4}$$

Comparative Statics of an Increase in Nonlabor Income   We can now consider the comparative statics effects of changes in nonlabor income and the wage rate on the optimal choices of consumption, leisure, and hours worked. To begin with, changes in nonlabor income act just like pure income effects in the standard utility-maximization model, developed in Sections 6.2 and 6.4. They result in parallel shifts in the budget line. To see this, we rewrite the budget equation (17.2) as

$$C = \frac{24w}{p} + \frac{I}{p} - \frac{w}{p}\ell. \tag{17.11}$$

Thus, the I in (17.11) acts just like a change in the income term (M) in the consumer problem (equations 5.4).

Figure 17.4 illustrates the effect of an increase in nonlabor income. The budget line shifts to the right, parallel, although there is still a time constraint of 24 hours. If both consumption goods and leisure can be represented as normal goods, the parallel shift in the budget line results in an increase in both consumption goods and leisure, and hence a decline in hours worked. Thus, when I increases from I_1 to I_2, consumption and leisure increase from (ℓ_1, C_1) to (ℓ_2, C_2) and labor falls from L_1 to L_2. At some point, however, further increases in nonlabor income would not result in further increases in leisure because of the time constraint. At I_3, for example, the consumer stops working altogether (leisure is 24 hours).[1]

Changes in the Wage Rate: Income and Substitution Effects   Analyzing the effect of an increase in the wage rate is somewhat more complicated. The problem is that there

---

[1] Notice that from this point on, the consumer is at a corner solution. In this case, the 24-hour constraint means that the consumer is not able to further increase leisure if income increases further. Thus, the consumer is not able to attain a combination such that the slope of the indifference curve is equal to the slope of the budget line.

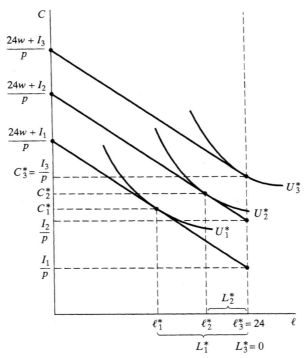

FIGURE 17.4 The Effect of an Increase in Nonlabor Income on the Allocation of Time

is a temptation to equate an increase in wages with an increase in income in the standard consumer model. However, we have already seen that I plays the role of M. The wage rate is actually a *price* in this model, the price of leisure expressed in forgone wages. Thus, changes in the wage rate change the slope of the budget line, and we can identify both income and substitution effects associated with changes in wages.

To complicate things even further, in contrast to the standard model of income and substitution effects developed in Sections 6.7 and 8.5, the income and substitution effects work in opposite directions when leisure is a normal good. This happens because an increase in wages raises the price of leisure, but *increases* the feasible set at the same time.[2] Thus, if leisure is a normal good, an increase in the wage rate reduces the optimal choice of leisure by the substitution effect (consume less of a good whose price has increased), but increases the optimal choice of leisure by the

---

[2]They worked in the same direction on normal goods in the consumption model because an increase in the price of a purchased good increases the price and *decreases* the feasible set.

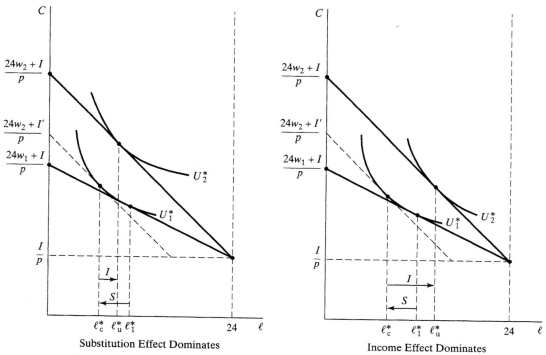

FIGURE 17.5 Increasing and Decreasing Leisure with an Increase in the Wage

income effect. The net effect is that leisure can increase or decrease as wages go up. The implication, then, is that the quantity of labor supplied can also increase or decrease as wages go up.

Figure 17.5 illustrates both possibilities. The left graph depicts a reduction in leisure (substitution effect dominates), and the right graph depicts an increase in leisure (income effect dominates) as wage increases. To begin, in both graphs, the effect of an increase in the wage rate is to increase the vertical intercept from

$$\frac{24w_1 + I}{p} \quad \text{to} \quad \frac{24w_2 + I}{p}.$$

The point $(24, I/p)$ is unchanged and the budget line becomes steeper: $(w_2/p) > (w_1/p)$. The substitution effect is to reduce leisure (increase labor) on both graphs: $\ell_c^* < \ell_1^*$. I' represents the minimum nonlabor income required to keep each consumer along his or her original indifference curve when the substitution effect is evaluated. On the left graph, the positive income effect is not enough to increase leisure overall: ℓ_u^* is still less than ℓ_1^*. But on the right graph, the positive income effect is enough to increase leisure overall.

17.3 ___ THE BACKWARD-BENDING LABOR SUPPLY CURVE

It is often assumed that individuals consume less leisure (work more) as wages go up when wages are low, but then consume more leisure (work less) when wages are high. This generates a *backward-bending* supply curve of labor, as illustrated in Figure 17.6. In the upper graph, the consumer consumes less leisure when the wage increases from w_1 to w_2 and then more leisure when the wage increases from w_2 to w_3. The wages depicted on the upper graph are plotted along the vertical axis of both lower graphs. The utility-maximizing choices for leisure (ℓ_1^*, ℓ_2^*, and ℓ_3^* are plotted along the lower left graph, and the consumer's demand curve for leisure connects the points (w_1, ℓ_1^*), (w_2, ℓ_2^*), and (w_3, ℓ_3^*). The difference between 24 and the utility-maximizing choices for leisure are the utility-maximizing choices for labor (L_1^*, L_2^*, and L_3^*), plotted along the horizontal axis of the lower right graph. The backward-bending labor supply curve connects the points (w_1, L_1^*), (w_2, L_2^*), and (w_3, L_3^*).

Evidence for a Backward-bending Labor Supply Curve   Evidence in favor of a backward-bending labor supply curve is quite strong. First, note that for some very low levels of income, the labor supply curve has to be upward sloping. When the wage goes from 0 to some positive amount, labor supply either stays at 0 (if there is some minimum wage before an individual begins working) or it increases from 0 to some positive amount. Leisure would not be a good if people worked when the wage was 0 and stopped working when it became positive. The question, then, is whether people actually do work less after some point as wages go up. Several different kinds of evidence suggest that they do. First, an important part of the union bargaining process over the past century has been to reduce the required number of hours. A century ago, the average work week was about 70 hours long. Today it is about 40 or fewer. Over time, as income and wages have risen, workers have clearly taken some of their increased earning power in shorter hours.

On a more microeconomic level, both survey data and experimental evidence support the backward-bending labor supply curve. Dunn[3] estimated a labor supply curve for 200 low-income textile workers in the southeastern United States from survey data. Her estimate yields a downward-sloping supply curve for labor over the entire wage range of her survey ($1 to $2.50 per hour). Her workers tried to maintain a target level of income, regardless of the wage, so they just said they would work fewer hours at a higher wage.

Battalio and Kagel and their associates[4] estimated labor supply curves in experimental environments. One study used rats and another used inmates in a mental hospital. For rats, the concept of a wage was operationalized as the number of lever presses required to get a drink of a 16% sucrose solution. For the human hospital patients, the wage was the number of tokens they could earn for doing various jobs around the hos-

---

[3]Lucia Dunn, "An Empirical Indifference Function for Income and Leisure," *Review of Economics and Statistics* 60 (1978):533–540.

[4]Raymond C. Battalio, John H. Kagel, and Leonard Green, "Labor Supply Behavior of Animal Workers: Towards an Experimental Analysis," in V. L. Smith, ed., *Research in Experimental Economics* (Greenwich, CT: JAI Press, 1979) 1:231–253; John H. Kagel, Raymond C. Battalio, R. Winkler, and E. J. Fisher, "Job Choice and Total Labor Supply: An Experimental Analysis," *Southern Economic Journal* (1977) 44:13–24.

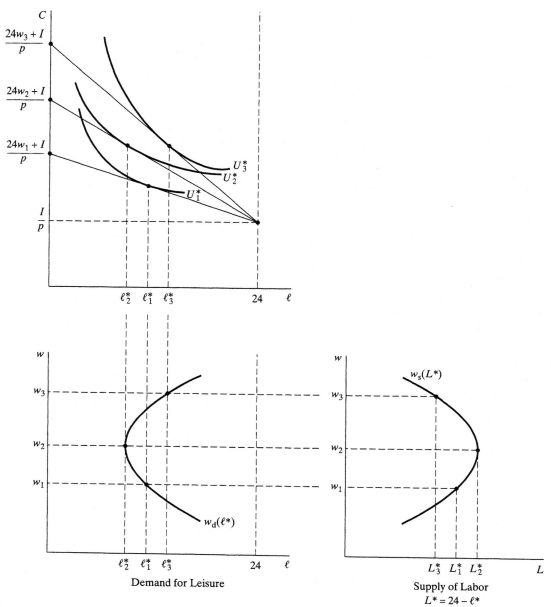

FIGURE 17.6 Derivation of a Backward-bending Labor Supply Curve

pital. The tokens could be redeemed for cigarettes, candy, and other small luxuries at the hospital store. For both groups of subjects, when wages were low, an increase in the real wage rate (fewer lever presses or more tokens) elicited more labor. But when the wage got high enough, higher wages implied that both groups of subjects worked less.

<u>17.4</u>   OVERTIME PAY: AN APPLICATION OF THE LABOR SUPPLY MODEL

The backward-bending labor supply curve presents a particular problem for employers who would like to get their experienced workers to work more hours. They could simply hire more workers, but often there are advantages to using an experienced crew for a few additional hours. The problem is that paying them higher wages for all the hours they work only encourages them to work less, but paying them less is likely to encourage them to find other jobs. The solution is to pay them more only for the additional hours they work (overtime pay). Thus, the only way they can increase their incomes is to work more hours.

Figure 17.7 illustrates how overtime pay elicits more hours. Suppose the normal work day is eight hours and workers are maximizing utility by working eight hours without overtime pay. The budget line without overtime is the line from $(24, I/p)$ to $(24w_1 + I)/p$. Overtime has the effect of putting a "kink" in the budget line at eight hours. Up to eight hours, the slope of the budget line is w_1/p. For additional hours worked, the budget line follows the higher line, with slope w_2/p. Since the second budget line does not start until eight hours, the only way to be on it is to reduce leisure (increase labor). Thus, leisure declines from 16 to ℓ_2^*, even though leisure would have increased if the higher wage had been applied to all hours worked. This has the effect

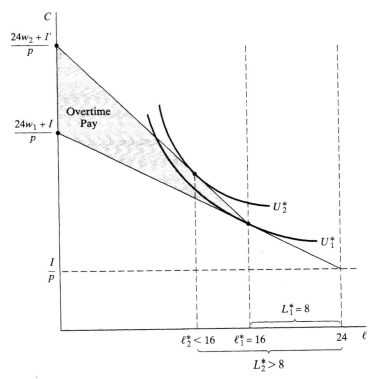

FIGURE 17.7 The Effect of Overtime Pay on Labor Supply

of removing most of the income effect associated with a wage increase, while taking advantage of the substitution effect.

17.5   THE HOUSEHOLD THEORY OF THE ALLOCATION OF TIME

Becker[5] has developed an alternative model of consumer behavior as an extension of the simple labor supply model developed above. He begins by suggesting that the distinction between consumption goods and leisure is artificial. A large segment of the population (homemakers) does not work for market wages but rather in *home production*. Moreover, all consumption requires some combination of purchased or home-produced goods and leisure. For example, we buy food and cook it in order to enjoy a gourmet meal. Even a fast-food hamburger requires some time for consumption.

He also models the character of consumption choices differently. Instead of having consumers choose bundles of purchased goods, he models the choice of a combination of purchased goods and time to satisfy a particular consumption desire. For example, food can be obtained with few purchases and much time if the homemaker grows a garden, keeps cows and chickens, and makes everything from scratch. The same calories and nutrients might be obtained from a purchased frozen dinner for more money and far less time.

The Choices of Home Production and Market Work   Becker assumes each consumer faces a home production possibilities frontier as well as a market wage budget line. Figure 17.8 provides a very simple graphical illustration of Becker's model. The horizontal axis is time and the vertical axis is consumption goods, just as in the labor supply model. For simplicity, we assume the price index is 1 and there is no nonlabor income. Starting at the point $(24, 0)$, the consumer can produce goods at home by exchanging time for goods along the concave production possibilities frontier. Alternatively, the consumer could work in the market for a wage of w.

One of the important insights from this model is that an individual will work at home as long as the marginal product of labor in home production exceeds the marginal product of market work (the wage). As soon as the marginal product of labor in home production falls below the market wage, the individual works some additional number of hours in the market. Thus, on the graph, the boldfaced frontier represents the consumer's actual consumption possibilities frontier. The individual works at home until the production possibilities frontier has the same slope as the market budget line. The number of hours of home work are shown from 24 to the point of tangency to the left. From that point on, the individual can get more consumption goods by working any additional hours in the market. In this case, the individual maximizes utility by working L_H^* hours at home and L_M^* hours in the labor market. The remaining hours (ℓ^*) represent the time for consumption of the produced and purchased goods (leisure).

---

[5]Becker, *Economic Approach to Human Behavior.* The actual presentation of Becker's model follows the development in Reuben Gronau, "The Effect of Children on the Housewife's Value of Time," *Journal of Political Economy* 81(March/April 1973): S168–S299.

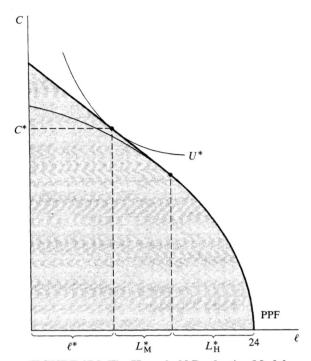

FIGURE 17.8 The Household Production Model

The beauty of this model is that it allows for an individual to do no home work or no market work. It also provides an understanding of when an individual who has been working exclusively at home will decide to enter the labor market, and it shows how the amount of time spent in home work will decline as a consequence of entering the labor market. Figure 17.9 illustrates the extreme cases of no home work and no market work and Figure 17.10 shows how an increase in the wage rate may lead to entry into the labor market and a decline in the time devoted to work at home.

In the left graph of Figure 17.9, the tangency between the indifference curve and the production possibilities frontier occurs along the homework portion of the curve. Thus, the individual works only at home. On the right graph, on the other hand, market wages are higher than the marginal product of home production at every point along the production possibilities frontier. Since the maximum attainable set is greater for market work than for non-market work, the individual works only in the labor market.

Comparative Statics of an Increase in the Wage Rate As Figure 17.10 shows, the effect of an increase in the wage rate is to move the point of tangency between the production possibilities frontier and the wage budget line to a point involving less home work. Individuals who remain at home would be unaffected by the wage increase, since they would stay on their household production possibilities frontiers anyway. Individuals who work in the labor market both before and after the wage increase would be modeled as in Section 17.2. But, as the left graph makes clear, they would

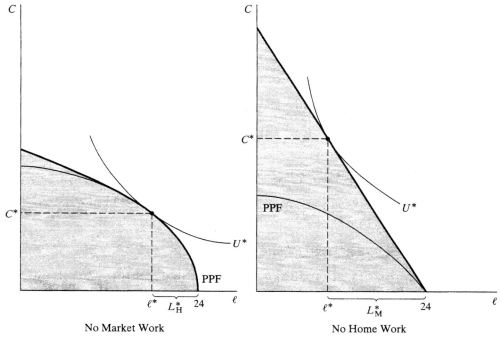

No Market Work   No Home Work

FIGURE 17.9 The Extremes of No Market Work and No Home Work

definitely work fewer hours at home as a result of the wage increase. Home work hours decline from L_H^* to L_{2H}^* for anyone who works some hours in the labor market. In addition, as the right graph shows, some people would actually start working as a result of the wage increase. They would also work fewer hours in the home as a result.

Applications of the Model   Becker has used this model to explain a variety of changes in the American family that have accompanied the recent rise in women's wages and the entry of women into the labor force in significant numbers. In the past 25 years, the labor force participation rate for women with small children has risen from under 10% to well over 50%. At the same time, average family size has fallen from over three children per family to under two children. The typical family no longer sits down to three meals a day prepared by a female homemaker. Instead, family members prepare their own breakfasts, eat lunch on the run, and may sit down to a prepared dinner together a couple of times a week. For the rest of the meals, they eat prepackaged convenience foods or they eat at restaurants or fast-food establishments.

In short, there has been a revolution in the amount of time the average adult female spends in homemaking tasks. At the same time, adult males and even young children have assumed more responsibility for homemaking. Becker argues that all these changes are directly related to the labor-force behavior and wages of women. In response to higher wages and more job opportunities, women have entered the labor force in unprecedented numbers and drastically reduced home production time as a result. Two of the most time-consuming tasks in home production are raising children

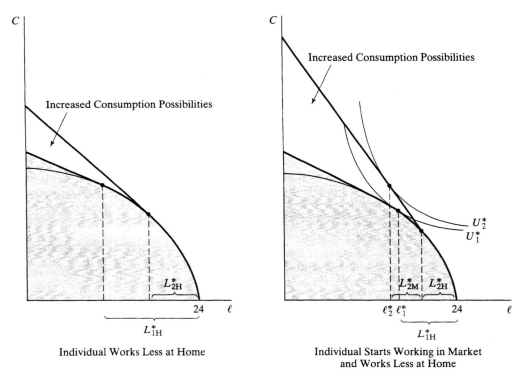

FIGURE 17.10 The Effect of an Increase in the Wage Rate

and preparing home-cooked food. Becker attributes both the decline in the number of children per family and the decline in time spent preparing food to the change in female labor-force behavior.

17.6 COMPETITIVE LABOR MARKET EQUILIBRIA

Returning to the individual labor supply function developed in Section 17.3, we can now combine individual labor supply curves and the individual firm labor demand curves developed in Chapter 12 (Figure 12.10) to construct market supply and demand curves for labor. Thus, just as with purchased goods, the **market labor demand function** is the schedule of the total quantities of labor demanded by all firms at each wage. The **market labor supply function** is the schedule of all the total quantities supplied by all workers at each wage.

The equilibrium market wage rate is found in exactly the same manner as the equilibrium price for a good. A **labor market equilibrium** is a wage and quantity of labor hired such that demand for labor equals supply of labor at that price. This is illustrated in Figure 17.11. Notice also that with a backward-bending supply curve for labor

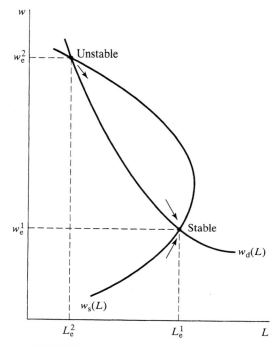

FIGURE 17.11 Labor Market Equilibria

there might be two equilibria: one at a low wage with more workers hired (L_e^1, w_e^1) and one at a high wage with fewer workers hired (L_e^2, w_e^2).[6]

Also, just as with the price for a consumption good, the equilibrium wage determined in this market becomes the wage parameter in competitive decisions. The firm takes the competitive wage as given in determining how much labor to hire, and the individual takes the competitive wage as given in determining how much labor to supply.

17.7   WAGE DIFFERENTIALS IN A COMPETITIVE MARKET

When we speak of a competitive labor market with an equilibrium wage, we are referring to a market for labor with a particular level of skill, performing a particular task, in a particular location. Different levels of skill translate into different marginal products of labor and different optimal combinations of capital and labor on the demand

---

[6]The low-wage, high-employment equilibrium (L_e^1, w_e^1) is actually more stable. To see that point, suppose wage falls a little below the higher-wage equilibrium. Workers would work a little more, because the labor supply curve is downward sloping at that point. Employers would hire a little more for the same reason. That would drive the wage down even further, instead of bringing it back to the equilibrium. The low-wage equilibrium, on the other hand, has the same properties as a competitive market equilibrium. If wage gets a little above equilibrium, excess supply drives it down; and if wage gets a little below, excess demand brings it back up. For that reason, economists often model market labor supply curves as if they were upward sloping: the observed equilibrium is likely to be on the upward-sloping portion of the curve.

side. On the supply side, different skills may be inherited or acquired through investment in *human capital* (discussed in more detail in Section 18.6). In the long run, the wage differentials between skilled and unskilled labor should be just enough to compensate workers for making the necessary investments in human capital.

Compensating Differentials   Different tasks that require the same skill may end up with different equilibrium wage rates because one job is deemed more interesting or enjoyable than another. The supply of labor in the more enjoyable job will be greater than in the less interesting job, and the equilibrium wage difference will be just enough to *compensate* workers in the less interesting job. We refer to the difference as a *compensating differential*. Put differently, workers in interesting jobs get **nonpecuniary benefits** from their work and are willing to accept less than they could earn at other jobs for which they are equally qualified. For example, college professors typically earn less than business executives with similar education and experience. It is often argued (by those same professors) that the life of a college professor is worth the difference in income.

From another perspective, workers in unpleasant or hazardous occupations typically earn more than other workers with comparable education or experience. For example, inner-city high school teachers often get "combat pay" and construction workers who build skyscrapers earn more than their counterparts who work closer to the ground. In these cases, the supply of labor available for work in these occupations is relatively low, and the equilibrium wage has to be high enough to compensate workers for subjecting themselves to occupational hazards.

Similarly, some geographical locations are more desirable places in which to live. Some people like to live on farms and continue farming, despite a substantial difference between farm earnings and urban wages, even taking account of the difference in the cost of living.

Factor Price Equalization   While some of these differences may persist over long periods of time, economists predict that factor prices for different occupations requiring the same skills and in different geographical locations will tend to equalize over time. If wages decline for one occupation or in one location relative to wages elsewhere, workers will move to other jobs in other locations and firms will move or hire different mixes of workers in order to utilize the lower-wage workers. The decrease in supply and the increase in demand will tend to raise wages in the previously low-wage occupations and locations. In the higher-wage occupations and locations, on the other hand, the influx of workers and the exit of firms will tend to lower equilibrium wages. Any wage differentials that persist in the long run will reflect the marginal value to the lower-paid workers of the quality of life in their communities, the marginal nonpecuniary benefits associated with their occupations, and the marginal value of any remaining skill differentials.

This theory of factor price equalization explains why U.S. workers want to keep the Mexican border closed and also why they resent the movement of U.S. firms to Mexico. Low wages in Mexico relative to those in the United States are currently encouraging hundreds of thousands of Mexican workers to cross the border illegally.

These same low wages are also encouraging U.S. manufacturers of a wide variety of different products to build plants just over the Mexican border. Both of these changes can only serve to reduce the equilibrium wages for U.S. workers at the same time that they raise the equilibrium wages for workers remaining in Mexico. The supply of labor is increasing in the United States and decreasing in Mexico, while the demand for labor is increasing in Mexico and decreasing in the United States.

17.8   IMPERFECT LABOR MARKETS: MONOPSONY

Not all labor markets are competitive. One particularly interesting kind of imperfectly competitive labor market is called a **monopsony:** one buyer of labor services in a particular labor market. Just as a monopolist in the output market treats the entire industry demand curve as its individual demand curve, the **monopsonist** in the labor market treats the entire supply curve for a particular kind of labor in a particular location as its individual supply curve. In a competitive market, the marginal cost of hiring an additional worker is equal to the wage, but, to a monopsonist, the marginal cost of hiring an additional worker is the wage paid to that worker plus the cost of raising the wages of all other workers (assuming an upward-sloping supply curve for labor). This can be seen by noting that the total cost of labor is $w(L)L$, where $w(L)$ is the supply curve (inverse supply function) of labor. Thus, we can derive the marginal cost of hiring another worker as

$$MC_L = \frac{d}{dL} TC_L = \frac{d}{dL}[w(L)L] = w + L\frac{dw}{dL} > w, \; \text{if} \frac{dw}{dL} > 0, \quad (17.12)$$

that is, if supply is upward sloping.

Equation 17.12 shows that the marginal cost curve for labor lies above the supply curve for labor. If the supply curve is linear, for example, the function for the curve can be written as

$$w = a + bL. \quad (17.13)$$

Differentiating (17.13) with respect to L,

$$\frac{dw}{dL} = b. \quad (17.14)$$

Substituting (17.13) and (17.14) in (17.12),

$$MC_L = a + bL + bL = a + 2bL. \quad (17.15)$$

Equation 17.15 indicates that the marginal cost curve will have the same wage intercept and twice the slope as the labor supply curve. This is illustrated in Figure 17.12.

Profit Maximization by a Monopsonist   The monopsonist's profit-maximization rule is the same as that of the firm operating in a competitive labor market: hire labor until the marginal revenue product is equal to the marginal cost of an additional worker.

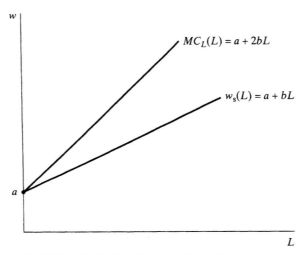

FIGURE 17.12 The Marginal Cost of Labor for a Monopsonist

This is illustrated in Figure 17.13. The quantity of labor that maximizes profits (L^*) equates marginal cost and the demand curve for labor, which is the marginal revenue product. With upward-sloping supply and downward-sloping demand, this quantity is always less than what would be the competitive quantity of labor (L_c). The firm then pays the wage that just calls forth L^* at w^* along the labor supply curve. Under the given assumptions, this wage is always less than the marginal cost of hiring the last worker $MC(L^*)$ and less than what the competitive wage would be (w_c).

To see how this result is derived mathematically, we write down the firm's short-run profit function in terms of the choice of labor, holding capital constant.

$$\pi = p_x x(L; \overline{K}) - w(L)L - r\overline{K}. \tag{17.16}$$

Assuming price is a parameter, the first-order condition is

$$\frac{d\pi}{dL} = p_x \frac{dx}{dL} - \left(w + \frac{dw}{dL}L\right) = 0 \quad \Rightarrow \quad MRP_L = MC_L. \tag{17.17}$$

Prevalence of Monopsony How prevalent is monopsony? This is a matter for some debate among economists. On the one hand, there still exist many small towns with only one or two substantial employers. On the other hand, the residents of those towns could leave to find work elsewhere. Thus, in some sense the employers in small towns compete with employers in other locations. Those who stay may work for lower wages, but is the difference due to monopsony or the value of community? These are difficult to separate empirically. A better case for monopsony can be made where there are real barriers to the movement of labor. For example, colleges and universities in small towns are often the sole source of market employment for the wives of male faculty and graduate students, who are not likely to move away from their husbands' place of

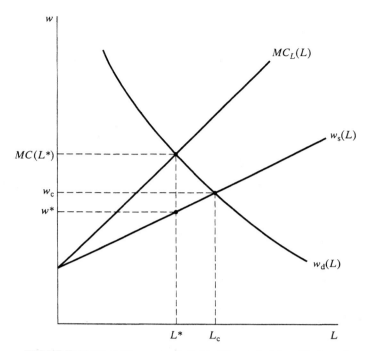

FIGURE 17.13 A Monopsonist's Profit-maximizing Choice of Labor

employment or education. It is argued that such colleges and universities can pay less than competitive market wages for secretaries, research support, and part-time teaching because they act as monopsonists in the market for educated (female) labor. This factor may have diminished recently as fewer wives are willing simply to follow their academic husbands wherever they go.

17.9   ECONOMIC RENT AND THE WELFARE IMPLICATIONS OF MONOPSONY

The welfare implications of monopsony are in some ways similar to, and in other ways different from, the welfare implications of monopoly. Recall that there is a loss of both consumer's and producer's surplus that is called the deadweight loss from monopoly. In factor markets, a concept analogous to consumer's and producer's surplus is called **economic rent** or **economic factor rent.** Looking at the supply side first, we can view each wage along the supply curve as the minimum wage necessary to get that many hours worked. However, if the market equilibrium wage is paid for all hours worked, workers earn more than is necessary to get them to supply each additional hour. Similarly, firms that pay only market wages for all the hours they hire earn rents on each hour equal to the difference between the marginal revenue product associated

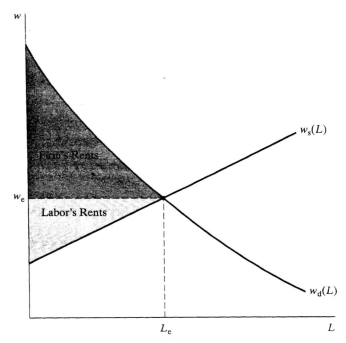

FIGURE 17.14 Economic Rents

with that hour and the market price.[7] This is illustrated in Figure 17.14. Like the representation of consumer's and producer's surplus, economic factor rent to the firm is the upper, darkly shaded area and economic factor rent to the workers is the lower, lightly shaded area.[8]

Deadweight Loss   Just as with a monopolist in the output market, the monopsonist in the labor market creates a **deadweight loss** of factor rents equal to the darkly outlined area in Figure 17.15. However, in contrast to the monopoly case, resources do not flow to the market production of other goods and services, since the monopsonist is the only employer of this particular kind of labor. Labor freed by the monopsonist does turn to home production, but the economy cannot be on its production possibilities frontier.

---

[7]At this point, we need to keep clear the difference between rents on capital (as used in Chapters 10 and 11) and economic rent as it is used here. Rent on capital, as used before, represents the market price that a firm pays for capital services. Economic rent, as used in this chapter, represents payments to factors of production *in excess* of what would be necessary to get the owners of the production to offer them to the marketplace. Thus, these are two quite different concepts.

[8]If there is only one variable factor, the firm's rents are simply equal to producer's surplus. If there is more than one variable factor, however, the rents on all of the variable factors combined equal the producer's surplus.

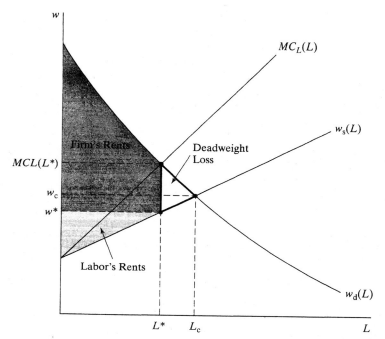

FIGURE 17.15 Deadweight Loss of Factor Rent from Monopsony

This is because the monopsonist does not satisfy the efficiency condition along the efficient production set; that is, for the monopsonist, $MP_L/MP_K \neq MC_L/MC_K$.

Perfect Wage Discrimination   One remedy, which is analogous to the monopolist practicing perfect discrimination, is for the monopsonist to practice perfect discrimination. If the monopsonist were to pay different workers different wages or different wages to the same workers for different numbers of hours worked, then it would hire additional hours until the marginal cost would be equal to the wage. The wage paid for the last hour hired would be the competitive wage, and the competitive number of hours would be hired. The cost of this remedy is, of course, that the owners of the monopsony firm collect all the economic factor rents shown in Figure 17.14 for themselves. The economy is back on its production possibilities frontier, but probably at a different point than what would have been the general competitive equilibrium.

17.10   UNIONS

Workers may also join together in unions and act as monopolists in their dealings with firms. Since a **union** is essentially a cartel of workers with the same prisoner's dilemma problem faced by an output cartel, it may or may not actually be able to act as a monopolist. Even if a union is successful, we do not know exactly what its objective function is. Maximizing total wages implies a very different strategy than does maximizing employment.

Wage Maximization and the Prisoner's Dilemma   Suppose, for example, the union tries to maximize total wages. In one sense, this is a reasonable strategy since if total wages are maximized, the total amount available for distribution among members is maximized. The problem is the same as that faced by the output cartel: how to divide up the payments. The problem is more difficult for the union, however, because some workers lose their jobs or work fewer hours when wages go up. To keep their allegiance and prevent cheating, the union has to compensate these workers in some way, which means collecting from the union members who keep their jobs at the higher pay. While each employed worker might agree with the principle, it is easier to enjoy the benefit while others pay. This is the free-rider problem, which we introduced in Section 4.6 and will develop in more detail in Sections 21.7 and 21.8.

Figure 17.16 illustrates the union's problem. Suppose the labor market is competitive to begin with. The wage is w_c and employment is L_c. Now, suppose a union forms and decides to maximize factor payments. Since factor payments in a labor market are equivalent to total revenue in the output market, the union chooses a wage and quantity of labor such that the elasticity of demand for labor is -1. (Such a choice maximized total revenue in a goods market.) Thus, maximum factor payments occur at w_u, with quantity of labor hired at L_u. The problem the union faces is that at w_u, L_u^s quantity of labor is actually willing to work. Unless the union achieves an acceptable rationing scheme and an acceptable means of compensation for all its members, some of the excess unemployed labor $(L_u^s - L_u)$ will offer to work for a lower wage and bid

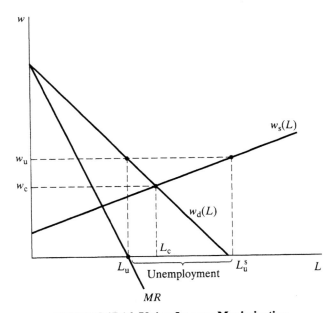

FIGURE 17.16 Union Income Maximization

down the price of labor. And even if an acceptable scheme is devised, the union must still enforce the agreement on its members (that is, keep workers from offering to work for a lower wage).

Union Bargaining with a Monopsonist   The above example assumes the union bargains with a competitive industry. However, when unions form, the argument often is made that workers need to join together because monopsonistic employers are paying them less than their marginal revenue products. If that is the case, then bilateral bargaining between union and monopsonist can actually be welfare improving if they are able to bargain to the joint maximum. This is illustrated in Figure 17.17. The joint maximum is the point where factor rents are maximized (where the competitive quantity of labor is hired). If the firm were a monopsonist, it would be paying w_m in wages and hiring L_m quantity of labor. Even if the union wins a wage increase, more workers may be hired, not fewer. In fact, if the union and the firm do reach the core of the "game," L_c would be hired.

The problem we face as analysts is that we do not know how the factor rents will be divided between the union and the firm. One efficient solution would be to pay workers the competitive wage (w_c) and give them a share of the firm's profits (if there are any). Profit sharing is actually a common outcome of union bargaining. However, just as in the duopoly models developed in Chapter 16, there are many possible solutions when a monopoly union bargains with a monopsonistic employer.

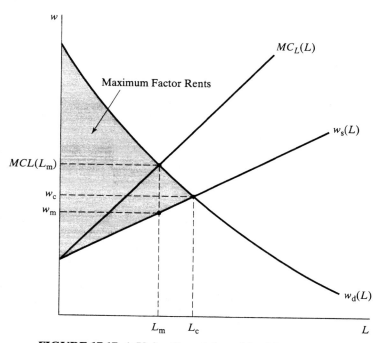

FIGURE 17.17 A Union Bargaining with a Monopsonist

17.11 UNIQUE FACTOR ENDOWMENTS

Some factors of production are unique and can act as monopolists in supplying their own factor markets. For example, there is only one Luciano Pavarotti or Fernando Valenzuela. Other opera stars or baseball players may be close substitutes, but superstars like these do have some monopoly power. Employers are willing to pay somewhat more than market wage to get the benefits of their superior talents.

The seller of a unique labor service can maximize his or her own factor payments just as a monopolistic union does. This is what an agent attempts to do for such a person: he or she bargains with employers (who may also be monopsonists) to try to get the income-maximizing wage for the star he or she represents.

Before the days of free agency, employers would sign long-term (sometimes lifetime) contracts with young performers and athletes before these performers and athletes were able to judge their own potential. The employer then became a monopsonist and paid the captive star just enough to keep him or her from leaving show business or sports to work in some other occupation. In other words, employers would pay stars the value of their next best alternative employment doing something else. This was typically much less than the values of their marginal revenue products if they continued to perform. The leagues in professional sports enforced noncompete agreements among the teams. As a result of this system, employers were able to capture a large portion of the economic rents attributable to their stars' unique talents. They typically even had the right to sell or trade their stars' labor services to other studios or teams. In this way an employer would actually collect in a lump sum the value of a star's rent.

The dramatic rise in performers' and athletes' salaries has resulted from court cases that declared many of the noncompete agreements to be in violation of the Sherman Antitrust Act. When performers could bargain with a number of potential employers, the result was to transfer a large portion of the factor rents owing to unique talents from the employers to the stars themselves.

17.12 REVIEW OF KEY CONCEPTS

This completes our survey of models of labor market decisions. Before going on to study capital markets and decisions over time, be sure you understand and can use the following key concepts.

Leisure time is a consumption good that is "purchased" by not working. The "price" of leisure is *forgone wages*.

The time budget constraint stipulates that expenditures on consumption goods cannot exceed labor plus nonlabor income, where labor income is measured as the wage rate times hours worked.

The ratio, the wage rate divided by the price of output, is called the *real wage*. It is an index of consumer purchasing power per hour of work.

At a utility-maximizing choice of consumption and leisure, the marginal rate of substitution between consumption and leisure is equal to the real wage.

An increase in nonlabor income results in a parallel shift in the time budget constraint. This implies that if leisure is a normal good, the consumer will consume more leisure (work less) as nonlabor income increases, until leisure equals 24 hours per day.

An increase in the wage rate increases both the slope of the time budget line and the feasible set. A decrease in the wage rate reduces both the slope of the budget line and feasible set.

If leisure is a normal good, an increase in the wage rate reduces the optimal choice of leisure by the substitution effect and then increases the optimal choice of leisure by the income effect.

If leisure is a normal good and the income effect outweighs the substitution effect, the consumer will consume more leisure (work less) as the wage rate increases. This implies that the labor supply curve may bend backward for a sufficiently high income.

Firms pay higher wages only for overtime work because some workers work less if wages increase. With overtime pay, the worker can increase income only by working additional hours.

The household theory of the allocation of time considers how a consumer allocates time between home and market production.

One of the predictions of the household theory of the allocation of time is that an individual will work at home as long as the marginal product of labor in home production exceeds the market wage rate.

The household theory of the allocation of time provides an explanation for the recent increase in female labor-force participation and decline in average family size. Increasing wages for women have raised the opportunity cost of home production and child rearing.

Market demand for labor is the total quantity demanded by all firms and *market supply* is the total quantity supplied by all workers at each wage.

An equilibrium in a competitive labor market is a wage rate and quantity of labor such that quantity demanded of labor equals quantity supplied at the equilibrium wage.

Differences in equilibrium wages among workers in different jobs may be due to different levels of skill (implying differences in marginal products) or to differences in qualities intrinsic to the jobs themselves. Workers in interesting jobs living in desirable locations may earn lower equilibrium wages because *nonpecuniary benefits* increase the supply curve of labor for those jobs in those locations. Workers in hazardous or unpleasant jobs may be *compensated*.

While wage differentials may persist in the long run, there is a tendency for wages to equalize across occupations requiring the same skill levels and across geographical areas, due to long-run changes in both demand and supply. Workers tend to leave low-wage areas and occupations and enter high-wage ones, while firms tend to relocate to take advantage of low wages and avoid high wages.

A labor market with only one buyer of labor is called a *monopsony* and the buyer is called a *monopsonist*.

A monopsonist facing an upward-sloping labor supply curve and a downward-sloping marginal revenue product curve pays a lower wage than the competitive wage and hires less labor than a competitive labor market would.

Economic rent in a factor market is analogous to consumer's and producer's surplus in a goods market. Workers earn economic rents when the market wage is higher than the minimum wages they would be willing to accept to work each additional hour, and firms earn economic rents when the market wage is lower than the marginal revenue product associated with each additional hour.

Since a monopsonist hires less labor than a competitive industry would, the existence of monopsony creates a *deadweight loss* of economic factor rents in the labor market.

A monopsonist practicing perfect wage discrimination would pay each worker the minimum required per hour to get him or her to work and would earn the total competitive factor rents.

A *union* is a group of workers who join together to bargain with employers as a monopoly.

A union faces a prisoner's dilemma in that maximizing total wages requires that workers agree to reduce either employment or hours worked. Some workers may have to be compensated to join the agreement, and the union has to prevent cheating on the agreement.

If a union bargains with a monopsonist, the result may be both higher wages and greater employment than if there were no union.

Some factors of production are unique and can act as monopolists in their own factor markets.

Bargaining between potentially monopsonistic employers and workers with unique skills leads to a (possibly nonunique) distribution of the factor rents from those unique skills.

17.13   QUESTIONS FOR DISCUSSION

1. In the nineteenth century, the managers of African mines had a difficult time getting enough native labor to work the mines. When they raised the wage, they found the workers worked for shorter stints before returning to their native villages. The Europeans attributed this behavior to laziness. Do you agree? Explain your answer.

2. Empirical evidence indicates that when wages increase, male workers work less on average and female workers work more. Female workers also make only about 50% of what male workers make on average. Can you conclude from this evidence that women like their jobs more than men do? Explain this difference in terms of the model developed in this chapter.

3. Use the evidence in Question 2 on the difference in female and male wages to explain why there are more females than males who work only at home. Assume for the purposes of this question that men and women have the same production possibilities frontiers.

4. Explain why women tend to have fewer children as their market wages increase.

5. During the nineteenth century, the United States allowed virtually unlimited immigration from Europe. During the 1890s, about 2% of the European population emigrated, most of them coming to the United States. Explain why this immigration took place and discuss what effects it must have had on the relative wages in Europe and the United States. Given that most immigrants are between 18 and 25, what positive effects did the migration have on the U.S. economy, and what negative effect did it have on the European economy?

6. You have been hired as a consultant to investigate a case of wage discrimination against educated minority workers brought against the only employer of educated minority workers in a medium-sized city. You find that it is true that minority workers are making significantly less than white male workers with the same education and experience. Can you conclude that the firm is discriminating on the basis of race or sex from this information? Why or why not? Assuming there are other employers of workers of the same education and experience who are not employing minorities, would forcing these employers to comply with the law be likely to end the wage discrimination? Explain.

7. You are a member of the United Auto Workers bargaining team, and the representative of the Big Three auto companies has just offered you a wage package that significantly increases the total wage bill, but also increases the chance that low-seniority workers will be laid off when business is slow. What factors do you and your team have to consider before deciding whether to try to sell the membership on this offer, and what problems are you likely to encounter in trying to sell it now and to enforce it later?

8. During the baseball and football antitrust cases, the owners argued that if the players were allowed to negotiate with different teams, player salaries would get so high that only rich teams would be able to afford good players. This would destroy the competitive balance and that would be "bad" for the game. If teams were already buying and selling the best players among themselves, would this change in the distribution of economic rents make any difference for the distribution of players among teams? Explain.

17.14   PROBLEMS

1. Suppose a consumer has the following utility function for consumption and leisure:

$$U = C\ell^2.$$

The wage rate is $10 per hour, the price of consumption is $5, and the consumer's nonlabor income is $50. What is the utility-maximizing choice of consumption and leisure? Show that at that choice, the marginal rate of substitution between consumption and leisure is equal to the real wage.

Problems 2–6 Suppose a firm faces a supply curve for labor

$$L = 1000w$$

and has a demand function for labor

$$L = 5000 - 50w.$$

2. How much labor would a monopsonist hire and what wage would it pay?

3. What wage and quantity of labor maximizes factor payments?

4. What are the competitive equilibrium wage and quantity of labor?

5. What are the total economic rents available for distribution in this labor market?

6. Do we know what the outcome will be if a monopolistic union faces a monopsonistic firm? Explain your answer.

Problems 7–9 A monopsonist faces two different labor supply curves for men and women. The supply curve for women is given by

$$L_f = 200w_f.$$

and the supply curve for men is given by

$$L_m = 10w_m^2,$$

where w_f and w_m are, respectively, the hourly wages for women and men.

7. Assume the monopsonist can sell output for $6 per unit and each worker's marginal product is three units per hour (both men and women). If the firm can pay different wages to men and women, how much will it pay each and how much of each will it hire?

8. Suppose a court case forces the firm to pay all workers the same, but the firm can still behave as a monopsonist. What nondiscriminatory monopsonistic wage would the firm pay and how many workers would it hire?

9. How many workers would the firm hire if it were constrained by market forces to pay all workers the value of their marginal revenue product? What wage would it pay?

17.15   LOGICAL AND MATHEMATICAL APPLICATIONS

1. The social security tax is levied as a percentage of a worker's wages up to a maximum tax. Assuming that workers are not paying the maximum tax, will an increase in the social security tax always increase the government's revenues from the tax? Explain your answer.

2. Show that if leisure is an inferior good, the labor supply curve is upward sloping.

3. Show that the introduction of a minimum wage above the equilibrium wage reduces employment of those subject to the minimum wage. Show also that it creates more unemployment than would be predicted by simply comparing the original employment and the new employment.

Chapter 18

INTERTEMPORAL DECISIONS AND COMPETITIVE CAPITAL MARKETS

18.1 WHAT YOU SHOULD LEARN FROM THIS CHAPTER

This chapter is devoted to an analysis of models of capital markets and decisions over time. We begin with a simple model of how consumers make choices between present and future consumption when there are only two time periods: today and tomorrow. In this model, consumers have preferences over consumption today and consumption tomorrow. They earn income each period, and they can either save today to consume more tomorrow or borrow against future consumption to consume more today. A consumer's combined intertemporal budget line is a function of income, the price of consumption each period, and the interest rate. Given the appropriate budget line and preferences, the consumer chooses a mix of present and future consumption to maximize utility. We show that, at that choice, the consumer equates the marginal rate of substitution between present and future consumption (called the **marginal rate of time preference**) and the inflation-adjusted return on savings (or borrowing rate). This consumption choice implies a choice of borrowing or saving, which will vary with the interest rate. This allows us to derive the supply of savings as a function of the interest rate, just as we derived the supply of labor as a function of the wage.

Consumer saving provides funds that can be used by firms to build new capital (machines, buildings, and roads, for example). By adding to the stock of capital, more consumption goods can be produced in the future and future production possibilities frontiers will shift out, but consumers must be willing to forgo some present consumption in order to supply the necessary funds.

The demand for funds to build capital comes from firms that make investments in capital goods. Moreover, since physical capital may last a long time, firms build capital today and then get a flow of *capital services* over time. In deciding whether to make such an investment, the firm compares the returns it will get from employing the capital to the interest it could earn if it simply put the funds in the bank. For the investment to be profitable, the flow of returns must be at least as good as the flow of interest from a bank. Using this rule, we develop the concept of the *discounted present value* of a flow of capital services over time. In a competitive capital market, the equilibrium price of new capital will turn out to equal the equilibrium discounted present value of the stream of capital services provided.

We next consider several important applications of the model of a capital market. First, we analyze the decision to invest in education (or *human capital*). Second, we analyze the optimal rate of exploitation of a nonrenewable natural resource, such as coal, oil, or gas. Third, we analyze the optimal exploitation of a renewable resource, such as trees or fish. In each example, making an optimal decision requires taking account of choices available over time.

18.2   THE TWO-PERIOD INTERTEMPORAL DECISION MODEL

In the context of the two-good model we have developed in this book, we can think of consumers as having preferences over present consumption (C_1) and future consumption (C_2), expressed as $U(C_1, C_2)$ and illustrated in Figure 18.1. In this model, we refer to the marginal rate of substitution between consumption today and consumption tomorrow as the **marginal rate of time preference:**

$$\text{marginal rate of time preference } (MRTP) = -\frac{dC_2}{dC_1} = \frac{\partial U/\partial C_1}{\partial U/\partial C_2} \qquad (18.1)$$

along an indifference curve.

The Intertemporal Budget Line   The consumer receives an income each period: M_1 in the present and M_2 in the future. Consumption in each period can be changed by borrowing at the market rate of interest in order to consume more today or saving at that rate of **interest** in order to consume more tomorrow. Anything borrowed in the present must be paid back out of future income, and anything saved in the present is added to future income. We can define **savings** as whatever is left over from present income after paying for present consumption:

$$S = M_1 - p_1 C_1 \qquad (18.2)$$

where p_1 is the price index for present consumption. Note from (18.2) that savings can be negative if the consumer borrows to consume relatively more in the present.

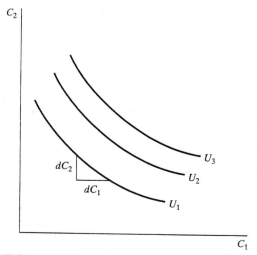

FIGURE 18.1   The Choice Between Present and Future Consumption

The amount available for future consumption is thus future income plus savings plus the amount of interest earned on savings. If savings are negative, the person is borrowing and must pay back the amount borrowed plus the interest in the second period. This has the effect of reducing future consumption. We can express future purchases as

$$p_2C_2 = M_2 + S + iS = M_2 + (1 + i)S, \tag{18.3}$$

where i is the market rate of interest. Substituting (18.2) in (18.3), we can rewrite (18.3) as

$$p_2C_2 = M_2 + (1 + i)(M_1 - p_1C_1) \tag{18.4}$$
$$= M_2 + (1 + i)M_1 - p_1(1 + i)C_1.$$

Rearranging (18.4), we can see that

$$p_2C_2 + p_1(1 + i)C_1 = M_2 + (1 + i)M_1 \tag{18.5}$$

is the consumer's budget constraint over the two periods. Expenditures, on the left-hand side of (18.5), equal the total income over both periods, on the right-hand side.

Now, we define a **rate of inflation** (d) as the percentage change in prices between the present and the future:

$$d = \frac{p_2 - p_1}{p_1}. \tag{18.6}$$

Rearranging (18.6),

$$p_2 = (1 + d)p_1. \tag{18.7}$$

Substituting (18.7) in (18.5),

$$p_1(1 + d)C_2 + p_1(1 + i)C_1 = M_2 + (1 + i)M_1. \tag{18.8}$$

Equation 18.8 shows that the two-period **intertemporal budget constraint** is a line with the following intercepts:

$$C_2 = \frac{M_2 + (1 + i)M_1}{(1 + d)p_1}, \quad \text{if } C_1 = 0 \tag{18.9}$$

$$C_1 = \frac{M_2 + (1 + i)M_1}{(1 + i)p_1}, \quad \text{if } C_2 = 0. \tag{18.10}$$

In constructing the budget line described by equation 18.8, we note that the consumer always has the choice of saving nothing and borrowing nothing: simply spending each period's income in that period. That would imply the following consumption pattern:

$$p_1C_1 = M_1 \tag{18.11}$$
$$p_2C_2 = M_2(1 + d)p_1C_2. \tag{18.12}$$

Rearranging (18.11) and (18.12),

$$C_1 = \frac{M_1}{p_1} \quad \text{and} \quad C_2 = \frac{M_2}{(1 + d)p_1} \tag{18.13}$$

is the combination of present and future consumption at which savings are 0. Any deviation from the point depicted in (18.13) and the consumer is a net borrower or a net saver. If $C_1 > M_1/p_1$, the consumer is consuming more than he or she is earning in the present and is a net borrower. In contrast, if $C_2 > M_2/[(1 + d)p_1]$, then the consumer is consuming more than he or she is earning in the future and is a net saver.

Figure 18.2 illustrates the intertemporal budget line. On the upper left portion of the curve, above the zero savings point, the consumer would be a net saver. On the lower right portion, below the zero savings point, the consumer would be a net borrower.

From the intercepts (equations 18.9 and 18.10), we can see that the slope of the intertemporal budget line (equation 18.8) is

$$\frac{dC_2}{dC_1} = -\frac{\dfrac{M_2 + (1 + i)M_1}{(1 + d)p_1}}{\dfrac{M_2 + (1 + i)M_1}{(1 + i)p_1}} = -\frac{1 + i}{1 + d}. \tag{18.14}$$

The ratio derived in equation 18.14 can be interpreted in several ways. We can call it the real cost of an additional unit of consumption today in terms of consumption tomorrow, the **intertemporal price ratio.** The idea is that if we buy something today, we forgo the interest we could earn, but that interest has to be *deflated* by the rate at which prices will increase or decrease between the present and the future. The slope of the intertemporal budget line can also be viewed as the real rate at which the purchasing power of savings increases. If the inflation rate is exactly equal to the interest rate, the ratio is 1, implying that the purchasing power of savings does not change, despite a positive interest rate. If the rate of interest is greater than the rate of inflation, the ratio is greater than 1, implying an increase in real purchasing power; but if the ratio is less than 1, real purchasing power declines.

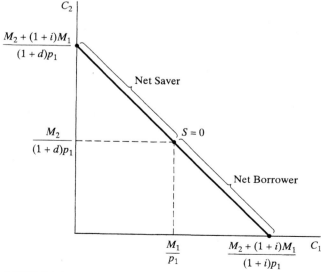

FIGURE 18.2   The Two-period Intertemporal Budget Line

Intertemporal Utility Maximization Putting Figures 18.1 and 18.2 together, we can see that the consumer chooses a combination of present and future consumption to maximize utility over the intertemporal budget constraint. This will imply the usual equal-slopes rule: the marginal rate of substitution (the internal price ratio) is equal to the external price ratio. In this case, the marginal rate of time preference equals the intertemporal price ratio:

$$MRTP = \frac{1 + i}{1 + d}.$$ (18.15)

The consumer's decision is illustrated in Figure 18.3 for net borrowers and net savers. In the left graph, the net borrower maximizes utility to the right of the zero savings point. In the right graph, the net saver maximizes utility to the left of the zero savings point.

An Increase in the Interest Rate Now, suppose the interest rate were to increase $(i_2 > i_1)$. The first thing we note is that the point at which savings are 0 is unaffected by the change in the interest rate. Thus, the new budget line has to go through the old zero-savings point, $C_1 = M_1/p_1, C_2 = M_2/[(1 + d)p_1]$ (equations 18.13). Therefore, the budget line pivots around that point. This implies that the vertical intercept (equation 18.9) increases:

$$\frac{M_2 + (1 + i_2)M_1}{(1 + d)p_1} > \frac{M_2 + (1 + i_1)M_1}{(1 + d)p_1};$$

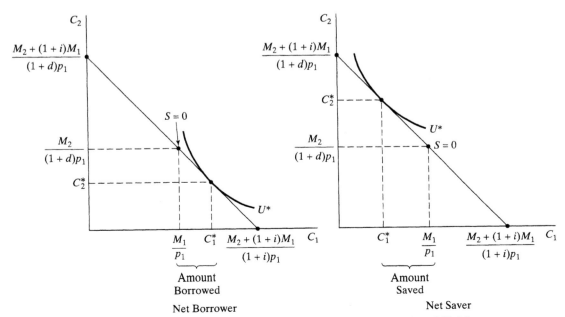

FIGURE 18.3 Utility Maximization by Net Borrowers and Net Savers

and the horizontal intercept (equation 18.10) decreases:

$$\frac{M_2 + (1 + i_2)M_1}{(1 + i_2)p_1} < \frac{M_2 + (1 + i_1)M_1}{(1 + i_1)p_1};$$

Figure 18.4 illustrates how the budget line rotates around the zero-savings point. The line AA', with a lower intercept along the C_2 axis and a higher intercept along the C_1 axis, represents the budget line before the increase in the interest rate. The line BB', with a higher intercept along the C_2 axis and a lower intercept along the C_1 axis, represents the budget line after the increase in the interest rate.

Comparative Statics of an Increase in the Interest Rate   Notice in Figure 18.4 that, because the budget line rotates, the increase in the interest rate affects net borrowers and net savers differently. The pure price effect (or substitution effect) is the same for both, since the budget line has become steeper. That means that the real price of present consumption (equation 18.14) has increased:

$$\frac{1 + i_2}{1 + d} > \frac{1 + i_1}{1 + d}.$$

Thus, the substitution effect for both net borrowers and net savers is to reduce present consumption.

The income effect of the increase in the interest rate on present consumption depends on each individual consumer's savings behavior, however. Net savers can potentially earn more income because the earnings on their savings have increased.

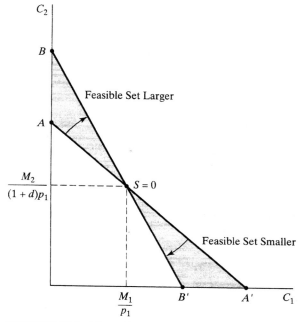

FIGURE 18.4   The Effect of an Increase in the Interest Rate on the Intertemporal Budget Line

Net borrowers, on the other hand, have potentially less income because the interest they have to pay to borrow for present consumption has increased. If present consumption is a normal good, net borrowers will always reduce consumption. This happens because the income effect as well as the substitution effect act to reduce consumption when the budget line rotates in. For net savers on the other hand, the income effect works to increase present consumption because the budget line has rotated out. Thus, net savers may consume less in the present if the substitution effect dominates the income effect, but they may also consume more in the present if the income effect dominates the substitution effect.

Figures 18.5 and 18.6 illustrate how an increase in the interest rate affects the utility-maximizing decision of a net borrower and two possible net savers. The net borrower in Figure 18.5 reduces present consumption, since the substitution effect and the income effect work in the same direction. The net saver in Figure 18.6 reduces present consumption if the substitution effect dominates (left graph) and increases present consumption if the income effect dominates (right graph).

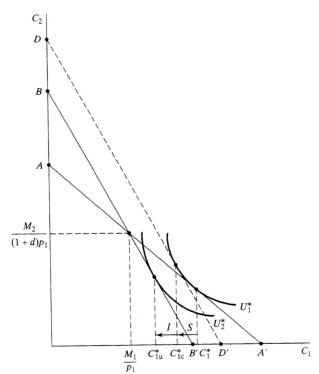

Key: AA' = original budget line
$\quad BB'$ = new budget line
$\quad DD'$ = new budget line with compensation

FIGURE 18.5   The Effect of an Increase in the Interest Rate on a Net Borrower

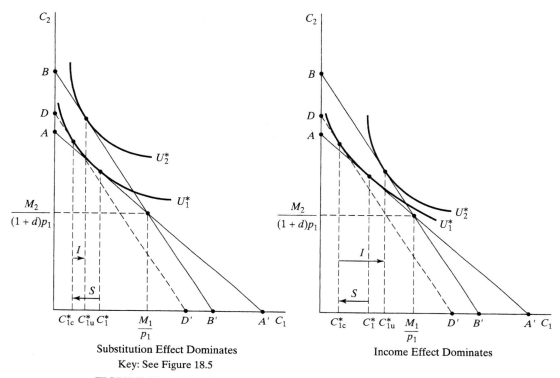

Substitution Effect Dominates
Key: See Figure 18.5

FIGURE 18.6   The Effect of an Increase in the Interest Rate on Two Net Savers

Income Effect Dominates

18.3   THE SUPPLY FUNCTION FOR SAVINGS

From the graphs showing the effects of an increase in the interest rate, we can construct demand curves for consumption today. Consumption today is a function of the
interest rate, holding present and future income, the price index for current consumption, and the inflation rate constant:

$$C_1 = C_1(i; \overline{M_1}, \overline{M_2}, \overline{p_1}, \overline{d}). \tag{18.16}$$

Then, substituting (18.16) in (18.2), we can construct functions for savings as
functions of the interest rate, holding the same variables constant:

$$S = S(i; \overline{M_1}, \overline{M_2}, \overline{p_1}, \overline{d}) = M_1 - p_1 C_1(i; \overline{M_1}, \overline{M_2}, \overline{p_1}, \overline{d}) \tag{18.17}$$

Figure 18.7 illustrates the derivation of the functions derived in equations 18.16
and 18.17 for a net borrower, if we assume present consumption is a normal good.
Since the substitution effect and the income effect work in the same direction, the
demand curve for present consumption is downward sloping. Subtracting price times
the present-consumption demand curve from M_1 yields a supply-of-savings function
which is negative but upward sloping. The net borrower borrows less (reduces present

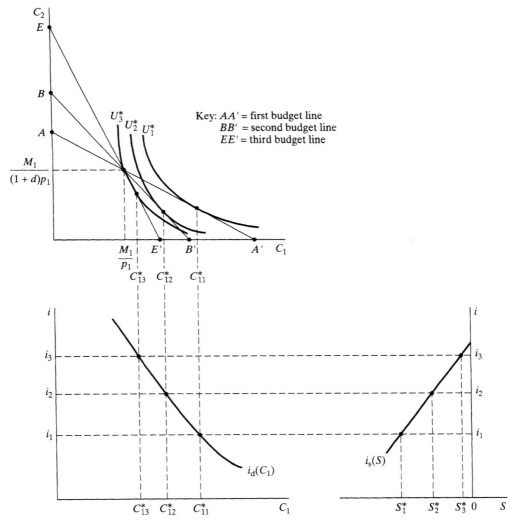

FIGURE 18.7   Demand for Present Consumption and Supply of Savings for a Net Borrower

consumption) as the interest rate increases. An analogous positive function would be a downward-sloping demand function for loans:

$$L_d = p_1 c_1 - M_1. \qquad (18.18)$$

Figure 18.8 illustrates the present-consumption demand and supply-of-savings functions for one possible net saver, assuming present consumption is a normal good. At some nonnegative interest rate, the consumer becomes a net saver instead of a net borrower and, at first, savings increase as the interest rate increases. The substitution effect dominates the income effect in this range. When the interest rate becomes high enough, however, the income effect dominates the substitution effect, and savings

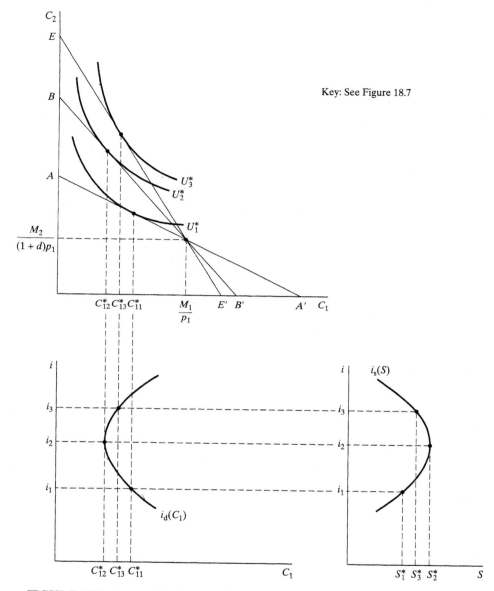

FIGURE 18.8   Demand for Present Consumption and Supply of Savings for a Net Saver

decrease as the interest rate continues to increase (the consumer purchases more in the present, despite the increase in the interest rate).

Putting the net borrower and the net saver graphs together, Figure 18.9 illustrates a savings supply function for a hypothetical consumer in both the borrowing and the savings ranges of interest rates. Present consumption is assumed to be a normal good, and the savings supply function is assumed to bend backward in the savings range.

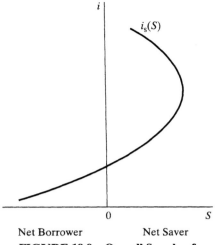

**FIGURE 18.9   Overall Supply of
Savings Curve over Borrowing and
Savings Ranges**

18.4   DISCOUNTED PRESENT VALUE

Having derived the supply of savings function, we now turn to an analysis of investment in new capital. Since machines, factories, and other forms of physical capital are generally employed by firms over many time periods, building and employing capital involves intertemporal decision making. In effect, new capital is projected to supply a flow of **capital services** over time. What a firm must decide is whether to build or purchase new capital or to simply lease it from other firms that own the capital. If a firm purchases new capital, it knows that the new capital will be used for a number of years into the future, even though it may have to pay the cost of the capital at the time of purchase. On the other hand, if the firm leases, it generally pays rent at specified time intervals over the life of the lease. In general, purchase requires either an up-front payment or a mortgage, while a lease only requires periodic payments. Since the time dimension of payment is different in the two cases, the firm needs some standard of comparison between the decision to buy and the decision to lease.

If the firm pays for the capital outright, it gets the use of the capital, the capital services, but it cannot earn bank interest on the funds used for purchase. If it rents or mortgages the capital, it pays some rental or mortgage rate per year, and the rest of the funds, which could have been used for outright purchase, can be earning the market rate of interest. The firm wants to pay no more to buy the capital outright than it would have to pay to lease it or mortgage it, including the interest forgone by tying up the funds in owned capital. This is not to say that this is simply a matter of adding up the lease payment each year and then comparing the sum to the purchase price. The appropriate way of making this comparison is derived below.

Mathematical Derivation of Discounted Present Value   To derive the appropriate basis for comparing a current payment and a stream of payments, we start by deriving the current cost of a stream of payments. To begin, we use the formula for compound interest. Let

i = market rate of interest, assumed constant for T years into the future;

D_T = some initial deposit, which will be untouched for T years;

V_T = the compound value of D_T after T years.

We can construct the value for D_T as follows:

$$V_1 = D_T(1 + i) \tag{18.19}$$
$$V_2 = V_1(1 + i) = D_T(1 + i)(1 + i) = D_T(1 + i)^2 \tag{18.20}$$
$$V_T = D_T(1 + i)^T. \tag{18.21}$$

Solving (18.21) for D_T,

$$D_T = \frac{V_T}{(1 + i)^T}. \tag{18.22}$$

Equation 18.22 shows that, in order to withdraw V_T at the end of T years when the interest rate is i, it is necessary to deposit D_T to begin with. We refer to the ratio $1/(1 + i)^T$ as the **discount factor** that should be applied to V_T; and we refer to D_T as the **discounted present value** of V_T.[1] In other words, having D_T today and putting it in the bank for T years is equivalent to getting V_T at the end of T years.

Now, suppose instead that you will withdraw a return (r_t) in each year t from a single initial deposit in your bank account. To withdraw r_1 in year 1, you must deposit the discounted present value of the compound value r_1 (call it D_1):

$$D_1 = \frac{r_1}{1 + i}. \tag{18.23}$$

To withdraw r_2 in year 2, you must deposit

$$D_2 = \frac{r_2}{(1 + i)^2}. \tag{18.24}$$

In fact, for each annual withdrawal, an appropriate D_t must be deposited in the beginning. Thus, the total amount to be deposited in order to withdraw r_t each year for T years is the sum of all the appropriate initial deposits (or discounted present values). Economists refer to this sum as the **discounted present value of a stream of returns:**

$$DPV_T = D_1 + D_2 + \cdots + D_T. \tag{18.25}$$

Thus, substituting (18.23), (18.24), and an analogous expression for D_T in (18.25),

$$DPV_T = \frac{r_1}{1 + i} + \frac{r_2}{(1 + i)^2} + \cdots + \frac{r_T}{(1 + i)^T}. \tag{18.26}$$

---

[1]This is sometimes also referred to as the present discounted value or, simply, the present value.

If r is a constant $(r_1 = r_2 = \cdots = r_T)$, then we can rewrite (18.26) as

$$DPV_T = \sum_{t=1}^{T} \frac{r}{(1 + i)^t}. \tag{18.27}$$

We can now derive a simple equation for the discounted present value of a stream of constant annual returns, where the time horizon is the entire future. The idea is to find what happens to discounted present value (equation 18.27) as the time horizon goes to infinity. To derive the discounted present value of an infinite stream, we begin by multiplying both sides of (18.27) by $1/(1 + i)$:

$$\frac{1}{1 + i} DPV_T = \frac{1}{1 + i}\left[\sum_{t=1}^{T} \frac{r}{(1 + i)^t} \right] \tag{18.28}$$

$$= \frac{r}{(1 + i)^2} + \frac{r}{(1 + i)^3} + \cdots + \frac{r}{(1 + i)^{T+1}}$$

$$= \sum_{t=1}^{T} \frac{r}{(1 + i)^{t+1}}.$$

Now, we subtract (18.28) from (18.27).

$$DPV_T - \frac{1}{1 + i} DPV_T = \sum_{t=1}^{T} \frac{r}{(1 + i)^t} - \sum_{t=1}^{T} \frac{r}{(1 + i)^{t+1}} \tag{18.29}$$

$$= \frac{r}{1 + i} + \frac{r}{(1 + i)^2} - \frac{r}{(1 + i)^2} + \frac{r}{(1 + i)^3} - \frac{r}{(1 + i)^3}$$

$$= + \cdots - \cdots - \frac{r}{(1 + i)^{T+1}}$$

Collecting terms in (18.29),

$$DPV_T\left(1 - \frac{1}{1 + i}\right) = \frac{r}{1 + i} - \frac{r}{(1 + i)^{T+1}} = \frac{r}{1 + i}\left(1 - \frac{1}{(1 + i)^T}\right). \tag{18.30}$$

Solving (18.30) for DPV_T,

$$DPV_T = \frac{r}{i}\left(1 - \frac{1}{(1 + i)^T}\right). \tag{18.31}$$

Now, if we let T go to infinity,

$$\lim_{T \to \infty} \frac{1}{(1 + i)^T} = 0. \tag{18.32}$$

Substituting (18.32) in (18.31),

$$\lim_{T \to \infty} DPV_T = \frac{r}{i}. \tag{18.33}$$

Equation 18.33 shows that in the limit as T goes to infinity, the discounted present value of a stream of returns of r per year is equal to r divided by the interest rate.

Alternatively, if a sum of money (DPV_T) is deposited in an interest-bearing account and left there forever, the annual interest payments that could be collected indefinitely would be

$$r = i \cdot DPV_T. \tag{18.34}$$

18.5   DETERMINING THE EQUILIBRIUM RATE OF INTEREST

In Section 18.4, we introduced a new good, capital, which is produced using resources today and which makes it possible to produce more consumption goods tomorrow. Expenditures on capital thus form part of the price of tomorrow's consumption in the model developed in Section 18.2. In a general equilibrium model, when consumers save in order to be able to consume more in the future, the funds they save are used by firms to produce new capital.[2] It is the coordination in **capital markets** of consumers who wish to save and firms that wish to borrow funds for investment that creates the market rate of interest. If there were no government intervention in the money market, the equilibrium rate of interest would equate the supply of savings and the demand for funds for investment.

Investment as a Function of the Interest Rate   To form a function that describes the relationship between investment and the interest rate, we first note that since the infinite-horizon discounted present value is equal to r divided by i (where r is an amount of withdrawal from savings), a competitive firm with an infinite time horizon will be indifferent between purchasing new capital at the discounted present value per unit and renting it at a rate of r per unit per year.[3] Thus, the competitive price per unit of new capital should be equal to the discounted present value per unit:

$$DPV = \frac{r}{i} = p_K. \tag{18.35}$$

If the price were higher than the discounted present value, firms would rent all their capital; if the price were lower, they would only purchase. When the price is equal to the discounted present value, firms are indifferent between purchasing and leasing capital.

Second, if new capital is produced and supplied in a competitive market, we can express the competitive market supply function for capital as

$$K_s = K_s(p_K), \tag{18.36}$$

where K_s represents the total quantity of capital that all firms producing capital goods are willing to supply at each possible discounted present value. Moreover, in a general

---

[2]This is usually referred to as investment, in macroeconomics.

[3]We assume there are no tax considerations in the decision to buy or rent.

equilibrium model, building new capital involves producing fewer goods for direct consumption today. If the production possibilities frontier bows out, then the general equilibrium long-run supply curve for new capital will be upward sloping.

Finally, total expenditures on new capital are equal to the unit price times the supply function:

$$E_K = p_K K_s(p_K). \qquad (18.37)$$

To find the relationship between the value of new capital and the interest rate, we note that if K_s is upward sloping in p_K, then E_K must also be increasing in p_K by equation 18.37. If the equilibrium price of capital increases, more capital is supplied and $p_K K_s$ must increase. Figure 18.10 translates an upward-sloping supply curve for

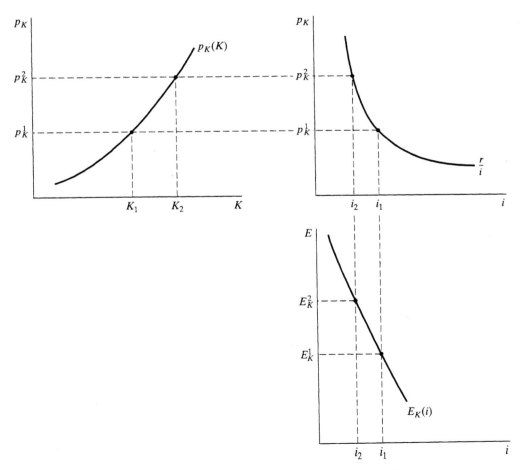

FIGURE 18.10   Derivation of a Downward-sloping $E_k(i)$ Function

capital into a function describing the relationship between the interest rate and expenditures on new capital. The upper left panel graphs the inverse of quantity supplied of capital as an upward-sloping function of the price of capital. The upper right panel translates that price, for a given r, into an interest rate along the rectangular hyperbola $p_K = r/i$. Finally, the lower panel graphs the price of capital times the quantity of capital ($E_K = p_K K$) from the upper left, against the interest rate from the upper right. For example, suppose we compare $p_K^2 > p_K^1$ along the supply curve. Since the supply curve is upward sloping, K_2 is also greater than K_1 and $p_K^2 K_2$ is greater than $p_K^1 K_1$. However, along the rectangular hyperbola, i_2 is less than i_1 if p_K^2 is greater than p_K^1. Thus, E_K^2 must be greater than E_K^1 when i_2 is less than i_1 and when the expenditure curve is downward sloping.

General Equilibrium in the Capital Market   The function $E_K(i)$ is not exactly a demand function in the usual sense, although one might argue that if the interest rate were to fall, some projects that were unprofitable would become profitable, and firms would demand more funds for investment. The problem with this approach is that equation 18.34 shows quite clearly that the interest rate cannot be determined independently of the price of capital in long-run equilibrium. A better approach is to note that in long-run equilibrium in a competitive market, the price of capital equals the long-run marginal cost of producing it. The quantity of capital produced represents an equilibrium in both the production market (where the quantity supplied of capital equals the quantity demanded at the long-run marginal cost (p_K^e) of producing that quantity) and the loanable-funds market. (Expenditures on investment, $E_K(i_e)$, equal the value of savings by consumers, $S(i_e)$, at the equilibrium rate of interest i_e.) The long-run equilibrium rental rate on capital is then determined by the long-run equilibrium price of capital and the equilibrium interest rate. Solving for r in equation 18.35,

$$r_e = i_e p_K^e. \tag{18.38}$$

18.6   HUMAN CAPITAL AND THE DEMAND FOR EDUCATIONAL SERVICES

The model of the capital market developed above can be used to understand how a number of different investment decisions are made. Any time that payment has to be made today for something that generates a stream of benefits over a period of time, we are dealing with a good that has characteristics similar to those of a capital good. One example of such a good is an education, which allows an individual to accumulate **human capital.**

Acquiring an education requires two different kinds of expenditures. There are the obvious direct costs of tuition, books, and supplies. In addition, getting an education almost always involves some reduction in the time spent working. Most students choose not to work at all while they are in school. Time spent not working results in an indirect cost of the forgone earnings. Economists refer to this as the opportunity cost of an education.

The Discounted Present Value of an Education   In return, graduates expect to earn higher lifetime earnings with an education than without.[4] But, these additional lifetime earnings accrue in the future, while the educational costs have to be paid today.[5] Thus, in order for the additional earnings to at least cover the cost of the education, the discounted present value of the additional earnings have to be greater than or equal to the full cost of the education. To illustrate this point, let

$$c_d = \text{direct cost (appropriately discounted)}$$

$$c_o = \text{opportunity cost (appropriately discounted)}$$

$$M_2 = \text{annual income with an education}$$

$$M_1 = \text{annual income without an education.}$$

Now, we can express the discounted present value of a four-year college education as the difference between the discounted present value of annual earnings with an education and without. In addition, the discounted present value of the income with an education has to be discounted back five years, since it will not begin to be earned until that time.[6]

$$DPV = \frac{M_2}{i}\left[\frac{1}{(1+i)^5}\right] - \frac{M_1}{i} \tag{18.39}$$

In long-run equilibrium in a perfect, competitive capital market, where an individual can borrow the full cost of an education, the discounted present value of the education (equation 18.39) should just equal the cost:

$$DPV = d_d + c_o. \tag{18.40}$$

Extensions of the Basic Model   In a more realistic version of this model, we can allow for the fact that earnings may differ from year to year both with and without an education and the rate of change may be different under the different regimes. For example, without education, earnings may rise quickly, but peak early at a relatively low annual income. With an education, earnings may rise more slowly, peaking later at a relatively high annual income. In this case, computing the discounted present value involves dis-

---

[4]For now, we ignore the possibility that a person might want to become educated even if he or she could not earn a higher income. For example, many students study art, history, English, and philosophy just because they enjoy those subjects, even though they know they could earn more in construction work without going to school. In this case, we say that an education is a consumption good as well as an investment decision. The return to investment in that kind of education will be lower by the price (appropriately discounted) that students are willing to pay to study those subjects.

[5]For simplicity, this model assumes costs are paid and earnings accrue on an annual basis.

[6]The equation uses the infinite-horizon approximation to the discounted present value, even though individuals clearly do not have infinite lives. It turns out, however, that the infinite-horizon equation is a very good approximation for time horizons of 30 years or more. Thus, since the average student probably will work for at least 30 years after college, this expression represents a reasonable approximation.

counting each year separately. To show this, let r_t be the additional income attributable to having an education in year t. Then the discounted present value is calculated just as in equation 18.27, where r varies from year to year:

$$DPV = \sum_{t=1}^{T} \frac{r_t}{(1 + i)^t},$$
(18.41)

where T would be the date of retirement. An additional factor that can be introduced is to recognize that the direct cost of the education is actually paid over several years and thus has to be discounted itself.

18.7   EXPLOITATION OF NONRENEWABLE NATURAL RESOURCES

The capital model developed above can also be used to analyze the optimal way to exploit a nonrenewable resource (like oil, gas, or minerals). Nonrenewable natural resources in the ground have economic characteristics similar to capital or money in the bank. Mining a resource today implies that it is not available to be mined tomorrow. Conversely, leaving it in the ground is like having money in the bank. Today, we have the choice of either mining all the resource or saving some to be mined tomorrow. If we mine it all today, we can take the proceeds and put them in the bank at the market rate of interest. In equilibrium, if all nonrenewable resources are privately owned and then sold in competitive markets, the amount that can be earned by leaving the resources in the ground must equal the returns that could be earned by selling the resources and putting the money in the bank. Thus, the returns to mining everything today must equal the discounted returns to mining tomorrow. If we let

$p_0 =$ the market price of the resource today,

$p_1 =$ the market price of the resource tomorrow, and

$LRMC =$ long-run marginal extraction cost,

then the relationship between mining today and mining tomorrow is stated as

$$p_0 - LRMC = \frac{p_1 - LRMC}{(1 + i)}.$$
(18.42)

Resource Rent   The difference between today's price and marginal extraction cost is called the opportunity cost of mining the resource today instead of leaving it in the ground. It can also be seen as the **economic rent** to the resource that is left in the ground (the value of the resource itself). In contrast to produced goods (where price is equal to the marginal cost of production in long-run equilibrium), in the case of exploitable resources currently under production, price exceeds long-run marginal extraction cost by the per-unit value of the resource remaining in the ground.

Just as returns in the next period after today have to be discounted back to the present, the returns in period 2 (and any period t) have to be appropriately discounted:

$$p_0 - LRMC = \frac{p_2 - LRMC}{(1 + i)^2}$$
(18.43)

$$p_0 - LRMC = \frac{p_t - LRMC}{(1 + i)^t}. \tag{18.44}$$

Rearranging terms in (18.44),

$$p_t = LRMC + (1 + i)^t(p_0 - LRMC). \tag{18.45}$$

Equation 18.45 shows that at any point in time, the (anticipated) price has to equal the long-run marginal cost plus the opportunity cost augmented at the compound rate of interest. An interpretation of (18.45) is that per-unit economic rent rises at the rate of interest as a resource is exploited.

Resource Substitution   If demand for the resource is downward sloping, as the price rises over time, the quantity demanded declines. In fact, if the demand curve has a price intercept, the quantity demanded eventually goes to 0. This would be likely to happen if there were close substitutes for the resource which could be used if its price became too high. This point is illustrated in Figure 18.11, with quantity extracted on the vertical axis (q) and price on the horizontal axis (p). The left graph shows the quantities demanded at different points in time as the price rises. Price and quantity are (p_1, q_1) at time 1, (p_2, q_2) at time 2, and (p_3, q_3) at time 3. The right graph then compares quantity demanded and time, taken from the left graph: q_1 at time 1, q_2 at time 2, and q_3 at time 3. Quantity extracted declines over time, eventually reaching 0, even though there may still be more of the resource available. If new sources of supply are developed, the curve describing the quantities extracted over time would shift out.

An important application of this model is to realize that we do not "run out" of resources as they are extracted over time. Rather, if no new sources of supply are discovered, the price simply rises until substitute resources become relatively inexpensive and are then used instead. For example, before the sixteenth century, coal was hardly used at all. It was considered a dirty, nasty-smelling fuel in contrast to wood charcoal, the fuel of choice for most uses. During the sixteenth century, however, the price of

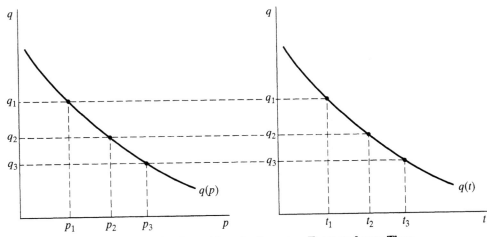

FIGURE 18.11   Quantities of a Resource Extracted over Time

charcoal rose dramatically in England because there were few forests left for charcoal production, and little attempt was being made to replant deforested areas. During the sixteenth, seventeenth, and eighteenth centuries, scientists and engineers worked to develop new technology to make it possible to substitute dirty coal for clean-burning charcoal in a wide variety of industrial uses. Their success made coal the fuel of the Industrial Revolution.

Today, doomsday theorists are predicting that our modern civilization must soon come to an end because we are going to run out of crucial resources such as oil and natural gas. As the above analysis makes clear, we will not actually ever run out of these resources. Rather, we can expect that their prices will rise over time, providing a strong incentive to develop the technology necessary for using substitutes. If that technology is not developed, the rate of economic growth may decline because of rising input costs; it is not likely, however, that our industrial civilization will collapse.

18.8   RENEWABLE NATURAL RESOURCES: TREES

With nonrenewable resources, there is some fixed supply at any time, which may or may not be augmented in the future by some new discovery. Renewable resources, on the other hand, grow at biologically determined rates and can be harvested, either in periodic, discrete amounts or continuously. In the "tree-growing problem," we consider a resource, trees, which will grow to maturity and then be harvested.[7] In the fisheries problem (Section 18.9), we consider a resource that is constantly being born and dying. It is harvested at some rate and allowed to replenish itself continuously. Both problems, however, involve decisions over time and are thus similar to capital decisions.

Biological Growth Patterns of Trees   In the tree-growing problem, we can think of a function $x(t)$ that describes the stock of wood available at each point in time. A typical biological growth pattern would be represented by the S curve shown in Figure 18.12. Growth is rapid at first and then slows down as the forest becomes crowded. The upper bound on the wood in the forest is $\bar{x}$.

The time derivative of $x(t)$ can be represented by another function,

$$f(x(t)) = \frac{d}{dt}x(t), \tag{18.46}$$

---

[7]This is only one possible, technological description of the tree-growing problem, however. It describes a management system in which trees are treated like wheat: an area is planted, it grows to maturity, and then it is cut down. While this technology is appropriate in areas not subject to erosion when a forest is cut down, it is not appropriate where erosion is a serious problem. In that case, efficient forestry management dictates that trees be planted and harvested continuously so that the forest is never "clear cut," leaving bare soil which can wash away. In that case, the forest always contains trees of all ages. Each year a few new seedlings are planted among the larger trees and the mature trees are harvested. While the second management system is clearly as economically interesting as the first, we focus on the first because it is easier to model and understand mathematically. Moreover, the second management system is actually quite similar to the management of a fishery, which we consider in Section 18.9. One major difference is that fish can often be left to replenish themselves, while a forest (which clearly can also replenish itself) generally grows better if new seedlings are actually planted each year.

which is positive and concave. As Figure 18.12 shows, the rate of growth increases and then decreases, eventually reaching 0 at $\bar{x}$. This is illustrated in Figure 18.13, which graphs the rate of growth against the stock of wood available.

Optimal Harvest Time   To find the optimal time to harvest a stock of wood, it is convenient to transform the capital problem developed above to a continuous-time problem. Then we can take a derivative with respect to t and find t^*. In the discrete-time capital problem, for a given nominal rate of interest, the appropriate discount factor is $1/(1 + i)^t$. For the same nominal rate of interest, the appropriate continuous-time discount factor is exponential:[8] e^{-it}. Thus, if there is no marginal cost to growing wood and the selling price is p, we can express the discounted present value of a stock of wood at time t as the price times the quantity of wood available, appropriately discounted:

$$V(t) = px(t)e^{-it}. \tag{18.47}$$

To find the optimal time to harvest the stock of wood, we maximize $V(t)$ by choosing t:

$$\frac{dV}{dt} = p\frac{dx}{dt}e^{-it^*} - ipx(t^*)e^{-it^*} = 0. \tag{18.48}$$

Substituting (18.46) in (18.48) and collecting terms,

$$pe^{-it^*}[f(x(t^*)) - ix(t^*)] = 0. \tag{18.49}$$

Solving (18.49) for $f(x(t^*))$,

$$f(x(t^*)) = ix(t^*). \tag{18.50}$$

The optimal decision characterized in (18.50) is illustrated in Figure 18.14. With x on the horizontal axis, ix is a linear function with slope i. The optimal decision is to

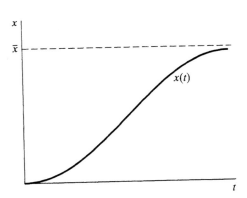

FIGURE 18.12   Growth Curve of Wood in a Forest

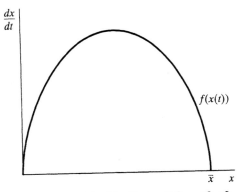

FIGURE 18.13   The Rate of Growth of a Stock of Wood

[8]See Chiang, *Fundamentals of Mathematical Economics*, pp. 274–281, for a discussion of how to transform the discount factor from discrete to continuous time.

allow the trees to grow as long as the rate of growth is faster than the stock of wood times the interest rate. The trees are harvested when the stock of wood is $x(t^*)$, growing at the rate of $f(x(t^*))$.

Comparative Statics of an Increase in the Interest Rate   An increase in the interest rate increases the cost of waiting to harvest the wood and should result in an earlier harvest of a smaller stock of wood. This is illustrated in Figure 18.15. An increase in the interest rate from i_1 to i_2 increases the slope of the ix function, which then intersects $f(x)$ at a smaller stock of wood (x_2 is less than x_1).

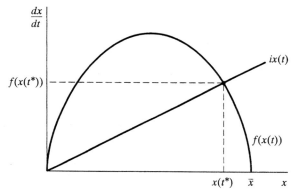

FIGURE 18.14   The Optimal Time to Harvest a Stock of Wood

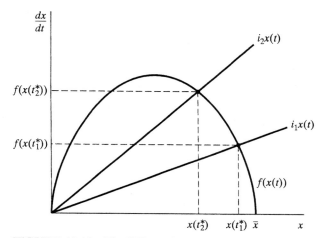

FIGURE 18.15   The Effect of an Increase in the Interest Rate on the Harvest Decision

18.9   OPTIMAL MANAGEMENT OF A FISHERY

Turning now to the fishery-management problem, we assume that fisheries are managed as private-property resources and that the fish are then sold in competitive markets.[9] We begin with a biological growth curve similar to that for the stock of wood, except that now we explicitly recognize that the stock is continuously replenishing itself. Here we compare the quantity of fish available and the amount being added to the stock each year. This gives us an amount that could be harvested and still keep the stock at a particular level. Biologists refer to this function as a *sustainable-yield* function, and the type of function usually used is illustrated in Figure 18.16.

If the stock of fish (F in Figure 18.16) is very small, the fish have few offspring and the yield (Y) is also small. At very low stocks, the rate of growth may be negative because the fish have difficulty finding each other in order to mate. As the stock size increases, so does the sustainable yield, but at a decreasing rate. This is because crowding tends to reduce the birthrate of most animal populations. At some point the stock size is such that the largest possible amount is being added and simultaneously harvested each year. This is referred to as the *maximum sustainable yield (MSY)*. If the stock size becomes larger, the yield falls due to crowding. If the stock size becomes large enough, births each year will exactly equal deaths, and there will be no excess to harvest if the stock is to remain at that size.

Sustainable Revenues   Now, suppose the quantity of fish that can be caught, given the technology and other resources available, is proportional to the stock of fish (that is, the more fish there are, the more that can be caught) and the amount of effort expended to catch the fish. Also, we have already assumed that fish are sold in a competitive market, so that market price is a constant and is independent of the quantity of fish caught. With output proportional to stock and price constant, the sustainable-yield function determines the shape of a function that indicates the sustainable revenues that can be obtained from the management of a fishery. As more and more fish are taken each year, at first the sustainable yield rises, increasing revenues. But once the maximum sustainable yield is achieved, the sustainable revenues start to fall as the sustainable yield falls.

A sustainable-revenues function is illustrated in Figure 18.17. The points along the horizontal axis are proportional to the points along the horizontal axis in Figure 18.16, and the points along the vertical axis are proportional to the points along the vertical axis in Figure 18.16. Since both axes are proportional, the maximum sustainable revenues are available at a point proportional to the maximum sustainable yield in Figure 18.16.

The Efficient Rate of Catch   To find the efficient catch for the fishery, we want to maximize the fishery's discounted profits. One approach to this problem is to find the

---

[9] Application 6 at the end of this chapter asks you to analyze what would happen if fisheries were common-property resources.

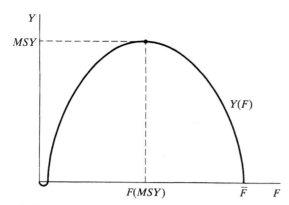

FIGURE 18.16   Sustainable Yield as a Function of the Stock of Fish

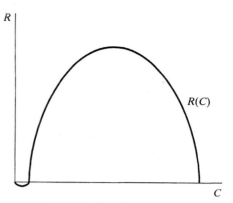

FIGURE 18.17   Sustainable Revenues as a Function of the Annual Catch

maximum sustainable profits. This would involve developing an appropriate discounted cost function, incorporating both the cost of capital and the cost of expending more effort for a given level of capital, and maximizing the difference between the sustainable revenue function and the cost function.

Figure 18.18 illustrates the determination of an efficient level of catch if the appropriate long-run total cost function is linear. The efficient catch is at C^*, where the slope of the total cost line is equal to the slope of the sustainable total revenue function. The maximum sustainable profits are thus

$$S\pi^* = STR(C^*) - LRMC \cdot C^*,$$

where $STR(C^*)$ equals the sustainable total revenue at C^*.

Notice in Figure 18.18 that the efficient level of catch is always to take less than the maximum sustainable yield each year, as long as long-run marginal cost is positive. This is one of the most important insights that economics can bring to the management of fisheries, and it is very similar to the observation that a monopolist always produces on the elastic portion of its demand curve. The intuition in both cases is that with positive marginal cost, it is never profit maximizing to maximize total revenue. While revenues may be higher at maximum total revenue than at maximum profits, the additional costs incurred to increase output to that point have the effect of lowering *profits*.

Comparative Statics of an Increase in the Interest Rate   Having determined the optimal level of catch, an interesting comparative-statics exercise is to analyze the effect of an increase in the interest rate on the optimal level of catch. One reason the analysis is interesting is because an increase in the interest rate has a (possibly) counterintuitive effect on the discounted long-run total cost. One of the components of cost to the management of a fishery has to be the opportunity cost of catching more fish today as opposed to leaving more fish to breed for the future. This is exactly analogous to the opportunity cost of mining a nonrenewable resource today instead of leaving it in the ground. If the interest rate increases, the opportunity cost of more quickly extracting any resource decreases. That is because profits earned

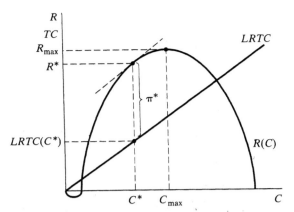

FIGURE 18.18 Maximizing Sustainable Profits

now and invested in the bank at the market rate of interest can earn more in the bank when the interest rate increases. A decrease in the opportunity cost of fishing more intensively today implies a reduction in the discounted long-run marginal cost, assuming the actual cost of fishing remains the same.

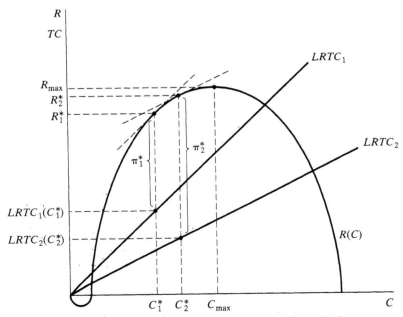

FIGURE 18.19 The Effect of an Increase in the Interest Rate on the Efficient Catch Level

The effect of a decrease in discounted long-run total cost is illustrated in Figure 18.19. The decrease in cost shifts the total cost curve down and results in an increase in the annual catch. As total cost shifts from TC_1 to TC_2, the efficient catch increases from C_1^* to C_2^*. Thus, the effect of an increase in the interest rate is to increase the efficient rate of catch.

18.10 REVIEW OF KEY CONCEPTS

This completes our introduction to theory and applications of intertemporal decision making. Before continuing on to the next chapter on decision making under uncertainty, be sure you understand and can use the following key concepts.

In an intertemporal decision problem, consumers are assumed to have preferences over consumption today and consumption tomorrow. The marginal rate of substitution between consumption today and consumption tomorrow is called the *marginal rate of time preference.*

The market rate of *interest (i)* is the price a consumer must pay to borrow against future income in order to consume more today. It is also the return to saving from current income in order to consume more in the future.

Savings are the amount of present income that is left after all spending for present consumption. If savings are positive, the consumer is a *net saver;* if savings are negative, the consumer is a net *borrower.*

The *inflation rate (d)* is the rate of increase (or decrease) in the price index between today and tomorrow.

The consumer's *intertemporal budget line* describes all the consumer's maximum consumption possibilities over time, given the price index in time period 1, the rate of inflation, the interest rate, and the consumer's income in each time period.

The consumer always has the option of just spending exactly his or her income in each time period and not borrowing or saving.

The slope of the intertemporal budget line is $1 + i$ divided by $1 + d$. This indicates the real rate at which the purchasing power of savings increases when the effect of inflation is taken into account. In other words, if this ratio is 1, implying the rate of interest is equal to the rate of inflation, then the purchasing power of savings stays the same. If it is greater than 1, net savers increase the purchasing power of their savings. If it is less than 1, the purchasing power of savings declines.

The slope of the intertemporal budget line is sometimes referred to as the *intertemporal price ratio.* The price of consumption today is forgone interest on savings and actual interest on borrowing; the price of waiting to consume tomorrow is the potential loss of purchasing power due to inflation.

At a utility-maximizing choice of consumption today and consumption tomorrow, the consumer's marginal rate of time preference is equal to the intertemporal price ratio. Net savers' points of tangency involve relatively more consumption tomorrow than if savings were 0; net borrowers' points of tangency involve relatively more consumption today than if savings were 0.

If the interest rate increases or decreases, the point on the budget line corresponding to zero savings is unaffected since it does not depend on the interest rate. This implies that the intertemporal budget line pivots on the zero-savings point as the interest rate changes. If the interest rate increases, net savers experience increases in their feasible sets, while net borrowers experience decreases.

An increase in the interest rate represents an increase in the price of current consumption in terms of forgone interest on savings and higher interest on anything borrowed from future income. Since the price of current consumption has increased, the substitution effect associated with an increase in the interest rate is *always* to reduce current consumption.

If current consumption is a normal good, the income effect of an increase in the interest rate depends on whether a consumer is a net borrower or a net saver. For a net borrower, the income effect is to reduce current consumption, since the feasible set has been reduced. For a net saver, however, the income effect is to increase current consumption, since the feasible set is larger.

The overall effect of an increase in the interest rate on current consumption combines the income effect and the substitution effect. Assuming current consumption is a normal good, net borrowers always reduce current consumption (and thus borrow less); net savers may increase current consumption (save less) if the income effect dominates, or reduce current consumption (save more) if the substitution effect dominates.

The possibility that net savers might save less as the interest rate increases generates a possibly backward-bending supply curve for savings.

Capital is productive over many time periods. In equilibrium, a competitive firm is indifferent between buying new capital (and using the *capital services* over time) and renting capital at the market rental rate, where the rental rate reflects the annualized value of the capital services.

If i is the interest rate, the ratio, 1 divided by $1 + i$, represents the rate at which income earned tomorrow has to be *discounted* to be equivalent to income earned today. If this income is to be earned several years in the future, the ratio is raised to a power equal to the number of years and is called the *discount factor*. The idea is to make income earned tomorrow equivalent to income that is earned today and deposited in the bank.

The *discounted present value* of an amount that will be paid T years in the future is that amount, divided by $(1 + i)$ raised to the power T. The discounted present value of a stream of returns to be paid annually in the future is the sum of the discounted present values of the individual annual returns.

The discounted present value of an infinite stream of returns that is constant at r each year is r divided by the interest rate.

The price of new capital equals the *discounted present value of the stream of returns* a firm

could earn from renting that capital to another firm.

Investments in new capital require that resources be diverted from current consumption to the production of capital. More capital then allows an economy to produce more consumption goods in the future.

Consumer savings out of current consumption become funds for investment in new capital by firms through the *capital market*.

At a general competitive equilibrium, the interest rate, the price of new capital, and the rental rate are jointly determined. The equilibrium price of new capital and the equilibrium interest rate represent simultaneous equilibria in the production market for new capital and in the market for funds to finance the building of new capital. The equilibrium rental rate is then the equilibrium price of capital times the equilibrium interest rate.

Human capital is produced when an individual forgoes present consumption in order to invest in getting an education.

The cost of an education includes both the explicit costs of tuition and books and the implicit cost of income forgone while in school.

The discounted present value of an education is the difference between the discounted present value of earnings with and without the education.

If capital markets are perfect so that an individual can borrow the full cost of an education, then in long-run equilibrium in a competitive market, the discounted present value of an education will exactly equal the sum of the explicit and implicit costs of obtaining it.

Exploiting a nonrenewable resource involves making a trade-off between mining today and putting the money in the bank and simply leaving the resource in the ground and mining it in the future.

The opportunity cost of mining a resource today instead of leaving it in the ground is called the resource's *economic rent*.

In equilibrium, the current price of a resource will equal the marginal extraction cost plus the compound value of leaving the resource in the ground. This implies that price rises over time as a resource is exploited. It can also be interpreted as implying that the economic rent for a resource rises at the rate of interest as a resource is exploited.

Over time, as a resource is exploited, price rises and market quantity demanded declines. Eventually, a resource will no longer be exploited, especially if some cheaper substitute becomes available.

If trees are planted, allowed to grow, and then harvested all at one time, the optimal time to harvest a forest (t^*) is found by equating the rate of growth of the forest at t^* and the size of the forest at t^* multiplied by the market rate of interest.

If the market rate of interest increases, the opportunity cost of allowing a forest to continue growing also increases. That implies that if the interest rate increases, a smaller forest should be harvested sooner. In the management of a fishery, with positive marginal cost, it is generally optimal to catch less than the maximum sustainable yield each year. This result is analogous to the result that a profit-maximizing monopolist with positive marginal cost does not maximize total revenues.

If the interest rate increases, the opportunity cost of leaving fish to breed also increases. This implies that if the interest rate increases, optimal fishery management dictates increasing the rate of catch.

18.11 QUESTIONS FOR DISCUSSION

1. Trees harvested continuously and fish are quite similar biologically, yet fisheries are much more difficult to manage efficiently than forests are. In particular, most logging forests are now managed by single firms that try to practice efficient management. In contrast, most fisheries are fished competitively and typically more fish are taken each year than is efficient, leading to problems of extinction in many areas. (See Application 6, below.) What differences between fish and trees would account for these management differences? Discuss in terms of the ability of a firm to claim the sole right to extract a particular resource.

2. Suppose we allow for the possibility that college students simply want to be educated in order to enjoy life more. How will this affect the equilibrium return to education and the equilibrium wages of college-educated workers as compared to those with only a high-school education? Compare this analysis to an analysis of equilibrium wage differences when some jobs or locations are simply more desirable than others.

3. Why is it necessary to save in order to invest in new capital?

4. Explain why not exploiting natural resources is like leaving money in the bank.

5. Explain why a firm that purchases capital outright would never pay more than the discounted present value of a stream of rental payments if the capital were leased.

6. What would happen to our capital resources over time if everyone were a net borrower? Is it possible in a general equilibrium framework for everyone to be a net borrower? Explain.

18.12 PROBLEMS

Problems 1–3 Calculate the discounted present values for the following assets, assuming the market rate of interest is 15%.

1. An acre of land yielding $500 per year in rent, after expenses, indefinitely into the future.

2. A loan that pays $1000 interest each year for three years, and then is paid off.

3. A building that will earn nothing for five years, and then will earn $5000 per year indefinitely into the future.

18.13 LOGICAL AND MATHEMATICAL APPLICATIONS

1. Suppose the rate of inflation were to increase. Show graphically the effect of that change on the savings behavior of both net borrowers and net savers. How does the supply of savings function shift as a result? What will be the effect on the equilibrium rate of interest?

2. Suppose we were to determine the equilibrium real rate of interest using a general equilibrium *tâtonnement* mechanism. Use an Edgeworth box to illustrate a competitive intertemporal equilibrium. What conditions will characterize an intertemporal Pareto optimum? Identify on your graph which consumer is the net borrower and which is the net saver and explain why there would have to be one of each in a two-person economy.

3. Show how an increase in the marginal cost of producing new capital raises the equilibrium rental rate on that same capital.

4. Suppose there are different rates for saving and borrowing. In particular, the interest rate for borrowing is higher than the interest rate for saving to cover the cost to the bank if a borrower defaults. Assuming the borrowing interest rate is higher and the saving interest rate is lower than if there were only one rate, analyze the effect of having two rates instead of one on the intertemporal budget line and on the amount of borrowing and lending.

5. Show that if consumption today is an inferior good for net savers and a normal good for net borrowers, the supply-of-savings curve is upward sloping.

6. Suppose a fishery were exploited competitively instead of as a monopoly. Identify the level of catch expected and analyze the resource-management problem as a prisoner's dilemma.

Chapter 19

Uncertainty: The Basics

19.1   WHAT YOU SHOULD LEARN FROM THIS CHAPTER

Up until now, we have assumed that the choices available and the consequences of consumer and firm decisions are always known with certainty. Of course, this assumption is rarely satisfied, especially when decisions are made over time. A more reasonable assumption is that producers and consumers have some idea of what the range of possible outcomes is and attach relative likelihoods to the different possible scenarios. Sometimes these likelihoods (or *probabilities*) are *objective*, as in the probability that a *fair coin* will come up heads 50% of the time. Other times they are *subjective*, as in a person's guess that a new product will be profitable. In that case, different analysts can reasonably differ about the probability to attach to such an event.

Whether the probabilities of events are objective or subjective, we can analyze *decisions under uncertainty* with models that are fairly simple extensions of the certainty models developed thus far. In this chapter, we develop the basic extension to uncertainty and some simple applications in which parties to a bargain can share risks with one another in markets. In the next chapter, then, we develop more complicated models in which buyers and sellers may have different kinds of information or in which more traditional kinds of markets do not exist for one reason or another.

In general, we will see that if consumers can purchase insurance to protect themselves in all future *states of the world,* the introduction of uncertainty has no effect on the basic model of efficient market transactions. All that is needed is to extend the set of commodities produced and consumed to include a specification of both the commodity and the state of the world in which it will be consumed.

Analysis of decisions under uncertainty will require the development of some new mathematical concepts. Thus, in order to make the discussion of the topics outlined above understandable, we begin the chapter with a brief introduction to probability theory and the development of utility functions under risk (*expected utility* functions). Having developed such utility functions, we can model decisions under risk as though the decision maker is maximizing expected utility.

19.2 INTRODUCTION TO PROBABILITY THEORY AND RISK PREFERENCE

Up until now, we have assumed that when a particular action is taken, a particular outcome is assumed to occur *with certainty*. We call an outcome that occurs with certainty a **certain outcome.** More often than not, however, a particular action can lead to a number of different possible outcomes: **uncertain outcomes.** When we can assign relative likelihoods to those outcomes, we can analyze decisions over risky actions in a way similar to that used to analyze decisions over lotteries or gambles (as in poker, blackjack, or roulette).

Objective and Subjective Probabilities Sometimes those likelihoods are **objective probabilities,** if they can be observed through experimentation and then agreed upon. For example, suppose a coin that has not been tampered with were to be tossed many times (1,000 times, 10,000 times). If the coin came up heads half the time and tails half the time, we would say that the coin was a **fair coin,** and we could describe the probability that each outcome will occur by setting up an objective **probability distribution** of outcomes.

$$\text{heads} \quad \text{with probability} \quad 1/2 \tag{19.1}$$
$$\text{tails} \qquad \text{with probability} \quad 1/2$$

Similarly, a fair, six-sided die has the following objective probability distribution.

$$\text{1 spot} \quad \text{with prob.} \quad 1/6 \tag{19.2}$$
$$\text{2 spots} \quad \text{with prob.} \quad 1/6$$
$$\text{3 spots} \quad \text{with prob.} \quad 1/6$$
$$\text{4 spots} \quad \text{with prob.} \quad 1/6$$
$$\text{5 spots} \quad \text{with prob.} \quad 1/6$$
$$\text{6 spots} \quad \text{with prob.} \quad 1/6$$

In many cases, however, we can only guess about the probability distribution, based on some prior information we might have about relative likelihoods. For example, you might be trying to decide between two stocks to buy or two jobs to take. Your stockbroker might tell you that one stock will pay $6 per share with probability 1/3 and nothing with probability 2/3, while the other stock pays $3 per share with probability 1/2 and $1 per share with probability 1/2. The stockbroker doesn't know for sure that those are the correct probabilities, but he or she makes an educated guess, based on research and experience. We call such probabilities **subjective probabilities.** Another stockbroker might have different information, experience, or prior beliefs, any one of which might lead him or her to give you another set of subjective probability estimates.

There are several things we should know about probabilities. First, note that in every example above (equations 19.1 and 19.2 and the stocks), the probabilities sum to 1:

$$\frac{1}{2} + \frac{1}{2} = 1 \tag{19.3}$$

$$\frac{1}{6} + \frac{1}{6} + \frac{1}{6} + \frac{1}{6} + \frac{1}{6} + \frac{1}{6} = 1 \tag{19.4}$$

$$\frac{1}{3} + \frac{2}{3} = 1. \tag{19.5}$$

In each case, the events are mutually exclusive and they exhaust all the possible outcomes. In other words, one and only one event will occur. Since probabilities represent relative likelihoods and one of the possible outcomes *will* eventually happen, the sum of the probabilities has to be 1.

Expected Value and Variance   Second, if a set of uncertain outcomes can be expressed in numerical terms, as in a **gamble** or a **lottery,** we calculate the average value of the possible outcomes by multiplying each outcome by its probability and then adding the products. The resulting sum is called the **expected value** of the gamble or lottery because if the gamble is played many times, the player's average payoff from playing the gamble will be that value. If the "price" to play a gamble (as in the price of a lottery ticket) is equal to the expected value of the gamble, we call it a **fair bet.** For example, the expected value of the two stocks is the same:

$$\left(\frac{1}{3}\right)(6) + \left(\frac{2}{3}\right)(0) = 2 \tag{19.6}$$

$$\left(\frac{1}{2}\right)(3) + \left(\frac{1}{2}\right)(1) = 2.$$

Thus, if they cost $2 each, they would be fair bets. Similarly, the expected value of an outcome that depends on getting "heads" from the toss of a fair coin is 1/2 times the value of the outcome. The expected value of a certain outcome (probability equals 1) is the value of the outcome itself.

Third, different gambles with the same expected value may differ in the amount of dispersion around the expected value. One common measure of dispersion is called the **variance.** It is measured as the sum of the squared differences between the possible outcomes in a lottery and the expected value of the lottery, each multiplied by its respective probability. The variance can be thought of as a measure of the average amount of dispersion in outcomes around the expected value. Thus, returning to the stocks whose expected values are calculated as equations 19.6, the variance of the first stock is

$$(6 - 2)^2 \left(\frac{1}{3}\right) + (0 - 2)^2 \left(\frac{2}{3}\right) = \frac{16}{3} + \frac{8}{3} = 8. \tag{19.7}$$

The variance of the second stock, on the other hand, is

$$(3 - 2)^2 \left(\frac{1}{2}\right) + (1 - 2)^2 \left(\frac{1}{2}\right) = 1. \tag{19.8}$$

Independence   Suppose now that a gamble is to be played several times in succession. If each time the gamble is played, the probability distribution over outcomes is the same as when the gamble is only played once, then we say that the possible outcomes are **independent** of one another. In other words, two probabilistic events are independent of one another if the occurrence of one event has no effect on the probability that the other event will occur. For example, the outcomes of the tosses of a fair coin are independent because every time a fair coin is tossed, the probability that heads will come up the next time is still $1/2$, no matter how many tails have come before.

If two events are independent, then the a priori probability[1] of both events occurring is simply the probabilities multiplied together. For example, the probability of getting heads-heads on two successive tosses is $(1/2)(1/2) = 1/4$. Similarly, the probabilities of getting heads-tails, tails-heads, and tails-tails are also each $1/4$. Each of the four possible combinations is equally likely with two tosses, just as each of the two possible single outcomes is equally likely on a single toss. If we toss three times, there are eight equally likely sequences of events. Each occurs with probability $(1/2)(1/2)(1/2) = (1/8)$. In general, if we toss n times, there are 2^n equally likely sequences, each occurring with probability $(1/2)^n$.

Formal Properties of Probabilities   To summarize the properties and definitions discussed informally above, suppose that each time an action is taken, the result will be one of n independent and different outcomes. Let

$$x_i = \text{the value of the } i\text{th outcome}$$

$$\rho_i = \text{the probability that the } i\text{th outcome will occur.}$$

Then, we can state the two properties of probabilities and the two definitions discussed above as

1. $\displaystyle\sum_{i=1}^{n} \rho_i = 1;$ (19.9)

2. the probability of x_i and x_j occurring in two "trials" $= (\rho_i)(\rho_j);$ (19.10)

3. expected value $= E\{x\} = \displaystyle\sum_{i=1}^{n} \rho_i x_i = \bar{x};$ (19.11)

4. variance $= \text{var}\{x\} = \displaystyle\sum_{i=1}^{n} \rho_i (x_i - \bar{x})^2.$ (19.12)

The St. Petersburg Paradox   Now, suppose you had the opportunity to pay $100 and then play any of the following gambles, each of which is a fair bet.

1. You get back $100. (19.13)

2. I toss a fair coin. You receive (19.14)
    $200 if heads
    0 if tails.

---

[1]When we say a priori probability, we mean before any steps have been taken to resolve the uncertainty. In this case, tossing the coin resolves the uncertainty.

3. I roll a fair die. You receive (19.15)
$400 if 1
70 if 2
55 if 3
25 if 4
40 if 5
10 if 6.

All the gambles described in (19.13–19.15) have expected values of $100, but would you be equally willing to play each one? For one thing, the variances are different:

1. 0 (19.16)

2. $\frac{1}{2}(200 - 100)^2 + \frac{1}{2}(0 - 100)^2 = 10,000$ (19.17)

3. $\frac{1}{6}(300^2 + 30^2 + 45^2 + 75^2 + 60^2 + 90^2)$ (19.18)

$$= \frac{9000 + 900 + 2025 + 5625 + 3600 + 8100}{6} = 18{,}375.$$

You might, for example, be more willing to play the gamble with the lower variance (19.13) than the one with the higher variance (19.15).

This point is illustrated by what is called the **St. Petersburg paradox.** This was noted by Bernoulli, a Swiss mathematician of the eighteenth century. He proposed a variation of the following gamble. Suppose a fair coin is tossed until it comes up heads. Your payoff depends on the number of tosses before heads appears for the first time. Recognizing that tosses of a fair coin are independent and that probabilities get multiplied together on successive tosses, your payoffs in Bernoulli's game are constructed as follows.

$2 if heads comes up first on the first try $(\rho = 1/2)$ (19.19)

$4 if heads comes up first on the second try $(\rho = 1/4)$

$8 if heads comes up first on the third try $(\rho = 1/8)$

$16 if heads comes up first on the fourth try $(\rho = 1/16)$

$\vdots$

2^n if heads comes up first on the nth try $(\rho = 1/(2^n))$

$\vdots$

The expected value of the gamble set out in (19.19) is

$$\left(\frac{1}{2}\right)2 + \left(\frac{1}{4}\right)4 + \left(\frac{1}{8}\right)8 + \cdots = \sum_{n=1}^{\infty} \frac{1}{2^n} 2^n = 1 + 1 + \cdots = \infty. \qquad (19.20)$$

But no one would pay an infinite amount to play this gamble. In fact, few would pay much more than a few dollars. One reason might be that the variance of this gamble is also infinite, and most people prefer lower variance (less uncertainty) to more.

19.3 EXPECTED UTILITY AND THE VON NEUMANN-MORGENSTERN UTILITY FUNCTION

The St. Petersburg paradox suggests that we need some concept other than expected value to analyze how people make decisions in risky situations. Von Neumann and Morgenstern used such a concept, called expected utility, in their book on game theory.[2] **Expected utility** is a representation of preferences under uncertainty in terms of the expected value of a set of utilities over possible outcomes, x_i:

$$E\{U\} = \sum_{i=1}^{n} \rho_i U(x_i), \qquad (19.21)$$

which is linear in the probabilities (ρ_i).

The Axioms of Expected Utility Before constructing a particular expected utility index, suppose we consider a set of reasonable assumptions which any expected utility index would satisfy, just as we set out the axioms of consumer preference in Section 5.3. The following axioms are generally used by economists who study decisions under uncertainty.

AXIOM E1 *Preferences over possible outcomes, $x_1, \ldots, x_n$, are complete, reflexive, and transitive.*

In other words, preferences over possible outcomes obey the first three axioms of consumer preference from Section 5.3. We will assume from now on that outcomes are ranked so that x_1 is the least-preferred alternative, x_n is the most-preferred alternative, and the subscripts in between reflect the order of preference.

AXIOM E2 *Compound lotteries can be reduced to simple lotteries,* where the compound lotteries have the same ultimate probabilities over outcomes as the simple lotteries.

This is best illustrated with an example. Suppose you were given a choice of playing the following two gambles. In the first gamble, you begin by tossing a coin. If heads come up, you toss another coin. If heads come up again you win $1 and if tails come up you win $0.75. If tails come up on the first toss on the other hand, you then roll a die. Your prize is $0.10 per "spot" on the up face ($0.10 for a 1, $0.20 for a 2, and so on up to $0.60 for a 6). This gamble is illustrated in Figure 19.1. First, you have a 50/50 chance of getting heads or tails. (This is shown as game 1.) If you get heads, you then have a 50/50 chance of getting $1 or $0.75. Thus, from the beginning, you have a 1/4 chance of getting either $1 or $0.75. If you get tails on the first toss, you then have a 1/6 chance of getting 10, 20, 30, 40, 50, or 60 cents. (This is shown as game 2.) Thus, from the beginning, you have a 1/12 chance of getting each of those. We can rewrite this gamble as the following lottery.

---

[2]Von Neumann and Morgenstern, *Theory of Games and Economic Behavior.*

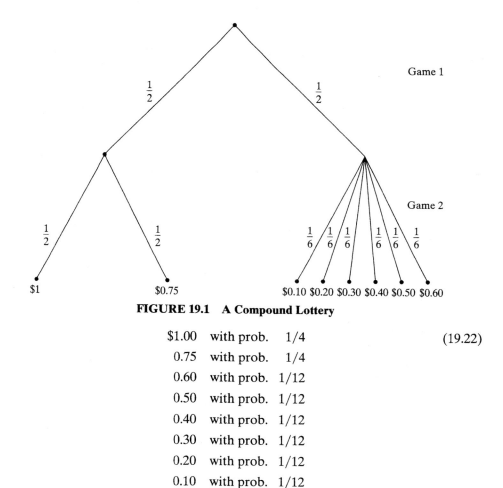

FIGURE 19.1   A Compound Lottery

$$
\begin{array}{lll}
\$1.00 & \text{with prob.} & 1/4 \\
0.75 & \text{with prob.} & 1/4 \\
0.60 & \text{with prob.} & 1/12 \\
0.50 & \text{with prob.} & 1/12 \\
0.40 & \text{with prob.} & 1/12 \\
0.30 & \text{with prob.} & 1/12 \\
0.20 & \text{with prob.} & 1/12 \\
0.10 & \text{with prob.} & 1/12
\end{array}
\qquad (19.22)
$$

In the second gamble, a wheel is spun and you win the prize associated with the amount shown where the pointer stops. The relative fractions of the wheel's circumference at which the pointer might stop are equal to the probabilities summarized in (19.22) and Figure 19.1 and the prizes are the associated outcomes of that lottery. Thus, 1/4 of the circumference wins $1.00, 1/4 wins $0.75, and 1/12 wins each of 10, 20, 30, 40, 50, and 60 cents. This gamble is illustrated in Figure 19.2.

To satisfy Axiom E2, the consumer has to be indifferent between playing gamble 1 and playing gamble 2.

AXIOM E3   *Continuity.* This axiom says that for each outcome x_i *between* x_1 and x_n, the consumer can name a probability, ρ_i, such that he or she is indifferent between getting x_i with certainty and playing a lottery (which involves getting x_n with probability ρ_i and x_1 with probability $(1 - \rho_i)$). We say that x_i is the **certainty equivalent** to the lottery, $\tilde{x}_i$, where

$$
\tilde{x}_i = (x_n \text{ with pr. } \rho_i \text{ and } x_1 \text{ with pr. } (1 - \rho_i)). \qquad (19.23)
$$

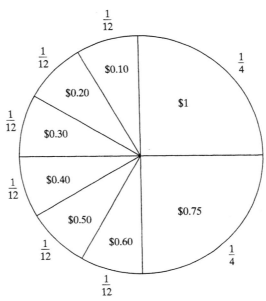

FIGURE 19.2 A Simple Lottery

The idea of certainty equivalence implies that $x_i^1 \tilde{x}_j$.

AXIOM E4 *Substitutability.* The lottery $\tilde{x}_i$ can always be substituted for its certainty equivalent x_i in any other lottery (since the consumer is indifferent between them).

AXIOM E5 *Transitivity.* Preferences over lotteries are transitive.

AXIOM E6 *Monotonicity.* If two lotteries with the same two alternatives each differ only in probabilities, then the lottery that gives higher probability to the most-preferred alternative is preferred to the other lottery.

$$[\rho x_n + (1 - \rho)x_1]^P [\rho' x_n + (1 - \rho')x_1] \quad \text{if and only if} \quad \rho > \rho' \qquad (19.24)$$

Now, if preferences over lotteries satisfy axioms E1–E6, then we can assign numbers $U(x_i)$ associated with the outcomes x_i, such that if we compare two lotteries L and L' which offer probabilities $(\rho_1, \ldots, \rho_n)$ and $(\rho'_1, \ldots, \rho'_n)$ of obtaining those outcomes, L will be preferred to L' if and only if

$$\sum_{i=1}^{n} \rho_i U(x_i) > \sum_{i=1}^{n} \rho'_i U(x_i).$$

This means that the rank order by expected utilities reflects the rank order of preference over the lotteries and that the rational individual will choose among risky alternatives as if he or she is maximizing expected utility.

The von Neumann-Morgenstern Utility Index   **The von Neumann-Morgenstern utility index** is constructed as follows. First, all possible outcomes are ranked as in the discussion of axiom E1: $x_1, \ldots, x_n$, where x_2 is preferred to x_1, x_3 is preferred to x_2, and x_n is preferred to x_{n-1}. Next, the least-preferred possible outcome is assigned a utility value of 0, the most preferred is assigned a utility value of 1, and every other possible outcome (x_i) is assigned a utility value equal to ρ_i, where x_i is the certainty equivalent of a lottery involving x_n with probability ρ_i and x_1 with probability $(1 - \rho_i)$:

$$U(x_1) \equiv 0, \; U(x_n) \equiv 1, \; U(x_i) \equiv \rho_i. \tag{19.25}$$

The utility index set out in (19.25) is equivalent to taking expected values of the utilities of x_n and x_1, using the probabilities ρ_i and $(1 - \rho_1)$ associated with the lottery for which x_i is the certainty equivalent, for every x_i, including x_1 and x_n:

$$U(x_i) = \rho_i U(x_n) + (1 - \rho_i)U(x_1) = \rho_i + 0 = \rho_i. \tag{19.26}$$

The utility index described by (19.25) and (19.26) is **unique up to linear transformations,** which means that we could have chosen any other nonnegative original values of the utilities for x_1 and x_n (as long as $U(x_n) > U(x_1)$) and then expressed $U(x_i)$ as the expected utility of the lottery. For example, the following index would be acceptable:

$$V(x_1) = a, \quad V(x_n) = b, \quad b > a \geq 0, \tag{19.27}$$
$$V(x_i) = \rho_1 b + (1 - \rho_i)a.$$

To see that a linear transformation *does* preserve the certainty equivalence, consider the original scaling set out in (19.25) to define $U(x)$. Now, let

$$V(x) = c + dU(x). \tag{19.28}$$

Substituting (19.25) in (19.28),

$$V(x_1) = c + d \cdot 0 = c \quad \text{and} \quad V(x_n) = c + d \cdot 1 = c + d. \tag{19.29}$$

From (19.29), the expected utility of x_i, given ρ_i, is

$$V(x_i) = \rho_i(c + d) + (1 - \rho_i)c = c + d\rho_i. \tag{19.30}$$

The value of $V(x_i)$ in equation 19.30 is thus the same as the transformed utility of x_i obtained by simply substituting for $U(x_i)$ from (19.25) in equation 19.28. Thus, equation 19.30 shows that when we evaluate the expected utility of x_i under the transformation on the utilities of x_1 and x_n, we get back the transformed utility of x_i. This implies that the transformation preserves the certainty equivalence relationship.

Risk Aversion, Risk Neutrality, and Risk Seeking   Expected utility functions are typically categorized in three ways. We say that an individual is **risk averse** if for constant wealth, a certain outcome is always preferred to a gamble with the same expected value but some positive variance. An individual is **risk neutral** if he or she is indifferent between the certain outcome and the gamble and is **risk seeking** if the gamble is preferred.

To illustrate risk aversion, suppose there are three possible outcomes and two actions which can be taken. Outcome 1 is $50 and the associated utility is 30; outcome 2 is $100 and the associated utility is 80; and outcome 3 is $150 and the associated utility is 110. Thus, we can summarize the utilities as

$$U(\$50) = 30, \quad U(\$100) = 80, \quad U(\$150) = 110. \tag{19.31}$$

The two different actions now yield these outcomes with different probabilities. Action A yields $100 with certainty and, from (19.31), has an expected utility of 80:

$$E\{U(A)\} = (1)U(100) = 80. \tag{19.32}$$

Action B yields $50 with probability $\frac{1}{2}$ and $150 with probability $\frac{1}{2}$. Thus, the expected utility is only 70:

$$E\{U(B)\} = \tfrac{1}{2}U(50) + \tfrac{1}{2}U(150) = \tfrac{1}{2}(30 + 110) = 70 < 80. \tag{19.33}$$

Equations 19.32 and 19.33 show that even though each action yields an expected payoff of $100, the expected utility of action B is less than the expected utility of action A.

The example set out in equations 19.32 and 19.33 is illustrated in Figure 19.3. $100 for certain yields a utility value of 80, while $50 and $150 yield utility values of 30 and 110, respectively, giving a concave utility function. The expected utility of the 50/50 gamble on $100 + 50$ and $100 - 50$ is at the midpoint of the linear combination of the utility of $50 and the utility of $150. This utility (70) is less than the utility of $100 for certain. Thus, we say that the individual having this utility function is risk averse.

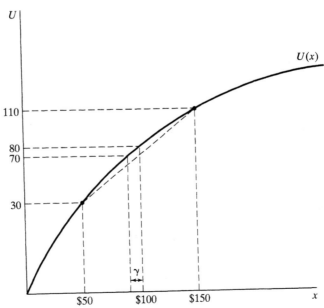

FIGURE 19.3   The Choice for a Risk-averse Individual Between a Certain Sum of Money and a Gamble

Moreover, this individual would be willing to pay the amount labeled γ to avoid playing the gamble altogether. At the lower payoff ($\$100 - \gamma$), the individual still gets utility of 70 and doesn't have to take any risk. We call the amount a risk-averse person is willing to pay to avoid risk the **risk premium.**

Figure 19.4 illustrates all three attitudes toward risk. In each case, we compare the utility of a certain sum $\bar{x}$ with the expected utility of a gamble that pays $\bar{x} - a$ with probability 1/2 and $\bar{x} + a$ with probability 1/2. In the left graph (risk neutrality), the utility function is a straight line, and the individual is indifferent between the certain prize and the gamble. In the middle graph (risk aversion), the utility function is concave, and the utility of the certain prize is always higher than the expected utility of the gamble. In the right graph (risk seeking), the utility function is convex, and the expected utility of the gamble is always higher than the utility of the certain prize.

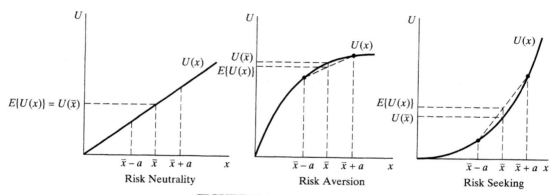

FIGURE 19.4   Attitudes Toward Risk

19.4   INSURANCE MARKETS

One important application of the theory of risk aversion is to the market for insurance. Insurance is protection against various forms of risk, and a risk-averse individual is willing to pay some risk premium to avoid taking risk.

An Example   To illustrate how a risk-averse individual benefits by buying insurance, consider the following simple example. Suppose you own a building that is worth $\$50,000$ and you have other assets worth $\$50,000$. There is a 10% chance that the building will be destroyed by fire, flood, or tornado, or collapse from snow or some other natural disaster. Thus, with 10% probability, you will have only your other $\$50,000$ in assets, and with 90% probability, you will have $\$100,000$ in assets (the building plus the other $\$50,000$). Assuming that your utility over the value of your assets is independent of the **state of the world** (defined as whether or not you suffer a loss), the expected utility of this gamble is

$$E\{U\} = (.10)U(50{,}000) + (.90)U(100{,}000);$$ (19.34)

and the expected value is

$$E\{x\} = .10(50,000) + .90(100,000) = 95,000. \qquad (19.35)$$

The gamble described by equations 19.34 and 19.35 is illustrated in Figure 19.5. The expected value of the gamble is $95,000. The expected utility of the gamble can be found by drawing a straight line between 50,000 and 100,000. The expected utility is 9/10 of the way from 50,000 to 100,000 along that line. Assuming risk aversion, the expected utility of the $95,000 gamble is less than having $95,000 for certain. Moreover, at the expected utility of the $95,000 gamble, you are willing to pay some risk premium (γ) to avoid the gamble altogether.

Now, if you are offered insurance, you can pay some **insurance premium**[3] and, if a loss occurs, the insurance company reimburses you some predetermined amount. Suppose that the premium is simply equal to the expected value of the loss. In equation 19.35, for example, the expected loss would be

$$.10(50,000) = \$5,000. \qquad (19.36)$$

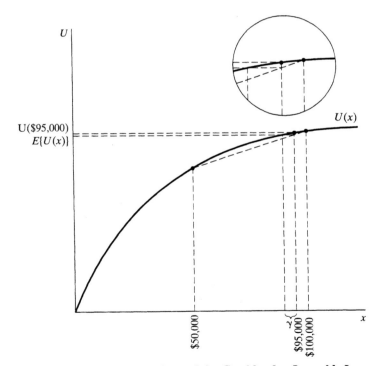

FIGURE 19.5   Risk Aversion and the Gamble of an Insurable Loss

---

[3]This is different from a risk premium.

We say that a premium is **actuarially fair** if it is equal to the expected value of the loss. In other words, purchasing the insurance is a fair bet. How much actuarially fair insurance will a risk-averse individual purchase?

A Model of Insurance Purchase   To answer that question, we develop a simple model of the insurance purchase decision. Let

$$x^0 = \text{income or assets without a loss}$$

$$L = \text{amount of loss}$$

$$\rho = \text{the probability of loss (on which consumer}$$
$$\text{and insurance company agree)}$$

$$A = \text{dollar amount of insurance coverage purchased}$$
$$\text{(reimbursement in case of loss).}$$

If the insurance premium is actuarially fair,

$$\rho A = \text{the expected reimbursement} = \text{the total insurance premium}$$

$$x^\ell = (x^0 - L + A - \rho A) = \text{income in the state of the world} \qquad (19.37)$$
$$\text{when a loss occurs}$$

$$x^n = (x^0 - \rho A) = \text{income in the state of the world} \qquad (19.38)$$
$$\text{when no loss occurs.}$$

Assuming once again that utility depends only on income, equations 19.37 and 19.38 indicate that expected utility with actuarially fair insurance is

$$E\{U\} = \rho U(x^\ell) + (1 - \rho)U(x^n). \qquad (19.39)$$

To find the optimal insurance coverage to purchase, we differentiate expected utility (19.39) with respect to A (using the chain rule) and set the derivative equal to 0:

$$\frac{\partial}{\partial A}E\{U\} = \rho(1 - \rho)\frac{\partial}{\partial A}U(x^\ell) - (1 - \rho)\rho\frac{\partial}{\partial A}U(x^n) = 0. \qquad (19.40)$$

Simplifying (19.40),

$$\frac{\partial}{\partial A}U(x^\ell) = \frac{\partial}{\partial A}U(x^n). \qquad (19.41)$$

With a strictly concave function, if the first derivatives are the same it must be because they are evaluated at the same net incomes, with and without the loss. Thus, equation 19.41 implies that the utilities and the net incomes must be the same, with and without the loss:

$$x^0 - L + A - \rho A = x^0 - \rho A. \qquad (19.42)$$

Solving 19.42 for A,

$$A^* = L. \qquad (19.43)$$

Equation 19.43 shows that the consumer buys full coverage insurance when insurance is actuarially fair. In other words, the consumer buys the amount of insurance that is equal to the full value of the potential loss.

Full Insurance Purchase and Certain Consumption   Notice that this result indicates that if insurance is actuarially fair, the consumer chooses to turn a random payoff (possible loss) into a certain payoff (assets will be the same whether there is a loss or not). This means that the expected utility will be equal to the utility of the expected value in this instance. This is illustrated in Figure 19.6. By buying full insurance at actuarially fair rates, the consumer is able to consume x^n in both states of the world. To see this point, substitute equation 19.43 in equation 19.37:

$$x^\ell = x^0 - A + A - pA = x^0 - pA = x^n. \tag{19.44}$$

Equation 19.44 shows that the consumer gets x^n with certainty. So, expected utility is simply the utility associated with x^n.

In the example developed in equations 19.34–19.36, the consumer pays an insurance premium of $5000 out of the original assets of $100,000, or out of the remaining $50,000 if a loss occurs. But, if a loss occurs, he or she also gets reimbursed $50,000. Thus, assets are $95,000, regardless of whether a loss does or does not occur.

Insurance and the Law of Large Numbers   Insurance companies can sell full insurance policies if the probabilities are known because they sell policies to many different individuals and can achieve an average return over all policies with virtual certainty. They can do this because of the law of large numbers. Basically, by **the law of large numbers,**

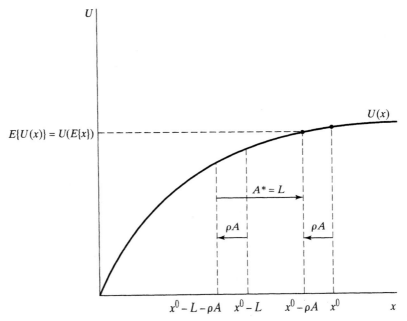

FIGURE 19.6   Certainty of Income and Utility with Full Insurance

if a sample drawn from a larger group (called a **population**) becomes large enough, the mean (expected value) of the sample becomes equal to the mean of the population, as long as the mean and variance of the underlying population distribution are finite.

This point is illustrated by thinking of drawing a series of samples of different sizes from the same underlying population. If samples of size $N = 1$ are drawn, the mean of each sample will be the value of each individual observation and there will be some probability distribution over those "means." As you increase the sample sizes however, the mean of each sample drawn is more and more likely to be close to the mean of the underlying distribution. Eventually, when the sample size is equal to the entire population size, the mean of the sample has to equal the underlying population mean. This is illustrated in Figure 19.7 with the familiar bell curve (or **normal distribution**). Mean values of samples are plotted along the horizontal axis and the probability of observing that mean from samples of a given size are plotted along the vertical axis. If samples of size $N = 1$ are drawn, the distribution of sample means forms the bell curve with the lowest peak at the underlying population mean value. As the sample sizes are increased, however, the probability of observing the underlying population mean ($E\{x\}$) as the mean of a sample becomes larger and larger.

Insurance companies benefit from the law of large numbers because their earnings depend upon the average value of the claims they process. At any point in time, most policy holders are filing no claims, but a few may be filing large claims. The companies use statistics from the larger population to estimate how much they will have to pay out in claims on average. If a company has enough policy holders (a large enough sample) and if that sample of policy holders is representative of the population as a whole, then the probability that the average claim will equal the estimate calculated from statistics on the larger population will be practically equal to 1. If that is the case, then the company can calculate its profits as if they are known with certainty. The firm may not always break even in a particular year, but it will almost always break even on average.

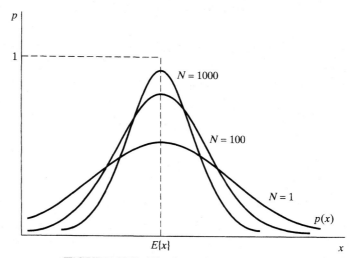

FIGURE 19.7   The Law of Large Numbers

19.5 FUTURES CONTRACTS AND OTHER LONG-TERM CONTRACTS AS INSURANCE

Consumers can purchase insurance in other ways than through formal insurance markets. For example, any transaction that specifies what price will be paid at some time or over some period in the future when prices are expected to be variable is a form of insurance. Two common examples are futures contracts (or forward contracts) for goods and long-term wage contracts.

Futures Contracts In a futures contract, a firm or consumer contracts to purchase a given quantity of a particular good at a stated price (called the **futures price**) at some time or over some period in the future. By doing so, the buyer avoids the implicit gamble if prices at that time (called **spot prices**) are not known with certainty. Assuming the buyer is risk averse, he or she will buy at the futures price as long as the difference between what he or she would pay at the futures price and at the mean of the spot prices is not greater than his or her risk premium.

This is illustrated for a one-unit purchase in Figure 19.8. The horizontal axis represents income or assets left over after a unit of the good has been purchased. The mean of the spot prices is $\bar{p}$ and the buyer has a 50/50 chance of getting p_1 or p_2, where $p_1 > p_2$. Since only one unit is purchased, the consumer has income $x^0 - p_1$ at price p_1 and $x^0 - p_2$ at price p_2, with mean income of $x^0 - \bar{p}$ and expected utility of $E\{U(x)\}$. If the consumer purchases the unit on the futures market at a price of P, on the other hand, he or she can attain the same utility with certainty:

$$U(x^0 - P) = E\{U(x)\}.$$

On the graph, the difference between the expected income and the certain income of the futures contract is the consumer's risk premium (γ):

$$(x^0 - \bar{p}) - (x^0 - P) = \gamma \implies P - \bar{p} = \gamma.$$

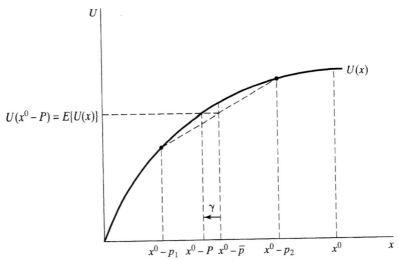

FIGURE 19.8 **Risk Aversion and the Purchase of a Futures Contract**

If P is any lower, the consumer is paying less than his or her risk premium and prefers the futures contract.

Long-term Labor Contracts   Turning now to long-term labor contracts, when a salaried worker signs a contract with an employer, he or she agrees to work so many hours per week or month, and the employer agrees to pay some wage for that time. There may also be provision made for overtime pay, typically up to some maximum number of hours per week. Without such a contract, the worker might earn a different wage each day if the spot price for labor were variable. In fact, in the past it was not uncommon for work to be available to anyone who showed up at the factory gates on a particular day, willing to work at the wage for that day. With a labor contract, a risk-averse worker gets a given wage for certain, instead of assuming the risk of getting high wages on some days and low wages or even no work on others. And just as in the futures market, the worker will accept any contract that pays no less than the average of the spot wages minus the risk premium.

19.6   CONTINGENT CLAIMS AND THE STATE-PREFERENCE MODEL

An alternative way of modeling decisions under uncertainty is called the state-preference model. Before the uncertainty is resolved (or *ex ante*), we can think of the different outcomes obtainable in different states of the world. Thus, in the insurance example, in one state of the world the consumer suffers a loss and in the other, he or she does not. *Ex ante,* the consumer doesn't know which state will occur, but wants to be sure to have consumption goods available in each state.

Contingent Commodities and Contingent Claims   Using the simple two-good model we have developed throughout this book, think of x_1 as consumption when state of the world 1 occurs and x_2 as consumption when state of the world 2 occurs. We call a commodity that is to be delivered in only one state of the world a **state-contingent commodity** (or just a contingent commodity). In actuality, if there are n different commodities and m states of the world, there will be $(n \times m)$ different contingent commodities. For now, we consider only one commodity (consumption) and two states of the world: "good" (1) and "bad" (2). Thus, in this case, there are two contingent commodities.

In the **state-preference model,** consumers trade **contingent claims,** which are rights to consumption, if, and only if, a particular state of the world occurs. Thus, in this framework, x_1 represents the amount of the good the consumer will receive if state 1 occurs and x_2 is the amount he or she will receive if state 2 occurs. If the consumer wants to be able to consume regardless of which state of the world occurs, he or she must own claims for both x_1 and x_2.

One way to imagine a contingent-claims market is to compare it to betting in a horse race. The states of the world correspond to how the various horses will place, and a claim corresponds, for example, to a bet that a horse will win. If your horse comes in, you get paid in proportion to the number of tickets you purchased. But the only way to guarantee payment in all states of the world is to bet on all the horses.

State-contingent Indifference Curves To analyze a contingent-claims market, we use the familiar approach of finding the highest possible indifference curve along a budget line. To construct the indifference map, we begin with the original, state-independent utility function $U(x)$. A point x^a along that function represents x^a for certain, and $U(x^a)$ is the utility associated with getting x^a for certain. This would be equivalent to getting x^a in both states of the world $(x_1^a = x_2^a)$. This equivalence is illustrated in Figure 19.9. In the left graph, x^a generates utility of $U(x^a)$ for certain. In the right graph, $x_1^a = x_2^a$ along the 45° line. This will eventually represent a point on an indifference curve such that

$$E\{U(x)\} = U(x^a), \tag{19.45}$$

and x^a will be the certainty equivalent for that indifference curve.

Now, suppose the probability of state 1 occurring is 2/3 and the probability of state 2 occurring is 1/3. We look for a combination of x_1 and x_2 (say x_1^b and x_2^b) such that the consumer is indifferent between x^a with certainty and a lottery that yields x_1^b with probability 2/3 and x_2^b with probability 1/3. And, since the consumer is indifferent between x^a and the lottery, the point (x_1^b, x_2^b) is also on the $U(x^a)$ indifference curve set out in equation 19.45. This is illustrated in Figure 19.10. In the left graph, the expected utility of the lottery is equal to the utility of x^a. We will refer to the expected utility as $V(x_1^a, x_2^a)$:

$$\tfrac{2}{3}U(x_1^b) + \tfrac{1}{3}U(x_2^b) = U(x^a) = V(x_1^a, x_2^a). \tag{19.46}$$

In the right graph, the point (x_1^b, x_2^b) is on the indifference curve defined by

$$V(x_1^a, x_2^a) = U(x^a). \tag{19.47}$$

To construct the indifference curve, we find all the possible combinations of quantities of goods consumed in states 1 and 2 such that the consumer is indifferent between x^a

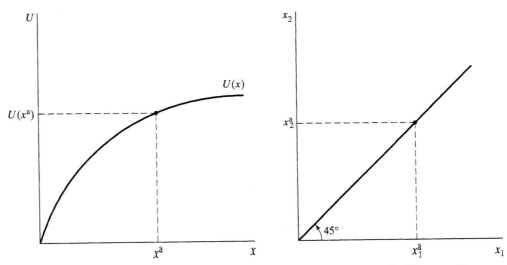

FIGURE 19.9   Identifying a Certainty Equivalent for a State-contingent Indifference Curve

with certainty and the lottery that yields state 1 with probability 2/3 and state 2 with probability 1/3.

Diminishing Marginal Rates of Substitution and Risk Aversion   Now, let's look at this indifference curve more closely. It consists of combinations of x_1 and x_2, such that

$$\rho U(x_1) + (1 - \rho)U(x_2) = U(x^a) = V(x_1^a, x_2^a), \tag{19.48}$$

where ρ is the probability of state 1 occurring. The marginal rate of substitution along the state-contingent indifference curve indicates the rate at which a consumer is willing to give up consumption in one state of the world in order to be able to consume more in the other state. To find the marginal rate of substitution, we totally differentiate equation 19.48 and set the total differential equal to 0, since $dV = 0$ along the indifference curve:

$$dV = 0 = \rho \frac{d}{dx}U(x_1)dx_1 + (1 - \rho)\frac{d}{dx}U(x_2)dx_2. \tag{19.49}$$

Solving (19.49) for the slope of the indifference curve,

$$\frac{dx_2}{dx_1} = -\frac{\rho[dU(x_1)/dx]}{(1 - \rho)[dU(x_2)/dx]} \tag{19.50}$$

$$= -\frac{\rho U'(x_1)}{(1 - \rho)U'(x_2)} < 0. \quad \text{by nonsatiation}$$

The first thing to note about the marginal rate of substitution is that along the 45° line, where $x_1 = x_2$,

$$MRS = \frac{\rho}{1 - \rho}, \tag{19.51}$$

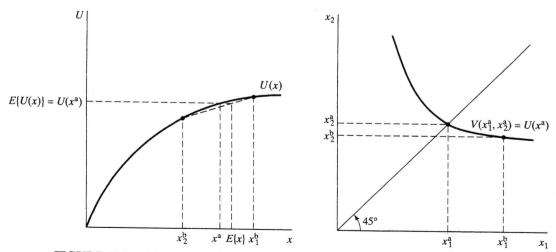

FIGURE 19.10   Identifying a Lottery as a Point on a State-contingent Indifference Curve

since $dU(x_1)/dx = dU(x_2)/dx$ when $x_1 = x_2$. Second, we want to look at the shape of the indifference curve. To do this, we take the second derivative:

$$\frac{d^2 x_2}{dx_1^2} = -\frac{\rho U''(x_1)[(1-\rho)U'(x_2)] - (1-\rho)U''(x_2)(dx_2/dx_1)[\rho U'(x_1)]}{[(1-\rho)U'(x_2)]^2}. \quad (19.52)$$

Since the first derivative of the utility function and the probabilities are all positive and the slope of the indifference curve is negative by equation 19.50, the expression in equation 19.52 will be positive at every point along every indifference curve (implying diminishing marginal rates of substitution) if, and only if, the second derivative of the utility function is negative at every point. That is, if the second derivative of the utility function is everywhere negative, (19.52) is positive; if the second derivative is everywhere 0, (19.52) is 0; and if the second derivative is everywhere positive, (19.52) is negative.

We have already seen, however, that a concave utility function (second derivative negative) implies that the individual is risk averse. Thus, the above argument shows that, in the state-preference model, risk aversion is a necessary and sufficient condition for state-contingent indifference curves to exhibit diminishing marginal rates of substitution. If an individual is risk neutral (second derivative 0), the indifference curve is linear (second derivative 0). If an individual is risk seeking (second derivative of utility function positive), the indifference curve bows out. The case of risk aversion is illustrated in Figure 19.11. A strictly concave utility function implies indifference curves that are strictly convex to the origin.

The State-contingent Budget Line and Utility Maximization   To construct the individual's budget line, we first note that the realization of state 1 or state 2 implies that some quantity of consumption goods will be available. By our calling state 1 "good" and state 2 "bad," we mean that the initial endowment in state 1 will be more than the initial endowment in state 2. That is, the initial endowment will fall below the 45° line.

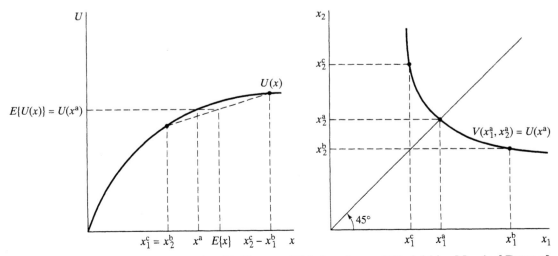

FIGURE 19.11   The Relationship Between Risk Aversion and Diminishing Marginal Rates of Substitution

Recognizing that we have initial endowments, we can construct the budget line just as we did in the pure-trade model introduced in Section 9.3. The value of contingent claims purchased cannot exceed the value of claims to the individual's initial endowment:

$$p_1 x_1 + p_2 x_2 \leq p_1 \bar{x}_1 + p_2 \bar{x}_2, \tag{19.53}$$

where p_1 and p_2 are the prices for contingent claims and $\bar{x}_1$ and $\bar{x}_2$ are the respective initial endowments. The budget line is thus just a straight line, with slope $-p_1/p_2$, going through the initial endowment. This is illustrated in Figure 19.12.

By utility maximization, then, we know that the marginal rate of substitution (equation 19.50) will be equal to the contingent price ratio:

$$MRS = \frac{\rho[U'(x_1)]}{(1 - \rho)[U'(x_2)]} = \frac{p_1}{p_2}. \tag{19.54}$$

Equation 19.54 tells us that the contingent price ratio is equal to the ratio of marginal utilities, weighted by the ratio of subjective probabilities.

Risk Sharing Between Consumers in a Contingent-claims Market Now, suppose there are two individuals with different risk preferences who are endowed with equal amounts of consumption goods in states 1 and 2. With a competitive market in contingent claims, the less risk-averse individual will be willing to sell claims in the "bad" state to the more risk-averse individual in return for the right to consume even more in the "good" state. Even though both may be risk averse, if their degree of risk aversion is different, the more risk-averse individual will be willing to pay enough to compensate the less risk-averse individual for giving up claims to consumption in the "bad" state.

Risk sharing is illustrated with an Edgeworth box, shown in Figure 19.13. The box is designed with less total amount available in state 2, reflecting that state 2 is the "bad" state. If both consumers are endowed with equal amounts, the initial endowment is in the center of the box (at *IE*). Consumer A is more risk averse than consumer B, implying that A's indifference curves are relatively more convex than B's. Both consumers'

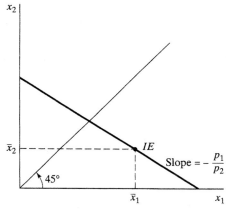

FIGURE 19.12 The Contingent-claims Budget Line

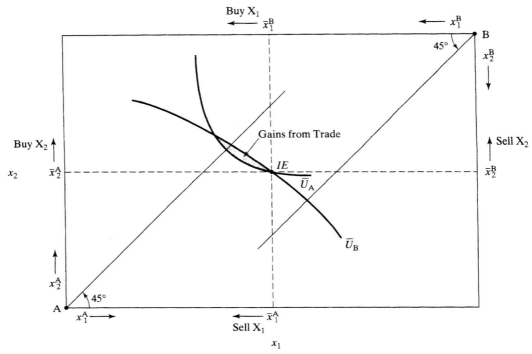

FIGURE 19.13 Gains from Trade in Contingent Claims When One Consumer Is More Risk Averse than the Other

indifference curves have marginal rates of substitution equal to their own subjective probability ratios along their respective 45° lines, as in equation 19.51.

Since consumer A's indifference curves are more convex, the area of gains from trade lies to the northwest of the equal initial endowment point. This means that at a Pareto optimal sharing of risk, the more risk-averse individual buys the right to consume more equally in the two states of the world. The less risk-averse individual, on the other hand, is willing to give up some consumption in state 2 (the bad state) for a relatively large transfer of state 1 contingent claims from the more risk-averse individual. The less risk-averse individual then consumes relatively more in state 1 (the good state).

Full Insurance When One Consumer Is Risk Neutral Figure 19.14 illustrates an optimal sharing of risk when one consumer is risk neutral, the other consumer is risk averse, and they agree on the subjective probability of loss. The risk-neutral consumer (consumer B) has a linear indifference curve through the initial endowment. B's marginal rate of substitution is simply equal to the ratio of probabilities. To see that, recall that a risk-neutral consumer is indifferent between a gamble and its expected value. Thus, we can write a risk-neutral consumer's expected utility function as

$$E\{U\} = \rho x_1 + (1 - \rho)x_2. \tag{19.55}$$

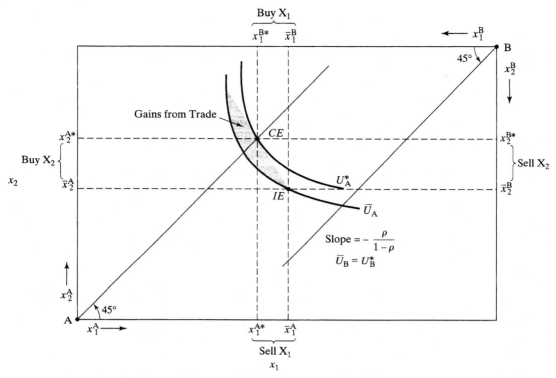

FIGURE 19.14 Optimal Allocation of Risk When One Individual Is Risk Neutral and Both Agree on the Probability of Loss

Equation 19.55 indicates that marginal rate of substitution is

$$MRS = \frac{\partial E\{U\}/\partial x_1}{\partial E\{U\}/\partial x_2} = \frac{\rho}{1 - \rho}. \tag{19.56}$$

Since the risk-neutral consumer's indifference curve is linear, the slope of the indifference curve, the ratio of objective probabilities, then becomes the price ratio for contingent claims. At a competitive equilibrium, the risk-averse consumer purchases as many claims as he or she wishes at that price ratio. Moreover, since the price ratio is equal to the ratio of probabilities, the risk-averse consumer maximizes utility by purchasing enough claims to ensure equal consumption in both states of the world. That is because the marginal rate of substitution is equal to the ratio of probabilities along the 45° line (equation 19.51).

Notice that this is exactly the result we obtained in the insurance market when an insurance company offered full insurance at actuarially fair rates. Here, equalizing consumption between the two states of the world is identical to buying full insurance. Thus, we see that purchase of full insurance at actuarially fair rates is a Pareto optimum if insurance companies are risk neutral and consumers are risk averse and if both agree on the probability of loss.

19.7 REVIEW OF KEY CONCEPTS

This completes our introduction to decision making under uncertainty. Before continuing to the next chapter on uncertainty models with incomplete or asymmetric information, be sure you understand the following key concepts.

Outcomes that occur with certainty are called *certain outcomes*. Outcomes which may or may not occur are called *uncertain outcomes*. The study of decision making when outcomes are uncertain is called decision making *under uncertainty*.

The likelihood that a particular uncertain outcome will occur is the *probability* of that outcome occurring.

If probabilities can be observed experimentally and then agreed upon, they are called *objective probabilities*.

If a coin is tossed many times and half the time it comes up heads and half the time tails, we say it is a *fair coin*.

The *probability distribution* over a set of uncertain outcomes describes the probability that each outcome will occur.

If the probability distribution over a set of uncertain outcomes cannot be verified experimentally but depends upon individuals' subjective beliefs, the probabilities are called *subjective probabilities*.

If a set of uncertain outcomes is mutually exclusive and exhausts all the possible outcomes in a particular situation, then the probabilities of each outcome occurring must sum to 1.

If a set of uncertain outcomes is given numerical values, as in a *gamble* or a *lottery*, then the average winnings from playing the lottery many times is called the *expected value* of the lottery. The expected value is found by multiplying the value of each outcome by its probability and then adding all the products.

If the price to play a gamble (as in the price of a lottery ticket) is equal to the expected value of the gamble, we say the gamble is a *fair bet*.

The *variance* of a lottery is the sum of the squared differences between the possible outcomes in a lottery and the expected value of the lottery, each multiplied by its respective probability. It can be thought of as a measure of the average amount of dispersion in outcomes around the expected value.

Two probabilistic events are *independent* of one another if one event's occurring has no effect on the probability that the other event will occur.

If a coin is tossed several times or a gamble is played several times and the outcomes are independent, then the a priori probability of two outcomes occurring in two successive trials is the individual probabilities multiplied together. For example, the probability of getting heads-heads on two successive tosses of a fair coin is $1/4$.

The *St. Petersburg paradox* refers to a gamble in which the probability of each of two outcomes is $1/2$ and the stakes are doubled each trial until a particular outcome occurs for the first time. Both the expected value and the variance of such a gamble are infinite. The paradox is that players will not pay an infinite amount to play such a gamble, even though that would be a fair bet.

Expected utility is a representation of preferences under uncertainty in terms of the expected value of a set of utilities over possible outcomes, which is linear in the probabilities (ρ_i).

An expected utility index will obey a set of axioms of expected utility. Axiom E1 is that preferences over possible outcomes are complete, reflexive, and transitive, as in the first three axioms of consumer preference from Section 5.3.

Axiom E2 states that consumers are always indifferent between a simple lottery and a compound lottery, where the ultimate probabilities over outcomes are the same in the two lotteries.

The *certainty equivalent* of a lottery that involves winning x_n with probability ρ_i and x_1 with probability $(1 - \rho_i)$ (where x_n is strictly preferred to x_1) is another outcome x_i, such that the individual is indifferent between getting x_i with certainty and playing the above lottery.

Axiom E3 states that for every outcome x_i, the consumer can name a probability ρ_i such that

x_i is the certainty equivalent to a lottery $\tilde{x}_i$ (which involves getting x_n with probability ρ_i and x_1 with probability $(1 - \rho_i)$).

By axiom E4 (*substitutability*), the lottery $\tilde{x}_i$ can always be substituted for its certainty equivalent, x_i, in any other lottery.

By axiom E5 (*transitivity*), preferences over lotteries are transitive.

By axiom E6 (*monotonicity*), if two lotteries have the same two possible outcomes, but one assigns a higher probability to the most-preferred outcome, then the lottery with that higher probability is preferred to the other lottery.

If preferences over lotteries satisfy axioms E1–E6, then we can assign numbers $U(x_i)$ associated with the outcomes x_i, such that if we compare two lotteries L and L' which offer probabilities $(\rho_1, \ldots, \rho_n)$ and $(\rho_1', \ldots, \rho_n')$ of obtaining those outcomes, L will be preferred to L' if and only if the expected utility of L is greater than the expected utility of L'.

If all possible outcomes are ranked, with the least-preferred (x_1) assigned a utility of 0 and the most-preferred (x_n) assigned a utility of 1, and if x_i is the certainty equivalent of a lottery which involves winning x_n with probability ρ_i and x_1 with probability $(1 - \rho_i)$, then the *von Neumann-Morgenstern utility index* assigns a value of ρ_i as the utility of x_i.

A von Neumann-Morgenstern utility index is *unique up to linear transformations.* In other words, any utility values can be assigned to x_1 and x_n, as long as the value assigned to x_n is greater than the value assigned to x_1 and both values are greater than or equal to 0. The utility value assigned to x_i is then the expectation over the utility values assigned to x_1 and x_n, where the probabilities are the probabilities from the lottery over x_1 and x_n, for which x_i is the certainty equivalent.

An individual is *risk averse* if, for constant wealth, a certain outcome is always preferred to a gamble with the same expected value but some positive variance, *risk neutral* if he or she is indifferent between the certain outcome and the gamble, and *risk seeking* if the gamble is preferred.

A *risk premium* is an amount of money a risk-averse individual is willing to pay to avoid a particular risk.

In decisions under uncertainty, a *state of the world* is a description of a situation in which some set of outcomes will occur with some probability. For example, in one state of the world, you may suffer a loss of some kind and in the other, you do not.

An *insurance premium* is an amount that a (probably risk-averse) individual will pay an insurance company in order to be reimbursed in the event of some specified, probabilistic loss.

An insurance premium is *actuarially fair* if it is equal to the expected value of the loss. In other words, buying actuarially fair insurance is a fair bet.

If insurance is actuarially fair, an expected-utility-maximizing, risk-averse consumer chooses to purchase full insurance coverage.

By the *law of large numbers,* if a sample drawn from a larger group (called a *population*) becomes large enough, the mean of the sample approaches the mean of the population, as long as the mean and variance of the underlying population distribution are finite.

A *normal distribution* is described by a bell-shaped curve. Outcomes at or near the expected value of the distribution of outcomes occur with the highest probability, while outcomes farther from the expected value occur with monotonically decreasing probability.

If an insurance company has enough policy holders (a large enough sample) and if that sample of policy holders is representative of the population as a whole, then by the law of large numbers, the probability that the average claim will equal an estimate calculated from statistics on the larger population will be practically equal to 1. If that is the case, then the company can calculate its profits as if they are known with certainty.

In a futures contract, a firm or consumer contracts to purchase a given quantity of a particular good at a stated price (called the *futures price*) at some time or over some period in the future. By doing so, the buyer avoids the implicit gamble if prices at that time (called *spot prices*) are not known with certainty.

Assuming risk aversion, an agent will buy at the futures price as long as the difference between what would be paid at the futures price and at the mean of the spot prices is not greater than the agent's risk premium.

Long-term labor contracts are like futures contracts and insurance. The firm agrees to pay the worker a certain amount per year, and the worker avoids the risk of always getting paid the spot wage. The risk-averse worker will accept any contract which pays no less than the average of the spot wages minus the risk premium.

In the *state-preference model* of decision making under uncertainty, economic agents trade *state-contingent claims* for consumption in different states of the world, where a state-contingent claim is a right to consume if and only if a particular state of the world occurs.

A *state-contingent commodity* is a commodity that will be delivered if a particular state of the world occurs.

With one commodity and two states of the world, a state-contingent indifference curve consists of all combinations of quantities of goods consumed in the two states of the world, given the probabilities of the two states occurring, such that the consumer is indifferent between a lottery over each of the specific combinations and getting the certainty equivalent of all the lotteries in both states of the world.

The marginal rate of substitution along a state-contingent indifference curve indicates the rate at which a consumer is willing to give up units of consumption in one state of the world in order to be able to consume more in another state.

Along the 45° line, the marginal rate of substitution is equal to the ratio of the probabilities that the states of the world will occur. That happens because the quantities of consumption are the same in both states along the 45° line.

State-contingent indifference curves are convex to the origin (diminishing marginal rates of substitution) if and only if the consumer is risk averse. State-contingent indifference curves are linear if a consumer is risk neutral and bowed out if a consumer is risk seeking.

A *state-contingent budget line* defines the feasible set over both states of the world, given a market in state-contingent claims. It is a straight line that goes through the consumer's initial endowment and has a slope equal to the ratio of prices for contingent claims.

If one consumer is more risk averse than another, the more risk-averse individual will be willing to pay the less risk-averse individual enough to make him or her willing to give up some claims to consumption in the "bad" state of the world. Thus, in effect, the less risk-averse individual sells some insurance to the more risk-averse individual, allowing the more risk-averse individual to consume relatively more equally in both states of the world.

If one consumer is risk neutral, the other is risk averse, and they agree on the probability of loss, then the competitive equilibrium and Pareto optimal sharing of risk involves the risk-neutral consumer selling full insurance coverage to the risk-averse individual at an actuarially fair rate in the form of contingent claims, allowing the risk-averse consumer to consume equal amounts in both states of the world.

19.8 _____ QUESTIONS FOR DISCUSSION

1. Under what conditions will risky occupations command higher wages than safe jobs at a competitive equilibrium if workers are risk averse? Explain.

2. Under what conditions will risk-averse individuals buy stocks with uncertain returns? Explain.

3. There are a number of kinds of losses for which market insurance is not available. Explain why the law of large numbers could not be applied in each of the following cases.

   (a) Earthquake insurance in California

   (b) Flood insurance for homes on the Mississippi flood plain

4. When a major snowstorm is predicted, people often go to the grocery store. Explain this behavior as a form of insurance. What are the appropriate states of the world and what are the outcomes in each state? What costs are people paying for this form of insurance? What types of people are more likely to shop before snowstorms?

19.9 ___ PROBLEMS

Problems 1–4 Suppose a lottery yields the following outcomes with the following probabilities.

$100   with probability   .2
$250   with probability   .5
$300   with probability   .3.

1. What is the expected value of the lottery?
2. What is the variance of the outcomes of the lottery?
3. Would a risk-averse person pay $235 to play the lottery? Explain.
4. Would a risk-averse person accept $235 instead of playing the lottery? Explain.

Problems 5–8 An individual has a utility function of the form

$$U = M^{1/2}$$

and faces a situation in which income is $36 with probability 1/2 and $100 with probability 1/2.

5. What payoff with certainty is indifferent to this gamble?
6. What is the risk premium associated with this gamble?
7. How much would the individual be willing to pay to avoid taking the risk?
8. Suppose the individual is offered, for $32, full insurance for the $64 (potential) loss. Will he or she buy it? Explain why or why not.

19.10 ___ LOGICAL AND MATHEMATICAL APPLICATIONS

1. Three individuals have initial wealth W and are offered the opportunity, at a cost of $10, to participate in a gamble that pays $20 with probability 1/2 and nothing with probability 1/2. Person A rejects the gamble, person B is indifferent, and person C accepts it. What can you say about each person's attitude toward risk? Explain.

2. Suppose there is an economy with one risk-averse individual and one risk-neutral individual, but they disagree about the probability of loss. In particular, the risk-neutral individual thinks it is higher than the risk-averse individual does. Use an Edgeworth box to show the market equilibrium in such a situation. Will the risk-averse individual still buy full insurance? Explain why or why not.

3. Suppose the government is trying to decide between increasing the fine associated with some illegal act (like parking illegally or driving too fast) or increasing the probability of being caught. Show that if all individuals are risk averse, increasing the fine is more of a deterrent to illegal activity than is increasing the probability of being caught. Assume the expected fine is the same in both cases.

Chapter 20

Applications of Uncertainty Models

20.1   WHAT YOU SHOULD LEARN FROM THIS CHAPTER

In the previous chapter, we assumed that economic agents who engaged in transactions under uncertainty agreed on the probability distribution over outcomes and on what outcomes would be observed in each state of the world. In reality, however, these assumptions are likely to be violated. First, individuals may have private information about their true probabilities of suffering losses, which is not available to insurance companies. Second, they may be able to take unobservable actions which can either affect the probability of a loss or affect the size of any loss that might occur. These examples introduce the possibility that competitive markets may not be efficient under uncertainty.

Most such inefficiencies stem from two basic problems associated with unobservability; moral hazard and adverse selection.[1] Using the insurance example, **moral hazard** occurs when the policy holder can take steps to reduce his or her probability of loss, but the insurance company cannot distinguish between loss due to carelessness and loss due to a random event which the policy holder could not have prevented. Moral hazard also occurs, for example, when a worker's output depends on some random event (like the weather) in addition to how hard he or she works. In that case, the worker has an incentive to work less hard, if the employer cannot distinguish between low output due to not working hard and low output due to a random event.

Adverse selection occurs when different groups of people have different intrinsic probabilities of sustaining losses, but the insurance company cannot distinguish one group from another. Both moral hazard and adverse selection also occur in markets when buyers cannot distinguish good workers from bad workers before they are hired. In the case of both goods and workers, the moral hazard occurs because producers could produce only good quality products and workers could all be hard working. Adverse selection occurs because once the decision has been made to be a "good" or "bad" product or worker, neither the consumer nor the hiring firm can distinguish one from the other.

---

[1]Kenneth Arrow, *Essays in the Theory of Risk-Bearing* (Amsterdam: North Holland, 1970) pp. 177–222, provides an introduction to the problems of moral hazard and adverse selection with medical insurance.

538

The existence of moral hazard means that full insurance is no longer Pareto optimal, even with risk-averse consumers and risk-neutral insurance companies. We will show that the more insurance an individual has, the less care he or she will take to prevent loss. This implies that insurance companies cannot offer full insurance at rates that would be actuarially fair, in the absence of moral hazard, and make nonnegative profits. With adverse selection, high-risk individuals try to represent themselves as low risk. To the extent they are successful, the insurance company ends up paying out more in claims, on average, than it collects in premiums. Moreover, there may not exist any set of competitive equilibrium insurance policies, separated by risk classes, that allows insurance companies to make nonnegative profits.

20.2   MORAL HAZARD IN INSURANCE MARKETS

The result that markets with uncertainty can achieve Pareto optimal allocations through full insurance and state-contingent claims (outlined in Sections 19.4 and 19.6) depends upon full information about the state of the world and the amount of loss (if any) being available to all economic agents after the uncertainty has been resolved. In addition, the law of large numbers, which allows insurance companies to behave as if they were risk neutral, depends on the population of insured people being a random sample from the population as a whole. In reality, however, these assumptions are not always satisfied.

Starting with moral hazard, in many cases, it is not easy to tell whether a loss could have been avoided if the policy holder had been more careful. Would you take more care to prevent an electrical fire if your house were not fully insured? Would you go to the doctor as often if you did not have insurance?

Suppose you own a home and there is no cost to you to making sure your home does not burn down. In that case, you will take care to prevent a fire. But there *are* costs. If, for example, you buy a smoke alarm or a sprinkler system, there will be less damage if you have a fire; if you build with fire-retardant materials, there is less chance of having a fire at all. The optimal investment in care will equate the marginal cost of care and the marginal reduction in the expected value of your loss as a result of making that investment.

Suppose you then purchase an actuarially fair homeowners' policy that guarantees your home will be fully rebuilt if it burns down. The loss you suffer in the case of a fire is reduced by the amount of insurance reimbursement. This means that the care you take has less effect on how much you will have to pay as a result of the loss. This implies that you will tend to take less care simply as a result of being insured. This point is illustrated with the following model of the decision of how much care to take to prevent a loss.

A Mathematical Model   If we assume that taking care reduces the probability of loss but at some positive marginal cost, we capture the essence of moral hazard, since the insurance company can only observe whether or not the consumer sustains a loss. It cannot observe the amount of care taken to try to prevent any particular loss. Introducing a new variable, z, the amount of care taken, the possibility of reducing the probability of loss by taking care would change our original model, outlined in equations 19.37–19.44, to make the probability of loss (ρ) a function of z:

$$\rho = \rho(z) \tag{20.1}$$

And, by assumption,

$$\frac{d\rho}{dz} < 0, \tag{20.2}$$

implying that taking more care reduces the probability of loss. The consumer's problem now is to choose a level of care so as to maximize expected utility. Moreover, in contrast to the model developed in equations 19.37–19.44, the probability of loss is a function of care, and the consumer pays for care as the total amount of care taken times the (constant) marginal cost of taking care (c). Because of moral hazard, we cannot be sure that the insurance company will be able to offer insurance at actuarially fair rates. This implies that the price of a unit of insurance coverage may not equal ρ. Consequently, we let p_A be the price per unit of insurance coverage. These changes in the model developed as equations 19.37–19.44 imply the following redefinitions for the values of x, with and without a loss (equations 19.37 and 19.38), and the expected utility function (equation 19.39):

$$x^\ell = x^0 - L - cz - p_A A + A \tag{20.3}$$
$$x^n = x^0 - cz - p_A A \tag{20.4}$$
$$EU = \rho(z')U^\ell + [1 - \rho(z)]U^n. \tag{20.5}$$

Now, suppose that A is fixed at some predetermined level ($\overline{A}$). To find the optimal level of care, we differentiate (20.5) with respect to z, set the derivative equal to 0, then interpret the resulting first-order condition.

$$\frac{d}{dz}E\{U\} = \rho'(z^*)U^\ell - \rho(z^*)c\frac{dU^\ell}{dx} - \rho'(z^*)U^n - [1 - \rho(z^*)]c\frac{dU^n}{dx} = 0 \tag{20.6}$$

Rearranging terms in (20.6),

$$\rho'(z)(U^\ell - U^n) = c\left\{\rho(z^*)\frac{dU^\ell}{dx} + [1 - \rho(z^*)]\frac{dU^n}{dx}\right\}. \tag{20.7}$$

To interpret the first-order condition (equation 20.7), we first note that the term in braces on the right-hand side is the expected marginal utility of income, given that the consumer has spent cz^* on taking care:

$$E\{MU_x(z^*)\} = \rho(z^*)\frac{dU^\ell}{dx} + [1 - \rho(z^*)]\frac{dU^n}{dx}. \tag{20.8}$$

Multiplying (20.8) by the marginal cost of taking care (c), the right-hand side of equation 20.7 can be interpreted as the expected marginal utility cost of taking care, evaluated at z^*. The term on the left-hand side of equation 20.7 represents the expected marginal benefit of taking an additional unit of care: the gain in utility from not suffering a loss times the marginal reduction in the probability of suffering a loss associated with the optimal level of care.

Now, to find how z^* changes as the amount of insurance changes, we would do a comparative statics analysis: totally differentiate equation 20.6, holding all variables except z^* and constant and then solve for the comparative statics term $\partial z^*/\partial A$.[2] The exercise is quite tedious and involves the use of concepts that we have not developed in this book, but the bottom line is that if there are "no income effects" in an individual's attitudes toward risk, we can say unequivocally that more insurance is always associated with taking less care to reduce the probability of loss:[3]

$$\frac{dz}{d\overline{A}} < 0. \tag{20.9}$$

This is the essence of moral hazard.

A Graphical Illustration   Translating this comparative statics result into the marginal benefit-marginal cost formulation developed in equations 20.6–20.8, equation 20.6 defines a marginal benefit function, which can be expressed as the demand for care as a function of the cost, parameterized by the amount of insurance ($\overline{A}$):

$$z_d^*(c; \overline{A}). \tag{20.10}$$

Assuming that the demand curve for care is downward sloping, equation 20.9 also tells us that an increase in $\overline{A}$ shifts the demand curve to the left: for every cost ($\overline{c}$), the consumer takes less care.

Figure 20.1 illustrates the effect of insurance on the decision to take care. The horizontal axis is the amount of care and the vertical axis is the marginal cost. The actual marginal cost is represented by the horizontal line at $\overline{c}$. The inverse of $z^*(c; \overline{A})$ is downward sloping and shifts in toward the origin as more insurance is purchased. Thus, z^* without insurance is greater than z^* with insurance.

Medical Insurance   While the analysis above applies to some homeowners' policies, the most widely studied form of moral hazard is in health insurance, which is administered quite differently from homeowners' insurance.[4] With health insurance, the individual (or his or her employer) pays a monthly premium. Payment of that premium in

---

[2]What we are doing here is allowing the insured to purchase a little more insurance (lifting the $\overline{A}$ constraint) and seeing if he or she takes more or less care to prevent loss. If the insured always takes less care, regardless of how much insurance there is to begin with, then we can say that having more insurance reduces the amount of care taken by the insured. In particular, if the insured is allowed to have all the insurance he or she desires instead of no insurance ($\overline{A} = 0$), having insurance reduces the amount of care taken.

[3]The proof of this proposition is available on request from the authors. A utility function that has "no income effects" is $U = -e^{-rx}$, where $r = -(U'', U')$ is a constant. $-(U'', U')$ is called the **Arrow-Pratt measure of absolute risk aversion**. (See Arrow, *Essays in the Theory of Risk-Bearing*, pp. 90–120; and J. W. Pratt, "Risk Aversion in the Small and the Large," *Econometrica* 32(1964):122–136.) If r is a constant for all possible $-(U'', U')$, then we say that the consumer's utility function exhibits *constant absolute risk aversion*. In other words, the degree of risk aversion is the same for all income levels (x), and there are no income effects in an individual's attitudes toward risk.

[4]See Mark V. Pauly, *Doctors and Their Workshops* (Chicago: University of Chicago Press, 1980).

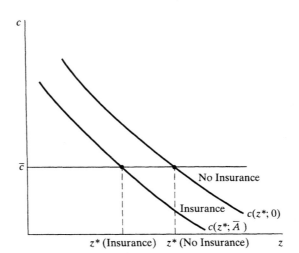

FIGURE 20.1   Moral Hazard Illustrated

turn guarantees the individual reimbursement for health care expenses after some annual minimum deductible is met. In addition, the individual may have to pay some fraction (usually 10% or 20%) of his or her medical bills up to some maximum. After that, the insurance company pays all bills for the remainder of that calendar year. In essence, therefore, medical insurance allows the individual to buy as much health care as he or she wants at a substantially reduced rate, after paying the premium and meeting the deductible.

We can analyze the effect of medical insurance by looking at what it does to an individual's budget line. Paying the premium is like a lump-sum reduction (the pure income effect). Then, once the deductible is met, the effect of the insurance is to substantially reduce the price of medical care as compared to other goods. Eventually, medical care becomes virtually free (if we ignore the cost of time spent going to the doctor). Assuming that medical care is a normal good, paying the premium first reduces the quantity demanded relative to the case without insurance, but the reduction in price then increases the quantity demanded, relative to the quantity demanded without insurance. The consumer's moral hazard associated with having medical insurance is that for most people, the effect of the price reduction outweighs any income effect associated with paying the premium.

This is illustrated in Figure 20.2 for purchases of medical services after the uncertainty has been resolved.[5] The straight budget line with intercepts M/p_x and M/p_y represents the original budget line for medical purchases (good X) and all other goods (good Y) before the purchase of insurance. The dashed budget line represents the situation after the purchase of medical insurance. The lower y intercept at $(M - p_A A)/p_y$ reflects the lump-sum payment of the premium $(p_A A)$. Until the deductible is met (at x_d) the slope is the same as that of the original budget line. Thereafter, the slope is

---

[5]Insurance is purchased under uncertainty, but medical services are purchased under certainty (after you know you are sick).

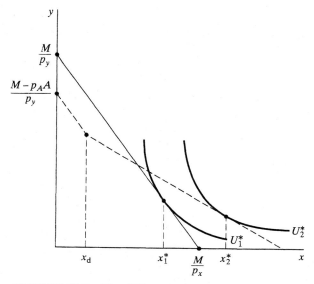

FIGURE 20.2   Moral Hazard with Medical Insurance

much less steep because the price of medical care is so much lower with insurance. For simplicity, we ignore the case when the price becomes 0. The individual whose choice is illustrated in this graph ends up choosing to purchase more medical care with insurance than without.

Moral Hazard in the Supply of Medical Services   A further consequence of medical insurance occurs on the supply side if the supply of medical services is upward sloping. Insurance acts as a subsidy over the price consumers actually pay. Just as a per-unit tax lowers the price producers receive and reduces the quantity demanded, a per-unit subsidy raises the price producers receive and increases the quantity demanded. This is illustrated in Figure 20.3. The original equilibrium is at (p_x^e, x_e). When the price consumers face declines to p_x^A, the quantity increases to x_A. This will be an equilibrium when the amount reimbursed just equals the difference between the supply price and the demand price at that quantity:

$$\text{per unit reimbursement} = p_x^s - p_x^A.$$

Notice, however, that if the supply curve for medical services is upward sloping, the price doctors receive actually increases at the same time that the price consumers pay declines. Thus, insurance has the effect of increasing both the quantity of medical services demanded and the unit price. The combination tends to substantially increase the total reimbursement over what would be expected on the basis of the market equilibrium without insurance.

Equilibria in Insurance Markets with Moral Hazard   The existence of moral hazard implies that insurance companies cannot make nonnegative profits if premiums are based on the expected amount of reimbursement in the absence of insurance.

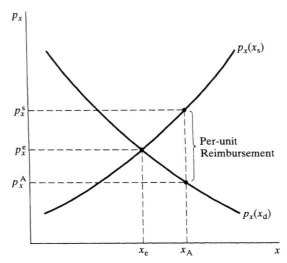

FIGURE 20.3   Moral Hazard in the Supply of Medical Services

Equilibria in insurance markets provide at least partial solutions to this problem in a variety of ways. One possible solution is for the insurance company to charge an additional premium over the actuarially fair premium (without insurance), to cover the cost of moral hazard. This has the effect of inducing risk-averse consumers to purchase less than full insurance.

The usual way that less than full insurance is sold in actual insurance markets is through *deductible clauses* and *coinsurance* (insurance only pays a fraction of each claim), which were discussed in the context of medical insurance. These also reduce certain kinds of moral hazard. For example, if consumers have to pay the first $100 after every automobile accident, they are more likely to take care to prevent minor accidents. Similarly, if consumers have to pay the first $100 of their medical expenses every year, they are more likely to take steps to prevent minor illnesses or to treat them themselves. In addition, if consumers have to pay even 10% of their own medical expenses, they are less likely to make frivolous trips to the doctor.

Insurance policies may also include *due care clauses*. These, in effect, specify the circumstances under which a claim may be paid. For example, a driver who is deemed "at fault" in an accident may not be able to collect on all of his or her claim and a car owner who does not lock up may not be able to collect on a car theft.

20.3   ADVERSE SELECTION

The second general incentive problem with insurance is called adverse selection. Insurance companies charge on the basis of the expected value of a loss over an entire population. Each individual, on the other hand, falls into a particular risk class, which may have a higher or a lower expected value than the population as a whole. Some

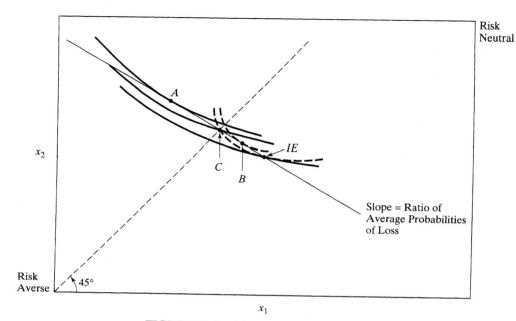

FIGURE 20.4   Adverse Selection Illustrated

people are simply healthier or better drivers or more careful than the average. If insurance companies could identify which people came from which risk classes and force them to pay different insurance premiums, there would be no problem.

A problem arises because individuals may know their own risk classes, but the insurance company may not be able to find out which risk class each individual fits into. If the insurance company offers one type of policy at a price equal to the average probability of loss over the whole population, high-risk individuals will buy full insurance and then file more claims than expected. However, sales of policies to low-risk individuals will not make up for the additional claims by high-risk individuals because the low-risk individuals will buy less than full insurance. That is because the price will be less than the expected value of loss for the high-risk group and more than the expected value of loss for the low-risk group.

A Contingent-claims Market with Adverse Selection   Adverse selection in a contingent-claims market is illustrated in Figure 20.4. In the Edgeworth box are the indifference curves of two individuals who have identical preferences but different probabilities of loss. This implies they have different marginal rates of substitution along the 45° line. In particular, the consumer with the higher probability of loss (the solid indifference curves) has a larger marginal rate of substitution along the 45° line. This is because along the 45° line, the individual's marginal rate of substitution is equal to the ratio of his or her true probabilities: $MRS_i = \rho_i/(1 - \rho_i)$ (equation 19.51). Suppose now that the risk-neutral insurance company offers policies at the average probability of loss (given by the slope of the line that goes through the initial endowment). By definition, the average probability of loss will be less than the high-risk individual's actual probability and greater than the low-risk individual's. The effect is that the high-risk individual actually wants to buy more than full insurance at that price, while the low-risk individual wants to buy less. The high-risk individual maximizes utility at point A, where x_2 is greater than x_1, while the low-risk-individual maximizes utility at point B, where x_1 is greater than x_2. Assuming that the insurance company does not offer more than full coverage, the high-risk individual ends up at point C along the 45° line, where the relative probability of loss exceeds the relative price paid for the insurance. This implies that the insurance company will lose money, on average, selling insurance to the high-risk group.

Separating Equilibria If there are only two (or a few) risk classes, an equilibrium in the insurance market involves different contracts being purchased by different risk classes (this is called a **separating equilibrium**). Ignoring moral hazard for a moment, one possible separating equilibrium involves full insurance for the high-risk group at a high price and insurance with a large deductible and a low price for the low-risk group. This separating equilibrium will exist if it is possible to design a premium-deductible combination for the low-risk group that is less attractive to the high-risk group than full insurance at the higher price. Otherwise, high-risk individuals will represent themselves as low risk, and the insurance company will lose on claims again.

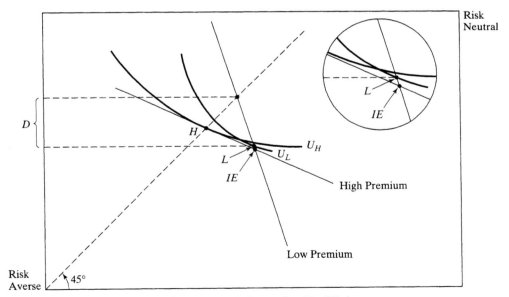

FIGURE 20.5 A Separating Equilibrium

---

[6]This graph is adapted from Michael Rothschild and Joseph Stiglitz, "Equilibrium in Competitive Insurance Markets: An Essay on the Economics of Imperfect Information," *The Quarterly Journal of Economics* 90(1976):629–650.

Such a separating equilibrium is illustrated in Figure 20.5.[6] Two insurance-deductible combinations are offered to consumers. One involves a relatively high premium and no deductible. This is represented by the less steep budget line through the initial endowment. (The line is less steep despite a high premium because the price of C_2 contingent claims is in the denominator.) The high-risk individual chooses full insurance at point H along that budget line. The other policy is designed so that the high-risk individual still prefers to be at point H. To guarantee that, the other premium is lower, represented by the steeper budget line (steeper, because the lower price, p_2, is in the denominator). But the lower price is only available with a deductible (D). Along that budget line, the low-risk individual is constrained by the insurance contract to be at point L, with the lower premium and the deductible. The high-risk individual, on the other hand, prefers point H to point L.

Other Kinds of Equilibria with Adverse Selection When there are many risk classes, however, Rothschild and Stiglitz argue that competitive separating equilibria may not exist because with more risk classes, it is more likely that a contract offered to one risk class will be acceptable to some other risk class. In addition, even when separating contracts do exist, new firms may enter, offering alternative contracts to profitable risk classes. Because these separating equilibria may be either nonexistent or unstable in the presence of entry, insurance companies deal with adverse selection in a variety of other ways. The most common is to try to assign people to risk classes on the basis of information that is associated with probability of loss. Thus, people with high blood pressure or a history of serious illness may have to pay higher market equilibrium prices for medical or life insurance premiums. Similarly, young, unmarried men (a group with high accident rates) pay very high car insurance rates. People who belong to groups with sufficiently high probabilities of loss may not be able to get insurance at all. For example, it is very difficult for the elderly to get medical or life insurance.

Group insurance offered to large companies has the effect of ensuring a statistically average population. If all employees of a large company or other large institution are required to have a certain kind of insurance coverage, then the insurance company can tailor the premiums to the average loss for that group and be sure that the low-risk individuals are going to remain in the group.

Because of both moral hazard and adverse selection, insurance companies commit substantial resources to investigating both potential policy holders and claims. A medical exam, usually paid for by the insurance company, is required in order to purchase most life insurance policies. Medical claims are carefully scrutinized by a staff that typically does nothing else. Suspicious deaths are investigated for suicide and suspicious fires are investigated for arson by the owner. Even so, it is not optimal to eliminate all sources of inefficiency. Using the appropriate marginal cost and marginal benefit calculation, the insurance company should investigate only until the marginal benefit from discovering fraudulent claims or high-risk individuals is equal to the marginal cost of investigation. That optimum will almost always leave some fraud undiscovered.

From a general equilibrium perspective, the existence of moral hazard and adverse selection and the amount spent on investigation and enforcement mean that a

Pareto optimal allocation of risk bearing, as described in Section 19.6, is rarely achieved. Even in long-run equilibrium, insurance is not generally actuarially fair because of the costs of investigation and enforcement. Even if it were actuarially fair, it would not be profit maximizing for insurance companies to offer full insurance, because of moral hazard. In addition, a substantial amount of insurance company revenues get paid for investigating fraud instead of for insuring risk.

20.4   THE PRINCIPAL-AGENT PROBLEM

Moral hazard and adverse selection are fundamental to markets under uncertainty in general, not just to insurance markets in particular. Other than the insurance market, the most widely studied application of moral hazard is called the **principal-agent problem.**[7] The principal-agent problem arises when one person (the agent) does a job for another person (the principal) in a situation in which differences due to quality of the work cannot be distinguished from random differences due to different states of the world.

For example, in agriculture, the weather is an important determinant of the size of a farmer's crop. However, if the size of the crop is not perfectly determined by specific weather conditions, the owner of a farm who hires someone to work the farm may not be able to tell whether a low yield occurs because of bad weather or because the worker did not work as hard as if the worker were to retain the crop for him- or herself. (This is referred to as **shirking** in the principal-agent literature.) As long as the principal cannot verify that bad outcomes are due to shirking, the agent has an incentive to shirk. This is analogous to the homeowner not taking care to prevent loss if the insurance company cannot verify that loss is due to poor care and not to a bad state of the world occurring.

Mathematical Model: Risk Sharing Without Moral Hazard   Just as in the insurance example outlined in Section 20.2, the existence of moral hazard means that the Pareto optimal sharing of risk cannot be achieved. To see this, consider the following mathematical model of the principal-agent problem.[8] Suppose there are two states of the world: state 1 is the bad state and state 2 is the good state. The agent produces output (x_1 or x_2) and then shares the output with the principal. The agent receives w_1 in state 1 and w_2 in state 2, and the principal receives $x_1 - w_1$ and $x_2 - w_2$, respectively. If there were no moral hazard, we could determine the optimal sharing rule (from the principal's point of view) by maximizing the principal's utility. In addition, we have to guarantee the agent some minimum level of utility, or the agent would never enter into

---

[7]See Bengt Holmstrom, "Moral Hazard and Observability," *The Bell Journal of Economics* 10(1979):74–91; S. Ross, "The Economic Theory of Agency: The Principal's Problem," *The American Economic Review* 63(1973):134–139; S. Shavell, "Risk Sharing and Incentives in the Principal and Agent Relationship," *The Bell Journal of Economics* 10(1979):55–73, for introductions to the principal-agent problem.

[8]This model is adapted from Holmstrom, "Moral Hazard and Observability."

such a contract. In other words, the agent's expected utility from the contract with the principal has to be at least as high as his or her opportunity cost associated with working in the next best alternative employment.

To summarize, the principal's problem is to maximize expected utility, subject to a minimum utility constraint for the agent:

$$\max E\{U_P\} = \rho U_P(x_1 - w_1) + (1 - \rho)U_P(x_2 - w_2) \tag{20.11}$$
$$\text{s.t. } E\{U_A\} = \rho U_A(w_1) + (1 - \rho)U_A(w_2) \geq \overline{U}_A.$$

The Lagrangian is

$$\mathcal{L} = \rho U_P(x_1 - w_1) + (1 - \rho)U_P(x_2 - w_2) \tag{20.12}$$
$$+ \lambda[\rho U_A(w_1) + (1 - \rho)U_A(w_2) - \overline{U}_A].$$

The relevant first-order conditions are

$$\frac{\partial \mathcal{L}}{\partial w_1} = -\rho MU_P(1) + \lambda \rho MU_A(1) = 0 \ \Rightarrow \ \lambda = \frac{MU_P(1)}{MU_A(1)} \tag{20.13}$$

$$\frac{\partial \mathcal{L}}{\partial w_2} = -(1 - \rho)MU_P(2) + \lambda(1 - \rho)MU_A(2) = 0 \ \Rightarrow \ \lambda = \frac{MU_P(2)}{MU_A(2)}. \tag{20.14}$$

Solving for λ from equations 20.13 and 20.14,

$$\lambda = \frac{MU_P(1)}{MU_A(1)} = \frac{MU_P(2)}{MU_A(2)}. \tag{20.15}$$

Equation 20.15 shows that the optimal sharing rule equates the marginal rates of substitution between states of the world of the principal and the agent. The condition described in equation 20.15 is identical to the condition describing optimal insurance, outlined in Section 19.6. If the principal is risk neutral and the agent is risk averse, the optimal sharing rule has the principal guarantee the agent a fixed income, regardless of the state of the world. This is equivalent to having the principal pay the agent a fixed wage. If the agent is risk neutral and the principal is risk averse, the optimal sharing rule has the agent guarantee the principal a fixed income, regardless of the state of the world. This is equivalent to having the agent pay a fixed rent to the principal. Finally, if both parties are risk averse, the optimal sharing rule pays some share to each party in each state of the world, where the actual shares depend on the parties' relative attitudes toward risk.

Second-best Risk Sharing with Moral Hazard   If there is moral hazard, the agent will choose an unobservable action, which affects either the probability of a particular state of the world occurring or the level of output obtainable in each state of the world. Moral hazard exists when taking action to raise expected output involves some cost to the agent. This gives the agent an incentive to shirk.

To keep this model similar to the insurance model in Section 20.2, assume the probability is a function of the action (a) and that there is some cost (ca), in utility terms, that is subtracted from the agent's expected utility of income. The probability function is such that taking more action (working harder) *lowers* the probability of observing the "bad" state, just as the insured's taking more care lowers the probability of sustaining a loss:

$$\frac{\partial \rho}{\partial a} < 0. \tag{20.16}$$

This makes the agent's expected utility function with moral hazard

$$E\{U_A\} = \rho(a)U_A(w_1) + [1 - \rho(a)]U_A(w_2) - ca. \tag{20.17}$$

The agent chooses a to maximize his expected utility:

$$\frac{\partial}{\partial a}E\{U_A\} = \frac{\partial \rho}{\partial a}U_A(w_1) - \frac{\partial \rho}{\partial a}U_A(w_2) - c = 0. \tag{20.18}$$

Equation 20.18, which characterizes the agent's choice of a, adds a further constraint to the principal's maximization problem. Equation 20.18 is referred to as the **incentive-compatibility constraint,** meaning any sharing rule has to be compatible with the agent's incentive to shirk.

We can now write the new Lagrangian (with moral hazard) as

$$\begin{aligned}\mathscr{L} = {} & \rho(a)U_P(x_1 - w_1) + [1 - \rho(a)]U_P(x_2 - w_2) \\ & + \lambda\{\rho(a)U_A(w_1) + [1 - \rho(a)]U_A(w_2) - ca - \overline{U}_A\} \\ & + \mu\left[\frac{\partial \rho}{\partial a}U_A(w_1) - \frac{\partial \rho}{\partial a}U_A(w_2) - c\right]. \end{aligned} \tag{20.19}$$

The relevant first-order conditions are

$$\frac{\partial \mathscr{L}}{\partial w_1} = -\rho MU_P(1) + \rho\lambda MU_A(1) + \mu MU_A(1)\frac{\partial \rho}{\partial a} = 0 \tag{20.20}$$

$$\frac{\partial \mathscr{L}}{\partial w_2} = -(1 - \rho)MU_P(2) + \lambda(1 - \rho)MU_A(2) - \mu MU_A(2)\frac{\partial \rho}{\partial a} = 0. \tag{20.21}$$

Collecting terms in equation 20.20,

$$\frac{MU_P(1)}{MU_A(1)} = \lambda + \frac{\mu}{\rho}\frac{\partial \rho}{\partial a}; \tag{20.22}$$

and collecting terms in equation 20.21,

$$\frac{MU_P(2)}{MU_A(2)} = \lambda - \frac{\mu}{1 - \rho}\frac{\partial \rho}{\partial a}. \tag{20.23}$$

Sharing Rules   Suppose now that the principal is risk neutral and the agent is risk averse. Equations 20.22 and 20.23 imply that the optimal sharing rule guarantees the agent a fixed payment, plus a variable payment which is a function of the amount of the observed output. The fixed payment represents less than full insurance provided by the principal. (If the agent were not risk averse, he or she would be willing to pay a

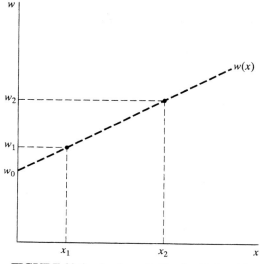

FIGURE 20.6   An Agent's Sharing Rule with Moral Hazard

fixed amount and absorb all the risk. That would solve the moral hazard problem and generate a Pareto optimal outcome.) With a risk-averse agent, some insurance may be Pareto superior to none, but moral hazard means that Pareto optimality cannot be achieved with full insurance, even if the principal is risk neutral. A sharing rule that gives the agent more if x_2 is observed than if x_1 is observed $[(\partial \rho / \partial a) < 0]$ reduces that moral hazard. Such a sharing rule is referred to as being **second best.** It is not Pareto optimal in the sense of Section 19.6, because both parties could be made better off if the agent's effort could be specified and enforced at no cost. But it does maximize the principal's utility, subject to the incentive-compatibility constraint and a minimum utility constraint for the agent.

Such a sharing rule is illustrated in Figure 20.6. The horizontal axis is output (x) and the vertical axis is the agent's payment (w). The agent gets w_1 if x_1 is observed and $w_2 > w_1$ if x_2 is observed. Using these points to derive a linear sharing rule (represented by the dashed line), which approximates the second-best rule, we see that if output were 0, the agent would still be paid $w_0 > 0$.

20.5   RISK SHARING AND THE PRINCIPAL-AGENT PROBLEM IN LABOR CONTRACTS

The principal-agent problem is a fundamental key to understanding the management of labor in situations in which the actual effort expended by workers cannot be observed and in which random events can affect output. Two examples, which have been widely studied in the economics literature, illustrate ways in which risk is shared and the principal-agent problem is dealt with as labor contracts are drawn. First, we will examine agriculture, in which weather is the random variable.[9] Then, we will examine textile manufacturing, in which random machine failure is the source of external variability.[10] In each case, it is possible to monitor how hard the agent works and to enforce standards, but only at some cost to the principal.

Agriculture In the case of agriculture, three distinct kinds of labor contracts are observed worldwide, in addition to the polar cases of owner-operators and slavery. Farms may be worked by hired labor with fixed wages under the supervision of a manager or owner; they may be rented out for a fixed rent; or they may be rented on a sharecropping basis, where the owner typically gets 1/3 or 1/2 of the tenant's crop. All of these contracts are observed simultaneously almost everywhere in the world.

If there were no moral hazard, we could analyze these contracts as reflecting different attitudes toward risk. As described above, the fixed wage is optimal when the worker is risk averse and the employer is risk neutral. Fixed rents are optimal when employers are risk averse and workers are risk neutral. And, sharecropping may approximate optimal risk sharing when both parties are risk averse.

With moral hazard, the actual set of equilibrium contracts observed depends upon risk sharing, the extent of moral hazard, and the cost of monitoring the workers' efforts. Fixed rents, for example, eliminate the moral hazard problem, but provide no insurance for risk-averse workers. In contrast, risk-averse workers are better off with the guaranteed wage, but moral hazard is worse. Employers can reduce moral hazard by monitoring workers' actions, but it may be costly to do so.

Sharecropping, it is argued, approximates the second-best solution when tenants are risk averse. Joint profits will not be maximized because of moral hazard, but risk can be shared between risk-averse parties, and moral hazard is reduced because the tenant's payment is a function of observed output. As we discussed above, if there were a minimum payment, it would also provide partial insurance. In addition, employers may further reduce moral hazard by monitoring the agents' efforts.

Much of the literature on sharecropping has focused on documenting either implicit minimum payments or consistent monitoring by owners. Studying southern agriculture after the Civil War, for example, Reid[11] finds that it is common for owners to give advice to sharecroppers regarding technology and to "make the rounds" of their tenants on a regular basis. In northern agriculture, it was common for a young

[9]See, for example, Steven N. S. Cheung, *The Theory of Share Tenancy* (Chicago: University of Chicago Press, 1969); Steven N. S. Cheung, "Transactions Costs, Risk Aversion, and the Choice of Contractual Arrangements," *Journal of Law and Economics* 7(1969):26; David Newberry, "Risk Sharing, Sharecropping and Uncertain Labour Markets," *Review of Economic Studies* 44(1977):585–594; Joseph D. Reid, "Sharecropping as an Understandable Market Response—The Post-Bellum South," The *Journal of Economic History* 33(1973):106–130; and Joseph Stiglitz, "Incentives and Risk Sharing in Sharecropping," *Review of Economic Studies* 41(1974):219–255.

[10]See, for example, Cathy McHugh, *The Family Labor System in The Southern Cotton Textile Industry, 1880–1915,* unpublished Ph.D. dissertation, Stanford University, Palo Alto, CA, 1982; and Caroline F. Ware, *The Early New England Cotton Manufacture: A Study in Industrial Beginnings* (Boston, 1931).

[11]Reid, "Sharecropping as an Understandable Market Response—The Post-Bellum South."

farmer to begin by sharecropping, under the constant supervision of the owner. Later, he might move to fixed-rent tenancy and later would purchase his own farm.

Implicit minimum payments are also widely observed, especially in Asian and European fixed tenancy and in sharecropping. The ultimate downside risk is total crop failure. With fixed-wage labor, the worker gets paid anyway, but with fixed rent and share tenancy, the tenant gets nothing and may not be able to pay the fixed rent if crops fail. It is widely observed in actual fixed rent and sharecropping situations, however, that owners (who are typically wealthier) will forgive rents and provide food for their tenants during such crises. It is only when landlords have some reason to get rid of their tenants that they do not provide that minimum subsistence protection.[12]

Textiles   In the cotton textile industry, the output of each worker can be easily observed, but effort is more difficult to observe since random differences in machines imply random differences in output. Once again, with risk sharing and moral hazard, we should observe contracts that provide a fixed minimum to workers plus a share which is a function of output. The piece-rate system is an example of such a sharing rule. Where work is done in the factory so that time spent working can be monitored inexpensively, wages have commonly been paid as a small hourly or daily wage plus an additional payment for each piece of output. Over time, the importance of the piece rates compared to the fixed wage has declined, as risk-averse workers have bargained for (and won) higher guaranteed wages. But in the nineteenth century, piece rates were very common, and they still exist today.

These kinds of sharing rules are widely observed in other industries as well, as long as the output of each worker can be identified. They are less valuable, however, when many workers combine in a team to produce a single item of output, such as on an automobile assembly line. In that case, the output of a single worker cannot be separated from the output produced by everyone else, and some other compensation scheme is needed.

20.6   THE MARKET FOR LEMONS

As an example of adverse selection, suppose that a particular good is available in two qualities, but consumers cannot verify quality before purchase. The example which often comes to mind is used cars. When you buy a particular make and model of a used car, you know that the car may be of good quality or it may be "a lemon."[13] There are some things you can do to check for lemons before purchase, but you won't be sure you didn't get a lemon until you have driven it for a while.

Sellers of used cars face a perverse set of incentives. Sellers of good-quality used cars would like to be able to distinguish their cars from lemons, but sellers of lemons have an incentive to represent their cars as being of good quality. This is analogous to high-risk individuals having an incentive to represent themselves as low risk in the

---

[12]See Joel Mokyr, *Why Ireland Starved* (Boston: Allen and Unwin, 1983), for a discussion of a scandalous failure to provide minimum subsistence protection.

[13]This example was made famous by Akerlof, "The Market for Lemons," *Quarterly Journal of Economics* 84(1970):488–500.

insurance example. Thus, when consumers buy cars represented as good quality, some fraction of them are actually lemons.

Assuming that the marginal cost of providing a lemon is less than the marginal cost of providing a good-quality car, a competitive market will price lemons at their marginal cost. But, as Akerlof points out, there may not exist a separating equilibrium price for good-quality used cars. In that case, buyers will only purchase lemons, because they will not be willing to pay a premium for cars which are represented as good quality but which might be lemons. If buyers express a demand only for lemons, only lemons will be sold, even though both buyers and sellers would be better off if good-quality used cars could be identified as such and sold for a higher price.

This is illustrated with the following simple mathematical example. Suppose a consumer can purchase one unit of a good that is available in two qualities: Q_1 (the lemon) and Q_2 (good quality). Quality is observable, but only after purchase. Utility is defined over quality and money, such that for a given amount of money, having higher quality increases the utility associated with having that amount of money:

$$U = U(M, Q), \tag{20.24}$$

such that

$$U(M; \overline{Q_2}) > U(M; \overline{Q_1}) > U(M; 0). \tag{20.25}$$

Now, suppose the consumer starts with M_0 and that the market price for Q_1 is p_1 and the market price for items represented as Q_2 is p_2, where $p_2 > p_1$. The consumer is then faced with the following choice. The consumer can pay p_1 and get Q_1 with certainty. The certain utility associated with that choice is

$$U(M_0 - p_1, Q_1). \tag{20.26}$$

The utility function described by equations 20.24 and 20.25 is illustrated in Figure 20.7 for a risk-averse customer. The parallel utility curves represent the utility of money at each of the consumer's quality levels: 0, Q_1, and Q_2.

Or, the consumer can pay p_2 for an item represented as being Q_2 and get Q_1 instead. The probability of getting Q_1 instead of Q_2 is ρ. The expected utility associated with that choice is

$$E\{U\} = \rho U(M_0 - p_2, Q_1) + (1 - \rho)U(M_0 - p_2, Q_2). \tag{20.27}$$

The consumer will only try to buy Q_2 if the expected utility of that action is greater than or equal to the certain utility from buying a Q_1 at p_1.

This decision is illustrated in Figure 20.8. First, we assume that purchasing an item of either quality gives higher utility after payment than not purchasing. This means that utility will be higher than $U(M_0; 0)$, which is identified as $\overline{U}$ on the graph. Given that assumption, the certain purchase of a lemon at price p_1 generates utility U_L and leaves income $M_0 - p_1$. The uncertain purchase of an item represented as Q_2 leaves income $M_0 - p_2$ and generates an expected utility between U_1 and U_2. If ρ is low enough, the resulting expected utility will be high enough to make the gamble over Q_2 attractive. This is represented by $E\{U\}_1$, which is greater than U_L. On the other hand, if ρ is high enough, the resulting expected utility, $E\{U\}_2$, will be less than U_L and the consumer only buys lemons.

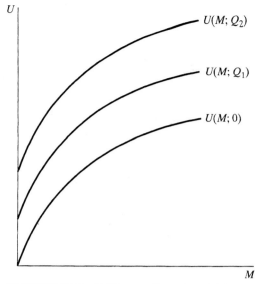

FIGURE 20.7   Utility as a Function of Money and Quality

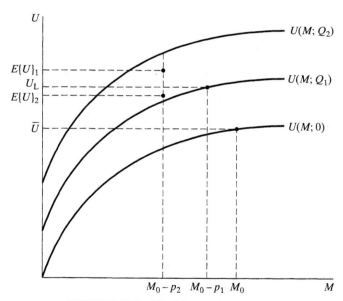

FIGURE 20.8   The Market for Lemons

20.7   REPUTATIONS, SIGNALLING, AND WARRANTIES

In the face of both the principal-agent problem and the lemons problem, those who offer high-quality work and high-quality goods would like to be able to distinguish themselves from shirking workers and their goods from lemons. There are several ways

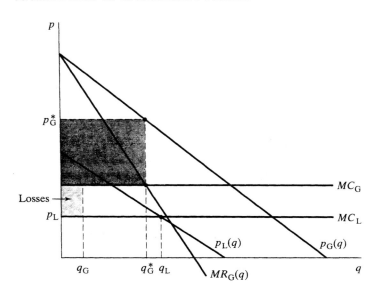

FIGURE 20.9   The Value of Building a Reputation

that this can be done, each of which involves some marginal cost. The three we consider here are reputation building, signalling, and warranties.

Sellers of Good-quality Merchandise   Suppose, for example, that you are an honest used-car dealer, who would like to be able to sell good-quality used cars as well as lemons. But the other dealers have misrepresented cars to customers so often that no one will pay enough for a car represented as good quality for you to make a profit on good-quality cars in the long run. What you may be able to do is sell good-quality used cars below long-run marginal cost today and build up a reputation for only selling good cars. You may then be able to gradually raise your prices until you are selling above long-run marginal cost (and profiting from your reputation) in the future. This will, of course, only be a profit-maximizing strategy if the discounted present value of the stream of profits you expect to make from reputation building exceeds the discounted present value of continuing to sell lemons. This will depend upon the relative marginal costs of providing lemons as compared to the cost of building the reputation and providing the good-quality cars, as well as the respective demand functions for lemons and good-quality cars.

Figure 20.9 illustrates how this strategy works in the first stage of this process. MC_L represents the marginal cost of lemons and MC_G represents the marginal cost of good-quality cars. $p_L(q)$ is the inverse demand curve for lemons and $p_G(q)$ is the inverse demand curve for good quality. Both demand and marginal cost are higher for good quality.

Because of the problem of the market for lemons, only lemons are currently being sold. The market for lemons is perfectly competitive, implying that the price is MC_L and the quantity is q_L. In order to establish a reputation during the current period, you offer some number of high-quality items (say q_G) for sale at MC_L and suffer a loss this period equal to $q_G(MC_G - MC_L)$. But if you are the only reputable supplier of high-quality goods, you will eventually be able to act as a monopolist. That implies that you charge p_G^* sell q_G^*, and make monopoly profits of

$$\pi_G^* = q_G(p_G - MC_G). \tag{20.28}$$

If other firms enter the reputation-building market, the long-run equilibrium maximum price of high-quality goods should equal the price that guarantees nonnegative discounted long-run profits.

An alternative to selling below cost today in order to build a reputation is to offer customers a **warranty** (a money-back guarantee) on the product. If it is costless to the seller to offer the warranty and make good on it, a competitive market in guaranteed products should sell high-quality goods at their marginal cost. In most such circumstances, however, it will be costly to offer a warranty and make good on it if the product fails. In that case, the long-run equilibrium price of a high-quality product will be its marginal production cost plus the marginal cost of providing the guarantee.

In some cases, a seller can also invest in a **signal** that is correlated with honesty. A used-car dealer might, for example, give a substantial amount of time and money to local charities. People who equate charitable work with honesty would begin to buy cars represented as high quality at high-quality prices. As long as the dealer actually did behave honestly, he or she could build a reputation for honesty by beginning with the signal for honesty.

When more than one strategy is available, a competitive market will generate a long-run equilibrium price for high-quality goods that minimizes the cost among building a reputation, investing in a signal, and providing a money-back guarantee. The price will be the marginal production cost plus the minimum marginal cost of guaranteeing the product.

Labor Markets   In Section 18.6, we analyzed the decision to invest in an education, and we concluded that an education is worthwhile if the discounted present value of the increase in earnings is greater than or equal to the discounted present value of the cost of the education itself. What we didn't analyze at that time is why a competitive market values an educated individual. In some fields, like science, engineering, and medicine, education imparts important skills that are necessary for adequate performance in those fields. In many cases, however, an individual does *not* learn any specific skills for a particular job. Still, many white-collar jobs require a college education. Why is it that qualified high-school (or even grade-school) graduates cannot find white-collar jobs, even if they offer to work for lower wages?

Education provides a signal to an employer that the educated individual is either intelligent or hardworking (or both). Without education as a signal, employers would be faced with trying to determine which workers were intelligent and hardworking out of the distribution of all workers, when all potential employees will try to represent themselves as having those characteristics.

In this example, there is both moral hazard and adverse selection. Shirking is the moral hazard. Adverse selection occurs because poor workers will try to represent themselves as good ones. At an average wage equal to the expected marginal revenue

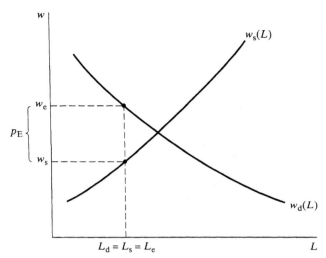

FIGURE 20.10 Equilibrium in the Market for Educated Workers

product of both kinds of workers, poor workers will be paid more than their marginal revenue products and good workers will be paid less. Without some way for good workers to distinguish themselves, a market for lemons in the labor market could develop, especially if the possibility of home production allows good workers to produce more at home than they can earn in a low-wage labor market. Education, because it requires intelligence or hard work sustained over a period of time, provides such a signal. Employers, by hiring only educated workers, screen out a high proportion of poor workers. In long-run equilibrium, wages paid to educated workers will compensate enough workers for the investment so as to equate the quantity of educated workers demanded and the quantity supplied at that price.

This equilibrium is illustrated in Figure 20.10. If the marginal cost of an education (calculated as in Section 18.6) is p_E, then workers would have to be paid p_E, in addition to the wage along the inverse supply curve (w_s) in order to invest in education. At a market wage of $w_e = p_E + w_s$, $L_e = L_d = L_s$ educated workers are employed. Each worker gets his or her supply price (w_s), plus the marginal return to his or her education (p_E). Even though wages are higher and some of the gains from trade are spent on a signal that may not raise the worker's intrinsic marginal revenue product, both employers and educated workers are better off. This happens simply because education allows the better workers to distinguish themselves from the "lemons."

20.8   REVIEW OF KEY CONCEPTS

This completes our introduction to markets under uncertainty where some actions are unobservable. Before continuing to the next chapter on externalities and public goods, be sure you understand and can use the following key concepts.

In an uncertain environment, if an economic agent can take an unobservable, costly action, which affects the probability distribution over outcomes or the actual outcomes themselves, then we say that *moral hazard* exists if the unobservable action affects the payoffs received by another agent or agents.

If different individuals have different intrinsic probabilities of sustaining losses, if there is no observable means of separating these individuals into separate risk classes, and if high-risk individuals represent themselves as low risk, thereby reducing the payoff to another agent or agents, then we say that *adverse selection* exists. In other words, the information required to distinguish among risk classes is unobservable.

If an individual can take a costly action (care) that reduces the probability of sustaining a loss, then the optimal level of care equates the marginal benefit of taking additional care and the marginal cost.

The *Arrow-Pratt measure of absolute risk aversion* is the ratio $-(U'', U')$.

If $-(U'', U')$ is a constant for all income levels, then we say that the utility function is characterized by *constant absolute risk aversion*. Constant absolute risk aversion is the equivalent, under uncertainty, of having no income effects in attitudes toward risk.

If a consumer is allowed to purchase more insurance and if there are no income effects in attitudes toward risk, the consumer takes less care as a result.

The moral hazard associated with having insurance is that by having any insurance at all, the consumer takes less care than if no insurance were available. This implies that the insurance company's true expected loss is greater than what would be anticipated from a study of losses in the absence of insurance.

Patients with medical insurance make more trips to the doctor on average than those who do not, because having medical insurance reduces the marginal cost of going to the doctor.

Medical insurance also tends to increase the equilibrium marginal cost of medical services if the supply of medical services is upward sloping. This happens because the insurance provides a per-unit subsidy to insured patients, effectively shifting the demand curve for medical services to the right.

The existence of moral hazard implies that insurance companies cannot make nonnegative profits if premiums are based on the expected amount of reimbursement in the absence of insurance.

Equilibria in insurance markets reduce the effects of moral hazard, allowing insurance companies to make nonnegative profits in several ways. A *deductible* clause requires the insured to pay the first x of any loss. *Coinsurance* requires the insured to pay some percentage of any loss. *Due care clauses* specify that the insured will only be reimbursed if some specified minimum level of care to prevent loss has been taken.

If individuals purchasing insurance fall into different risk classes and one premium is charged, high-risk individuals will want to buy more than full insurance and low-risk individuals will buy less than full insurance. Assuming the insurance company sells full insurance to the high-risk group, it loses money, on average, if it sells the insurance at the expected value of loss over the whole population.

An equilibrium that involves different insurance contracts being purchased by different risk classes is called a *separating equilibrium*.

One possible separating equilibrium involves charging a high premium for full insurance and a low premium only with a substantial amount deductible. It is a separating equilibrium if only high-risk individuals buy the high-priced insurance and only low-risk individuals buy the low-priced insurance.

Separating equilibria may not exist or may be unstable in the presence of entry by competing firms.

Group insurance for a large company, which requires that all employees be insured, eliminates the adverse selection problem by requiring that low-risk individuals purchase the same insurance as high-risk individuals at the expected value of loss for the whole group.

Insurance companies reduce the effects of moral hazard and adverse selection by investigating potential policy holders and claims. The optimal level of investigation equates the marginal benefit from reducing losses and the marginal cost of carrying out the investigation.

When a *principal* hires an *agent* to do a job, the agent may have an incentive to shirk (or work less hard than if he or she were to get the profits) if the principal cannot distinguish between random bad outcomes and bad outcomes due to the agent's shirking. This is referred to as the *principal-agent problem* and it is basically a problem of moral hazard.

In the absence of moral hazard, an optimal sharing of risk between principal and agent takes the form of an optimal insurance contract. If the principal is risk neutral and the agent is risk averse, the principal provides full insurance to the agent in the form of a fixed wage; if the principal is risk averse and the agent is risk neutral, the agent provides full insurance in the form of a fixed rent; if both are risk averse, they share the profits according to some contractual agreement.

When the agent has an incentive to shirk, he or she chooses a utility-maximizing, unobservable action that affects the outcome, either by affecting the probability of the occurrence of different states of the world or by affecting the outcome in each state of the world.

The first-order condition of the agent's decision problem becomes an *incentive-compatibility constraint* in the principal's decision problem. In other words, an optimal decision by the principal, given the existence of moral hazard, has to take the agent's actions into account.

If the agent is risk neutral, there is no principal-agent problem, because the optimal sharing of risk involves the agent paying a fixed rent and then retaining the full residual. In that case, there is no incentive to shirk.

If the principal is risk neutral and the agent is risk averse, the principal-agent problem implies that it is not Pareto optimal for the principal to pay a fixed wage. Instead, the optimal contract involves paying the agent some fixed minimum amount as insurance and then sharing additional output as an incentive for the agent to shirk less. Such a contract is said to be *second best*.

An important application of the principal-agent model is to a labor market in which workers have an incentive to shirk on the job.

The used-car market represents a possible application of adverse selection, since there are used cars of different quality, and sellers of "lemons" may be able to present their cars as being of good quality.

The *market for lemons* refers to a situation in which no separating equilibrium exists and, consequently, only lemons are bought and sold.

One way for a seller of good-quality merchandise to overcome the problem of the market for lemons is to provide a *warranty*. Such a seller might also invest in building a reputation or in a *signal* of quality.

Education may act as a signal that a worker is intelligent and hardworking. If education is simply a signal and does not impart useful skills, an equilibrium in which good-quality workers have to be educated in order to get high-paying jobs may develop, even though real resources are being invested in the acquisition of skills that do not actually raise the marginal product of the better-quality workers.

20.9 QUESTIONS FOR DISCUSSION

1. There is considerable concern in government and in the insurance industry that doctors are contributing to the rise in health-care costs by prescribing unnecessary tests and performing unnecessary surgery. Leaving aside the severe liability problems associated with medical malpractice for the moment, explain why nearly universal health insurance coverage would contribute to this trend.

2. Explain why it is virtually impossible to fully insure against any risk. In other words, why is there a deductible clause in almost every insurance policy?

3. When Medicare and Medicaid (government medical insurance programs) were proposed, the projected cost was based upon medical expenses at that time (that is, when these programs did not exist). After they had been in

effect for several years, it was clear they were far more costly than expected, even allowing for rising prices due to inflation. Explain why these programs turned out to be much more expensive than expected.

4. In the analysis of the principal-agent problem, we found that the optimal sharing rule depended on the risk preferences of both principal and agent as described by their marginal utilities of income. In practice, however, sharing rules tend to be very simple—they are typically linear and the same across individuals. For example, real estate commissions are typically 6% or 7% of the sale price of the building, and share tenancies typically specify that one-third or one-half of the crop goes to the landlord. Why do you think a market equilibrium principal-agent contract would be likely to reduce to a simple, linear sharing rule that is the same for everyone?

5. Can you think of other examples of valuable market signals that individuals might profitably invest in? Explain your choices.

6. Can you think of potential markets for lemons (other than the used-car example developed above)? Justify your choices.

7. Can you think of ways of building a reputation (other than those already outlined in the text)? Explain your choices.

8. Under what circumstances will it not be profitable to invest in building a reputation or in providing a market signal? Explain.

Chapter 21

EXTERNALITIES, PUBLIC GOODS, AND PUBLIC DECISION MAKING

21.1 WHAT YOU SHOULD LEARN FROM THIS CHAPTER

This chapter considers the implications of the existence of *externalities* and *public goods* for the efficiency of competitive markets. Recall from Section 4.6 that an externality exists when the consumption or production decisions made by one agent affect the utility or production attainable by another agent or agents through some channel other than market price. Air and water *pollution* are the most commonly cited examples. A *public good* is a good that can be jointly consumed by a number of consumers without reducing any one consumer's ability to enjoy that consumption. Indeed, a public good can be viewed as providing a positive externality: if one person provides a public good, others can enjoy consuming it without having to pay for its provision. For example, if you pay for public TV, I can enjoy it for free.

The conditions for a Pareto optimal allocation of resources are different in the presence of externalities and public goods than when the competitive assumptions are satisfied. This means that competitive markets do not allocate externalities and public goods efficiently. In general, too little of a public good will be supplied by a competitive market, and too many negative externalities will be produced.

Analyzing the optimal allocation in the presence of an externality can be somewhat complicated, since there are several different approaches one can take. The appropriate approach in any given situation depends on the nature of the externality and who, in particular, is affected by it. To begin with, we make the analysis simple by assuming that one firm pollutes the production of another firm and that no consumers and no other firms are directly affected. This allows us to identify very clearly the cost of pollution to the polluted firm and the effect of a production externality on the production possibilities frontier. We then consider another simple situation comprising one consumer, two goods, and one source of pollution. This allows us to identify the conditions that characterize a Pareto optimal allocation of pollution when a consumer is directly affected by an externality. Extensions to situations involving several firms and several consumers follow logically, but the analyses are considerably more complicated and we do not develop them in detail.

These models are, by necessity, very simple and must ignore many of the realities of production and consumption externalities involving many firms and consumers simultaneously. For that reason, we view them as introductions to modeling the allocation of an externality in the general equilibrium case. To provide some more insight into the general case, we also include a partial equilibrium marginal-benefit/marginal-cost analysis to illustrate optimal allocation with large numbers of consumers and firms operating in a market.

After developing the optimality conditions with both externalities and public goods, we then consider several mechanisms that might be employed to "solve" the resource allocation problem posed by the presence of externalities and public goods. No one mechanism is ideal, however, because it is never possible to completely solve the allocation problem. There are many such mechanisms, and economists disagree among themselves as to which are most appropriate in specific circumstances. Consequently, in order to show the range of mechanisms and to indicate the problems associated with each, this chapter surveys a wide variety of them. To organize the presentation, we take a somewhat historical perspective, starting with the mechanisms first proposed in the early twentieth century and working forward to some of those proposed most recently. We conclude by returning to the distributional problem discussed in Section 9.5 to show why some public decision problems can never be resolved so that everyone is made better off than they would have been at the status quo.

21.2   OPTIMAL LEVELS OF EXTERNALITIES WHEN ONLY FIRMS ARE AFFECTED BY THE EXTERNALITIES

To begin our analysis of the optimal allocation of an externality, we assume there are two firms operating side by side and employing labor as their only variable factor of production. Pollution from the firm producing X reduces the output of the firm producing Y, but does not directly affect any other firms or consumers. Basically, the more X produced, the less Y for any given set of inputs employed in the production of Y:

$$\frac{\partial y}{\partial x} < 0. \tag{21.1}$$

We can write these production functions in the following form, assuming labor is the only factor of production:

$$y = y(L_y, x) \tag{21.2}$$
$$x = x(L_x). \tag{21.3}$$

Internalizing Externalities   While it might seem intuitive to simply ban production by the polluting firm, the efficient allocation of production between the two firms generally allows some positive production of X and, therefore, some residual pollution. One approach to analyzing the efficient production of X and Y is to consider a situation in which the firms are merged and one management chooses an output level of each firm to maximize the joint profits from producing both goods. This joint decision, then, takes into account the effect of producing more X on the production of Y. When no other firms or consumers are directly affected by the pollution and when the merged firm has optimized internally, we say that the merged firm has **internalized the externality** produced by firm X. We can then infer the characteristics of the efficient production set from the production behavior of the merged firm.

To analyze this internal allocation problem mathematically, we write the merged firm's profit function as the sum of the revenues it earns from the two operations minus the labor cost:

$$\pi = p_x x(L_x) + p_y y(L_y, x(L_x)) - w(L_x + L_y). \tag{21.4}$$

To find the profit-maximizing combination of x and y, we evaluate the first-order conditions from maximizing (21.4) with respect to the labor inputs:

$$\frac{\partial \pi}{\partial L_x} = p_x MP_{Lx} + p_y \frac{\partial y}{\partial x} MP_{Lx} - w = 0 \tag{21.5}$$

$$\frac{\partial \pi}{\partial L_y} = p_y MP_{Ly} - w = 0. \tag{21.6}$$

Solving both (21.5) and (21.6) for w,

$$w = p_x MP_{Lx} + p_y \frac{\partial y}{\partial x} MP_{Lx} \tag{21.7}$$

and

$$w = p_y MP_{Ly}. \tag{21.8}$$

Equation 21.8 indicates that the firm will employ labor in the production of Y until the wage rate is equal to the marginal revenue product of labor (as in any competitive firm). But, as equation 21.7 shows, the firm will only employ labor in X until the wage is equal to the difference between the marginal revenue product and the value of the *marginal damage* to Y of employing more labor in X. If we solve (21.7) for the price of X, we see that it is equal to the sum of the marginal cost without damages and the marginal damage term (the damage term is negative):

$$p_x = \frac{w}{MP_{Lx}} - p_y \frac{\partial y}{\partial x}. \tag{21.9}$$

Equation 21.8 shows that the price of Y is simply equal to the competitive price:

$$p_y = \frac{w}{MP_{Ly}}. \tag{21.10}$$

Equations 21.9 and 21.10 tell us that if the production externality is internalized, the price ratio p_x/p_y which *correctly* internalizes the externality, is *higher* than the competitive price ratio. If the externality is not internalized, the price of X will not correctly reflect the opportunity cost imposed on firm Y of producing more X, and *too much* X will be produced as a result. Merged firms would produce less X and more Y than unmerged competitive firms would; and if all producers of X and Y were merged, there would be a reduction in the market supply of X and an increase in the market supply of Y. This change would have the effect of raising the relative price of X to reflect the true opportunity cost of producing it.

A Graphical Illustration   Figure 21.1 now illustrates the effect of this externality on the production possibilities frontier between X and Y for the merged firm, using a two-good general equilibrium approach. The upper left graph is the production function for Y, and the lower right graph is the production function for X (shown as its inverse, $L(x)$). The lower left graph illustrates a certain amount of labor, $\overline{L} = L_x + L_y$, available for allocation in this economy. The function is a straight line with slope -1. Given $\overline{L}$, the upper right graph constructs the production possibilities frontier by mapping points on the respective production functions to the xy graph.

Looking first at the production function for Y, the top curve represents attainable outputs of Y if X were not produced close enough to pollute Y. Using only that total product curve for Y, we can construct a production possibilities frontier without pollution. The intercepts are $(0, y_1)$ and $(x_3, 0)$ and an intermediate point is (x_2, y_2). The effect of the externality is to reduce the total product curve for Y every time the output of X is increased. Clearly, if x is 0, we are still at the same y intercept. And, if y is 0, we

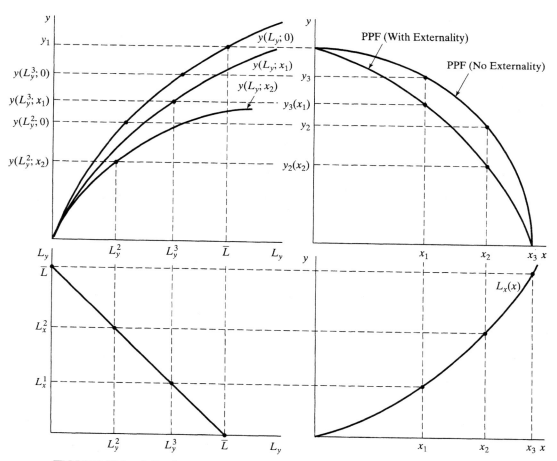

FIGURE 21.1   A Production Possibilities Frontier with an Externality

are at the same x intercept, since Y does not pollute X to begin with. In between, however, for a given output of X, less Y can be produced than without pollution. Thus, if x_2 is produced, the total product curve is lower ($y(L_y; x_2)$) and the point on the pollution production possibilities frontier is *inside* the no pollution frontier.

Pareto Optimality If we now introduce a consumer into this model, we can see that the effect of not internalizing the externality is similar to the effect of having a monopoly in the production of one good. The economy may be on its production possibilities frontier (including the externality), but in this case, the price of the good that produces the externality is too low. The consumer maximizes utility (so that the marginal rate of substitution equals the price ratio), but the marginal rate of substitution is not equal to the marginal rate of transformation. The consumer could be made better off if less of the good that pollutes were produced and if the relative price of that good were higher. In other words, the Pareto optimal allocation of the externality occurs where the consumer's marginal rate of substitution is equal to the true marginal rate of transformation (including the marginal damage that firm X imposes on firm Y).

This improvement in efficiency is illustrated in Figure 21.2. At point *A* the consumer is maximizing utility subject to the price ratio that prevails if the externality is

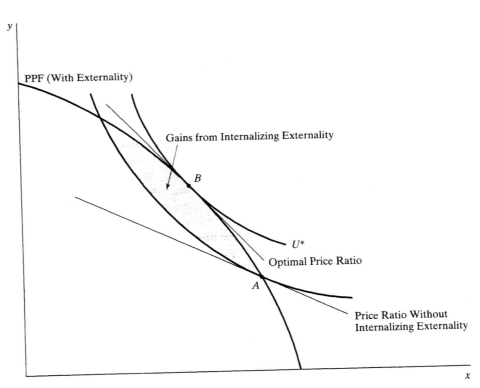

FIGURE 21.2 Optimal Allocation of a Negative Externality in a General Equilibrium Context

not internalized. However, the consumer would prefer to be at point B, with less X and more Y being produced and with the relative price of X higher than at point A.

Positive Externalities We should note at this point that externalities can be positive as well as negative. The most famous example of a positive externality was suggested by Meade.[1] In his example, there are two firms; one produces apples and the other produces honey. The honey producer keeps bees, which pollinate the apple orchard, and the apple blossoms provide nectar, from which the bees make their honey. Thus, each firm provides a positive externality to the other firm. In that case, the partial derivative of y with respect to x (and of x with respect to y, since both provide benefits) would be positive instead of negative. That would mean, in the above analysis, that the true opportunity costs of both honey and apples would be less than their respective marginal costs that were figured without taking account of the positive externalities. If positive externalities are ignored, fewer apples and less honey would be produced than would be socially optimal.

Many Consumers and Firms in a Partial Equilibrium Analysis The model developed above only allows pollution to affect one firm. If more than one firm is affected, then damages have to be calculated as the sum of the marginal damages imposed on all affected parties simultaneously. Section 21.4 develops this idea for the allocation of public goods, which can be viewed as providing positive externalities. For now, however, we use the following partial equilibrium analysis to analyze the optimal allocation of an externality in a market framework.

In equation 21.9, we identified a full marginal cost with an externality (including both the input costs and the marginal damage or benefit, depending on whether the externality is negative or positive). Economists distinguish between the **marginal private cost,** which just includes input costs, and the **marginal social cost,** which includes the opportunity cost associated with the externality. Marginal social cost is higher than marginal private cost for a negative externality and lower for a beneficial externality. The socially optimal amount of the externality is produced when the marginal social cost of the good associated with the externality is equal to the price along the inverse demand function associated with that optimum quantity.

This optimum is illustrated in Figure 21.3 for a negative externality. The input costs are represented by the marginal private cost curve (MPC), and the full marginal cost is represented by the higher marginal social cost (MSC). The optimal quantity is x^*, where $p_x(x^*)$ is equal to MSC. Marginal private cost is $MC(x^*)$ and the marginal damage associated with the externality at that quantity is $p_x(x^*) - MC(x^*)$. Notice also that the optimal quantity is less than the quantity that would be produced in the absence of the externality, and the optimal price is higher. This is what we found in the general equilibrium analysis described in Figure 21.2.

Pollution-control Technology For simplicity, we have analyzed pollution control as reducing the output of the good that pollutes. In actuality, much pollution is reduced by

[1]J. Meade, "External Economies and Diseconomies in a Competitive Situation," *Economic Journal* 62(1952):54–67.

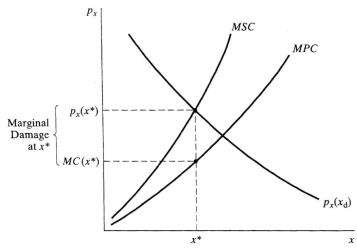

FIGURE 21.3   Optimal Allocation of a Negative Externality in a Partial Equilibrium Context

installing pollution-control equipment, such as scrubbers for smokestacks. When pollution-control equipment is available at some cost, the optimal way to reduce pollution involves using the least-cost method (which might reduce output) of achieving whatever is the optimal level of pollution. Moreover, that optimal level depends upon that least-cost method. Basically, the optimal level is achieved when the marginal cost of reducing pollution by the least-cost method is equal to the marginal benefit from further reductions in pollution. In addition, if the marginal cost of reducing pollution is lowered (say by some new pollution-control technology), then it is optimal to reduce pollution at the margin.

21.3   OPTIMAL ALLOCATION OF AN EXTERNALITY THAT AFFECTS CONSUMER UTILITY

Externalities among firms are relatively easy to model as an introduction to the subject, but most pollution directly affects consumers as well as (or more than) it does other firms. The air pollution in Los Angeles, for example, does not seriously affect the productivity of most businesses, but it significantly reduces the utility of many consumers. In that case, the relative prices and the allocation should reflect the marginal damage to consumers.

Pollution in a Robinson Crusoe Economy   To illustrate the Pareto optimal allocation, suppose we consider a Robinson Crusoe economy, like the one we analyzed in Section 14.3, only now we include pollution. In this model, Robinson produces goods X and Y with labor as the only input, and good X produces smoke as a by-product. Robinson doesn't like smoke (s), but he does like X and he does not have any smoke control technology, so he has to produce some smoke in order to consume X. Robinson's problem is to maximize utility:

$$U = U(x, y, s),$$ (21.11)

subject to his production constraints

$$x = x(L_x)$$ (21.12)

$$y = y(L_y)$$ (21.13)

$$s = s(x)$$ (21.14)

$$L_x + L_y = \bar{L} \Rightarrow L_y = \bar{L} - L_x,$$ (21.15)

where

$$\frac{\partial U}{\partial x} > 0, \quad \frac{\partial U}{\partial y} > 0, \quad \frac{\partial U}{\partial s} < 0.$$ (21.16)

Substituting x, y, L_y, and s from equations 21.12–21.15 in the utility function (equation 21.11), Robinson's maximization problem becomes

$$\max U(x(L_x), y(\bar{L} - L_x), s(x(L_x))).$$ (21.17)

The first-order condition for the optimal choice of L_x is

$$\frac{dU}{dL_x} = \frac{\partial U}{\partial x}\frac{dx}{dL} - \frac{\partial U}{\partial y}\frac{dy}{dL} + \frac{\partial U}{\partial s}\frac{ds}{dx}\frac{dx}{dL} = 0.$$ (21.18)

Combining terms in (21.18) around the marginal products of labor,

$$MP_{LX}\left(\frac{\partial U}{\partial x} + \frac{\partial U}{\partial s}\frac{ds}{dx}\right) = MP_{Ly}\frac{\partial U}{\partial y}.$$ (21.19)

Rearranging equation 21.19,

$$\frac{MP_{Ly}}{MP_{Lx}} = \frac{\dfrac{\partial U}{\partial x} + \dfrac{\partial U}{\partial s}\dfrac{ds}{dx}}{\partial U/\partial y}.$$ (21.20)

Expressing equation 21.20 in terms of marginal rates of substitution and marginal rate of transformation,

$$MRT = MRS_{yx} + MRS_{ys}\frac{ds}{dx}.$$ (21.21)

Rearranging terms in (21.21),

$$MRS_{yx} = MRT - MRS_{ys}\frac{ds}{dx}.$$ (21.22)

Equation 21.22 defines an implicit price ratio equal to the marginal rate of substitution, as in Section 14.3:

$$\frac{p_x}{p_y} = MRS_{yx} = MRT - MRS_{ys}\frac{ds}{dx}.$$ (21.23)

Equation 21.23 tells us that the optimal amount of X to produce is such that the consumer's marginal rate of substitution equals the marginal rate of product transformation *plus* (since the marginal utility of s is negative) the marginal rate of substitution between y and s times the marginal productivity of X in the production of s. Thus, as we saw in equation 21.9 where only firms are affected, if the externality is not internalized, the relative price of X will be too low, implying too much X and too little Y will be produced. To achieve a Pareto optimum, the economy needs to produce less X at a higher relative price, reflecting the damage from smoke pollution.

21.4   OPTIMAL PROVISION OF PURE PUBLIC GOODS

Public goods (such as TV signals and national defense) can be understood as being essentially equivalent to positive consumption externalities. In the previous example of a negative consumption externality, we found that the optimal level of the externality is characterized by equating the marginal rate of transformation and the sum of the marginal rates of substitution (where the ratio involving the externality is negative). If there were more than one consumer, the condition would include the sum of the marginal rates of substitution between y and s across all consumers. The same kind of condition appears in the description of the optimal provision of public goods, only the marginal rates of substitution will generally be positive.

A Mathematical Model   To characterize the optimal provision of a public good, we construct a simple model with a **pure public good.** A pure public good has the property that all consumers can enjoy it jointly, without any one person's consumption reducing others' ability to consume. Thus, there is no crowding if more and more people consume it, and no one need be excluded from consuming it.[2] National defense, information, and broadcast signals are good examples.

In this model, there are two consumers, A and B, who produce and consume X and Y, using a given amount of labor. Good Y is a private good, but X is a public good. This means that output of Y will be divided between A and B, but all the output of X will be consumed jointly. The utility functions can be written as

$$U_A = U_A(x, y_A) \quad \text{and} \quad U_B = U_B(x, y_B). \tag{21.24}$$

The production constraints are

$$x = x(L_x), \quad y_A + y_B = y(L_y), \quad \text{and} \quad L_x + L_y = \overline{L}. \tag{21.25}$$

To find a Pareto optimum, we maximize A's utility subject to a given utility level for B and the production constraints. Using four constraints, the Lagrangian is

---

[2]Most public goods are not *pure*. If too many people try to enjoy them, the use value declines because of crowding, and new or larger facilities need to be built. Obvious examples are parks, roads, bridges, and public swimming pools. These types of public goods are studied with slightly more complicated models, but the basic result, that the sum of the marginal rates of substitution should equal the marginal rate of transformation, is fundamental to the optimal provision of public goods.

$$\mathcal{L} = U_A(x, y_A) + \lambda_1(\overline{U}_B - U_B(x, y_B)) + \lambda_2(x - x(L_x)) \qquad (21.26)$$
$$+ \lambda_3(y_A + y_B - y(L_y)) + \lambda_4(\overline{L} - L_x - L_y).$$

The relevant first-order conditions are

$$\frac{\partial \mathcal{L}}{\partial x} = MU_x^A - \lambda_1 MU_x^B + \lambda_2 = 0 \qquad (21.27)$$

$$\frac{\partial \mathcal{L}}{\partial y_A} = MU_y^A + \lambda_3 = 0 \qquad (21.28)$$

$$\frac{\partial \mathcal{L}}{\partial y_B} = -\lambda_1 MU_y^B + \lambda_3 = 0 \qquad (21.29)$$

$$\frac{\partial \mathcal{L}}{\partial L_x} = -\lambda_2 MP_{Lx} - \lambda_4 = 0 \qquad (21.30)$$

$$\frac{\partial \mathcal{L}}{\partial L_y} = -\lambda_3 MP_{Ly} - \lambda_4 = 0. \qquad (21.31)$$

Combining equations 21.30 and 21.31,

$$\lambda_4 = -\lambda_2 MP_{Lx} = -\lambda_3 MP_{Ly}. \qquad (21.32)$$

Rearranging terms in equation 21.32,

$$\frac{\lambda_2}{\lambda_3} = \frac{MP_{Ly}}{MP_{Lx}} = MRT. \qquad (21.33)$$

From equations 21.28 and 21.29,

$$\lambda_1 = \frac{\lambda_3}{MU_y^B} = \frac{-MU_y^A}{MU_y^B}. \qquad (21.34)$$

Substituting (21.34) in (21.27),

$$\lambda_2 = -MU_x^A + MU_x^B \frac{-MU_y^A}{MU_y^B}. \qquad (21.35)$$

Combining (21.35) and (21.28) with (21.33),

$$\frac{\lambda_2}{\lambda_3} = \frac{-MU_x^A + MU_x^B \dfrac{-MU_y^A}{MU_y^B}}{-MU_y^A} \qquad (21.36)$$

$$= \frac{MU_x^A}{MU_y^A} + \frac{MU_x^B}{MU_y^B} = MRS_{yx}^A + MRS_{yx}^B = MRT.$$

Equation 21.36 indicates that the optimal provision of a pure public good equates the marginal rate of transformation and the sum of the marginal rates of substitution.

The condition that the optimal provision of a public good equates the marginal rate of transformation and the sum of the marginal rates of substitution across consumers, summarized in equation 21.36, also carries over to the optimal provision of an externality when more than one consumer is affected. This is because we can view reducing a negative externality as providing a public good to those affected by that externality and because we can view a produced public good (like national defense) as providing positive externalities to all those who consume it jointly. Carrying through the analogy, the optimal level of a negative externality is achieved when the marginal rate of transformation is equal to the marginal rate of substitution between the goods (which will be the same across consumers) *plus* the sum of the marginal damages imposed on each of the affected consumers. For example, in the Robinson Crusoe economy analyzed in the previous section, we found in equation 21.21 that $MRT = MRS_{yx} + MRS_{ys}(ds/dx)$. If there had been two consumers (A and B), we would have found the following conditions:

1. $MRS_{yx}^A = MRS_{yx}^B = MRS_{yx}$ (21.37)

2. $MRT = MRS_{yx} + (MRS_{ys}^A + MRS_{ys}^B)(ds/dx)$.   (21.38)

A Graphical Illustration of a General Equilibrium   The construction of a Pareto optimum for a pure public good is illustrated in Samuelson's diagram,[3] shown as Figure 21.4. In the upper graph, person B's given utility level $\overline{U}_B$ is shown with the production possibilities frontier. The vertical axis is the private good Y and the horizontal axis is the public good X. If person B enjoys $\overline{U}_B$ utility, person A can maximize A's utility over what is left of good Y and over the same amount of good X that B consumes. The concave curve in the lower graph represents the amounts of Y that are left over for A to consume for given amounts of joint consumption of X. This is simply the difference between the production of Y along the production possibilities frontier and the amount consumed by B at each level of production of X, given $\overline{U}_B$. In other words, A's consumption possibilities are constructed as the vertical difference between B's indifference curve and the production possibilities frontier.

A then maximizes utility over this set. A and B jointly consume the quantity of X chosen by $A(X^*)$, and the total Y produced (Y^*) is the sum of y_A^* and y_B. In addition, by the construction of the lower graph, the slope of A's indifference curve is equal to the difference between the slope of the production possibilities frontier and the slope of B's indifference curve. This guarantees that, at X^*, we get the optimality condition that the sum of the marginal rates of substitution (the sum of the slopes of the indifference curves) equals the marginal rate of transformation (the slope of the production possibilities frontier).

A Partial Equilibrium Graphical Illustration   The optimal provision of a public good can also be analyzed in a partial equilibrium context, using individual demand curves for the public good.[4] Recall that when we analyzed the market for a private

---

[3]Paul Samuelson, "Diagrammatic Exposition of a Theory of Public Expenditure," *Review of Economics and Statistics* 37(1955):350–356.

[4]When we use demand curves in a partial equilibrium framework, we are implicitly assuming that there is *one* optimal quantity of a public good. However, as we show below, unless there are no income effects, the optimal quantity is not independent of the distribution of income across consumers. Thus, the use of a partial equilibrium analysis also implicitly assumes either that there are no income effects, or that there is a given distribution of income and that individual demand curves are well defined given that distribution.

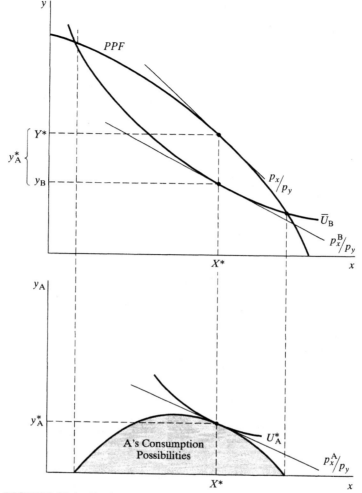

FIGURE 21.4   Derivation of the Optimal Provision of a Public Good

good, we assumed that all consumers faced the same price and each then purchased a different quantity, the utility-maximizing quantity, given that single market price. The optimal quantity is produced when the total quantity consumers wish to purchase is equal to the total quantity firms will offer for sale at a market price equal to marginal cost. With a public good, the constant is quantity, since all consumers enjoy the same quantity of a public good jointly. Given a single quantity, the inverse demand price for each consumer indicates that consumer's marginal willingness to pay to consume that quantity of the public good. The optimal quantity is achieved when the sum of every consumer's marginal willingness to pay is equal to the marginal cost of producing that many units of the public good. Unless all consumers are identical, each consumer will pay a different, **personalized price** when the efficient quantity is provided.

This optimum is illustrated in Figure 21.5 for two consumers. The lower two graphs represent the individual inverse demand functions for consumers A and B, and the upper graph shows a demand curve that is the sum of the inverse demand prices at each quantity. The constant marginal cost (MC) is also shown on the upper graph. Thus, at x_1, consumer A's marginal willingness to pay is p_A^1 and consumer B's marginal willingness to pay is p_B^1, for a total inverse demand price for x_1 of $p_1 = p_A^1 + p_B^1$. Similarly, at x_2, consumer A would pay p_A^2 per unit of the public good and consumer B would pay p_B^2, for a total inverse demand price of $p_2 = p_A^2 + p_B^2$. The optimum quantity is X^*, where the vertically summed "market" demand curve intersects the marginal cost curve. At X^*, consumer A would pay p_A^* per unit and consumer B would pay p_B^* per unit, where $p_A^* + p_B^* = MC$.

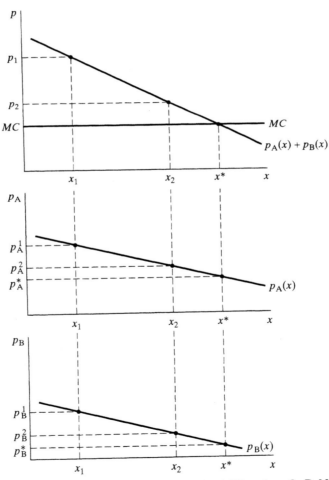

FIGURE 21.5 Derivation of the Optimal Allocation of a Public Good in a Partial Equilibrium Context

Income Effects and the Optimal Provision of a Public Good   We should note at this point that if consumer preferences do allow for income effects, the optimal provision of a public good will depend on consumer endowments, just as the competitive equilibrium and the core in a private-goods economy depend on the endowments. Thus, we cannot refer to *the* optimal provision. The best we can do is characterize the conditions for optimal provision by taking different utility levels for B in Samuelson's diagram (Figure 21.4).

To see this point, consider two simple utility functions. The Cobb-Douglas utility function, introduced as equation 6.15, allows for income effects. Assuming that the *i*th consumer has an individual exponential parameter and that $\alpha + \beta = 1$ for all consumers, we write the individual Cobb-Douglas utility function with private good Y_i and public good X as

$$U_i = x^{\beta_i} y_i^{1-\beta_i}. \tag{21.39}$$

The other utility function is referred to as a **quasilinear** utility function. The general form is

$$U_i = f_i(x) + y_i. \tag{21.40}$$

One specific example of (21.40) is often expressed in natural logs:

$$U_i = \beta_i \ln(x) + y_i. \tag{21.41}$$

Beginning with the Cobb-Douglas utility function and assuming for simplicity that both marginal costs are equal to 1, if β is the coefficient for x and $1 - \beta$ is the coefficient for y in equation 6.22, then the individual demand function for good X for person i, given a personalized price of p_i, would be

$$x^* = \frac{\beta_i M_i}{p_i} \quad \Rightarrow \quad p_i = \frac{\beta_i M_i}{x}. \tag{21.42}$$

Now, if we sum the personalized prices in (21.42) and set them equal to the marginal cost (which is 1), we can derive the optimal X, recalling that in equilibrium, the x_i^*'s are all equal to one another:

$$\sum_{i=1}^{n} p_i = \sum_{i=1}^{n} \frac{\beta_i M_i}{X^*} = 1. \tag{21.43}$$

Solving (21.43) for X^*,

$$X^* = \sum_{i=1}^{n} \beta_i M_i. \tag{21.44}$$

Equation 21.44 indicates that, unless the β_i's are identical, X^* clearly depends on the distribution of income across consumers with different utility parameters.

Now, let's consider the utility function in equation 21.41. To find the personalized prices for X, we set up the consumer's Lagrangian, assuming the price of Y is 1:

$$\mathcal{L}_i = \beta_i \ln(x) + y_i + \lambda_i (M_i - p_i x - y_i). \tag{21.45}$$

The relevant first-order conditions are

$$\frac{\partial \mathcal{L}_i}{\partial x} = \frac{\beta_i}{x^*} - \lambda_i^* p_i = 0 \tag{21.46}$$

$$\frac{\partial \mathcal{L}_i}{\partial y_i} = 1 - \lambda_i^* = 0. \tag{21.47}$$

Solving (21.46) and (21.47) for λ_i^* and collecting terms,

$$p_i = \frac{\beta_i}{x^*}. \tag{21.48}$$

Summing (21.48) over p_i as in equation 21.43,

$$\sum_{i=1}^{n} p_i = \sum_{i=1}^{n} \frac{\beta_i}{X^*} = 1. \tag{21.49}$$

Solving (21.49) for X^*,

$$X^* = \sum_{i=1}^{n} \beta_i. \tag{21.50}$$

Equation 21.50 illustrates how, if there are no income effects in the consumption of the public good by any consumer, the optimal provision of the public good is independent of consumer incomes. This implies that if consumer utility functions are as given in equation 21.41, there is only one optimal quantity of the public good for each set of consumer preferences. In the case of the Cobb-Douglas utility function, on the other hand, there will be different optimal quantities for different income distributions.

21.5   EXTERNALITIES AND PUBLIC GOODS IN COMPETITIVE MARKETS

We have just seen that the optimal level of an externality or a public good involves choosing a quantity of output such that the sum of the marginal benefits and costs is equal to the marginal rate of transformation. We have also seen in Sections 7.2 and 14.4, however, that competitive markets work to equate individual marginal rates of substitution to the marginal rate of transformation. They do this by establishing a single equilibrium price at which the sum of individual, private quantities demanded is equal to the sum of individual, private firm supplies at that price. At that price, marginal private benefit is equal to marginal private cost. This is appropriate when the consequences of all private decisions are also private. But when there are public consequences of private decisions, the usual competitive market setup has no mechanism for incorporating the costs or benefits of those public consequences.

To see this point, consider the case of production externalities. The competitive firm that produces externalities, either positive or negative, but does not internalize them, faces a market price and chooses a profit-maximizing quantity that equates the input price for each input and the private marginal revenue product of that input. Equivalently, the price of output will be equal to the input price divided by the marginal product of that input at that output level: $w = pMP \Rightarrow p = w/MP$. However, there is no market mechanism by which a firm producing a negative externality incorporates the damages it imposes on other firms into its private decision. Neither is there any mechanism by which firms that provide a positive externality can be compensated for providing it. The result will be that too much negative externality and too little positive externality will be provided through competitive markets. We say that the producer of a negative externality is imposing **external costs** on others, while the producer of a positive externality (or the provider of a public good) is providing **external benefits.**

Similarly, if provision of public goods or other positive consumption externalities is left to the private competitive market, each consumer will take account of what everyone else has provided and then provide him- or herself with additional amounts of public goods until the individual marginal rates of substitution are equal to the market price ratio. Since the optimal allocation equates the marginal cost of provision and the *sum* of the marginal rates of substitution, a single price equal to marginal cost will be "too high" to generate the optimal allocation, and too little of the public good will be provided. It is this inability of competitive markets to force individuals to internalize external costs and benefits that constitutes the "problem" of externalities and public goods.

21.6   PIGOUVIAN TAXES AND LINDAHL PRICES

In theory, the problem of externalities and public goods can be "solved" by an appropriate set of taxes that forces firms and consumers to internalize the externalities they are creating. Three classic works in economics proposed such solutions: Pigou dealt with externalities (particularly negative externalities), and Lindahl and Wicksell dealt with public goods.[5]

Pigouvian Taxes   Pigou suggested that firms that created negative externalities should be taxed the difference between marginal social cost and marginal private cost for each additional unit of output they produced. These taxes would force the firms to internalize those external costs and produce the socially optimal amount of pollution. He illustrated his point by considering a factory that emitted smoke and made everything around it dirtier than was socially optimal. Residents around the factory paid for that smoke in much higher laundry costs. (Today we would add the health costs associated with most factory smoke and the aesthetic costs of having to look at dirty smoke.) The State, he said, should impose a tax on each unit of output equal to the marginal external cost associated with that output level. This solution is already illustrated in Figure 21.3. The optimal output level is x^*, where the price of output includes both the marginal input costs and the social opportunity cost of the pollution created at that output level. Pigou's scheme is to tax the firm that social opportunity cost for each unit of output produced. That would force the firm to pay the full marginal cost and would induce it to produce x^*.

[5]A. C. Pigou, *The Economics of Welfare,* 4th ed. (London: Macmillan & Company, 1932); E. Lindahl, "Just Taxation–A Positive Solution," (originally published in German in 1919); and K. Wicksell, "A New Principle of Just Taxation," (originally published in German in 1896). Both Lindahl and Wicksell have been translated and reprinted in R. A. Musgrave and A. T. Peacock, eds., *Classics in the Theory of Public Finance* (New York: Macmillan and Company, 1958).

This can also be illustrated mathematically with the two-firm model (goods X and Y) developed as equations 21.1–21.10. Suppose the government were to impose the following tax on firm X for each unit of output produced:

$$t_x = -p_y \frac{\partial}{\partial x} y(x^*).$$
(21.51)

This is, of course, the marginal damage imposed by firm X on firm Y at the optimal output level, from equation 21.9. Firm X now maximizes profits, including this tax in its costs:

$$\max \pi_x = p_x x - C(x) - t_x x,$$
(21.52)

where $C(x)$ is the firm's cost function.

$$\frac{d\pi}{dx} = p_x - MC - t_x = 0.$$
(21.53)

Solving (21.53) for p_x,

$$p_x = MC + t_x = MC - p_y \frac{\partial y}{\partial x}.$$
(21.54)

Now, if we compare equations 21.9 and 21.54, the **Pigouvian tax** leads to the same characterization of the allocation of X as the characterization of the optimal allocation where the externality is internalized. The difference is that in equation 21.9, a merged firm internalizes the externality naturally and pays for it implicitly, whereas in equation 21.54, firm X is being forced to pay the marginal damage.

Lindahl Prices   Regarding public goods, Wicksell first proposed that individuals should only have to pay for public goods according to their individual benefits from consuming them. Lindahl then suggested that the personalized prices proposed by Wicksell could be generated as the equilibrium of a *tâtonnement* process, similar to the private goods process outlined in Section 9.3. The idea is to adjust individual price ratios between the public good and a private good used for normalization (as in Section 9.3) until all consumers demand the same quantity of the public good at those price ratios.

Samuelson later showed that if all consumers behaved competitively at each iteration of the **Lindahl *tâtonnement* mechanism** (that is, if they took announced price ratios *as given*), the **Lindahl prices** would generate a Pareto optimal allocation of the public good, with the sum of the marginal rates of substitution equal to the marginal rate of transformation.[6] Figure 21.4 illustrates Lindahl prices in a partial equilibrium context. We saw that if each consumer pays his or her marginal value as the personalized price at the optimal quantity, then the sum of the personalized prices equals the

---

[6]P. Samuelson, "The Pure Theory of Public Expenditures," *Review of Economics and Statistics* (November 1954), pp. 387–389.

marginal cost of providing that quantity. In the Wicksell-Lindahl scheme, consumers are individually taxed those personalized prices that are generated by the *tâtonnement* mechanism outlined above.

The following simple mathematical model also illustrates the optimality of the Wicksell-Lindahl scheme. Suppose each consumer (i) has an individual utility function defined over Y_i (private consumption of the private good) and X (the public good), and an initial endowment, which we simply designate M_i. Suppose also that the production possibilities frontier is linear, so that the marginal rate of transformation, p_x/p_y, is known with certainty. In that case, the auctioneer calls out personalized prices (p_i) for the public good and prices for Y (p_y), making sure at each iteration that the sum of the personalized price ratios is equal to the marginal rate of transformation:

$$\sum_{i=1}^{n} \frac{p_i}{p_y} = \frac{p_x}{p_y}. \tag{21.55}$$

The participants then respond with utility-maximizing quantities demanded, given those prices, and the auctioneer adjusts the personalized price *ratios* until all the participants demand the same quantity of the public good.

Now, putting the consumer's decision problem in this mechanism into formal terms, the utility-maximization problem can be represented as

$$\max U_i(x, y_i) \tag{21.56}$$
$$\text{s.t. } M_i = p_i x + p_y y_i.$$

The Lagrangian for each consumer is

$$\mathcal{L}_i = U_i(x, y_i) + \lambda_i(M_i - p_i x - p_y y_i). \tag{21.57}$$

The relevant first-order conditions are

$$\frac{\partial \mathcal{L}_i}{\partial x} = \frac{\partial U_i}{\partial x_i} - \lambda_i^* p_i = 0, \quad \text{for all } i \tag{21.58}$$

$$\frac{\partial \mathcal{L}_i}{\partial y_i} = \frac{\partial U_i}{\partial y_i} - \lambda_i^* p_y = 0, \quad \text{for all } i. \tag{21.59}$$

Solving equations 21.58 and 21.59 for λ_i^* for each consumer:

$$\lambda_i^* = \frac{\partial U_i/\partial x}{p_i} = \frac{\partial U_i/y_i}{p_y}. \tag{21.60}$$

Collecting terms in (21.60),

$$\frac{MU_x^i}{MU_y^i} = \frac{p_i}{p_y} = MRS_i. \tag{21.61}$$

To judge whether the resulting equilibrium of X is Pareto optimal, we sum the marginal rates of substitution given in equation 21.61:

$$\sum_{i=1}^{n} MRS_i = \sum_{i=1}^{n} \frac{p_i}{p_y} = \frac{p_x}{p_y}. \tag{21.62}$$

Equation 21.62 shows that the sum of the marginal rates of substitution is equal to the price ratio, and the allocation is Pareto optimal. This is often referred to as the **Lindahl-Samuelson condition** for Pareto optimality.

21.7   PROBLEMS WITH THE IMPLEMENTATION OF OPTIMAL TAXES

While Pigouvian taxes and Lindahl prices may lead to Pareto optimality if the "correct" taxes are identified, there is a fundamental problem associated with identifying those taxes: the information needed to identify them is private and the individuals having that information have no incentive to reveal it truthfully. In fact, it is generally in their interest to misrepresent the information (in predictable directions). Moreover, if there are income effects, the optimal allocation of the externality may not actually be achieved if the proceeds of the tax go toward the general tax fund instead of toward compensation for damages.

In regard to the problem of misrepresentation, suppose the government is trying to determine a correct Pigouvian tax. That requires determining the actual marginal damages imposed on other firms and consumers, information available only to those other firms and consumers. If the government asks them how much they are damaged, they have an obvious incentive to overestimate that damage in an attempt to force the factory to reduce output (and pollution) by even more. The polluting firm, on the other hand, will try to discredit that information, in an attempt to make its tax as low as possible. Thus, both sides will misrepresent in opposite directions, and the government will still not be able to determine the correct tax.

Operation of the Lindahl* Tâtonnement *Mechanism   A similar thing happens when the government tries to determine the correct Lindahl prices. If a *tâtonnement* mechanism were used, as suggested by Lindahl for example, the mechanism would tend to reduce the personalized prices of those who demanded less than the average quantity and raise the personalized prices of those who demanded more. This would happen because a person who demands less than everyone else would have to pay a low price to be encouraged to demand more, and the person who demands more would have to pay a higher price to be induced to demand less. The object of the Lindahl mechanism is to find a set of personalized prices such that everyone demands the same quantity of the public good at those prices.

This is illustrated in Figure 21.6. The average quantity proposed by all participants on the previous iteration is shown as $\bar{x}$ on both graphs. Person 1 on the left, however, had been given personalized price $\hat{p}_1$ and had responded $\hat{x}_1^*$, larger than $\bar{x}$. To get his or her response closer to the average, the auctioneer raises the personalized price and encourages person 1 to move back up along the demand curve, as the arrow shows. Person 2 on the right, on the other hand, responded $\hat{x}_2^*$, less than $\bar{x}$, when presented with personalized price $\hat{p}_2$. To increase the response on the next round, the auctioneer lowers person 2's price and moves him or her down along the demand curve, in the direction of the arrow.

The Free-rider Problem and Strategic Underrevelation   Suppose now that you were participating in a Lindahl *tâtonnement* mechanism. How would you actually respond?

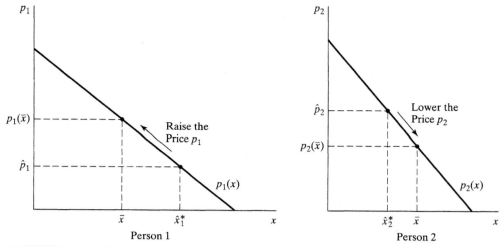

FIGURE 21.6   Using Excess Demand to Adjust Personalized Prices in a Lindahl *Tâtonnement* Process

Since the good in question is a public good, you know that if everyone else were to pay for it, you could consume it at zero cost. Even if you do contribute, you have an incentive to try to pay less than the most you are willing to and let everyone else contribute more. In other words, you would like to *free ride* on everyone else's provision. We refer to this incentive problem as the **free-rider problem.** Put into a Lindahl mechanism, your strategy is clear. You want to underreveal your demand for the public good relative to your true demand, in order to get a lower personalized price on the final iteration. Unfortunately, if everyone adopts the same strategy, the mean demand revealed will be less than the optimal quantity, implying an equilibrium that is also less than the optimal quantity.

We can use the utility function with no income effects, which we introduced above, to illustrate this point. Suppose everyone had the utility function introduced as equation 21.41: $U_i = \beta_i \ln(x) + y_i$. We have already seen in equations 21.50 and 21.48 that if both marginal costs are equal to 1, the optimal x is $X^* = \sum_{i=1}^{n} \beta_i$ (equation 21.50), and the Lindahl prices are $p_i = \beta_i / X^*$ (equation 21.48).

Substituting (21.50) in (21.48), we can rewrite the Lindahl prices as

$$p_i = \frac{\beta_i}{\sum_{j=1}^{n} \beta_j}. \tag{21.63}$$

We assume now that each consumer maximizes utility, subject to a budget constraint:

$$\max U_i = \beta_i \ln(x) + y_i \tag{21.64}$$

$$\text{s.t. } M_i = p_i x + y_i \implies y_i = M_i - p_i x.$$

Substituting for y_i from the constraint in equations 21.64, p_i from equation 21.63, and X^* from equation 21.50 in the objective function in equations 21.64,

$$U_i = \beta_i \ln \sum_{j=1}^{n} \beta_j + M_i - \frac{\beta_i}{\sum_{j=1}^{n} \beta_j} \sum_{j=1}^{n} \beta_j \tag{21.65}$$

$$= \beta_i \ln \sum_{j=1}^{n} \beta_j + M_i - \beta_i.$$

Now, suppose that participant i decides to misrepresent preferences by behaving as if he or she had a different β_i, the marginal valuation for the public good. The lower the revealed β_i, the less of the public good he or she will appear to demand. We let b_i signify the β_i he or she pretends to have.

To find the effect of i's misrepresentation, let's assume that i knows the other participants' utility functions and believes that all other participants will tell the truth. The strategy, then, is to find i's misrepresentation strategy that maximizes utility, assuming everyone else tells the truth. To find that, we substitute b_i for β_i in the value for x and in the tax, as they are incorporated in i's utility function as given in equation 21.65. The only place where β_i remains is as the coefficient for $\ln(x)$

$$U_i = \beta_i \ln\left(b_i + \sum_{j \neq i} \beta_j\right) + M_i - b_i, \tag{21.66}$$

where $\sum_{j \neq i} \beta_j$ is the sum of the β's of everyone but person i. We now choose b_i to maximize utility:

$$\frac{\partial U_i}{\partial b_i} = \frac{\beta_i}{b_i^* + \sum_{j \neq i} \beta_j} - 1 = 0. \tag{21.67}$$

Solving 21.67 for b_i^*,

$$b_i^* = \beta_i - \sum_{j \neq i} \beta_j. \tag{21.68}$$

Equation 21.68 indicates that the utility-maximizing "lie" under the Lindahl mechanism is to significantly underreport relative to the true β_i. In fact, if everyone had identical, quasilinear preferences as in (21.64), one Nash equilibrium in such sophisticated strategies is for everyone to report β/n, instead of β, implying that the quantity provided would be only x^*/n.

21.8 _EVIDENCE ON FREE RIDING

It is somewhat difficult to determine whether people are actually free riding in naturally occurring situations, because we do not know their true marginal valuation functions, but there are a number of examples that suggest that free riding may be a significant problem. One of the first that comes to mind is funding for public television and public radio. Millions of people watch public television and listen to public radio, but never contribute during the fund drives. If asked, they would tell you that public broadcasting is valuable and that they derive pleasure from the programs. Thus, the benefit they receive is clearly greater than 0, but they are paying 0. Since 0 is the marginal cost of providing the broadcast to one more person, individuals who do not contribute are simply behaving rationally in what looks to them like a competitive private-goods market. The broadcast is available at a zero price, so they consume it without paying. The stations appeal to morality and offer private incentives, such as special recordings and program guides, to get people to subscribe, but contributions still fall short of the cost of providing the programming.

Experimental Evidence   While it is fairly clear that free riding exists, it is very difficult to determine the extent of free riding without knowing peoples' utility functions. Because of this difficulty, economists have turned to laboratory experiments to test for free riding. As we showed in Section 13.4 on experimental markets, the experimenter can induce preferences and profit functions with monetary payoffs. Thus, in the public goods framework, the experimenter can induce a set of monetary parameters such that all participants earn the highest profits at some particular level of provision of a public good. The experimenter can then see if subjects in an experiment provide that level, either by voluntary means or through some allocation mechanism. While no one has yet tested the specific Lindahl mechanisms outlined above, there have been several tests of both voluntary provision and of mechanisms somewhat like the Lindahl mechanism.

One of the first experimental studies of free riding was by two sociologists, Marwell and Ames.[7] They gave subjects tokens which they could contribute to either a private good or a public good. Tokens contributed to the private good returned a certain dollar amount per token in profit. Tokens contributed to the public good returned a profit as a function of the total contributions by everyone else participating in the experiment. They found that, while subjects did not typically contribute enough to provide an optimal amount of the public good, they did not contribute 0 either. In fact, very few subjects exhibited **strong free riding**—zero contribution. Most contributed something, but less than the optimum.

Isaac, McCue, and Plott, and Isaac, Walker, and Thomas[8] criticized Marwell and Ames for not using an iterative process, such as a Lindahl mechanism, for finding an equilibrium level of provision. Both of these studies retained the voluntary provision feature of Marwell and Ames, but they added the feature that subjects were informed at each iteration what they would have been paid at the group's provision level for that iteration. What they found was that provision was relatively high the first iteration (as Marwell and Ames found in their one-shot experiment), but less than optimal. But when subjects who had contributed generously saw how little others had contributed, they contributed less the next iteration. After several iterations, total provision converged to a very low, but still positive, level. They were able to reduce the amount of

---

[7]Gerald Marwell and Ruth Ames, "Experiments on the Provision of Public Goods I: Resources, Interest, Group Size, and the Free Rider Problem," *American Journal of Sociology* 84(1979):1335; and "Experiments on the Provision of Public Goods II: Provision Point, Stakes, Experience, and the Free Rider Problem," *American Journal of Sociology* 85(1980):926.

[8]R. Mark Isaac, Ken McCue, and Charles R. Plott, "Public Goods Provision in an Experimental Environment," *Journal of Public Economics* 26(1985):51; and R. Mark Isaac, James M. Walker, and Susan H. Thomas, "Divergent Evidence on Free Riding: An Experimental Examination of Possible Explanations," *Public Choice* 43(1984):113–149.

free riding by making individual returns rise faster as a function of total contributions, but they still only got contributions totaling 45% of the optimum. They concluded that, while strong free riding appears to be refuted by theirs and Marwell and Ames' results, **weak free riding** is a serious problem for any voluntary public-goods provision scheme. That is to say, people *will* contribute, but total contributions will be less than necessary to provide the optimal quantity of a public good.[9] This is consistent with the Nash equilibrium of the Lindahl mechanism, outlined in equation 21.68. Participants in both the Lindahl and the voluntary provision mechanisms have incentives to reveal nonzero demands; however, these revealed demands may be considerably less than their actual demands. Consequently, the total quantity of the public good provided may be less than the optimal quantity.

21.9 _____ COASIAN BARGAINING

In 1960, Ronald Coase[10] criticized the Pigouvian approach to external costs and went so far as to suggest that a "solution" to the problem of externalities and public goods was unnecessary. His critique and, in fact, his entire alternative approach focus on the importance of property rights in analyzing the allocation of externalities and public goods.

Coase's Critique of Pigou   Using Pigou's own example, the air which is being dirtied with smoke from the factory is an important factor of production for the factory. If the factory has a legal **right to pollute,** then it *owns* a property right in that air. Individuals who wish to reduce that pollution would be willing to compensate the factory owner for giving up some of his legal right to produce output and pollute the air. If the benefits they would receive from reducing pollution are not sufficient to compensate the factory owner, then it would not be efficient to reduce the pollution. A Pigouvian tax would simply add up the marginal damages without considering whether the resulting allocation was both Pareto optimal and Pareto superior, given the prior distribution of property rights. If the factory owner did have a clearly defined property right, for example, giving up that right without compensation would not be Pareto superior.

On the other hand, the government and the courts might deem that individual homeowners have the legal right to breathe clean air. In that case, the factory owner would have to pay for the right to dirty the air, just as he would have to pay for the right to use any other valuable factor of production. He will, thus, "hire" units of air until the marginal cost of using that air equals its marginal revenue product. But if the cost of using that air is so high that the firm cannot make nonnegative profits, it will cease operation altogether.

The Coase Theorem and Coase's Illustration   Assuming that middle ground exists—so that homeowners can compensate (some say "bribe") the firm to reduce output and

---

[9]Vernon Smith, "Incentive Compatible Experimental Processes for the Provision of Public Goods," *Research in Experimental Economics* 1(1979):59, also found weak free riding in a bidding version of the Lindahl mechanism.

[10]R. Coase, "The Problem of Social Cost," *Journal of Law and Economics* 3(1960):1.

the firm can pay the homeowners to allow it to expand output—Coase came to the somewhat surprising conclusion that the *same amount of output and pollution would be produced,* regardless of which side owned the rights to the air. If the firm owned the right, homeowners would pay until the marginal benefit from pollution reduction equalled the marginal cost. If homeowners owned the right, the firm would pay until the marginal cost of air equalled the marginal benefit of less pollution. In the absence of obstacles to bargaining or significant costs associated with bargaining (called *transactions costs*), these two marginal cost and marginal benefit calculations would lead to the same (Pareto optimal) level of pollution. The only difference would be an *equity* issue: who pays whom for the right to use the air.

Coase illustrated his proposition with examples that have since become classics in the economics literature. One involves a farmer and a rancher; the farmer grows grain and the rancher runs cows. The cows would get fat on the farmer's grain, but the farmer makes more profits if the cows are kept from the grain. The question is how many cows will there be and how much grain will be grown if the farmer and the rancher come to an agreement through bargaining.

Coase argues that if the rancher has the unrestricted right to run cows, the farmer will pay the rancher to reduce the herd, relative to some initial position, or to be allowed to fence off some land. If the farmer has the right to grow crops without having them trampled by cows, the rancher will pay to be allowed to increase the herd, relative to the initial position, or to use some land for pasture. However, the most important conclusion is that the same number of cows will run and the same amount of grain will be produced, regardless of which side has the right. The statement that the outcome is *invariant* to the prior assignment of rights is known as the **Coase theorem.**

Mathematical Model of a Market in Rights to Pollute   Coase's point is illustrated with the simple two-firm model developed in equations 21.1–21.10. Suppose first that firm Y has the right to be free from pollution and agrees to let firm X pollute for a price (t), to be determined by a competitive market. This is called an **auxiliary market** in pollution rights. Given output and input prices and the competitively determined per-unit tax paid by firm X to firm Y, firm Y simultaneously chooses its own labor input, and a quantity demanded in the auxiliary market for firm X's output, such that the firm's profits are maximized:

$$\max \pi_y = p_y y(L_y, x) - wL_y + tx. \tag{21.69}$$

The first-order conditions are

$$\frac{\partial \pi_y}{\partial x} = p_y \frac{\partial y}{\partial x} + t = 0 \tag{21.70}$$

$$\frac{\partial \pi_y}{\partial L_y} = p_y \frac{\partial y}{\partial L} - w = 0. \tag{21.71}$$

Solving (21.70) for t,

$$t = -p_y \frac{\partial y}{\partial x}, \tag{21.72}$$

which describes Y's inverse supply for the increments in X's output in the auxiliary market.

Firm X also maximizes profits, given prices and the tax:

$$\max \pi_x = p_x x(L_x) - tx(L_x) - wL_x. \tag{21.73}$$

Firm X's first-order condition is

$$\frac{\partial \pi_x}{\partial L_x} = (p_x - t)\frac{\partial x}{\partial L} - w = 0. \tag{21.74}$$

Equation 21.74, in turn, implies firm X's inverse demand for rights to increase production in the auxiliary market:

$$t = p_x - \frac{w}{MP_{L_x}}. \tag{21.75}$$

To find the equilibrium value for t, we equate inverse demand (21.75) and inverse supply (21.72):

$$t = p_x - \frac{w}{MP_{L_x}} = -p_y \frac{\partial y}{\partial x}. \tag{21.76}$$

Solving (21.76) for p_x,

$$p_x = \frac{w}{MP_{L_x}} - p_y \frac{\partial y}{\partial x}. \tag{21.77}$$

Notice that equation 21.77 is the same as equation 21.9, which characterized the optimal price of X.

Now, suppose firm X has the right to pollute and firm Y pays firm X a competitively determined bribe (b) per unit of reduction in firm X's output, relative to some agreed upon initial output (call it $\tilde{x}$). Firm Y's problem is to choose labor and a demanded reduction in firm X's output, given the wage, the price of output, and the bribe:

$$\max \pi_y = p_y y(L_y, x) - wL_y - b(\tilde{x} - x). \tag{21.78}$$

The first-order conditions are

$$\frac{\partial \pi_y}{\partial x} = p_y \frac{\partial y}{\partial x} + b = 0 \tag{21.79}$$

$$\frac{\partial \pi_y}{\partial L_y} = p_y \frac{\partial y}{\partial L} - w = 0. \tag{21.80}$$

Solving equation 21.79 for b, Y's inverse demand for firm X's reductions in output is

$$b = -p_y \frac{\partial y}{\partial x}. \tag{21.81}$$

Firm X also maximizes profits, taking output price, the wage, and the bribe as given:

$$\max \pi_x = p_x x(L_x) - wL_x + b[\tilde{x} - x(L_x)]. \tag{21.82}$$

The first-order condition is

$$\frac{\partial \pi_x}{\partial L_x} = (p_x - b)\frac{\partial x}{\partial L} - w = 0. \tag{21.83}$$

Solving equation 21.83 for b, the inverse supply curve is

$$b = p_x - \frac{w}{MP_{Lx}}. \tag{21.84}$$

To find the equilibrium bribe, we set the inverse supply (equation 21.84) equal to the inverse demand (equation 21.81):

$$b = p_x - \frac{w}{MP_{Lx}} = -p_y \frac{\partial y}{\partial x}. \tag{21.85}$$

Solving (21.85) for the price of X,

$$p_x = \frac{w}{MP_{Lx}} - p_y \frac{\partial y}{\partial x} = (21.77) = (21.9). \tag{21.86}$$

Equations 21.9, 21.77, and 21.86 show that the optimality conditions are satisfied at a competitive equilibrium in the auxiliary market, implying that the outputs of the merged firm are the same as the outputs produced with both auxiliary markets (Coase's invariance prediction). Given that the outputs are the same, equations 21.76 and 21.85 show that equilibrium *tax* is equal to the equilibrium *bribe*. Moreover, the tax and bribe are both equal to the optimal Pigouvian tax. (Compare equations 21.77 and 21.86 with equation 21.51.)

Coase and the Core of a Cooperative Game   Coase's argument rests on the theoretical concept of the core in cooperative games, developed in Section 16.2. At the core, it is not possible for any individual or coalition to unilaterally improve its position by taking some other action. With two parties to a bargain, that is the same as the definition of an allocation that is both Pareto optimal and Pareto superior, relative to some initial allocation. In effect, what Coase is arguing is that there is a *unique* core to such a bargaining game and that individuals faced with such a cooperative game situation will always bargain to that core—an allocation which is, by definition, Pareto optimal.

Tradable Pollution Permits   An application of the Coase theorem is to allow a market in tradable pollution permits.[11] The idea is that firms will only be able to emit as much pollution as they have permits to do so, and those permits can be bought and sold in a competitive market. This means that consumer groups who want to reduce pollution can buy up permits and retire them from use, and firms that want to increase pollution have to buy them from consumers or other firms. Firms that must reduce pollution

---

[11]See, for example, William D. Montgomery, "Markets in Licenses and Efficient Pollution Control Programs," *Journal of Economic Theory* 5(1972):395–418.

to meet the limits imposed by their permits will then use least-cost methods of doing so. That can mean either reducing output or installing pollution control equipment.

Applying the Coase theorem, we can conjecture that it does not matter who is granted the permits to begin with: permits can be given to firms or consumers or both. Firms and consumers will trade the permits among themselves until the optimal level of pollution is achieved, and the equilibrium market price for the permits will equal the marginal damage from pollution at the optimal level. That is, a competitive market in tradable permits will yield results identical to an optimal Pigouvian tax or a competitive Coasian bargain.

What Montgomery showed was that that conjecture was basically true, as long as the number of permits issued was within certain bounds. Clearly, if the number of permits to pollute is less than the optimal level of pollution, the resulting level cannot be optimal. On the other side, the number of permits cannot be so large that they no longer have value in a competitive market. Thus, the government would have to know something about the optimal level of pollution in order to administer an efficient market in pollution permits, but it would not have to choose the number of permits to exactly equal the optimal number.

Criticisms of the Coase Theorem   Criticisms of the bargaining version of the Coase theorem are analogous to the criticisms of cartel theory, developed in Section 16.2: every cooperative game has an inherent prisoner's dilemma problem.[12] Basically, most critics would agree that if the following conditions hold, the Coase theorem predicts correctly. First, there are only two parties to a bargain (as in the above example) and property rights are well defined. Second, the bargainers have perfect knowledge of one another's profit or utility functions, and all the assumptions of the competitive model are satisfied, including the assumption that the bargainers behave competitively. In the context of the above model, for example, both firms take prices as given; firm Y charges firm X exactly Y's marginal damage and firm X takes firm Y's damage charge as given. Third, there are no costs or impediments to bargaining and the courts will costlessly enforce any bargain the parties strike. Fourth, agents strike advantageous bargains and do not persist in strategic behavior to the point of bargaining breakdown in the absence of transactions costs.

Finally, there are no income effects. That is to say, if one side pays the other, that does not change the demand or supply functions relative to what they would have been if there had been no payment. If there are income effects, bargaining may still be efficient, but the level of pollution may be different if one side has the right as opposed to the other. For example, if a homeowner is bargaining with a power plant, the homeowner may demand more clean air the higher his or her income level (that is, clean air is a normal good). If the homeowner has the right to clean air and gets compensated by the power plant, he or she may demand cleaner air than if the power plant has the right and the homeowner compensates. That would happen simply because the homeowner ends up richer with the right than when the power plant has the right.

---

[12]See Elizabeth Hoffman and Matthew L. Spitzer, "The Coase Theorem: Some Experimental Tests," *Journal of Law and Economics* 25(1982):73–98; and Donald H. Regan, "The Problem of Social Cost Revisited," *Journal of Law and Economics* 15(1972):427, for discussions of the criticisms.

The problem with the Coase theorem, say the critics, is that in most naturally occurring pollution disputes, one or more of these assumptions is violated. For example, most pollution disputes involve many (perhaps thousands) of consumers and generally more than one firm. The transactions costs associated with bargaining under those circumstances can be very high. Some person or group has to take the time and perhaps pay a substantial monetary cost to organize and inform both sides and to get them together for the purpose of bargaining. At this point, from the point of view of the consumers, getting cleaner air becomes a public good and thus is subject to all the problems associated with the provision of public goods. Moreover, even if the bargain actually did involve only two people, the assumption of competitive behavior would probably be violated. With only one party to each side of a bargain, each party has an incentive to act as a monopolist or a monopsonist instead of as a competitor.

Even if the sides can be brought together, the bargaining process itself is fraught with danger. One of the most serious problems is that the right to use the air is not clearly defined almost anywhere in the world. Thus, each case has to be argued on individual grounds. This means public hearings and potentially costly court battles as each side tries to avoid being the one to pay for pollution control. Even if they can agree without a court battle, they cannot be sure the courts will enforce their agreement, because it is not clear a priori which side has the right.

Finally, even if the rights are established, the existence of more than one party to each side of the bargain introduces the possibility of free-rider problems and what are called hold-out effects. For example, suppose the power plant has the right and consumers must agree to pay the plant to reduce pollution. Since the reduction in pollution is a public good, each consumer will contribute less than his or her true willingness to pay and will try to free ride on everyone else's provision. The result will be a less than optimal reduction in pollution. On the other hand, if the consumers have the right and the power plant has to secure the right to pollute by paying the consumers, individuals can demand more than their true values by threatening to ask for an injunction to stop the plant from operating. In fact, since the consent of all affected consumers must be secured, the last consumer can demand all remaining firm profits as compensation and still leave the firm indifferent between continuing to operate and shutting down. In the end, if the consent of all consumers is obtained, there will be more pollution control than would be socially optimal.

21.10   EVIDENCE ON THE USEFULNESS OF THE COASE THEOREM

There is considerable evidence both for and against the usefulness of the Coase theorem. On the one hand, private contracting to internalize externalities is the basis for much of contract and tort law. Many of the cases that are law-school classics involve one party being damaged by another party's action. In fact, without such private contracting, our complicated economy would have difficulty functioning.[13]

---

[13]See Victor Goldberg, "Regulation and Administered Contracts," *Bell Journal of Economics* 7(1976):426–452, for a discussion of the economic importance of private contracting; and Richard Posner, *Economic Analysis of Law* (Chicago: University of Chicago Press, 1977), for a discussion of the legal importance of private contracting.

Acid Rain   On the other hand, there are numerous examples of externalities and public goods that have not been corrected or provided by private contracting. A recent example is the controversy over acid rain. This is an important example of a pollution problem that violates all the assumptions of the Coase theorem. Acid rain is largely produced by power plants in the Midwest that burn coal with a high sulfur content and deposit it into the atmosphere from very high smokestacks. The emissions from these plants get caught in higher altitude wind patterns and may "stream" for hundreds of miles. When the stream passes through moisture-laden clouds, the sulfur dioxide in the emissions combines with water to produce a weak sulfuric acid. This falls as rain and may ruin vegetation hundreds of miles from the original pollution site. In fact, some of the worst acid rain has fallen in northeastern Canada and in Maine. Thus, we have pollution produced by numerous power plants in different states causing damage to hundreds of thousands of widely scattered consumers, some of whom even live in a different country. It is very difficult to even determine who is polluting whom, although atmospheric physicists are collecting data on streaming patterns from specific power plants. And even if that could be determined, those who are damaged would have to bring suit across state, and even national boundaries. This issue has not yet been resolved, and an international commission is studying centralized means by which the United States and Canada can resolve it.

Management of Common Resources   Regarding contracting to provide public goods, Libecap and Wiggins[14] have studied the failure of private contracting to solve problems associated with the common ownership and exploitation of oil fields. This is an example of the **common property problem** or the **commons dilemma**.[15] Basically, the problem in oil exploitation is that oil is often trapped in pools in subsurface rock formations that may lie under property owned or leased by many different individuals and firms. Thus, if one firm extracts faster than the optimal rate characterized in Section 18.7, it takes oil away from those drilling on neighboring land. This happens because, as oil is removed from one area, oil from other areas "migrates" to that area to maintain the same level of the pool. In a competitive extraction environment, each driller has a dominant strategy to extract faster than the optimum rate.

The result is a classic prisoner's dilemma problem. All firms extract too much oil today, leaving too little for later extraction. They then either sell it today, depressing today's price, or store it above ground at considerable cost, when they could have "stored" it in the ground at zero input cost. In addition, the faster rate of extraction inefficiently reduces the subsurface oil pressure, making it more costly to recover all the oil actually available. As in any prisoner's dilemma, all firms would be better off if they could agree to manage the common pool jointly and extract the oil at the rate that

---

[14]Gary D. Libecap and Steven N. Wiggins, "The Influence of Private Contractual Failure on Regulation: the Case of Oil Field Unitization," *Journal of Political Economy* 93(1985):690–714; and Steven N. Wiggins and Gary D. Libecap, "Oil Field Unitization: Contractual Failure in the Presence of Imperfect Information," *American Economic Review* 75(1985):368–385.

[15]Another classic common property problem, which has not often been successfully solved by bargaining, is the problem of managing ocean fisheries. If no one *owns* the fish in the ocean, then everyone's catch rate is higher than the socially optimal rate identified in Section 18.9.

maximizes the discounted present value of profits from that management. Thus, we can think of the output reduction that would come about as a result of joint management of an oil reservoir as a public good.

In this example, there is no problem with the definition of rights and there are not many parties to each bargain. Typically, no more than 15 clearly identified firms are involved, and the courts have upheld those "unitization" (joint management) contracts that have been negotiated. The U.S. Bureau of Mines has been encouraging unitization since at least 1916. Moreover, most oil experts agree that unitization is the right way to manage an oil field. Despite this agreement, however, as late as 1975, only 40% of the production in Oklahoma and Texas came from jointly managed oil fields.

Libecap and Wiggins tried to find out why there has been so little unitization. One problem is that firms hold out strategically, trying to get a higher share of the joint profits. This problem had already been identified by McDonald.[16] A much more serious problem seems to be that there is not enough information about the actual size of reserves in a pool and the location of those reserves (that is, under whose property?) to determine an acceptable division of the joint profits. First, each firm has its own method for estimating the total reserves available and the estimates may differ substantially. Second, each firm has private, imperfect information about its own reserves and (usually) worse information about other firms' reserves. The result is that much of the time preparing to bargain is spent trying to reach agreement about contradictory information. In many cases, the information cost precludes bargaining to begin with. In other cases, no agreement is ever reached at the preliminary, information aggregation stage. What looks like strategic holding out may simply be honest differences of opinion about uncertain information.

Experimental Results   In an effort to try to separate out these different possible explanations for contractual failure, economists have turned, once again, to laboratory experiments. A number of experimental studies have examined Coasian bargaining in both simple and more complex environments. The original papers in this area were by Hoffman and Spitzer[17] and Prudencio.[18] Both of these papers tested the Coase theorem in very simple environments. The object was to see first whether the theorem had predictive power in environments closely paralleling the assumptions of the model.

In the Hoffman and Spitzer experiments, there were two parties to a bargain presented with the following payoff sheet, which told both parties how much each would earn if the group choice was one of the numbers listed in Table 21.1.

Table 21.1 shows that if 1 were chosen, A would get $0.00 and B would get $12.00; and if 2 were chosen, A would get $4.00 and B would get $10.00. Notice that joint profits are maximized at number 2, with a total of $14.00 available for distribution.

Before the decision process began, one subject was designated *controller.* The controller had the power to choose the group number without consulting the other

---

[16]Stephen McDonald, *The Leasing of Federal Lands for Fossil Fuel Production* (Baltimore: Johns Hopkins University Press, 1979).

[17]Hoffman and Spitzer, "The Coase Theorem: Some Experimental Tests."

[18]Yves C. Prudencio, "The Voluntary Approach to Externality Problems: An Experimental Test," *Journal of Environmental Economics and Management* 9(1982):213–228.

TABLE 21.1 Payoffs in Hoffman and Spitzer Coase Experiments

Outcome Number	Subject A	Subject B
1	$ 0.00	$12.00
2	4.00	10.00
3	6.00	6.00
4	7.50	4.00
5	9.00	2.50
6	10.50	1.00
7	12.00	0.00

participant. Thus, A could choose 7, leaving B with nothing; and B could choose 1, leaving A with nothing. The joint maximum (number 2) is the prediction of the Coase theorem. The controller's right paralleled the right to pollute or the right to enjoy clean air implicit in pollution cases. In addition, the party which was not controller could offer to pay something to the controller to get him or her to agree (in writing) to another number. This models the compensation feature of the Coase theorem.

In this simple, full-information experiment, Hoffman and Spitzer found that 100% of the bargaining pairs chose the efficient outcome. Thus, the efficiency prediction of the Coase theorem was strongly supported in the environment first modeled in the theorem. But they also found that many of the bargaining pairs split the profits $7.00 each, violating the prediction that the outcome will be an allocation in the core. Subsequent experiments involving from 2 parties up to 20 parties to a bargain and considerably more complicated environments have confirmed the efficiency results and generated allocations in the core.[19] Plott has shown that tradable permits are also efficient.[20]

What do these experimental results tell us about the applicability of the Coase theorem? Most importantly, they suggest that if parties to a bargain that can do harm to one another are brought together for the purpose of bargaining and the information needed to come to an agreement is not difficult to figure out, the parties will reach

---

[19]Don L. Coursey, Elizabeth Hoffman, and Matthew L. Spitzer, "Fear and Loathing in the Coase Theorem: Experiments Involving Physical Discomfort," *Journal of Legal Studies* 16(1987):217–248; Glenn W. Harrison, Elizabeth Hoffman, E. E. Rutstrom, and Matthew L. Spitzer, "Coasian Solutions to the Externality Problem in Experimental Markets," *Economic Journal* 97(1987):388–402; Glenn W. Harrison and Michael McKee, "Experimental Evaluation of the Coase Theorem," *Journal of Law and Economics* 28(1985):653–670; Elizabeth Hoffman and Matthew L. Spitzer, "Entitlements, Rights and Fairness: An Experimental Examination of Subjects' Concepts of Distributive Justice," *Journal of Legal Studies* 14(1985):259–297; Elizabeth Hoffman and Matthew L. Spitzer, "Experimental Tests of the Coase Theorem with Large Bargaining Groups," *Journal of Legal Studies* 15(1986):149–171.

[20]Charles R. Plott, "Externalities and Corrective Policies in Experimental Markets," *Economic Journal* 93(1983):106–127.

agreement in the manner predicted by Coase, *even if there are a number of parties to the bargain and if information is initially private.*

Reasons for Bargaining Breakdown   Why then do we still have documented cases of bargaining breakdown and contractual failure? Three important factors in the acid-rain and the oil-unitization cases have not been and (perhaps) cannot be modeled experimentally. First, by bringing the parties together *for the purpose of bargaining,* we have circumvented a major barrier to the resolution of the acid-rain case. The cost of locating all the affected consumers and polluting firms, transporting them to a central location, and keeping them together long enough to bargain would be prohibitive. Second, in the experiments, property rights were clearly defined and subjects knew that written and signed agreements would be strictly enforced. Such rights are still vague in the acid-rain case.

While the unitization case did not suffer from the first two problems, both cases suffer from the third; information is complicated, costly to obtain, and not very reliable. Parties to a bargain cannot simply sit down, agree on the joint profit maximum and then get down to the business of bargaining over the distribution of profits. Much time gets spent arguing over whose information about those profits is correct. If the parties do not reach an agreement on that issue, they will never get to address the distributional issue. The experimental results support Libecap's and Wiggins's contention that informational problems are more important for contractual failure than holding out is, since holding out was not a serious problem in the experiment.

We should not conclude that holding out never occurs, however. All we know is that it does not seem to be a problem when parties sit down together at the bargaining table and can agree about what the relevant profit information is. When firms must go one by one to individual households to buy the right to do something, holding out can be a serious problem. It is so serious, in fact, that large firms negotiating real estate deals do so in great secrecy, so as not to alert landowners to hold out on selling their land.

21.11   INCENTIVE-COMPATIBLE ALLOCATION MECHANISMS

Dissatisfaction with Lindahl and voluntary-provision processes, Pigouvian taxes, and Coasian bargaining has led economists to explore ways to get people to truthfully reveal their demands for public goods and damages from pollution. Most of the approaches that have been developed utilize insights gained from studying the second-price auction, which we outlined in Section 15.6 when we discussed franchise regulation of monopolies. Recall that one of the regulation schemes involved selling the right to the profits of a perfectly discriminating monopolist in an auction in which the highest bidder won the right but only had to pay the second highest bid price. We argued at that time that it was a dominant strategy to bid your true value because you did not have to pay what you bid. This insight is extended to public-goods allocation mechanisms and damage assessment mechanisms by having an individual's taxes not be a function of the marginal valuation he or she reveals. By an analogous argument, there are some mechanisms for which it is a dominant strategy to reveal your true demand for the public good or your damage function. For that reason, these mechanisms are referred to as **demand-revealing** or **incentive-compatible** mechanisms.

The Clarke Tax   The first application of the second-price auction to public goods was done independently by Clarke[21] and Groves.[22] The following simple example of the **Clarke tax** illustrates how a demand-revealing mechanism works and when telling the truth is a dominant strategy.[23]

Suppose all consumers have the following quasilinear utility function:

$$U_i = 2\beta_i x^{1/2} + y_i. \tag{21.87}$$

The marginal rate of substitution is

$$MRS_i = \frac{\beta_i x^{-1/2}}{1}. \tag{21.88}$$

Assume also that both prices are equal to 1, implying that the marginal rate of transformation is 1. Summing (21.88) and setting the sum equal to the marginal rate of transformation, the condition for a Pareto optimal provision of X is

$$\sum_{i=1}^{n} \beta_i x^{-1/2} = 1. \tag{21.89}$$

Solving (21.89) for X^*,

$$X^* = \left(\sum_{i=1}^{n} \beta_i \right)^2. \tag{21.90}$$

The way the mechanism works is that the government asks each consumer for a schedule, which tells the total amount he or she is willing to pay for different quantities of the public good that the government might provide. With the utility function given in equation 21.87, this is equivalent to reporting the function $2b_i x^{1/2}$, where b_i represents i's reported value for β. The government then finds the value for x (call it $\hat{x}$, since we are not yet sure it is Pareto optimal) that satisfies the Lindahl-Samuelson condition, given the reported valuation functions. This is the condition summarized in equation 21.90 and illustrated graphically in Figure 21.3. The government then charges each consumer a total contribution equal to the difference between the total cost of providing $\hat{x}$ and the sum of everyone else's reported willingness to pay for $\hat{x}$

$$T_i = \hat{x} - \sum_{j \neq i} 2b_j \hat{x}^{1/2} = i\text{'s tax for } \hat{x}. \tag{21.91}$$

---

[21]Edward H. Clarke, "Multipart Pricing of Public Goods," *Public Choice* 11(1971):17–33.

[22]Theodore Groves, "Information, Incentives, and the Internalization of Production Externalities," in S. A. Y. Lin, ed., *Theory and Measurement of Economic Externalities* (New York: Academic Press, 1976), pp. 65–86. "Groves mechanisms" are also discussed in Jerald Green and Jean-Jacques Laffont, *Incentives in Public Decision-Making* (Amsterdam: North-Holland, 1980).

[23]For a more complete discussion of demand-revealing mechanisms, see Alan M. Feldman, *Welfare Economics and Social Choice Theory* (Boston: Kluwer Nijhoff Publishing, 1980), Chapter 6 (on public goods).

To see how this mechanism works, suppose we have three individuals with the following β_i's:

$$\beta_1 = 1, \quad \beta_2 = 3, \quad \text{and} \quad \beta_3 = 10. \tag{21.92}$$

The sum of the β's is 14, and substituting 14 for the sum of the β's in equation 21.90, the optimal quantity of X is $(14)^2$, or 196. If everyone reports truthfully, the government provides 196 units of the public good and charges the following taxes:

$$T_1 = 196 - 2(3)(196)^{1/2} - 2(10)(196)^{1/2} = -168 \tag{21.93}$$
$$T_2 = 196 - 2(1)(196)^{1/2} - 2(10)(196)^{1/2} = -112$$
$$T_3 = 196 - 2(1)(196)^{1/2} - 2(3)(196)^{1/2} = 84.$$

Equations 21.93 indicate that person 1 gets paid 168, person 2 gets paid 112, and person 3 pays 84, for a total, net collection of -196.

We will have to worry about making up this budget deficit later[24], but for now, we should verify that this scheme does have a dominant strategy to tell the truth (assuming the quasilinear utility functions set out in equation 21.87). To do this, we consider what valuation person i wants to report, assuming a set of reports by everyone else. Thus, given the reported b_j for $j \neq i$, i maximizes equation 21.87, subject to a budget constraint that includes the Clarke tax:

$$M_i = y_i + T_i \quad \Rightarrow \quad y_i = M_i - T_i. \tag{21.94}$$

Substituting (21.94) in (21.87),

$$U_i = 2\beta_i \hat{x}^{1/2} + M_i - T_i. \tag{21.95}$$

But, person i knows the government will set T_i by the formula given in equation 21.91. Substituting for x from equation 21.90 in (21.91),

$$T_i = \left(\sum_{j=1}^{n} b_j \right)^2 - \sum_{j \neq i} 2b_j \left[\left(\sum_{j=1}^{n} b_j \right)^2 \right]^{1/2}. \tag{21.96}$$

Substituting (21.96) in (21.95) and writing the β_i's in terms of the reported b_i's,

$$U_i = 2\beta_i \left(b_i + \sum_{j \neq i} b_j \right) - \left(b_i + \sum_{j \neq i} b_j \right)^2 + \sum_{j \neq i} 2b_j \left(b_i + \sum_{j \neq i} b_j \right). \tag{21.97}$$

Now, to find the optimal reported b_i for each individual, we differentiate with respect to b_i:

$$\frac{\partial U_i}{\partial b_i} = 2\beta_i - 2 \left(b_i + \sum_{j \neq i} b_j \right) + \sum_{j \neq i} 2b_j = 0. \tag{21.98}$$

Solving (21.98) for b_i,

$$b_i^* = \beta_i. \tag{21.99}$$

---

[24] The result is only equal to the negative of the total cost by accident. The result could be any number less than the total cost.

Equation 21.99 shows that person i reports β_i, the true utility parameter, no matter what each other person reports. In other words, it is a dominant strategy to report one's true β_i.[25]

Groves Mechanisms: Deficits and Surpluses   We still have not dealt with the deficit problem, however. Even if this scheme does choose the Pareto optimal level of the public good, it clearly does not generate enough tax revenue to actually build it. Groves therefore created a new mechanism (called a **Groves mechanism**), in which he added another term to T_i that also depended only on what others reported. Basically, any function will do, as long as it does not depend on what the individual reports. This term can turn a deficit into a surplus, but it can only balance the budget by accident if the incentive to report truthfully is to be preserved. In fact, it can be shown, through some complicated mathematics, that it is impossible to create a mechanism which both balances the budget reliably and has a dominant strategy to tell the truth.[26]

Thus, with a Groves mechanism, we can guarantee that we collect enough revenue to build the public good, but there will be a surplus instead of a deficit. The obvious solution would be to simply return the surplus to the participants, but if they knew that was to happen, they would report differently to begin with. So, we cannot do that and preserve the dominant strategy property. If we do not return the surplus to consumers, on the other hand, the sum of consumer purchases of both the private and the public good is less than the sum of their incomes, since some of what they have to spend is (essentially) being thrown away:

$$\hat{x} + \sum_{i=1}^{n} y_i < \sum_{i=1}^{n} M_i.$$

Thus, because we cannot balance the budget, the resulting allocation (including payment) cannot be Pareto optimal, even though the Lindahl-Samuelson conditions are satisfied. The Pareto optimal amount is provided, but resources are thrown away in the process of providing it. We would like to avoid that problem and still get truthful revelation, but the Hurwicz theorem, alluded to above, tells us that is impossible.

The Groves-Ledyard Mechanism   Given that we cannot have a balanced budget, the Pareto optimal provision, *and* dominant strategy simultaneously, the question becomes: which goal will we sacrifice in designing a demand-revealing mechanism? One approach tries to find mechanisms that balance the budget and try to get people to reveal truthfully somewhat reliably, even though truth is not a dominant strategy. The basic idea is to try to design a mechanism that has truth as a weak Nash equilibrium.

---

[25]This result also generalizes to other utility functions with no income effects. While the proof is more advanced, the intuition is the same as in the second-price auction. Since your tax does not depend on what you report, the best you can do is report your true value.

[26]Green and Laffont, *Incentives in Public Decision-Making,* presents the proof of this proposition. It was originally developed by Leonid Hurwicz, "On Allocations Attainable Through Nash Equilibria," in J. J. Laffont, ed. *Aggregation and Revelation of Preferences* (Amsterdam: North-Holland, 1979), pp. 397–419.

The first mechanism to combine Nash-equilibrium demand revelation and budget balance was designed by Groves and Ledyard.[27] Their idea was to have each participant propose an additional amount of the public good (possibly negative) that he or she would like to see provided, given a set of provisions already proposed by everyone else. For example, you might be asked, if everyone else were to provide a certain amount of a public good, how much more would you be willing to provide?

The **Groves-Ledyard mechanism** works as follows. Each participant sends a message to the government, specifying his or her proposed incremental provision, x_i. The government then sums those incremental provisions to find the total proposed contributions:

$$\hat{x} = \sum_{i=1}^{n} x_i. \tag{21.100}$$

The government then sets taxes by a complicated rule that does not provide a dominant strategy to tell the truth, but that does have truth telling as one possible weak Nash equilibrium. Moreover, at such a Nash equilibrium, the resulting allocation of the public good is Pareto optimal.

A serious problem with the Groves-Ledyard mechanism, however, is that if participants use more sophisticated strategies that, for example, take account of the effects of their reports on what others might report, the outcome is not necessarily Pareto optimal. The budget will still balance, but the Lindahl-Samuelson conditions may not be satisfied. But, since we cannot have both budget balance and dominant strategy to tell the truth, we can start with the Cournot-Nash assumption and then see whether it actually describes peoples' behavior. Section 21.12 outlines experimental results on the efficiency of such mechanisms.

There has been less work on incentive-compatible methods for determining optimal levels of pollution or for assessing damages from pollution, but two approaches have been proposed. Kwerel[28] and Roberts and Spence[29] have suggested using both permits and charges to get firms to reveal their true costs for reducing pollution. Brookshire, Coursey, and Schulze[30] suggest using a second-price auction to get people to reveal their true damage from pollution. The actual details of the technique suggested by Brookshire, Coursey, and Schulze are described at the end of Section 21.12, which deals with experimental work on incentive-compatible mechanisms.

---

[27]Theodore Groves and John Ledyard, "Optimal Allocation of Public Goods: A Solution to the 'Free Rider' Problem," *Econometrica* 45(1977):783–809.

[28]Evan Kwerel, "To Tell the Truth: Imperfect Information and Optimal Pollution Control," *Review of Economic Studies* 44(1977):595–601.

[29]Marc J. Roberts and Michael Spence, "Effluent Charges and Licenses Under Uncertainty," *Journal of Public Economics* 5(1976):193–208.

[30]David S. Brookshire, Don L. Coursey, and William D. Schulze, "Experiments in the Solicitation of Private and Public Values: An Overview," in L. Green and J. Kagel, eds. *Advances in Behavioral Economics* (Greenwich, CT: JAI Press, forthcoming); and Don L. Coursey and William D. Schulze, "The Application of Laboratory Experimental Economics to the Contingent Valuation of Public Goods," *Public Choice* (1987).

21.12 EXPERIMENTS ON INCENTIVE-COMPATIBLE ALLOCATION MECHANISMS

Vernon Smith pioneered experimental work on the implementability of incentive-compatible mechanisms with experiments comparing a bidding version of the Lindahl mechanism (described above) and an iterative version of the Groves-Ledyard mechanism.[31] The experimental design for the iterative Groves-Ledyard mechanism can be briefly described as follows. First, each subject was given a payoff function, specifying how much money would be earned for different group choices of a public good (X), which cost q per unit to produce:

$$U_i = V_i(X) = \text{amount of money } i \text{ will earn if} \qquad (21.101)$$
$$X \text{ is the group choice.}$$

At the beginning of each iteration (t), each participant was then asked to choose an integer $(x_i(t))$ from some given range, and the participants were told that the value for $X(t)$ would be the sum of those integers, as in the statement of responses in the Groves-Ledyard mechanism given in equation (21.100),

$$\sum_{i=1}^{n} x_i(t) = X(t). \qquad (21.102)$$

After each participant had reported an x_i, a tax for each participant was determined, based on the Groves-Ledyard tax formulation. Each participant's payoff in period t was the difference between V_i, evaluated at $X(t)$ and $T_i(t)$:

$$v_i(t) = V_i(X(t)) - T_i(t). \qquad (21.103)$$

Each subject was then given a chance to change his or her x_i report on the next round if he or she did not like the payoff $v_i(t)$ given in equation (21.103). Agreement could be signalled by reporting the same x_i at $t + 1$

$$x_i(t) = x_i(t + 1). \qquad (21.104)$$

The process stopped either when everyone repeated two times (defined as t^*), or after a set number of iterations. Subjects were paid $v_i(t^*)$ if they reached agreement within the set number of trials, or some minimal payment if they did not.

The Smith Auction Mechanism Having run experiments with this version of the Groves-Ledyard mechanism, Smith found it to be somewhat unstable and designed another mechanism which he called the **auction mechanism.** This has since become a standard experimental mechanism, largely because it is relatively simple for participants to understand and because it seems to work. He defined the per-unit tax in his

---

[31]Smith, "Incentive Compatible Experimental Processes."

version of the Groves-Ledyard mechanism as an implicit bid or contribution to the public good, given what everyone else was bidding. The implicit bids in the Groves-Ledyard mechanism were each equal to the marginal cost minus the sum of everyone else's bids.

This suggested another mechanism, in which participants signal a bid and a proposed quantity of the public good each round. The auctioneer computes the average quantity proposed and then sends back to each participant a proposed cost share equal to the difference between the marginal cost and the sum of everyone else's bids. At the next round, the participant could change his or her proposed quantity and bid, or signal agreement by repeating the average quantity and the proposed cost share from the previous round. The mechanism stops when everyone has repeated his or her proposed cost share at least twice. One Nash equilibrium of this mechanism is the set of Groves-Ledyard taxes, as described above.

Smith's first experimental test of this mechanism was quite successful, at least in generating the Pareto optimal outcome. It does not always generate true Lindahl prices, however. Since those preliminary experiments, however, variations of this mechanism have been used fairly successfully in a variety of experimental tests and applications to actual public-goods decision problems.[32] The only problem with the mechanism seems to be that it sometimes fails to generate agreement within the prescribed number of trials. This is shown by Banks, Plott, and Porter. But when agreement is reached, the outcome is almost always the Pareto optimal quantity of the public good.

Demand Revelation and Pollution Damage   Turning now to the experimental work on incentive-compatible methods for determining marginal damage from pollution, the only work so far is that by Brookshire, Coursey, and Schulze, mentioned above.[33] In their experiments, they operationalized pollution with a harmless but very bitter tasting substance called sucrose octa-acetate (SOA); subjects who would be polluted would have to hold SOA in their mouths for 20 seconds. The experimental subjects were divided into two groups; one group was asked how much they would be willing to pay to avoid having to taste SOA, and the other group was asked how much they would have to be paid to agree to taste it. This captures the essence of the incentive problem associated with asking people their marginal damages from pollution: they

---

[32]See, for example, Jeffrey S. Banks, Charles R. Plott, and David P. Porter, "Public Goods Pricing Mechanisms: Experimental Analysis for Space Station Pricing Policies," Econometric Society Meetings, December 1985; Brookshire, Coursey, and Schulze, "Experiments in the Solicitation of Private and Public Values"; David S. Brookshire and Don L. Coursey, "Measuring the Value of a Public Good: An Empirical Comparison of Elicitation Procedures," *The American Economic Review* 77(1987):554–566; Don L. Coursey and Vernon L. Smith, "Experimental Tests of a Mechanism for Private, Public, and Externality Goods," *Scandinavian Journal of Economics* 86(1984):468–484; Vernon L. Smith, "An Experimental Comparison of Three Public Good Decision Mechanisms, *Scandinavian Journal of Economics* 81(1979):198; Vernon L. Smith, "Experiments With a Decentralized Mechanism for Public Good Decisions," *American Economic Review* 70(1980):584.

[33]See note 30.

typically understate how much they would be willing to pay and overstate how much they would have to be paid.[34]

In the Brookshire, Coursey, and Schulze experiments, they first asked the respective subject groups the hypothetical question how much they would pay or have to be paid. The responses were very different, as the incentives would suggest. The average willingness to pay was about $4 and the average willingness to accept was about $15. They then allowed each subject to sample a drop of SOA and asked the hypothetical question again. The responses changed very little. Finally, they "sold" the right not to be polluted in an auction similar to a second-price auction. In the willingness to pay group, they asked eight subjects to bid for how much they would pay not to taste. The top four bids "won" the right not to taste, but they only had to pay the fifth highest bid price. Thus, they did not have to pay what they bid, so the dominant strategy was to reveal truthfully. The four lowest bidders then had to taste.

In the willingness-to-accept group, eight subjects bid for how much they would have to be paid in order to be willing to taste. In this case, the four lowest bidders purchased the right not to taste, but they were paid the next higher bid, making it a dominant strategy for them to reveal truthfully. The four highest bidders had to taste. In addition, the subjects were given several trial bidding periods before their decision was binding, and the subjects who ultimately had to taste had to agree to the group decision unanimously.

The results suggest strongly that some kind of second-price (or, more generally nth price) auction might be used to elicit marginal damages from pollution. The bidding started out near the $15 and $4 hypothetical values, but converged over time. The average final willingness-to-accept value was still slightly higher than the willingness-to-pay value, but the difference was not statistically significant. Moreover, the final average willingness to pay and willingness to accept was about $4, almost identical to the hypothetical willingness to pay: all the convergence occurred in willingness-to-accept values being bid down by the auction process. Brookshire, Coursey, and Schulze conclude that these results suggest a place for willingness-to-pay survey techniques, which are validated by experimental auctions, using a random sample of the people being surveyed. They have since tried this technique as part of the planning for a public park in Fort Collins, Colorado.[35]

21.13 THE ARROW PROBLEM IN PUBLIC DECISION MAKING

All of the public decision making problems discussed in this chapter so far involve situations in which there is some *market failure* if competitive markets are used as the allocation mechanism. This implies that without some other mechanism for allocating externalities or public goods (like taxes, bargaining, or incentive-compatible mechanisms), the competitive allocation will not be Pareto optimal. That means, in turn, that

---

[34]See, for example, Jack L. Knetsch and J. A. Sinden, "Willingness to Pay and Compensation Demanded: Experimental Evidence of an Unexpected Disparity in Measures of Value," *Quarterly Journal of Economics* 99(1984):507.

[35]Brookshire and Coursey, "Measuring the Value of a Public Good."

there will still exist gains from trade either among firms, among consumers, or among *consumers and firms*. When there exist gains from trade it is possible, in principle, to find an allocation that everyone *would prefer to the* status quo competitive allocation. In other words, everyone would *unanimously* agree to implement *a core allocation* or an allocation that is both Pareto optimal and Pareto superior to the status quo.

The Distribution Problem Revisited   Unfortunately for the public decision-making process, however, most public decisions do not involve determining allocations that are Pareto optimal and Pareto superior to the status quo. Most involve questions of redistribution. Even when public goods are being funded, they are generally funded through general revenue taxes on goods and income, where these taxes have the effect of distorting choices among goods (as discussed in Section 13.9 on the welfare effects of per-unit taxes) or the choice between consumption and leisure (in the case of the income tax). In addition, many taxes are developed as part of a tax and transfer program that redistributes income from those who are taxed to those who benefit by means of subsidies and transfer programs.

As we have said earlier in Sections 4.3 and 7.5, redistribution always reduces the welfare of some groups in society and increases the welfare of others. In such a situation it is never possible to get unanimous agreement to enact a particular policy. In fact, as we showed in Section 4.4, it may not be possible to make any internally consistent policy decisions if different groups in society support different policy alternatives.

Voting Cycles and Agenda Manipulation   Recall from Section 4.4 that we introduced the idea of a voting cycle, in which three different voters had different preferences and the outcome of the majority voting process was indeterminate. To reiterate that example in a slightly different context, suppose Congress is preparing a tax reform bill and there are currently three competing versions of the bill. One version gives subsidies to dairy farmers but takes them away from home builders and shoe manufacturers. Another gives the subsidies to home builders and takes them away from the other two groups. The third favors only shoe manufacturers. Congressmen align themselves into three approximately equal groups, depending on whether their constituencies are farmers, home builders, or in manufacturing. If we call the three alternatives X, Y, and Z and the three groups of congressmen A, B, and C, then one possible set of preferences over the alternatives could be represented as in Table 21.2. (Table 21.2 is

TABLE 21.2   Preference of Voters over Alternatives

	Voters	
A	B	C
X	Y	Z
Y	Z	X
Z	X	Y

actually a review of Table 4.1, where we introduced the *Arrow problem,* and the following discussion reviews the discussion surrounding Table 4.1.) Thus, voters in group A prefer X to Y to Z; voters in group B prefer Y to Z to X; and voters in group C prefer Z to X to Y. Whatever outcome is chosen will hurt two groups and help only one.

Now, consider a majority-rule voting process with this set of preferences. Two groups of voters prefer X to Y, so X would win against Y. Two groups of voters prefer Y to Z, so Y wins against Z. But, two groups of voters also prefer Z to X; so Z wins against X, and the social preferences are not transitive. In fact, depending on the order in which outcomes are voted on, any of the three possibilities might be chosen. For example, if the agenda is to compare X to Y and then the winner of that vote to Z, the outcome will be Z. But if the agenda starts by comparing Z to X and then the winner of that vote to Y, the outcome will be Y. Finally, if the agenda starts by comparing Y to Z and the winner of that vote to X, the outcome will be X. In such a situation, there is no "solution" to the public decision making problem in the sense that we have proposed "solutions" to the problem of allocating externalities and public goods in the rest of this chapter. Depending on the agenda, there will be an outcome, but it will not be an "optimal" outcome in any sense of that word.

While this example may seem extreme, it is actually representative of many public decision-making problems. The problem was first identified by an eighteenth-century French political thinker and politician, the Marquis de Condorcet.[36] In the nineteenth century, it was revived by Lewis Carroll, who was a political thinker in addition to being a writer of children's books. In the modern era, it was first discussed by Duncan Black[37] and then made famous by Kenneth Arrow.[38] It has since become known as the **Arrow problem** in the public choice literature. Basically, the Arrow problem is that the only public decision process that can be counted on to make consistent public choices is a dictatorship, where the dictator simply imposes his or her own preferences. Since we would like to rule out such a decision process as not being responsive to voter preferences, there simply does not exist a consistent decision process for issues involving redistribution.

Inconsistency and Instability of Public Decision Processes This lack of consistency in public decisions has profound implications for public decision making.[39] For example, as the discussion of Table 21.1 illustrates, control of the agenda is a very powerful tool for getting one's own preferred alternatives enacted.[40] Thus, much of the real power in Congress resides in the committee chairmen who control the agendas.

---

[36]M. de Condorcet, *Essai sur L'Application de L'Analyse à la Probabilité des Decisions Rendues à la Pluraliste des Vois* (Paris, 1785).

[37]D. Black, *The Theory of Elections and Committees* (London: Cambridge University Press, 1958).

[38]K. J. Arrow, *Social Choice and Individual Values* (New York: John Wiley, 1963).

[39]For an excellent introduction to voting, see William H. Riker, *Liberalism Against Populism* (San Francisco: W. H. Freeman, 1982).

[40]This point was first made clear by Charles Plott and Michael Levine, "A Model of Agenda Influence on Committee Decisions," *American Economic Review* 68(1978):146–160.

Similarly, different voting rules yield different outcomes with the same set of underlying preferences, and the way is left open for individuals and groups to manipulate voting outcomes by misrepresenting their preferences in the voting process or by proposing alternative voting procedures.

What all this adds up to is the potential for public decisions to be highly unstable and certainly not defensible from a welfare-improvement perspective. What does get enacted depends upon the voting rule used and who wrote the agenda, not on what is "best" for society, even if some "best" alternative could be identified. Moreover, when a group that has been out of power regains some control of the selection of alternatives to be voted on, public policy can shift dramatically with no change in underlying consumer preferences.[41]

Because of all these public decision-making problems, economists continue to search for implementable decentralized means of allocating externalities and public goods. For example, if some kind of modified market or a Coasian bargain were used, it is possible that a Pareto optimal and Pareto superior allocation might be identified and implemented when it exists. (The political process, on the other hand, is not so likely to identify welfare-improving outcomes, even when they exist.) If externalities and public goods are allocated by decentralized means, the scope for public decision making through voting would be limited to issues involving redistribution instead of welfare improvement. In the case of redistribution issues, we either come to an agreement as a society that we will abide by the outcomes of a process that we consider to be fair (even though it can be shown that the outcomes themselves are not necessarily fair), or we run the risk of revolution.

Stability, despite the fact that outcomes may be unfair, is essentially what we have opted for in the United States. Most Americans support the outcomes of majority rule, even when they disagree with those outcomes, because they believe in the *principle* of one person–one vote.

21.14   REVIEW OF KEY CONCEPTS

This completes our discussion of externalities and public goods. Be sure you understand and can use the following key concepts.

An *externality* exists when the actions taken by an individual firm or consumer directly affect the profits or utilities attainable by other firms or consumers, respectively. Externalities can be either positive (beneficial) or negative (harmful).

One kind of negative externality is air or water *pollution.*

Public goods are goods that are jointly consumed. Public goods can be thought of as providing positive externalities.

If a polluting firm absorbs all the costs of its pollution internally, including the *marginal damages* imposed on other firms or consumers, we say the firm has *internalized the externality.*

An externality that reduces the output of one particular good, but does not affect other goods or consumers, has the effect of shifting the production possibilities frontier between

---

[41]Riker, *Liberalism Against Populism,* presents numerous examples from the history of American politics.

the two goods towards the origin, without changing the intercepts.

Marginal private cost refers solely to the opportunity cost of input costs used to produce a particular product.

In addition to input costs, *marginal social cost* includes the positive or negative opportunity cost (marginal benefit or damage) associated with an externality. With a positive externality, marginal social cost is less than marginal private cost; with a negative externality, marginal social cost is greater than marginal private cost.

A socially optimal quantity of an externality is produced when the market price of the polluting firms' product is equal to the product's marginal social cost.

Depending on the state of pollution-control technology, pollution reduction may be achieved by reducing output or by reducing pollution at every output level.

When pollution reduces consumer utility but does not affect the production of other firms, the production possibilities frontier is unaffected, but, if the externality is not internalized, the economy will produce too much of the good producing the externality at too low a price. An optimal amount of the polluting good will be produced when its price reflects both the marginal rate of transformation and the marginal utility damage from pollution.

A *pure public good* has the property that all consumers can enjoy it jointly, without any one person's consumption reducing others' ability to consume. Thus, there is no crowding if more and more people consume it, and no one need be excluded from consuming it.

Most public goods are not pure. If too many people try to enjoy them, the use value declines because of crowding. Obvious examples are parks, roads, bridges, and public swimming pools.

At a Pareto optimal allocation of a pure public good, the sum of the consumer marginal rates of substitution is equal to the marginal rate of transformation.

When there is more than one consumer affected by an externality, the optimal allocation of that externality is achieved when the marginal rate of transformation is equal to the marginal rate of substitution between goods plus the sum of the marginal damages imposed on the individual consumers.

With private goods, at a Pareto optimal allocation in a competitive market, consumers pay the same (market) price for the good. In contrast, at a Pareto optimal allocation of a public good, each consumer would pay a different (*personalized*) *price* that reflects his or her marginal willingness to pay for the public good. Such a personalized price would not be the outcome of a competitive market process.

In a partial equilibrium setting, an optimal quantity of a public good is provided when the sum of the consumers' personalized prices is equal to the marginal cost of providing the public good.

If consumer utility functions have no income effects in the consumption of the public good, the optimal quantity of the public good will be a constant, independent of the distribution of consumer incomes. If there are income effects, however, there may be many possible Pareto optimal quantities, depending on the distribution of income among consumers.

Competitive markets yield equilibria that equate the marginal private benefit each consumer gets from consuming a good and the marginal private cost of producing it. There is no mechanism to force firms to internalize *external costs* or to subsidize those who provide *external benefits*.

An optimal *Pigouvian tax* is equal to the marginal damage imposed by a polluting firm. Pigou proposed that externalities could be internalized if all polluting firms were charged such taxes.

A consumer's *Lindahl price* is his or her optimal personalized price to participate in the consumption of a public good. If each consumer is charged his or her Lindahl price per unit of a public good provided, then the sum of the personalized prices can be used to provide each unit of the public good at marginal cost, and the optimal quantity will be provided.

The condition that the sum of the marginal rates of substitution equals the price ratio is called the *Lindahl-Samuelson condition* for the Pareto optimal provision of a public good.

In a *Lindahl tâtonnement mechanism,* an auction-eer adjusts individual personalized prices until all consumers demand the same quantity of a public good.

Determining Pigouvian taxes and Lindahl prices involves obtaining private information on costs, damages from pollution and benefits from the provision of public goods—all of which firms and consumers have incentives to misrepresent. In the case of pollution, polluting firms have an incentive to overestimate the costs of reducing pollution, and affected firms and consumers have an incentive to overestimate the damages.

In determining *Lindahl prices,* each consumer has an incentive to underreveal how much he or she is willing to pay. This happens because if others pay, a consumer can then enjoy some of the benefits from consuming a public good for free. This phenomenon is referred to as the *free-rider problem.*

A utility function of the form $U_i = f(x) + y_i$ is said to be *quasilinear.* Moreover, if x is a public good and y_i is consumption of a private good, then these quasilinear preferences have no income effects associated with the consumption of the public good.

Individuals are said to exhibit *strong free riding* behavior if they contribute $0 to the provision of a public good. They are said to exhibit *weak free riding* behavior if they contribute a positive amount which is less than the optimum.

One approach to internalizing externalities is to assign property rights in air and water, for example. In this formulation, a *right to pollute* would be a right to use the air or water as a productive input and a right to breathe clean air would be a right to bar firms from using the air as a productive input.

The *Coase theorem* states that in situations involving externalities, it does not matter whether firms have the right to pollute or consumers have the right to clean air or water—the same (optimal) level of pollution will emerge as the result of a bargain between firms and consumers. If firms have the right to pollute, consumers will pay for cleaner air. If consumers have the right to breathe clean air, firms will pay for the right to use the air as a productive input.

An *auxiliary market* in pollution rights is a market in rights to pollute or be free from pollution.

At a competitive equilibrium in an auxiliary market, the equilibrium *bribe* (if firms have the right) will equal both the equilibrium tax (if consumers have the right) and the Pigouvian tax.

The Coase theorem can be reinterpreted as a statement that there always exists a unique core in a game between polluters and those who suffer from pollution and that both groups will always play that game as a cooperative game. As such, it ignores the prisoner's dilemma problem inherent in any cooperative game.

The Coase theorem assumes that two parties to a bargain with perfect information behave competitively in an auxiliary market which determines taxes or bribes. There are no income effects in the consumption of the public good; there are no impediments to bargaining (no *transactions costs*); property rights are well defined; and contracts are strictly enforced.

In most cases of pollution, one or more of the assumptions of the Coase theorem are violated, and the prisoner's dilemma problem is likely to be serious.

The *common property problem* or *commons dilemma* occurs when a resource is jointly owned and joint owners compete to use it. It is essentially a prisoner's dilemma, in that all producers could be better off if the resource were managed as a monopoly, but for each individual it is a dominant strategy to exploit the resource more rapidly than a monopolist would.

Experimental results support the Coase theorem in situations in which parties to a bargain are brought together for the purpose of bargaining, contracts are enforced, and information is either perfect or easily obtained.

Demand-revealing or *incentive-compatible* mechanisms for the provision of public goods and the allocation of externalities induce revelation by charging individual agents as a function of what other agents respond and not as a function of what they respond themselves. This is somewhat analogous to a second-price auction, in which the highest bidder wins the auction, but only pays the second highest bid price.

The *Clarke tax* is a demand-revealing mechanism that charges each individual the total cost of the public good minus the sum of what all other participants report they are willing to pay. With quasilinear preferences, it is a dominant strategy to reveal truthfully, but the Clarke tax never collects enough revenue to finance the building of the public good.

A *Groves mechanism* is a Clarke tax with an added term on each person's tax (which does not depend on that individual's response) to make up the deficit inherent in the Clarke tax. The Groves mechanism always collects *more* than enough to finance the building of the public good.

It is impossible to create a mechanism that always chooses a Pareto optimum, balances the budget, and also provides a dominant strategy for participants in the mechanism to reveal truthfully.

In the *Groves-Ledyard* mechanism, demand revelation is a weak Nash equilibrium. Each participant reports an additional amount of the public good, given reports by all other participants.

The *Smith auction mechanism* is a version of the Groves-Ledyard mechanism that has been widely used in laboratory experiments.

The *Arrow problem* in public decision making refers to the fact that when distributional decisions are being made, there may be no consistent social ordering over alternatives. This occurs because distributional decisions involve movements along the production possibilities frontier, hurting some groups and helping others.

Because of the Arrow problem, voting mechanisms for making redistributional decisions tend to be unstable and vulnerable to manipulation of the agenda and manipulation of the voting process itself. Among Americans, it is generally accepted that the process, one man–one vote by majority rule, is fair, even though it can be shown that the outcomes of that process are neither consistent nor stable.

21.15   QUESTIONS FOR DISCUSSION

1. Under what circumstances do you think free riding is likely to be more or less prevalent? Explain why free riding is likely to be less of a problem in certain circumstances.

2. Some economists argue that the amount of pollution we have in our economy must be optimal. On what argument do they base their claim and is it reasonable?

3. How feasible do you think it is to use incentive-compatible mechanisms to provide public goods? What pitfalls do planners face if they use them?

4. Some economists argue that a natural monopoly provides a public good and that we should, therefore, regulate monopoly in such a way as to provide the optimal amount of that public good. Present an argument in defense of that position. Do you think this is a reasonable position to take and why?

5. Why do many economists focus their attention on finding mechanisms that identify and implement outcomes that are Pareto optimal and Pareto superior to some status quo point instead of on government corrective policies? Are there ways that economists can inform the decision process when the issue is redistribution? (Hint: Think about consumer's surplus analysis and tax incidence.)

6. Think of one example of an externality that is likely to be resolved through bargaining among the parties and one that is not. Explain your choice in terms of the assumptions underlying the application of the Coase theorem.

7. In medieval England, village grazing land was held in common, but the right to graze animals was restricted by what were known as "stint rights," which specified how many animals a particular household was allowed to graze. Explain the origins of stint rights with reference to the concepts developed in this chapter.

8. Suppose you are working for your state's department of environmental quality and a

smelting plant applies for a license to produce. You have to decide how much output you are going to allow the plant to produce over a specified period of time. What infor-

mation would you need to determine the optimal level of pollution and output? Draw a graph to illustrate how you would use that information if you could obtain it.

21.16   PROBLEMS

Problems 1–4   Suppose firms X and Y have the following production functions,

$$y = L_y - x$$
$$x = (L_x)^{1/2},$$

and there are 100 units of labor available in this two-good economy.

1. Find an equation for and graph the production possibilities frontier.

2. Find an expression for the marginal rate of transformation.

Problems 3–4   Now suppose there is one consumer in the economy depicted in Problems 1 and 2, who has utility function

$$U = xy.$$

3. What will be the optimal combination of x and y for the economy to produce and what will be the optimal price ratio?

4. Suppose the externality were not internalized. What output combination would be produced and what would be the price ratio?

Problems 5–6   Suppose all consumers had the following utility function over a public good (X) and a private good (Y):

$$U_i = 8\alpha_i x^{1/4} + y_i,$$

and that both p_x and p_y are equal to 1.

5. Find the optimal quantity of X to produce and the Lindahl prices.

6. Now suppose that $\alpha_1 = 1$, $\alpha_2 = 4$, and $\alpha_3 = 12$. Find the Clarke taxes and the amount of the deficit under a Clarke tax for this three-person economy.

21.17   LOGICAL AND MATHEMATICAL APPLICATIONS

1. Set up an economy with two consumers and two firms, one of which pollutes both consumers and the other firm. Solve for the characteristics of the Pareto optimal allocation and identify the marginal damages that would have to be accounted for in designing an optimal tax or bribe scheme. Show that the competitive equilibrium is not Pareto optimal.

2. Suppose consumer utility functions include income effects. Illustrate graphically why Coasian bargaining would no longer lead to the same allocation of an externality regard-

less of which side had the right to pollute or be free from pollution.

3. Suppose that members of a community are voting on a school bond issue and each person has one ideal amount he or she wishes to see spent. Moreover, for each individual, suppose that preferences decline monotonically away from the ideal point. Show that in this case a majority-rule process does choose a winning alternative in a consistent manner. (This is called the case of *single-peaked preferences* and it was first identified by Duncan Black.)

Answers to Selected Odd-Numbered Problems

Chapter 1 (page 25)

7. $x = 2 - \frac{1}{2}y$

9. $x = \dfrac{2}{y}$

11. 1) $\dfrac{dy}{dx} = -2, \dfrac{d^2y}{dx^2} = 0$

   3) $\dfrac{dy}{dx} = -\dfrac{2}{x^2}, \dfrac{d^2y}{dx^2} = \dfrac{4}{x^3}$

   5) $\dfrac{dy}{dx} = 16 - 2x, \dfrac{d^2y}{dx^2} = -2$

13. $\dfrac{dy}{dx} = 2 + 10x - 12x^2$,

   $\dfrac{d^2y}{dx^2} = 10 - 24x$

15. $\dfrac{dy}{dx} = 72(8x^3 - x^2)(6x - 2)^4$

   $\dfrac{d^2y}{dx^2} = 288x(6x - 2)^3(84x^2 - 21x + 1)$

17. $\dfrac{\partial z}{\partial x} = 6x - 1, \dfrac{\partial z}{\partial y} = 30y - 3$

   $dz = (6x - 1)\,dx + (30y - 3)\,dy$

19. $\dfrac{\partial z}{\partial x} = -\dfrac{1}{x^2}, \dfrac{\partial z}{\partial y} = -\dfrac{1}{y^2}$,

   $dz = -\dfrac{1}{x^2}dx - \dfrac{1}{y^2}dy$

Chapter 2 (page 53)

1. Average: $\dfrac{y}{x} = \dfrac{25}{x} - 5$; Marginal: $\dfrac{dy}{dx} = -5$

3. Average: $\dfrac{y}{x} = 10x + \dfrac{5}{x}$; Marginal: $\dfrac{dy}{dx} = 20x$

5. Average: $\dfrac{y}{x} = 100 + \dfrac{1}{x^2}$;

   Marginal: $\dfrac{dy}{dx} = 100 - \dfrac{1}{x^2}$

7. $x^* = \dfrac{1}{10}, y^* = 20$, minimum

9. $x^*\left(\dfrac{1}{10}\right)^{1/2} \approx 0.3162$,

   $y^* = 8(10)^{1/2} \approx 25.2982$, minimum

11. $x^* = \frac{1}{2}, y^* = \frac{1}{5}, z^* = 1.65$, maximum

Chapter 3 (page 87)

1. $x^* = 4, y^* = \dfrac{24}{5}$,

   $z^* = \dfrac{221184}{125} = 1769.472$,

   $\lambda^* = \dfrac{27648}{125} = 221.184$

3. $x^* = 30, y^* = 15$,

   $z^* = 10, \lambda^* = \dfrac{225}{2025} = 0.11$

5. $x^* = 2.77778, y^* = 4.44444$,

   $z^* = 347.22222, \lambda^* = 11.11111$

7. $x^* = 5, y^* = 5$,

   $z^* = 375, \lambda^* = 0$

Chapter 5 (page 131)

1. Satisfies

3. Satisfies

5. Satisfies

608

7. 1) $\dfrac{y}{x}$, **3)** $\dfrac{y}{2x}$, **5)** $\dfrac{y^2}{x^2}$

Chapter 6 (page 161)

1. (a) $y = \frac{2}{3}x$,

   (b) $y = \frac{2}{3}x$,

   (c) $y = \frac{4}{3}x$

5. (a) $\lambda = \dfrac{M^7}{32(p_x p_y)^4}$,

   (b) $\lambda = (2)^{-3/2} \dfrac{1}{M^{1/2}(p_x p_y)^4}$

7. (a) $x^* = \dfrac{M}{2p_x}, y^* = \dfrac{M}{2p_y}$,

   (b) $x^* = \dfrac{M}{2p_x}, y^* = \dfrac{M}{2p_y}$

11. 0, neither a substitute nor a complement

13. $+1$

Chapter 7 (page 182)

1. $x_A^* = 180.39215, y_A^* = 204.44444,$

   $x_B^* = 69.60784, y_B^* = 315.55556,$

   $\tilde{p}_x = 2.26667$

   (Follow the outline in Section 7.3.)

3. $x_A^* = 155.89985, y_A^* = 152.29720$

   $x_B^* = 94.10032, y_B^* = 367.70280$

   $\tilde{p}_x = 1.95378$

   (Use the answers to Problem 1 as new initial endowments.)

5. $x_A^* = 131.86022, y_A^* = 186.25331$

   $x_B^* = 118.13995, y_B^* = 333.74669$

   $\tilde{p}_x = 1.41251$

   (Use the answers to Problem 3 as new initial endowments.)

Chapter 8 (page 214)

1. $U^*(p_x, p_y, M) = \dfrac{4M^3}{27 p_x (p_y)^2}$

(Find the generalized, uncompensated demand functions first.)

3. $M^*(p_x, p_y, U) = 1.88988[p_x(p_y)^2 U]^{1/3}$

5. $x^* = 33.33333, y^* = 44.44444$

7. $\sigma = 1$ (Section 8.7)

9. $\displaystyle\int_2^4 \dfrac{M}{2p_x} dp_x = 46.20981$

   (Should be less than ΔCS_c.)

Chapter 9 (page 228)

1. $X_d = \dfrac{2,000,000}{3p_x}$

3. $X^* = \dfrac{\sum_{i=1}^n M_i}{6}, \epsilon_M = +1$

5. (a) $TR = 5x - 0.1x^2$,

   $MR = 5 - 0.2x$

   (b) $TR = 100, MR = 0$

Chapter 10 (page 246)

3. Functions (a), (c), and (d) exhibit diminishing marginal rates of technical substitution. (See equations 10.3–10.7.)

5. Functions (a) and (c) exhibit diminishing marginal products of labor. (See equations 10.26–10.29.)

Chapter 11 (page 286)

1. (a) $K^* = \dfrac{w}{r}L^*$,

   (c) $K^* = \left(\dfrac{w}{r}\right)^{1/2} L^*$,

   (e) $K^* = \frac{4}{3}L^*$

3. (a) $K^* = \dfrac{5}{4}, L^* = 5$,

   (c) $K^* = \dfrac{3}{2}, L^* = 3$

   (e) $K^* = \dfrac{10}{3}, L^* = \dfrac{5}{2}$

5. $LRTC = TC^*(w, r, x) = \dfrac{(w^{1/2} + r^{1/2})^2 x}{10}$

$LRMC = LRAC = \dfrac{(w^{1/2} + r^{1/2})^2}{10}$

7. $\lambda^* = LRMC$

(Find λ as a function of w and r and show it is equal to long-run marginal cost.)

9. $SRVC = \dfrac{4x}{40 - x}$, $SRAVC = \dfrac{4}{40 - x}$,

$SRTC = \dfrac{4x}{40 - x} + 16$,

$SRATC = \dfrac{4}{40 - x} + \dfrac{16}{x}$,

$SRMC = \dfrac{160}{(40 - x)^2}$

11. Solve this problem as if you were finding $LRTC$.

min $SRTC = 2L + 4m + 8$

s.t. $x = 8^{1/4}L^{1/4}m^{1/4}$

$\mathcal{L} = 2L + 4m + 8 + \lambda(x - 8^{1/4}L^{1/4}m^{1/4})$

The short-run cost functions are $SRVC = 2x^2$,

$SRAVC = 2x$, $SRTC = 2x^2 + 8$,

$SRATC = 2x + 8/x$, $SRMC = 4x$.

Chapter 12 (page 314)

1. $x^*(p_x) = 100 - 10(10)^{1/2}(p_x)^{-1/2}$

$100 - 31.62278(p_x)^{-1/2}$

3. Neutral technological change

(Show that the $MRTS$ stays the same.)

5. $L^*(w) = 10(50)^{1/2}w^{1/2} - 10$

$\approx 70.710678w^{1/2} - 10$,

$MRP_L = \dfrac{5000}{(10 + L)^2}$,

$ARP_L = \dfrac{500}{10 + L}$

Chapter 13 (page 343)

1. Short-run supply is $x_j^*(p_x) = \frac{81}{8}p_x$.

Long-run supply is perfectly elastic at

$p_x = LRMC = \$4$.

3. $SRp_x^e = \$16.23$, $SRX_e = 3{,}286{,}335$,

$LRp_x^e = \$4$, $LRX_e = 13{,}333{,}333$

7. $x_j^* = \dfrac{13{,}333{,}333}{20{,}000} = 666.66667$,

$K_j = \frac{2}{9}x_j = 148.14814$

$x_j^*(p_x) = 166.66667p_x$

9. $X_S(p_x) = \sum_{j \neq k} x_j^*(p_x) + x_k^*(p_x)$

$= 3{,}333{,}463p_x$

11. $\pi_k = \$1037.04$, $\pi_j = \$0$, $j \neq k$

13. $LRp_x^e = \$3$, $LRX_e = 17{,}777{,}778$

15. $p_x^d = \$5.67$, $p_x^s = \$4.67$,

$X_t = 943.33333$

17. Consumers pay 96%, Producers pay 4%

19. Short-run: $DWL = 4.766$;

Long-run: $DWL = 5$

(Long-run supply is perfectly elastic and price rises to \$5.71.)

Chapter 14 (page 373)

1. To solve this problem, first find an expression for F in terms of the labor used to produce C, where $L_F + L_C = 6$:

$L_F = 6 - L_C \Rightarrow F = 6(6 - L_C)$.

Next, solve for L_C in terms of F and substitute in the production function for C:

$L_C = 6 - F/6 \Rightarrow C = 5(6 - F6)^{1/2}$.

Now solve for F as a function of C:

$F(C) = 36 - \dfrac{6C^2}{25}$,

which is the production possibilities frontier.

3. $MRS = MRT = 2.62907$. (Solve Problem 2 for C^* and F^*.)

$MRS = \dfrac{MU_C}{MU_F} = \dfrac{F}{2C}$, $MRT = -\dfrac{dF}{dC} = \dfrac{12C}{25}$

5. To solve this problem, first note that both production functions are Cobb-Douglas production functions with constant returns to

scale, and they are monotonic transformations of one another. This means that the production possiblities frontier will be linear and that $y = 4x$, implying $p_x = 4p_y$. Moreover, the marginal rate of technical substitution can be found by rearranging equation 11.44 and substituting for $\alpha = \beta = 1/2$. That gives you the wage-rental ratio; and the price of X can then be found from equation 11.31 after normalizing on one of the input prices. Once you have all the prices, you can evaluate consumer incomes and then solve for the utility-maximizing choices. Check your answer for feasibility. A solution that normalizes on the rental rate is

$\tilde{r} = 1, w = 4, \tilde{p}_x = 4, \tilde{p}_y = 1,$

$x_A^* = 100, x_B^* = 200,$

$y_A^* = 800, y_B^* = 400,$

$L_x = 150, L_y = 150,$

$K_x = 600, K_y = 600.$

Chapter 15 (page 401)

1. To solve this problem, first find the short-run total cost function, $wL(x) + \tilde{r}K$, and then set up the short-run profit function:

   $SR\pi = p_x(x)x - SRTC$. The solution is found by maximizing short-run profits:

   $x^* = 120.19231, p_x^* = \$129.81.$

3. $SR\pi^* = \$14,924.04$
5. $LR\pi^* = \$15,129.00$
7. $p_x^c = \$4, x_c = 246$
9. $K_c = 123, L_c = 492$

   (Use the conditional input demands derived as equations 11.24 and 11.25.)

11. Lowest price $= LRMC = \$4,$

$$\pi = \int_4^{250} (250 - p_x)\,dp_x$$

$$= \$30,258.00$$

13. $x_1^* = 15, p_x^{1*} = \$34,$

    $x_2^* = 19, p_x^{2*} = \$23$

15. $x_j^* = 34, p_x^{j*} = \$26.67$

Chapter 16 (page 436)

1. $x_1 = 123 - \frac{1}{2}x_2, x_2 = 123 - \frac{1}{2}x_1$
3. $p_x = \$4, x = 246$
5. $p_x = \$4, x = 246$

Chapter 17 (page 462)

1. $C^* = \ell^* = 19.33,$

   $MRS = w/p = 2$
3. $w = \$4.76, L = 4762$
5. $238,100$ (Rounded)
7. $w_f = \$9, L_f = 1800,$

   $w_m = \$12, L_m = 1440$
9. $w = MRP = \$18,$

   $L_f + L_m = 6840$

Chapter 18 (page 491)

1. $3,333.33
3. $16,572.56

   (You have to discount the infinite stream of payments back 5 years.)

Chapter 19 (page 518)

1. $235
3. No
5. $64

   (Find the expected utility and then find the income associated with getting the expected utility with certainty.)
7. $4

Chapter 21 (page 586)

1. $y = 100 - x^2 - x$
3. $X^* = 5.44978, Y^* = 64.85008,$

   $MRS = MRT = 11.89956$
5. $x^* = \left(2\sum_{i=1}^{n} \alpha_i\right)^{4/3},$

   $p_i = 2\alpha_i(x^*)^{-3/4}$

Author Index

Subject Index

Acid rain, 590, 593
Actuarially fair insurance, 523-24, 533, 535
    adverse selection and, 547-48
    moral hazard and, 539, 544
Additivity of cardinal utility functions, 132
Additivity of utility functions, 108
Adverse selection, 538, 539, 544-48
    educational signalling and, 558
    inefficiency in insurance markets and, 544-48, 559
    market for lemons and, 553-55, 560
    separating equilibria in a contingent claims market and, 539, 546-47, 559
Advertising, U-shaped long-run average cost and, 441-42
Agenda, 100, 105
Agenda manipulation, 601-2, 606
Agent. *See* Principal-agent problem
Agriculture and the principal-problem, 548, 552-53
Allocation. *See also* Coase theorem
    competitive equilibrium, 234-35
    efficient allocation of inputs, 361
    efficient allocation of production externality, 562-70, 577-78, 587, 604
    incentive-compatible allocation mechanisms, 593-600, 604-5
    initial allocation, defined, 97, 105
    Pareto optimal allocation of externalities, 103, 566-70, 604
    Pareto optimal allocation of public goods, 103, 562-63, 570-76, 604
    resource allocation, 95-97, 104
    of time, 455-61, 464-68, 479
Altruism, 99
Anchoring technique in compensated demand, 187-91, 211
    anchor point, 188, 205, 207
Antiderivative, 20-24
Antitrust
    cartels and, 423
    experimental markets and, 450
    unique factor endowments and, 478
A priori probability, 514, 534
Arc elasticity, 161
Arrow paradox (or problem), 100, 105, 600-603, 606
Arrow-Pratt measure of absolute risk aversion, 541n, 559
"As given" assumptions, 101
"As if" assumptions, 94-95, 104, 107
    utility maximization and, 119, 123

Assumptions in economic theory, 92-94, 104. *See also* Competitive assumptions; Cournot-Nash behavioral assumptions; Price taking assumption
    "as if" assumptions, 94-95, 104, 107, 119, 123
    private ownership assumption, 98
    self-interest assumption, 98-99, 105
    small economy assumption, 100-101
Attitudes towards risk. *See* Constant absolute risk aversion; Risk aversion; Risk neutrality; Risk seeking
Auction. *See* Double oral auction in experimental markets; Second-price auction
Auctioneer
    in *tâtonnement* process, 239-40
    trade and price determination facilitated by, 223-25, 239
Auction mechanism, 598-99, 606
Auxiliary markets in rights to pollute, 585-87, 605
Average cost regulation of natural monopolies, 413, 414
Average costs
    average fixed cost, 282, 299
    average variable cost, 303n, 312, 313, 327
    long-run, 271, 298
    short-run average total cost, 282-88, 299
    short-run average variable cost, 282-88, 299, 312, 327
Average fixed cost, 282, 299
Average functions, general description, 34, 36-41, 53
Average (physical) product of capital, 251
Average (physical) product of labor, 251, 253, 257
    input demand and, 316-17, 327
Average revenue, 166, 171
Average revenue product, 316-17, 318, 327
Average variable cost
    short-run, 282-88, 299
    short-run shutdown and, 303n, 312, 313, 327
Averch-Johnson effect, 413-16, 417
Axioms of consumer preference, 109-18, 141-42
Axioms of expected utility theory, 516-18, 534-35
Axioms of revealed preference, 123, 132

Baby boom, 155-56
Baby bust, 155
Backward-bending labor supply curve, 462-63, 479
    overtime pay and, 464-65, 479
Backward-bending savings supply curve, 491-92, 508
Backward induction and finitely repeated games, 447, 452
Bargaining
    Coasian, 584-93, 605
    Nash bargaining solution, 422n, 451
    union, 455, 462, 475-77, 479
    unique factor endowments and, 455, 478, 479
Bargaining breakdown (and Coase theorem), 593
Barriers to entry, 337-38
Bell curve, 525, 535
Benefits
    external, 577, 604
    marginal private, 103
    marginal social, 102, 103
    nonpecuniary, 470, 479
Benthamite cardinal utility, 108
Bertrand model, 433-34, 448, 449, 451